Handbook of Qualitative Organizational Research

This handbook provides a comprehensive overview of state-of-the-art, innovative approaches to qualitative research for organizational scholars. Individual chapters in each area are written by experts in a variety of fields, who have contributed some of the most innovative studies themselves in recent years. An indispensable reference guide to anyone conducting high-impact organizational research, this handbook includes innovative approaches to research problems, data collection, data analysis and interpretation, and application of research findings. The book will be of interest to scholars and graduate students in a wide variety of disciplines, including anthropology, organizational behavior, organizational theory, social psychology, and sociology.

Kimberly D. Elsbach is Professor of Management, Stephen G. Newberry Chair in Leadership, and Associate Dean for Instruction at the Graduate School of Management, University of California, Davis. She is also an International Research Fellow at the Center for Corporate Reputation, Oxford University, and the co-founder and organizer of the Davis Conference on Qualitative Research. She has published over 60 scholarly articles and 6 books, focusing on the study of individual and organizational perceptions.

Roderick M. Kramer is the William R. Kimball Professor of Organizational Behavior at Stanford University's Graduate School of Business. He is the author of more than 150 scholarly articles, and his work has appeared in leading academic journals such as *Administrative Science Quarterly*, as well as in practitioner-oriented magazines such as the *Harvard Business Review*. He is also the author or co-author of 17 books.

Handbook of Qualitative Organizational Research

Innovative Pathways and Methods

Edited by Kimberly D. Elsbach and Roderick M. Kramer

Routledge
Taylor & Francis Group

NEW YORK AND LONDON

First published 2016
by Routledge
711 Third Avenue, New York, NY 10017

and by Routledge
2 Park Square, Milton Park, Abingdon, Oxon, OX14 4RN

Routledge is an imprint of the Taylor & Francis Group, an informa business

Library of Congress Cataloging-in-Publication Data
Handbook of qualitative organizational research : innovative pathways and ideas / edited by Kimberly D. Elsbach and Roderick M. Kramer.
     pages cm
   Includes bibliographical references and index.
  1. Organizational sociology—Research.   2. Organizational behavior—
Research.   3. Management—Research.   4. Qualitative research.   I. Elsbach,
Kimberly D.   II. Kramer, Roderick M. (Roderick Moreland), 1950–
   HM786.H365 2015
   302.35—dc23
   2015004478

ISBN: 978-1-84872-509-6 (hbk)
ISBN: 978-1-84872-510-2 (pbk)
ISBN: 978-1-3158-4907-2 (ebk)

Typeset in Bembo
by Apex CoVantage, LLC

Contents

List of Figures   *xi*
List of Tables   *xiii*
About the Editors   *xv*
About the Contributors   *xvii*

PART I
Introduction, History, and Context of Qualitative Methods   **1**

1 Introduction: In Search of Innovative Pathways and
   Methods in Qualitative Research   3
   Kimberly D. Elsbach and Roderick M. Kramer

2 Qualitative Research: It Just Keeps Getting More Interesting!   9
   Sara L. Rynes and Jean M. Bartunek

3 Ups and Downs: Trends in the Development and
   Reception of Qualitative Methods   24
   Michael Mauskapf and Paul Hirsch

PART II
Innovative Research Settings   **31**

4 Using Extreme Cases to Understand Organizations   33
   Katherine K. Chen

5 Contract Ethnography in Corporate Settings:
   Innovation From Entanglement   45
   Anne-Laure Fayard, John Van Maanen, and John Weeks

6 Studying Elites in Institutions of Higher Education   54
   Scott Snook and Rakesh Khurana

Contents

7   Drawing Fine Lines Behind Bars: Pushing the Boundaries of
    Researcher Neutrality in Unconventional Contexts   66
    Kristie M. Rogers, Madeline Toubiana, and Katherine A. DeCelles

8   Why Is That Interesting? Finding the Meanings of
    Unexplored Phenomena   77
    Ian J. Walsh and Jean M. Bartunek

9   Studying Organizational Fields Through Ethnography   86
    Tammar B. Zilber

PART III
Innovative Research Designs   **97**

10 How to Look Two Ways at Once: Research Strategies
    for Inhabited Institutionalism   99
    Michael A. Haedicke and Tim Hallett

11 Using Qualitative Methods to Track Evolving Entrepreneurial Identities   112
    Philip Anderson

12 From What Happened to What Happens: Using Microhistorical
    Case Studies to Build Grounded Theory in Organization Studies   122
    Andrew Hargadon

13 Immersion Ethnography of Elites   134
    Brooke Harrington

14 Accounting for Accounts: Crafting Ethnographic Validity Through
    Team Ethnography   143
    Joelle Evans, Ruthanne Huising, and Susan S. Silbey

15 Qualitative Comparative Analysis: Opportunities for Case-Based Research   156
    *Reut Livne-Tarandach, Benjamin Hawbaker, Brooke
    Lahneman Boren, and Candace Jones*

16 Leveraging Comparative Field Data for Theory Generation   168
    Beth A. Bechky and Siobhan O'Mahony

17 Crafting and Selecting Research Questions and
    Contexts in Qualitative Research   177
    Michael G. Pratt

18 A Practice Approach to the Study of Social Networks   186
    Maria Christina Binz-Scharf

PART IV
Unique Forms of Qualitative Data   **195**

19 Denials, Obstructions, and Silences: Lessons from
    Repertoires of Field Resistance (and Embrace)   197
    Michel Anteby

20 The Aesthetics of Data: Qualitative Analysis of Visual and
    Other Nontextual Forms of Data   206
    Simona Giorgi and Mary Ann Glynn

21 Leveraging Archival Data from Online Communities
    for Grounded Process Theorizing   215
    Natalia Levina and Emmanuelle Vaast

22 Analyzing Visual Rhetoric in Organizational Research   225
    Lianne Lefsrud, Heather Graves, and Nelson Phillips

23 Markers, Metaphors, and Meaning: Drawings as a Visual and
    Creative Qualitative Research Methodology in Organizations   238
    Sarah J. Tracy and Shawna Malvini Redden

PART V
Unique Data Collection Methods   **249**

24 Structural Sampling: A Technique for Illuminating Social Systems   251
    Sonali K. Shah and Andreea D. Gorbatai

25 Ethnography Across the Work Boundary: Benefits and
    Considerations for Organizational Studies   262
    Melissa Mazmanian, Christine M. Beckman, and Ellie Harmon

26 Strategic Conversations: Methods for Data Collection and Analysis   272
    Christina Kyprianou, Melissa E. Graebner, and Violina Rindova

27 Triangulate and Expand: Using Multiple Sources of Data for
    Convergence and Expansion to Enrich Inductive Theorizing   286
    Elizabeth D. Rouse and Spencer H. Harrison

Contents

28 "What's Cooking?" Serendipitous Opportunities and
Creative Action in Data Collection   298
Silviya Svejenova

PART VI
Innovative Forms of Analysis   **309**

29 Adventures in Qualitative Research   311
Connie J. G. Gersick

30 Concept Mapping as a Methodical and Transparent Data Analysis Process   318
Peter Balan, Eva Balan-Vnuk, Mike Metcalfe, and Noel Lindsay

31 Innovation Through Collaboration: Working Together
on Data Analysis and Interpretation   331
Kevin G. Corley, Courtney R. Masterson, and Beth S. Schinoff

32 Multilevel Discourse Analysis: A Structured Approach
to Analyzing Longitudinal Data   341
Steven J. Kahl and Stine Grodal

33 *Tabula Geminus*: A "Both/And" Approach to Coding and Theorizing   350
Glen E. Kreiner

34 Using Qualitative Comparative Analysis (QCA) as a Descriptive
Numerical Method in Support of Narrative Methods   362
Rodney Lacey and Lisa Cohen

35 Discovery, Validation, and Live Coding   371
Karen Locke, Martha S. Feldman, and Karen Golden-Biddle

36 Between Text and Context: Innovative Approaches
to the Qualitative Analysis of Online Data   381
Anca Metiu and Anne-Laure Fayard

37 Documenting Work: From Participant Observation to Participant Tracing   391
Carsten Østerlund, Jaime Snyder, Steve Sawyer, Sarika Sharma, and Matt Willis

38 The Journey From Data to Qualitative Inductive Paper:
Who Helps and How?   401
Špela Trefalt and Marya L. Besharov

39 Worth a Second Look? Exploring the Power of
Post-Mortems on Post-Mortems   411
Roderick M. Kramer

PART VII
Multimethods Approaches   **421**

40 Mixing Quantitative and Qualitative Research   423
    Sarah Kaplan

41 Counting Qualitative Data   434
    Chad Michael McPherson and Michael Sauder

42 Combining Qualitative Methods to Study Collective
    Cognition in Organizations   444
    Ileana Stigliani and Davide Ravasi

43 Highlights of the Hybrid Method   454
    Charles Galunic

PART VIII
Challenges and Opportunities in Qualitative Methods   **463**

44 Confessions of a Mad Ethnographer   465
    Stephen R. Barley

Index   477

Figures

4.1	Undertaking Research on Extreme Cases	39
8.1	Finding the Meaning in Unexplored Phenomena	84
9.1	Basic Steps in Conducting Field-Level Ethnography	87
10.1	Analysis as a Ball on a Teeter-Totter, Rolling between Quasi-Deduction and Responsive Induction, with Surprise as the Abductive Shift-Point	104
10.2	Ideas Coming to Ground Force a Reckoning as the Empirical Data Push Back Against Informing Theories	105
10.3	Misfitting and Surprising Empirical Findings Serve as an Abductive Shift-Point as the Weight of the Analysis Rolls Towards Responsive Induction	105
10.4	Reconsideration of the Data and the Search for Empirical Patterns and Insights Provide Another Push	105
10.5	Recognition of Theoretical Surprise and Insight, Creation of New Concepts That Can Serve as the Basis of Quasi-Deduction in Further Research	106
11.1	Blending Qualitative Methods to Track Evolving Entrepreneurial Identities	115
12.1	Cognition and Action Acting Within and Upon the Institutional Context	128
13.1	Process Characteristics of Immersion Ethnography of Elites	138
14.1	Collecting, Analyzing, and Theorizing Accounts Through Team Ethnography	148
15.1	QCA Analytical Process	159
17.1	A Linear Understanding of Selecting Research Questions and Contexts in Inductive Research	178
17.2	Circular Process of Selecting Research Question and Context	180
18.1	Using a Practice Approach to Study Social Networks	189
19.1	Combining Novel and Traditional Data Sources	203
20.1	The Coupling Between the Visual and the Textual	210
21.1	Identifying Key Concepts and Their Evolution Over Time in the Discourse Archive (DA)	217
22.1	Analyzing Visual Rhetoric	228
22.2	Ethical Oil Institute's Conflict Oil, Ethical Oil Advertisement	233
23.1	Value of Drawing and Metaphor Analysis	239
23.2	Drawing from Target of Workplace Bullying Responding to the Question "What Does Workplace Bullying Feel Like?"	241

23.3	Drawing from a Student in Response to the Question "What Does Graduate School Feel Like?"	245
23.4	Drawing from a Student in Response to the Prompt "Draw an Ideal Leader."	246
24.1	Structural Sampling: Purpose, Benefits, and Technique	252
25.1	Ethnography Across the Work Boundary	266
26.1	Research Topics and Methods Suitable for Strategic Conversation Data	283
27.1	Four-Step Process for Data Triangulation and Expansion	287
27.2	Schematic of Data Sources for Expansion	292
28.1	Elements and Workings of the Approach	302
29.1	Two Examples Showing How to Read the Career Trajectories	315
29.2	Illustration of Four Career Trajectories	316
30.1	Research Overview	320
30.2	IC Dimensions Concept Map	323
30.3	Textbox Summarizing the Innovation	327
31.1	Innovative Analysis Through Collaboration	333
32.1	The Five Steps in Multilevel Discourse Analysis	343
33.1	The *Tabula Geminus* Process	353
34.1	Using QCA as Descriptive Numerical Analysis to Support Narrative Qualitative Research	363
37.1	Document-centric Data Gathering Strategy	394
38.1	Types of Helpers and the Help They Provide	403
39.1	Conducting Second-Look Decision Analyses	414
40.1	Relationship Between Qualitative and Quantitative Research	424
41.1	Combined Qualitative and Counting Data Analysis	440
42.1	A Visual Representation of Our Method	447

Tables

2.1	Citations to Editorial Essays on Qualitative Research in *AMJ* (2004–2012)	10
2.2	Qualitative Best Paper Winners: *Academy of Management Journal* (2003–2012) and *Administrative Science Quarterly* (2003–2013)	15
3.1	Trends in Qualitative Organizational Research	26
4.1	Extreme Cases That Examine How the Extraordinary Handle the Mundanity of Organizing Dilemmas	35
4.2	Extreme Cases That Show How Organizations Pursue Values via Their Organizing Practices and Forms	37
4.3	Extreme Cases That Delve into How Organizations Concentrate Power and Reproduce the Status Quo	38
5.1	Similarities and Differences: Traditional and Contract Ethnography	48
7.1	Key Features of Unconventional Contexts	70
7.2	Distinctions between Traditional Methods and Alternative Methods	75
7.3	Use of Alternative Methods in Qualitative Organizational Research	75
8.1	Exemplary Papers	84
9.1	The Use of Field-Level Ethnography	91
10.1	Examples of Inhabited Institutions Research Design in Organizational Analysis	101
11.1	Examples of Qualitative Methods Drawn upon in This Study	116
12.1	Use of Microhistorical Methods in Qualitative Research	126
13.1	Use of Immersion Ethnography in Recent Research on Elites	137
14.1	Examples of Team Ethnographies	152
15.1	Use of QCA in Qualitative Research Methods	162
16.1	Use of Comparative Designs in Qualitative Field Research Methods	175
17.1	Use of a Nonlinear Process for Selecting Research Questions and Contexts	181
18.1	Examples of Projects Using a Relational Practice Approach	188
19.1	Use of Forms of Field Resistance (and Embrace★) in Qualitative Research	201
21.1	Use of Online Community Discourse for Process Theory Building	222
22.1	Coding Scheme for Analyzing Words and Images in Multimodal Messages	230

22.2	Analysis of Conflict Oil, Ethical Oil Advertisement	232
22.3	Syllogistic Argument Presented in Ethical Oil Advertisement	234
22.4	Use of Visual Rhetoric in Qualitative Research Methods	235
23.1	Empirical Studies Featuring Drawing Analysis in Organizational Studies	242
24.1	Examples of Structural Sampling in Management and Social Science Research	257
25.1	Ethnographies of Work and Private Space	263
26.1	Use of Strategic Conversations in Strategy Research	275
26.2	Data Collection and Analysis of Strategic Conversations	279
27.1	Use of Data Expansion in Qualitative Research Methods	294
30.1	IC Dimensions Identified from the Matrix Analysis	321
30.2	IC Dimension Concept Map Clusters	323
30.3	Comparison of IC Dimensions Generated From Both Methods	324
30.4	Use of Concept Mapping for Grounded Data Analysis in Qualitative Research	328
31.1	Examples of Collaboration in Qualitative Research Methods	338
32.1	Examples of Articles Using Elements of Multilevel Discourse Analysis	347
33.1	Use of *Tabula Geminus* in Qualitative Research Methods	358
34.1	QCA Research of Interest to Researchers Using Narrative Methods	364
34.2	Truth Table for QCA Analysis of Fact Checker Coping Strategies	366
34.3	QCA Truth Table Reduction of Fact Checker Coping Strategies	367
35.1	Comparing Live and Inert Coding	373
35.2	Illustrations of Live Coding	378
36.1	The Contextual Challenge in Qualitative Research	384
36.2	Innovative Strategies for Analyzing Online Data and Exemplars	385
37.1	Use of Document-centric Participant Tracing in Qualitative Research Methods	393
37.2	Methodological Implications	396
38.1	Use of "Travel Companions" and Other Helpers in Qualitative, Inductive Research	408
39.1	Examples of Second-Look Studies of Decision-Making Fiascoes	418
40.1	Examples of Mixed-Methods Papers and Research Programs	424
41.1	Uses of Quantification in Qualitative Research Methods	437
42.1	A List of Past Studies Combining Different Qualitative Research Methods	448
43.1	Highlights of the Hybrid Method	461

About the Editors

Kimberly D. Elsbach is professor of management, Stephen G. Newberry chair in leadership, and Associate Dean for instruction at the Graduate School of Management, University of California, Davis, and international research fellow at the Center for Corporate Reputation, Oxford University. She is also the co-founder and organizer of the Davis Conference on Qualitative Research and the Davis Workshop on Qualitative Research Methods. Kim's research focuses on perception, specifically how people perceive each other and their organizations. She has studied these perceptual processes in a variety of contexts ranging from the California cattle industry and the National Rifle Association to Hollywood screenwriters. She is currently studying how crying at work affects perceptions of professional women and why fans identify with NASCAR. Her book *Organizational Perception Management* was recently published by Lawrence-Erlbaum as part of its Organization and Management Series.

Roderick M. Kramer is the William R. Kimball professor of organizational behavior at Stanford University's Graduate School of Business, where he has been a professor since 1985. He is the author of more than 150 scholarly articles, and his work has appeared in leading academic journals such as *Administrative Science Quarterly*, as well as in practitioner-oriented magazines such as the *Harvard Business Review*. He is also the author or co-author of 17 books, including *Restoring Trust in Organizations and Leaders, Contemporary Conceptions of Leadership*. and the forthcoming *Handbook of Heroism and Heroic Leadership Research*. Professor Kramer has been a visiting scholar at numerous institutions, including the Bellagio Center, London Business School, Oxford University, Harvard Business School, Harvard Kennedy School, and Stanford's Hoover Institution.

About the Contributors

Philip Anderson is the INSEAD alumni fund professor of entrepreneurship at INSEAD in Singapore. He is the co-author of *Managing Strategic Innovation and Change: A Collection of Readings* (with Michael Tushman) published in 2004 (second edition) and *Inside the Kaisha: Demystifying Japanese Business Behavior* (with Noboru Yoshimura) published in 1997. *Inside the Kaisha* was named 1997 Booz Allen Hamilton/Financial Times Global business book of the year for industry analysis/business context. He has been an associate editor of *Administrative Science Quarterly* and a senior editor at *Organization Science*.

Michel Anteby is an associate professor of organizational behavior at Boston University. He has taught for several years a "Design of Field Research Methods" doctoral seminar. His research looks at how individuals relate to their work, their occupations, and the organizations they belong to. He examines more specifically how the practices people engage in at work help them sustain their chosen cultures or identities. In doing so, his research contributes to a better understanding of how these cultures and identities come to be and manifest themselves. Michel holds a joint PhD in management from New York University and in sociology from the Ecole des Hautes Etudes en Sciences Sociales (EHESS, Paris). His latest book titled *Manufacturing Morals: The Values of Silence in Business School Education* (2013) was a finalist for the 2015 AOM George R. Terry Award.

Peter Balan started as a quantitative researcher but has more recently used both NVivo and concept mapping in numerous grounded research projects to explore the factors underlying a range of phenomena in business as well as in education. He joined the University of South Australia following a career in market research, marketing, and management in France, Germany, Switzerland, the UK, and Australia. He was the foundation head of the university's school of marketing and the foundation director of his university's Centre for the Development of Entrepreneurs. His research is in innovation capability and entrepreneurial orientation, as well as in entrepreneurship education.

Eva Balan-Vnuk combines qualitative and quantitative methods, namely concept mapping and Qualitative Comparative Analysis (QCA), in her research to investigate aspects of innovation and entrepreneurship. Prior to academia, Eva spent 9 years working for Microsoft in Europe, the Middle East, Africa, and Asia in a variety of sales, marketing, strategy, and management roles. After having completed her PhD to better understand the business model strategies of sustainable social enterprises, she now works for Microsoft in Australia, working with corporate clients to help them become more innovative. Eva is a visiting research fellow at the University of Adelaide, South Australia.

Stephen R. Barley is the Richard W. Weiland Professor of Management Science and Engineering, the associate chair of Stanford's Department of Management Science and Engineering, and the co-director of the Center for Work, Technology and Organization at Stanford's School of

Engineering. He holds a BA in English from the College of William and Mary, a masters in education from the Ohio State University, and a PhD in organization studies from the Massachusetts Institute of Technology.

Jean M. Bartunek is the Robert A. and Evelyn J. Ferris chair and professor of management and organization at Boston College. Her PhD in social and organizational psychology is from the University of Illinois at Chicago. She is a past president and fellow of the Academy of Management, and in 2009 she won the academy's Career Distinguished Service Award. Her research interests center around organizational change and academic–practitioner relationships. Jean is currently an associate editor of the *Journal of Applied Behavioral Science* and will be an associate editor of the *Academy of Management Review* from 2015 to 2017.

Beth A. Bechky is the Jacob B. Melnick term professor of management of organizations and professor of sociology (by courtesy) at New York University. Her primary research interest is the micro-sociology of work, and she focuses her attention on interactions and dynamics at organizational and occupational boundaries. She studies how occupational groups in organizations collaborate to solve problems, coordinate their activities, respond to surprises, and innovate. She is the author of numerous articles in journals such as *Administrative Science Quarterly, Academy of Management Journal, Organization Science*, and *American Journal of Sociology*. Her most recent project is an ethnographic study of a crime laboratory. Professor Bechky received a BS (with honors) from the School of Industrial and Labor Relations at Cornell University and an MA in sociology and a PhD in industrial engineering and engineering management from Stanford University.

Christine M. Beckman is an associate professor of management and organization at The Paul Merage School of Business, University of California, Irvine, and The Robert H. Smith School of Business, University of Maryland. Her research has focused on organizational learning, interorganizational networks, and entrepreneurship, particularly on how collaborative relationships facilitate organizational change. Recent work examines how new forms of organizational control operate in a technology-enabled world where boundaries between the personal and the professional are blurred. She received her PhD in organizational behavior from the Graduate School of Business at Stanford University.

Marya L. Besharov is an assistant professor of organizational behavior at the ILR School at Cornell University. An organizational theorist with a background in organizational sociology, she studies how organizations and their leaders navigate competing goals. Much of her research focuses on social-business hybrid organizations such as social enterprises and mission-driven businesses. Drawing on institutional and identity theories, Marya investigates the structures and practices that enable hybrids to sustain their often competing social and commercial goals. Her research has been published and is forthcoming in journals such as *Academy of Management Journal, Academy of Management Review, Business Ethics Quarterly, Academy of Management Learning and Education, Research in Organizational Behavior, Research in the Sociology of Organizations*, and *Industrial and Corporate Change*. Marya received a BA in social studies, an MA in sociology, and a PhD in organizational behavior from Harvard University. She also holds an MBA from Stanford.

Maria Christina Binz-Scharf is associate professor of management in the Colin Powell School for Civic and Global Leadership at CUNY City College. Her research examines how individuals search for and share knowledge to accomplish work. In particular, she is interested in understanding the role technology plays in processes of knowledge sharing and innovation. With the support of grants from the National Science Foundation and National Institutes of Health, she has studied the knowledge networks of biologists, government workers, primary care physicians, and DNA forensic scientists. Before joining the faculty at City College, Dr. Binz-Scharf was a postdoctoral fellow at the Harvard Kennedy School. Prior to her academic career, she worked at the European Commission and the International Road Transport Union in Brussels, Belgium. Dr. Binz-Scharf holds a PhD in business economics from the University of St. Gallen and a BA from Bocconi University in Milan, Italy.

Brooke Lahneman Boren is a PhD candidate in management at the University of Oregon. Brooke researches the development and change of organizational cultures, identities, and practices. She is particularly interested in cultural issues regarding sustainable operations and practices. Brooke's primary research integrates aspects of culture, identity, and strategy surrounding the adoption of environmental certifications in organizations, and utilizes mixed methodological approaches. In her dissertation, Brooke investigates how organizations understand and use shared industry level conceptions of sustainability, using cultural consensus modeling to measure the exchange of cultural knowledge between organizations and environmental certified management standards in the wine industry.

Katherine K. Chen, PhD, is assistant professor in the department of sociology at the City College of New York and the Graduate Center, CUNY. Her publications include the award-winning book *Enabling Creative Chaos: The Organization Behind the Burning Man Event* and journal articles in *American Behavioral Scientist, Nonprofit and Voluntary Sector Quarterly, Qualitative Sociology*, and *Research in the Sociology of Organizations*. Her current research examines how organizations innovate and coordinate under uncertainty.

Lisa Cohen is an associate professor of organizational behavior at the Desautels Faculty of Management at McGill. She received her PhD from the University of California, Berkeley. Her current research focuses on jobs (the set of tasks assembled under an administrative job title) and job structures (the set of jobs assembled into organizational hierarchies, functions, and departments). She uses both qualitative and quantitative methods to answer questions such as: How tasks are bundled into and across jobs? When are new jobs added to or removed from organizational structures? What are the implications of a shifting job structure for organizations?

Kevin G. Corley is a professor in the management department at the W.P. Carey School of Business at Arizona State University. His research interests focus on sensemaking and organizing processes, especially as they pertain to organizational change. He has applied this focus to areas of organizational identity, image, identification, culture, and knowledge. His research has recently appeared in the *Academy of Management Journal, Academy of Management Review, Administrative Science Quarterly, Organization Science*, and *Academy of Management Annals*. His 2004 *ASQ* article with Gioia received the 2010 *ASQ* Award for Scholarly Contribution.

Katherine A. DeCelles is an assistant professor in organizational behavior at the Rotman School of Management at the University of Toronto. Her research examines topics at the intersection of ethics, emotion, and the organizational context. She is passionate about field research and the study of prison as a workplace. Katy received her PhD from the University of Maryland and completed a postdoctoral fellowship at the University of Michigan.

Joelle Evans is an assistant professor at HEC Paris. She received her PhD from the Massachusetts Institute of Technology, Sloan School of Management. She uses qualitative and ethnographic approaches to study how organizational and expert communities respond to moral challenges related to their activities. Her research interests include the social implications of new technologies, the structuring of work in socially contested areas, and regulation in practice.

Anne-Laure Fayard is associate professor of management in the department of technology management and innovation at NYU Polytechnic School of Engineering and is affiliated with the department of management and organizations at NYU Stern Business School. Her research interests involve communication, collaboration, culture, and space, with a focus on interactions, particularly those between people and technology. Her work has been published in several leading journals such as *Organization Science and Organization Studies*. She is also the author with Anca Metiu of *The Power of Writing in Organizations* (Routledge, 2012). Prior to joining NYU Polytechnic, Fayard was a faculty member at INSEAD in Singapore and France. She holds a PhD in cognitive science from the Ecole des Hautes-Etudes en Sciences Sociales (Paris), an MA in cognitive science from Ecole Polytechnique (Paris), and a BA and an MA in philosophy from La Sorbonne (Paris).

Martha S. Feldman is the Johnson chair for civic governance and public management and professor of social ecology, business, political science and sociology at the University of California, Irvine. She has written four books and dozens of articles on the topics of organization theory, public management, and qualitative research methods. Her current research on organizational routines explores the role of performance and agency in creating, maintaining, and altering these fundamental organizational phenomena. She is a senior editor for *Organization Science* and also serves on the editorial boards of the *Academy of Management Journal, Academy of Management Discoveries, International Public Management Journal, Journal of Management Studies, Organization Studies, Public Administration Review*, and *Qualitative Research in Organizations and Management*. She received *Administrative Science Quarterly*'s 2009 award for scholarly contribution, the 2011 Academy of Management Practice Scholarship Award, and in 2014, she received an honorary doctorate in economics from St. Gallen University Business School and was listed by Thompson Reuters as a highly cited author.

Charles Galunic is a Canadian professor of organizational behaviour and the AVIVA chair in leadership and responsibility at INSEAD residing in Fontainebleau, France. He received his PhD from Stanford University, BA from Oxford (politics, philosophy, economics, Rhodes Scholar from Ontario), and BSc from Queen's University (chemical engineering). His research interests are at the crossroads of organization and management theory and strategy, exploring the micro-foundations of strategic advantage with a concern for the performance implications and benefits of structures (e.g., social networks) and processes (e.g., innovation through recombinations) within organizations. He has published in top academic and practitioner-oriented journals, including *Administrative Science Quarterly, Journal of Managerial and Decision Economics, Academy of Management Journal, Organisation Science, Strategic Management Journal, Harvard Business Review*, and *Research in Organisational Behaviour*. Charles also works with numerous companies across the globe in developing their leadership and organizational capabilities.

Andreea D. Gorbatai is an assistant professor in management of organizations at the Haas School of Business at University of California at Berkeley. Her research is nested in the field of organization theory, concentrating on the structural characteristics of new forms of organizing and on the social mechanisms linking organization structure, participant behavior, and performance outcomes in these settings. Most recently, Andreea has been employing natural language processing techniques to evaluate the role of language, framing, and emotion in emergent computer-mediated markets such as crowdfunding and bitcoin. Additionally, she has been examining the Maker Movement and entrepreneurial ventures coming out of makerspaces. She holds a master's degree in sociology and a PhD in organizational behavior from Harvard University.

Connie J. G. Gersick spent 16 years on the faculty of human resources and organizational behavior at UCLA's Graduate School of Management and a year as a visiting scholar at Harvard Business

School. Gersick's research for over a decade has centered on women's lives and careers. Most recently, she co-authored a study on women in Asian enterprise families. She has won a number of national awards for her publications on group work and change processes. Dr. Gersick was the founding faculty director of the Women's Leadership Institute, an executive education workshop at UCLA, and she continues to teach high-potential women from all over the world through UCLA's programs. Her chapter describes work she did while at Yale University, first as a doctoral student, and much later as a visiting scholar.

Simona Giorgi is an assistant professor of management and organization at the Carroll School of Management, Boston College. Her research uses cultural and institutional analysis to examine social evaluations, framing, and change in a wide variety of contexts, including financial analysts, food movements, environmental nonprofits, the Catholic Church, and the automobile industry. She received her PhD from the Kellogg School of Management at Northwestern University.

Mary Ann Glynn is the Joseph F. Cotter professor of management and organization at the Carroll School of Management, Boston College. Mary Ann's research focuses on social cognition writ large—organizational identity, learning, intelligence, and leadership—as well as its social embeddedness in larger systems of meaning arising from organizational fields, market categories, institutional systems, and cultural forces. She is the vice president-elect and program chair-elect of the Academy of Management. She received her PhD from the Graduate School of Business at Columbia University.

Karen Golden-Biddle is the Questrom professor in management at Boston University's School of Management. Working in the areas of organizational change and theorizing in research, she has a keen interest in the cultural and relational micro-processes constituting and motivating active, engaged change efforts that enrich human lives at work and improve society. She has received the Douglas McGregor Award for her work on change and the Academy of Management's Robert McDonald Award for the Advancement of Organizational Research Methodology. Her book, *Composing Qualitative Research* (with Karen Locke), is in its second edition and has been widely used in doctoral programs across the world.

Heather Graves is associate professor of English and film studies at the University of Alberta, Edmonton, where she teaches academic and technical and business communication. Her research interests include argument in academic discourse, visual rhetoric, and the rhetoric of science. She has published three academic books: *Rhetoric in(to) Science: Style as Invention in Inquiry* in 2005; *Writing Centres, Writing Seminars, Writing Culture: Writing Instruction in Anglo-Canadian Universities*, edited with Roger Graves, in 2006; and *Interdisciplinarity: Thinking and Writing Beyond Borders*, edited with Roger Graves, in 2010; and four writing textbooks: *A Strategic Guide to Technical Communication* with Roger Graves (2007/2012); *The Brief Penguin Handbook* with Lester Faigley and Roger Graves (2008/2011/2014); *The Little Penguin Handbook* with Lester Faigley and Roger Graves (2009/2012/2015); and *Dynamics of Business and Professional Communication: A Case-Based Approach* with Roger Graves (2015).

Melissa E. Graebner is associate professor of management and CBA foundation advisory council centennial fellow at the McCombs School of Business, University of Texas at Austin. She received her PhD in strategy and organizations from the department of management science and engineering at Stanford University. Her work has been published in *Administrative Science Quarterly, Academy of Management Journal, Strategic Management Journal, Strategic Organization*, and *Academy of Management Perspectives*. Her research interests include mergers and acquisitions, strategy in entrepreneurial ventures, and interorganizational trust. She has published two articles on qualitative research methods and received the *Academy of Management Journal*'s Best Paper Award for her 2009 article "Caveat Venditor: Trust

Asymmetries in Acquisitions of Entrepreneurial Firms." Her research has received media coverage in outlets including the *New York Times* Dealbook, Forbes.com, and *Le Monde*.

Stine Grodal is an assistant professor at Boston University. She received her PhD from Stanford University in management science and engineering. Her research focuses on the emergence and evolution of markets, industries, and organizational fields with a specific focus on the role categories and their associated labels play in this process. In particular, her work explores the strategic actions that market participants take to shape and exploit categorical structures. Her work has received numerous awards including the EGOS Best Paper Award and has been published across a variety of journals including *Organization Science*, *Academy of Management Journal*, and *American Sociological Review*.

Michael A. Haedicke is associate professor of sociology at Drake University. His research has examined alternative economic and organizational arrangements within the North American food industry, including natural foods co-ops and ethical certification programs. His book *Growing Markets, Cultivating Change: Conflict and Compromise in the Organic Foods Sector* (forthcoming in the spring of 2016) brings an "inhabited institutions" perspective to bear on the organic sector's history and on the ideologies and activities of its current members.

Tim Hallett is associate professor of sociology at Indiana University. He is most known for his research on inhabited institutions (*American Sociological Review*, 2010; *Theory and Society*, 2006, with Marc Ventresca). His most recent project seeks to build an inhabited institutional approach to understanding professional socialization and the learning of accountability rationales, based on a 2-year ethnographic study of a cohort of students in a masters of public affairs program.

Andrew Hargadon is the Charles J. Soderquist chair in entrepreneurship and a professor of technology management at the Graduate School of Management at University of California, Davis. He is the author of *How Breakthroughs Happen: The Surprising Truth About How Companies Innovate* (Harvard Business School Press, 2003) and *Sustainable Innovation: Build Your Company's Capacity to Change the World* (forthcoming, Stanford University Press). Professor Hargadon's research combines historical methods with qualitative case studies and focuses on the context and management of innovation and entrepreneurship. He received his PhD from the management science and engineering department in Stanford University's School of Engineering and his BS and MS in Stanford University's product design program in the mechanical engineering department.

Ellie Harmon is a PhD candidate in the department of informatics at the University of California, Irvine. Her research focuses on the centrality of ubiquitous personal computing—devices like smartphones, tablets, and laptops—to the mundane practices of daily living and working. She is especially interested in how these devices further entrench a diffuse and systemic ethos of limitlessness—a striving toward, and belief in the possibility of, always doing more. She holds an MS in human-computer interaction and BS in computer science, both from Georgia Tech. See http://ellieharmon.com.

Brooke Harrington is associate professor of economic sociology at the Copenhagen Business School in Denmark. Her research examines the social underpinnings of finance; methodologically, she has specialized in qualitative methods and published several articles on the social psychological dynamics of ethnographic research. Her books include *Pop Finance: Investment Clubs and Stock Market Populism* (Princeton, 2008) and *Deception: From Ancient Empires to Internet Dating* (Stanford, 2009), and she currently has a third book forthcoming with Harvard University Press based on her 7-year ethnography of the elite wealth management profession. Her research has received grants and awards from the National Science Foundation, the Academy of Management, and the American Sociological Association. Professor Harrington holds an MA and PhD in Sociology from Harvard University and a BA in English literature from Stanford University.

Spencer H. Harrison is an assistant professor of management at the Carroll School of Management at Boston College. He received his PhD from Arizona State University. His research explores the interplay of individual strengths and organizational processes, focusing on the concepts of curiosity, hope, passion, and creativity.

Benjamin Hawbaker earned his BS from the U.S. Naval Academy with distinction, and a Naval Engineer's Degree and MS in Engineering and Management from the Massachusetts Institute of Technology. He is currently a PhD student in the organization studies program at Boston College. His research interests include technology, innovation, materiality, entrepreneurship and business ethics.

Paul Hirsch is the James Allen professor of strategy and organization at Northwestern University's Kellogg School of Management. A longtime supporter of qualitative research, he has analyzed accounts of corporate takeovers, interviewed Studs Terkel, and contributed essays on "Qualitative Sociology and Good Journalism As Demystifiers" and "Tales From The Field: Learning From Researchers' Accounts." Hirsch has served as co-editor of the *Journal of Management Inquiry*, a showcase for nontraditional and qualitative research. He is a fellow of the Academy of Management and has been president of the Western Academy of Management.

Ruthanne Huising is an assistant professor in the Desautels faculty of management at McGill University. She received her PhD from the Sloan School of Management at the Massachusetts Institute of Technology. She uses ethnographic methods to analyze organizational change processes and their implications for work, professions, and control.

Candace Jones received her BA from Smith College with honors, and a master's in human resource management (Phi Beta Kappa) and PhD in business administration from the University of Utah. She is a chaired professor in the strategy department at University of Edinburgh Business School. Her research interests include institutional logics, networks, vocabularies and materiality. In 2015, she won an outstanding reviewer award from *AMR*. She has published in top journals, serves on editorial review boards, and is currently division chair for Organization and Management Theory Division, Academy of Management.

Steven J. Kahl is an associate professor at the Tuck School of Business at Dartmouth College. Prior to Tuck, Steve was an assistant professor of organizations and strategy at the University of Chicago Booth School of Business. He received his PhD from the MIT Sloan School of Management. Steve's research examines how new markets emerge through sociological and cognitive perspectives. He examines how markets come to understand new firms and innovations through historically grounded discursive analysis. His research has been published (or is forthcoming) in *Academy of Management Journal, Management Science, Strategic Management Journal, Strategic Entrepreneurship Journal, Advances in Strategic Management*, and *Research in the Sociology of Organizations*.

Sarah Kaplan is professor of strategic management at the Rotman School of Management, University of Toronto. She is a multimethod researcher exploring how organizations participate in and respond to the emergence of new technologies and fields, with a particular focus on the interpretive processes that shape choice and action. Her studies examine the biotechnology, fiber optics, personal digital assistant, and nanotechnology fields. Most recently, she has turned her attention to the new field emerging at the nexus of gender and finance. She received her PhD from MIT's Sloan School of Management and previously served on the faculty of the Wharton School, University of Pennsylvania, where she remains a senior fellow. She is senior editor at *Organization Science*, guest editor for the special issue on new research methods for the *Strategic Management Journal*, and formerly associate editor for the *Academy of Management Annals*.

Rakesh Khurana is the Marvin Bower professor of leadership development at Harvard Business School and professor of sociology, Harvard University. His research focuses on the elite labor markets, institutions, and networks.

Glen E. Kreiner is associate professor of management and organization in the Smeal College of Business at The Pennsylvania State University. He received his PhD from Arizona State University. His research focuses on identity-related challenges and opportunities as experienced at the organizational, professional, and individual levels. Primarily a grounded theorist, he examines linkages between identity and such topics as work–home dynamics, stigma, dirty work, emotions, ethics, and workers with disabilities. At work, he enjoys evangelizing the virtues of qualitative research methods and the power of positive identity. Outside of work he qualitatively enjoys his positive identities of husband, parent, gardener, and musical theatre fan.

Christina Kyprianou is a PhD candidate in strategic management at the McCombs School of Business, University of Texas at Austin. Her research focuses on strategy making in entrepreneurial firms and the role of customers, users, advisors and other external stakeholders in this process. Her dissertation examines the strategies that support the creation and growth of peer-to-peer marketplaces, and in particular, how early-stage strategies leverage marketplace participants' knowledge and voluntary efforts as growth resources. She has presented her work at conferences such as the Academy of Management, the Strategic Management Society, and the European Group of Organization Studies.

Rodney Lacey is an assistant professor of practice at the Goizueta Business School at Emory University. He received his PhD from Northwestern University in organization behavior and sociology in 2000. One of his main scholarly interests is in the further development of set-theoretic and comparative methods in general, and QCA in specific. He has co-authored research on the use of QCA with large-N datasets in the field of strategy and the use of QCA in comparative multilevel research. He has also worked with a team of QCA scholars to provide professional development workshops on the use of QCA for the last decade.

Lianne Lefsrud is an assistant professor of engineering safety and risk management at the University of Alberta. She uses mixed methods to study the actors' use of persuasive language and visuals to shape conceptions of technology, the environment, and regulation. Her work has won the EGOS Best Paper Award and Most Read from *Organization Studies*. As a personal reminder of the power of images: "I know this to be good art, for it causes me to stand erect and feel equal to high and splendid braveries" (Emily Murphy).

Natalia Levina has received her PhD in information technology from MIT's Sloan School of Management (2001) and is an associate professor at New York University Stern School of Business. She uses practice theory to understanding how people span organizational, professional, cultural, and other boundaries in the process of building and using new technology and the social dynamics that ensures. Her current research focuses on open innovation and crowdsourcing. She has been active contributor to the research methods discussions. She has co-founded the Association of Information Systems (AIS) special interest group on grounded theory method and has co-edited the special issue of the *European Journal of Information Systems* on grounded theory. She frequently leads seminars on philosophical underpinnings of qualitative methods and on pragmatic issues in conducting fieldwork. Her recent interest has been in combining quantitative and qualitative data within the realm of grounded theorizing, which is a topic she has discussed in a forthcoming paper in the *Organizational Research Methods* journal. Her research appeared in *Information Systems Research, MIS Quarterly, Organization Science*, and *Academy of Management Journal*, among others. She serves as a senior editor of *Information Systems Research* and on the editorial board of *Information and Organization*.

Noel Lindsay is the director of the Entrepreneurship, Commercialisation and Innovation Centre and the academic director of Singapore Operations, The University of Adelaide, where he is the professor of entrepreneurship and commercialisation. Noel's research embraces both business and social entrepreneurship. More recently, he has been involved in evaluative projects that involve the use of technology including 3-D virtual-learning environments to assist socially and economically disadvantaged and high-functioning intellectually disabled young people to engage in more entrepreneurial behavior. Within this context, he has found longitudinal studies to be particularly useful in providing insight into behavioral variables that have a tendency to be changeable over time and/or after being exposed to particular interventions.

Reut Livne-Tarandach is an assistant professor of management at the University of Oregon. She received her BA in behavioral science from Ben-Gurion University, her MSc in organization research from the Technion Israel Institute of Technology, and a PhD in organizational studies from Boston College. Her research explores the phenomenon of re-emergence within and of organizations, a paradox of learning that requires individuals, teams, and/or organizations to simultaneously build on and transcend their past. Her research has been published in outlets such as the *Journal of Academy of Management, Journal of Organizational Behavior*, and *Research in Organizational Change and Development*.

Karen Locke is the W. Brooks George professor of business administration at the College of William and Mary's school of business. She joined the faculty there in 1989 after earning her PhD in organizational behavior from Case Western Reserve University. Dr. Locke's work focuses on developing a sociology of knowledge in organizational studies and on the use of qualitative research for the investigation of organizational phenomena. Her work appears in journals such as *Academy of Management Journal, Organization Science, Journal of Organizational Behavior, Journal of Management Inquiry, Organizational Research Methods*, and *Studies in Organization, Culture and Society*. In addition, she authored *Grounded Theory in Management Research* and co-authored *Composing Qualitative Research* (with Karen Golden-Biddle). She is a recipient of the Academy of Management's Robert McDonald Award for the Advancement of Organizational Research Methodology.

Courtney R. Masterson is a PhD candidate at the University of Illinois at Chicago's department of managerial studies. Prior to joining UIC's PhD program, Courtney spent 10 years in marketing and communications, working with organizations to address issues related to corporate reputation and stakeholder engagement. During this time, she also developed a deep curiosity for the societal impact of businesses. Building upon these interests, Courtney currently draws upon qualitative and quantitative methods to examine issues of justice, ethics, and inequality in organizations.

Michael Mauskapf is a doctoral candidate at Northwestern University's Kellogg School of Management, where his research employs and develops organizational theories to understand cultural products, organizations, and industries. Trained first as a music historian at the University of Pennsylvania

(BA) and the University of Michigan (MA, PhD), he has presented his research at national meetings of the Academy of Management and the American Musicological Society, and his work has been published in scholarly journals and industry outlets. His dissertation utilizes both quantitative and qualitative methods to study innovation, influence, and competition dynamics in the production and consumption of popular music.

Melissa Mazmanian is an assistant professor in the department of informatics at the Donald Bren School of Information and Computer Sciences at the University of California, Irvine. Dr. Mazmanian's interests revolve around on the use of communication technologies and workflow systems in personal and organizational contexts. She is currently engaged in ethnographic research that examines how busy professionals and their families balance work and life and negotiate communication technologies during personal time. Melissa has published in the *Academy of Management Journal, Organization Science, MIS Quarterly*, and the ACM Computer Human Interaction and Computer Supported Cooperative Work conferences. She earned a PhD in organization studies from the MIT Sloan School of Management and a master's in information economics, management and policy from the University of Michigan, School of Information.

Chad Michael McPherson is a doctoral candidate in sociology at the University of Iowa. His research interests include the influence of institutional demands on local organizational decision making, how the study of institutional logics can be forwarded by examining micro-level interactions and practices, how organizations manage institutional complexity and competing institutional demands, how workgroups made up of multiple professions and different professionals collaborate and accomplish collective action and, of course, qualitative methods. His dissertation examines the role and influence of trustees of nonprofit colleges and universities, as professionals and outsiders; what it means to "govern" in higher education; and the ways in which external pressures bleed into higher education through trustees' decision making.

Mike Metcalfe's main expertise is in managerial problem solving. He has published extensively on this topic. His pragmatic pluralism comes from a lifetime of engaging with change from the contraction of the British Empire through the IT revolution, to careers in the Merchant Navy, being a British Army Parachute Regiment Reservist; working in industry and government; and as a lecturer at Universities in England, New Zealand, and Australia. At one time, he was a senior policy adviser to the deputy premier and treasurer of South Australia.

Anca Metiu is a professor of management at ESSEC Business School. She earned her PhD from the Wharton School of the University of Pennsylvania, and her MBA from the University of Illinois at Urbana-Champaign. Her research examines collaboration, problem solving, and communication processes in collocated and distributed teams. Some of her current research projects examine the role of written communication in virtual collaboration, the process of knowledge transformation in a development context, and the gender dynamics in the free and open source software community. Her book (with Anne-Laure Fayard), *The Power of Writing and Organizational Communication: From Letters to Online Interactions*, appeared in 2012. Her research has been published in the leading management journals: *Administrative Science Quarterly, Organization Science, Organization Studies*, and *Oxford Review of Economic Policy*. She is a senior editor at *Organization Studies* and a member of the editorial board of *Organization Science*.

Siobhan O'Mahony is a tenured associate professor at the Boston University School of Management and chair of the strategy and innovation department. Professor O'Mahony studies how technical and creative projects and communities organize. In her research, Professor O'Mahony has examined high technology contractors, open source programmers, music producers, scientists and engineers, Internet startups, incubators, and corporate consortiums. She is interested in how people organize for innovation, creativity, and growth without replicating the bureaucratic structures they strive to avoid. Much of her work examines how innovative projects manage the tension between maintaining open, participatory, and pluralistic organizing approaches and preserving project boundaries and contributing to corporate goals. Professor O'Mahony received her PhD in management science and engineering from Stanford University, an MPA from the Cornell Institute of Public Affairs, and a BS in industrial labor relations from Cornell University.

Carsten Østerlund is an associate professor at the iSchool at Syracuse University. His research explores the organization, creation, and use of documents in distributed environments where people's daily practices are characterized by high mobility. He is particularly interested in the interplay between social and material structures and how they together facilitate distributed work, play, and learning. Empirically, he studies these issues through in-depth qualitative studies of everyday work practices in range of settings including health care, citizen science, distributed science teams, and game design. He earned a PhD in management from Massachusetts Institute of Technology and is a former student of UC Berkeley, University of Århus, and University of Copenhagen, Denmark. He has been affiliated with the Work Practice and Technology Group at Xerox PARC. For more information, see: http://carsten.syr.edu.

Nelson Phillips is professor of strategy and organizational behaviour at Imperial College London. His research interests include various aspects of organization theory, technology strategy, innovation, and entrepreneurship, often studied from an institutional theory perspective. He has published four books: *Discourse Analysis* with Cynthia Hardy (2002), *Power and Organizations* with Stewart Clegg and David Courpasson (2006), *Technology and Organization* with Graham Sewell and Dorothy Griffiths (2010), and the *Oxford Handbook of Innovation Management* with David Gann and Mark Dodgson (2014). He is also the editor-in-chief of the *Journal of Management Inquiry*.

Michael G. Pratt received his PhD from the University of Michigan and is the O'Connor Family professor in the management and organization department at Boston College. Mike has been conducting and publishing qualitative research in our field for about two decades, and his ethnography "The Good, the Bad, and the Ambivalent . . ." was named to a list of the 17 "most interesting publications in the organizational and management literature from the past 100 years" in an *Academy of Management Journal* editorial board survey. Mike's qualitative research has not only appeared in our field's top journals, but he also evaluates qualitative research for such journals. He was the inaugural qualitative research associate editor at *AMJ*, and he currently plays a similar role at the *Administrative Science Quarterly*.

Davide Ravasi is professor of strategic and entrepreneurial management at the Cass Business School, London. His research examines interrelations between organizational identity, culture, and strategy in times of change, and how discursive and material artifacts influence sensemaking. He is interested more generally in cultural processes influencing how new objects and new practices come to be, and whether and how they are adopted by individuals and organizations. He received his PhD in management from Bocconi University.

Shawna Malvini Redden received her PhD from Arizona State University and is an award-winning author and teacher who specializes in organizational communication research, teaching, and consulting. She studies a constellation of organizational issues including sensemaking, identity, emotion, organizational change, and workplace wellness. When she's not instructing classes at Sacramento

State University or researching with the Center for Applied Behavioral Health Policy at Arizona State University, she can be found working on her first book *101 Pat-downs*, an insider's exploration of the Transportation Security Administration based upon her dissertation research. In addition to academic writing, she maintains a blog called "The Bluest Muse," where she writes about life, cooking, attempts at gardening, and her pursuit of a pilot's license.

Violina Rindova is the Zlotnick Family chair in entrepreneurship and the Herb Kelleher chair in entrepreneurship at the McCombs School of Business, University of Texas at Austin. Her research focusing on the sociocognitive processes through which firms build competitive advantage, create intangible assets, and discover and shape new market opportunities has been published in the premier journals in management. She is the recipient of Thought Leadership Award from the Entrepreneurship Division of the Academy of Management and a best paper award from *Strategic Organization*. She received her PhD from New York University.

Kristie M. Rogers is an assistant professor of organizational behavior at the University of Kansas, School of Business. Her research focuses on identity, respect, and stigma in organizations. She greatly enjoys qualitative field research, especially in unconventional organizational settings. Most notably, Kristie led a longitudinal qualitative study of respect and identity in an organization that employs inmates inside a prison. Kristie earned her PhD from the W.P. Carey School of Business at Arizona State University.

Elizabeth D. Rouse is an assistant professor of organizational behavior at Boston University School of Management. She received her PhD from Boston College. Her research focuses on creativity at work to understand the role of social interactions in the creative process and how creative workers psychologically attach to and detach from the products they make.

Sara L. Rynes is the John Murray professor of management and organizations in the University of Iowa's Tippie College of Business. Her research interests are the academic-practice gap, management education, recruitment, and compensation. She was editor-in-chief for *The Academy of Management Journal* from 2005 to 2007. She is a fellow of the Academy of Management, the American Psychological Association, the Management Education Research Institute, and the Society for Industrial and Organizational Psychology. She received the Academy of Management's Herbert Heneman Career Achievement Award for Research in Human Resource Management in 2006 and the 2011 Society of Human Resource Management's Michael Losey Human Resource Management Career Research Award. She earned her PhD in industrial relations from the University of Wisconsin–Madison.

Michael Sauder is associate professor of sociology at the University of Iowa and the editor of *Contemporary Sociology*. His research interests include organizational status, the effects of quantification, and the processes by which third-party assessments influence organizational activity.

Steve Sawyer is on the faculty of Syracuse University's School of Information Studies and is a research fellow at the Center for Technology and Information Policy. His research focuses on the sociotechnical relationships among changing forms of work and organizing enabled through uses of information and communication technologies. This is done through detailed field-based studies of scientific collaborators, software developers, real estate agents, police officers, organizational technologists, and other information-intensive work settings. Sawyer's work is published in a range of venues and supported by funds from the National Science Foundation, IBM, Corning, and a number of other public and private sponsors. Prior to returning to Syracuse, Steve was a founding faculty member of the Pennsylvania State University's College of Information Sciences and Technology. He earned his doctorate from Boston University in 1995.

Beth S. Schinoff is a management PhD student in the W.P. Carey School of Business at Arizona State University. Her research focuses on individual and organizational identity, identification, and relationships in organizations. She believes there is great potential in better understanding how the people around us shape who we are as well as how we experience our work.

Sonali K. Shah is an assistant professor of strategy and entrepreneurship at the University of Illinois at Urbana-Champaign. Drawing on rich, primary source data her research examines new forms of organizing for innovation and the emergence of these forms of organizing. In one stream of research, she examines collaborative models of innovation development by users, focusing on the interplay between social structure, individual motivation and behavior, and innovation outcomes. In another stream, she examines the differential benefits of knowledge drawn from use, employment, and academic research on the strategies and performance of both startup and incumbent firms. These streams are coming together in a project examining the Maker Movement and startups emerging from makerspaces. She has examined these patterns in the software, medical device, scientific instrument, sports equipment, and juvenile products industries. Her research has been recognized with an Alfred P. Sloan Foundation Fellowship. She holds a PhD in management from MIT's Sloan School of Management.

Sarika Sharma is a third-year doctoral student at Syracuse University and an eScience fellow at the Institute for Museum and Library Services. Her research focuses on the long-term digital preservation of cultural and scientific artifacts, the governance of knowledge commons, and information and communications technology in scientific work. She earned a master's degree in library and information studies at University of Pittsburgh and her undergraduate degree from the University of Wisconsin–Madison.

Susan S. Silbey is the Leon and Anne Goldberg professor of sociology and anthropology, School of Humanities, Arts and Social Sciences and professor of behavioral and policy sciences at Sloan School of Management at MIT. She is interested in the governance, regulatory, risk management, and audit processes in complex organizations.

Ileana Stigliani is assistant professor of design and innovation at the innovation and entrepreneurship department of Imperial Business School, London. Her current research focuses on how material artifacts and practices influence cognitive processes—including sensemaking and sensegiving, and perceptions of organizational and professional identities—within organizations. She received her PhD in management from Bocconi University.

Scott Snook is the MBA class of 1958 senior lecturer of business administration at Harvard Business School. His research focuses on authentic leadership and development.

Jaime Snyder is an assistant professor at the University of Washington's Information School. Dr. Snyder's research focuses on the visual representation of information in social and interactive contexts, including ethics and values in the design of visualizations. In examining visualization activities as sociotechnical practice, her work addresses issues of representation, communication, and agency related to visual communication technologies. Snyder has explored the ways in which the visual representation of digital trace data can be used as an elicitation technique in ethnographic research. She also recently completed a collaborative study examining dynamics of automatic disclosure and self-revelation resulting from the visual display of biosensor data through personal informatics systems. Snyder received a PhD in information science and technology from Syracuse University and an MFA in Visual Art from Stanford University. Snyder recently completed a a 2-year postdoctoral research fellowship at the School of Information Studies, Syracuse University, and a 1-year postdoctoral research appointment with Dr. Geri Gay in the Interaction Design Lab at Cornell University.

Silviya Svejenova is professor of leadership and innovation at the department of organization, Copenhagen Business School, Denmark. Silviya's research is on organizing and managing for creativity and innovation, with emphasis on creative industries and power structures. She has examined the work and careers of creatives and executives, the emergence of novelty, and the role of entrepreneurs and business models in it. Her current work is on the transformation of executive power structures and on the visual and material dimensions of innovation in the creative industries. At present, she is the chair of EGOS, the European Group of Organizational Studies.

Madeline Toubiana is a PhD candidate at the Schulich School of Business at York University. Her research focuses on individual and organizational responses to complexity and how complexity influences processes of change, development, and agency. She is specifically interested in using qualitative methodology to connect macro-level institutional constructs to the actors inhabiting those institutional spaces, such as prison contexts and former inmates who once inhabited them.

Sarah J. Tracy is a professor and co-director of the Transformation Project in the Hugh Downs School of Human Communication at Arizona State University–Tempe. She studies stressful workplace issues such as burnout, work–life balance, emotional labor, and workplace bullying, as well as positive types of communication such as compassion, engagement, and generosity. She has provided qualitative insight on correctional officers, cruise ship activity directors, 911 call takers, and medical staff, and she is the author of *Qualitative Research Methods* (Wiley-Blackwell). Her favorite courses to teach include "Communication and the Art of Happiness," "Emotion and Organizations," and "Advanced Qualitative Research Methods." Sarah aims to develop students' on-the-court practice in their work, scholarship, and life, where people not only learn *about* but also learn *to be*. In her free time, she practices yoga, enjoys her partner's killer sense of humor, and creates tasty Crock-Pot concoctions.

Špela Trefalt is an assistant professor of organizational behavior at the School of Management at Simmons College. Her predominantly qualitative inductive research examines individuals' approaches and experiences in combining their work and life outside of work, with a particular focus on the role of interpersonal relationships in this process. Her research includes publications in *Academy of Management Journal*, *European Management Journal*, *Journal of Management Education*, and *Journal of Business Ethics Education*. She earned her doctorate from the Harvard Business School, her MBA from the University of Kansas, and her BA in law from the University of Ljubljana, Slovenia. Špela is also a coach, certified by the Coaches Training Institute and the International Coaching Federation.

John Van Maanen is the Erwin Schell professor of organization studies in the Sloan School of Management at MIT. He is an ethnographer of occupations and organizations focusing on work socialization practices, careers, and cultures. The settings in which he has worked include police organizations, fisheries, educational institutions, Disneyland, and business firms. Van Maanen is the author of numerous articles and books including, most recently, *Tales of the Field* (University of Chicago Press, 2011, 2nd edition) and, with Edgar Schein, *Career Anchors* (Wiley, 2013, 4th edition). He holds an MS and PhD in social administration for the University of California Irvine and a BA in political science and sociology from California State University at Long Beach.

Emmanuelle Vaast is an associate professor of information systems at the Desautels faculty of management of McGill University. Her research examines how social practices emerge and change with the implementation and use of new technologies and how these new practices are associated with organizational and change dynamics. In particular, she has investigated the learning and knowledge dynamics taking place at different levels (communities and networks of practice, for instance) and the boundary spanning involved in these dynamics when new information systems get implemented and used. Emmanuelle has been fascinated by the new practices and social and societal changes associated with social media, such as blogs and microblogs. Some of the themes she has especially been interested in deal with the emergence of new organizational forms and with new dynamics associated with organizational and occupational identification, cognition, as well as institutional dynamics and mindfulness. Emmanuelle is fascinated by methodological questions. Most of her research so far has been qualitative, relying upon case-based evidence analyzed from an interpretive perspective. She has become increasingly intrigued by the potential for innovation in qualitative and mixed-methods research with electronically collected data.

Ian J. Walsh is an assistant professor of management at the University of Massachusetts Amherst. He received his PhD in organization studies from Boston College. His research focuses on the themes of persistence and regeneration, and it explores the role of social identity, sensemaking, and leadership in experiences of organizational change. His work has appeared in *Academy of Management Journal*, *Human Relations, Management and Organization Review, Corporate Reputation Review*, and *Organizational Dynamics*.

John Weeks is professor of leadership and organizational behavior at IMD in Lausanne, Switzerland. His research focuses on issues of organizational culture, leadership, and change. He is particularly interested in how organizational cultures evolve, and how effective leadership is shaped by culture while at the same time changing the culture. His academic writing has appeared in *Academy of Management Review, Human Relations, Journal of Organizational Behavior*, and *Organization Studies*. His book, *Unpopular Culture: The Ritual of Complaint in a British Bank*, was published in 2004 by University of Chicago Press. His practitioner-oriented work has been published in the *Financial Times, Harvard Business Review, Spectator*, and *Academy of Management Learning and Education*. Before joining IMD in 2007, Professor Weeks spent 11 years at INSEAD in Fontainebleau, France. He holds a PhD in management from the MIT Sloan School of Management, an MPhil in Management from Oxford University, and a B.A. in computer science from the University of California, Berkeley.

Matt Willis is a doctoral candidate in the School of Information Studies at Syracuse University. His dissertation research explores the distributed cognition of health information management and how patients form sociotechnical assemblages that support their care. Other research interests include participatory medicine, sociotechnical health-care systems, computer-supported cooperative work, digital infrastructures, social shaping of technology, and video game design and development. Matthew received his master's degree in health communication from the department of communication at the University of New Mexico. He has been affiliated with interdisciplinary research groups at both the Center for Alcoholism, Substance Abuse, and Addictions and at Sandia National Laboratories.

Tammar B. Zilber is an associate professor of organization theory at the Jerusalem School of Business Administration of Hebrew University, Israel. She studies the ideational and micro-level dynamics of institutional processes.

Part I
Introduction, History, and Context of Qualitative Methods

1

Introduction

In Search of Innovative Pathways and Methods in Qualitative Research

Kimberly D. Elsbach and Roderick M. Kramer

It is our pleasure to introduce this collection of 43 original essays, all of which focus on the most innovative qualitative methods currently in use in the organizational sciences. This is the first handbook to provide a comprehensive compilation and overview of the latest innovative approaches to qualitative research specifically aimed at organizational scholars.

Inspiration for the Volume

There were several sources of inspiration that motivated this volume. First and foremost was a thoughtful and provocative article by Jean Bartunek, Sara Rynes, and Duane Ireland that appeared in the *Academy of Management Journal* in 2006. This article published a list of the 17 most *interesting* organizational papers published in the last 100 years. These papers were identified by *Academy of Management Journal* board members—all of whom are leading organizational scholars cognizant of the best work being done in their respective areas. A total of 67 board members nominated 160 articles as exceptionally interesting; those articles that received two or more nominations were deemed the most interesting. Of these exceptional articles, 12 (71%) involved qualitative methods.

This result strongly mirrors our own experience as organizational researchers. Although both of us have used a variety of methods in our organizational research (ranging from experimental lab studies and surveys to computer-based, agent simulations), our favorite studies by far have been our qualitative studies (including those we have done together). One of the qualities we have come to most appreciate, even cherish, about qualitative research is the sense of discovery and the opportunity for genuine intellectual surprise. Rather than merely seeking to confirm a preordained hypothesis or "nail down" an extrapolation drawn from the extant literature, our inductive studies, we found, invariably opened up exciting, unexpected intellectual doors and pointed us toward fruitful empirical paths for further investigation. In short, if life is largely all about the journey rather than destination, as the adage asserts, we've found qualitative research most often gave us a road we wanted to follow.

Together, then, our own experiences, along with the findings of Bartunek, Rynes, and Ireland, led us to wonder about the use of qualitative methods to produce such an overrepresentation of stimulating and thought-provoking papers. In particular, we were interested in learning more about how purveyors of qualitative methods used innovative approaches to data collection, design, analysis, and interpretation on the way to their discoveries.

To help us pursue this objective, we enlisted the aid of over 80 scholars—each an expert in a particular qualitative method or approach. These scholars, who include both seasoned veterans of the methodology as well as those new to the practice, represent the cutting edge in qualitative organizational research. Each of these experts has published empirical articles using his or her particular methods, and, as a collection, these articles are at the vanguard of new and creative methodological approaches that have not (yet) been recognized in the mainstream literature. Thus, they are uniquely suited to provide insight on how qualitative methods can best serve those who, like them, seek pathways to cool ideas and interesting papers.

Organization of the Volume

The volume is organized around a variety of broad, major themes suggested to us by the contributors. These include innovations in *research settings*, *research designs*, *forms of data*, *data collection*, *data analysis*, and *multimethod approaches*. The volume also includes an introductory section providing a rich *history and context* for these methods, as well as a final chapter outlining the *challenges and opportunities* facing qualitative researchers in the years to come. We briefly describe these book sections next.

The history and context of qualitative organizational research. This section includes two chapters that set the stage for the volume by providing up-to-date accounts of how and where qualitative methods have been used in organizational scholarship. Chapter 2, by Rynes and Bartunek, picks up where their original *AMJ* article left off and provides convincing evidence that qualitative methods continue to produce some of the most innovative and interesting papers in organizational research. Chapter 3, by Mauskapf and Hirsch, provides a detailed historical account of the trajectory of qualitative methods, reflecting trends in opportunities, agendas, and technologies available to organizational scholars. Both of these chapters help to validate the notion that qualitative methods do, in fact, produce cool ideas and interesting papers. The following sections of the book illustrate the specific ways in which that may be done.

Innovative research settings. This section includes six chapters that describe how researchers may leverage innovative research settings through qualitative methods. Chapter 4, by Chen, examines the use of extreme cases in qualitative research, addressing some common criticisms of their use and providing guidance in how best to leverage them in developing theory. Chapter 5, by Fayard, Van Maanen, and Weeks, explores the use of corporate settings for conducting contract ethnography (i.e., ethnography that is sponsored by the corporation being studied) and argues that the entanglements that arise from such arrangements (e.g., diverging interests of ethnographer and corporation) may actually provide unique insights and open up innovative ways of doing ethnography. Chapter 6, by Snook and Khurana, describes how the elite business school is an apt setting for studying leaders (whom they call "elites") and may fill important gaps in our understanding of how and why leaders act. Chapter 7, by Rogers, Toubiana, and DeCelles, examines unconventional research contexts (e.g., prisons) and discusses how some "less objective" approaches to data collection (such as feeling emotion and showing encouragement) might be useful in gaining insight in these settings. Chapter 8, by Walsh and Bartunek, discusses the value in studying novel phenomena (i.e., phenomena that one encounters that currently are undefined or unexplored—such as the authors' encounters with organizations that have an "afterlife") and provides a set of tools for gaining the most from such studies. Finally, Chapter 9, by Zilber, provides an ethnographic technique for examining organizational fields (i.e., the social space between organizations and societies), which should help researchers gain insight about this elusive, interorganizational phenomena. Together, these chapters provide guidance to researchers studying problems that are often only observable in unique (and at times, intractable) research contexts.

Innovative research designs. This section includes nine chapters that focus on creative research designs that may be used with qualitative methods. Chapter 10, by Haedicke and Hallet, describes how qualitative research designs may be the key to uncovering the recursive relationships identified by researchers of "inhabited institutionalism." They identify how a move toward inductive research is critical to understanding the *process* of institutionalism that defines this new perspective. Chapter 11, by Anderson, illustrates how a multipronged research design that includes a number of qualitative data collection and analysis techniques (e.g., narrative analysis, visual sorting, and repertory grid analysis) may be ideally suited to the study of entrepreneurial firms that are highly dynamic and informal. Chapter 12, by Hargadon, outlines how the construction of microhistorical case studies (i.e., case studies of the thoughts and actions of individuals in the past) may be an effective research design for exploring larger historical phenomena (e.g., how breakthroughs unfolded in scientific communities). Chapter 13, by Harrington, describes how the research design of "immersion ethnography" may be effective, where less intensive methods fail, in studying the behavior of elites (e.g., CEOs) in organizations. Chapter 14, by Evans, Huising, and Silbey, discusses how research designs that involve "team ethnography" (i.e., in-place data collection by a team of individuals) may improve descriptive, interpretive, and theoretical validity beyond that achieved through individual ethnography. Chapter 15, by Livne-Tarandach, Hawbaker, Lahneman Boren, and Jones, presents a framework for using Qualitative Comparative Analysis (i.e., a method of comparing numerous case studies or dealing with large amounts of qualitative data) as a research design to provide validity to qualitative findings and to connect qualitative and quantitative data in theory development. Chapter 16, by Bechky and O'Mahony, examines how research designs involving comparative qualitative field studies (i.e., multiple studies of the same general phenomena across distinct contexts) may be exceptionally useful for developing novel insight about processes, improving the generalizability of findings, and linking organizational and institutional processes in theorizing. Chapter 17, by Pratt, prescribes a "circular process" for selecting research questions in the design of qualitative studies, suggesting that research questions do not drive research designs, but rather evolve in a recursive relationship with the selection of real-world problems and research contexts. Finally, Chapter 18, by Binz-Scharf, discusses how a "practice approach" (i.e., a focus on studying doing vs. being) may extend network studies in organizations by forcing researchers to examine both micro- and macro-level dynamics that comprise organizational networks. Together, these nine chapters provide a set of innovative templates for designing research projects that leverage the strengths of qualitative methods.

Innovative forms of data. This section includes five chapters that discuss how qualitative researchers may use unique and innovative forms of data in their studies. Chapter 19, by Anteby, examines how participants' resistance to research inquiries (e.g., through denials, obstructions, and silence in response to research questions) may serve as an important form of data (providing insight about participants that they may not openly disclose) that is not available via quantitative methods. Chapter 20, by Giorgi and Glynn, explores how the aesthetic content of texts (e.g., graphs, illustrations, font choice) provides important information—separate from the content of text itself—based on its level of coupling or alignment with the text content. Chapter 21, by Levina and Vaast, discusses how archival data from online communities (e.g., blogs for professional groups or technology designers) may provide a way to develop longitudinal process theory that is free from recollection bias and provides more naturally occurring (vs. more scripted) discourse about events over time. Chapter 22, by Lefsrud, Graves, and Phillips, presents a detailed discussion regarding the use of images (e.g., illustrations and photographs) as data sources for understanding how emotion is generated and strategically used in organizational communication. Finally, Chapter 23, by Tracy and Redden, outlines a method of creating data, relevant to metaphor analysis, by asking participants to craft artistic drawings in response to researcher questions (e.g., What does a leader look like?). As a group, these five chapters provide a set of highly creative avenues for using data forms that may be uniquely available to qualitative researchers.

Innovative data collection. This section includes five chapters that describe innovative techniques for gathering qualitative data. Chapter 24, by Shah and Gorbatai, discusses how the use of "structural sampling" (i.e., sampling across *all* roles involved in a social system vs. sampling only selected actors and roles) may provide a more complete understanding of a social system and its many functions than do traditional sampling techniques. Chapter 25, by Mazmanian, Beckman, and Harmon, presents a framework for collecting data on workers in nonwork settings (e.g., intensive fieldwork engagements at workers' homes with their families) as a means of examining the multiple roles that workers occupy (e.g., colleague, spouse, parent) as well as the relationships between work and nonwork roles. Chapter 26, by Kyprianou, Graebner, and Rindova, outlines a method for collecting "strategic conversation data" (i.e., data about naturally occurring interpersonal interactions that are focused on strategic issues) as a means of gaining insight about the links between strategic behavior and cognition. Chapter 27, by Rouse and Harrison, presents a method for attaining "data expansion" (i.e., the use of multiple sources of data to reveal divergence and, thus, gain new insights about a phenomena) that may help scholars to develop more sophisticated theory by complementing their findings of data convergence. Finally, Chapter 28, by Svejenova, describes a technique for capitalizing on serendipitous opportunities in data collection by following up on interesting leads, negotiating entrance to intriguing and relevant roles, and "trespassing" into tangentially related contexts as opportunities arise. Together, these chapters extend options for data collection beyond the already rich set of contexts and forms available to qualitative researchers, and they showcase the truly innovative nature of data collection occurring among our colleagues.

Innovative data analysis. This largest section of the volume includes 11 chapters outlining innovative approaches to data analysis that may be used by qualitative researchers. Chapter 29, by Gersick, relates the value of an "inventive" approach to data analysis (i.e., not using tried and true methods as a matter of course) and describes how this approach led her to develop an innovative visual mapping technique for data analysis. Chapter 30, by Balan, Balan-Vnuk, Metcalfe, and Lindsay, explains the use of "concept mapping" software for qualitative data analysis and demonstrates how this method may provide similar results to NVivo analysis while offering some advantages over this more common methodology (e.g., a visual representation of the data, time savings, and no requirement for a priori identification of categories). Chapter 31, by Corley, Masterson, and Schinoff, offers a detailed look at the use of collaborative analysis (i.e., analysis by a team of researchers) and suggests how two specific types of collaborations (i.e., advisor–student and researcher–practitioner) may produce more innovative insights through cognitive, emotional, and physiological processes. Chapter 32, by Kahl and Grodal presents a framework for using multilevel discourse analysis (i.e., a method of identifying relationships across texts—such as texts from members of an emerging scientific community—by decomposing them into their sematic relationships) as a means of utilizing large amounts of textual data in longitudinal studies. Chapter 33, by Kreiner, describes the use of a *tabula geminus*, or twin slate, approach to data coding, which involves having two co-authors simultaneously code and interpret data while overtly and reflexively drawing on both data and theory during analysis. Chapter 34, by Lacey and Cohen, examines how Qualitative Comparative Analysis (discussed earlier in Chapter 15 as a research design tactic) may be used, specifically, in support of narrative data analysis through its ability to numerically describe and illustrate qualitative data. Chapter 35, by Locke, Feldman, and Golden-Biddle, explicates a "live coding" process in which the coding process and the data mutually shape each other (e.g., coders arrive at multiple meanings for codes and learn about their data through the evolution of code meanings), which contributes to a more organic and trial-and-error approach to theorizing. Chapter 36, by Metiu and Fayard, describes a set of innovative techniques (e.g., looking at evolution in language and definitions of events over time) for gleaning context information about phenomena that are primarily evident in online data (e.g., online gaming communities, open source software communities). Chapter 37, by Østerlund, Snyder, Sawyer, Sharma, and Willis, explores the study of distributed work through the analysis of documents and prescribes a number of practices (e.g., when analyzing documents, it is best to view them as snapshots in time rather than as stable information artifacts) that may help researchers gain reliable insights from this type of data source. Chapter 38, by Trefalt and Besharov, discusses the roles and benefits of nonauthor collaborators (e.g., colleagues, informants, editors) in analyzing and building theory from qualitative data and offers tips for how to leverage the help of these unsung heroes. Finally, Chapter 39, by Kramer, introduces the practice of doing post-mortem post-mortems (i.e., second looks at case studies that examined historical events, such as the Bay of Pigs fiasco) and describes some useful methods (e.g., adding newly acquired empirical evidence to the original evidence to get a more complete picture of the case) for conducting such second-look analyses. In sum, this important section of the volume provides a number of never-seen-before insights from the experts about how to tackle tough analysis problems and further leverage the value of qualitative data.

Innovations in multimethod approaches. This section of the book includes four chapters discussing the combination of multiple methodological approaches (both qualitative and quantitative) in organizational research and theory building. Chapter 40, by Kaplan, offers a number of strategies for integrating qualitative and quantitative methods in a single research design, including sequential approaches (e.g., using qualitative methods to develop hypotheses that are tested via quantitative methods) and simultaneous approaches (e.g., quantifying qualitative data for analysis). Chapter 41, by McPherson and Sauder, provides a methodology for quantifying qualitative data through counting the amount and type of data collected (e.g., hours of interviews, categories of interviews) or the prevalence, frequency, or pattern of specific instances (e.g., most common behavior) and discusses the potential benefits and risks of adopting such an approach. Chapter 42, by Stigliani and Ravasi, presents a framework for combining a number of different qualitative methodologies (i.e., ethnography, grounded theory building, and visual narrative analysis) that may be useful in the study of collective cognition in organizations and illustrates this framework through a description of several empirical studies of designers. Finally, Chapter 43, by Galunic, examines a number of published papers using hybrid methodologies that combine inductive (mostly qualitative) and deductive (mostly quantitative) approaches to research and comments on why these exemplars were especially effective in their hybrid approach. Together, the chapters in this section provide strategies for researchers seeking to take on the full benefits of using both qualitative and quantitative methods.

Challenges and opportunities in qualitative organizational research. In the final section of the volume, qualitative research pioneer Steve Barley comments on some of the challenges and opportunities facing today's qualitative researchers, particularly those engaged in ethnography. In Chapter 44, Barley relates his discontent with the current state of ethnographic research and urges researchers to take a different path. He focuses on several unsettling trends in our field, including (a) demands for a uniform approach to ethnography, including specification of a right and wrong way to collect and analyze ethnographic data; (b) the expectation that ethnographers should be willing to reframe their papers around completely different theories because reviewers think the data is about X and not Y (even though they did not collect or analyze the data); and (c) an overreliance on interviews versus observation as a data source. Barley describes how each of these trends pulls us further away from the core benefits of ethnography—that is, telling stories about life *in situ*—and suggests that ethnographers resist pressures to conform to these trends. This chapter makes clear that the innovations described in this book should be implemented with an eye on both the future and the past, lest we forget why we got interested in qualitative methods in the first place.

Use of the Volume

We intend this handbook as a valuable reference for students, scholars, educators, and managers, including doctoral students and faculty in the fields of anthropology, organizational behavior, organizational theory, social psychology, and sociology. We also think the handbook will also appeal to scholars in education, political science, public policy, and history who study organizations and/or institutions using qualitative methodologies.

We hope this handbook will accomplish more, however, than the simple assembling of these diverse methodologies in one volume as a reference book. We hope it will accomplish something *generative*. Specifically, by placing these articles together—in a sense, side-by-side, for the discerning reader—we believe the handbook will allow researchers to see more clearly the range of options available to them as they approach their own research interests and opportunities. Viewed in aggregate, the chapters herein provide powerful contrasts as well as commonalities that may point creative researchers toward significant lacunae in the literature with respect to extant methodologies. Finally, we believe, by placing all of these methodologies together in one volume, there is the possibility that researchers may identify some exciting new prospects for additional, innovative combinatorial or hybrid approaches to future qualitative studies.

We view methodological innovation, broadly construed, as just as important as theory development in the organizational sciences. This is especially true because advances in technology, changing laws and reporting requirements, and shifting public concerns and interests guarantee that new forms of data (their collection, modes of storage, transmission, etc.) will continue to present themselves. Along similar lines, we expect that as new organizational forms and problems emerge to engage scholars' interests, so should there be a parallel, evolving process in which new forms of data collection and analysis become available to researchers. As the organizational world evolves, so must the methodologies used to study it. Our hope, in short, is that this handbook will help stimulate that evolution.

Reference

Bartunek, J.M., Rynes, S.L., & Ireland, R.D. (2006). What makes management research interesting, and why does it matter? *Academy of Management Journal, 49*, 9–15.

2

Qualitative Research
It Just Keeps Getting More Interesting!

Sara L. Rynes and Jean M. Bartunek

We developed our curiosity about interesting research—and particularly, interesting qualitative research—in a roundabout way. In 2004, each of us had just taken on a significant editorial role with the *Academy of Management Journal* (*AMJ*)—Rynes as incoming editor and Bartunek as incoming chair of the *AMJ* advisory committee. Prior to becoming editor, Rynes conducted a survey of the editorial board, asking (among other things) what board members thought was the single most important change to make at the journal. The most frequent answers were varied: accept less formulaic, more innovative research (17%); relax the theory requirement (10%); keep a balanced, broad base of appeal and remain open to all (8%); increase methodological rigor (6%); aim for higher impact and address more socially important issues (5%); and eliminate research notes (5%) (Rynes, 2005).

Noting that the most oft-mentioned category seemed to center on producing research that was somehow more "interesting" than current publications, Bartunek suggested conducting a second survey to see what board members considered to be interesting research, and why. Using a variant of the critical incident methodology, respondents were invited to nominate up to three empirical articles related to management from any academic journal over the past 100 years that they regarded as particularly interesting and to describe what it was about them that they saw as interesting. The results of this survey were published in an *AMJ* Editorial Forum on Interesting Research that featured not only the survey results (Bartunek, Rynes, & Ireland, 2006), but also two essays by authors regarded to have produced particularly interesting research (Barley, 2006; Dutton & Dukerich, 2006).

Fifty-seven percent of respondents indicated that they regarded a chosen article as interesting because it was counterintuitive in some way—it challenged some sort of wisdom, be it folk wisdom, consultant wisdom, or theory, or it produced an "aha" moment. This response was similar to Murray Davis's (1971) influential claim that what makes research interesting is that it challenges some (though not too many) of readers' assumptions. Fifty-seven percent also mentioned characteristics associated with high quality, such as well-crafted theory, strong methods, good fit between theory and methods, or making something complex seem simple and elegant. Good writing (e.g., builds momentum, provides good examples or rich descriptions, is clear and engaging) figured in 48% of responses, while strong theoretical contribution figured in 46%. Two other mentioned characteristics were practical implications (31%) and impact on future research (28%).

Examination of the 17 articles that were nominated as the "most interesting" by at least two board members revealed that nine used solely qualitative methods, five used solely quantitative methods, and the other three included both qualitative and quantitative approaches. This was a rather striking finding, since qualitative papers were dramatically underrepresented in the management and organization science literatures (e.g., only 5% of *AMJ* articles were qualitative at the time of the survey). Another striking finding was that all but one of the most interesting papers had been published in either *Administrative Science Quarterly* (nine articles) or *AMJ* (seven articles). In its guidelines for contributors, *ASQ* had already been placing an emphasis on interesting work (according to Davis's 1971 definition) for several years by the time we conducted our survey, and it appears that this emphasis had paid dividends.

As a result of both of these surveys (Bartunek, et al., 2006; Rynes, 2005), *AMJ* picked up its efforts (which were already underway during Tom Lee's editorship; see, e.g., Gephart, 2004) to encourage more qualitative work. This was done primarily by putting more qualitative researchers on the editorial board and writing a series of editorial essays designed to help authors succeed with qualitative research. When we heard that Kim and Rod were editing this handbook, we proposed to examine how qualitative research has fared at *AMJ* and *ASQ* in the decade since our initial forays into encouraging both qualitative and interesting research. This chapter is the result.

As will become obvious, our investigation has led us to conclude that qualitative research is more prominent, admired, and impactful than it was a decade ago. We document the interest in, and impact of, qualitative research in two primary ways: (1) by reviewing editorial essays and editors' forums appearing in *AMJ*[1] on qualitative research and their citation impact over the past decade, and (2) by documenting the predominance of qualitative research in the annual "best paper" selections at *AMJ* and *ASQ*. We turn first to editorial essays and editors' forums.

Editorial Essays and Editors' Forums on Qualitative Research

One marker of the expanding impact of qualitative research in management and the organization sciences is the number of citations to *AMJ*'s "From the Editors" pieces involving qualitative research and to their two editorial forums (on "Interesting Research" and "The Power of Rich"). Table 2.1 shows citations to the editorial essays involving qualitative research, as well the five invited essays for the editorial forums. As the table makes evident, these essays have had considerable impact.

In the first editorial essay, published under the editorship of Thomas Lee, Robert Gephart (2004) was invited to provide a mini-tutorial on qualitative research for aspiring qualitative researchers and

Table 2.1 Citations to Editorial Essays on Qualitative Research in *AMJ* (2004–2012)

Author & Year	Google Scholar Citations	Web of Science Citations
Gephart 2004	769	198
Suddaby 2006	1,436	363
Bartunek et al. 2006	257	89
Barley 2006	81	35
Dutton & Dukerich 2006	58	22
Eisenhardt & Graebner 2007	5,495	1,519
Siggelkow 2007	1,719	501
Weick 2007	341	103
Pratt 2009	485	152
Bansal & Corley 2011	75	31
Bansal & Corley 2012	70	9

reviewers. His essay covered such topics as the nature of qualitative research and why it is important, the link between alternative theoretical positions and appropriate methodologies, and descriptions of various qualitative methods. These sections were followed by a discussion of common problems observed in qualitative research submissions, as well as possible solutions to these problems. Two years after the publication of Gephart's 2004 essay, the number of submissions to and acceptances of qualitative research at *AMJ* had both increased.

During the first year of Rynes's editorial term, *AMJ*'s editors noticed that one of the most common problems in submitted qualitative manuscripts was that authors inappropriately claimed to have used "grounded theory." To address this issue, Roy Suddaby (2006) was invited to write a follow-up editorial essay. Drawing on Gephart (2004, p. 457), he began by providing a precise description of what grounded theory (GT) *is*: "a practical method for conducting research that focuses on the interpretive process by analyzing the actual production of meanings and concepts used by social actors in real settings" (p. 633). He further indicated that GT, as conceptualized by Glaser and Strauss (1967), was built upon two constructs: constant comparison and theoretical sampling, both of which "violate longstanding positivist assumptions about how the research process should work" (p. 634).

From there, Suddaby proceeded to outline six common misconceptions that he observed as a reviewer of manuscript submissions claiming to use GT methods. Specifically, he asserted that GT is *not*: (1) an excuse to ignore the literature; (2) presentation of raw data; (3) theory testing, content analysis, or word counts; (4) routine application of formulaic techniques to data; (5) perfect; or (6) easy. As editors and observers of top-tier research journals over the past decade, we believe that Suddaby's "What Grounded Theory Is *Not*" essay has had a significant effect in terms of reducing the number of manuscripts erroneously claiming to have applied GT and in motivating authors to seek the kind of closer theoretical and methodological fit recommended by Gephart (2004).

Concomitant with the Bartunek et al. (2006) survey on interesting research, *AMJ* also published two essays by researchers whose qualitative work was regarded as the "most interesting" by board members. In "When I Write My Masterpiece," Stephen Barley offered several thoughts on what makes a paper interesting. Drawing on analogies from rock and roll, he argued that whether or not a paper (or musician) is regarded as interesting is a matter of taste, and that tastes vary widely. He also argued that few if any authors "can will themselves to write interesting papers. . . . The most any scholar can do is describe the broad attributes of papers that he or she has found interesting and then provide examples" (p. 16). With that said, the common denominator of interestingness for Barley is *difference*: "The otherwise diverse papers that I have found interesting over the years have one common denominator: they differed in some significant and striking way from most of the other papers in academic journals. For this reason they captured my attention, like scarlet begonias against a sea of gray" (pp. 16–17).

In the second essay that was deemed most interesting, Jane Dutton and Janet Dukerich (2006) discussed *relational foundations* as an underappreciated underpinning of interesting research. They defined relational foundations as the "set of interaction partners whom one encounters in the course of doing research," such as "co-members of a research team, people whom one is studying, and individuals who are neither researchers nor participants, but who, through their direct or indirect contributions to the research, affect its quality" (p. 21). They go on to describe how various relationships were important to the quality of their landmark paper on the homeless in the Port Authority of New York and New Jersey, and they suggest ways of increasing the relational foundations of one's research. These include allowing oneself to be vulnerable, being genuinely interested in the topic and people, being open to experience, seeking feedback, and being trustworthy and trusting.

The 2006 editor's forum on interesting research was followed with one on "The Power of Rich." This editor's forum grew out of a 2006 professional development workshop (PDW) at the 2006 Academy of Management meeting whose purpose was to try to remedy the paucity of formal instruction in qualitative methods at many universities. According to the PDW's organizers, Diana

Day and J. Peter Murmann, the idea was "to have the best of the best in each of the qualitative methodologies talk about them and to have editors explain the problems they see and possible ways to overcome them" (Rynes, 2007, p. 13). Enthusiasm for the topic was extraordinary, participants overflowed into the hallways, and extra audiovisual equipment was brought in to broadcast to those who couldn't fit into the room.

In "The Generative Properties of Richness," Karl Weick (2007) used his personal experiences in studying firefighters and the teaching methods of zoologist and geologist Jean Louis Rodolphe Agassiz to generate five lessons for building richness: (1) reading builds richness; (2) read with theories in hand because theories increase requisite variety; (3) rich comparisons breed further richness; (4) simple accounts mean you're not paying attention; and (5) adopt an e-prime (saying things without the verb "to be") mindset. He summed up his essay as "an argument for detail, for thoroughness, for prototypical narratives, and an argument against formulations that strip out most of what matters. It is an argument that the power of richness lies in the fact that it feeds on itself in ways that enlarge our understanding of the human condition" (p. 18).

In the second essay, Nicolaj Siggelkow (2007) memorably addressed the question of what makes a case study persuasive. Drawing on a story by neurologist V.S. Ramachandran, he argued that one can address the common "small sample" critique of case research by having a particularly striking case:

> You cart a pig into my living room and tell me that it can talk. I say, "Oh, really? Show me." You snap with your fingers and the pig starts talking. I say, "Wow, you should write a paper about this." You write up your case report and send it to a journal. What will the reviewers say? Will the reviewers respond with "Interesting, but that's just one pig. Show me a few more and then I might believe you"? I think we would agree that that would be a silly response. A single case can be a very powerful example. (p. 20)

He uses a second memorable case—that of Phineas Gage, who had a complete personality change as a result of major damage to his frontal lobe—as an illustration of how single cases can also address the potential criticism of nonrepresentativeness.

He then makes the important point that both of these cases are so striking that they can they can "stand on their descriptive feet." However, with most cases, new conceptual insight is also needed, so Siggelkow spends the rest of the paper talking about three ways that cases can provide insight above and beyond the internal logic of the theoretical insight: (1) by being an exciting way to motivate a research question, (2) by providing inspiration for new ideas, and (3) by providing an illustration of the concept. He then uses two very different cases of his own—Liz Claiborne (Siggelkow, 2001) and Vanguard (Siggelkow, 2002, a best paper winner at *Administrative Science Quarterly*) to illustrate his points.

In another highly influential essay, Kathleen Eisenhardt and Melissa Graebner (2007) address the topic of building theory from multiple cases. They indicate that although theory-building from cases is sometimes seen as subjective,

> well-done theory building from cases is surprisingly "objective," because its close adherence to the data keeps researchers "honest." The data provide the discipline that mathematics does in formal analytic modelling. . . . A particular advantage of theory developed from multiple cases is that it is one of the best (if not the best) of the bridges from rich qualitative evidence to mainstream deductive research. (p. 25)

Despite these strengths, Eisenhardt and Graebner acknowledge that multicase qualitative research sometimes runs into a variety of problems in the journal review phase. These include reviewers who are unfamiliar with or have negative attitudes toward case research, or those who are sympathetic to thick description but have less interest in generalizable theory-building. In light of these challenges, they discuss different ways to justify case-based theory building, explain the advantages of theoretical sampling, and make suggestions for dealing with interview data, presenting one's evidence, and writing the emergent theory. Clearly, this has been a helpful and inspirational essay for many qualitative researchers, having been cited nearly 5,500 times (according to Google Scholar) in less than 8 years!

In "For the Lack of a Boilerplate: Tips on Writing Up (and Reviewing) Qualitative Research," Michael Pratt (2009) homes in on what he believes to be the central problem for inductive qualitative researchers: there is no accepted "boilerplate" for writing up qualitative methods and determining their quality. Based on his own and others' experiences (e.g., Golden-Biddle & Locke, 2007; Pratt, 2008), he describes two "dangerous paths" for qualitative research. The first is having a lack of balance between theory and data—either telling too much about the data while showing too little of it, or showing too much data without sufficiently interpreting it. The second dangerous path is making qualitative research appear quantitative. Again, this can be done in more than one way: for example, using rhetorical tactics that try to make the paper more acceptable to quantitatively oriented reviewers; quantifying qualitative data; and inappropriately mixing inductive and deductive strategies.

To avoid such problems, Pratt provides readers with five pieces of advice: (1) Make sure the methods section includes the basics (why the research is needed, whether you are building or elaborating theory, why you chose the particular context and level of analysis, and how you got from the data to your conclusions); (2) show data in a smart fashion (usually several revisions are necessary before this is achieved); (3) use organizing figures where appropriate; (4) think about telling a story; and (5) consider modeling your style after someone who consistently produces high-quality qualitative research, particularly when you are just beginning.

Most recently, Bansal and Corley produced two editorial essays (2011, 2012) designed to help readers improve their chances of successfully publishing qualitative research. In the first, the two authors/editors (one macro, one micro) carry on a dialog about their personal experiences as qualitative researchers, as well as the evolution of qualitative research at *AMJ*. They note that from 2001 to 2010, the percentage of published *AMJ* articles that were entirely qualitative rose from around 3% to 11%, with the percentage of qualitative submissions in the second half of 2010 coming in at 12%. Thus, qualitative article acceptances appear to be roughly proportionate to their submission rates. Despite these encouraging trends, however, they worry that qualitative manuscripts are perhaps becoming too similarly structured, coded, tabled, graphed, diagrammed, and "propositioned" (to show theoretical contribution). They close by encouraging authors to be as creative as possible and assuring them that editors will support such efforts.

In their second article, Bansal and Corley (2012) focus on the major differences in the requirements for qualitative versus quantitative research and the implications of those differences for authors. First, they argue that qualitative researchers often have to work harder to establish the need for their research, and they suggest that this requirement favors a short, multipurpose front end followed by a long, robust back end. They cite Plowman et al.'s 2007 description of how small changes at an urban church led to radical change as an exemplary piece in this regard. They also recommend a comprehensive, transparent, and personal description of the journey from research initiation to manuscript submission, drawing on Dutton and Dukerich's (1991) examination of the Port Authority's reaction to homelessness as an exemplar. They also suggest creative data displays, citing Gersick's (1989) use of asterisks in a diagram showing each team's transition points in her study of teams completing a creative task. Like Pratt (2009), they recommend creating a two-strand narrative that creates appropriate tension between data and theory (e.g., Elsbach & Kramer, 2003). Finally, they suggest embracing the process, not the plan, of qualitative research, reminding readers that it is a highly iterative process in which submission of the manuscript might best be thought of as just another beginning.

To this point, we have shown that attempts by *AMJ* editors and invited editorial essayists to stimulate the production of high-quality qualitative research have been widely cited and have succeeded in producing more qualitative submissions and acceptances at *AMJ*. We now turn to evidence indicating that over the past decade, qualitative research has continued to be disproportionately recognized as the highest quality research in both *AMJ* and *ASQ*.

Best Papers

An examination of best papers from the *AMJ* and *ASQ* websites shows that over the past 10 years[2], 8 of the 11 best paper winners at *AMJ*[3] were qualitative studies. Similarly, a majority (6 of 10) of best papers at *ASQ* used qualitative methods. Major characteristics of the qualitative award-winning papers are presented in Table 2.2.

Of course, we cannot definitively say that these articles won best paper awards solely, or even primarily, because judges found them "interesting." Other factors such as solid methodology, good writing, and perceived importance of the topic undoubtedly also played a role. However, interestingness would seem to be a prerequisite for making it to the top of a "short list" in two elite journals such as *AMJ* and *ASQ*, especially given *ASQ*'s stated requirements and recent emphasis on interestingness in *AMJ*. Moreover, the table allows us to make some reasoned speculation as to why these articles might be regarded as interesting.

Several current and former editors have made the observation that studying unusual (Barley, 2006) or socially important settings (e.g., Bamberger & Pratt, 2010) can make research more interesting. Table 2.2 shows that many of the research settings of award-winning papers were unusual: Hollywood pitch meetings (Elsbach & Kramer, 2003), acute care settings in British and U.S. health care systems (Ferlie et al., 2005; Klein et al., 2006), establishment of new online publishing ventures (Gilbert, 2005), a declining urban church in a southern U.S. city (Plowman et al., 2007), and spin-off of the top-performing unit of a *Fortune* 100 company (Corley & Gioia, 2004). Some settings were not only unusual, but also likely to grow in importance, such as digital publishing (Gilbert, 2005), multidisciplinary or international professional practices (Ferlie et al., 2005; Smets et al., 2012), extreme action teams (e.g., Klein et al., 2006), and acquisitions of high-tech entrepreneurial ventures (e.g., Graebner, 2009).

As indicated earlier, the characteristic that has most often been associated with interesting research is counterintuitiveness or violation of prior assumptions (e.g., Bartunek et al., 2006; Davis, 1971). Our evaluation of the best papers suggests that many of them clearly contained such violations (column 7 in Table 2.2). For example, Plowman et al. (2007) showed that radical change could emerge through small, incremental changes, and Ferlie et al. (2005) found that high degrees of professionalization do not necessarily speed adoption of scientifically validated innovations. With some papers, however, counterintuitiveness or violation of assumptions were not obvious. However, all the papers produced findings that would be regarded as novel in some way. For example, although it might not be counterintuitive to suggest that having different perspectives on diversity might affect diverse groups' processes and outcomes, Ely and Thomas's (2001) finding to that effect was both new and interesting.

Another finding shown in Table 2.2 (column 4) is that a majority of the best papers pursued theory elaboration rather than theory generation. According to Lee, Mitchell, and Sablynski (1999), theory generation occurs when the inquiry's design produces formal and testable hypotheses. Similarly, according to Eisenhardt (1989), theory building includes shaping hypotheses—a process similar to hypothesis-testing research, but relying more on the judgment of the researcher(s) since there are no statistical tests available (p. 543)—to provide exact tests. Theory elaboration, on the other hand, occurs when preexisting conceptual ideas or a preexisting model drive a study's design (Lee et al., 1999, p. 164). Using these definitions, none of the best papers had the purpose of theory generation! However, we believe this is a rather narrow description of theory generation. As a result, articles in our table that are described as generating theory are ones whose designs did not draw heavily on preexisting concepts or models (e.g., Siggelkow, 2002; Smets et al., 2012). In terms of theory elaboration, some authors explicitly described their papers that way, citing Lee et al.'s definition (e.g.,

Table 2.2 Qualitative Best Paper Winners: *Academy of Management Journal* (2003–2012) and *Administrative Science Quarterly* (2003–2013)

Article	Setting	Research Question	Research Purpose	Methods & Data	Outcomes	Novel or Counterintuitive Findings/Violations of Assumptions	Citations (Google Scholar, Web of Science)
Elsbach & Kramer, *AMJ*, 2003	Hollywood screenwriters' "pitch" meetings	How do experts assess the creativity of unknown writers?	Theory elaboration	Interviews, observation of pitches; archival data	A dual-process social judgment model of the creativity assessment process	Some traits evaluated as positive signals of creativity were not supported by prior empirical evidence	195 84
Ferlie, Fitzgerald, Wood & Hawkins, *AMJ*, 2005	British health care system	Why do evidence-based innovations spread rapidly (or not) in health care?	Theory elaboration	Eight case studies of innovation adoption/ nonadoption in acute care and primary care settings; semistructured interviews	Elaboration of *why* innovation adoption is "messy;" i.e., social and cognitive boundaries between professions impede spread	Counter to previous assumptions, high professionalization does not necessarily speed adoption of scientifically validated innovations	639 269
Gilbert, *AMJ*, 2005	Establishment of U.S. newspapers' online ventures in response to digital publishing	How does perception of threat affect organizational inertia/ action in the face of external change?	Theory elaboration	Eight case studies; interviews, observation, archival documents	Interpretive model of inertia in response to discontinuous external change	Perception of threat produces paradoxical outcomes: reduction in resource rigidity but increase in routine rigidity	604 200
Greenwood & Suddaby, 2006	Emergence of multidisciplinary practices in professional business service firms in Canada	How can actors envision and enact changes to the contexts in which they are embedded?	Theory elaboration	Case study; interviews in three global accounting firms and one global law firm and five types of archival records	Process model of elite institutional entrepreneurship	Counter to prior theory, network centrality of elite institutions can increase, rather than decrease, the possibility of change	1066 390

Table 2.2 Continued

Article	Setting	Research Question	Research Purpose	Methods & Data	Outcomes	Novel or Counterintuitive Findings/Violations of Assumptions	Citations (Google Scholar, Web of Science)
Plowman et al., AMJ, 2007	Urban church in a southern U.S. city	How and why did an initial small change result in unintended radical change?	Theory elaboration	Case study; interviews and archival sources	Complexity theory explanations for emergence of radical change	Radical change emerged in a way not previously theorized (through small, continuous rather than episodic changes)	262 99
Graebner, AMJ, 2009	Buying and selling of entrepreneurial technology firms	How do trust and deception play out in acquisitions?	Theory elaboration	Eight case studies; interviews and archival records	Explanation of how trust and deception coexist among buyers and sellers as a result of asymmetries and errors on both sides	Found asymmetries in dyadic interorganizational trust where symmetries had been previously assumed	105 42
Detert & Edmondson, AMJ, 2011	Decisions to remain silent or speak up in a complex high-technology company	What implicit theories drive self-protective silence among employees?	Theory elaboration	Multiple studies, the first of which employed exploratory interviews	Identification of five implicit voice theories	Challenges leader-centric models that emphasize how employee silence depends on immediate leader and develops a follower-centric view	71 28
Smets, Morris & Greenwood, AMJ, 2012	English and German banking lawyers in a new international law firm	How can field-level change arise in the course of everyday practice?	Theory generation	Case study; interviews, observation, and archival records	Multilevel model of practice-driven institutional change	Practice-driven institutional change differs from existing field-level accounts in terms of its initial locus, its mechanisms, and its unfolding	61 1⁓

Reference	Context	Research question	Theory type	Data/Methods	Contribution	Key findings	Citations
Zbaracki, 1998 (best paper, 2004)	Five diverse organizations in various stages of implementing TQM	How do institutional processes shape the technical reality of TQM?	Theory elaboration	Five case studies; interviews, observations, participation in TQM training, and archival materials	A process model of how the rhetoric and technical reality of TQM diverge through cycles of variation, selection, and retention	Derived model deviated from institutional theory in three ways	831 264
Ely & Thomas, ASQ, 2001 (BP, 2007)	Three multicultural small firms: a nonprofit law firm, a for-profit financial services firm, and a nonprofit consulting firm	What factors determine whether cultural diversity leads to positive or negative group performance outcomes?	Theory elaboration	Interviews and observations	Identification of three perspectives on diversity; model of how diversity perspectives influence performance via three intervening variables	Showed that within highly diverse firms, successful group processes and outcomes were obtained only under beliefs and expectations that diverse cultural perspectives and identities are assets that can create value	1348 422
Siggelkow, ASQ, 2002 (BP, 2008)	The Vanguard Group	What developmental processes lead to internal organizational fit? What are the core elements of an organization and how can you determine them?	Theory generation	Longitudinal case study; archival and secondary data, interviews	Creation of a grammar to describe the core elements and developmental paths of different organizations; identification of four (organizational) developmental processes	Created a methodology and a grammar for identifying core organizational elements and their associated change processes	586 175

(*Continued*)

Table 2.2 Continued

Article	Setting	Research Question	Research Purpose	Methods & Data	Outcomes	Novel or Counterintuitive Findings/Violations of Assumptions	Citations (Google Scholar, Web of Science)
Corley & Gioia, ASQ, 2004 (BP, 2010)	Spin-off of the top-performing unit of a Fortune 100 company	How does organizational identity change during a process of organizational subtraction (e.g., spin-off)?	Theory elaboration	Longitudinal case study; interviews, identity and image artifacts and documentation, nonparticipant observation	Process model of identity change that revolves around identity ambiguity	Challenges prior taken-for-granted assumptions about the role of identity in complex organizational change	701 252
Suddaby & Greenwood, 2005 (BP, 2011)	Acquisition of a law firm by a big-five accounting firm	What are the rhetorical processes by which new organizational forms get legitimized?	Theory elaboration	Two-stage content analysis of transcripts of two commissions designed to examine the appropriateness of multidisciplinary practices	Model of how new organizational forms are enabled by shifts in logics; identification of two elements of rhetorical strategies (institutional vocabularies and theorizations of change) and their sub-elements	Shows how institutional assumptions may be challenged and changed by rhetorical strategies	1230 459
Klein, Ziegert, Knight, & Xiao, 2006 (BP, 2012)	Medical teams in an emergency trauma center	How does leadership occur in action teams whose goals may conflict, whose tasks are urgent, complex, and interdependent, and whose membership changes frequently?	Theory elaboration	Grounded theory; interviews, observation, and archival data	Model of hierarchical, deindividualized system of shared leadership based on dynamic delegation. Combination of hierarchical and bureaucratic role-based structures with dynamic processes	Found violations of some previous assumptions about shared team leadership and delegation	303 138

Elsbach & Kramer, 2003; Gilbert, 2005). In other cases, we made the evaluation based on the clear presence of a driving model, theory, or typology for situating the study (e.g., Detert & Edmondson, 2011; Ely & Thomas, 2001).

In general, papers that elaborated on prior theory were more likely to produce counterintuitive findings or violations of previous assumptions than were papers that generated theory. For example, Elsbach and Kramer (2003) found that some Hollywood producers' implicit theories of creativity emphasized traits that had previously been found not to be predictive of creativity, while Graebner (2009) found asymmetries in dyadic interorganizational trust relations where symmetries previously had been assumed. Theory elaboration studies also resolve existing puzzles in the literature. For example, elaborating on prior research regarding threat rigidity, Gilbert (2005) focused on two different types of rigidity (resource and routine) to show why threats sometimes lead to observed overall rigidity (Staw, Sandelands, & Dutton, 1981) and other times to adaptability (Lant, Milliken, & Batra, 1992). Similarly, Ely and Thomas (2001) showed how adoption of an "integrate and learn" perspective toward diversity leads to positive group processes and outcomes while "access and legitimacy" and "fairness and discrimination" perspectives do not.

With respect to methodology and data collection, nearly all the studies used some combination of interviews, written and electronic documents or records, and (usually nonparticipant) observation. In this sense, they are quite different from most quantitative research in the extent to which they draw on multiple types of data to develop and triangulate their findings. However, what really stands out in most of these papers is the sheer amount of time and effort that went into creating the results. For example, Klein and her colleagues (2006) spent more than 250 hours observing the treatment of more than 175 unique patients in a trauma care center. In addition, they conducted interviews with 33 surgeons, residents, fellows, anesthesiologists, and nurses in two phases, resulting in a data set that produced 1,430 chunks of related sentences or "thought units" during initial coding. Similarly, Smets and colleagues (2012) spent approximately 130 hours closely observing lawyers' daily work practices, attended two full-day workshops, and conducted 77 interviews lasting between 30 and 140 minutes each. Both sets of authors also checked their emerging theories with interviewees to gain additional nuance and understanding—a practice that was followed by many, if not most, of the authors. And all this effort takes place before the writing even begins. A recent "From the Editors" column by Adam Grant and Timothy Pollock (2011) reported that best paper winners in *AMJ* rewrite the introductions to their articles an average of 10 times!

In a recent Exemplary Contribution essay in the *Academy of Management Learning and Education*, Susan Ashford (2013) discusses four articles (Bunderson & Thompson, 2009; Edmondson, 1999; Ibarra, 1999; Morrison & Milliken, 2000) that she considers to be exemplars of academic "home runs."[4,5] Drawing on analogies to the creation of the 1991 blockbuster movie *Thelma and Louise* (as documented by Weller, 2011), Ashford argues that the four exemplar papers and the movie have several characteristics in common. Above all, however, she argues that their main commonality is that they didn't "settle": "Not on artistic, commercial, emotional, or sociopolitical grounds did *Thelma and Louse* settle. That is why in just two decades, it has become a classic." The same can be said of the best papers reflected in Table 2.2. Because the data for these studies were generally personally collected, theoretically sampled, and then analyzed over a period of years, the final products are not only highly valid (Eisenhardt & Graebner, 2007), but also simple, communicable, timely, and fundamental (Ashford, 2013).

Final Thoughts: Can "Being Interesting" Become Too Much of a Good Thing?

By now, it is probably clear that we mainly view interesting research as a positive thing. In our earlier editorial essay on this topic (Bartunek et al., 2006), we advanced a number of reasons that we felt "being interesting" mattered. First, we noted that researchers who produce interesting research have a higher probability of influencing others. This is something that most academics want to do when they begin their careers (Vermeulen, 2007). It is also something that most of us believe would improve public discourse and managerial decision making if we were to achieve it (e.g., Abrahamson & Eisenman, 2001; Pfeffer 2012; Rousseau, 2006). Second, we cited psychological research suggesting that materials that are perceived as interesting produce a higher degree of learning, in part because interest seems to stimulate deeper levels of processing the meanings of textual material (e.g., Bartunek, 2013; Sansone & Thoman, 2005; Silvia, 2006). Third, producing interesting research may be important to attracting, retaining, and inspiring doctoral students. For example, one of our students who read two of the "most interesting" articles by Barley (1986) and Dutton and Dukerich (1991) said, "Both articles give me *hope*. These are among the articles that I consider as models for what I want to do later on. With many other articles, I sometimes have doubts as to whether this (i.e., academics) is what I want to do with my life."

Recently, however, there have been a growing number of voices—in the organizational sciences and elsewhere—questioning the wisdom of encouraging novel and interesting research. One big concern is that we may be placing more emphasis on what is interesting or new than on what is true (e.g., Miner, 1984; Pfeffer, 2007). Epidemiologist John Ioannidis (2005a, 2005b) and various social scientists (e.g., Nosek, Spies, & Motyl, 2012) have reported "a pervasive bias favouring publication of claims to have found something new" ("Trouble at the Lab," 2013), as well as studies that report positive rather than null results. Another concern is that placing too much emphasis on novelty discourages the important scientific task of replication (Kepes, Bennett, & McDaniel, 2014).

As these concerns escalate, it is worth noting that novel and interesting qualitative work is less likely than quantitative research to create most of the problems mentioned.[6] This is because qualitative research is generally designed to answer fundamentally different kinds of questions (i.e., how and why) than quantitative research, which is designed to answer "how much, how many, or how big" types of questions (Lee et al., 1999).

For the most part, these criticisms have come from researchers with a positivist bent. Still, even excellent qualitative researchers have pondered the question of whether we might be placing too much emphasis on interesting research:

> If being interesting requires a paper to be different, before long the field would be a mess. Every paper would take on a new topic, devise a new method, or offer a new way of seeing things. With all of us so busily striving for the next interesting paper, no subjects would be studied more than once, no methods would be refined, and no ideas would be worked though. The development of knowledge, at least in any scientific sense, would all but cease. (Barley 2006, p. 20)

In the end, however, Barley concludes that we are not in much danger, since "interesting papers only come along every so often" and "no one can tell us how to write more interestingly" (Barley 2006, p. 20). Our own view is that although we certainly need to make sure that we do all we can to answer "how much, how many, and how big" questions in a more trustworthy fashion (Kepes et al., 2014), we are in little danger of being led astray—or becoming bored—by interesting qualitative research that helps us better understand how and why things happen.

In their note to contributors for this book, Kim Elsbach and Rod Kramer noted that the

> over-representation of qualitative methods in producing interesting research suggests that there is something about these methods that lend themselves to interesting findings. We suggest that this "something" is the set of innovative approaches to data collection, analysis, and interpretation that qualitative organizational scholars have developed and used over the past several decades.

Yet, to date, no organizational book has examined and discussed these innovative research methods. . . . This book will provide a comprehensive overview of "state of the art" innovative approaches to qualitative research for organizational scholars, and thus, provide insight about doing really interesting research.

As we have made evident in this chapter, qualitative research continues to be overrepresented in measures of interesting research, even more so than before. We have suggested a few reasons for this—reasons that we hope will whet readers' appetites for the more detailed explorations of what makes for interesting qualitative research that follow in subsequent chapters.

Notes

1 Until very recently, *ASQ* did not contain a similar column.
2 Best paper awards for *Administrative Science Quarterly* (called scholarly contribution awards) are given to "the most significant paper published in ASQ five years earlier." Thus, the best *ASQ* papers for 2004–2013 were actually published between 1998 and 2007.
3 There were two *AMJ* best paper winners in 2005; also, Detert and Edmondson (2011) employed both qualitative and quantitative methods.
4 For a detailed description of the game of baseball, see http://en.wikipedia.org/wiki/Baseball. For present purposes, suffice it to say that home runs are the most valuable kinds of "hits" a baseball player can make.
5 Interestingly, two of these articles (Ibarra; Bunderson & Thompson) are purely qualitative, while Edmondson is mixed quantitative/qualitative and Morrison and Milliken is nonempirical. Thus, once again, qualitative research stands out as being disproportionately memorable.
6 It is not completely exempt from them, however. Consider, for example, reviewer biases toward positive rather than null results. It is unlikely that Ely and Thomas's (2001) study would have generated as much interest as it did if none of the three diversity perspectives had had differential effects on group processes and outcomes.

References

Abrahamson, E.C., & Eisenman, M. (2001). Why management scholars must intervene strategically in the management knowledge market. *Human Relations, 54*, 67–75.

Ashford, S.E. (2013). Having scholarly impact: The art of hitting academic home runs. *Academy of Learning & Education, 12*, 623–633.

Bamberger, P.A., & Pratt, M.G. (2010). Moving forward by looking back: Reclaiming unconventional research contexts and samples in organizational scholarship. *Academy of Management Journal, 53*, 665–671.

Bansal, P., & Corley, K. (2011). The coming of age of qualitative research. *Academy of Management Journal, 54*, 233–237.

Bansal, P., & Corley, K. (2012). Publishing in *AMJ*—part 7: What's different about qualitative research? *Academy of Management Journal, 55*, 509–513.

Barley, S.R. (1986). Technology as an occasion for brokering: Evidence from observations of CT Scanners and the social order of radiology departments. *Administrative Science Quarterly, 3*, 78–108.

Barley, S.R. (2006). When I write my masterpiece: Thoughts on what makes a paper interesting. *Academy of Management Journal, 49*, 16–20.

Bartunek, J.M. (2013). Theory of the interesting. In E.H. Kessler (Ed.), *Encyclopedia of management theory* (Vol. 2, pp. 870–872). Thousand Oaks, CA: Sage.

Bartunek, J.M., Rynes, S.L., & Ireland, R.D. (2006). What makes management research interesting, and why does it matter? *Academy of Management Journal, 49*, 9–15.

Bunderson, J.S., & Thompson, J.A. (2009). The call of the wild: Zookeepers, callings, and the double-edged sword of deeply meaningful work. *Administrative Science Quarterly, 54*, 32–57.

Corley, K.G., & Gioia, D.A. (2004). Identity ambiguity and change in the wake of a corporate spin-off. *Administrative Science Quarterly, 49*, 173–208.

Davis, M.S. (1971). That's interesting! Towards a phenomenology of sociology and a sociology of phenomenology. *Philosophy of the Social Sciences, 1*, 309–344.

Detert, J.R., & Edmondson, A.C. (2011). Implicit voice theories: Taken-for-granted rules of self-censorship at work. *Academy of Management Journal, 54*, 461–488.

Dutton, J.E., & Dukerich, J.M. (1991). Keeping an eye on the mirror: Image and identity in organizational adaptation. *Academy of Management Journal, 34*, 517–554.

Dutton, J.E., & Dukerich, J.M. (2006). The relational foundation of research: An underappreciated dimension of interesting research. *Academy of Management Journal, 49*, 21–26.

Edmondson, A. (1999). Psychological safety and learning behavior in work teams. *Administrative Science Quarterly, 44*, 350–383.

Eisenhardt, K.M. (1989). Building theories from case study research. *Academy of Management Review, 14*, 532–550.

Eisenhardt, K.M., & Graebner, M. E. (2007) Theory building from cases: Opportunities and challenges. *Academy of Management Journal, 50*, 25–32.

Elsbach, K.D., & Kramer, R.M. (2003). Assessing creativity in Hollywood pitch meetings: Evidence for a dual-process model of creativity judgments. *Academy of Management Journal, 46*, 283–301.

Ely, R.J., & Thomas, D.A. (2001). Cultural diversity at work: The effects of diversity perspectives on work group processes and outcomes. *Administrative Science Quarterly, 46*, 229–273.

Ferlie, E., FitzGerald, L., Wood, M., & Hawkins, C. (2005). The non-spread of innovations: The mediating role of professionals. *Academy of Management Journal, 48*, 117–134.

Gephart, R. (2004). Qualitative research and the *Academy of Management Journal*. *Academy of Management Journal, 47*, 454–462. doi:10.5465/AMJ.2004.14438580

Gersick, C.J. (1989). Marking time: Predictable transitions in task groups. *Academy of Management Journal, 32*, 274–309.

Gilbert, C. (2005). Unbundling the structure of inertia: Resource versus routine rigidity. *Academy of Management Journal, 48*, 741–763.

Glaser, B.G., & Anselm L.S. (1967). *The Discovery of Grounded Theory: Strategies for Qualitative Research*. Chicago: Aldine Publishing Co.

Golden-Biddle, K., & Locke, K. (2007). *Composing qualitative research* (2nd ed.). Thousand Oaks, CA: Sage.

Graebner, M.E. (2009). Caveat venditor: Trust asymmetries in acquisitions of entrepreneurial firms. *Academy of Management Journal, 52*, 435–472.

Grant, A. M., & Pollock, T.G. (2011). From the editors: Publishing in *AMJ*—Part 3: Setting the hook. *Academy of Management Journal, 54*, 873–879.

Greenwood, R., & Suddaby, R. (2006). Institutional entrepreneurship in mature fields: The big five accounting firms. *Academy of Management Journal, 49*, 27–48.

Ibarra, H. (1999). Provisional selves: Experimenting with image and identity in professional adaptation. *Administrative Science Quarterly, 44*, 764–791.

Ioannidis, J. P. (2005a). Contradicted and initially stronger effects in highly cited clinical research. *Journal of the American Medical Association, 294*, 218–228.

Ioannidis, J.P.A. (2005b). Why most research findings are false. *Plos Medicine, 2*(8), e124. doi:10.1371/journal.pmed.0020124.

Kepes, S., Bennett, A., & McDaniel, M.A. (2014). Evidence-based management and the trustworthiness of our cumulative scientific knowledge: Implications for teaching, research, and practice. *Academy of Management Learning and Education, 13*, 446–466.

Klein, K.J., Ziegert, J.C., Knight, A.P., & Xiao, Y. (2006). Dynamic delegation: Shared, hierarchical, and de-individualized leadership in extreme action teams. *Administrative Science Quarterly, 51*, 590–621.

Lant, T. K., Milliken, F.J., & Batra, B. (1992). The role of managerial learning and interpretation in strategic reorientation. *Strategic Management Journal, 13*, 585–608.

Lee, T.W., Mitchell, T.R., & Sablinsky, C.J. (1999). Qualitative research in organizational and vocational psychology: 1979–1999. *Journal of Vocational Behavior, 55*, 161–187.

Miner, J.B. (1984). The validity and usefulness of theories in an emerging organizational science. *Academy of Management Review, 9*, 296–306.

Morrison, E.W., & Milliken, F.J. (2000). Organizational silence: A barrier to change and development in a pluralistic world. *Academy of Management Review, 25*, 706–725.

Nosek, B.A., Spies, J.R., & Motyl, M. (2012). Scientific utopia: II. Restructuring incentives and practices to promote truth over publishability. *Perspectives on Psychological Science, 7*, 615–631.

Pfeffer, J. (2007). A modest proposal: How we might change the process and product of managerial research. *Academy of Management Journal, 50*, 1344–1345.

Pfeffer, J. (2012). Foreword. In D.M. Rousseau (Ed.), *The Oxford handbook of evidence-based management* (pp. vii–x). New York, NY: Oxford University Press.

Plowman, D.A., Baker, L.T., Beck, T.E., Kulkarni, M., Solansky, S.T., & Travis, D.V. (2007). Radical change accidentally: The emergence and amplification of small change. *Academy of Management Journal, 52*, 515–543.

Pratt, M.G. (2008). Fitting oval pegs into round holes: Tensions in evaluating and publishing qualitative research in top-tier North American journals. *Organizational Research Methods, 11*, 481–509. doi:10.1177/1094428107303349

Pratt, M. G. (2009). For the lack of a boilerplate: Tips on writing up (and reviewing) qualitative research. *Academy of Management Journal, 52*, 856–862.

Rousseau, D.M. (2006). Is there such a thing as evidence-based management? *Academy of Management Journal, 31*, 256–269.

Rynes, S.L. (2005). From the editors: Taking stock and looking ahead. *Academy of Management Journal, 48*, 9–15.

Rynes, S.L. (2007). Editor's foreword: *Academy of Management Journal* editor's forum on rich research. *Academy of Management Journal, 50*, 13.

Sansone, C., & Thoman, D.B. (2005). Interest as the missing motivator in self-regulation. *European Psychologist, 10*, 175–186.

Siggelkow, N. (2001). Change in the presence of fit: The rise, the fall, and the renaissance of Liz Claiborne. *Academy of Management Journal, 44*, 838–857.

Siggelkow, N. (2002). Evolution toward fit. *Administrative Science Quarterly, 47*, 125–159.

Siggelkow, N. (2007). Persuasion with case studies. *Academy of Management Journal, 50*, 20–24.

Silvia, P.J. (2006). *Exploring the psychology of interest.* New York, NY: Oxford University Press.

Smets, M., Morris, T., & Greenwood, R. (2012). From practice to field: A multi-level model of practice-driven institutional change. *Academy of Management Journal, 55*, 877–904. http://dx.doi.org/10.5465/amj.2010.0013

Staw, B.M., Sandelands, L.E., and Dutton, J.E. (1981). Threat rigidity effects in organizational behavior: A multilevel perspective. *Administrative Science Quarterly, 26*, 501–524.

Suddaby, R. (2006). From the editors: What grounded theory is not. *Academy of Management Journal, 49*, 633–642.

Suddaby, R., & Greenwood, R. (2005). Rhetorical strategies of legitimacy. *Administrative Science Quarterly, 50*, 35–67.

Trouble at the lab. (2013, October 19). *The Economist.* Retrieved from www.economist.com/news/briefing/21588057-scientists-think-science-self-correcting-alarming-degree-it-not-trouble

Vermeulen, F. (2007). "I shall not remain insignificant": Adding a second loop to matter more. *Academy of Management Journal, 50*, 754–761.

Weick, K. E. (2007). The generative properties of richness. *Academy of Management Journal, 50*, 14–19.

Weller, S. (2011, March). The ride of a lifetime. *Vanity Fair*, 315–351.

Zbaracki, M.J. (1998). The rhetoric and reality of total quality management. *Administrative Science Quarterly, 43*, 602–636.

3

Ups and Downs

Trends in the Development and Reception of Qualitative Methods

Michael Mauskapf and Paul Hirsch

The trajectory of qualitative methods in social and organizational research features moments of high praise, strong attacks, benign neglect, and unexpected revivals. In this chapter, we analyze this turbulent history by charting shifts in the way qualitative scholars have framed their research and interpreted and presented their findings. Focusing on the ways in which qualitative research and methods have been framed, deployed, and legitimated suggests a sequential but rarely linear history that reflects different ontologies, perspectives, and agendas over time. These differences exist not only between qualitative research and other forms of social inquiry but within qualitative research itself, playing a critical role in shaping how qualitative researchers frame and defend their identities today.

The chapters in this handbook document how researchers conducting qualitative research in organization and management have succeeded in making the work more rigorous and relevant to 21st-century scholarship. Indeed, the social sciences have experienced a "qualitative revolution" in recent years, producing more high-quality and innovative research than ever before (Denzin & Lincoln, 2003). Within the field of organization and management, the quality and diversity of qualitative research is outstanding, receiving disproportionate accolades from our top journals (Rynes-Weller & Bartunek, this volume; Bansal & Corley, 2011) and inspiring new peer-reviewed publications featuring qualitative research (Cassell & Symon, 2006). While its traditional definitions often invoke phrases like "case-based," "process-oriented," and "thick description" and emphasize the interpretive and inductive rather than the statistical relationship between some set of variables, the developments in qualitative research discussed in this handbook suggest a blurring of lines that makes a simple definition hard to pin down. To be sure, "qualitative methods are many, they are everywhere, and they do not easily boil down to formula" (Van Mannen, 1998: *x*). While much qualitative research remains interpretive in some fundamental way, the development of Qualitative Comparative Analysis (QCA) and other set-analytic methods indicates some reorientations around scientific inference and causal claims (Goertz & Mahoney, 2012). While we will ultimately conclude that the state of the field may still retain its "let a thousand flowers bloom" characterization, much qualitative research produced today is more deductive in flavor, often emphasizing generalizable claims rather than case-specific insights. Is this simply the logical evolution of a more systematic approach to qualitative research, or the result of qualitative researchers adopting the norms of some real or perceived quantitative mainstream? Advanced research designs, standardized analysis techniques, and new technologies have led some to celebrated gains in scientific rigor, while others decry the loss of contextual richness.

In this essay, we provide a historical context though which to understand the origins and implications of these developments. We focus on variation within the field of qualitative organizational research over time, highlighting distinct value systems (e.g., positivist vs. constructivist), preferred data collection and analysis methods (e.g., ethnographies vs. interviews, inductive description vs. deductive coding), and modes of presentation (e.g., narrative vs. tables). While these dualities represent an obvious but necessary simplification of questions facing qualitative researchers, we argue that they reflect fundamental elements in the norms of qualitative research practice and influence the relative position of qualitative research in organization and management studies more broadly. We conclude by discussing the implications of the increased diversity of qualitative methods on contemporary research practice and their potential costs and benefits for the future.

Mapping the Terrain

The designation "qualitative research" encompasses a diversity of methods, including historical analysis based on archival records, analysis of spoken or written texts, interviews that may be more or less structured, and observations of people and their surroundings (Van Mannen, 1998). When applied to the study of organizations, its reach is especially broad, in part due to management's position at the intersection of multiple disciplines, including sociology, psychology, economics, political science, anthropology, and history. The boundaries of what constitutes normative qualitative organizational research are historically contingent. Although there is some consistency concerning what is and is not qualitative research over time, there is also meaningful divergence across historical periods. While most work in this vein focuses on the specific nature of individual cases rather than on generalizations drawn from some statistically significant sample, whether a researcher employed a particular method or assumption is considerably less determined.

Dominant paradigms and practices in qualitative organizational research emerged and evolved over time. Here we review five time periods during which the typical qualitative research conducted shared similarities that differ from research conducted in the others. These periods—pre–1950, 1950–1970, 1970–1985, 1985–2000, 2000–present—were selected jointly through our reading of works on the history of qualitative research and a consideration of punctuating events generally considered to have shaped the evolution of organizational theories and research.[1] Each period reflects a prevailing system of values and norms that are at least partially distinct; what exactly qualitative research "means" is contingent on the period and category in question. We then trace shifts in the content of five categories (i.e., method of data collection, method of data analysis, focus of interpretation, method of data presentation, relative position in organizational research) across each time period. These categories loosely imitate the research design-and-execution scheme used by most qualitative methods textbooks, and they roughly follow this handbook's basic organizing principles. Table 3.1 summarizes the historical shifts of qualitative research across these categories. The clean edges and apparent simplicity of this table reflect the reductionist nature of this summary chapter. Indeed, the explanation that follows does not presume to be complete or systematic, but instead focuses on evocative and consequential shifts in qualitative methodology that helped to shape—and continues to shape—the future of organizational research.

Pre-1950

In the first half of the 20th century, nearly all behavioral research that occurred outside of the lab was qualitative in nature. Indeed, most scholars in the fields of sociology, anthropology, and political science at the time might be subsumed under the rubric of "qualitative researcher," championing a

Table 3.1 Trends in Qualitative Organizational Research

Period	Period Method of Data Collection	Method of Data Analysis	Focus of Interpretation	Method of Data Presentation	Relative Position in Organizational Research
pre-1950	Case studies, ethnography, interviews	Intuition and description	Face validity	Narrative	Dominant
1950–1970	Case studies, ethnography, interviews, archival	Inductive manual coding	Internal and external validity	Narrative	One of several prominent streams
1970–1985	Single and comparative case studies	Inductive manual coding	Internal and external validity, reflexivity	Narrative	Increasingly marginalized
1985–2000	Single and comparative case studies, ethnography	Inductive and deductive coding (by hand or computer); QCA	Internal and external validity, reflexivity, generalizability	Narrative, coding manuals, tables	Gradual return to (minority) mainstream
2000–2014	Single and comparative case studies, ethnography, digital and mixed methods	Multiple-stage computer coding, text and discourse analysis, QCA, and other set analyses	Validity, generalizability, replicability, causation	Narrative, coding manuals, tables, process diagrams, decision trees, network maps	Fragmented but influential; ever-increasing quantity and diversity

brand of research focused on observing and describing the lives of "others" via ethnographies and interviews (e.g., Park, Burgess, & McKenzie, 1925). Rooted in intuitive discovery, their research efforts aimed to unearth and describe the world around them rather than to draw generalizable conclusions. The boundary between those doing the investigating and those being investigated remained fixed, and findings were organized and presented using relatively easy-to-understand language and a story-telling narrative comparable to the good writing in contemporary issues of *The New Yorker* or *The New York Times Magazine*. Subsequently, a common critique leveled against this type of qualitative research was that "it's nothing more than journalism." Organizational sociology and related disciplines continue to devalue journalism and vice versa. Hirsch (1999) later noted that journalists and social scientists still have a great deal to learn from one another, even as "too academic" remains a pejorative term among journalists, while academics often "mystify" their work through the use of jargon and other devices of obfuscation veiled as markers of scientific rigor.[2]

1950–1970

After World War II, qualitative research in the social sciences took on a decidedly modernist flavor, favoring a more theory- and method-oriented approach. Influential qualitative scholars active in organizational research during this period (e.g., Becker, 1961) began to explicitly distance their research from the work of journalists, who they argued did not engage with social theory, collect appropriate amounts of evidence, or incorporate systematic data analysis to generate defendable conclusions (Ragin, 1994). Unlike their predecessors, this generation of qualitative researchers engaged critically with their observations, cultivating an implicit dialogue between empirical evidence and analytical frames informed by existing theory (e.g., Dalton, 1959). With the founding of *Administrative Science Quarterly* in 1958 and an increased interest in the influence of the environment on organizational outcomes, qualitative researchers began to develop systematic coding schemes to analyze their data. These schemes were developed inductively at first, helping scholars address issues of internal or concept validity without abandoning their interest in generating theoretical insights through the description of empirical phenomena. These developments were accompanied or surpassed by gains in other methods of organizational inquiry, including quantitative and action research. While qualitative methods remained a significant means by which to study organizational behavior, their singular foothold on the field was quickly being eroded by advancements in other areas.

1970–1985

After several decades in which qualitative research methods were well represented in studies of management and organizations, the 1970s and early 1980s saw a decline in their relative popularity. This trend can be attributed to several factors. First, the development and funding of sophisticated quantitative methods and computer software for statistical analysis generated renewed interest in cutting-edge quantitative methods. When asked in 1983 why qualitative research was appearing less frequently and seemed to be on the defensive, James Coleman, a pioneer in quantitative studies who also supported qualitative research, replied: "The rise of the National Science Foundation and the funding it provides."[3] In addition, the rise of critical theory and its emphasis on historical, cultural, and political contingencies led to a blurring of the distinctions between humanistic scholarship and social science. Many of original assumptions associated with qualitative research were challenged by a more critical stance following postmodern critiques of objectivity (Marshall & Rossman, 1999). For example, rather than being viewed as neutral observers seeking to understand others' behavior, ethnographers increasingly engaged in a dialectical and reflexive relationship with those that they studied. This critical stance was exacerbated by the assumptions and values supported by the linguistic, cultural, and historical turns in social science, each of which enriched qualitative research by providing it with a post-modernist foundation but also marginalized it from other more positivist strains of organizational research. Despite their similarities, some have argued that qualitative and quantitative research comprise two distinct cultures that vary in their methodological orientations and research properties (Goertz & Mahoney, 2012; Miles & Huberman, 1994; Ragin, 1994). Work within the qualitative realm continued to be concerned primarily with small-N, within-case analyses that employed a logic of necessary and sufficient conditions, rather than statistical inference. While much of the research in this tradition has traditionally been driven by phenomenological concerns and been guided by the principles of analytic induction, description, and temporal sensitivity, it also signaled the increasingly fragmented nature of qualitative research itself (Van Mannen, 1983). Such internal diversity affected the identity and reception of this work as a coherent body of scholarship.

1985–2000

In the last decades of the 20th century, qualitative research experienced a revival. A growing interest in producing generalizable insights was enhanced with the appearance of new methods and reporting conventions. Although single ethnographic and historical case studies continued to serve an important function in qualitative research, multicase comparisons became a more common way to draw defensible conclusions about organizational processes and outcomes that reached beyond the limits of an individual empirical context (see Dyer & Wilkins, 1991, and Eisenhardt, 1991 on the merits of single vs. comparative case studies). Qualitative scholars began to explicitly state theoretical propositions in their papers, which were increasingly generated through a process that was at last partially deductive. Nevertheless, translating qualitative findings into generalizable processes still remained a tricky and potentially misguided exercise, given the inherent differences between logical and statistical inference (Small, 2009).

The shift toward theoretical deduction and empirical generalizability was strongly reinforced by advancements in analysis techniques and technologies made possible by the personal computer. The appearance of new and more rigorous methods was aided by the development QCA (Ragin, 1987) and computer-based software that enabled automated coding (Dohan & Sanchez- Jankowski, 1998). These advances were instituted into standardized research practice through authoritative and widely distributed texts such as Miles and Huberman's *Qualitative Data Analysis*, now in its third edition. They built a bridge between qualitative and quantitative research traditions, aiding the effort to introduce more and different kinds of qualitative research in the field's top journals (Lofland et al., 2006; Van Mannen, 1998). Lessons from feminist, queer, and gender studies; linguistics; and a host of other perspectives also began to appear in the work of organizational researchers, highlighting the role qualitative methods could play in building new theory.

2000–2014

As with (almost) anything, empirical research can be understood as a competitive marketplace, and our collective concern over issues of reflexivity, reliability, and generalizability can be viewed in part as a consequence of our struggle to stay relevant—even central—to mainstream social science. Over the last 15 years, this has led to (a) an increased diversity of legitimate qualitative methods (Hannah, 2012) and (b) a mutually understood (if not agreed upon) standard of rigor that is applied to most, if not all, modes of qualitative research. An informal review conducted by the then-editors of the *Academy of Management Journal* found that "there is increasing consistency in the structure of published qualitative papers. . . . STATA analyses increasingly rely on coding data, findings are illustrated in increasingly detailed tables, graphs, and diagrams . . . [and] propositions are increasingly used to show a theoretical contribution" (Bansal & Corley, 2011: 234). Their assessment suggests that while our field supports more and different kinds of qualitative research than ever before, there is a greater expectation of theoretical engagement and methodological rigor and transparency.

The continued advancements made possible by computer-aided technologies and cross-field conversations have yielded additional innovations. More so today than ever before, mixed methods—qualitative, quantitative, or some combination of both—are used to conduct sophisticated, multipronged analyses of emergent or complex phenomena (e.g., Kaplan, this volume; Weber, Heiner, & DeSoucey, 2008). New and diverse forms of data and data analysis have resulted in new norms of data (re)presentation (Phillips, this volume). For example, although "big data" is often associated with sweeping quantitative analyses and sophisticated modeling techniques, its fine-grained nature enables qualitative researchers to generate rich, contextual explanations of social phenomena. Although narrative still serves as a primary means through which qualitative data is introduced, researchers often employ tables, process diagrams, and decision trees to make sense of their data and generate more causal claims (Goertz & Mahoney, 2012; Small, 2013). To control for researcher bias, contemporary scholars employ multistage coding techniques that systematically differentiate informant-generated codes and researcher-created concepts (Gioia, Corley, & Hamilton, 2013). These and other advancements may not have been possible in the past, but they are nonetheless historically contingent, suggesting that the innovations contained within this handbook will serve as a guide to future directions in qualitative organizational research.

Future Directions: What's Past Is Prologue

Qualitative research makes for more than just interesting reading; primed for empirical discovery and theory building, it helps us understand the world in new ways. Work in this domain is also increasingly rigorous and of generally high quality—while only 11% of the articles published in *AMJ* between 2000 and 2010 were based solely on qualitative data, they were the winners of six of its last eight best article awards (Bansal & Corley, 2011). The innovations charted herein have helped to move our field forward, even though qualitative research remains underrepresented in our flagship journals.

The blurring of these lines, and the lack of a unified qualitative paradigm (at least methodologically speaking), may be seen as a double-edged sword (cf. Sauder, this volume). Within-category fragmentation has made it difficult for traditional qualitative methods to gain a majority stake in organizational research. Yet, for the goal of advancing our understanding of the social world through rigorous and reproducible modes of inquiry, the evolution of qualitative research methods suggests continued growth and promise. In July of 2003, a group of the country's most accomplished social scientists gathered in Arlington, Virginia, to discuss what constitutes good qualitative research and determine how scholars might improve upon existing methods to advance scientific discourse and public policy. The conveners and participants of the National Science Foundation–sponsored workshop came to the conclusion that, while the state of qualitative research was more vibrant than it had ever been, room for further development remained (Ragin, Nagel, & White, 2004). Embracing a diversity of methods that address concerns about reliability, standardization, and generalizability without losing sight of a shared commitment to description and discovery will ensure qualitative methods continue to flourish in organization and management research. If we agree that methods are powerful tools rather than ends unto themselves, and that no single study can address all possible questions or critics, the future of qualitative organizational research remains bright indeed.

Notes

1 Our periodization is also aided and loosely informed by Denzin and Lincoln (2003), who denote seven historical periods of qualitative research that demarcate its development.
2 Such inaccessibility is paradoxically reinforced through the publication and editing process: "professionally, it is less harmful to be told that one's writing is unclear or filled with jargon than that it is accessible and (too) clean." (Hirsch, 1999: 253).
3 Personal communication with Paul Hirsch.

References

Bansal, P., & Corley, K. A. (2011). The coming of age for qualitative research: Embracing the diversity of qualitative methods. *Academy of Management Journal, 54*(2), 233–237.

Becker, H. S., Geer, B., Hughes, E. C., & Strauss, A. L. (1961). *Boys in white: Student culture in a medical school.* Chicago: University of Chicago Press.

Cassell, C., & Symon, G. (2006). Taking qualitative methods in organization and management research seriously. *Qualitative Research in Organizations and Management, 1*, 4–12.

Dalton, M. (1959). *Men who manage.* Hoboken, NJ: Wiley.

Denzin, N. K., & Lincoln, Y. S. (Eds.). (2003). *The landscape of qualitative research: Theories and issues* (2nd ed.). Thousand Oaks, CA: Sage.

Dohan, D., & Sanchez-Jankowski, M. (1998). Using computers to analyze ethnographic field data: Theoretical & practical considerations. *Annual Review of Sociology, 24*, 477–498.

Dyer, W. G., & Wilkins, A. L. (1991). Better stories, not better constructs, to generate better theory: A rejoinder to Eisenhardt. *Academy of Management Review, 16*(3), 613–619.

Eisenhardt, K. M. (1991). Better stories and better constructs: The case for rigor and comparative logic. *Academy of Management Review, 16*(3), 620–627.

Gioia, D., Corley, K. A., & Hamilton, A. L. (2013). Seeking qualitative rigor in inductive research: Notes on the Gioia methodology. *Organizational Research Methods, 16*, 15–31.

Goertz, G., & Mahoney, J. (2012). *A tale of two cultures: Qualitative and quantitative research in the social sciences.* Princeton, NJ: Princeton University Press.

Hannah, D. (2012). An accounting of counting as a means of qualitative data analysis. Working paper. Beadie School of Business, Simon Fraser University.

Hirsch, P. M., & Cornfield, D. (1999). Qualitative sociology and good journalism as demystifiers. In B. Glassner & R. Hertz (Eds.), *Qualitative sociology as everyday life* (pp. 251–259). Thousand Oaks, CA: Sage.

Lofland, J., Snow, D., Anderson, L., & Lofland, L. (2006). *Analyzing social settings: A guide to qualitative observation and analysis.* Belmont, CA: Wadsworth.

Marshall, C., & Rossman, G.B. (1999). Designing qualitative research (3rd ed.). Thousand Oaks, CA: Sage.

Miles, M., & Huberman, M. (1994). *Qualitative data analysis.* Thousand Oaks, CA: Sage.

Park, R. E., Burgess, E. W., & McKenzie, R. D. (1925). *The city: Suggestions for investigation of human behavior in the urban environment.* Chicago, IL: University of Chicago Press.

Ragin, C. (1987). *The Comparative Method: Moving Beyond Qualitative and Quantitative Strategies.* Berkeley, CA: University of California Press.

Ragin, C. (1994). *Constructing social research.* Thousand Oaks, CA: Pine Forge Press.

Ragin, C., & Becker, H. (Eds.) (1992). *What is a case? Exploring the foundations of social inquiry.* Cambridge, UK: Cambridge University Press.

Ragin, C., Nagel, J., & White, P. (2004). *Report for workshop on scientific foundations of qualitative research.* Arlington, VA: National Science Foundation.

Small, M. L. (2009). How many cases do I need?: On science and the logic of case selection in field-based research. *Ethnography, 10*(1), 5–38.

Small, M. L. (Ed.). (2013). Causal thinking and ethnographic research. Symposium in the *American Journal of Sociology, 119*(3), 597–714.

Van Maanen, J. (Ed.). (1983). *Qualitative methodology.* Newbury Park, CA: Sage.

Van Maanen, J. (1995). Style as theory. *Organization Science, 6*(1), 133–143.

Van Maanen, J. (1998). Different strokes: Qualitative research in the Administrative Science Quarterly from 1956 to 1996. In J. Van Mannen (Ed.), *Qualitative studies of organizations* (pp. ix–xxxii). Thousand Oaks, CA: Sage.

Weber, K., Heinze, K., & DeSoucey, M. 2008. Forage for thought: Mobilizing codes in the movement for grass-fed meat and dairy products. *Administrative Science Quarterly, 53*, 529–567.1. Note that table is edited in the supplied PDF file.

Part II
Innovative Research Settings

4

Using Extreme Cases to Understand Organizations

Katherine K. Chen

Introduction

Drawing on the insights of organizational studies and sociology, this chapter examines the study and use of "extreme" or atypical cases. These include single case studies, comparative cases, and cases aggregated from prior research. Because of the features of the sites studied, extreme cases can reveal more about a phenomenon than so-called average or typical cases (Flyvberg, 2006). Extreme cases also aid reflexive reflection of how we study organizations and phenomena. In other words, extreme cases can encourage reflexivity (i.e., Bourdieu & Wacquant, 1992; Kleinman, 1996) by revealing normative assumptions about appropriate sites of study and methods. I first address objections commonly raised about qualitative research methodologies, including extreme cases. Misconceptions include concerns about generalizability and representativeness; researchers not only must underscore the strengths of qualitative research, but also explain "what is this a case of?" Then, using examples from journal articles and monographs, I show how extreme cases excel at shedding insight into various organizational phenomena, including issues common to all organizations. Finally, I discuss how when conducting such studies researchers must consider how to negotiate access and undertake analysis, as well as how to effectively present findings and claims.

Misconceptions About Research Designs

With extreme cases, researchers must identify and explicitly state what is taken for granted in typical cases: what can an intensive, in-depth study of a particular organization teach us about other organizations? In more general terms, researchers must articulate, "what is this a case of?" This explication usually requires additional effort, especially when addressing misconceptions raised by those who are less familiar with how to undertake qualitative research such as observations, interviews, focus groups, and content analysis. When justifying how their studies follow "scientific" or quantitative conventions for generalizability and representativeness, researchers may fail to explicate the strengths of qualitative research and inadvertently reify narrow standards for research (Small, 2009).[1] Confusion over deductive versus inductive research has pressured some researchers into applying sampling and analytic approaches that are more appropriate to deductive rather than inductive research.

Various guides to research have extensively discussed how the case study method excels in inductive research in which researchers build up theory by repeatedly testing ideas in the field (Eisenhardt & Graebner, 2007; Small, 2009; Yin, 1994) and multiple settings (e.g., Burowoy, 1998). To deepen understanding of a phenomenon, we should first "identify the case that is likely to upset thinking and look for it" (Becker, 1998, p. 87). By following up on "unexpected observations in the field," intrepid researchers can engage in novel theory-building (Becker, 2009, p. 4). Furthermore, an extreme case can serve as the "black swan" that helps reject or falsify assumptions (Flyvberg, 2006). As Buroway (2009) states, "theory exists to be extended in the face of external anomalies and internal contradictions" (p. 13), and cases allow us to explore such issues in intensive detail.

The case study approach relies upon theoretical sampling that leads to saturation rather than generalization (Small, 2009). Past studies have shown the pitfalls of pursuing generalizability in organizational studies. When attempting to identify and quantify the features of an "average" organization, researchers can too tightly focus their data collection and inadvertently limit their claims. For example, by studying two or three variables thought to be generalizable across organizations, contingency theorists' quest to explain all types of organizations dulled their attention to distinctive organizational aspects that could have better explained organizational practices (Starbuck, 2008). The "average" does not afford the depth of rich data offered by extreme cases (Stinchcombe, 2005). Researchers may use averages to downplay ambiguous data, including interesting contradictions that enhance organizations' abilities to function (Starbuck, 2004b). Moreover, although averages offer an appealing and reassuring analytic construction, they can jettison wide swaths of the population (Igo, 2007; Starbuck, 1993).

Just as informative claims can be curbed by a search for an average, studies can be derailed by efforts to construct a random sample in order to take a representative sample. Generating a comprehensive list of organizations is difficult and labor intensive. For example, smaller, younger, and less formalized organizations may not appear on IRS lists (Smith, 1997) or other directories (Kalleberg, Marsden, Aldrich, & Cassell, 1990). While researchers can canvass for these organizations by foot or web, they may still overlook smaller organizations that lack the resources or wherewithal to have an active web presence, office space, or staff who can answer questions. Because of these issues, older, more well-established, and larger organizations are typically overrepresented in studies while newer, emergent, and smaller organizations are underrepresented. Thus, we have studies of certain organization processes and practices, such as rationalization and institutional maintenance. However, we have a shallower understanding of other phenomenon, such as the emergence of new organizing practices and experimentation.

Calls for comparative cases can also misguide research. Some cases can be matched or compared, strengthening studies. But for other cases, particularly extreme cases, comparative cases do not yet exist, or they may exist in attenuated forms. For example, during the years when I conducted my research, the Burning Man organization was in the process of formalizing from an ad hoc to a year-round organization (Chen, 2009). Comparable cases of growing organizations that coordinated temporary arts communities were not available for study, as the Burning Man phenomenon had not yet disseminated worldwide. Thus, I followed Isaac Newton's maxim to "stand on the shoulders of giants." I built on others' research on similar organizations, including extreme cases of organizations with collectivist practices (i.e., communes, cooperatives, and kibbutzim), to help identify conditions for my phenomena. Now, others can build on my research by studying Burning Man–inspired events and their organizations.

Challenges of Researching Extreme Cases

Research design principles emphasize validity, reliability, and generalizability as essential to knowledge-building. But when such principles are applied without regard to the research question and context, norms about research design reveal more about myth and ceremony, or taken-for-granted beliefs (i.e., Meyer & Rowan, 1977), than thoughtful consideration of how to conduct and present research. In particular, certain groups or sites are treated as "model systems" for understanding phenomena. These attract inordinate focus in studies, at least until researchers or advocates raise other possibilities. In doing so, proponents of alternate sites articulate why these are appropriate, thereby unveiling taken-for-granted assumptions. For example, until challenged with alternatives, Chicago was the city to study among sociologists; car factories were considered "typical" organizations; and middle-class women were the locus of study for gender issues (Guggenheim & Krause, 2012).

Rather than rationalizing research designs to a few narrow standards or restricting study to certain sites, colleagues advocate that we deploy a variety of research methods toward understanding phenomena (Small, 2009; Starbuck, 2004a, 2007, 2008). Here, I focus on the challenges of researching extreme cases and highlight past contributions. Several of these studies have become "frame-breaking" memorable works that not only are often cited (Bamberger & Pratt, 2010, p. 666), but also are widely taught to illustrate organizing dilemmas and possibilities.

Understanding "What Is This a Case Of?"

When conducting and writing up research, researchers must consider how the object of study relates to a larger phenomenon. For some, especially those undertaking inductive research, this may not be readily apparent or settled until later phases of the study when researchers can test and revise assumptions and hypotheses (Becker, 2009; Ragin, 1992). In particular, extreme cases excel at rendering visible what is taken for granted. In organizational studies, this is most apparent in ethnographic research of how seemingly extraordinary organizations confront organizing dilemmas common to all organizations. In addition, extreme cases reveal how organizations pursue values in their organizational forms and practices, including not yet taken-for-granted organizing practices. Extreme cases are also ideal for identifying conditions under which groups can sustain their practices despite internal and external pressures to follow conventions. Moreover, extreme cases can also highlight how organizations or particular practices emerge, particularly when the market and state and civil sectors are not present to shape activities. Finally, extreme cases unveil the black box of how organizations concentrate and wield power.

How the Extraordinary Handle the Mundanity of Organizing Dilemmas

Extreme cases show how the seemingly most extraordinary organizations must contend with mundane organizing dilemmas: recruiting and retaining members, coordinating efforts, tracking activities, and expanding efforts. As shown in Table 4.1, examples of recently studied extreme cases include organizations composed of pirates and privateers (government-sanctioned sailors who preyed upon

Table 4.1 Extreme Cases That Examine How the Extraordinary Handle the Mundanity of Organizing Dilemmas

Reference	Research Context	How Innovation Was Studied	Outcomes/Results of Innovation
Leeson (2007)	17th and 18th century pirate and privateer ships	Archival research	Application of bureaucratic practices to principal/agent problems
Gambetta (2009)	Contemporary mafia/mob	Interviews	Managing trust through signaling
Varese (2011)	Contemporary mafia/mob	Interviews	Expanding territory
Shapiro (2013)	Contemporary terrorist groups	Content analysis of documents	Managing principal/agent problems

the ships of enemy nations) during the 17th and 18th centuries (Leeson, 2007), mafioso (Gambetta, 2009; Varese, 2011), and terrorists (Shapiro, 2013). Because these organizations are considered illegitimate by the state, they cannot turn to the state or its institutions to adjudicate matters.

Organizing dilemmas such as how to wield authority or motivate members appear in greater relief in such extreme cases. For example, according to Shapiro (2013), terrorist groups prefer conventional top-down bureaucratic practices; however, a bureaucratic paper trail can attract scrutiny and suppression by the state and intelligence agencies. Terrorist groups thus decentralize networks to coordinate activities, but this exacerbates tensions between rank-and-file members and leaders over everyday matters such as appropriate expenditures and reimbursements (Shapiro, 2013). In contrast, because 17th and 18th century pirate ship crew members lived and worked in close proximity, they could apply and enforce bureaucratic practices, such as relying upon written codes of conduct to specify booty-sharing, compensation for injuries, and judicial review of disputes (Leeson, 2007). These extreme cases offer insights into principal/agent problems and conflicts over authority.

How Organizations Pursue Values via Their Organizing Practices and Forms

Even for the most conventional organizations, organizational forms and practices are not only a means to an end, but also instantiations of preferred values such as bureaucratic efficiency or democratic inclusiveness (Chen, Lune, & Queen, 2013). This expressive dimension was most apparent in recent social movement groups including Occupy (Gitlin, 2012; Graeber, 2013; Milkman, Lewis, & Luce, 2013; Razsa & Kurnik, 2012) and transnational economic justice gatherings (Smith & Glidden, 2012). How these organizations are perceived reveals deep-seated assumptions about appropriate organizing practices. When discussing Occupy's unfamiliar participatory organizing practices, unions, the media, and the general public have expressed puzzlement and even hostility. Such reactions indicate the degree to which Occupy has threatened and violated otherwise unquestioned beliefs about how organizations should look and operate. For example, Occupy participants rejected hierarchy by refusing to appoint leaders or spokespersons to communicate with elected officials and the media. When pressed by their city's mayor to send a representative, Occupy Denver selected Shelby, a dog, as their leader to question the state's designation of corporations as having the rights of human persons.[2] Defying the expectations for a few clearly stated goals, Occupy participants supported a multiplicity of goals and encouraged the proliferation of affinity groups to explore the myriad issues raised.

Occupy's seemingly novel participatory practices and values have a long legacy of predecessors documented by research. Several decades of studies have examined how such organizations enact prefigurative practices that embody desired values and goals (e.g., Breines, 1982). In particular, studies have sought to understand how groups can introduce and sustain collectivist or democratic practices in which members have a say in decision-making and organizing matters. Organizations have implemented these practices in the hopes of realizing utopist or democratic aims of integrating collective and individual interests; others sought to combat the ills of existing institutions and bureaucratic practices (Rothschild & Whitt, 1986). Studies of communes (Kanter, 1972) and kibbutzim (Simons & Ingram, 2003) explicated how the most intensive of collectivist/democratic organizations enhance member commitment. Other studies examined internally and externally imposed tensions over decision-making and authority in worker cooperatives (Brecher, 2011; Rothschild & Whitt, 1986; Whyte & Whyte, 1988), free schools where students and teachers collaboratively shaped the curriculum (Swidler, 1979), and alternative health clinics that sought to eliminate hierarchies among members with different professional credentials (Kleinman, 1996). In addition, researchers have examined the tensions between collectivist practices and pressures to bureaucratize in various social movement organizations such as civil rights (Polletta, 2002) and women's groups (Bordt, 1997).

While much of the research on collectivist practices focuses on organizations originating in the 1960s and 1970s countercultural ferment, recent research has examined contemporary applications of participatory practices in other contexts. The original extreme cases offer a foil against which we can compare the consequences of decoupling organizing practices from their original values and goals. For example, in the pursuit of efficiency gains, workplaces such as factories introduced "high performance" participatory teamwork. In such organizations, managers do not share authority or ownership among members (Rothschild, 2000; Vallas, 2006). Instead, participatory practices offer a more internalized form of control (Barker, 1993, 1999), albeit one that workers resist (Graham, 1995) or use to challenge management (Vallas, 2006). Similarly, studies of cities and civic groups' experimentation with deliberative practices, guided by professional facilitators, have revealed how this latest trend in governance failed to induce structural changes (Lee & Romano, 2013) and diminished individuals' enthusiasm for trying participatory practices in the future (Lee & Lingo, 2011).

In contrast, research on expanding contemporary organizations that produce collective goods, such as open source projects (Chen & O'Mahony, 2009) and the annual, week-long arts community Burning Man (Chen, 2009), highlights the trade-offs of organizing practices, as shown in Table 4.2. When combined with research on Occupy and its precursor, the Direct Action Network (Graeber, 2009), such studies of extreme cases show how increasing scale is not necessarily inimical to collectivist practices and goals. By aggregating this and related research (e.g., Vail & Hollands, 2012, 2013), we can see how values help groups to more mindfully make decisions about expansion and resources that are otherwise taken for granted in more conventional organizations.

When aggregating cases, knowing what research on similar organizations has already been conducted is crucial. This may be more difficult because mainstream class syllabi or conventional literature reviews often overlook extreme cases; thus, pursuing knowledgeable recommendations and undertaking thorough literature searches are key. If a number of cases are available, researchers can conduct a meta-analysis, as exemplified by Hodson's (2001) aggregation of ethnographies to identify commonalities of abuses and mismanagement across workplaces, as well as strategies by which workers defended their dignity through personal routines and even sabotage. Such meta-analyses have revealed the extensiveness of organizational practices across organizations, including the prevalence of patrimonialism, that previously were considered anomalous (Hodson, Martin, Lopez, and Roscigno 2012). Meta-analysis and other forms of aggregating cases can promote more robust theory-building.

Table 4.2 Extreme Cases That Show How Organizations Pursue Values via Their Organizing Practices and Forms

Reference	Research Context	How Innovation Was Studied	Outcomes/Results of Innovation
Rothschild & Whitt (1986)	Communes, cooperatives, and other collectivist organizations	Identified typology of organizations that rely upon collectivist practices	Proposed conditions that enhance likelihood that organizations can maintain collectivist practices
Chen (2009)	Contemporary organization that coordinates an annual week-long arts festival	Examined how values helped organization select and retain practices despite pressures to drop these practices	Showed how an organization can sustain desired organizing practices despite internal and external pressures
Chen & O'Mahony (2009)	Comparison of open source projects and an organization that coordinates an annual week-long arts festival	Studied how collectivities differentiated themselves from conventional organizing practices	Demonstrated how reference groups serve as foils

How Organizations Engage in Emergent Action When the Market and State and Civil Sectors Are Absent

The extreme cases of ephemeral organizations also help us understand how ad hoc organizing practices emerge, as well as how other organizations and the state can suppress such activities. For example, the study of how temporary organizations arise during disasters, when the state and other organizations are not yet able to react, enhances our knowledge of the development of routines. Moreover, these studies demonstrate how reestablishment of conventional state and organizational activities can dampen ad hoc organizing efforts (Kendra & Wachtendorf, 2003; Lanzara, 1983).

By examining organizations in countries with governance structures and norms about appropriate organizational forms that differ from North American standards, we gain a wider perspective on the diversity of organizing activities worldwide (Clegg, 1990; Ibarra-Colado, 2006). For example, studies of nongovernmental organizations in China show how these collectivities skirt governmental regulations that constrain their activities (Spires, 2011). Similarly, anarchist collectivities offer for study alternate ways of coordinating activities in areas where the state and civil sectors cannot or will not operate (Graeber, 2007; Mandiberg & Sakamoto, 2013; Scott, 2010). In these and similar settings, researchers can more easily identify necessary conditions that support coordinated activities, such as the development and enforcement of norms and guidelines (Ostrom, 2008 [1990]). Similarly, how organizations are able to regenerate, even after catastrophic circumstances like 9/11 when the state and other institutions are in disarray (Beunza & Stark, 2003), offer important insights into organizing practices.

How Organizations Concentrate Power and Reproduce the Status Quo

Classic studies of total institutions such as mental institutions (e.g., Goffman, 1961; Rosenhan, 1973), as well as recent analysis of World War II concentration camps (Martí & Fernández, 2013), reveal the depth to which routines can elicit unthinking obedience and concentrate and sustain power despite members' resistance. More recent studies of varieties of workplace surveillance illustrate workers' reluctant acceptance of eroding autonomy (Anteby & Chan, 2014; Sallaz, 2009). Such extreme cases render visible the invisible: the concentration of power in our everyday organizations, particularly hierarchical ones, and our acceptance of this as normal or even desirable (Perrow, 1986).

As Table 4.3 shows, such embedded power helps reproduce the status quo by making the uncertain certain via routines and smoothing over potential threats to institutional activities. Using archival documents, Vaughan (1997) traced how NASA's normalization of deviance enabled managers'

Table 4.3 Extreme Cases That Delve into How Organizations Concentrate Power and Reproduce the Status Quo

Reference	Research Context	How Innovation Was Studied	Outcomes/Results of Innovation
Chen (2012)	Contemporary organization that coordinates an annual week-long arts festival	Focused on use of storytelling	Linked how storytelling helped charismatize the routine by inspiring agency and delineating appropriate from inappropriate activities
Lok & de Rond (2013)	Sports team participating in a traditional event	Examined how organization dealt with challenges to institution of racing	Showed micro-processes that smooth over potential damage to institutions
Vaughan (1997)	Governmental agency responsible for space exploration	Studied how organization made deviance acceptable	Illustrated how internal and external pressures commit organizations to risky actions

disastrous decision to launch the *Challenger* shuttle despite engineers' protests. By studying the Cambridge University Boat Club crew team's efforts to prepare for an annual race between Cambridge and Oxford Universities, researchers illuminated how maintenance efforts repair minor and major breakdowns that could undermine long-standing institutions (Lok & De Rond, 2013). While routinization constitutes the everyday life of conventional organizations (Leidner, 1993), the formation and enactment of routines are easier to identify in extreme cases. Exemplar studies include how ritualistic routines contribute to the institutional maintenance of status and privilege at Cambridge Colleges and beyond (Dacin, Munir, & Tracey, 2010) and the annual reformation of a summer camp by new and returning campers (Birnholtz, Cohen, & Hoch, 2007). "Softer" forms of power are evident in organizations that harness the extraordinary to sustain the everyday, as shown by storytelling efforts to inspire unfamiliar activities at Burning Man (Chen, 2012) and rituals in universities (Clark, 2005).

Extreme cases show how other organizations can challenge the status quo through their practices. To call attention to their causes and power arrangements, some organizations, particularly social movement groups, have used tactics that have been deemed by others as illegitimate or disruptive. This includes civil disobedience such as occupying businesses and governmental offices, as practiced by civil rights groups (Polletta, 2002), and even destruction of property, as done by environmental activist groups (Elsbach & Sutton, 1992). Recent organizational theories such as strategic action fields may foster more research in this area (Fligstein & McAdam, 2011, 2012).

How to Undertake Research Using Extreme Cases

When studying extreme cases, researchers may encounter hurdles with negotiating access, analyzing data, and presenting the data, as indicated in Figure 4.1. Researchers may thus have to expend more time and effort to continuously revisit research stages rather than undertaking a linear path (Starbuck, 2004a).

Negotiating Access and Collecting Data

When identifying potential cases, researchers may soon realize that the needed data may not be easy to gather. For example, historical records may not exist if the organizations did not have the capacity or priority to make and keep these records or if they have no place to store them. Here, governmental organizations and entities with record-keeping repositories, such as universities, may be useful. For those conducting interviews and/or observations, time is also an issue because researchers may need to expend months or even years cultivating relationships with gatekeepers to gain or retain access.

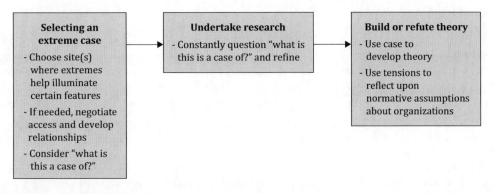

Figure 4.1 Undertaking Research on Extreme Cases

Katherine K. Chen

Increasingly, researchers face more hurdles in launching and publishing organizational research. These include attempts to standardize documents for use with human subjects (Becker, 2009). In addition, some institutional review boards' (IRBs), human subjects committees, and publishers demand documentation regarding access to organizations. These have raised concerns that researchers will eschew undertaking studies on human subjects (Babb, 2013).

Analyzing Data

Extreme cases require more processing time during data analysis. Researchers may have to take additional steps to help with data analysis, including repeatedly presenting or workshopping a paper to hone arguments for "what is this a case of?" Tensions about this can reflect how a site of study may question deeply held beliefs about what organizations should do, thereby constructing a strong case.[3] In addition, researchers have to do extra work to convince potential audiences why they should care—efforts that may not be as strenuous for cases that are viewed as legitimate sites of study.

Presenting Claims and Data

Researchers who use extreme cases must devote more effort and space in presentations and publications to explaining their organizations and how these shed insight into particular phenomena. The ability to foreground the most relevant details while relegating other details to the background is paramount. Disciplinary standards and publication venues differ in their norms for how these are conveyed. For example, anthropologists can reproduce pages of field notes verbatim per thick description, whereas sociologists prefer shorter quotes extracted from field notes, often interspersed with analysis, to support their points. In journal articles with strict word limits, tables can quickly provide examples of quotes, but they run the risk of decontextualizing data. Narrative presentations allow for greater reader involvement by fostering more active consideration of alternative explanations; this format also conveys the ambiguity of organizing situations (Flyvberg, 2006).[4]

Without an explicit statement of what a case shares in common with other organizations or phenomena, the audience may not be able to make such connections. Instead, they may conclude that the case is an odd, unusual organization and, because of the case's seemingly unique features, that the findings have limited contributions.[5] As stated earlier, by explaining "what is this a case of?" researchers can "normalize" the data by explicitly specifying how the study sheds insight into larger phenomena (Bamberger & Pratt, 2010, p. 669). Additional tips on how to navigate such waters include the *Administrative Science Quarterly* blog (http://asqblog.com) and advice to would-be manuscript submitters and reviewers from journal editors (i.e., Pratt, 2009).

Conclusion

Undertaking extreme case research is challenging but offers high payoffs. Challenges include defending study design against misguided calls for "typical" or average organizations, representative sampling, and comparative cases. When arguing for the merits of their research, researchers must thoroughly explain "what is this a case of?" To illustrate how to do this, I described how studies of extreme cases help us understand four phenomena. First, researchers of seemingly unusual organizations, including terrorist groups and pirate crews, have examined how the extraordinary handle the mundanity of organizing dilemmas such as coordination and decision-making. Second, studies of organizations that have adopted participatory or democratic practices show how organizations pursue values via their organizing practices and forms. Third, studies of anarchist groups and organizations recovering from mass disasters have illuminated how organizations undertake emergent action when the market and state and civil sectors are disabled or absent. Fourth, extreme cases of organizations ranging from the

Cambridge University boat club to NASA have revealed how organizations concentrate power and reproduce the status quo.

Returning to this chapter's larger theme, extreme cases can benefit knowledge-building by helping researchers cultivate greater reflexivity. For example, neoinstitutionalist theory (DiMaggio & Powell, 1983) and research have extensively documented how organizations tend to adopt similar practices via three isomorphic processes. However, scholars rarely acknowledge their part in promoting convergence through their choice of study and recommendations. As professionals who import norms via teaching, publications, and advice, scholars can reinforce and even propagate the phenomena that they laud or critique. Rather than advocating just a few approaches, researchers could instead document the variety of practices that organizations engage in (Starbuck, 2004a) and question taken-for-granted norms (Eikenberry, 2009).

Organizational studies and society would benefit from a wider understanding of a variety of organizations, especially as organizations are increasingly granted more powerful rights than individual human beings. Identifying and documenting a spectrum of organizational forms, practices, and consequences is of growing importance. In particular, this knowledge would allow individuals and collectives to more mindfully consider organizing possibilities and trade-offs, rather than resorting to familiar conventions. Extreme cases help round out our abilities to delve into organizational phenomena, as well as question deeply held assumptions about how organizations should look and operate.

Notes

1 Critics have complained that gatekeepers, such as grant agencies and reviewers, promote a circumscribed conception of research. For example, the National Science Foundation (NSF) has tended to fund studies that build large datasets and undertake hypothesis testing over other research designs (Becker, 2009). Prompted by concerns about how reviewers have incorrectly applied positivist expectations to deductive research proposals, researchers have offered guidelines on how to give useful feedback (e.g., Bashi, 2004).
2 http://occupydenver.org/occupy-denver-elects-leader/
3 See Thacher's (2006) discussion of the normative case, for instance.
4 The narrative style of Jackall's (1997) ethnography *Wild Cowboys* underscores how law enforcement pieces together investigations of seemingly unrelated crimes under gang activities.
5 In addition, according to Bamberger and Pratt (2010), the researcher may suffer from a spoiled identity.

References

Anteby, M. & Chan, C. K. (2014). Job task segregation: A mechanism for work inequality at the Transportation Security Administration. Presentation at Eastern Sociological Society annual meeting.

Babb, S. (2013). Beyond the horror stories: Non-experimental social researchers' encounters with Institutional Review Boards (IRB). Presentation at the Graduate Center, CUNY, Sociology Colloquim.

Bamberger, P.A. & Pratt, M. G. (2010). Moving forward by looking back: Reclaiming unconventional research contexts and samples in organizational scholarship. *Academy of Management Journal*, 53, 665–671.

Barker, J.R. (1993). Tightening the iron cage: Concertive control in self-managing teams. *Administrative Science Quarterly*, 38(3), 408–437.

Barker, J.R. (1999). *The discipline of teamwork: Participation and concertive control.* Thousand Oaks, CA: Sage.

Bashi, V. (2004). Improving qualitative research proposal evaluation. In C.C. Ragin, J. Nagel, and P. White for the National Science Foundation, Workshop on scientific foundations of qualitative research report (pp. 39–43). www.nsf.gov/pubs/2004/nsf04219/nsf04219.pdf

Becker, H.S. (1998). *Tricks of the trade: How to think about your research while you're doing it.* Chicago, IL: University of Chicago Press.

Becker, H.S. (2009). How to find out to do qualitative research. http://home.earthlink.net/~hsbecker/articles/NSF.html

Beunza, D. & Stark, D. (2003). The organization of responsiveness: Innovation and recovery in the trading rooms of Lower Manhattan. *Socio-Economic Review*, 1(2), 135–164.

Birnholtz, J. P., Cohen, M.D. & Hoch, S.V. (2007). Organizational character: On the regeneration of Camp Poplar Grove. *Organization Science*, 18, 315–332.

Bordt, R.L. (1997). *The structure of women's nonprofit organizations*. Bloomington: Indiana University Press.

Bourdieu, P. & Wacquant, L. J. D. (1992). *An invitation to reflexive sociology*. Chicago, IL: University of Chicago Press.

Brecher, J. (2011). *Banded together: Economic democratization in the Brass Valley*. Urbana, IL: University of Illinois Press.

Breines, W. (1982). *Community and organization in the New Left: 1962–1968: The great refusal*. New York, NY: Praeger.

Burawoy, M. (1998). The extended case method. *Sociological Theory*, 16(1), 4–33.

Burawoy, M. (2009). *The extended case method: Four countries, four decades, four great transformations, and one theoretical tradition*. Berkeley: University of California Press.

Chen, K.K. (2009). *Enabling creative chaos: The organization behind the Burning Man event*. Chicago, IL: University of Chicago Press.

Chen, K.K. (2012). Charismatizing the routine: Storytelling for meaning and agency in the Burning Man organization. *Qualitative Sociology*, 35(3), 311–334.

Chen, K.K., Lune, H. & Queen, II, E.L. (2013). How values shape and are shaped by nonprofit and voluntary organizations: The current state of the field. *Nonprofit and Voluntary Sector Quarterly*, 42(5), 856–885.

Chen, K.K. & O'Mahony, S. (2009). Differentiating organizational boundaries. *Research in the Sociology of Organizations*, 26, 183–220.

Clark, W. (2005). *Academic charisma and the origins of the research university*. Chicago, IL: University of Chicago Press.

Clegg, S.R. (1990). *Modern organizations: Organization studies in the postmodern world*. London, UK: Sage.

Dacin, M. T., Munir, K. & Tracey, P. (2010). Formal dining at Cambridge Colleges: Linking ritual performance and institutional maintenance. *Academy of Management Journal*, 53(6), 1393–1418.

DiMaggio, P.J. & Powell, W.W. (1983). The iron cage revisited: Institutional isomorphism and collective rationality in organizational fields. *American Sociological Review*, 48(2), 147–160.

Eikenberry, A. (2009). Refusing the market: A democratic discourse for voluntary and nonprofit organizations. *Nonprofit and Voluntary Sector Quarterly*, 38(4), 582–596.

Eisenhardt, K.M. & Graebner, M.E. (2007). Theory building from cases: Opportunities and challenges. *Academy of Management Journal*, 50(1), 25–32.

Elsbach, K.D. & Sutton, R.I. (1992). Acquiring organizational legitimacy through illegitimate actions: A marriage of institutional and impression management theories. *Academy of Management Journal*, 35(4), 699–738.

Fligstein, N. & McAdam, D. (2011). Toward a general theory of strategic action fields. *Sociological Theory*, 29(1), 1–26.

Fligstein, N. & McAdam, D. (2012). *A theory of fields*. New York, NY: Oxford University Press.

Flyvberg, B. (2006). Five misunderstandings about case-study research. *Qualitative Inquiry*, 12(2), 219–245.

Gambetta, D. (2009). *Codes of the underworld: How criminals communicate*. Princeton, NJ: Princeton University Press.

Gitlin, T. (2012). *Occupy nation: The roots, the spirit, and the promise of Occupy Wall Street*. New York, NY: HarperCollins.

Goffman, E. (1961). *Asylums: Essays on the social situation of mental patients and other inmates*. Garden City, NY: Anchor Books.

Graeber, D. (2007). *Lost people: Magic and the legacy of slavery in Madagascar*. Bloomington: Indiana University Press.

Graeber, D. (2009). *Direct action: An ethnography*. Oakland, CA: AK Press.

Graeber, D. (2013). *The democracy project: A history, a crisis, a movement*. New York, NY: Random House.

Graham, L. (1995). *On the line at Subaru-Isuzu: The Japanese model and the American worker*. Ithaca, NY: ILR Press.

Guggenheim, M. & Krause, M. (2012). How facts travel: The model systems of sociology. *Poetics*, 40, 101–117.

Hodson, R. (2001). *Dignity at work*. New York, NY: Cambridge University Press.

Hodson, R., Martin, A.W., Lopez, S.H. & Roscigno, V.J. (2012). Rules don't apply: Kafka's insights on bureaucracy. *Organization*, 20(2), 256–278.

Ibarra-Colado, E. (2006). Organization studies and epistemic coloniality in Latin America: Thinking otherness from the margins. *Organization*, 13(4), 463–488.

Igo, S. (2007). *The averaged American: Surveys, citizens, and the making of the mass public*. Cambridge, MA: Harvard University Press.

Jackall, R. (1997). *Wild cowboys: Urban marauders & the forces of order*. Cambridge, MA: Harvard University Press.

Kalleberg, A.L., Marsden, P.V., Aldrich, H.E. & Cassell, J.W. (1990). Comparing organizational sampling frames. *Administrative Science Quarterly*, 35, 658–688.

Kanter, R.M. (1972). *Commitment and community: Communes and utopias in sociological perspective*. Cambridge, MA: Harvard University Press.

Kendra, J.M. & Wachtendorf, T. (2003). Reconsidering convergence and converger legitimacy in response to the World Trade Center disaster. *Research in Social Problems and Public Policy*, 11, 97–122.

Kleinman, S. (1996). *Opposing ambitions: Gender and identity in an alternative organization*. Chicago, IL: University of Chicago Press.

Lanzara, G.F. (1983). Ephemeral organizations in extreme environments: Emergence, strategy, extinction. *Journal of Management Studies*, 20(1), 71–95.

Lee, C.W. & Lingo, E.L. (2011). The "got art?" paradox: Questioning the value of art in collective action. *Poetics*, 39(4), 316–335.

Lee, C.W. & Romano, Z. (2013). Democracy's new discipline: Public deliberation as organizational strategy. *Organization Studies*, 34(5–6), 733–753.

Leeson, P.T. (2007). An-*arrgh*-chy: The law and economics of pirate organization. *Journal of Political Economy*, 115(6), 1049–1094.

Leidner, R. (1993). *Fast food, fast talk*. Berkeley: University of California Press.

Lok, J. & de Rond, M. (2013). On the plasticity of institutions: Containing and restoring breakdowns at the Cambridge University Boat Club. *Academy of Management Journal*, 56(1), 185–207.

Mandiberg, J. & Sakamoto, I. (2013). Alternative social services or alternative to social services? Unpublished manuscript.

Martí, I. & Fernández, P. (2013). The institutional work of oppression and resistance: Learning from the Holocaust. *Organization Studies*, 34(8), 1195–1223.

Meyer, J.W. & Rowan, B. (1977). Institutionalized organizations: Formal structure as myth and ceremony. *American Journal of Sociology*, 83(2), 340–363.

Milkman, R., Lewis, P. & Luce, S. (2013). The genie's out of the bottle: Insiders' perspectives on Occupy Wall Street. *Sociological Quarterly*, 54(2), 194–198.

Ostrom, E. (2008 [1990]). *Governing the commons*. New York, NY: Cambridge University Press.

Perrow, C. (1986). *Complex organizations: A critical essay* (3rd ed.). New York, NY: McGraw-Hill.

Polletta, F. (2002). *Freedom is an endless meeting: Democracy in American social movements*. Chicago, IL: University of Chicago Press.

Pratt, M. (2009). For the lack of a boilerplate: Tips on writing up (and reviewing) qualitative research. *Academy of Management Journal*, 52(5), 856–862.

Ragin, C.C. (1992). Introduction: Cases of "what is a case?" In C.C. Ragin & H.S. Becker (Eds.), *What is a case? Exploring the foundations of social inquiry* (pp. 1–17). New York, NY: Cambridge University Press.

Razsa, M. & Kurnik, A. (2012). The Occupy movement in Žižek's hometown: Direct democracy and a politics of becoming. *American Ethnologist*, 39(2), 238–258.

Rosenhan, D.L. (1973). On being sane in insane places. *Science*, 179(4070), 250–258.

Rothschild, J. (2000). Creating a just and democratic workplace: More engagement, less hierarchy. *Contemporary Society*, 29(1), 195–213.

Rothschild, J. & Whitt, J.A. (1986). *The cooperative workplace: Potentials and dilemmas of organizational democracy and participation*. New York, NY: Cambridge University Press.

Sallaz, J. (2009). *The labor of luck: Casino capitalism in the United States and South Africa*. Berkeley: University of California Press.

Scott, J.C. (2010). *The art of not being governed: An anarchist history of upland Southeast Asia*. New Haven, CT: Yale University Press.

Shapiro, J.N. (2013). *The terrorist's dilemma: Managing violent covert organizations*. Princeton, NJ: Princeton University Press.

Simons, T. & Ingram, P. (2003). Enemies of the state: The interdependence of institutional forms and the ecology of the kibbutz, 1910–1997. *Administrative Science Quarterly*, 48(4), 592–621.

Small, M. L. (2009). "How many cases do I need?" On science and the logic of case selection in field-based research. *Ethnography*, 10(1), 5–38.

Smith, D.H. (1997). Rest of the nonprofit sector: Grassroots associations as the dark matter ignored in prevailing "flat Earth" maps of the sector. *Nonprofit and Voluntary Sector Quarterly*, 26, 114–131.

Smith, J. & Glidden, B. (2012) Occupy Pittsburgh and the challenges of participatory democracy. *Social Movement Studies*, 11(3–4), 288–294.

Spires, A.J. (2011). Contingent symbiosis and civil society in an authoritarian state: Understanding the survival of China's grassroots NGOs. *American Journal of Sociology*, 117(1), 1–45.

Starbuck, W.H. (1993). Keeping a butterfly and an elephant in a house of cards: The elements of exceptional success. *Journal of Management Studies*, 30(6), 885–921.

Starbuck, W.H. (2004a). Learning from extreme cases. Presentation at Lancaster University Management School. http://pages.stern.nyu.edu/~wstarbuc/extreweb/Extreweb_files/v3_document.htm

Starbuck, W.H. (2004b). Vita contemplativa: Why I stopped trying to understand the *real* world. *Organization Studies*, 25(7), 1233–1254.

Starbuck, W.H. (2007). Living in mythical spaces. *Organization Studies*, 28(1), 21–25.

Starbuck, W.H. (2008). Constant causes of never-ending faddishness in the behavioral and social sciences. *Scandinavian Journal of Management*, 25, 108–116.

Stinchcombe, A. (2005). *The logic of social research*. Chicago, IL: University of Chicago Press.

Swidler, A. (1979). *Organization without authority*. Cambridge, MA: Harvard University Press.

Thacher, D. (2006). The normative case study. *American Journal of Sociology*, 111(6), 1631–1676.

Vail, J. & Hollands, R.G. (2012). Cultural work and transformative arts. *Journal of Cultural Economy*, 5(3), 337–353.

Vail, J. & Hollands, R.G. (2013). Creative democracy and the arts: The participatory democracy of the Amber Collective. *Cultural Sociology*, 7(3), 352–367.

Vallas, S.P. (2006). Empowerment redux: Structure, agency, and the remaking of managerial authority. *American Journal of Sociology*, 111(6), 1677–1717.

Varese, F. (2011). *Mafias on the move: How organized crime conquers new territories*. Princeton, NJ: Princeton University Press.

Vaughan, D. (1997). *The Challenger launch decision: Risky technology, culture, and deviance at NASA*. Chicago, IL: University of Chicago Press.

Whyte, W.F. & Whyte, K.K. (1988). *Making Mondragón: The growth and dynamics of the worker cooperative complex*. Ithaca, NY: ILR Press.

Yin, R.K. (1994). *Case study research design and methods*. Thousand Oaks, CA: Sage.

5

Contract Ethnography in Corporate Settings

Innovation From Entanglement

Anne-Laure Fayard, John Van Maanen, and John Weeks

Introduction

Organizational culture has been a topic of interest for practitioners and academics since anthropologist William Lloyd Warner joined the Harvard Business School study team (headed by Elton Mayo) that engaged in the Hawthorne experiments of the 1920s (Gillespie, 1991; Luthans et al., 2013). Warner was a "hired hand" brought in during the late stages of the project to design and oversee the observations and interviews in the famous (or infamous) Bank Wiring Room of the Hawthorne plant. While Warner's cultural interpretation of the results of that phase of the study were discounted by Mayo and others directing the project, anthropology and the quasi-ethnographic perspective Warner brought to Hawthorne left a mark on organization studies that persists to this day.[1]

Today, corporate ethnography is something of a field in its own right. Two journals have recently been established—the *Journal of Organizational Ethnography* and the *Journal of Business Anthropology*. Alongside the steady accumulation of research monographs representing organizational culture (e.g., Nagle, 2013; Krause-Jensen, 2010; Sarfaty, 2012), specialized "how to" or methods books on organizational ethnography are appearing (e.g., Atkinson et al., 2007; Neyland, 2008; Pelto, 2013). Increasingly, discipline-based ethnographers are entering organizations worldwide as traditional (unsponsored) university-affiliated researchers, as temporary contract researchers (with or without university affiliations), or as full-time employees (Cefkin, 2009b; Jordan, 2013). Interest in representing organizational culture seems to have spread to corporate managers who say they hire ethnographers—novices and veterans—to help them "discover, decode or otherwise decipher their company's culture."[2]

While academically trained ethnographic researchers still manage by hook or crook to gain unsponsored access to a company (and remain in the field for a year or more), growing numbers of ethnographers are paid to work as culture consultants to an organization advising executive-level managers on a variety of topics or to work solo or as members of internal project teams (guiding the team or not) charged, for example, with studying organizational culture(s), customer thought, behavior and habits, and how brands are managed, or assessing the likely integration of an acquisition. Some are hired as full-time members of the organization. A few companies have maintained an "ethnographic unit" for a number of years (e.g., General Motors, General Electric, Coca-Cola, Ikea, Intel, Xerox).

We argue here—and try to demonstrate—that what we call "contract ethnography" offers considerable opportunities to do serious and innovative scholarly work. Some might contend that contract work severely compromises various respected conventions surrounding adequate ethnographic representation since, for example, it may be done swiftly (*fly-by ethnography*), it can privilege the voice of those who do the hiring (*top-down ethnography*), it may allow the researcher little autonomy or independence in the field or analytically in terms of interpretation (*captive ethnography*), and the results of the work might remain restricted as a corporate rather than public property (*private ethnography*). These matters are no doubt worrisome, but we believe they are neither inevitable nor insurmountable. Contract work, like any ethnographic encounter, occasions an ever-changing entanglement of differing interests, practices, points of view, and shifts in the relationships that develop both in and out of the field.

How these entanglements both help and hinder a contract ethnographer is what we explore in this chapter. Critical features include openness to an unfolding research design, candid conversations with a variety of others unlike ourselves about ideas not our own, continual dialogue and negotiation with sponsors, cycles of withdrawal (and reentry), learning from the reactions of others to our "deliverables," and of course the wee bit of luck that attends to a progressively extensive and expansive study.[3] These are features that we take as modestly innovative in regard to the doing of organizational ethnography generally as well as its contract varieties. We will shortly turn to just how we approached such entanglements, sorted them out, and attended to the opportunities and challenges they posed in one particular example drawn from our own work. But first, we have a few remarks on our own understandings of and approach to contract ethnography.

Ethnography as Epistemology

Our view is that ethnography is a stance rather than a given method or any particular type of study. It names an epistemology—a way of knowing and the kind of knowledge that results. It is anything but a recipe. It involves fieldwork, headwork, and text work and results typically in a written representation of the cultural understandings (meanings in context)—always provisional and partial—held by others. It is both dynamic and recursive, and the encounter with the "foreign" is the very essence of ethnography (Agar, 1980). We spend, for instance, a few days in the field or talk to few people quite different from ourselves, learn what we can, and then alter the questions we ask or the way we ask them and spend a few more days in the field and talk to more people. And on and on it goes. Those who revere standardization break out in hives when ethnographers hold forth about their craft.

Ethnography is improvisational, not procedural. It is path dependent because we learn more about the subjectivity and intentionality of those we encounter in the field after our work has begun, and the longer we are at it, the more we learn about what we need to learn next. Our knowledge accumulates and changes over time as we come closer to understanding the perspectives—the points of view—of the people from whom we are learning. Knowledge accumulates in large part because surprise—in some sense the Holy Grail of ethnography—is inevitable and taken seriously. When people do or say what we least expect, explanations are called for, however limited and tentative they may be at the moment. It is the creative reaction to surprise that fuels ethnography such that often the early days in the field are the most exciting and the most creative periods of study because the learning curve for the ethnographer is rapidly accelerating. Yet, as we have discovered in all our ethnographic work, cultural learning curves rarely if ever flatline. There is always more to learn and another surprise just around the bend. Exit is then largely arbitrary, having little to do with either theoretical or empirical saturation.

Contract ethnography is a specific kind of work that is sponsored by the organization being studied for the purpose—explicit or implicit—of helping the sponsoring managers make more informed decisions. There are three key elements to this definition, all of which must be present. First, contract ethnography is ethnography. The characteristics of ethnography that we outlined previously may make other forms of contract research rest easier with sponsors, especially what Westney and Van Maanen (2011) call *casual ethnography*, which is exemplified in the works of Bartlett and Ghoshal (1998), Doz and Hamel (1998), and Prahalad and Doz (1987) whose work also involves spending a long period of time in the company being studied but taking a different epistemological stance.

Second, contract ethnography is sponsored by the organization being studied. The ethnographers may be scholars brought in on a part-time basis; they may be full-time employees of the organization doing ethnography, either as part or all of their job; or, as in our case, a mix of the two. It should be noted that it is not uncommon in what we would call "traditional ethnography" for the organization to provide some form of sponsorship and assistance, or at a minimum for the organization to expect something from the ethnographer in return for granting access. So sponsored ethnography doesn't fully capture the entanglement of contract ethnography.

Contract ethnography also requires a third element, which is that its purpose is to help the sponsors make more informed—and one hopes, of course, wiser—decisions. The organization wants to understand its culture better for some practical reasons defined by them. Those in the organization itself form the primary audience of the ethnography. Scholarly publication is secondary and may be constrained by confidentiality concerns. The contract ethnographer is often granted easier access than the traditional ethnographer but can publish less of what he or she learns. The contract ethnographer is writing culture first and foremost for the people enacting that culture themselves and not merely to represent it but perhaps to influence it. It is this practical and in some ways postmodern aspect of the work that we argue gives contract ethnography its sharp edge. Table 5.1 highlights these differences (and similarities) between traditional and contract ethnography.

Into the Field: The Trifecta Studies

Our work with Trifecta (a pseudonym) began in 2005 and continues in a limited fashion to this day. The company is a profitable, privately held, growing international firm with 50,000 employees operating in over 50 countries. Trifecta was founded over 100 years ago, and it commands a leadership position in several highly competitive consumer categories. Impetus, a relatively small internal research group within the company, solicited and sponsored our work, and we considered it—and Eli, the executive in charge of the unit, in particular—our primary client. They provided the funds for the research along with access to various parts of the company. As contract ethnographers, we were paid by Trifecta on a per diem basis. Our research expenses that were covered by the company included all site visits and the days we put to planning, analysis, writing, editing, presentations, meetings, and so forth. Several post-docs from Anne-Laure's university department were hired as research assistants to do both field and analytic work during the later stages of the studies. They were paid through a grant sponsored by Trifecta. There were budgetary constraints on both sides of course. Impetus did not have unlimited funds, nor did we have unlimited time given our academic day jobs.

Our involvement with Trifecta began with a series of conversations initiated by Eli about organizational culture generally and Trifecta's culture specifically. These conversations took place individually in our respective academic quarters and, beyond their ostensible purpose of talking about culture, they were important for establishing an initial degree of trust and a mutual sense that we could work comfortably together. Eventually we agreed to be part of a culture study, each playing quite different roles. Anne-Laure played the leading part in all the field studies, interpretive analysis, and write-ups; the two Johns acted largely as distant, behind-the-scenes supporters,[4] readers, editors,

Table 5.1 Similarities and Differences: Traditional and Contract Ethnography

	Traditional Ethnography	Contract Ethnography
Who is doing the work?	Individual outsider or team of outsiders	Individual or team of outsiders and/or insiders
Who is sponsoring the work?	Possibly the company, possibly not	The company
Who is the audience of the work?	Primary audience is scholarly; secondary audience is the organization being studied	Primary audience is the organization being studied; secondary audience is scholarly
What is the intended use of the research?	To broaden our empirical understanding of different cultural settings and deepen our theoretical understanding of how culture works	To provide a cultural description of the organization that will inform decisions of senior management
What are the outputs of the research?	Primary outputs are scholarly monographs and articles; secondary outputs are materials presented to the organization and informants	Primary outputs are reports and workshops delivered to the organization; secondary outputs are scholarly monographs and articles
Who determines access and the scope of the research?	This is negotiated. The researchers are independent but may be reliant upon the organization for access and funding. It is a periodic struggle to preserve the integrity of the researchers' vision for the work given the constraints they face	This is negotiated. The researchers are being paid by the organization and the organization has laid out the goals of the research, but has hired the researchers for their presumed expertise in how best those goals can be achieved. It is a periodic struggle to preserve the integrity of the researchers' vision for the work given the constraints they face
Examples	Kellogg (2011) Kunda (1992) Krause-Jensen (2010) Desmond (2009) Pachirat (2013)	Baba (2006) Jordan & Lambert (2009) Cefkin (2009a) Flynn (2009) Suchman (1987)

advisors, critics, and nudges who periodically took part in meetings about the studies with both sponsors and senior managers. That they as "insiders" came to us as "outsiders" suggests that from the outset of our work they not only believed we were in possession of the sorts of research skills and expertise—both analytic and practical—that they lacked, but that we also carried a certain amount of symbolic capital they felt would help legitimize the Impetus-sponsored culture study of the firm.[5]

Originally, the official goal of our work was to help Impetus and, by implication, help senior managers in the company develop a "deeper understanding of the corporate culture." One of our sponsors at Impetus put this a bit more prosaically: "Tell us who we are. What is the culture of Trifecta?" Our contract work began as a single site study, conducted by Anne-Laure, intended to provide Impetus with a "quick read" of the company's culture in a time that was described to us as marked by major changes in the firm. Worries were expressed by those we spoke with at Impetus about many matters, including the rapid growth and increased globalization of the firm, ongoing (and perpetual) structural segmentation (and resegmentation) that split loyalties and interests, the decreased involvement by members of the founding family who were seen as the "guardians of the culture," and the possible influence potential acquisitions could have on the company. All of these things, according to our sponsors, might "weaken the culture."

This "quick read" of 2005 turned into what is now an ongoing research project that that has produced more than 30 studies in the firm. More than 500 interviews have taken place and 350 days were spent in the proverbial field.[6] Much of this was unplanned but apparently due to the interest our first study triggered. The research team grew slowly over time as we were provided with access to multiple sites in North America, Europe, and Asia. Our sponsors said they wanted to learn more about their culture in different sites (as did we). Five years after our first study (and after a dozen individual site studies in various locations and in varied business segments), we were asked to trace cultural shifts in the company over time and location plus produce several new studies of complementary sites that would provide an increasingly broad account of Trifecta's culture. This set of studies took 18 months to complete and led to a comparative analysis on our part of Trifecta culture(s) across time and space. In all, we studied 17 sites.

Entry to and exit from all sites was determined and facilitated by the Impetus group, reacting to requests from various Trifecta business unit managers; however, we had considerable freedom in the broad design of the studies, but not a free hand. Entanglement with the ideas and wishes of our sponsors and our own sensibilities as to what kind of contract work we were willing to do was always present, as was a degree of tension. For example, in the first study, which became known to us and those in the company as the "original study," after several give-and-take conversations, we were able to convince our Impetus sponsors that their idea of interviewing only the 15 most senior managers at the site was hardly a proper or indeed "serious" ethnographic approach. Anne-Laure was then able to interview—both formally and informally—a much larger and more diverse group at the site in terms of tenure and rank. She was also able to accomplish some observational fieldwork. The multisite comparative project undertaken much later in our studies provides another example (among many possible) of entanglement. Some of the sites chosen were based on previous studies, in part to look for changes, if any. Other sites were added because the Impetus team said senior executives in the firm considered them critical (perhaps both in the sense of importance and of being seen as most problematic by those at headquarters). We pushed for a wider, more representative sample. Not all our recommendations were acceptable, but some were.

Written accounts of each study (about 25–35 pages apiece) were produced and shared with the Impetus team and the site manager who internally sponsored the work. In some cases, we helped Impetus develop brief company reports (summaries provided in the ubiquitous form of slide decks) of our work that were presented to senior management in meetings and several workshops in which we all participated. Through such continual conversations, we were able to track how senior managers—in the so-called executive suite—were interpreting our work as well as gain an appreciation for just how they understood and tried to use Trifecta culture to accomplish their aims.

This ongoing dialogue with the Impetus team and senior management made us quite conscious of slipping into what Davis (1973) called the "convert" role. Even though we were treated as researchers and we were valued, we were told, as "outsiders" who brought a "fresh perspective" into the firm, how could we not be influenced by our sponsor's point of view? And no doubt we were as our stay lengthened. This was subtle because we continued to have creative disagreements with Eli and the other Impetus managers about how best to conduct the studies, interpret the results, and move forward. Yet, this back-and-forth dialogue led also to shared understandings of the work. Over time, we found ourselves slowly adopting some of their evolving goals for the project as our own and wanting to help them solve the problems those goals presented. Just how this creeping entanglement of perspectives occurred is difficult to precisely pin down, but this was something we continually asked ourselves (and wrote about extensively to one another).[7]

As ethnographers, we tried to disengage ourselves from ideas—theirs and ours—about what was "natural" about culture and what we were learning. Some help in this regard came from our repeated cycling in and out of Trifecta. Work would periodically become intensive and then retreat, giving us time to reflect on and adjust to what we had learned before a new round of study began. This built in reflexive time in which we could read, converse, and question one another led to a sharpening of our cultural accounts. Meetings with senior managers and sponsors were treated as episodes of fieldwork, not as simply planning or report-out meetings. We learned much from them in terms of contrasting their interpretations of our work with our own. These were opportunities to see what in our data or interpretations they ignored, resisted, or rejected; what surprised them; and what they wanted to change. This was yet another experienced version of Trifecta culture enacted in part as a response to our work. For instance, on reading one of our reports, senior management was rather pleased to see that many of our studies emphasized how the "push for performance" had emerged as a rather obvious theme in our interviews across sites. What they failed to hear in our narratives or notice in our writings—despite our emphasis—were the negative implications this push generated among many employees.

We found on occasion that our findings were taken well out of context and used in ways seemingly designed to accomplish managerial ends. For example, our first study pointed out that many, if not most, Trifecta employees with whom we interacted seemed to be what we called "past oriented"—employees talking eagerly about the "good old days." Changes (and there were many, in strategy, in operations, in technology, etc.) were usually seen by them as negative unless they interpreted such changes as a return to something they associated with the golden age of Trifecta. After our report was circulated, several managers told Anne-Laure that our remarks about the time orientation of Trifecta employees made perfect sense to them. Several said they now tried to frame projects and programs they were trying to implement in terms of "going back to the roots of the company." In a like fashion, a corporate branding effort at Trifecta that was initiated after some of our reports were circulated—originally to be propagated as a "new and different" direction for the company—was recast in terms of the Trifecta going "back to its roots."

This is entanglement squared. Our public articulation of culture puts it into play within the organization, and it comes back to us as our studies continue, thus producing more surprise in need of reflection and tentative explanation. This looping occurred on many fronts. Every report we generated, formal or informal, produced feedback that potentially could endorse our cultural representations or dispute them. What such interaction allows—and, in some sense, creates—is what we believe to be an altogether useful discourse that both expands our own and their own cultural learning and knowledge of Trifecta.

On Entanglement and Innovation

On the surface, the appeal and the perils of contract ethnography seem clear. The ethnographers get funding for the research and—even more valuable—the access to do it. In return, they sell a little bit of their scholarly souls to the devil. In Trifecta, because of the contract, we had unprecedented (though far from unlimited) access to all levels of the company across geographies over a long period of time and funding to allow us at one point to employ a team of ethnographers to take advantage of this access. In return, we accepted constraints on the scope and focus of the study; on where we would go, when, and for how long; and on how much we could reveal in what we publish, and we had also to accept our sponsor's goal (increasingly, goals) for the study. When we started our work, this seemed like a fair trade: We would learn a lot and maybe publish a little and we would get a chance to test our half-serious idea (or conceit) that if managers thought more like ethnographers, the organizations they run would be better off. Over the course of this long study, though, two surprising things happened.

First, we came to realize that the constraints we were under as contract ethnographers were different only in degree, not in kind, to the constraints we had faced in the traditional ethnographic work we had done before. We came to know that access is always negotiated; there is a moral obligation to give back to those that help you in your studies; organizations providing access always have some expectation surrounding deliverables and the utility of your work; and "going native" is an omnipresent concern and is to some extent unavoidable. In this regard, ethnography is always a little deal with the devil. It comes from using yourself and your subjectivity as your primary research instrument, of not hiding behind a white lab coat or sterilized set of testable hypotheses, of forging the relationships necessary to try to learn how other people see their world. The issue is how aware you are of the impact of these constraints on your work and how well you negotiate them. Contract ethnography has the advantage of making these issues so plain and stark that they are impossible to ignore, but it also affords some leverage across these entanglements because the sponsors want the work done.

Second, we realized that the possibilities of contract ethnography go beyond simply finding ways around the constraints to do ethnography. Contract work allows you do different kinds of ethnography. Several points are particularly relevant here. One of them concerns fieldwork. Contract ethnography doesn't just potentially provide more access, it provides a different kind of access because conversations with those you are learning from in the field are different when you are collaborating with them to solve a problem, when they view the work as helpful, and when you are asked in, not merely tolerated. Another is that there is a difference between writing an account for academic colleagues and writing an account for them, about them, and with them. The chance to go beyond merely getting the reactions of insiders to what we have written and to notice that what we have written influences—if only modestly—certain ways of thinking, talking, and acting in the organization (and then take this into account in subsequent loops of ethnography) is we think uncommon, but of considerable interest. This is neither a hypothesis test nor an experiment, but it shares characteristics of both and provides an acute awareness into how culture operates in organizations.

Treating contract ethnography as entanglement makes apparent that work of this sort provokes reactions and reflections on the part of all those involved about taken-for-granted assumptions, the ever-present set of shifting and multiple meanings, and of course ongoing problems—both theirs and ours. This is unsettlement, but of a sort that is not simply an unwanted accomplice to an ethnographic encounter but we think positively productive of an ethnographic account. And this is why we argue that it is not only possible for contract ethnography to produce serious work but also to produce innovative work.

Notes

1 The interest in the origins of organizational ethnography is now a crowded domain. Numerous fine accounts are available. A small sample would include: Baba (2006, 2012), Bate (1997), Buroway (1979), Cefkin (2009a), Schwartzman (1993), and Wright (1994). On the Hawthorne Studies, Gillespie (1991) is magisterial. On the contribution of anthropologist W. Lloyd Warner to the Hawthorne studies, Baba (2006) has much to say. Not to be missed either is the spritely—if snarky—treatment of Hawthorne (and the role of Elton Mayo) by Stewart (2009).

2 See, for example, a number of the chapters appearing in Ybema et al. (2009), Garsten and Nyqvist (2013) and Geller and Hirsch (2001) that put forth the varied interests organizational members have in sponsoring cultural studies—contractual or otherwise—of their respective organizations. Generalizing shamelessly from these accounts suggests that ethnography is in demand when new ways of approaching problems are desperately needed. The inelegant question "what the hell is going on here (or there)?" seems to motivate some organizational members to seek ethnographic help. One of the most detailed and explicit stories of contract research undertaken at the bequest of an organization is Schein's (1996) depiction in *Strategic Pragmatism: The Culture of Singapore's Economic Development Board*.

3 "Deliverables" is of course jargon, bureaucratic in origin and associated tightly with contract work, but it applies to all ethnographers. What have you promised or what must you deliver in return for the support to do the work? Considerable interest now surrounds finding ways to do ethnography—contractual or not—with a greater degree of reciprocity and reflexivity. Sending back a copy of a report, article, or book after a study has been completed is no longer adequate—and probably never was adequate (See, for example, Holmes and Marcus, 2005; Bartunek, 2007; Van Maanen, 2010).

4 Of importance and considerable value to any ethnographer are those close connections they are able to establish and maintain with at least a few "outsiders" who are both knowledgeable about ethnographic aims and traditions and deeply interested in, yet removed from, the everyday field and representation work involved in a given study. They serve as empathetic listening (and questioning) supporters with whom the ethnographer can periodically and comfortably share concerns about the direction the work is taking, the personal entanglements emerging in the field, the practical and moral difficulties encountered at various times throughout a study, and so forth. Peter and Patricia Adler (1991) provide one of the few detailed accounts of how such reflective practices, which they called "debriefing sessions," became routine and worked for them over the course of an intense and lengthy study of a big-time college basketball program—a program in which Peter was deeply embedded as a "motivational coach" on the team. Our "debriefing" sessions during the Trifecta studies began well after most of Anne-Laure's fieldwork had been completed and were, in comparison to the Adlers', sporadic and far less frequent. We were, however, struggling with the same ethnographic problem: namely, figuring out on what grounds our learning stood. In Fred Davis's (1973) terms, were we Martians or were we converts (or just where in-between did we stand)?

5 Whatever symbolic capital we carried—as outside researchers associated with universities—was made quite apparent to us because research participants and senior managers were always told explicitly and with some zest that all interviews, field visits, analysis, and report-writing were done by "academics." We were never referred to as consultants, contractors, or employees. We should note, too, that the Impetus team told us that we were sought and hired as "academic researchers" and explicitly not as management consultants with whom they had worked a good deal in the past (and are still working). As our and their entanglement wound tighter across the years, the distinction between providing "knowledge" and providing "advice" blurred considerably, although the contrast they made between consulting and research served and remained a framing device for our work.

6 Fieldwork consisted of shadowing, observation (participant observation when—alas, infrequently—permitted), interviews, and informal interaction with employees in factories and sales teams across the company and with senior managers in meetings. It also included participation in numerous meetings, presentations, workshops, and conference calls and regular communication via phone, text, email, and face-to-face encounters with different members of the organization across all ranks. Also of note is that Eli and eventually other managers at Impetus who sponsored our work and with whom we developed rather close and valued relationships over time were our "key informants" on most matters.

7 This gradual sharing of goals that we note in the text does not imply that we slowly adopted or inadvertently absorbed the perspectives and practices of our sponsors. Rather, our deepening engagement led to our sense that we could argue with our sponsors in ways akin to how insiders argue with each other rather than as an outsider might. Our conversation such as it was took shape around being drawn into their problem-solving tasks, not their worldviews. It meant putting forth our own views on how a particular problem might be best addressed, views that our sponsors sometimes found helpful, sometimes not.

References

Adler, P.A. & Adler, P. (1991). *Backboards and blackboards: College athletes and role engulfment*. New York: Columbia University Press.

Agar, M. (1980). *The professional stranger: An informal introduction to ethnography*. New York: Academic Press.

Atkinson, P., Delamont, S. & Housley, W. (2007). *Contours of culture: Complex ethnography and the ethnography of complexity*. Walnut Creek, CA: AltaMira Press.

Baba, M.L. (2006). Anthropology and business. In H. James Birx (ed.), *Encyclopedia of anthropology, Vol. 1*. Newbury Park, CA: Sage, pp. 83–117.

Baba, M. L. (2012). Anthropology and business: Influence and interests. *Journal of Business Anthropology*. 1:1, pp. 1–52.

Bartlett, C. A. & Ghoshal, S. (1998). *Managing across borders: The transnational solution* (2nd ed.). Boston, MA: Harvard Business School Press.

Bartunek, J.M. (2007). Academic-practitioner collaboration need not require joint or relevant research: Toward a relational scholarship of integration. *Academy of Management Journal*. 50:6, pp. 1323–1333.

Bate, P.S. (1997). What ever happened to organizational anthropology? A review of the field of organizational ethnography and anthropological studies. *Human Relations*. 50:9, pp. 1147–1175.

Buroway, M. (1979). The anthropology of industrial work. *Annual Review of Anthropology*. 8, pp. 231–266.

Cefkin, M. (2009a). Introduction: Business, anthropology, and the growth of corporate ethnography. In M. Chefkin (ed.), *Ethnography and the corporate encounter: Reflections on research in and of corporations*. Oxford: Berghahn.

Cefkin, M. (2009b). *Ethnography and the corporate encounter: Reflections on research in and of corporations*. Oxford: Berghahn, pp. 1–37.

Davis, F. (1973). The Martian and the convert: Ontological polarities in social research. *Journal of Contemporary Ethnography*. 2:3, pp. 333–342.

Desmond, M. (2009). *On the fireline: Living and dying with wild land firefighters*. Chicago, IL: University of Chicago Press.

Doz, Y.L. & Hamel, G. (1998). *Alliance advantage: The art of creating value through partnering*. Boston, MA: Harvard Business School Press.

Flynn, D.K. (2009). "My customers are different!" Identity, difference and the political economy of design. In M. Cefkin (ed.), *Ethnography and the corporate encounter*. Oxford: Berghahn, pp. 41–57.

Garsten, C. & Nyqvist, A., eds. (2013). *Organizational anthropology: Doing ethnography in and among complex organizations*. London: Pluto Press.

Gellner, D.N. & Hirsch, E., eds. (2001). *Inside organizations: Anthropologists at work*. New York: Berg.

Gillespie, R. (1991). *Manufacturing knowledge: A history of the Hawthorne experiments*. Cambridge: Cambridge University Press.

Holmes, D.R. & Marcus, G. (2005). Cultures of expertise and the management of globalization: Toward the re-functioning of ethnography. In A. Ong and S. J. Collier (eds.), *Global assemblages: Technology, politics and ethics as anthropological problems*. Oxford: Blackwell, pp. 235–252.

Jordan, B., ed. (2013). *Advancing ethnography in corporate environments*. Walnut Creek, CA: Left Coast Press.

Jordan, B. & Lambert, M. (2009). Working in corporate jungles: Reflections on ethnographic praxis in industry. In M. Cefkin (ed.), *Ethnography and the corporate encounter*. Oxford: Berghahn, pp. 95–133.

Kellogg, K.C. (2011). *Challenging operations: Medical reform and resistance in surgery*. Chicago, IL: University of Chicago Press.

Krause-Jensen, J. (2010). *Flexible firm: The design of culture at Bang & Olufsen*. New York: Berghahn Books.

Kunda, G. (1992). *Engineering culture: Control and commitment in a high tech corporation*. Philadelphia, PA: Temple University Press.

Luthans, F., Milosevic, I., Bechky, B. A., Schein, E. H., Wright, S., Van Maanen, J. & Greenwood, D. (2013). Revisiting the past: Reclaiming anthropology: The forgotten behavioral science in management history—commentaries. *Journal of Organizational Ethnography*. 2:1, pp. 92–116.

Nagle, R. (2013). *Picking up: On the streets and behind the trucks with the sanitation workers of New York City*. New York: Farrar, Straus and Giroux.

Neyland, D. (2008). *Handbook of ethnography*. London: Sage.

Pachirat, M. (2013). *Every twelve seconds: Industrial slaughter and the politics of sight*. New Haven, CT: Yale University Press.

Pelto, P.J. (2013). *Applied ethnography: Guidelines for field research*. Walnut Creek, CA: Left Coast Press.

Prahalad, C.K., & Doz, Y.L. (1987). *The multinational mission: Balancing local demands and global vision*. New York: Free Press.

Sarfaty, G.A. (2012). *Values in translation: Human rights and the culture of the World Bank*. Stanford, CA: University of Stanford Press.

Schein, E. H. (1996). *Strategic pragmatism: The culture of Singapore's Economic Development Board*. Cambridge, MA: MIT Press.

Schwartzman, H. (1993). *Ethnography in organizations*. Newbury Park, CA: Sage.

Stewart, M. (2009). *The management myth: Debunking modern business philosophy*. New York: Norton.

Suchman, L. (1987). *Plans and situated actions: The problem of human-machine communication*. New York: Cambridge University Press.

Van Maanen, J. (2010). A song for my supper: More tales of the field. *Organization Research Journal*. 12:2, pp. 240–255.

Westney, D.E., & Van Maanen, J. (2011). The casual ethnography of the executive suite. *Journal of International Business Studies*. 42, pp. 602–609.

Wright, S., ed. (1994). *Anthropology of organizations*. London: Routledge.

Ybema, S., Yanow, D., Wels, H. & Kamsteeg, F. K., eds. (2009). *Organizational ethnography: Studying the complexity of everyday life*. London: Sage.

6

Studying Elites in Institutions of Higher Education

Scott Snook and Rakesh Khurana

As educators at one of our nation's most selective business schools, we find ourselves obsessed with a troubling contradiction. We teach at an institution intended to produce, in its own words, "leaders who make a difference in the world," and yet we live in a world that, by many economic and social measures, is in decline. If our country's universities—including our own—are among the best, then we should expect our graduates to be among the most effective at leading our most important political, economic, and social institutions. Yet, our political institutions are increasingly captured by special interests (Carpenter & Moss, 2013), our civic leaders are not trusted (Kellerman, 2012), and our business leaders seem incapable of creating broad-based prosperity (Piketty, 2014; Porter & Rivkin, 2012). Why can't they do better? Why can't we do better? For us, studying these leaders—or *elites*, as we will call them—has never been more important. Studying the role we play in creating them is a professional obligation.

Both of us have conducted studies of elites in institutions of higher education (Khurana, 2007; Snook, Nohria, & Khurana, 2012). Our work, which is largely situated in the domain of organizational behavior, is part of a growing literature that looks not only at the impact these educational institutions have on our students, but also the role they play in our broader society (Khan, 2011; Petriglieri & Petriglieri, 2015; Stevens, 2007). In this chapter we highlight a few of the more novel methods we used to examine the intricate dance between the development of elite institutions and those who flow through them.

Studying elites is conceptually, empirically, and politically complex (for a review of some of the challenges, see Hertz & Imber, 1995). Some studies are theoretically and conceptually interesting, but empirically weak. Because elites are a nonrepresentative group of society, some of the more customary methods for studying social groups are difficult to apply. It is hard, for example, to apply traditional tools for stratification research to a group that is so few in number and often quite effective at camouflaging characteristics that are of particular interest, such as income and informal social networks. Elites do not generally flock to fill out surveys.

Qualitative research is also difficult. Ideally, qualitative data is collected over a relatively long period, but getting regular face-to-face time with elites—individually or as a group—for prolonged observation or interviews is challenging; they are busy people, and they tend to avoid extended contact with a social science researcher, surmising that their lives will be under particular scrutiny or subject to critical analysis.

Even when these limitations are overcome, studying elites is politically charged work, particularly in a country founded on the belief that "all *men* are created equal." At a time when inequality in the United States has reached levels not seen since the early 20th century, Americans are particularly reluctant to talk about elites because it often leads them to the idea of class—an uncomfortable construct for a supposedly classless society. Witness, for example, the recent backlash against Thomas Piketty's book, *Capital in the Twenty-First Century*. Piketty offers one of the most comprehensive analyses of the growth of inequality in the 20th century, yet he has been accused of socialism just for identifying uncomfortable facts. In short, the nature of contemporary elites is a complex and difficult subject for social scientists to approach, but it has perhaps never been more important to try.

Our focus is the modern elite business school. We argue that a principle advantage of studying this setting is that it gives us extensive access to people—MBA students—who are likely to become elites in our economic and social institutions. The problems of access are reduced since MBA students can be studied by researchers before they fully perceive themselves and are perceived by others as elites and before they become embedded in more formal elite structures, such as corporate top managements, where they will be protected by a phalanx of lawyers, tax accountants, and public relations experts. Finally, such a focus allows for a variety of theoretical approaches, including institutional, social psychological, and developmental. An institution that educates future elites is an ideal setting in which to investigate the process by which they are socialized, the content of the ideas they are internalizing, and the networks of relations they are forming.

The remainder of this chapter is organized into three parts. The first part provides a brief summary of the link between education and elites; specifically, how elite schools produce an elite class. The second part delves deeper into the process of elite education, offering a historically informed narrative suggesting that business schools have evolved through three phases to arrive at the market-based values and practices that today's business leaders take for granted: Managers are agents of shareholders, and the purpose of the corporation is to maximize shareholder value. The third part introduces an individual level of analysis to the study of elites in a developmental setting by highlighting selected portions of a longitudinal study titled "Becoming a Harvard MBA."

Elites and Elite Education

Elites can be defined in various ways, but most definitions—including ours—agree that elites are people with relatively high power and control of resources (Khan, 2011). In the United States, three groups have been singled out as elites: intellectuals/professionals (Bell, 1973), owners/managers of large corporations (Useem, 1984), and senior government officials (Mills, 1956). Our focus here is mostly on business elites.

As a society changes, the processes by which its elites are selected and developed changes, as does the cultural logic that justifies their privileged position; that is, there is an evolution of both *how* they are chosen and *why* they are chosen. Writing in 1956, sociologist C. Wright Mills argued that the growth of large organizations, such as corporations and government, during the 20th century had replaced a decentralized, local system of elite power in the United States with one that "for the first time had become truly national in scope" (Mills, 1956, p. 28). Robber-baron capitalism had filled its top positions through entrepreneurship, inheritance, pluck, luck, and cunning and was justified on a cultural logic blending self-determination and social Darwinism. Managerial capitalism—based on the separation of ownership and control (that is, the managers who run the company are generally not the people who own it) had created, in its later phase, a new system of allocating opportunities. This new manager was "not the individualist," as William Whyte put it, but someone "who works through others for others" (Whyte, 1956, p. 21). His values and motives were not those of his owner-manager predecessors. For the executive operating in the era of managerial capitalism, "never has the imputation of a profit motive been further from the real motives of men than it is for modern bureaucratic managers" (Dahrendorf, 1959, p. 46).

Education played a critical role in this shift. With the expansion of higher education and advanced degrees in business, a different cultural logic of meritocracy emerged to justify how executives often acquired their positions and their rewards. Elite status was the result of a combination of individual effort and natural ability. Managers were no longer people who had started their careers on the factory floor. Instead, they were products of a meritocracy: college graduates, engineers, and business school graduates who often had entered into management training programs immediately after school (Mayo & Nohria, 2005). A bureaucratic career process of internal succession—rooted in competence, administrative expertise, and loyalty to the organization—supposedly determined who got ahead (Khurana, 2002). The widely accepted belief in the fairness of this system contributed to its broad acceptance and legitimacy in the United States.

Highly selective educational institutions play a particularly critical role in allocating people to society's most powerful and highly compensated positions. Admission rates at schools like Harvard, Princeton, and Yale now hover between 5% and 10%, with many of the same students accepted to multiple elite schools. The top 25 most selective colleges in the United States are important feeders into the nation's top graduate schools, which have themselves become critical in selecting and shaping our nation's elites (Bok, 2013).

The ethos of meritocracy that had arisen in business also took root in business schools, with effects that reached well beyond those intended. Elite schools generally admit students through a rigorous process that differentiates and elevates individuals, thereby allocating "the best and the brightest" to important social and economic positions. Schools' institutional narratives and rituals—such as standardized exams, interviews for admissions, academic honors, recommendations, application-based fellowships, and merit scholarships—are meant to evoke reverence for meritocratic values. At the most selective business schools, case studies, brochures, and alumni awards preach entrepreneurship and lionize great business leaders. But in so doing, they explicitly and implicitly promote public policies that support the well-off over the poor. The outcomes they emphasize are efficiency and profits. Very rarely do elite business school courses examine how the American economic system favors the haves over the have-nots; very rarely do they explicitly evaluate business, economic, and social policies from the perspective of how they affect the least advantaged. Faculty feel more comfortable promoting probusiness arguments. Even if their research uncovers potential downsides to our current form of capitalism, they are careful not to be seen as "antibusiness." Although courses on organizational behavior typically consider the durable inequalities associated with race and ethnicity in America, few other courses raise questions about those who may suffer rather than benefit from contemporary business practices. It is power, not powerlessness, that excites students in elite MBA programs.

Business schools, then, as one of the most significant parts of the higher education system, are an ideal place to examine the formation of America's elites. Many of America's current and future business elites have been and are being trained there, bringing about an assimilation of meanings and concepts that shape these students' identities and subsequent behaviors. American elite business schools have thus helped create and continue to maintain our broader national business culture (Ferraro, Pfeffer, & Sutton, 2005).

Today, business schools do more than generate ideas and technical tools for business. They not only reflect the business climate, but they also help produce and reproduce our larger culture itself. They are the wellspring from which business elite norms and values flow. They are the arenas in which students struggle to construct their professional identities. They are the institutions that articulate, legitimize, and then reproduce the aspirations of practitioners. They are the crucibles in which students' expectations and standards of practice are forged. For practicing MBAs, the elite business school is *the* institution that defines business culture and practice. It is the place where students learn the meaning of success and failure; how to talk, dress, and act; and, perhaps most importantly, what is valued and what is not. Clearly, not all business practitioners earn an MBA. However, as society's single sanctioned socializing mechanism for business professionals, elite business schools are by default the primary guardians and collective conscience of acceptable business practice.

Elite Business Schools: A Historical Level of Analysis

The use of historical archives is an underutilized approach in the study of elites. However, there are instances that have shown the power of such methods to uncover important social processes. Karabel's (2005) masterful study of the admission processes at Harvard, Yale, and Princeton is one example. Dimaggio's (1982) study of social elites in the creation of modern museums is another. In both cases, this type of scholarship moves us away from a fixation on the present to an understanding of how today's taken-for-granted values and practices emerged.

To give a sense of how such a historical approach can be used to understand elite business education and to provide a context for Snook's study of Harvard Business School students, it is useful to have a sense of the institutional history of business schools. (Institutional history is in itself a good way to study elites.) Around the time of Snook's study, Khurana (2007) had also undertaken an institutional history of business education that examined how business schools evolved and how they adapted to changes in the business, national, and international contexts. A central finding was the identification of three successive definitions of the goal of business education. For the purposes of this chapter, we can consider the conditions that led to the founding of university-based business schools and how the social context at the time influenced their creation and diffusion. The remainder of this section relies heavily on Khurana (2007) and his co-authors' previously published work.

It is critical to note that the university-based business school in America arose in the context of what one historian has called the "search for order" in American society in the last quarter of the 19th century and the first two decades of the 20th century (Wiebe, 1967). The disruption of the social order occasioned by the rise of the large corporation in America and its attendant economic and social phenomena was profoundly troubling to the nation's established social and economic elites. The appearance, at this time, of a new class of aspiring elites known as managers occurred in a context in which industrialization, urbanization, increased mobility, and the absorption of local economies into what was increasingly a single national economy dominated by large corporations had all helped deinstitutionalize traditional authority structures.

In this destabilized context, three institutions—science, the professions, and the university—offered alternative structures and rationales on which to erect a new social order and create a new class of elites that, according to their proponents, were more suited to the new social conditions. Amid the sometimes violent clashes of interests (particularly between capital and labor) attending the rise of the new industrial order, science, the professions, and the university presented themselves as disinterested communities possessing both expertise and commitment to the common good. The novel institution of the university-based business school—which made its first appearance with the founding of the Wharton School at the University of Pennsylvania in 1881—drew upon the prestige of science, the professions, and the university in arguing that management could be conceived as a science; that it could be transformed into a profession on the model of the "high" professions—medicine, law, and divinity—which had been part of the Western university from its medieval origins; and that it should therefore be taught by professors in universities. The traditional high professions—particularly medicine and law as they were being reconstructed in late 19th-century America—provided a rhetoric of social duty that could be used to frame business education as possessing a higher purpose than mere "moneymaking," thus rendering it more palatable to academics who opposed its inclusion within the university.

Such a historical analysis also reveals that changes in business schools are not arbitrary, but rather are rooted in concrete and evolving institutional contexts. In the postwar period, for example, the shift in focus from professionalizing management to professionalizing faculty, along the lines of the postwar social sciences, can be linked to changes in the nature of corporations and the relative prestige of disciplinary social science. It was the widespread belief that American business schools lacked the necessary intellectual rigor that—along with Cold War fervor—motivated the Ford Foundation to spend what would eventually amount to over $35 million to remake business education in the United States in the 1950s and 1960s. This concerted effort to transform American business schools was driven by a two-part premise about how best to increase the intellectual quality of business education and to make it a truly "professional" academic field. First, the reasoning went, business schools must increase the proportion of faculty with doctorates in existing academic disciplines, primarily the social sciences and various quantitative fields. Second, MBA students must be extensively trained in quantitative analysis and the behavioral sciences. The new emphasis on hiring business school faculty from the quantitative disciplines dovetailed perfectly with the new conception of the rational manager that came out of the American war effort and became established in the corporate world by the rise of the conglomerate form of organization. The appearance of the postwar industrial conglomerate, with its multiplicity of managers increasingly removed from hands-on operations, made the sophisticated quantitative tools developed during the war seem increasingly applicable to corporate management. As a result of their diversification orientation and because, in a conglomerate, a single executive was often responsible for 10 or 12 businesses, corporate management in these companies devalued concrete, industry- or firm-specific knowledge and skills in favor of the new and more abstract and analytical tools and techniques that could be applied without regard to industry distinctions. Meanwhile, the idea of the professional—with its emphasis on a self-governing body with an explicit duty to society—seemed less and less suited to the conglomerate environment.

In the early 1970s, stagflation and the declining competitiveness of American firms led business schools to abandon any notion of professionalism in business schools; the ethos of professional management was held by some to have been responsible for America's economic problems. Drawing on the legitimacy of economics—a discipline that had become ensconced in business schools through the Ford Foundation reforms—economic theories, specifically agency theory, came to characterize managerial action and managerial character.

This was not an innocent academic exercise. The intimate bonding of disciplinary knowledge and its implications for professional identity are fundamental postulates in the social sciences. Of course, people actively use knowledge to advance their influence and privilege. But as Michel Foucault has noted, the process is more profound, since the classification of knowledge—grounded in behavioral science—creates distinctions we come to see as *natural*, thus limiting our thinking by providing scripts and preconstituted habits of thought. The classifications we create to organize our lives come to control our lives. Any theory of what *should* be will not only explicitly define what *should not* be, but will also implicitly make it difficult or even impossible to imagine certain alternatives that *could* be.

What gave particular power to agency scholars like Michael Jensen and his colleagues was that, unlike many of their disciplinary brethren, they made a considerable effort to disseminate their ideas and findings not only through traditional academic channels, such as journals and professional meetings, but also into the business school classroom and the wider world of practice. The acids of this new model could not help but eat into the traditional conceptions and legitimacy of managerialism. Jensen and his colleagues, by writing both prolifically and vividly, breathed life into the too-often sterile mathematical gymnastics of modern economic theory. As academic experts, they invoked their critical authority—a symbolic power—to define a framework that, when applied to ambiguous and contested events like hostile takeovers or executive compensation, exerted a powerful cognitive hold in shaping the interpretation of those events. Jensen and his colleagues skillfully connected their ideas both to illuminate and explain the changing corporate environment and to offer prescriptive approaches to improving corporate profitability. They assembled a rhetorical apparatus for agency theory that significantly influenced the interpretation and legitimation of a variety of new corporate practices. For example, Jensen authored or coauthored several articles and editorials in highly influential and authoritative outlets like the *Harvard Business Review* and the *Wall Street Journal* that helped legitimate the takeover movement, encouraged the proliferation of executive stock options to align incentives between executives and shareholders, and argued that leveraging corporations with debt was the best way to discipline supposedly wasteful managers. *Institutional Investor* remarked in 1985 on the economic sensemaking that Jensen provided for the hostile takeover movement, writing that Jensen "has come out in favor of corporate raiders and greenmailers to the point of developing an economic rationale for takeovers." Jensen argued that the deregulation that enabled hostile takeovers had resulted in a more efficient market within the U.S. economy for the right to control corporate assets. He stated that managers who are unable to keep their companies efficient, as measured primarily by the firm's stock price, will suffer the consequences in the form of a takeover. Jensen framed the market for corporate control as one in which alternative managerial teams compete for the right to manage corporate resources, stating that takeover entrepreneurs and imaginative investment bankers will continue to prosper. He described takeover artists, like T. Boone Pickens, not as financial speculators, but as "inventors." Dobbin and Zorn (2005, p. 187) suggest that Jensen's article on the takeover movement helped legitimize takeover activity by characterizing its perpetrators not as rapacious takeover artists but as providers of a societal service that "convinced the world that what they did for a living, far from threatening the corporation, was efficient: that it was in the interest of the shareholder and the broader public interest." Even after the recent financial crisis, this model has maintained an intellectual hold in business school research and business school education.

Elite Business Schools: An Individual Level of Analysis

In the context of a business culture and a business education culture strongly influenced by agency theory, we now turn our attention to a fairly ambitious attempt to study elites in a novel setting.

Over a period of 5 years, Snook and a team of researchers followed approximately 50 Harvard MBA students in the class of 2006 from just prior to entry (summer of 2004) through several years following graduation. Using a variety of methods ranging across organizational and individual levels of analysis, he drew from several disciplines to explore what it means to become a Harvard MBA. This was a longitudinal, qualitative, exploratory field study of 50 clinical cases for the purpose of building grounded theory.

Research Questions

Given that the Harvard MBA program claims to be a transformational leadership development experience, this study was designed to address two central research questions. The first was: What changes? That is, how are students different as a result of their time at Harvard Business School (HBS)? Is it a *transformational* experience? If so, for whom and in what direction? The second question was: How does it happen? That is, what is it about the experience that students find transformative? What are the central mechanisms of change? What experiences are most salient? What are the key components of the developmental curriculum?

Research Team

Due to the magnitude of this project (managing more than 50 individual case studies over 5 years) and the importance of timing (each set of interviews had to be completed in a relatively narrow window of time), Snook formed a research team to help him interview participants, manage administrative tasks, and conduct rough initial coding. Supported by the HBS Division of Research and the Leadership Initiative, he trained a total of nine researchers over the course of 5 years in the techniques of semistructured interviewing from an ethnographic perspective. Throughout the project, he also managed to include on his team at least one member who had just completed the Harvard MBA program the previous year. These recent graduates acted as "trusted informants" and "cultural translators," not only helping him make sense of his data from a student's perspective, but also helping to ensure that the team didn't miss any key elements of the experience itself.[1] Finally, he enlisted two long-time research colleagues to help him study the experience from an adult development perspective.[2]

Pilot Study

In the spring of 2003, Snook conducted a pilot study to inform the initial design and scope of the project. Following a review of the leadership, education, and development literature, he interviewed 30 second-year MBA students who were nearing the end of their 2 years at HBS. Using semistructured interviews, he explored both research questions—what changes, and how? Analysis of these interviews confirmed that, while the depth and specific nature of "transformation" varied from student to student, most reported experiencing significant change beyond the expected accumulation of technical knowledge and skills. This pilot study not only helped clarify *what* might be changing, but also informed the research team about how to go about gathering data on the *how*—that is, the *process* of transformation. For example, pilot study participants helped researchers create a developmental map identifying key events and transition points throughout the 2-year experience. The team relied heavily on this map to design their initial interview schedule.

Participants

Based on lessons gleaned from the pilot study, 75 students were randomly selected from the incoming HBS MBA class of 2006 (accepted and confirmed), and they were mailed solicitation letters during the summer of 2004 (about two months before their scheduled arrival at HBS). Fifty-four students agreed to participate, a response rate of 72%. Of those 54 students, 49 remained active in the study for all 3 years.

Methods

Multiple methods were used to gather a wide variety of potentially relevant data to address both research questions. In choosing these methods, earlier projects facing similar challenges were consulted.[3] Snook, like most who conduct exploratory longitudinal studies, adapted his approach along the way in response to what the team was learning (and not learning) from its ongoing analysis. For example, his original design called for administering only one Kegan Subject-Object Interview (SOI), scheduled for the fall of the first semester and included only as a measure of individual differences to add depth and breadth to the team's understanding of each student's level of psychosocial development. However, after scoring the initial interviews, Snook was surprised to learn how widely spread his participants were across three levels of development. As a result, he modified the original design and added a second set of SOIs just prior to graduation to see if they could detect any movement as a result of students' time at HBS.

While a complete description of each method is beyond the scope of this chapter, what follows is a brief outline of a few of the more important methods and techniques.

Interviews

The overarching goal was to gain students' perspectives of *their* holistic experience of the Harvard MBA experience and how it changed them. As a result, the team adopted a decidedly ethnographic stance in their interviews. Spradley (1979) describes the essence of ethnography this way:

The essential core of this activity aims to understand another way of life from the native point of view. The goal of ethnography, as Malinowski put it, is "to grasp the native's point of view, his relation to life, to realize *his* vision of *his* world." . . . The essential core of ethnography is this concern with the meaning of actions and events to the people we seek to understand. (p. 3)

Since the primary goal here was to learn how students experienced their time at HBS—the team wanted *the students'* vision of *their* world—all interviewers were trained to conduct semistructured interviews from an ethnographic perspective. (See www.hbs.edu/faculty/Pages/profile.aspx?-facId=164841 for examples of two interview guides.[4])

Informants

Consistent with adopting an ethnographic stance, in which the researchers were the students and the students were their teachers, MBA study participants were treated as informants. They were not merely *subjects* selected to test previously generated hypotheses, *respondents* recruited to complete surveys, or *actors* being observed from afar. Rather, they were trusted informants enlisted to teach the researchers about their world.

Timing and Context

Based on what Snook learned during the pilot study, his team conducted eight semistructured interviews over the course of 3 years. Each interview was timed to follow a significant event or milestone in a student's educational career at HBS. Interview 1 took place right after students arrived on campus, but before they began formal classes. Interview 2 was scheduled just after midterm exams in the middle of the first term. Interview 3 took place in January, just after the holiday break. Interview 4 caught them at the end of the first year and just before their departure for summer internships. Interview 5 took place shortly after they returned for their second year. Interview 6 was scheduled just after "hell week" in late February of their final semester. Interview 7 was the final on-campus interview, just before graduation in the spring of 2006. Approximately one year after graduation, each of the 49 remaining participants participated in a phone interview (8), lasting between 90 and 120 minutes. Each interview took place in a private location and was digitally recorded and transcribed.

Evolution

Data collection and analysis was an iterative and evolving process. Following each interview, the entire research team met to compare field notes. Not only did they begin to code what they had learned, but, based on each interview, they also identified gaps to fill and promising paths to pursue. The written guide for each ensuing interview was a collective effort based on the entire research team's accumulated experience from previous interviews. This evolution can be observed in the significant shift from Interview 1 Guide to Interview 7 Guide (see www.hbs.edu/faculty/Pages/profile.aspx?facId=164841), as the team began to dedicate portions of successive interviews for rough "hypothesis testing" and to gather more quantitative data to supplement what had been learned from preliminary analyses.

Psychological Instruments

Qualitative interviews were supplemented by several psychological instruments to further assess the influence of individual differences. Personality was assessed using a standard NEO PI-R

(Neuroticism-Extroversion-Openness Personality Inventory-Revised) instrument to assess differences along each of the commonly accepted "big five" personality dimensions.[5] A web-based picture story exercise (PSE)—a refinement of the Thematic Apperception Test—was administered to uncover students' dominant patterns of social motives (needs for achievement, affiliation, and power).[6] Participants' "hardiness" (Maddi, 2002) was also assessed to gain a general sense of how well they respond to adversity. Finally, researchers applied Robert Kegan's (1982) theory of adult development to evaluate students' general levels of psychological maturity. Rigorous subject-object interviews (Lahey, Souvain, Kegan, Goodman, & Felix, 1988) were conducted twice with a subset ($N = 26$) of participants—the first just after entry and the second just prior to graduation—in an attempt to assess deep, structural change in students' world views.

Before/After Pictures

Not surprisingly, students struggled to articulate how they were changing while caught up in the middle of it. During the final interview on campus, researchers asked participants to draw a set of "before" and "after" self-portraits[7] and then to explain what they had drawn. By engaging their "right brains," highly verbal and extremely analytical students were able to communicate with pictures—in a way that few had been able to do before this exercise—the essence of how they had changed while at HBS. (See www.hbs.edu/faculty/Pages/profile.aspx?facId=164841 for examples.)

Analysis

As mentioned previously, analysis was a continuous process. As a general rule, the team followed standard coding procedures for building grounded theory as described by Strauss and Corbin (1990). Multiple iterations of open, axial, and selective coding were conducted both collectively as a research team and then individually by Snook. For each psychological instrument used, researchers followed commonly accepted procedures for coding and analyzing the resulting data. For example, both NEO PI-Rs and picture story exercises were scored by external experts and results were integrated into each case study. In addition to standard field notes and periodic theoretical memoranda, the following additional techniques were used to help make sense of such an extensive body of qualitative and quantitative data (over 14,000 pages of transcripts were generated during this study).

Data Displays

All poll results were integrated into large visual data displays on single Excel spreadsheets that allowed for easier comparison and coding. Standard responses from many sections of semistructured interviews were electronically searched, tagged, transferred, and displayed in a similar manner.

Descriptive Statistics

Quantitative and, where possible, qualitative data were translated into counts and displayed as descriptive statistics for ease of analysis and comparison across cases.

Thumbnail sketches

To summarize individual cases, researchers constructed and continuously updated one-page thumbnail sketches for each participant in the study (see www.hbs.edu/faculty/Pages/profile.aspx?-facId=164841 for examples).

Summary

Studying individuals while passing through institutions designed to change them is tricky business. When both the individuals and institutions themselves are elite, the challenge becomes even more daunting. Doing this at a time when these institutions, the fields they occupy, and the very notion of what it means to be an elite in our broader society is increasingly contested requires some creativity.

In the last two decades, the study of elites has advanced by applying innovative methods of qualitative research that pay increased attention to unconventional settings and data. This is only the beginning. Recent investigations, such as those summarized in this chapter, illustrate the potential of focusing on how elites are formed and—lying causally behind that—how the institutions which form them were themselves formed. To accomplish this challenging work, scholars interested in elites must continue to develop and apply increasingly novel methods of qualitative research. The stakes are high. Given the pervasive and everyday influence that America's business elite have on practically all Americans and on the world at large, society cannot know too much about these people, including the forces that put them where they are and that allow and encourage them to do what they do.

Notes

1 The team was an intentionally diverse group of scholars who not only had the technical skills required to gather, manage, and analyze the particular types of data collected, but also could offer various disciplinary insights and a mix of insider and outsider perspectives. Sarah Kauss (HBS/MBA 2003) and George Karris (HBS/MBA 2005) were full-time research associates who sequentially filled the roles of trusted informants. Tony Mayo (HBS/MBA 1988) and Laura Singleton (HBS/MBA 1988) were not only team members who had the Harvard MBA experience themselves, but also were actively reengaged as informal "participant ob-servers" of the institution (as members of the HBS staff) during the study. The primary researcher, Scott Snook, experienced HBS not only as an MBA student (1985–87), but also as a doctoral candidate (1992–96) and finally as a faculty member since 2002. Balancing out his team over the 5 years were several research as-sociates with PhDs in the social sciences and extensive experience in qualitative interview techniques. They provided key insights by playing the valuable role of "true outsiders."

2 Barney Forsythe (PhD in education, President of Westminster College), Philip Lewis (PhD in clinical psy-chology, Auburn University), and Snook have applied Robert Kegan's theory of adult development to the study of leadership in various domains for over 15 years. Snook enlisted both scholars to conduct Kegan subject-object interviews for approximately half the students in this study at the start of the program and just before graduation. Each 90-minute interview was recorded, transcribed, and coded to obtain developmental scores indicating each individual's level of psychosocial development.

3 In this regard, Snook drew heavily from the experience of Howard Becker, Blanche Geer, Everett C. Hughes, and Anselm Strauss, as summarized in their classic study of how medical students become doctors, *Boys in White* (1961). Guided by similar research questions, both projects attempted to study emerging elites and the role that their respective professional schools played in creating them:

> The problem we began with was to discover what medical school did to medical students other than giving them a technical education. . . . In one sense our study had no design. That is, we had no well-worked out set of hypotheses to be tested, no data-gathering instruments purposely designed to secure information relevant to these hypotheses, no set of analytic procedures specified in advance. Insofar as the term "design" implies these features of elaborate prior planning, our study had none. (p. 17)

As the Harvard MBA study progressed, Snook and his team adopted an iterative approach to data gathering and analysis similar to the one Becker and his colleagues (1961) described:

> We carried on a running analysis of the materials gathered and as we became aware of certain problems made a greater effort to include materials which bore on those problems and tended to prove or disprove provisional hypotheses we were entertaining. (p. 27)

In the end, even the goals of the Harvard MBA study were similar to those of Becker and his team (1961): "to build and progressively refine models of the school as a social organization and of the process of development of the student moving through that organization" (p. 25).

4 Due to space constraints, a complete rendering of referenced appendices could not be published in this book. For readers interested in reviewing these supplemental documents, a PDF copy can be found on Scott Snook's faculty homepage, www.hbs.edu/faculty/Pages/profile.aspx?facId=164841.

5 Until the early 1980s, there was little consensus among psychologists as to the major personality traits. Today, however, there is general agreement on what is called the "big five model" or "five factor model" of personality. See McCrae and Costa (1990) for a summary of the evolution of personality inventories.

6 Based on Harvard psychologist David McClelland's groundbreaking research (1987), the picture story exercise is an assessment instrument that requires respondents to write stories based upon several pictures that are presented to them online. See www.hbs.edu/faculty/Pages/profile.aspx?facId=164841 for a sample PSE completed by one of our informants. According to Ruth Jacobs of the Hay Group's McClelland Center for Research and Innovation, the PSE is "based on more than 30 years of research demonstrating that motivation can be understood and measured through a detailed analysis of a person's spontaneous imaginative thoughts." The MBA research team worked with Jacobs and her colleagues to code and make sense of students' patterns of motivation and how these affected their HBS experiences.

7 This novel method was applied by Shoshana Zuboff (1984) in her work exploring how the introduction of technology fundamentally changes the nature of work and power in the workplace. According to Zuboff:

> During my discussions with these office workers, I sometimes asked them to draw pictures that represented their "felt sense" of their job experience before and after the conversion to the new computer system. Frequently these pictures functioned as a catalyst, helping them to articulate feelings that had been implicit and hard to define. (p. 141)

References

Becker, H., Blanche, G., Hughes, E. C., & Strauss, A. (1961). *Boys in white: Student culture in medical school*. Chicago, IL: University of Chicago Press.

Bell, D. (1973). *The coming of post-industrial society: A venture in social forecasting*. New York, NY: Basic.

Bok, D. C. (2013). *Higher education in America*. Princeton, NJ: Princeton University Press.

Carpenter, D. P., & Moss, D. A. (2013). Introduction. In D. Carpenter & D. A. Moss (Eds.), *Preventing regulatory capture: Special interest influence and how to limit it*. New York, NY: Cambridge University Press.

Dahrendorf, R. (1959). *Class and class conflict in industrial society*. Stanford, CA: Stanford University Press.

Dimaggio, P. (1982). Cultural entrepreneurship in nineteenth-century Boston: The creation of an organizational base for high culture in America. *Media, Culture & Society*, *4*(1), 33–50.

Dobbin, F., & Zorn, D. (2005). Corporate malfeasance and the myth of shareholder value. *Political Power and Social Theory*, *17*, 179–98.

Ferraro, F., Pfeffer, J., & Sutton, R. (2005). Economics language and assumptions: How theories can become self-fulfilling. *Academy of Management Review*, *30*(1), 8–24.

Hertz, R., & Imber, J. B. (1995). *Studying elites using qualitative methods*. Thousand Oaks, CA: Sage Publications.

Karabel, J. (2005). *The chosen: The hidden history of admission and exclusion at Harvard, Yale, and Princeton*. Boston, MA: Houghton Mifflin.

Kegan, R. (1982). *The evolving self*. Cambridge, MA: Harvard University Press.

Kellerman, B. (2012). *The end of leadership*. New York, NY: Harper Business.

Khan, S. R. (2011). *Privilege: The making of an adolescent elite at St. Paul's School*. Princeton, NJ: Princeton University Press.

Khurana, R. (2002). *Searching for a corporate savior: The irrational quest for charismatic CEOs*. Princeton, NJ: Princeton University Press.

Khurana, R. (2007). *From higher aims to hired hands: The social transformation of American business schools and the unfulfilled promise of management as a profession*. Princeton, NJ: Princeton University Press.

Lahey, L., Souvaine, E., Kegan, R., Goodman, R., & Felix, S. (1988). *A guide to the subject-object interview: Its administration and interpretation*. Cambridge, MA: Harvard University School of Education, Subject-Object Research Group.

Maddi, S. R. (2002). The story of hardiness: Twenty years of theorizing, research, and practice. *Consulting Psychology Journal: Practice and Research*, *54*(3), 173–185.

Mayo, A. J., & Nohria, N. (2005). *In their time: The greatest business leaders of the twentieth century*. Boston, MA: Harvard Business School Press.

McClelland, D. C. (1987). *Human motivation*. New York, NY: Cambridge University Press.

McCrae, R. R., & Costa, P. T. (1990). *Personality in adulthood*. New York, NY: Guilford.

Mills, C. W. (1956). *The power elite*. New York, NY: Oxford University Press.

Petriglieri, G., & Petriglieri, J. (2015). Can business schools humanize leadership? *Academy of Management Learning & Education, 14*(1).

Piketty, T. (2014). *Capital in the twenty-first century*. Cambridge, MA: Harvard University Press.

Porter, M., & Rivkin, J. (2012). The looming challenge to U.S. competitiveness. *Harvard Business Review, 90*(3), 54–61.

Snook, S. A., Nohria, N., & Khurana, R. (2012). *The handbook for teaching leadership: Knowing, doing, and being*. Thousand Oaks, CA: Sage Publications.

Spradley, J. P. (1979). *The ethnographic interview*. Fort Worth, TX: Harcourt Brace Jovanovich College Publishers.

Stevens, M. L. (2007). *Creating a class: College admissions and the education of elites*. Cambridge, MA: Harvard University Press.

Strauss, A., & Corbin, J. (1990). *Basics of qualitative research: Grounded theory procedures and techniques*. Newbury Park, CA: Sage Publications.

Useem, M. (1984). *The inner circle: Large corporations and the rise of business political activity in the U.S. and U.K*. New York, NY: Oxford University Press.

Whyte, W. H. (1956). *The organization man*. New York, NY: Simon and Schuster.

Wiebe, R. H. (1967). *The search for order, 1877–1920*. New York, NY: Hill and Wang.

Zuboff, S. (1984). *In the age of the smart machine*. New York, NY: Basic Books.

7

Drawing Fine Lines Behind Bars

Pushing the Boundaries of Researcher Neutrality in Unconventional Contexts

Kristie M. Rogers, Madeline Toubiana, and Katherine A. DeCelles

---

The guard says, "It's just like the airport except we need you to turn your pockets inside out too." After passing through security, I hear a guard requesting that the toddler behind me remove her shoes. The accompanying adult gives the guard an inquisitive look, to which the guard responds, "Well, that's where I'd hide it." We situate our pockets, shoes, and belts and grab our green laminated "visitor" passes before we are free to enter the Sally port with the VP of the on-site company. We walk in and press our visitor badges against the glass for the guard to see. I take a deep breath as the metal door behind us closes completely, locks, and then the one in front of us opens. We step out to see gray cinder block walls topped with spirals of barbed wire and walk forward, as the second metal door closes behind us. I feel sure of only one thing: the door that was keeping us out of the prison is once again securely locked, but this time, with us inside. (Day 1 field notes: description of author's initial prison visit)

Context is central to qualitative research because it directs the researcher's attention and facilitates the creation of theories that are "specific, explanatory, and relevant" for organizational scholars (Elsbach & Bechky, 2009, p. 4). We define context as the surroundings of organizational phenomena of interest (Cappelli & Sherer, 1991), including the circumstances surrounding the research project, the physical locations in which studies are embedded, and the populations under study. Within the domain of organizational research, context varies greatly, and some of the most novel and innovative advancements in organizational research come from studies in unconventional contexts (i.e., those that are unusual or extreme: Bamberger & Pratt, 2010). However, such unconventional contexts are rare partly because they are often exceptionally difficult for researchers to access, and they come with additional unique challenges for high-quality data collection.

Each author of this chapter independently led qualitative research projects that were in the prison context, examining phenomena involving former or current inmates and/or correctional officers. As the opening excerpt illustrates, the prison context can often be highly foreign to researchers, who experience it as jarring, uncomfortable, and emotionally evocative (Jewkes, 2014), all of which could interfere with high-quality data collection and thwart the researcher's role as an objective "scientist" (McCracken, 1988, p. 28). While contexts such as these may be particularly illuminating for understanding organizational phenomena of interest, there is little discussion in the organizational literature about the challenges such settings can pose for researchers when collecting data.

When the three of us discussed our independent data collections, a theme emerged that we wished we had known prior to beginning our research: Unconventional contexts may require researchers to break methodological "rules" for remaining neutral, formal, and objective in order to collect the most meaningful and accurate qualitative data, which is what we wish to articulate in this chapter. In particular, we center our chapter on qualitative researchers' interviewing practices in unconventional contexts such as prisons. We focus on the interview because it is likely more common than other forms of qualitative research in these contexts (e.g., ethnography) given safety concerns to researchers, as well as logistical difficulties.

For many qualitative researchers, conducting interviews is "exciting and enriching" and central to understanding context, as well as seeing the phenomenon of interest through the eyes of those living it (Kvale & Brinkmann, 2009, p. 123). However, researchers' specific behaviors that facilitate this exciting and enriching interpersonal exchange likely vary by context, and methodological guidance about *how* these concrete behaviors vary is limited. In our experiences, much of the qualitative research guidance for approaching interviews in organizational research favor a neutral approach characterized by nondirection in questioning (e.g., McCracken, 1988; Patton, 2002). This perspective advises interviewer formality, objectivity, and neutrality and maintenance of social distance when interacting with informants. For example, McCracken (1988) advised that "a certain formality in dress, demeanor, and speech is useful because it helps the respondent cast the investigator in the role of a 'scientist'" (p. 26) and notes that "unambiguous social distance between respondent and interviewer is especially necessary when 'tough' questions must be asked and 'delicate' analysis undertaken" (p. 27).

Furthermore, given that the majority of organizational scholars and published research in our field are positivist and quantitative in nature, qualitative researchers often face reviewers who expect a relatively more straightforward, unbiased, and consistent approach than more constructivist- and feminist-based disciplines (see Pratt, 2008). In our common experience as organizational researchers in the prison context, we found that acting with neutral manners (e.g., Patton, 2002; Singleton & Straits, 2005), or presenting ourselves as formal, objective scientists (e.g., McCracken, 1988), was nearly impossible and unproductive. We found that such an approach only increased the psychological distance between ourselves and our informants, which actually jeopardized our ability to collect relevant data. Instead, we found ourselves bending the rules, blurring the lines between the very stark "us" and "them" divide when possible, and drawing on our own emotions as cues for appropriate interview behavior. But how and when might traditional qualitative interview practices be modified in order to maximize the value of interviews? And with what potential risks?

Our chapter is organized as follows: first, we discuss the features of unconventional research contexts that may signal to scholars that adaptation of more traditional and objective interviewing tactics might be necessary. Second, we describe the nontraditional tactics we used and our experiences during data collection that we believe helped to produce novel theoretical insights: emotion, encouragement, and sensitivity. Finally, we identify the potential risks and trade-offs of these modifications.

Key Features of Unconventional Research Contexts

We wish to clarify distinguishing features of the prison context that could be shared with other unconventional or extreme organizational settings and that could indicate to the researcher that adaptation of traditional methodology may be needed. Based on our experiences, we articulate four key contextual features: (1) the gap in experience between the researcher and informants, (2) the strong and unfamiliar culture for researchers, (3) perceived power and privilege differences between the researcher and a marginalized or disenfranchised population of study, and (4) salient demographic differences separating the in-group from the out-groups.

Researcher–Informant Experience Gap

The first contextual feature we wish to highlight is the researchers' inability to share the experience of the informant. By this, we refer to contexts wherein the informants have experienced some sort of crisis or tragedy (Charmaz, 2006) or are so far removed from the researchers' day-to-day reality that it is difficult to imagine their experiences. None of us has been incarcerated or formally worked at a prison, and thus we could not realistically understand or relate to the experiences of our participants in a truly authentic way. For example, in response to general questions about what their work was like, correctional officers replied by describing emotionally evocative experiences of a prison riot, being stabbed or taken hostage by inmates, protecting inmates from violent assault and rape, and encountering the dead body of an inmate for whom they had been responsible. Inmates described similarly harsh tragedies, including growing up in extreme poverty, homelessness, abuse, drug addiction, suicide, rape, violent assault, and losing custody of children. Hearing about these events firsthand, especially when informants become emotional during their narratives, is exceptionally shocking and emotional for researchers as well.

Corbin and Strauss provided the example of studying individuals who experienced an unwanted divorce and suggested trying to relate to their loss by recalling the death of a loved one. They stated, "In the end, only the data themselves are significant, but it helps to have a little insight to start with" (p. 34). However, while we often experienced overwhelming shock, sadness, and compassion for our informants during interviews, it was also very clear that we did *not* share the same difficult experiences or anything similar enough to directly relate.

Strong and Unfamiliar Culture

A second difference that was apparent in our research was related to the strong and relatively novel culture of prisons. Prisons are, by definition, total institutions (Goffman, 1961), and with that comes jargon and belief systems that can be completely foreign to institutional outsiders, leading to difficulties in communication. In interviews, it became apparent to us that informants used many institutional terms (e.g., "boss chair," the tool for metal detection inside a human being; "Home in Virginia" for HIV status; "yard birds" for inmates who did not hold jobs while incarcerated) and had certain cultural belief systems (e.g., highly masculine and sexualized in a male prison) that were foreign and sometimes uncomfortable for us. The dynamics of the culture accompanying a total institution were important to consider as we attempted to maximize the flow of information during interviews.

Perceived Power and Privilege Differences

A third feature of our unconventional setting that challenged the objective nature of our interviews was the salient power and privilege differences between us and our informants. We, as White, relatively well-paid, highly educated, professional researchers could be perceived as far more powerful than the often minority, poor, disenfranchised inmates or often marginalized, minority officer informants, making them potentially uncomfortable in speaking openly with us. This was particularly true when informants were uncertain about our relationships with prison officials and administrators. Given the extensive bureaucracy and hierarchical structure of the prison context, informants were especially attentive to such issues. In our research, this meant that inmates were curious about our intent (e.g., asking us "is this a setup to get me in trouble?") or asking whether we could help them in various ways by influencing officers and administration. It also impacted officers' propensity to believe us when we assured the inmates that we were not there to find out information to aid prison administration, and it made the officers wonder whether we had the ability to actually affect change in their organization as a result of their shared ideas and experiences.

Salient Demographic Differences Separating the In-Group from the Out-Groups

Finally, demographic differences such as age, race, and gender played important roles in our research, as they were largely responsible for the stark in-group versus out-group contrast. When building rapport with informants, salient demographic differences between the interviewer and informant sometimes made it challenging to communicate that it was safe to share feelings, thoughts, and sensitive information without judgment. For example, in male prisons, race, sex and gender are frequent themes in interviews given (a) many inmates are deprived of sex, (b) the prison bias against homosexuality, (c) racial tensions among inmates and officers, and (d) the highly masculine culture. Thus, in our interviews we often heard highly graphic, sexist, and racist comments, which might come as a shock to a researcher and have the potential to thwart an interview.

As a result of these differences, we noted great divides between in-group (them) and the out-group (us) in the prison context, and the highly salient markers of this division. For example, upon entering the prison context, it was immediately evident that the researcher is not an inmate or a correctional officer, but an outsider (i.e., researchers being the only ones not wearing uniforms). Even outside the prison, however, former inmates described knowing the markers of who was "one of them," as one interviewee noted: "you can always tell, you can just walk and I can tell, I can look around and see if someone has been there just by the way they move and stuff like that." Furthermore, even within a prison there were inmate-versus-officer dynamics and officer-versus-supervisor and officer-versus-administration dynamics that required complex navigation in order to gain trust from informants without being insincere or misleading.

Jointly Considering the Key Features of Unconventional Research Contexts

Although the prison context is certainly unique in many ways, we see these four contextual features appearing in other settings for organizational researchers. For example, the extreme gap in our lived experiences could be equally true for researchers studying populations who have experienced similar tragedies, such as extreme discrimination or bullying (e.g., Lutgen-Sandvik, 2008) or informants who have been enmeshed in other total institutions that the researcher has not experienced on an equal level (e.g., Ebaugh, 1977, 1988). Regarding power differences between the researcher and informants, other unconventional organizational contexts where these dynamics are prevalent may include work with nonmanagerial or blue-collar employees (Bamberger & Pratt, 2010) who might fear speaking with more powerful actors with unclear relationships to the organization or those in control (e.g., Scott, 1985). There are also many situations in which the cultural and demographic differences could create in-group/out-group barriers for researchers, such as those studying dirty work occupations (e.g., "I've gotten a lot of variations on the 'What's a nice girl like you doing studying truckers?' theme question over the years" as described by Drew and Mills, 2007, p. 218) or highly masculine organizations (such as firefighters, the military, or police, e.g., Van Maanen, 1978). Whether in the prison context or another context that shares these features, it is our suggestion that the cumulative effects of these four contextual features may require adaptations to more traditional qualitative methods, which we describe in the next section.

Pushing the Boundaries of Neutrality

The ideas for this chapter evolved from discussions regarding each author's independent methodological adaptations to data collection practices throughout our research projects. We revealed three common elements that we had used to address the extreme contexts with which we were engaged, and we often felt during the process that this went against some of the training we had received as qualitative researchers. Through our discussion, we realized that we were not neutral investigators; rather, our alternative process centered around emotion, encouragement, and sensitivity. In what follows, we explain these techniques and the insights and advantages they afforded us (see Table 7.1 for a summary of the techniques matched to contextual features).

Emotion

The conventional approach to managing emotions and personal feelings in data collection suggests that:

> As an interviewer, I want to establish rapport with the person I am questioning, but that rapport must be established in such a way that it does not undermine my neutrality . . . I cannot be shocked; I cannot be angered; I cannot be embarrassed; I cannot be saddened. (Patton, 2002, p. 365)

Table 7.1 Key Features of Unconventional Contexts

Key Features of Context	Description	Suggested Interview Techniques
Researcher–informant experience gap	The researcher cannot reasonably experience or imagine the lived experiences of the informant	*Emotion*: Use felt emotion as a guide for appropriate response; mirror emotions *Encouragement*: Be informal and sensitive; allow for informants' voices and catharsis; go "off script"
Strong and unfamiliar culture	Research site has strong jargon and belief systems that are foreign to the researcher	*Emotion*: Mirror informants' jargon and beliefs; withhold and regulate emotions inconsistent with the context *Encouragement*: Investigate how to phrase questions to signal familiarity with the context; use encouragement and examples *Sensitivity*: Attempt to experience the unfamiliar culture to glean informants' perspectives and potential theoretical insights
Perceived power and privilege differences	There is a gap between the marginalized/disenfranchised population and the status of the researcher	*Emotion*: Treat informant as expert/educator; mirror jargon and beliefs *Encouragement*: Demonstrate openness; use encouragement and examples of responses
Salient demographic differences separating the in-group from out-groups	There are significant differences between the researcher and informant on a number of demographic traits such as age, race, gender, religion, and education; the context is riddled with salient markers of group status, and "us versus them" mentality	*Emotion*: Mirror jargon and beliefs *Encouragement*: Build camaraderie and send signals of taking sides; investigate how to phrase questions to signal familiarity with the context *Sensitivity*: Try to build trust and find similarity

Regardless of the context or content of the interview, this approach would say that the researcher's goal should be "to maintain an even emotional balance—not too excited, but interested" (Singleton & Straits, 2005, p. 321), as this neutrality constitutes a successful interview. However, emotions can be intense and salient in extreme contexts such as prison research; they can direct researchers' attention in important theoretical ways and impact interactions with informants. This reflects the sentiment recently expressed by some involved in prison research who say it is critical to be attentive to emotions and transparent about these realities for the sake of future researchers (Jewkes, 2014).

In our experiences, we felt that our data collection, and especially interviews, in the prison context demanded our emotional involvement and labor. We had to continually regulate our emotions in terms of deeming what was and was not appropriate to express, and when. In many ways we felt unprepared for this component of our research and improvised our way through it. However, our reflections indicate that remaining neutral throughout data collection would have been a detriment to the quality of data we obtained and also difficult to sustain personally as we experienced intense emotions through the process.

We suggest that rather than being a neutral scientist, researchers in contexts such as these need to form a permeable emotional boundary and identify when it is appropriate to withhold emotion, mirror emotions and beliefs of the informant, or express genuine emotions in ways that maximize the exchange quality between the researcher and informant. Given the cultural, demographic, and power/privilege differences between us and our informants, it was critical to overcome the "you're not one of us" skepticism, which was especially prevalent in the paranoia-ridden prison environment.

Mirroring Informants' Emotions, Jargon, and Beliefs

We found that one way to maintain and develop the connection between the informants and the researcher, despite the many salient differences, involved mirroring their emotions, jargon, and beliefs, even if we did not necessary feel that way; and thus, we could "talk the talk" of our informants. We believe that this helped to give legitimacy to the informants as the directors and leaders in the interviews, and it helped make informants comfortable that we understood where they were coming from and helped them believe that we were "on their side" of the many potential in-group/out-group divides. For example, many of the convicts interviewed were angry at the system and blamed various parties for the trouble they were in. Sometimes the researcher did not personally agree with the outrage or characterization they made, but he or she feigned and mirrored outrage the inmates expressed. For example, in one interview a man said, "Women have, in my opinion, way too much power," and looked to the researcher to see her reaction. Her nodding in agreement and expression of compassion for his experience was likely necessary for him to feel safe sharing. Others discussed corrupt police, correctional officers, administrators, and inmates. In these cases, the expression of shock or outrage conveyed that the informants had information the researchers did not have, and thus gave them a feeling of legitimacy and value in telling the interviewer something important and unknown. Thus, treating informants as educators rather than subjects was often a helpful way to bridge differences, help informants feel comfortable sharing strong opinions, establish rapport as though the researcher took their side, and feel a sense of worth in helping teach researchers about their context.

Expressing Authentic Emotions

At other times, it was most appropriate to express authentic emotions. For example, one informant had masked her pregnancy with baggy clothes until volunteering this information in her third interview. She said that her C-section birth was scheduled the next week, and the baby would be turned over to the state because she did not have a family member able to care for the baby while she was incarcerated. She was dreading the two weeks of recovery until she could work again because she knew the down time would be heartbreaking. Seeing how much she needed support, the researcher came out of her role and expressed authentic empathy. Similarly, when some informants shared stories of sexual and physical abuse, showing authentic compassion was a way of building the interviewer–interviewee relationship. Relating on a human level was important and meaningful; it allowed us to connect to the inmates experiences and understand them more deeply. Furthermore, responding appropriately to the first disclosure of something personal and/or painful established trust that characterized remaining exchanges.

Regulating Emotions

Yet sometimes showing emotion needed to be paired with the regulation and withholding of other emotions and beliefs. For example, interviewing convicted criminals meant that judgment about their crimes needed to be contained, and officers often would admit to inappropriate behavior toward which we could not readily signal disapproval. More pointedly, getting legitimacy and breaking down us-versus-them boundaries sometimes demanded that we hide our authentic emotions and beliefs. For example, in one prison where there had been a riot, correctional officers took the researcher on a prison tour. During the tour, the officers took her into the busy dining hall, telling her that is where the riot had started. The inmates all turned to look, and a busy, loud meal quickly turned into a deathly silent room with hundreds of maximum security inmates watching her. While her heart pounded, the researcher did not display fear, and instead commented that it was the quietest she had ever heard inmates. The officers laughed, patting her on the back and telling her she could have a job there if she wanted. In this situation, masking fear was critical to help demonstrate toughness in the highly mas-culine prison culture, and thus bridge the differences to establish camaraderie by "walking the walk."

Encouragement

One of the most common rules for qualitative interviewing is ensuring that questions are balanced and not leading. This is important because it ensures that the researcher does not ask a question and "supply the terms of the answer" (McCracken, 1988, p. 34). What we found, however, is that this approach to questioning did not always work well in our interviews. Instead, we often had to encourage our informants so that they knew what was being asked, and we let them know that it was appropriate to respond authentically.

The Role of Examples

We often realized during the data collection process that we had to give examples of others' responses. For instance, a researcher might say, "Some people I have spoken with have said they have had real difficulty relating to others upon their release, while others have not had any trouble. What has your experience been like?" When the question was originally framed as, "Can you tell me about your experiences relating to other people since your release?" there was often no response. In the latter cases, responses were much more informative. This tactic likely helped informants to feel the legitimacy to talk about a particular issue or opinion.

Modifying Questions

Encouragement was also important. We all noted throughout our interviews that interviewees tended to be less reflective and theoretical and more matter-of-fact and literal than you may find in more traditional organizational contexts. This could be because informants have very real day-to-day concerns about their safety and well-being that occupy their thoughts, and also because of the salient demographic differences, such as educational differences, that were inherent in our exchanges. One way to deal with this was by encouraging response through examples, as noted previously, and the other was to encourage through making questions more relatable, legitimate, or understandable. Before we learned much of the prison jargon, the language we used often seemed to shut down conversations. We learned over time that terms like "prison," "inmate," "offender," "officer," and "guard" all had symbolic value that signaled whose "side" the user of the term was on. By educating ourselves regarding these granularities, we were better able to use this terminology to send signals that fostered better responses. This sensitization to their language and experience was not like "playing dumb" (McCracken, 1988), as has been recognized in traditional approaches, but about building a sense of trust for informants that we were sensitive to their perspectives and perhaps even "on their side," rather than neutral outsiders.

Thus, while traditional interviewing tactics might call this leading or directive, we found these data were richer when examples and encouragement were provided. The several options that were given as possible answers likely fostered understanding and legitimacy among respondents, which aided in data collection. We worked to ensure that our examples and encouragement did not lead the informants to one type of response. To be sure, we checked for variance in responses across informants (which each of us were able to clearly see in our data).

Sensitivity

As we have suggested, two features of unconventional contexts that might require adaptations are, first, that the researcher cannot inherently relate to the experience of the informant and, second, that strong in-group/out-group boundaries act as a barrier. We found sensitivity to the context gave us experiences, language, and reflexivity that enhanced both the relationships with our informants and also our ability to generate novel theoretical insights. Corbin and Strauss (2008) have suggested, "Sensitivity stands in contrast to objectivity. It requires that a researcher put him- or herself into the research. Sensitivity means having insight, being tuned in to, being able to pick up on relevant issues, events, and happenings in data" (p. 32). This notion of practicing sensitivity, or putting oneself into the research, resonates with us and our experiences in the prison environment. In a 2014 special issue on conducting qualitative prison research, Jewkes described prison researchers' experience well:

> Researchers nonetheless cannot help but be touched, if not deeply affected, by the cultural isolation and emotional intensity of confinement, even though they are largely experiencing it at one step removed and in relatively short doses. Prisons are *intensely* human environments, giving rise to *acute* difficulties, dilemmas, complexities, and contradictions. They are peculiar places from a sensory perspective, managing to deny and deprive while, sometimes simultaneously, overloading the sense. (pp. 388–389)

Throughout data collection, each of us allowed ourselves and our experiences to be part of the research, and this enabled us "to see the issues and problems from the perspectives of participants" (Corbin & Strauss, 2008, p. 32) as much as possible. This involved purposeful work to reflect upon the context. We next provide some examples to show how allowing ourselves to be part of our research facilitated making connections with informants and, ultimately, theoretical insights.

Practicing Sensitivity: Attention to Our Own Experiences of the Context

One example comes from the researchers' experiences with the correctional officers, as they controlled access to the data site and informants. Each day of data collection, researchers passed through a security point and had research equipment (notebook, pen, voice recorder, laptop) inspected. The equipment, badge, and approval documents were the same each day, yet the inspections would be thorough at times and superficial at others. One of us was even turned away one day because a correctional officer decided the documents were not sufficient; another was almost turned away for wearing "inappropriate" clothing (a white dress shirt) that she had worn many times before. Thus, our experiences of the correctional officers being unpredictable and inconsistent were important because similar experiences were echoed both in officers' and inmates' interviews, fostering several theoretical insights. First, when one researcher contrasted her stress of these officer interactions with her experiences inside the offices of the onsite company where data collection took place, she realized that the offices felt safe in comparison. This helped her see the work environment as a safe space for inmate employees to construct their evolving personal and professional identities, a theoretical insight that may have remained buried in the data had the researcher not experienced the rapid transition from correctional officer interactions to work-environment interactions for herself and considered them in relation to the data.

Another author's experience with this inconsistency allowed insight into the large amount of discretion that officers had to enforce the rules, despite the fact that prison is a command-and-control, paramilitary organization. In officers' use of this discretion, she found that officers could either better establish or damage their rapport with inmates, which has implications not only for officers' safety and well-being, but also for more therapeutic and caring relationships between officers and inmates. In sum, we found that practicing sensitivity improved the quality of the data collected, the depth of theoretical insights, and ultimately the richness of resulting theories.

Discussion of Risks and Conclusion

The suggestions we make could mean that boundaries between involvement and observation can be difficult to navigate. Thus, one inherent risk to this approach is becoming too emotionally invested in the participants' perspectives and/or actually getting involved and influencing their decisions and states of mind. At times we felt more like therapists than researchers, and it was difficult to disentangle our roles when emotions were very real. For example, one of us responded to an informant's expressed desire to commit suicide rather than continue working at the prison with an acknowledgement that no job was worth her level of stress and encouraged the informant to quit the job. Other risks of this approach include being less than "objective" as interviewers and struggling to justify this unconventional approach to editors and reviewers when attempting to publish the work in top-tier, North American management journals. Finally, we acknowledge that while some of our advice could be seen as suggestions for how to be manipulative, we intend it as quite the opposite: collegial insights on how to best navigate real, often emotional and difficult tensions that occur when conducting interview-based research in unconventional contexts that produce the best outcomes for both the researchers and those being researched.

In this chapter, we have sought to specify an innovative alternative to the traditional qualitative approaches espoused as norms in our field (see Table 7.2 for a summary). While various research paradigms have placed different value on the role and appropriateness of objectivity in qualitative research (cf. Lincoln & Guba, 1985; Morgan, 1983), we suggest that the context, not necessarily the paradigm, can indicate how to best gather qualitative interview data. We ground our discussion of contextual features and alternative techniques in prison research, but as noted, we see the techniques as broadly applicable to unconventional organizational settings that share the contextual features highlighted (see Table 7.3 for examples). We suggest that researchers spend time considering the influence of context before and during data collection and pay attention to the potential for methodological modifications through emotion, encouragement, and sensitivity when warranted by contextual features.

Table 7.2 Distinctions between Traditional Methods and Alternative Methods

	Traditional Methods	Alternative Methods
Relationship between interviewer and interviewee	Formal, professional	Personal, human
Tone	Neutral	Emotion laden
Framing and questions	"Law of non-direction"; unbiased, balanced	Encouraging, sensitive
Basis of rapport	Giving voice (i.e., interviewer as listener, reporter of their story)	Giving legitimacy (i.e., interviewer feels and expresses validation and empathy)

Table 7.3 Use of Alternative Methods in Qualitative Organizational Research

Reference	Research Context	Alternative Method Used	Outcomes/Results of Innovation
Ebaugh (1988)	Ex-nuns, transsexuals, ex-convicts	Emotion, encouragement	Interviewees used the interview as a site to talk through their challenges in transition, leading to rich introspective data.
Zilber (2002)	Rape crisis center	Emotion, sensitivity	Human encounter with those at research site, the establishment of trust that allowed connection and sharing with members over the 15-month ethnography.
Creed, DeJordy, & Lok (2010)	LGTB ministers	Emotion, encouragement	Sharing of personal and painful experiences by participants, in-depth reflections, and novel theoretical insights.
Drew, Mills, & Gassaway (2007)	Numerous "dirty work" occupations (e.g., truck drivers)	Emotion, sensitivity	Bridging the highly salient us-versus-them divide with individuals in "dirty work" occupations.

References

Bamberger, P.A., & Pratt, M.G. (2010). Moving forward by looking back: Reclaiming unconventional research contexts and samples in organizational scholarship. *Academy of Management Journal, 53*, 665–671.

Cappelli, P., & Sherer, P.D. (1991). The missing role of context in OB: The need for a meso-level approach. *Research in Organizational Behavior, 13*, 55–110.

Charmaz, K. (2006). *Constructing grounded theory: A practical guide through qualitative analysis.* Los Angeles, CA: Sage.

Corbin, J., & Strauss, A. (2008). *Basics of qualitative research: Techniques and procedures for developing grounded theory* (3rd ed.). Los Angeles, CA: Sage.

Creed, W.E.D., DeJordy, R., & Lok, J. (2010). Being the change: Resolving institutional contradiction through identity work. *Academy of Management Journal, 53*, 1336–1364.

Drew, S.K., & Mills, M. (2007). Ethnography as dirty work. In S.K. Drew, M.B. Mills, & B.M. Gassaway (Eds.), *Dirty work* (pp. 217–231). Waco, TX: Baylor University Press.

Drew, S.K., Mills, M.B., & Gassaway, B.M. (2007). *Dirty work.* Waco, TX: Baylor University Press.

Ebaugh, H.R.F. (1977). *Out of the cloister: A study of organizational dilemmas.* Austin: University of Texas Press.

Ebaugh, H.R.F. (1988). *Becoming an ex: The process of role exit.* Chicago, IL: University of Chicago Press.

Elsbach, K., & Bechky, B.A. (2009). Introduction: Research context and attention of the qualitative researcher. In K.D. Elsbach & B.A. Bechky (Eds.), *Qualitative organizational research: Best papers from the Davis Conference on Qualitative Research* (Vol. 2). Greenwich, CT: Information Age Publishing.

Goffman, E. (1961). *Asylums: Essays on the social situation of mental patients and other inmates.* Garden City, NY: Doubleday.

Jewkes, Y. (2014). An introduction to "Doing Prison Research Differently." *Qualitative Inquiry, 20*, 387–391.

Kvale, S., & Brinkmann, S. (2009). *Interviews: Learning the craft of qualitative research interviewing* (2nd ed.). Thousand Oaks, CA: Sage.

Lincoln, Y.S., & Guba, E.G. (1985). *Naturalistic inquiry*. Beverly Hills, CA: Sage.

Lutgen-Sandvik, P. (2008). Intensive remedial identity work: Responses to workplace bullying trauma and stigmatization. *Organization, 15*, 97–119.

McCracken, G. (1988). *The long interview*. Thousand Oaks, CA: Sage.

Morgan, G. (Ed.). (1983). *Beyond method: Strategies for social research*. Beverly Hills, CA: Sage.

Patton, M.Q. (2002). *Qualitative research & evaluation methods* (3rd ed.). Thousand Oaks, CA: Sage.

Pratt, M.G. (2008). Fitting oval pegs into round holes: Tensions in evaluating and publishing qualitative research in top-tier North American journals. *Organizational Research Methods, 11*, 481–509.

Scott, J.C. (1985). *Weapons of the weak: Everyday forms of peasant resistance*. New Haven, CT: Yale University Press.

Singleton, R.A., Jr., & Straits, B. C. (2005). *Approaches to social research* (4th ed.). New York, NY: Oxford University Press.

Van Maanen, J. (1978). The asshole. In P.K. Manning & J. Van Maanen (Eds.), *Policing: A view from the street* (pp. 231–238). Santa Monica, CA: Goodyear.

Zilber, T.B. (2002). Institutionalization as an interplay between actions, meanings, and actors: The case of a rape crisis center in Israel. *Academy of Management Journal, 45*, 234–254.

8

Why Is That Interesting?

Finding the Meanings of Unexplored Phenomena

Ian J. Walsh and Jean M. Bartunek

Introduction

Among the many benefits of qualitative research is its capacity to develop and advance scholarly understanding of organizations through an exploration of emergent or overlooked phenomena. While some qualitative inquiries commence with well-defined research questions that are grounded in ongoing theoretical conversations, scholars may also be confronted with meaningful questions that arise from their engagement in field work (Golden-Biddle & Locke, 2006). Some of our experience with qualitative research has led us to recognize that scholars may also sometimes find themselves exposed to research contexts they were neither planning to study nor initially knew how to describe in any scholarly way.

We certainly recognize the importance of defining one's research focus as a prelude to meaningful qualitative analysis (Corbin & Strauss, 2008), and this challenge can be particularly arduous in studying novel contexts. While unexpected phenomena can fuel groundbreaking research, scholars' capacities to study them in ways that build meaningful connections to extant research provide an important basis for framing the contribution of a qualitative study. In this chapter, we seek to illuminate an approach by which scholars can discern theoretical and practical contributions from unusual situations they encounter in the field. The primary contribution of the chapter is a presentation of an innovative approach to defining, exploring, and explaining novel phenomena in ways that situate their meaning in the broader literature. We draw on our personal experiences in developing such projects and supplement our reflections with illustrations drawn from other exemplars of the types of approaches we have employed in our own research.

Why Is This Chapter Important?

Before describing our approach, it is important to offer a brief explanation about why this innovation warrants scholars' attention. Indeed, there is a substantive body of work that has already provided great insight into how to design qualitative studies and about how to establish the "interestingness" of one's research (e.g., Bartunek, Rynes, & Ireland, 2006; Corbin & Strauss, 2008; Golden-Biddle & Locke, 2006). Most of these processes assume a planned and intentional foray into the field, with researchers having a general, if fuzzy, map of some terrain they seek to examine. Yet, in our own experience, scholars may sometimes stumble upon unexpected situations that they cannot readily categorize or describe. Such opportunities are rife with potentially "weird ideas" or counterintuitive theoretical discoveries that can be effectively clarified though the deft application of qualitative methods (Elsbach, 2005). We thus believe it is important for scholars to have a plan of attack for those unplanned moments that hold so much potential for developing new theory. Our goal in this chapter is to expand the tool kit of qualitative research to facilitate scholarly inquiry into newly encountered contexts that seem unexplainable at first glance but may hold great potential for unlocking powerful insights about organizational life.

Studying Unexplored Phenomena

In this chapter, we are explaining an approach to conducting research on unexplored phenomena. The "data" from which we developed this approach are our experiences in conducting two qualitative studies that both addressed issues previously unconsidered in organizational research. In both cases, our inquiries commenced with general awareness of distinctive phenomena that we could not define with any ready-made labels. We supplemented our personal dataset by taking into account some influential qualitative studies that have also illuminated important phenomena in organizational contexts, and these papers are listed in the table. While we make no claims that our research process mirrors the manner in which these authors conducted their research, our reading of their papers gave us some sense that our suggested practices reflect the spirit of their work. In our reflections herein, we thus draw on this broader body of work to illustrate some of the ways in which scholars can explore and explain novel phenomena amidst the backdrop of extant scholarship. As is the case with many processes, the approach we describe, which is depicted in the figure, is not strictly linear in nature. While we present a sequence of activities in the order in which they generally take place, we feel it is important to recognize that the approach to studying novel phenomena that we describe has a recursive character. At certain points, scholars studying unexplored phenomena may find it important to revisit earlier points in the research process.

Sharpening Our Focus

Inquiry into unexplored phenomena generally commences with an observation of conditions that foster bouts of head-scratching. For instance, Harris and Sutton (1986: 5) noted that, amidst an investigation into the dynamics of organizational death, "we were struck by the prevalence of parties, picnics, and other social occasions." In our own research on collective turnover (Bartunek, Huang, & Walsh, 2008), one of us was perplexed when witnessing an episode of multiple organization members choosing to quit in ways that seemed particularly interconnected and coordinated. While theoretically grounded scholarship should provide some explanation of why or how experiences occur as they do, early encounters with novel phenomena force scholars to confront a more general question about "what is the experience that is happening here?" To develop a conceptual understanding of novel phenomena, three particular techniques may be particularly helpful, and we will now explore each of them.

Finding Instances

At early stages in the study of novel phenomena, there may be great value in exploring anecdotal evidence of unexpected conditions. In their research on organizational disidentification, Elsbach and Bhattacharya (2001) noted how stories from the news media helped them clarify their awareness of individuals defining themselves through their nonmembership in social groups. Prior to starting our research on postdeath organizing (Walsh & Bartunek, 2011), one of us attended a gathering of former employees of a defunct organization and puzzled over the seeming reenactment of organizational life that was taking place. Developing an initial understanding of a novel phenomenon may be facilitated by finding more examples of it. Following our participation in the former employee gathering, we conducted an extensive search of the popular press and the Internet to find examples of defunct organizations being "reborn" in various ways. We discovered a range of stories, one of which was a small chain of retail stores that had been "permanently" shut down only to be reopened by its founders more than a decade later. We ultimately derived an extensive and diverse inventory of examples from a broad range of industries and time periods, many of which seemed to involve former members convening to rebuild certain elements of organizational life.

Other scholars have used comparable techniques to establish a sense of the phenomena they have noticed. For instance, Elsbach and Bhattacharya (2001: 395) employed in-class discussions and student-run projects to conduct some "preliminary, informal data collection" about instances of disidentification. Harris and Sutton (1986) scanned the geographic region of southeastern Michigan to develop a list of 20 organizations whose experience seemed to reflect the phenomenon that they were exploring. We also recognize that scholars can sometimes develop rich theoretical insight from a single, extensive observation of a phenomenon, as Plowman and colleagues (2007) did in their research on emergent, radical change. Indeed, the benefits of individual "extreme cases" are well documented (Yin, 2009). However, efforts to enumerate multiple examples of a novel phenomenon may have both short-term and longer-term benefits. For instance, our reviewers for our collective turnover paper (Bartunek et al., 2008) ultimately urged us to include multiple cases in our study, leading us to reconsider this technique of finding more instances later in our subsequent research.

Free-Form Writing

Developing an understanding of a phenomenon may also be facilitated by open-ended written reflections on what seems important about it and what questions it conjures. Corbin and Strauss (2008) point to the importance of memoing as a means to track insights that emerge through the data collection process. Our suggestion mirrors the spirit of this idea at an earlier point in time, before plans to collect data are even formulated. In our study of postdeath organizing, we examined the list of instances of the phenomenon (for which we had yet to form even a working label or definition) and wrote a brief essay that attempted to capture the essence of what we thought we were seeing in this preliminary data. Instead of reviewing the literature, this essay instead summarized and interpreted our observations of the phenomenon. Without much forethought, we wrote this essay with a heavy dose of death-related language; we noted how our examples showed ways in which some organizational elements were "embalmed" for indefinite preservation and other organizations were "resurrected" after some period of time.

While this writing did not directly appear in any drafts of our paper, it helped us to clarify our conceptual understanding. In particular, it enabled us to develop a more concrete typology of the specific elements of organizational life that individuals preserved through what we would come to identify as postdeath organizing. Some of the cases we had previously identified turned out to be more relevant examples of this phenomenon than others. For instance, we had initially considered the preservation of former Shaker communities to be instances of postdeath organizing, but our free-form writing exercise helped us to recognize the crucial role of former members as active agents in the phenomenon, thus making it a less instructive example. Whether it is written or verbal, reflection on initial observations can prove extremely useful in making phenomena more readily recognizable and explainable. For instance, Plowman et al. (2007) explained how their active reflection on observations from their visits to Mission Church ultimately led them to identify a type of radical change that was not initially transparent when their first encountered their research context.

Discovering Boundaries

Searching for instances of a phenomenon and writing about what it entails can certainly draw one's focus onto its important characteristics. However, we believe that it is equally important to bound a phenomenon to ensure its clarity to guide and focus scholarly inquiry about it. As was the case in Harris and Sutton's (1986) research on parting ceremonies, we found ourselves taking great efforts to explain what constituted organizational death and the forms it took. However, we also found it important to identify situations that did not constitute death, such as Chapter 11 bankruptcy reorganizing efforts. Doing so ultimately helped us to exclude potential research sites that did not involve the same behaviors, motives, and experiences as those that occurred in situations where organizations were unambiguously closed. Efforts to discover boundaries at an early stage can serve an important purpose in subsequent efforts to collect data about your phenomenon. Gioia and Chittipeddi (1991) recognized the potential for exploring the symbolic character of strategic change, and their explicit focus on the role of CEOs in this process ultimately fostered their awareness of the process of "sensegiving." Being explicit up front about conceptual boundaries can also help scholars as they write their manuscripts. For instance, Elsbach and Bhattacharya (2001) point out the ways in which disidentification differs from cognitive apathy and other negatively framed organizational attributions. This clarity can facilitate thoughtful engagement in the field and credible theorizing about the phenomena being observed.

Selecting Your Approach

When initial exploration of a phenomenon has provided some rudimentary awareness of its general character and boundaries, more formal inquiry can provide a solid foundation for developing a theory about it. In this short chapter, we will make no effort to provide an overview of the vast array of qualitative research methods available to organizational scholars. Instead, we would like to suggest two particular methodological considerations that confront investigators of novel phenomena before they commence their data collection campaigns.

Making Choices About Your Modes of Reasoning

First, explorations of novel phenomena require a decision about the modes of reasoning that will guide the inquiry. While the differences between various modes of reasoning and their application to the research process have been well covered in prior writing (e.g. Van de Ven, 2007), we contribute to this knowledge by suggesting how scholars might select from among them when exploring novel phenomena. The techniques we associate with sharpening one's focus depend in some ways on an initial adoption of a logic of abduction, which Locke, Golden-Biddle, and Feldman (2008: 907–908) describe as an "ampliative and conjectural mode of inquiry through which we engender and entertain hunches, explanatory propositions, ideas, and theoretical elements." We believe that the willingness to explore unusual or counterintuitive observations that is emblematic of abduction serves an important purpose in establishing an open-minded engagement with a newly encountered phenomenon. An abductive mindset allows scholars to give ample consideration to the potentially diverse range of ways in which a phenomenon could be defined and understood.

As studies of novel phenomena progress, scholars are likely to sense a need to transition from the divergent thought patterns associated with abduction to more convergent ways of thinking that facilitate theory development. In particular, choices must be made between whether to adopt a methodological approach grounded in inductive or deductive reasoning. In studies of novel phenomena, we suggest that scholars should consider the extent to which the initial stages of their research have pointed to substantive links with other well-established constructs and theories. In some cases, the nature of a phenomenon may be quite distinctive and thus lend itself to an approach that is broadly inductive in nature. Gioia and Chittipeddi (1991: 434) recognized the merits of prior scholarship on strategic change, but "wondered if some viable alternative approach of viewing the initiation of strategic change might emerge by using a grounded approach." In this case, the authors were seeking to unearth a new way of thinking of strategic change that was not conceptually anchored to prior work, thus making an inductive logic quite appropriate. Harris and Sutton's (1986) research followed a similar approach in light of the authors' treatment of parting ceremonies as a distinctive phenomenon.

In other cases, scholars may recognize their phenomena of interest are quite novel but still best understood when considered in relationship to established constructs or theories. We believe that such situations call for cycles of inductive- and deductive-oriented inquiry. For instance, in our research on postdeath organizing, we quickly realized that we were exploring a form of organizational death that had not been explored but that could be best understood when taking into account other types of death that had been studied (e.g., Sutton, 1987). So we chose an approach that involved movement back and forth between induction and deduction. Similarly, Elsbach and Bhattacharya (2001) brought attention to the concept of disidentification, which could be more thoroughly clarified by taking into account prior research on the related topic of organizational identification. They thus planned two discrete studies, the first of which took an exploratory approach consistent with an inductive logic. They followed this work with a second, deduction-driven study that showcased the antecedents and consequences of the construct they had fleshed out more fully through their earlier inductive research.

Finding Informants

Adoption of specific modes of reasoning then prompts scholars to give consideration to how and from whom they will collect data about their novel phenomena. In our experience, studying novel phenomena can pose unique challenges to scholars seeking to collect data about them. Indeed, difficulties with gaining appropriate access to data may well be one of the reasons why scholars have not previously studied a topic. In our experience, keeping two issues in mind may facilitate efforts to gather data about novel phenomena.

First, studies of novel phenomena can entail complications in tracking down suitable informants that are less salient in more traditional qualitative studies. In particular, the range of potential research sites, and thus the set of individuals from whom data can be collected, can be quite constrained, leading to heightened concerns about gaining access to specific individuals who appear to play crucial roles in a phenomenon. In our research on collective turnover, the number of suitable participants (i.e., individuals who had participated in an episode of collective turnover) to whom we could actually gain access in a timely fashion was somewhat limited, thus making each individual's actual participation quite important. This risk can be particularly high in studies of single cases (e.g., Plowman et al., 2007). Finding informants can also be challenging when studying cases that unfold over an extended period of time, as was the case in our research on postdeath organizing. To emphasize the lasting character of postdeath organizing, we limited our possible sites to cases that had been initiated at least 5 years prior to our data collection. As a result, some of the individuals with whom we spoke identified others who had seemingly played crucial roles in the process many years earlier but were now difficult or impossible to track down. While many qualitative studies use a snowball sampling approach to develop samples, episodes of novel phenomena may not lend themselves to strictly referral-based approaches when substantial time has elapsed. Interviews and archival records may reveal names of individuals for whom no current contact information is available. Our experience suggests that scholars preparing for studies of novel phenomena should hone their sleuthing skills as they prepare for the process of finding informants. In our research, we were confronted with this challenge on several occasions and resorted to using online search services, social media, and even phone directories to ascertain the whereabouts of central actors in our cases. In some cases, these searches revealed the names of additional individuals who had not been suggested to us by our prior informants and turned out to have valuable insight to share.

Second, individuals who have been part of some unusual experience may have some apprehension about discussing it. In some cases, the situation may harken some harrowing memories that individuals would rather not revisit. For instance, in our study of postdeath organizing, more than one interview evoked tears, with one respondent in particular saying, "I'm not ready to talk about that. Maybe in a few years." In other cases, the novelty of the phenomenon may make individuals worry that their identities could not be concealed despite standard assurances of anonymity. For instance, in our research on collective turnover, the perceived distinctiveness of the situation raised fears among some prospective study participants that their identities could not be credibly concealed if they were quoted in our paper. In both of these research projects, the eventual inclusion of multiple cases allayed lingering fears among our informants about their anonymity. However, we believe it is important to recognize and manage these fears before and as they arise through tactful and gentle engagement with potential informants.

Connecting Our Findings

As data collection processes progress, the prospect of writing about novel phenomena in ways that make them accessible and interesting to scholars and practitioners becomes particularly important. While the novel phenomenon may inspire a qualitative study that produces seemingly rich data, its capacity to create a meaningful contribution depends in large part on authors' abilities to connect their findings with ongoing scholarly conversations within the field. A theory that deeply explains a particular phenomenon runs the risk of being accurate but lacking in either the simplicity or generality needed for it to be impactful (Weick, 1979). As scholars attempt to build connections between their research on novel phenomena and broader areas of scholarly inquiry, a couple of procedures can be particularly useful.

Building a Vocabulary

Well-defined constructs provide a necessary, but insufficient, foundation for developing robust theoretical explanations. Good theories provide explanations of the relationships among constructs (Bacharach, 1989), thus making it important for scholars to have clear and meaningful labels to express the constructs about which they are writing. In the case of novel phenomena, scholars may find themselves confronted with the need to build a working "vocabulary" that expresses the constructs in which they are interested and provides important building blocks for creating a theoretical explanation. In some cases, this vocabulary is not routinely or consistently available. For instance, in our research on postdeath organizing, we found ourselves searching for ways to represent what we were studying in language that both evoked the meaning our informants were conveying to us and could be understood by scholars who had not witnessed the experiences we discovered through our research. In effect, scholars exploring unstudied phenomena face the challenge of making the novel more familiar. In some situations, emerging links to other streams of research can provide a means to communicate the rich meaning of novel phenomena in an accessible manner. For instance, Gioia and Chittipeddi's (1991) creation of the label *sensegiving* contributed to a vocabulary for explaining the phenomenon they studied. It both acknowledged the experience they observed among leaders in a strategic change episode and demonstrated how the phenomena could be understood in the context of the developing stream of research on sensemaking. Comparably, Elsbach and Bhattacharya (2001) deftly coined the meaning-laden label of *disidentification* to describe the unexplored phenomena they observed in ways that made transparent its links to the identification literature. Harris and Sutton

(1986) conceptualized parting ceremonies as an additional form of organizational rituals, thereby demonstrating both the uniqueness and the connectedness of the phenomenon they studied.

In other cases, the vocabulary may not be so readily available. As we developed our research on postdeath organizing, we found ourselves moving back and forth between two approaches to building a vocabulary. First, we attuned ourselves to the messages conveyed by our first-order codes and searched for language that could convey their meaning in "scholarly" terms. For instance, we found repeated, tongue-in-cheek statements from individuals claiming a shared sense of livelihood despite an organization's definitive death (cf. Sutton, 1987). One of us recalls being told, "We're not as dead as people think." These quotes initially led us to label our phenomenon of interest as organizational "afterlife" (Walsh & Bartunek, 2009). However, the vocabulary we ultimately developed was also influenced by ongoing conversations with other scholars. As we presented our findings or more informally spoke individually with peers, we gained an appreciation for content in our data that was not initially apparent to either of us.

For example, we recall a meeting where one of our colleagues, who had expressed a sense of confusion about our work at an earlier time, listened to a more developed account of our coding and suggested to us that there was an important entrepreneurship-related theme that was not captured by the label of *afterlife*. Indeed, we came to realize that the phenomenon was more than just a forum for reminiscing, but actually involved former members creating new ventures out of the "ashes" of their defunct organizations. Through cycles of interrogating our coding and speaking with peers, we were better able to capture the true meaning of our phenomenon in ways that expressed its links to existing areas of scholarly research. Specifically, we developed the term *ex morte* ventures to establish a meaningful contrast with *de novo* and *de alio* forms of entrepreneurship that were discussed in prior research.

Piloting Multiple Provisional Framings

During our research on postdeath organizing, our conversations with other scholars led us to recognize that there may be more than one viable way to frame the meaning of a novel phenomenon. Indeed, the schemas we develop through our own cumulative experience as scholars may predispose us to see different "stories" in a given dataset (Corbin & Strauss, 2008). Our experience with studying novel phenomena has led us to recognize the importance of piloting multiple provisional framings as a means to maximize the potential theoretical contribution of such research. For instance, our study of collective turnover initially focused on those involved being new recruits, but the eventual theoretical model in our published paper emphasized the nature of their shared cognition and affect. During the writing of our research on postdeath organizing, we explored at least four very different theoretical foundations on which to base our paper. In one of our initial revisions of our manuscript, we discussed our phenomenon (which we had ultimately started calling *postdeath organizing*) as an unstudied period of the organizational life cycle, bridging periods of death and birth. Around the same time, we explored the ways in which our phenomenon of interest shed light on the generativity of doubt amidst experiences of organizational change (Walsh, 2010). Some of these framings were explored in parallel, and others were explored in a sequential manner, as our conversations with peers and comments from reviewers guided us toward our ultimate framing grounded in the literature on new venture creation.

While we fully admit that the frequent shifts in the theoretical orientation of the paper were both dizzying and nerve-wracking, our experience has led us to realize that these provisional framings were important milestones in the trajectory of this research study. Each framing illuminated crucial characteristics of our phenomenon that informed our subsequent iterations of our theoretical storyline. While the polished quality of a published qualitative study can provide a worthy role model for in-process projects, it can also overstate the definitiveness of foresight that inspired it. Provisional

Ian J. Walsh and Jean M. Bartunek

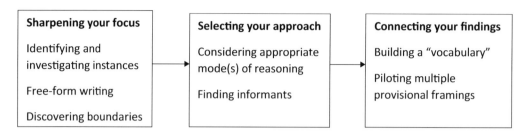

Sharpening your focus	→	Selecting your approach	→	Connecting your findings
Identifying and investigating instances Free-form writing Discovering boundaries		Considering appropriate mode(s) of reasoning Finding informants		Building a "vocabulary" Piloting multiple provisional framings

Figure 8.1 Finding the Meaning in Unexplored Phenomena

Table 8.1 Exemplary Papers

Citation	Novel Phenomenon of Interest
Bartunek, Huang, & Walsh (2008)	Collective turnover
Elsbach & Bhattacharya (2001)	Disidentification
Gioia & Chittipeddi (1991)	Sensegiving
Harris & Sutton (1986)	Parting ceremonies
Plowman, Baker, Beck, Kulkarni, Solansky, & Travis (2007)	Radical, emergent change
Walsh & Bartunek (2011)	Postdeath organizing

framings provide valuable "rest stops" to reflect on and re-route journeys to study and publish scholarship on novel phenomena, for which scholars must construct maps as they navigate their way through an uncharted research context.

Conclusion

Much like new organizations, studies of novel phenomena face a "liability of newness" (Stinchcombe, 1965). Compared to research on well-established topics, such inquiries face "a greater risk of failure ... because they depend on the cooperation of strangers, have low levels of legitimacy, and are unable to compete effectively" (Freeman, Carroll, & Hannan, 1983: 692), at least at the outset. However, as the exemplars we have highlighted in this chapter make clear, a thoughtful approach to research on novel phenomena holds great promise to open new avenues for scholarly inquiry and to redirect long-held assumptions about extant organizational theories in the long term. In this chapter, we have attempted to illuminate some ways that qualitative methods can be used constructively to develop effective studies of novel phenomena, and we hope our suggestions spur further thought about the unique challenges and opportunities such moments present.

References

Bacharach, S. B. (1989). Organizational theories: Some criteria for evaluation. *Academy of Management Review*, 14, 496–515.

Bartunek, J. M., Huang, Z., & Walsh, I. J. (2008). The development of a process model of collective turnover. *Human Relations*, 61, 5–38.

Bartunek, J. M., Rynes, S. L., & Ireland, R. D. (2006). What makes management research interesting, and why does it matter? *Academy of Management Journal*, 49, 9–15.

Corbin, J., & Strauss, A. (2008). *Basics of qualitative research: techniques and procedures for developing grounded theory*. Thousand Oaks, CA: Sage.

Elsbach, K. D. (2005). Weird ideas from qualitative research. In K. D. Elsbach (Ed.), *Qualitative Organizational Research: Best Papers from the Davis Conference on Qualitative Research* (first edition, pp. 1–13). Charlotte, NC: Information Age Publishing.

Elsbach, K. D., & Bhattacharya, C. B. (2001). Defining who you are by what you're not: Organizational disidentification and the National Rifle Association. *Organization Science*, 12, 393–413.

Freeman, J., Carroll, G. R., & Hannan, M. T. (1983). The liability of newness: Age dependence in organizational death rates. *American Sociological Review*, 48, 692–710.

Gioia, D.A., & Chittipeddi, K. (1991). Sensemaking and sensegiving in strategic change initiation. *Strategic Management Journal*, 12, 433–448.

Golden-Biddle, K., & Locke, K. D. (2006). *Composing qualitative research.* Thousand Oaks, CA: Sage.

Harris, S.G., & Sutton, R.I. (1986). Functions of parting ceremonies in dying organizations. *Academy of Management Journal*, 29, 5–30.

Locke, K., Golden-Biddle, K., & Feldman, M. S. (2008). Making doubt generative: Rethinking the role of doubt in the research process. *Organization Science*, 19, 907–918.

Plowman, D.A., Baker, L.T., Beck, T.E., Kulkarni, M., Solansky, S.T., & Travis, D.A. (2007). Radical change accidentally: The emergence and amplification of small change. *Academy of Management Journal*, 50, 515–543.

Stinchcombe, A.L. (1965). Social structure and organizations. In J.G. March (Ed.), *Handbook of organizations* (first edition, pp. 142–193). Chicago, IL: Rand McNally.

Sutton, R.I. (1987). The process of organization death: Disbanding and reconnecting. *Administrative Science Quarterly*, 32, 542–569.

Van de Ven, A.H. (2007). *Engaged scholarship: A guide for organizational and social research.* Oxford, UK: Oxford University Press.

Walsh, I. J. (2010). The generativity of doubt in episodes of organizational change. In L.A. Toombs (Ed.), *Proceedings of the Seventieth Annual Meeting of the Academy of Management* (CD), ISSN 1543–8643.

Walsh, I. J., & Bartunek, J. M. (2009). Rescue and recovery: The role of sensemaking and affect in experiences of organizational death. In K. D. Elsbach & B. A. Bechky (Eds.), *Qualitative Organizational Research: Best Papers from the Davis Conference on Qualitative Research* (second edition, pp. 221–251). Charlotte, NC: Information Age Publishing.

Walsh, I. J., & Bartunek, J. M. (2011). Cheating the fates: Organizational foundings in the wake of demise. *Academy of Management Journal*, 54, 1017–1044.

Weick, K. (1979). *The social psychology of organizing.* New York, NY: Random House.

Yin, R.K. (2009). *Case study research: Design and methods.* Thousand Oaks, CA: Sage.

9

Studying Organizational Fields Through Ethnography

Tammar B. Zilber

The interorganizational social sphere has attracted much interest in recent years (Baum & Rowley, 2005). According to open-system approaches like Institutional Theory, this social sphere—the organizational field[1]—is where much of the drama of organizational reality takes place (Wooten & Hoffman, 2008). Organizational fields are networks of actors (individuals and organizations; DiMaggio & Powell, 1991), who negotiate the meanings they share or contest (Scott, 1994) through various channels of communication (Hoffman, 1999). These meaning are worked out within an ongoing, political (Brint & Karabel, 1991), and context-bound effort to form collective understanding (Wooten & Hoffman, 2008). Accordingly, organizational "reality," the "natural" ways of thinking, structures, norms of conduct, and practices are neither usually born within the organization itself nor are they taken up by direct imitation of other organizations alone or from the society within which an organization resides. Rather this taken-for-granted reality of organizations is borrowed and translated from a mediating sphere—the organizational field—that is analytically and socially discerned between organizations and societies.

At the same time, some meanings, structures, and practices originating from within organizations diffuse across fields and are adopted and adapted by other organizations (Czarniawska & Joerges, 1996; Strang & Soule, 1998). Organizations and fields, then, constitute each other in an ongoing process (Lawrence & Suddaby, 2006). To fully understand organizations, we need to also explore the fields within which they are embedded.

Most studies of organizational fields, however, take a macro-level approach and they follow changes in the field over time (see, for example, Thornton, Ocasio, & Lounsbury's 2012 review of the institutional logics perspective, and see Scott, 2014, for a more general review). On the other hand, common methodologies that allow for the exploration of micro-level processes—like ethnography—are not usually harnessed for the study of fields, but rather focus on organizations (for a recent review, see Locke, 2011). As a result, we do not know enough about the micro-foundations of field-level effects (Powell & Colyvas, 2008)—how meanings are negotiated, how roles and interrelations are formed, and how rules and norms are set. In this chapter, accordingly, I offer guidelines for the application of ethnography on the field level. I explore the challenges involved in doing ethnographic study to uncover the micro-dynamics of organizational fields.

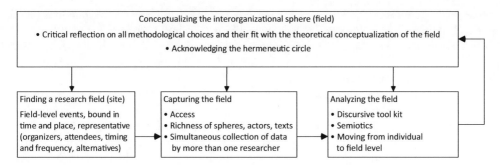

Figure 9.1   Basic Steps in Conducting Field-Level Ethnography

As a research method, ethnography highlights the "extraordinary-in-the-ordinary" (Ybema, Yanow, Wels, & Kamsteeg, 2009, p. 2). It uncovers "what actually happens" (Watson, 2011) within social spheres because it focuses our attention on the implicit and hidden (at times concealed) aspects of lived experiences within them. Ethnography is based on a constructivist paradigmatic stance (Guba & Lincoln, 1994), so it fits nicely with the understanding of both fields and organizations as mutually constructed.

This perspective also integrates well with another perspective that can be very helpful for ethnographers: the discursive approach to institutions, which argues that the shared meanings that constitute the field are all linguistic constructs—that is, fields are socially constructed through the production, dissemination, and consumption of texts (Phillips, Lawrence, & Hardy, 2004). *Texts* are defined here in a broad sense to include written and oral texts, but also spatial (room arrangement), material (artifacts like logos), and performative (behaviors, interactions) texts. All these texts are not merely one sample of practices and objects to be found in organizations and fields. Rather, the very negotiations and deliberations over these texts constitute the field (Wooten & Hoffman, 2008). Texts carry this burden by shaping understandings and behaviors (Phillips, Lawrence, & Hardy, 2004), setting up a space of possibilities and constraints on actors' actions (Hall, 2001) and the redistributing of power (Fairclough, 1992). The ethnographer's challenge is how to capture and represent the organizational field through its diverse texts and discursive practices.

In the following, I detail three analytic steps in the pursuit of organizational field ethnography. The depiction I offer here (see Figure 9.1) is seemingly straightforward and linear, but I would like to underscore that ethnographic inquiries are usually messy, involving relapses and diversions. Still, it is my belief that these analytical steps need to be covered sometime along the research process, and probably more than once.

Finding a Site

In comparison to organizations, organizational fields seem to be much harder to delineate. They have no clear boundaries, and it is not always clear where exactly they reside. If we conceive fields as an ongoing conversation between interested constituencies (Wooten & Hoffman, 2008), then the challenge is to find, empirically, the various sites and channels through which this conversation proceeds.

One possibility would be to follow the traces, effects, and preconditions of organizational fields within organizations, on the one hand, and within societies, on the other. But prior research also offers some directions and clues as to where organizational fields in themselves are to be found. Organizational fields materialize in various social sites and through actual social happenings. According to the discursive approach, one should look for social arenas in which one can follow the textual activity that constitutes the field (Phillips, Lawrence, & Hardy, 2004). These sites include, in particular, field-wide organizations, field-wide agreements, and field-wide events (for details, see Zilber, 2014).

Whereas field-wide organizations and agreements leave much "archival residue" (Gephart, 1993, p. 1469), field-wide events seem the most suitable for a classic ethnographic inquiry. Field-wide events such as conferences, committees, tournament rituals, certification competitions, and training courses allow for the *in vivo* and *in situ* observation of field-level dynamics. These are "temporal organizations" in which "people from diverse organizations and with diverse purposes assemble periodically or on a one-time basis" (Lampel & Meyer, 2008, p. 1026). If indeed the conversation that constitutes the fields unfolds within field-level events (among other places), than those events are, potentially, field-configuring events (Lampel & Meyer, 2008; see also other papers in that *Journal of Management Studies* special issue). No one event encompasses the wholeness of the conversation that constitutes the field. In fact, fields can never be captured in their entirety because they are ongoing achievements, going on simultaneously over long periods of time in multiple locations. Still, field-level events are condensed social events, bound in time and place, which bring into one space all or most of the significant field members. In such events, many texts are produced and disseminated—key note addresses, workshops, presentations, handouts. Moreover, interactions in the events are also texts that can be observed and recorded. Finally, the events themselves—their spatial arrangements, artifacts, logos, and the like—are texts. Thus, field-level events allow the ethnographer to collect rich textual data that may be analyzed to explore field-level dynamics (Lampel & Meyer, 2008).

Since any one event represents only a small chunk of field-level activity, when choosing a research site, we need to make sure the events we observe and study are representative enough of the field and its micro-level dynamics. This means paying attention to the event's organizers and attendees and the frequency and timing of the event(s). No less important is the need to map the event(s) we set up to explore within the entire set of events taking place in the field. We need to be aware of the alternative event(s) not covered by our particular inquiry.

When looking into the events we explore closely, we first need to contextualize them within the broader institutional order. Accordingly, to begin with, we need to find out who organize the event(s) and what their interests are. Organizers may be central or peripheral actors in the field, they may have explicit interests (e.g., financial) and implicit interests (e.g., positioning themselves in the field), and all this may impact the depiction of the field that the events (try to) construct and offer. For example, organizers may limit the audience allowed into the event or given voice at the event (e.g., giving talks or distributing marketing material), excluding competitors or adversaries. The researcher, then, needs to be critical in assessing how representative the event is. To what extent is the event inclusive or alternatively selective, and to what extent does it aim at making certain actors visible and more powerful (Zilber & Gross-Friedenberg, 2014)?

In addition, a specific conference may be part of a series of events, or it may spearhead further events (like training courses or field-level competitions). The timing and frequency of the event may help us determine its centrality to the field and the interests behind it.

Finally, there are usually multiple actors and multiple events in any given field. As researchers, we may not be able to cover them all. Being familiar with the entire array of events in the field will help us to place the ones we attend in this wider context. Another interesting possibility is to cover more than one type of event. At times it's impossible to have them all within our research project, but comparing between carefully selected events may highlight taken-for granted dimensions of the field (see Zilber, 2011).

Using significant-enough field-level events to study the field, and positioning them within their wider context, means that we build on a bottom-up, empirical definition of the field (e.g., who are the central players, what are the vital processes) rather than assuming this definition in advance. Such an inductive approach fits well with qualitative studies (Guba & Lincoln, 1994), ethnography (Locke, 2011), and an understanding of the field as an ongoing construction (Wooten & Hoffman, 2008).

Capturing the Field

As with all ethnographic studies, field-level ethnography involves issues of accessibility. Field-level events are often public events that anyone can attend (with or without attendance fee), which makes access easy. In those circumstances, given that the researcher blends with the crowds, issues of positioning are less troubling. Ethical issues are also less problematic because the ethnographer collects publicly available data. However, field-level events may also be closed events with selective attendance. In these circumstances, the researcher needs to obtain formal agreement with the organizers and balance between collecting as much data as possible and ethical considerations in relation to specific participants and their private affairs.

Once access is given, other challenges begin. Collecting data in field-level events with so much going on, at times within a very short time frame, poses unique challenges (e.g., think about a conference with parallel sessions carried out simultaneously). Events are very rich and condensed. Whereas when conducting organizational level ethnography one can take her time and focus her attention on different (often repeated) activities over the course of the study, in field-level events there is often only one, usually short, shot at data collection. The short time frame is balanced by the richness of the event, but if the researcher cannot cover this richness, she will get a very partial depiction of the event. Moreover, when events are comprised by simultaneous activities, it often reflects not only ways of offering meaningful activities to a vast volume of attendees, but also various deliberate divisions in the field (Zilber, 2011). Such divisions of labor within the formal structures of events make it even harder on the researcher to capture everything that is going on.

Further, events produce many kinds of texts. For instance, participants may talk and give presentations that can be recorded and later transcribed. Oftentimes the presentations are made available for downloading from the conference website. Usually, many written materials are distributed in the conference package and during the event. And, using a broad discursive approach, the event itself may be considered as a text, including the choice of location, the spatial arrangement of the various conference rooms, the behaviors of participants and organizers, the technological equipment, and more. It is hard, once again, to pay attention to and document all these varieties of texts. For these reasons, a fruitful research strategy would be to build up a large enough research team. In particular, it is advisable to enlist research assistance that will help to collect as much data in different arenas and various activities within the course of the event. Later on, the various field notes and the various materials collected can be combined to form the corpus of data.

Even with a large enough research team, it is important to note the epistemological conundrum such ethnography faces. One simply cannot capture the event in its entirety, just as there is no way to capture the field as a whole. Part of the difficulty is quite tangible. For example, any event contains both front stage and backstage occurrences, and it is often quite challenging to observe backstage dynamics and negotiations (Hardy & Maguire, 2010). What we are aspiring to do, then, is to capture a big enough and rich enough slice of the happenings in the event. If we choose the event wisely, and carry out within it a broad enough ethnographic inquiry, this piece will teach us something significant enough about the field as a whole (e.g., Hardy & Maguire, 2010; Mair & Hehenberger, 2014; Schufler, Ruling, & Wittneben, 2014; Zilber, 2007, 2011).

Analysis

The analysis of field-level events, based on ethnographic data, is principally not much different than the analysis of ethnographic data collected on an organizational level. The "conceptual leap" it requires (Klag & Langley, 2013) is as daunting and challenging. Still, some unique features of organizational fields and some features of the theoretical approach one takes are worth noting in analyzing the data.

First, as noted previously, the definition of a field, as well as the basis of the ethnographic method, both fit nicely with a discursive approach that assumes the social construction of reality (Phillips & Hardy, 2002). The discursive approach offers not only an ontological and epistemological basis, but also a more specific methodological tool kit that may be enlisted and used in the analysis (e.g., Gee, 2011; Phillips & Hardy, 2002; Wodak & Meyer, 2009). Discourse directs researchers to pay attention, then, to notions like narratives, genres, intertextuality, subject position, discursive spaces, and the way texts construct subjects and objects (Phillips, Lawrence, & Hardy, 2004; for empirical examples, see Hardy & Maguire, 2010; Maguire, Hardy, & Lawrence, 2004).

Second, given the richness of different kinds of texts—oral, spatial, visual, and performative—one may want to consider the use of semiotics as well, for this approach points to a comprehensive and systematic way to decode the meanings of these varied texts (Barthes, 1967), treating the various characteristics of the conferences as signs. Decoding such signs using knowledge of the interpretative community that constitutes the organizational field may turn out to be fruitful in understanding its micro-dynamics. Specifically drawing attention to "signs" (made up of a "signifier" and the "signified") points not only to words but also to visual images, spatial arrangements, and artifacts. The meaning attached to these signs within a particular historical, social, and cultural context form together the construction of the institutions (which is the *signified* in semiotic terms). The semiotic approach also allows for more complex understanding of the construction of the ideational in the event because it includes both denotative (literal and commonsense) and connotative (metaphorical, implicit) meanings of the signifiers (see Gottdiener, 1995; Hawkes, 1977; Manning & Cullum-Swan, 1998; Woollacott, 1982). A semiotic analysis allows the ethnographer then to decode spatial, visual, and behavioral artifacts and integrate their interpretation with content analysis of the conference's transcripts. These various data sources and analytical moves enable the use of "triangulation" in the service of interpretation (Denzin, 1978) and allow one to check the integrity of the reading by examining how various datasets and various interpretations relate to each other (for an empirical example, see Zilber, 2011).

Finally, field-level ethnography aims at crossing levels of analysis—observing people and their talk and action, but also interpreting their behaviors and words as field-level actors. Most field-level events are public, large-scale gatherings that do not allow for the fuller understanding of individual actors and their actions. This is a shortcoming of field-level ethnography (unlike the more longitudinal organizational-level ethnography that usually involves close relations, conversations, and interviews with organization members over a long period of time). But it is also its advantage, as it directs our attention at the similarities and differences between participants based on their social categories and social positions as representatives of specific subpopulations within the field.

Closing the Hermeneutic Circle: The Role of Conceptualizations

Any ethnography is based on a set of assumptions, often implicit, about the nature of the reality we set out to explore. Organizational ethnography is by now very well established, so we take these assumptions for granted (Czarniawska-Joerges, 1992; Down, 2012; Kosteva, 2007; Neyland, 2008; Schwartzman, 1993; Smith, 2001; Van Maanen, 2011; Yanow, 2012; Yanow, Ybema, & Van Hulst, 2012; Ybema, Yanow, Wels, & Kamsteeg, 2009). Organizational field ethnography, on the contrary, is still new, and hence demands a reflective effort to decipher those assumptions, refine them, and consider their implications (Alvesson & Skoldberg, 2000; Alvesson, Hardy, & Harley, 2008).

The road map I offered here aims at helping to carefully navigate the various considerations involved in forming the organizational field as a field of inquiry. In Table 9.1, I offer some detailed empirical examples. My arguments are based on a specific definition of a *field* as grounded within institutional theory (Wooten & Hoffman, 2008) and further articulated by a discourse analysis (Phillips, Lawrence, & Hardy, 2004). This is but one available definition. Whatever definition one enlists

Table 9.1 The Use of Field-Level Ethnography

Reference	Research Context	Use of Ethnography	Findings
Zilber (2007)	Examine the role and usage of stories in the discursive dynamics of institutional entrepreneurship.	"In depth analysis of one field-wide high-tech conference held in Israel after the dot-com crash of 2000. With the help of a research assistant, I conducted field work during the day-long conference. We collected various types of data: recordings of talks, PowerPoint presentations, handouts, and observations. We attended various activities—plenary welcoming, concluding, and keynote addresses, discussion panels, workshops, and social gatherings (breakfast, lunch, coffee breaks and closing reception). Three rounds of four parallel workshops were held, half of which were documented (we tried to attend workshops with more general themes, based on title and list of participants). When appropriate, we recorded the proceedings, which were later transcribed. Fifteen out of 21 different events were so documented, occupying some 250 double-spaced pages. I also examined PowerPoint presentations that were posted on the conference website after the conference, holding some 380 slides. We collected all materials distributed in the exhibition hall (brochures and little souvenirs), and one of us wandered around documenting informal activities. We wrote detailed field notes, complementing the verbal texts of the presentations and official documents with observations of space and place (location of the conference, spatial arrangement of the event), actors (number, gender, age, dress codes), and social practices (use of technology, exchange of business cards). For analyzing the subject position of actors and its relation to their discursive practices, I collected, from the internet, data on the participants and their affiliated organizations." (p. 1040) Narrative analysis to explore explicit and implicit texts.	"Actors who represented different groups in the field were engaged in constructing a shared story of the crisis that reflected and further strengthened the established institutional order. Concurrently, the same actors were also each telling a counter-story of indictment, blaming other groups for the crisis and calling for changes in the institutional order. Institutional entrepreneurship, then, centered on efforts of sense-making through the narration of stories. The three accounts of the high-tech 2000 fall reflected simultaneous efforts of both collaboration in maintaining the institutional order and contestation that could potentially disrupt it. The delicate balance between these contradictory orientations was carried out by the skillful manipulation of explicit and implicit meanings, which was made possible by the use of stories as the medium of, and resource for, institutional entrepreneurship." (from abstract, p. 1035)
Zilber (2011)	Examine how diverse institutions are discursively handled in field-configuring events. Uncover the	A comparative study of the two high-tech conferences held in Israel in 2002. "Through participant observation, with the help of two research assistants, each attending different conferences or parts thereof, I closely observed how each conference was configured and collected all the texts produced, disseminated, and consumed within their boundaries. We observed the formations of space and place (e.g., spatial arrangements, equipment, and decor),	"Institutional multiplicity was expressed at this site through two identity discourses, one that situated the industry within a national context and another that oriented it toward the global markets. In addition, the conferences were constructed

(Continued)

Table 9.1 Continued

Reference	Research Context	Use of Ethnography	Findings
	routine, ongoing practices that sustain institutional multiplicity on the field level.	actors (class, gender, dress code), and practices (planned activities, participation in Q&A). We attended and recorded all plenary activities and about half of parallel sessions. Recordings were later transcribed, comprising approximately 350 double-spaced pages of text. Informal social events (meals, coffee breaks, and activities in the exhibition hall, taking place in between the meeting rooms) were observed as well and documented in detailed field journals. Handouts and other materials distributed throughout the events were also collected." (p. 1543) Semiotic analysis allowed me to compare different kinds of texts (spoken, visual, spatial, etc.).	around different best-practice discourses that focused on guidelines for either investment or management. These four discourses reflected and further affected power relations between the field's actors, and they were differentially distributed across separate social spaces between the conferences and within them. The contribution of this study to our understanding of institutional multiplicity lies in demonstrating how it is maintained in practice, politically negotiated between actors, and refracted across separate social spaces." (from abstract, p. 1539)
Zilber & Gross-Friedenberg (2014)	Examine the practices invested in organizing field-level events and how they offer a specific construction of the field.	Based on a narrative analysis of two annual conferences in the Israeli healthcare industry. Participant observations allowed us to follow narratives not only as meanings carriers but also as part of social action, including the way stories are produced and performed. We could thus take into account the contexts, settings, narrators' and listeners' roles, and other paralinguistic dimensions of stories and storytelling. The second author conducted participant observation during these day-long conferences, closely observing and documenting the formation of space and place, actors, and practices. The majority of activities were attended, including plenary welcoming and keynote addresses, discussion panels, and workshops. While we observed the nonformal parts of the conferences (breakfast, lunch, coffee breaks, and cocktail receptions), our analysis is mainly based on the formal parts. These were the larger parts, and they were fully accessible to us as participant observers in a public event, unlike the one-on-one, face-to-face nonformal interactions. All the formal activities were recorded and later transcribed. These included seven	Our study shed new light on field-level events by going beyond issues of their effects and focusing instead on the multifaceted mechanisms by which they are configured. The organization of the conferences set the stage for specific stories and their telling and enactment. These practices involve the creative construction and utilization of actors' resources and work through different channels, spanning beyond the cognitive to include the material, emotional, and corporeal. These seemingly trivial practices, we argue, allow organizers to offer a self-serving depiction of the field: Casting actors in specific roles

formal events, with 26 presenters altogether. The transcriptions occupy about 250 double-spaced pages and some 150 pages of slides (made available to the audience through a website). The second author also wrote detailed field notes of her observations of the setting (including spatial arrangements of the sessions), the actors (number, gender, age, dress codes), and the social practices (like the use of technology such as short movies or requests for business cards), and she documented the behaviors of presenters and the audience, as well as her thoughts, experiences, and emotions. Narrative analysis of both story content and story as action.

and interrelations, constructing understandings to be shared by all participants, and pointing to lines of action appropriate for each actor.

Zilber (2014)

Theoretically, examine how institutional maintenance is carried out at the organizational field level.

Empirically, explore how the field of Israeli high-tech coped with the 2000 crisis.

Based on the analysis of four consecutive annual conferences held in the Israeli high-tech industry between the years 2001–2004. My longitudinal approach allowed for comparing the four conferences and appreciating the maintenance work in each year, relative to the other events.

With the help of research assistants, I conducted participant observation in the conferences throughout the entire event, from the welcoming breakfast through plenary and parallel sessions, as well as the various coffee breaks, lunch, and the "happy hour" at the end. All attended sessions were recorded and later transcribed, producing more than 650 double-spaced pages. In three conferences (2001, 2003, and 2004), most PowerPoint presentations were made available to participants via the web, adding more than 740 slides to my data. We also collected all the materials distributed throughout the conferences (e.g., conference package, advertisement materials). In addition, we kept detailed field journals, noting setting (e.g., spatial arrangements of the event, the music played), actors (e.g., age, gender, attire), and behaviors (e.g., language use).

Analysis involved looking at both the texts of the conferences and at the conferences themselves as texts, including the physical setting and artifacts (e.g., location, size, and shape of rooms; room's adornment; lights; background music; availability of food and drinks), social setting (number, gender, and age of attendees and speakers; various social arenas and different formats of events within the conference), interactions among participants, and performance (language use, use of technology). I used semiotics which allows for the treatment of different kinds of texts (oral, spatial, visual, performative) as signs.

Moving from grandiose to disconsolate to balanced conceptions of time and place, actors were engaged in a collective effort to reestablish their understanding of themselves. The data suggests that maintenance involves working through the field's identity; it relates to fundamental tensions in the symbolic institutional order, and these issues are delicately realigned over time. Institutional work is related, I suggest, to cognitive, emotional, and material factors at the intersection of inner- and outer-field pressures.

when considering a social space between organizations and societies—be it field, market, network, or social movement (to mention just a few)—one needs to be reflective about it and make sure all subsequent decisions made throughout the research process fit together to create a coherent project. I hope this chapter will be helpful in that endeavor.

Acknowledgment

This writing was supported by the Recanati Center at the Jerusalem Business School, Hebrew University, Israel. Thanks to Rod Kramer and Ian Walsh for their comments on an earlier version of this chapter. Special thanks to Yehuda Goodman for the ongoing discussion of this chapter.

Note

1 Sometimes called the "institutional field."

References

Alvesson, M., Hardy, C., & Harley, B. (2008). Reflecting on reflexivity: Reflexive textual practices in organization and management theory." *Journal of Management Studies*, *45*(3), 480–501.

Alvesson, M., & Skoldberg, K. (2000). *Reflexive methodology: New vistas for Qualitative Research*. London, UK: Sage.

Barthes, R. (1967). *Elements of semiology*. New York, NY: Hill & Wang.

Baum, J.A.C., & Rowley, T.J.R. (2005). Companion to organizations: An introduction. In J. A. C. Baum (Ed.), *The Blackwell companion to organizations* (pp. 1–34). Oxford, UK: Blackwell.

Brint, S., & Karabel, J. (1991). Institutional origins and transformations: The case of American community colleges. In W. W. Powell & P. J. DiMaggio (Eds.), *The new institutionalism in organizational analysis* (pp. 337–360). Chicago, IL: University of Chicago Press.

Czarniawska, B., & Joerges, B. (1996). Travels of ideas. In B. Czarniawska & G. Sevon (Eds.), *Translating organizational change* (pp. 13–48). Berlin, Germany: Walter de Gruyter.

Czarniawska-Joerges, B. (1992). *Exploring complex organizations: A cultural perspective*. Newbury Park, CA: Sage.

Denzin, N.K. (1978). *The research act*. New York, NY: McGraw-Hill.

DiMaggio, P. J., & Powell, W. W. (1991). The iron cage revisited: Institutional isomorphism and collective rationality in organizational fields. In W. W. Powell & P. J. DiMaggio (Eds.), *The new institutionalism in organizational analysis* (pp. 63–82). Chicago, IL: University of Chicago Press.

Down, S. (2012). A historiographical account of workplace and organizational ethnography. *Journal of Organizational Ethnography*, *1*(1), 72–82.

Fairclough, N. (1992). *Discourse and social change*. London, UK: Polity.

Gee, J.P. (2011). *An introduction to discourse analysis: Theory and method*. New York, NY: Routledge.

Gephart, R. P. (1993). The textual approach: Risk and blame in disaster sensemaking. *Academy of Management Journal*, *36*(6), 1465–1514.

Gottdiener, M. (1995). *Postmodern semiotics: Material culture and the forms of postmodern life*. Oxford, UK: Blackwell.

Guba, E.G., & Lincoln, Y.S. (1994). Competing paradigms in qualitative research. In N. Denzin & Y.S. Lincoln (Eds.), *Handbook of qualitative research* (pp. 105–117). Thousand Oaks, CA: Sage.

Hall, S. (2001). Foucault: Power, knowledge and discourse. In M. Wetherell, S. Taylor, & S. J. Yates (Eds.), *Discourse theory and practice: A reader* (pp. 72–81). London, UK: Sage.

Hardy, C., & Maguire, S. (2010). Discourse, field-configuring events, and change in organizations and institutional fields: Narratives of DDT and the Stockholm convention. *Academy of Management Journal*, *53*(6), 1365–1392.

Hawkes, T. (1977). *Structuralism and semiotics*. Berkeley, CA: University of California Press.

Hoffman, A.J. (1999). Institutional evolution and change: Environmentalism and the US chemical industry. *Academy of Management Journal*, *42*(4), 351–371.

Klag, M., & Langley, A. (2013). Approaching the conceptual leap in qualitative research. *International Journal of Management Reviews*, *15*, 149–166.

Kosteva, M. (2007). *Organizational ethnography: Methods and inspirations*. Lund, Sweden: Studentlitterature AB.

Lampel, J., & Meyer, A. D. (2008). Field-configuring events as structuring mechanisms: How conferences, ceremonies, and trade shows constitute new technologies, industries, and markets—Introduction. *Journal of Management Studies*, *45*(6), 1025–1035.

Lawrence, T.B., & Suddaby, R. (2006). Institutions and institutional work. In S. R. Clegg, C. Hardy, W. R. Nord, & T. Lawrence (Eds.), *Handbook of organization studies* (pp. 215–254). Thousand Oaks, CA: Sage.

Locke, K. (2011). Field research practice in management and organization studies: Reclaiming its tradition of discovery. *Academy of Management Annals, 5*, 613–652.

Maguire, S., Hardy, C., & Lawrence, T.B. (2004). Institutional entrepreneurship in emerging fields: HIV/AIDS treatment advocacy in Canada. *Academy of Management Journal, 47*(5), 657–679.

Mair, J., & Hehenberger, L. (2014). Front-stage and backstage convening: The transition from opposition to mutualistic coexistence in organizational philanthropy. *Academy of Management Journal, 57*(4), 1174–1200.

Manning, P. K., & Cullum-Swan, B. (1998). Narrative, content and semiotic analysis. In N. K. Denzin & Y. S. Lincoln (Eds.), *Collecting and interpreting qualitative materials* (pp. 246–273). Thousand Oaks, CA: Sage.

Neyland, D. (2008). *Organizational ethnography*. London, UK: Sage.

Phillips, N., & Hardy, C. (2002). *Discourse analysis: Investigating processes of social construction*. Thousand Oaks, CA: Sage.

Phillips, N., Lawrence, T.B., & Hardy, C. (2004). Discourse and institutions. *Academy of Management Review, 29*(4), 635–652.

Powell, W.W., & Colyvas, J.A. (2008). Microfoundations of institutional theory. In R. Greenwood, C. Oliver, K. Sahlin, & R. Suddaby (Eds.), *Sage handbook of organizational institutionalism* (pp. 276–298). Los Angeles, CA: Sage.

Schufler, E., Ruling, C., & Wittneben, B. B. F. (2014). Om melting summits: The limitations of field-configuring events as catalysts of change in transnational climate policy. *Academy of Management Journal, 57*(1), 140–171.

Schwartzman, H.B. (1993). *Ethnography in organizations*. Newbury Park, CA: Sage.

Scott, W. R. (1994). Institutions and organizations: Towards a theoretical synthesis. In W. R. Scott & J. W. Meyer (Eds.), *Institutional environments and organizations: Structural complexity and individualism* (pp. 55–80). Thousand Oaks, CA: Sage.

Scott, W.R. (2014). *Institutions and organizations: Ideas, interests and identity*. Thousand Oaks, CA: Sage.

Smith, V. (2001). Ethnographies of work and the work of ethnographers. In P. Atkinson, A. Coffey, S. Delamont, J. Lofland & L. Lofland (Eds.), *Handbook of ethnography* (pp. 220–233). Thousand Oaks, CA: Sage.

Strang, D., & Soule, S. A. (1998). Diffusion in organizations and social movements: From Hybrid corn to poison pills. *Annual Review of Sociology, 24*, 265–290.

Thornton, P.H., Ocasio, W., & Lounsbury, M. (2012). *The institutional logics perspective: A new approach to culture, structure, and process*. Oxford, UK: Oxford University Press.

Van Maanen, J. (2011). Ethnography as work: Some rules of engagement. *Journal of Management Studies, 48*(1), 218–234.

Watson, T.J. (2011). Ethnography, reality, and truth: The vital need for studies of "how things work" in organizations and management. *Journal of Management Studies, 48*(1), 202–217.

Wodak, R., & Meyer, M. (Eds.). (2009). *Methods of critical discourse analysis*. London, UK: Sage.

Woollacott, J. (1982). Messages and meanings. In M. Gurevitch, T. Bennett, J. Curran, & J. Woollacott (Eds.), *Culture, society and the media* (pp. 91–111). London, UK: Routledge.

Wooten, M., & Hoffman, A. J. (2008). Organizational fields: Past, present and future. In R. Greenwood, C. Oliver, K. Sahlin-Andersson, & R. Suddaby (Eds.), *The Sage handbook of organizational institutionalism* (pp. 130–147). Los Angeles, CA: Sage.

Yanow, D. (2012). Organizational ethnography between toolbox and world-making. *Journal of Organizational Ethnography, 1*(1), 31–42.

Yanow, D., Ybema, S., & Van Hulst, M. (2012). Practising organizational ethnography. In G. Symon & C. Cassell (Eds.), *The practice of qualitative organizational research: Core methods and current challenges* (pp. 331–350). London, UK: Sage.

Ybema, S., Yanow, D., Wels, H., & Kamsteeg, F. H. (2009). Studying everyday organizational life. In S. Ybema, D. Yanow, F. H. Kamsteeg, & H. Wels (Eds.), *Organizational ethnography: Studying the complexity of everyday life* (pp. 1–20). London, UK: Sage.

Zilber, T. B. (2007). Stories and the discursive dynamics of institutional entrepreneurship: The case of Israeli high-tech after the bubble. *Organization Studies, 28*(7), 1035–1054.

Zilber, T. B. (2011). Institutional multiplicity in practice: A tale of two high-tech conferences in Israel. *Organization Science, 22*(6) 1539–1559.

Zilber, T. B. (2014). Beyond a single organization: Challenges and opportunities in doing field level ethnography. *Journal of Organizational Ethnography, 3*(1), 96–113.

Zilber, T. B., & Gross-Friedenberg, T. (2014). *Staging, telling, and enacting self-serving stories: The configuration of field-level events*. Unpublished manuscript.

Part III
Innovative Research Designs

10

How to Look Two Ways at Once

Research Strategies for Inhabited Institutionalism[1]

Michael A. Haedicke and Tim Hallett

Introduction

How do institutionalized meanings and the environments in which organizations operate influence culture and action within organizations? How do people in organizations reproduce, disrupt, and recreate meanings that are institutionalized in organizational fields? These questions guide the growing stream of research that is coming to be known as *inhabited institutionalism* (II). In its questions and its methodological design, II research is Janus-faced. Methodologically, researchers look outward to the broader relationships and understandings that condition organizational life, and inward toward the construction of meaning in organizational settings. Analytically, they move between quasi-deductive moments and more inductive moments, with the moments of surprise that inevitably arise in qualitative research serving as a shifting point between these positions.

In this chapter, we unpack the methodological choices and analytic stances that characterize qualitative research in the II stream. Since theory and method are linked, we begin by situating II in the context of related approaches to organizational research. We trace II's connections to interactionist studies of work[2] and other approaches that examine the informal side of organizational life. We also distinguish the model of social action that lies at the heart of II research from models that derive from the "new institutional" turn in organizational sociology.

Next, we turn to a close examination of the methodological choices that characterize recent II studies. We discuss why II researchers tend to focus on "unsettled" (Swidler 1986) organizational environments and how they combine ethnographic research techniques with other methodologies to collect data about local organizational dynamics and field-level meanings. We also trace how II researchers slide between moments of reasoning that are more or less deductive and inductive and consider how this analytic flexibility shapes II's contributions to organizational studies. We conclude with a sympathetic critique of this research, which describes tensions that exist between ethnographic methods and systematic knowledge production and also challenges the organization-centric tendencies of II scholarship.

Inhabited Institutionalism's Genealogy

II research employs a fine-grained, multilevel methodological approach to understanding institutional effects and processes of institutional reproduction and change (Clemens and Cook 1999;

Jepperson 1991). Its genealogy includes interactionist studies of work as well as institutional scholarship about organizational life.

From interactionist research, II inherits a focus on interpersonal relationships and group cultures in organizational life (Blumer 1969; Fine 1996; Glaser and Strauss 1965). In contrast to formal organizational theory, interactionists contended that negotiations, conflicts, work routines, and collective interpretations expressed through gossip, joking, and shop talk were the stuff from which organizational life was made (Becker, Geer, Hughes, and Strauss 1962; Fine 1984; Strauss 1978). These scholars depicted organizations as richly textured settings in which people produced and reproduced complex meanings and relationships on a daily basis. Ethnography was their methodology of choice. By immersing themselves in workplaces, documenting the minutia of daily life, and speaking at length to workers, they pursued a view of organizations that was holistic, but built from its interactionist parts and the perspective of the "folk." Ethnography yielded portraits of organizations as messy places full of competing interests, divergent interpretations, and crosscutting relationships, and it provided a means for observing how the social processes of organization life unfolded over time (Goffman 1961; Hughes 1962).

While interactionists directed their attention to life within organizations, institutional researchers concentrated on the effects of organizational environments. Early versions of sociological institutionalism described organizational efforts to pursue goals in the context of the divergent interests and shifting coalitions that affected organizations from the outside (Clark 1956; Messinger 1955; Selznick [1949] 1966; Zald and Denton 1963). The "new institutional" (NI) scholarship of the early 1980s and subsequent years, in contrast, directed attention to the cultural dimensions of organizational environments. Organizations were understood to seek legitimacy—and to enhance their likelihood of survival—by conforming to the expectations that were institutionalized within the societies and organizational fields that surrounded them (DiMaggio and Powell 1983; Meyer and Rowan 1977).

Although there are important exceptions (DiMaggio 1982; Elsbach and Sutton 1992; Powell 1985), NI tended to rely on large-N datasets and quantitative techniques to track the convergence of organizational forms over time and the diffusion of cultural expectations within populations of similar organizations and networks of interacting organizations (Chaves 1996; Sutton, Dobbin, Meyer, and Scott 1994; Westphal and Zajac 1994). This macro focus treats social action inside organizations as a secondary concern, and indeed, its methodologies of choice usually render such action unobservable. Theoretically, NI has portrayed people as carriers of taken-for-granted institutional ideas (Meyer, Boli, and Thomas 1987; Powell and DiMaggio 1991; Scott 2007). As Schneiberg and Clemens (2006:195) summarized: "The behavior of actors—whether individuals or social entities—is attributed not to the characteristics or motives of that entity, but to its context or to higher-order factors." In this way, NI held that the concerns that were central to interactionist research distracted from the task of understanding institutional effects.

The different methodologies and theoretical commitments of interactionist and institutional research about organizations also contributed to divergent analytic stances. Interactionists tended toward analytic induction, a stance most evident in their advocacy of grounded theory (Glaser and Strauss 1967). As Tavory and Timmermans (2009:246) explained, "[Grounded theory] encourages an in-depth familiarity and granular analysis of micro data to produce empirically backed-up, generalizable theoretical claims." Most NI research, on the other hand, went in a logico-deductive direction, formulating testable hypotheses from the approach's theoretical core. Scholars designed empirical projects and selected cases for research mainly as a means of evaluating these hypotheses, which necessarily involved abstractions away from the details of social action (Orru, Biggart, and Hamilton 1991; Singh, Tucker, and Meinhard 1991).

II calls for renewed attention to the lived experience of people within organizations to remedy NI's tendency to "de-people" organizations, but it does not abandon NI's insights (Hallett, Shulman, and Fine 2009). II researchers examine how political and cultural environments influence organizational life from the outside in and focus on how the collective interpretations of creative, multidimensional organizational inhabitants rework and channel these institutional effects.[3] II thus embraces the interactionist tradition to gain leverage on core questions in sociological institutionalism. Its emphasis on social *interaction* and meanings at the institutional and intraorganizational levels also distinguishes II from recent research about "institutional entrepreneurship" and "institutional work" that emphasizes strategic, interest-driven actions (Battilana, Leca, and Boxenbaum 2009; Hardy and Maguire 2008; Lawrence, Suddaby, and Leca 2009). By extending NI's cultural analysis to also include local dynamics of meaning, II expands NI's important critique of overly utilitarian, rationalist models of action (Powell and DiMaggio 1991).

Designing Research for Inhabited Institutionalism

In their empirical studies (see Table 10.1), II researchers look simultaneously at the world of locally situated interactions and the extra-local world of institutionalized meanings and patterns of organization, and they seek to understand the influence that each exerts upon the other (Hallett and Ventresca

Table 10.1 Examples of Inhabited Institutions Research Design in Organizational Analysis

Reference	Research Context	How II Design Was Used	Key Findings
Haedicke (2012)	Natural/ organic foods co-op stores	To investigate responses to increased competition in the natural/organic foods market	Translation: Organizational leaders adapt to a new institutional environment by revising narratives of organizational identity to accommodate institutionally enforced practices
Hallett (2010)	Public elementary school	To examine the principal's effort to make teachers accountable for externally mandated student learning outcomes	Recoupling and turmoil: Organizational leaders try to enforce members' compliance with external mandates through surveillance and coercion, but members mobilize local meanings to justify resistance
Binder (2007)	Nonprofit transitional housing agency	To analyze influence of federal funding and reporting requirements on client–staff relationships	Bricolage: Members of organizations strategically combine different cultural ideas in order to pursue goals
Everitt (2012)	Three public and private high schools	To examine teachers' understanding of the nature of secondary education	Arsenals of practice: Professionals make sense of institutional mandates by reflecting on accumulated personal experiences in organizational settings
Everitt (2013)	Teacher training program at a public university	To study teacher candidates' interpretations of conflicting professional mandates	Interpretive reproduction: Organizational incumbents reproduce (and customize) institutional logics as they make sense of professional roles and identities
Aurini (2012)	For-profit learning center	To scrutinize tutors' use of proprietary curricula and teaching practices in their interactions with pupils	Patterns of coupling: Different forms of tight and loose coupling to institutional requirements emerge as organizational members interpret the informal expectations of clients

2006). That is, neither the local "folk" account of the organization nor the extra-local institutional account are to be taken at face value. Instead, these accounts are to be interrogated by each other. This multidirectional gaze sets the stage for methodological and analytical pluralism. Researchers use a range of strategies to collect data about these dynamics, including ethnography, interviewing, archival, and artifact analysis.

II studies also slide between analytic positions and reject the opposition of deduction and induction.[4] In II research, what amounts to quasi-deductive reasoning tends to influence the selection of research sites and initial research questions. However, data is collected with eyes open wide and with special attention to unexpected findings. The discovery of surprising data shifts the analysis toward a more inductive approach and the generation of new insights.

Site Selection and Research Questions

II scholars tend to examine sites of institutional "pluralism" and contradiction, where rapid changes or competing expectations push people to articulate and renegotiate implicit understandings (Heimer 1999; Kraatz and Block 2008). For example, Everitt (2012, 2013) investigates the professional socialization of aspiring teachers at a university school of education who face the unsettling requirement of teaching a standardized curriculum to students with different backgrounds and skill levels. Haedicke (2012) examines the work of natural food co-op managers who find that increasing competition with mainstream retailers has disrupted their ability to pursue deeply held goals of community empowerment and food system reform. Aurini (2012) considers private learning centers where semi-professional tutors struggle to conform to the parent company's trademarked procedures while also ensuring that their students feel nurtured and supported as individuals. In all of these cases, researchers examine settings where conditions make it difficult for people to settle comfortably into routines and where understandings of purpose and legitimate activity are challenged.

It is at this initial stage of a project that II research is closest to the deductive end of the spectrum, as researchers draw from organizational theory to identify cases of interest and to craft initial expectations. The goal is not to empirically refute or prove a theory in a logico-deductive sense, but rather to collect data that speak to questions of interest. This quasi-deductive moment appears clearly in the work of Binder (2007), who begins her examination of a transitional housing organization by asking how three schools of organizational theory—resource dependency, contingency theory, and new institutionalism—would expect increasing reliance on federal dollars to shape work in this non-profit organization. This kind of framing creates a baseline by providing a set of theoretically relevant expectations against which data can be compared.

However, II scholars avoid constructing formal, testable hypotheses, as often occurs in new institutional research. Moreover, these guiding questions do not represent strong theoretical commitments as they do in the extended case method (Burawoy 1998). Rather, theories provide conceptual buoys that help the scholar stay afloat, keeping his or her head above water when flooded with qualitative data, until he or she can understand where the empirical current leads. At this point, the scholar can abandon the buoy to swim with confidence toward the fresh insight. Certainly, the direction of the research is shaped by the placing of the initial buoys, but the buoys themselves do not drive the analysis.

Orientation and Multilevel Analysis

As they begin to collect data, II researchers direct their gaze outward, toward the social relationships and meaning systems in which organizations are embedded, and inward, toward the ways that members of the setting interpret and transform those meanings and relationships. Researchers also use original qualitative data to make sense of these contexts. For example, Binder and Haedicke use interviews to collect information about the relationships between social service departments and external funders, in the first case, and natural foods co-ops and local competitors, in the second. Everitt and Aurini mine documents, such as lesson plans, policy manuals, web pages, and assignments given to teacher candidates to understand the institutional logics of public and private schooling systems (Thornton, Ocasio, and Lounsbury 2012).

II researchers also use ethnographic methods to map out meanings and relationships within the organization that diverge from those that that are institutionalized in the surrounding environment. In his study of a public elementary school, Hallett collects information from interviews with teachers to describe an earlier period in the school's history when principals zealously defended the autonomy of teachers and sheltered them from surveillance by the school board. At the time of his research, accountability oriented reforms had largely undermined this culture of professional freedom, although it continued to exist in an idealized form in teachers' memories. Similarly, Haedicke pairs retrospective interviews with an archival examination of trade magazines to describe the democratic practices and ideologies that characterized the natural foods co-op world during its adolescence in the 1970s. These meanings, he points out, are increasingly called into question as co-ops compete with profit-oriented supermarkets that sell organic and natural foods.

Finally, researchers link these portraits of institutionalized meanings and relationships with close analysis of patterns of interaction and emergent understandings within organizations. Influenced by their interactionist forerunners, II researchers spend extended periods of time immersed in the organizational settings that they study in order to "become saturated with first-hand knowledge," and they use a variety of techniques for collecting and logging data (Morrill and Fine 1997:425). During the nearly two years that Hallett spent at Costen Elementary, he shadowed administrators, observed classrooms, videotaped staff meetings, and participated in lunchroom conversations with teachers while also conducting more formal interviews with teachers and administrators. Aurini, in order to collect data for her study of a Canadian for-profit learning center, took a year-long position that involved teaching small groups of students for 6 hours each week. In addition to observing her students and colleagues, Aurini recorded her own experiences and challenges, and these records were also part of the analysis.

Through the collection of rich and voluminous data, researchers discover discrepancies between institutionalized meanings and local practices, as well as between predicted and observed patterns of action. These surprises play a key role in II research. Epistemologically, researchers shift from the quasi-deductive stance that characterized the moment of site selection to an "abductive" sensibility: one that treats anomalies and unexpected findings as keys to understanding how the cultural creativity of organizational inhabitants shapes and is shaped by the institutional environment (Timmermans and Tavory 2012). These "abductive" moments in II research focus the investigation and often form the germ of theoretical elaboration.

Focusing the Research and Elaborating Theory

Abductive surprises highlight aspects of the setting that capture the researcher's attention and create an agenda for continued data collection. Here, the II project is at its most inductive, but not in a pure sense because the scholar does not (and probably never could) "ignore the literature of theory" (Glaser and Strauss 1967:37). Instead, it is a kind of responsive induction: responsive not only to the data, in a classic grounded theory sense, but also and inevitably to the surprising misfit between the data and prior ideas. Staying close to the data, researchers aim to "thickly describe" the nature of institutional effects in the setting and focus on making sense of why patterns of action diverge from theoretical expectations (Geertz 1973). They are attuned to local nomenclature, to the concerns and aspirations of organizational members, and to the informal social structures that emerged over time. By concentrating on features of the institutional environment that organizational inhabitants define as important, meaningful, or problematic, researchers aim to understand how "the social grammar of everyday life" in the setting is conditioned by institutional forces (Tavory and Timmermans 2009:256). These inductive efforts allow researchers to gauge the extent to which observed anomalies are sustained and deeply embedded in the life of the setting under study. They reveal new surprises as researchers uncover other features of action and interaction in the setting that diverge from the initial expectations.

As the empirical data accumulates, researchers also move from inductive data collection and analysis to the development of concepts that offer more general insight into institutional effects. Investigating the work of staff at a transitional housing center who face competing expectations from funders, clients, and professional peers, Binder (2007) imports the concept of "bricolage" from scholarship on subcultures (Hebdige 1979). She refines this concept to capture the ability of institutional members to pursue their goals by creatively combining different institutional logics. Studying teachers at various career stages, Everitt (2012) points out that instead of relying on a general cultural tool kit (Swidler 1986), professionals develop more refined "arsenals of practice" as they create routines that bridge institutional expectations and the demands of local populations. On the basis of his examination of institutional changes in the natural foods co-op sector, Haedicke extends the notion of "translation" processes in organizational studies (Sahlin and Wedlin 2008) by showing that co-op leaders draw on existing identities and understandings to make sense of institutionally imposed practices. This conceptual work elaborates theory by creating a vocabulary for describing how institutional effects are jointly constituted by the interpretive interactions of members of organizations and the cultural and political pressures of the surrounding environment. It also offers a starting point for subsequent research, since these concepts become the grist for the quasi-deductions that occur in the initial phase of later projects.

We can depict this research cycle visually by envisioning analysis as a ball on a teeter-totter, rolling between quasi-deduction and responsive induction, with surprise as the abductive shift point. The surface beneath the teeter-totter is the empirical ground, comprised of data on local interactions and activity as well as broader extra-local context and institutions (see Figures 10.1–10.5).

In Figure 10.1, the analysis sits near quasi-deduction, but the weight of analysis creates downward movement, leading to Figure 10.2.

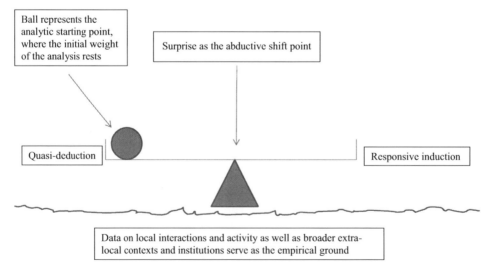

Figure 10.1 Existing Theory Informs Case Selection and Analytic Expectations During Initial Stage of Research

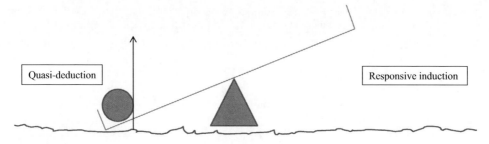

Figure 10.2   Ideas Coming to Ground Force a Reckoning as the Empirical Data Push Back Against Informing Theories

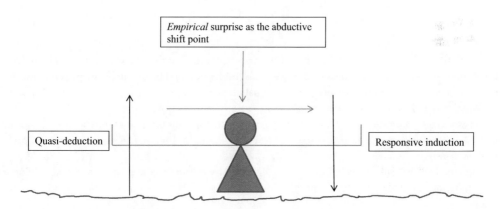

Figure 10.3   Misfitting and Surprising Empirical Findings Serve as an Abductive Shift-Point as the Weight of the Analysis Rolls Towards Responsive Induction

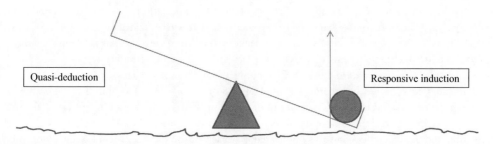

Figure 10.4   Reconsideration of the Data and the Search for Empirical Patterns and Insights Provide Another Push

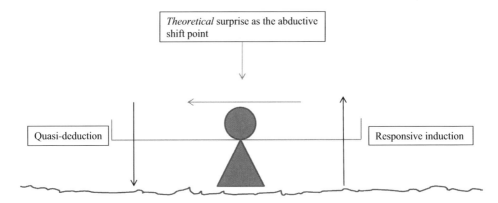

Figure 10.5 Recognition of Theoretical Surprise and Insight, Creation of New Concepts That Can Serve as the Basis of Quasi-Deduction in Further Research

In Figure 10.2, the guiding ideas come to empirical ground. This forces a reckoning as the empirical data push back against the ideas (pushing upward in the figure). The inevitable surprise and misfit between theory and data that comes with any qualitative project provides the abductive shift point as the analysis rolls from quasi-deduction toward responsive induction.

As the weight of the analysis moves further toward induction, it comes to empirical ground again, in the weeds of data. Again, in time the empirical ground pushes back in the form of observed patterns and insight.

Informed by the data, the scholar can recognize theoretical surprise, constituting another abductive shift point and revealing concepts that can serve as the basis of quasi-deduction in further research.

The II Research Cycle

This cycle appears clearly in the example of how one II project unfolded over time. Haedicke began research about natural foods co-operatives with the (deductive) expectation—derived mainly from new institutionalist studies of organizational isomorphism—that increasing market competition within the field of natural and organic foods retailing would have forced these stores to abandon countercultural practices and conform to the rationalized models of the mainstream supermarket industry. His initial observations appeared to confirm this expectation. Co-ops had shifted from volunteer to professional staff; abandoned the collective, democratic management approaches that characterized earlier years; and devoted a great deal of attention to customer satisfaction. Yet, he also noticed that despite the new similarity to market-oriented competitors, leaders of co-ops continued to define their work in terms of community empowerment and social change.

This (abductive) anomaly became a central puzzle of the research. Combing through archival sources, interview transcripts, and observations of co-op practices, Haedicke (inductively) catalogued the ways that co-ops had become more similar to mainstream stores in terms of their organizational structures and daily practices. He also discovered that each of these changes had been accompanied by the development of collective accounts within the co-op world that asserted the legitimacy of the new structures and practices within democratic, change-oriented organizations. In short, he argued, co-op leaders had "translated" the meaning of these new practices in ways that minimized the contradictions with countercultural ideologies.

Moving Forward With Inhabited Institutional Research: Case Comparison and Field-Level Ethnography

By paying attention to *both* institutional pressures *and* local interactions, II researchers have gained insight into the character of intraorganizational power struggles, the interpretive work of organizational members, the variety of connections that may exist between institutional expectations and situated practices, and the incorporation of institutionalized meanings into professional identities. However, the approach's methodological tendencies may also limit its vision and influence. In this concluding section, we discuss two of these limits—the difficult relationship between ethnographic research and systematic knowledge production and the organization-centric character of II research—as a way to spur methodological innovation.

Ethnographic research techniques provide II researchers with access to the informal dimensions of organizational life, including the friendship groups, ad hoc task forces, and sideline conversations in which people more openly discuss their goals and concerns. This enables researchers to observe how cultural institutions influence and challenge organizational members in ways that are simultaneously cognitive, practical, and emotional. Using ethnography, II documents how people in organizational settings interpret, react to, and affect institutionalized meanings in diverse and creative ways. But ethnography alone may not be well positioned to generate rigorous typologies of the sorts of responses that may occur or of the conditions under which one or another sort of response might prevail. How can II move past the (by now, well-established) assertions that "people are creative" and that "local interactions matter" to a more systematic analysis of the pathways that creativity and interactions might follow?

In our view, comparative approaches have a great potential for moving inhabited institutional research forward. The comparative approach allows for the collection of rich, qualitative data and the abductive analysis that has characterized II research up to this point, but it also offers leverage for creating systematic accounts of why members of different organizations may react to institutional expectations in different ways (Ragin 2013). Nunn's (2014) examination of meanings of student success at three public high schools and Binder and Wood's (2013) study of conservative student activism on two university campuses illustrate the potential of a comparative approach. Both studies document how organizational members in different settings interpret widely shared cultural meanings (read: institutional logics) in divergent ways, and they point to systematic principles of variation. Nunn demonstrates that students and faculty at the vocationally oriented Alternative High tend to think that school success is a function of motivation and effort, while those at the high-performing (and affluent) Elite Charter High attribute success to innate and fixed intelligence. Binder and Wood explain that the culture of anonymity at a large, state university encourages a flamboyant and confrontational style of conservative activism, while the intellectual reputation and collegiality of an elite, private campus encourage more respectful, deliberate arguments. Such findings present II researchers with the ability to construct more refined understandings about how organizational settings influence local interpretations of and responses to institutional environments.

A second limit, also linked to II's reliance on ethnography, is the organization-centric character of most studies. In a sense, the methodological tools that have been employed by II researchers so far fall short of the approach's theoretical ambitions. Although inhabited institutions researchers argue that people in organizational settings both "modify" institutionalized ideas (within organizations) and also "carry forward" those modifications into larger organizational environments, researchers have in practice halted their investigations at the boundary between the organization and the larger world (Hallett and Ventresca 2006). This means that the research has generated a range of empirical accounts of how institutionalized meanings are interpreted, resisted, or transformed within organizations, but very little information about how these innovations are "carried forward" into organizational fields and about how they might influence practices in other settings.[5]

Practical considerations help to account for II's organization-centric tendencies: It is easier to do ethnographic research in a bounded, localized environment. Few models exist of ethnographies at the level of organizational fields (although see Zilber, this volume, on this possibility). Yet, there are ways that II researchers could examine the flow of cultural innovations from organizational settings to larger fields. One would be to extend ethnographic research to settings—such as trade and professional conferences, political meetings, or courtrooms—where field-level meanings are constructed and contested. A researcher might accompany members of an organization to a national convention, for example, to observe how they interact with peers from other organizations and recognized authorities in their fields.[6] II researchers could also use discourse analytic methods to examine the influence of locally produced ideas on field-level meanings.[7] Both strategies would enable II scholars to engage with new institutionalist models that portray field-level meanings as diffusing out from centers of authority and to make the case that these meanings may also percolate up from local social settings.

These strategies would preserve the bidirectional gaze and the analytic flexibility that distinguish II. By examining meanings that are both publicly available and locally constructed and by sliding between moments of quasi-deduction and responsive inductive, II researchers are building a rich conceptual and empirical understanding of institutional effects. Comparative and field-level approaches would enable researchers to chart variation in these effects across organizational environments and to understand how organization members' creative interpretations of institutional logics ripple outward through organizational fields. The time is ripe for II research to move in these directions, as scholars pursue the project of "re-peopling" institutional analysis with the complex and creative inhabitants of organizational life.

Notes

1 We thank Matt Gougherty for providing comments.
2 We use the general term *interactionist* in lieu of the more specific term *symbolic interaction* because scholars in the microsociological tradition make fine distinctions between symbolic interaction, Goffman's ritualism, Goffman's dramaturgy, and ethnomethodology. II draws from all of these traditions, not as a synthesis but in different ways and at different times. For a fuller discussion, see Hallett, Shulman, and Fine (2009).
3 In a recent piece, McGinty (2014:11) writes that II insists that "the most salient contributions of interactionism within organizational studies are ethnographies that attend to organizational culture, interaction, and the construction of meaning." While II does use ethnographic research methods, this characterization misses the way the approach foregrounds the question of institutional effects. This focus distinguishes II ethnographies from classic interactionist studies of organizations.
4 The II stance is similar to that of Fine, who argues that the distinction between deduction and induction "that has been propounded both by qualitative and quantitative researchers is fundamentally at odds with the way that people experience and generalize from their worlds." This is necessarily so, because "as 'natural persons,' we are continually learning from our situational exposure and from what we have been assured by others. *We are inductive theorists.* But we then use this learning to assume and to create expectations about how the world operates. *We are deductive theorists.*" (Fine 2004:11; see also Fine and Hallett 2014).
5 The spread of meanings from local settings to organizational fields is sometimes implied in inhabited institutions work, even if it is not directly studied. For example, Hallett notes in his study of Costen Elementary that

> turmoil is a local outcome, but it could have larger consequences. . . . In April 2008, a Seattle teacher was suspended for refusing to administer standardized tests. . . . More than 140 organizations representing 50 million members signed the Joint Organizational Statement on No Child Left Behind, calling for major changes to NCLB. . . . Accountability lives, but when Congress debates reauthorization of NCLB, it will be in an environment where its legitimacy is no longer taken for granted, but is negotiable. [2010:70]

6 In his study of homeschooling parents, Stevens (2001) offers an example of this sort of ethnographic approach.
7 Examples of this approach might include Zilber (2006) and Meanwell and Hallett (2011).

References

Aurini, Janice Danielle. 2012. "Patterns of Tight and Loose Coupling in a Competitive Marketplace: The Case of Learning Center Franchises." *Sociology of Education* 85:373–387.

Battilana, Julie, Bernard Leca, and Eva Boxenbaum. 2009. "How Actors Change Institutions: Towards a Theory of Institutional Entrepreneurship." *Academy of Management Annals* 3: 65–107.

Becker, Howard S., Blanche Geer, C. Everett Hughes, and Anselm L. Strauss. 1962. *Boys in White: Student Culture in Medical School*. New Brunswick, NJ: Transaction Books.

Binder, Amy J. 2007. "For Love and Money: Organizations' Creative Responses to Multiple Environmental Logics." *Theory and Society* 36:547–571.

Binder, Amy J. and Kate Wood. 2013. *Becoming Right: How Campuses Shape Young Conservatives*. Princeton, NJ: Princeton University Press.

Blumer, Herbert. 1969. *Symbolic Interactionism: Perspective and Method*. Berkeley: University of California Press.

Burawoy, Michael. 1998. "The Extended Case Method." *Sociological Theory* 16:5–32.

Chaves, Mark. 1996. "Ordaining Women: The Diffusion of an Organizational Innovation." *American Journal of Sociology* 101:840–873.

Clark, Burton R. 1956. "Organizational Adaptation and Precarious Values: A Case Study." *American Sociological Review* 21:327–336.

Clemens, Elizabeth S. and James M. Cook. 1999. "Politics and Institutionalism: Explaining Durability and Change." *Annual Review of Sociology* 25:441–466.

DiMaggio, Paul. 1982. "Cultural Entrepreneurship in Nineteenth-Century Boston." *Media, Culture, and Society* 4:33–50.

DiMaggio, Paul and Walter W. Powell. 1983. "The Iron Cage Revisited: Institutional Isomorphism and Collective Rationality in Organizational Fields." *American Sociological Review* 48:147–160.

Elsbach, Kimberly and Robert I. Sutton. 1992. "Acquiring Organizational Legitimacy Through Illegitimate Action." *Academy of Management Journal* 35:699–738.

Everitt, Judson G. 2012. "Teacher Careers and Inhabited Institutions: Sense-Making and Arsenals of Teaching Practice in Educational Institutions." *Symbolic Interaction* 35:203–220.

Everitt, Judson G. 2013. "Inhabitants Moving In: Prospective Sensemaking and the Reproduction of Inhabited Institutions in Teacher Education." *Symbolic Interaction* 36:177–196.

Fine, Gary Alan. 1984. "Negotiated Orders and Organizational Cultures." *Annual Review of Sociology* 10:239–262.

Fine, Gary Alan. 1996. *Kitchens: The Culture of Restaurant Work*. Berkeley: University of California Press.

Fine, Gary Alan. 2004. "The When of Ethnographic Theory." *Perspectives: Newsletter of the ASA Theory Section* 27:4–5, 11.

Fine, Gary Alan and Tim Hallett. 2014. "Stranger and Stranger: Creating Theory Through Ethnographic Distance and Authority." *Journal of Organizational Ethnography* 3(2):188–203.

Geertz, Clifford. 1973. *The Interpretation of Cultures*. New York: Basic Books.

Glaser, Barney G. and Anselm L. Strauss. 1965. *Awareness of Dying*. Chicago: Aldine.

Glaser, Barney G. and Anselm L. Strauss. 1967. *The Discovery of Grounded Theory: Strategies for Qualitative Research*. Chicago: Aldine Publishing Co.

Goffman, Erving. 1961. *Asylums: Essays on the Social Situation of Mental Patients and Other Inmates*. Garden City, NY: Doubleday and Company, Inc.

Haedicke, Michael. 2012. "'Keeping Our Mission, Changing Our System': Translation and Organizational Change in Natural Foods Co-ops." *The Sociological Quarterly* 53:44–67.

Hallett, Tim. 2010. "The Myth Incarnate: Recoupling Processes, Turmoil and Inhabited Institutions in an Urban Elementary School." *American Sociological Review* 75:52–74.

Hallett, Tim, David Shulman, and Gary Alan Fine. 2009. "Peopling Organizations: The Promise of Classic Symbolic Interactionism for an Inhabited Institutionalism." Pp. 486–509 in *The Oxford Handbook of Sociology and Organization Studies*, edited by P.S. Adler. Oxford: Oxford University Press.

Hallett, Tim and Marc Ventresca. 2006. "Inhabited Institutions: Social Interactions and Organizational Forms in Gouldner's *Patterns of Industrial Bureaucracy*." *Theory and Society* 35:213–236.

Hardy, Cynthia, and Steve Maguire. 2008. "Institutional Entrepreneurship." In *The SAGE Handbook of Organizational Institutionalism*, edited by Royston Greenwood, Christine Oliver, Roy Suddaby, and Kirsten Sahlin-Andersson. Thousand Oaks, CA: Sage.

Hebdige, Dick. 1979. *Subculture: The Meaning of Style*. London: Routledge.

Heimer, Carol A. 1999. "Competing Institutions: Law, Medicine, and Family in Neonatal Intensive Care." *Law and Society Review* 33:17–66.

Hughes, Everett C. 1962 (1984). "Good People and Dirty Work." Pp. 87–97 in *The Sociological Eye: Selected Papers*. Edited by Everett C. Hughes. NJ: Transaction Press.

Jepperson, Ronald. 1991. "Institutions, Institutional Effects and Institutionalism." Pp. 143–163 in *The New Institutionalism in Organizational Analysis*, edited by W.W. Powell and P. DiMaggio. Chicago: University of Chicago Press.

Kraatz, Matthew S. and Emily S. Block. 2008. "Organizational Implications of Institutional Pluralism." Pp. 243–275 in *The SAGE Handbook of Organizational Institutionalism*, edited by S.R. Clegg, C. Hardy, T.B. Lawrence, and W.R. Nord. London: Sage.

Lawrence, Thomas, Roy Suddaby, and Bernard Leca. 2009. "Introduction: Theorizing and Studying Institutional Work." In *Institutional Work: Actors and Agency in Institutional Studies of Organizations*, edited by Thomas Lawrence, Roy Suddaby, and Bernard Leca. Cambridge, UK: Cambridge University Press.

McGinty, Patrick J.W. 2014. "Divided and Drifting: Interactionism and the Neglect of Social Organizational Analysis in Organization Studies." *Symbolic Interaction* 37:1–32.

Meanwell, Emily and Tim Hallett. 2011. "Accountability as an Inhabited Institution: Contested Meanings and the Symbolic Politics of Reform." Section on the Sociology of Education Invited Session: "Challenging Toward Utopia: Education Reform in the Contemporary United States." American Sociological Association Meetings, Las Vegas, NV, August 21.

Messinger, Sheldon. 1955. "Organizational Transformation: A Case Study of a Declining Social Movement." *American Sociological Review* 20:3–10.

Meyer, John W., J. Boli, and George M. Thomas. 1987. "Ontology and Rationalization in the Western Cultural Account." In *Institutional structure: Constituting state, society, and the individual*, edited by G.M. Thomas, J.W. Meyer, F. Ramirez, and J. Boli. Newberry Park, CA: Sage Publications.

Meyer, John W. and Brian Rowan. 1977. "Institutionalized Organizations: Formal Structures as Myth and Ceremony." *American Journal of Sociology* 83:340–363.

Morrill, Calvin and Gary Alan Fine. 1997. "Ethnographic Contributions to Organizational Sociology." *Sociological Methods and Research* 25:424–451.

Nunn, Lisa M. 2014. *Defining Student Success: The Role of School and Culture*. New Brunswick, NJ: Rutgers University Press.

Orru, Marco, Nicole Woolsey Biggart, and Gary G. Hamilton. 1991. "Organizational Isomorphism in East Asia." Pp. 361–389 in *The New Institutionalism in Organizational Analysis*, edited by W.W. Powell and P.J. DiMaggio. Chicago: University of Chicago Press.

Powell, Walter W. 1985. *Getting Into Print*. Chicago: University of Chicago Press.

Powell, Walter W. and Paul J. DiMaggio. 1991. "Introduction." Pp. 1–40 in *The New Institutionalism in Organizational Analysis*, edited by W.W. Powell and P.J. DiMaggio. Chicago: University of Chicago Press.

Ragin, Charles. 2013. *The Comparative Method: Moving Beyond Qualitative and Quantitative Strategies*. Berkeley: University of California Press.

Sahlin, Kerstin and Linda Wedlin. 2008. "Circulating Ideas: Imitation, Translation, and Editing." Pp. 218–242 in *The Sage Handbook of Organizational Institutionalism*, edited by R. Greenwood, C. Oliver, K. Sahlin, and R. Suddaby. Thousand Oaks, CA: Sage.

Schneiberg, Marc and Elizabeth S. Clemens. 2006. "The Typical Tools for the Job: Research Strategies in Institutional Analysis." *Sociological Theory* 24:195–227.

Scott, W. Richard. 2007. *Institutions and Organizations: Ideas and Interests*. Thousand Oaks, CA: Sage.

Selznick, Philip. [1949] 1966. *TVA and the Grass Roots: A Study in the Sociology of Formal Organization*. New York: Harper & Row.

Singh, Jitendra V., David J. Tucker, and Agnes G. Meinhard. 1991. "Institutional Change and Ecological Dynamics." Pp. 390–422 in *The New Institutionalism in Organizational Analysis*, edited by W.W. Powell and P.J. DiMaggio. Chicago: University of Chicago Press.

Stevens, Mitchell L. 2001. Kingdom of Children: Culture and Controversy in the Homeschooling Movement. Princeton, NJ: Princeton University Press.

Strauss, Anselm L. 1978. *Negotiations: Varieties, Processes, Context, and Social Order*. San Francisco: Jossey-Bass.

Sutton, John R., Frank Dobbin, John W. Meyer, and W. Richard Scott. 1994. "The Legalization of the Workplace." *American Journal of Sociology* 99:944–971.

Swidler, Ann. 1986. "Culture in Action: Symbols and Strategies." *American Sociological Review* 51:273–286.

Tavory, Iddo and Stefan Timmermans. 2009. "Two Cases of Ethnography: Grounded Theory and the Extended Case Method." *Ethnography* 10:243–263.

Thornton, Patricia H., William Ocasio, and Michael Lounsbury. 2012. *The Institutional Logics Perspective*. New York: Oxford University Press.

Timmermans, Stefan and Iddo Tavory. 2012. "Theory Construction in Qualitative Research: From Grounded Theory to Abductive Analysis." *Sociological Theory* 30:167–186.

Westphal, James D. and Edward J. Zajac. 1994. "Substance and Symbolism in CEO's Long-Term Incentive Plans." *Administrative Science Quarterly* 39:367–390.

Zald, Mayer and Patricia Denton. 1963. "From Evangelism to General Service: The Transformation of the YMCA." *Administrative Science Quarterly* 8:214–234.

Zilber, Tammar B. 2006. "The Work of the Symbolic in Institutional Processes: Translations of Rational Myths in Israeli High Tech." *Academy of Management Journal* 49:281–303.

11

Using Qualitative Methods to Track Evolving Entrepreneurial Identities

Philip Anderson

Introduction

Qualitative research methods are especially important in the study of entrepreneurship because firms typically enter archival datasets only after they have achieved a certain degree of maturity. For example, industry trade directories usually include new firms only when they first begin selling a product or service, excluding startups that never reach that stage of development. Entrepreneurial organizations are usually not yet formalized, so data from documents, statistics, or organizational information and control systems are seldom available.

Because entrepreneurial firms change so rapidly, dynamic methods are needed to track their fluid life courses. Cross-sectional investigations or panel studies with infrequent observations miss important shifts in young firms, which can lead to spurious causal inferences. Progress in understanding how new ventures evolve can by accelerated by new ways to study unfolding processes that are not yet regularized or routinized. A process study uses detailed descriptions of events that constitute change in the development of the entity being studied in order to discover event sequences that are linked by a theoretically coherent narrative (Poole et al., 2000). The emphasis is not on variables but on progressions: the nature, sequence, and order of events than an entity undergoes as it changes over time.

In recent years, the most popular method for developing process theories about young firms has been single-case or multiple-case qualitative studies that typically draw on a combination of structured interviews, archival data, and occasionally questionnaires to build an event history. Eisenhardt and Graebner (2007) urge case-study researchers to iterate between theory and data to generate constructs that are supported empirically by a mixture of selected text from interviews with a construct table that assembles narrative evidence supporting each construct. For example, the Stanford Project on Emerging Companies focused on a sample of firms less than 10 years old that had fewer than 10 employees. A retrospective history of the firm was constructed by asking founders how they had thought about the organization-building process and whether they had an organizational model or blueprint for employee relations in mind when founding the company. Responses were content analyzed to develop a typology of organizational blueprints that have been analyzed in various ways (e.g., Baron, Hannan, & Burton, 1999).

Although the rigorous application of these techniques in inductive case studies has generated many novel and heavily cited process models, case studies are subject to several limitations that may be addressed by supplementing them with a combination of other qualitative methods. One drawback is that articles must deploy small samples of the concrete evidence that was gathered. Without access to the hundreds of pages of documents generated through structured interviews, it can be difficult for others to replicate methods and findings so that theory and empirical results cumulate across studies. Another limitation is that more often than not, scholars have not confirmed in a rigorous or replicable way that the process theories they induce are congruent with the subjective meanings (verstehen) that actors attributed to their experiences, as recommended by Miles and Huberman (1984). We cannot be sure whether we are observing the mental models of the actors or of the investigators, or perhaps a complex hybrid of both.

This chapter will illustrate how scholars may study unfolding processes in entrepreneurial organizations by combining a number of well-established qualitative techniques—including narrative analysis, visual sorting, repertory grid analysis, and causal mapping—in a multiwave panel study design. The innovativeness of this approach rests on the combination of methods more than the introduction of new methods. Used together at regular intervals to probe how meanings and the causal structure of entrepreneurs over time, they may help us understand evolving entrepreneurial identities in a replicable way that facilitates comparison across cases.

The Research Question: How Do Entrepreneurial Identities Form and Develop?

Entrepreneurs face the challenge of creating a self-fulfilling prophecy (Merton, 1968) in order to survive. They must persuade different actors that the fledgling enterprise is viable in order to acquire from them the resources that make them viable. A young organization can survive only if investors, employees, customers, vendors, distribution channels, partners, and the like believe that the enterprise is a going concern with a good chance to survive. They must have confidence in the entrepreneur's story. Lounsbury and Glynn (2001) define this process of storytelling as "cultural entrepreneurship." They argue that entrepreneurial stories facilitate the crafting of a new venture identity that serves as a touchstone on which legitimacy may be conferred by stakeholders. Legitimacy in this sense goes beyond conformity to norms and regulations; it also means other actors will transact with a young firm because they believe it will survive long enough to fulfill its end of a bargain.

Lounsbury and Glynn provide several anecdotal examples of entrepreneurial stories, but they do not study the process by which such stories morph. In order to launch a company, an entrepreneur must start out with a founding story, which in Western cultures is often formalized in the form of a business plan or standard presentation (typically a "pitch deck" of computer slides). This story must evolve as the fledgling organization finds out what works and what doesn't in its efforts to acquire resources, partners, and people. The challenge an entrepreneur faces is sustaining the coherence of the story even though it must shift from time to time as the firm tests its hypotheses and learns how to thrive. The story cannot be consistent over time, but it must remain intelligible to those who have heard previous versions, in order to sustain their confidence.

A number of scholars have studied how the storytelling process produces an evolving identity for a firm. For example, Rindova and Kotha (2001) studied how the dot-com ventures Excite and Yahoo continually adapted their forms and functions in search of competitive advantage from 1994 to 1998. From archival materials validated by an interview with one of Yahoo's founders, they concluded that the self-described identity of these young companies shifted from "Internet search engine" (1994–1995) to "Internet destination site" (1996–1997) to "Internet portal" (1998–early 1999).

Santos and Eisenhardt (2009) conducted a multiple-case inductive study using archival and field data to track how entrepreneurs at five new firms in different nascent markets shaped their organizational boundaries during their initial years of organizational life. They defined *claiming* as the process by which entrepreneurs in nascent markets define a distinct identity for both the firm and market, ideally so they become synonymous. Describing one firm in their sample, they noted, "executives spent considerable time trying to hone this idea by grappling with questions such as: What are we selling? Who are we? Who's the customer? In particular, they debated 'security' versus 'trust' as the core element of their identity."

Tripsas (2009) viewed identity as comprised of perceptions of what is core about an organization. It helps insiders answer such questions as "Who are we? What kind of business are we in?" and guides key strategic decisions. In an inductive field-based study of the entire life of a single firm, she found that it changed its identity three times in 10 years, from "the digital photography company" (1996–2001), to a period of ambiguous identity from 2001 to 2005, to "the flash memory company" from 2005 to 2006.

As they describe their changing identity to audiences both inside and outside an enterprise, entrepreneurs are also learning how customers perceive their offerings relative to viable substitutes. To sustain confidence, the entrepreneurial story must explain not only "who we are," but also why others choose to transact with us instead of alternative actors. Rosa et al. (1999) argued that market sense-making is also story based. They conducted a case study of how an emerging product market category (minivans) was socially constructed through waves of stories that help create and affirm collective beliefs about current category boundaries and quality orderings. Entrepreneurs must create a belief through their evolving stories that they inhabit a viable (preferably attractive) space in the markets they define themselves as serving (Santos & Eisenhardt, 2009).

An organization's identity tells others what kind of actor it is. As Scott and Meyer (1994) argue, much of the coherence of social life is due to the creation of categories of social actors. Other actors recognize and can take meaningful action with respect to a firm when they place it in a category they understand, such as school, restaurant, or hospital. They decide whether to support or transact with an organization based on its position within the category they perceive it to occupy. Such positioning is the essence of strategy, and for entrepreneurial firms it can require a delicate balancing act. On the one hand, firms lose support if prospective employees, partners, or resource providers cannot place them in a comprehensible category. On the other hand, they may lose support if they appear too similar to others in the category, especially others who are more established and can provide similar offerings.

As an entrepreneurial firm grows and acquires employees, investors, advisors, and the like, its identity becomes a collectively shared construct. Yet the entrepreneurial leader of a firm retains a distinctive role. Selznick (1984) viewed the leader as an institutionalization agent who shapes the character and identity of the organization as its mission and identity emerge over time. An organization limits its own future freedom of choice by making character-defining commitments to develop its own identity. These commitments are chosen to align with the evolving identity narrative that the leader must continually develop and tell.

An entrepreneur's evolving conception of, and story about, what his/her firm is and does, why it is chosen, and why others should believe it is viable is encapsulated in a mental model. Over time, through trial and error, success and failure, the entrepreneur develops a set of causal connections that explain what has worked and what has not. This mental model underpins and rationalizes the entrepreneur's identity narrative and helps determine what character-defining commitments to make, based on the lessons of experience. Salancik and Porac (1986) refer to this model as a *distilled ideology*—a set of causal conclusions about the likelihood of a connection between two elements of the environment.

Clearly these factors intertwine. To win support and create a self-fulfilling prophecy of success, an entrepreneur must tell again and again a coherent identity narrative that occasionally shifts in a believably consistent way. The story must position a nascent venture, showing what other actors

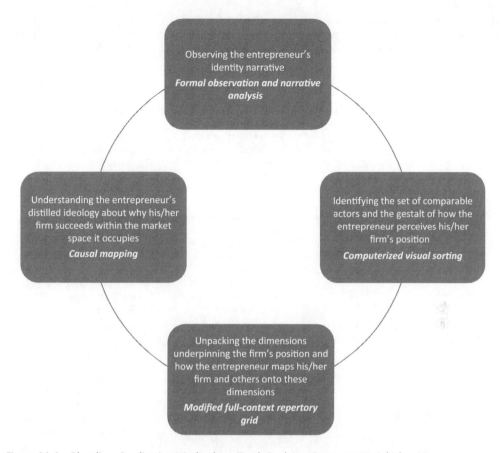

Figure 11.1   Blending Qualitative Methods to Track Evolving Entrepreneurial Identities

it should be compared to and how it is both similar to yet different from them. The entrepreneur must develop from experience a causal map that explains why it succeeds within the market space it occupies, given that its clientele could instead choose the offerings of other, comparable actors. As this causal map changes through lessons learned, and the entrepreneur's distilled ideology then informs the next iteration of the narrative that explains to self and others why the organization is viable and likely to thrive in the future. This process and the combination of qualitative methods we use to examine it are described in Figure 11.1.

Research Design for a Qualitative Panel Study of Evolving Entrepreneurial Identities

Fiol and Huff (1992) suggested that the broad strategic concerns of managers are best examined through a portfolio of different kinds of cognitive maps. They argued that the interactions among different maps are as important as the function of each map separately. Accordingly, my INSEAD colleague Rolf Hoefer and I are employing four different yet linked and complementary methods to understand the evolving identity of entrepreneurial firms. Table 11.1 outlines the methods used and representative earlier studies that employ comparable methods.

We are interviewing a panel of 50 entrepreneurs once per month in order to understand how they portray their identity narratives, view potential competitors, and make sense of what they must

Table 11.1 Examples of Qualitative Methods Drawn upon in This Study

Reference	Research Context	How Innovation Was Used	Outcomes/Results of Innovation
Down (2006)	Long-term ethnographic study of two UK-based entrepreneurs using an array of narrative analysis techniques	Repeated observations of how two co-founders created an entrepreneurial identity for themselves by crafting various justificatory and motivating stories in different settings	Identification of four themes for self-identity-building narratives: relationships, generations, space, and clichés. Entrepreneurs selectively alter narratives to suit the context and dynamically shift their narratives over time.
Johnson, Daniels, & Asch (1998)	Three organizations in the international automotive industry	Managers used a visual card sort technique to name all perceived competing organizations, then arrayed cards on a surface to reflect the manner in which these organizations compete with each other	Considerable heterogeneity in how managers map competitors in the same industry. Executives of the same nationality and hierarchical level have more similar knowledge structures but those from the same organization or function do not.
Ng, Westgren, & Sonka (2009)	Veterinarians as intermediaries in the swine genetics value chain	Respondents listed swine genetics firms with which they were familiar. A list of 16 attributes that define the key constructs used to distinguish similar firms was derived using the triadic form of the repertory grid	Perceptions about competitive attributes and groupings of a sector depend on a firm's location in the sector's value chain. Firms that are more distant in cognitive space have more different beliefs about competitive attributes and groupings.
Barr (1998)	Letters to shareholders from pharmaceutical firms from 1960–1968, studying the impact of a 1962 legislative change	Building and comparing causal maps within firms and comparing maps from year to year to identify new or deleted concepts, new or changed linkages, or changed concept meanings	Interpretations of unfamiliar events depend less on disconfirming past beliefs and more on accumulated information and comparison to past experiences. Interpretations of what the firm is doing change over time as organizations adapt to environmental change.

do in order to differentiate themselves successfully from such rivals. Each entrepreneur is a member of The Hub, a co-working space and trusted community for "purpose-driven" entrepreneurs who typically are building ventures to address social needs (in whole or in part). Because members pay a monthly fee for access to the facilities, events, and the network of The Hub, most have already launched their ventures and are building them into viable, self-sustaining enterprises.

The Hub's members come from a variety of sectors, and many have difficulty placing their ventures neatly into a single, well-defined category (e.g., telecommunications or health care). All of the ventures in our sample are less than two years old, and their founders say they are still actively developing their firms' identities and the definitions of the niches they inhabit. Our sample is limited to members whose firms serve and aim to derive revenues from a clientele instead of subsisting on grants or state aid. Some define themselves as social entrepreneurs, while others prefer to avoid such labels.

Instead of conducting the type of inductive case analysis described by Eisenhardt and Graebner, we analyze our subjects using four qualitative research techniques we have chosen because they elicit cognitive information for each observation period from each subject in a standard, replicable way. This facilitates the comparison of successive observations from the same entrepreneur, often in ways that allow us to falsify hypotheses. It also makes feasible comparisons across entrepreneurs because the method of gathering and coding data is the same for each case.

Observing the Entrepreneur's Identity Narratives

Method: Formal Observation and Narrative Analysis

We begin by asking each entrepreneur, "Have you in the past month had to describe your firm's story to relevant outside actors?" If so, we ask them to replay as closely as possible how they portrayed their firm's story, in a manner similar to the "concept pitches" studied by Elsbach and Kramer (2003). If not, we ask them how they would describe their story to a relevant outside actor if they were called upon to do that within the next week. Similar to Elsbach and Kramer, we have found that respondents are quite engaged in this activity and relate rich, vivid narratives.

The entrepreneurs in our sample have no difficulty understanding what we mean by describing their firm's story, and they report that they are frequently called upon to do so. However, they do not use a shared template for such storytelling, and individual approaches to narratives often differ considerably. Sometimes, entrepreneurs report that they would tell a different version of the story to different stakeholders (e.g., investors vs. prospective customers). In such cases, we ask them to relate each version of the story, one at a time, with as much verisimilitude as possible.

Because we use other, more formal means of tapping into the respondents' mental models, we do not probe the stories unless the meaning of a term or phrase is unclear. To analyze stories, we use an interpretive approach similar to that described by Eisenhardt and Graebner (2007) while also drawing on techniques for thematic and structural analysis of narratives explained by Riessman (2008). Consequently, the insights we draw from this first step of a monthly interview are similar in kind and quality to those derived from inductive case studies. They allow us to identify ways in which the narrative changes or remains stable from one time period to the next, tracking changes in the concepts employed and linkages between them; the richness and complexity of the narrative; the points it emphasizes; and where they are located in the narrative.

Identifying the Set of Comparable Actors and the Gestalt of How the Entrepreneur Perceives His/Her Firm's Position

Method: Computerized Visual Sorting

Next, we use a computerized version of a visual card sort technique, comparable to that employed by Johnson, Daniels, and Asch (1998). First, each entrepreneur is asked to list all firms to which the focal firm is compared by self or others and that provide offerings that might be substituted for those of the focal firm. Sometimes, respondents name an "ideal type" (e.g., "low-cost Taiwanese manufacturers") instead of enumerating specific organizations. Each response is entered into a computer, which generates one "virtual card" for each. Respondents drag and drop these cards on a two-dimensional surface without labeled axes, placing them as close together or as far apart as they deem appropriate. This generates a gestalt depiction of the respondent's mental map of competition that is congruent with the suggestion of Meyer (1991) that in many cases, visual data may more effectively capture a subject's verstehen than verbal data.

Our procedure is conceptually similar to that used by Lant and Baum (1995), who had hotel managers spatially arrange on a large sheet of paper a set of Post-It notes, one per relevant competitor. Lant and Baum were able to enumerate all the hotels in Manhattan; while we cannot identify in advance all potential competitors that Hub members might cite, the principle is similar. One advantage of computerizing the procedure is that, behind the scenes, software computes the Euclidean distance between all pairs of cards once the respondent has finished arranging them to his/her satisfaction. Within subjects at different time periods, we can examine how the set of competitors changes, how the adjacency matrix describing the distances between pairs of rivals shifts, and how the firm's positioning is perceived to be more or less distinctive compared to specific comparable others or the entire set of potential rivals.

Unpacking the Dimensions Underpinning the Firm's Position and How the Entrepreneur Maps His/Her Firm and Others onto These Dimensions

Method: Modified Full-Context Repertory Grid

Next, we wish to investigate the dimensions that underpin this gestalt picture of where an entrepreneurial venture is located relative to comparable actors. To uncover the dimensions of this construct space, we use the well-established repertory grid technique (Fransella, Bell, & Bannister, 2004). Repertory grids have frequently been used to identify the dimensions of the implicit theories individuals use to classify the elements of a set of entities as similar or dissimilar. Rooted in Kelly's personal construct theory, a repertory grid analysis extracts opposing poles for each construct (e.g., good–bad or expensive–inexpensive) and shows where a respondent locates each object or event in the set along those poles. Quantitative analysis of these data can help clarify not only how similar or dissimilar the set elements are relative to each other, but why.

One drawback of repertory grid analysis has been the tradition of presenting every possible triad of actors to the respondent, asking which two are similar and why, then how the third differs. Because we already know from the visual sort analysis which pairs of firms are perceived to be most similar, we instead present each pair to the respondent in descending order, starting with the most similar. As is standard in repertory grid studies, we ask, "In what ways are these two organizations alike?" We then ask what the opposite of the stated likeness relationship is. We continue until each element has been compared to its nearest neighbor and three consecutive comparisons yield no new constructs explaining how a pair of elements is similar. This dramatically reduces the time required to elicit concepts, alleviating the problem of respondent fatigue that others who have used triadic techniques report.

On a computer, the constructs (dimensions) elicited are listed in random order, and respondents are asked to position each firm along an 11-point scale for each dimension, anchored by the opposite poles. Previous studies have shown that respondents tend to place individual observations nearer the poles instead of clustering them in the middle when the opposite of each construct is elicited directly, instead of asking how the third member of each triad differs from the first two.

The arrangement of firms in the comparable set along these construct dimensions provides a rich source of data that can be analyzed quantitatively. For example, changes in the constructs elicited from period to period are apparent, allowing us to assess the appearance, disappearance, merging, or reconceptualization of concepts over time. Principal components can be extracted, showing how over time the respondent's mental model becomes more or less complex. The distance between constructs and the centrality of constructs (degree of correlation with other constructs) can be compared from one period to the next. By comparing the Euclidean distance of firms in construct space to their distance in the visual sort, we can infer the implied weighting of constructs for each respondent and can examine how this changes over time. We can also examine how the entrepreneur's perception of his/her firm's position in construct space changes over time and can identify those dimensions on which he/she perceives his/her firm to be most distinctive.

Understanding the Entrepreneur's Distilled Ideology About Why His/Her Firm Succeeds Within the Market Space It Occupies

Method: Causal Mapping

A causal map represents the structure and content of a respondent's mental models, focusing on perceived cause–effect linkages (Armstrong, 2004). It is a network of assertions about causes, effects, and the links between them. Causal maps have been employed in many organizational studies. For example, Nadkarni and Narayanan (2007) used textual analysis of letters to shareholders to identify 214 cause–effect linkages, classified into 35 broad categories. Using a matrix linking cause labels with effect labels, they derived maps showing the causal chains by which firms such as Microsoft or Boeing explained their performance. Diesner and Carley (2004) show how cause–effect concepts can be organized into an adjacency matrix where the value of each cell depends on whether (or how often) a specific cause is linked to a specific effect. This allows scholars to apply the entire methodological apparatus of social network analysis to causal maps.

We present one at a time to each respondent the firms he or she selected earlier as comparable actors who provide offerings that might be substituted for those of the focal firm. We then ask the respondent to complete as many sentences as he/she likes of the form "If ____, then a prospective customer would be more likely to transact with us than with them." For example, a respondent might reply, "If it is not price sensitive, then a prospective customer would be more likely to transact with us than with them." The result is a set of if-then statements explaining the mental model an entrepreneur uses to explain why his/her firm succeeds within the market space it occupies, given that its clientele could instead choose the offerings of the other. With repeated observations, we can understand how this mental model changes over time. At the level of individual causal linkages, we can identify when and how convictions emerge, disappear, combine, or are transformed. At the level of the causal map as a whole, we can examine how the number of concepts, the centrality of specific concepts, and associations between concepts shift.

Conclusion and Future Directions

We believe that by collecting all four types of data, we will be able in the future to develop a better theory of how changing identity narratives are related to shifts in the mental models entrepreneurs create in order to make sense of their experience. Over time, an entrepreneur's perceptions change. His/her notions about whom a venture competes with, how it is positioned against potential rivals, why it is similar to or different from them, and why it succeeds or fails in winning customers evolve through direct and vicarious experience. These conceptual shifts inform an evolving narrative about what the firm is and why it can be expected to survive and thrive. In turn, the narrative integrates elements of a distilled ideology and tests the mental model because the entrepreneur observes whether the story is more or less successful from period to period in winning support and creating a self-fulfilling prophecy that the firm will succeed. We do not yet understand the process by which narratives and causal conceptions unfold, but we believe the research design we have outlined provides clear guidelines that will promote the accumulation of theory and data as others undertake panel studies of entrepreneurs and their ventures.

Because this line of research is relatively nascent, we can foresee but not yet address a number of important future extensions to the design described in this chapter. First, at present we are only interviewing the founder of each firm. In some cases, the founder is the only employee, but over time we hope to add multiple informants. This will allow us to understand narratives and mental maps as fuzzy, imperfectly shared, collective constructs. Second, we would like to extend our understanding of how the narrative influences the committing decisions and enduring structures that lead to institutionalization and imprinting. At present, we focus on what Scott and Meyer (1994) have termed *representational rules*, which define what categories an object belongs to and what properties characterize that category. Meaning systems that quality as institutions also incorporate constitutive rules (defining the nature of actors and their capacity for action) and normative rules, prescribing how actors in a certain category should act. Third, we can extend our depiction of a venture's environment beyond potential competitors, taking in a broader constellation of actors (e.g., partners or regulators) whose actions can affect or need to be influenced by an evolving narrative. Finally, we intend to study how the members' collective, shared perceptions of The Hub itself change over time, allowing us to link their individual narratives to their evolving perceptions of what it means for them to belong to The Hub and how that becomes more or less congruent with their shifting individual identities.

It should be emphasized in closing that this chapter is not meant to question the utility or importance of inductive case studies. Rather, it is our intention to show that a panel study using a complementary combination of previously tested qualitative research methods can provide a rich depiction of an unfolding process in a way that may be easier for scholars to replicate. We hope to encourage others to push forward the study of entrepreneurial identity formation as a vibrant research stream within organization theory and strategy.

References

Armstrong, D. (2004). Causal mapping: A discussion and demonstration. In V.K. Narayanan and D. Armstrong (Eds.), *Causal mapping for research in information technology* (pp. 20–45). Hershey, PA: Idea Group Publishing

Baron, J.N., Hannan, M.T., & Burton, M.D. (1999). Building the iron cage: Determinants of managerial intensity in the early years of organizations. *American Sociological Review, 64*, 527–547.

Barr, P.S. (1998). Adapting to unfamiliar environmental events: A look at the evolution of interpretation and its role in strategic change. *Organization Science, 9*, 644–669.

Diesner, J., & Carley, K. M. (2004). Revealing social structure from texts: Meta-matrix text analysis as a novel method for network text analysis. In V.K. Narayanan and D. Armstrong (Eds.), *Causal mapping for research in information technology* (pp. 20–45). Hershey, PA: Idea Group Publishing

Down, S. (2006). *Narratives of enterprise: Crafting entrepreneurial self-identity in a small firm.* Cheltenham, UK: Edward Elgar Publishing.

Eisenhardt, K.M., & Graebnerm M. E. (2007). Theory building from cases: Opportunities and challenges. *Academy of Management Journal, 50*, 25–32.

Elsbach, K. D., & Kramer, R. M. (2003). Assessing creativity in Hollywood pitch meetings: Evidence for a dual-process model of creativity judgments. *Academy of Management Journal, 46*, 283–301.

Fiol, C.M., & Huff, A. S. (1992). Maps for managers: Where are we? Where do we go from here? *Journal of Management Studies, 29*, 267–285.

Fransella, F., Bell, R., & Bannister, D. (2004). *A manual for repertory grid technique* (2nd ed.). Chichester, England: Wiley.

Johnson, P., Daniels, K., & Asch, R. (1998). Mental models of competition. In C. Eden & J.-C. Spender (Eds.), *Managerial and organizational cognition: Theory, methods and research* (pp. 130–146). London, England: Sage.

Lant, T.K., & Baum, J.A. C. (1995). Cognitive sources of socially constructed competitive groups: Examples from the Manhattan hotel industry. In W. Richard Scott & S. M. Christensen (Eds.), *The institutional construction of organizations: International and longitudinal studies* (pp. 31–47). Los Angeles, CA: Sage.

Lounsbury, M. & Glynn, M.A. (2001). Cultural entrepreneurship: stories, legitimacy, and the acquisition of resources. *Strategic Management Journal, 22*, 545–564.

Merton, R. (1968). *Social theory and social structure.* New York, NY: Free Press.

Meyer, A. D. (1991). Visual data in organizational research. *Organization Science, 2,* 218–236.

Miles, M.B., & Huberman, M. (1984). *Qualitative data analysis: A sourcebook of new methods.* Thousand Oaks, CA: Sage.

Nadkarni, S., & Narayanan, V. K. (2007). Strategic schemas, strategic flexibility, and firm performance: The moderating role of industry clockspeed. *Strategic Management Journal, 28,* 243–270.

Ng, D., Westgren, R., & Sonka. S. (2009). Competitive blind spots in an institutional field. *Strategic Management Journal, 30,* 349–369.

Poole, M.S., Dooley, K., Van de Ven, A. H., & Holmes, M. E. (2000). *Organizational change and innovation processes: Theory and methods for research.* New York, NY: Oxford University Press.

Riessman, C.K. (2008). *Narrative methods for the human sciences.* Los Angeles, CA: Sage.

Rindova, V.P., & Kotha, S. (2001). Continuous "morphing": Competing through dynamic capabilities, form, and function. *Academy of Management Journal, 44,* 1263–1280.

Rosa, J.A., Porac, J. F., Runser-Spanjol, J., & Saxon, M. S. (1999). Sociocognitive dynamics in a product market. *Journal of Marketing, 63,* 64–77.

Salancik, G.R., & Porac, J. F. (1986). Distilled ideologies: Values derived from causal reasoning in complex environments. In H. P. Sims, Jr., D. Gioia & Associates (Eds.), *The thinking organization* (pp. 75–101). San Francisco, CA: Jossey-Bass.

Santos, F.M., & Eisenhardt, K. M. (2009). Constructing markets and shaping boundaries: Entrepreneurial power in nascent fields. *Academy of Management Journal, 52,* 643–671.

Selznick, P. (1984). *Leadership in administration: A sociological interpretation.* Berkeley: University of California Press.

Scott, W.R., & Meyer, J.W. (1994). *Institutional environments and organizations: Structural complexity and individualism.* Thousand Oaks, CA: Sage.

Tripsas, M. (2009). Technology, identity and inertia through the lens of "the digital photography company." *Organization Science, 20,* 441–460.

12

From What Happened to What Happens

Using Microhistorical Case Studies to Build Grounded Theory in Organization Studies

Andrew Hargadon

History in Organization Studies

The role of history in both research and teaching organization studies has reemerged in the past several decades.[1] Its dominant use today lies in methodologies that pursue the discovery of general patterns or universal laws that can be empirically validated through the acquisition and testing of data (Zald, 1991) and employ historical data primarily to test hypotheses over extended time periods (see, for example, population ecology and institutional theory, e.g., Hannan & Freeman, 1977; DiMaggio & Powell, 1983). By looking at processes that unfolded over time, this work is historical, yet at the same time, it is ahistorical in that it employs historical data to test general patterns or universal laws of individual and organizational behavior independent of the cultural context of its time and place.

An alternative approach builds on the rise of cultural history and its roots in sociology and anthropology. To study culture, business historians have looked back to the verstehen tradition of Weber and the German historical school, to the Annales School of France (Leblebici, 2013), to the grounded theory and thick description of cultural anthropology (Geertz, 1973), and, most recently, to structuration (Giddens, 1979). This return to the study of culture in history more generally has fostered a theoretical and methodological approach labeled *microhistory*, an approach that blends historical and qualitative research methods.

Microhistory

Microhistory describes the intensive study of particular lives, artifacts, events, or places with the objective of revealing the fundamental experiences, cognition, and action of the people involved (Clark, 2004; Lepore, 2001; Rowlinson et al., 2014). It is, in the words of historian Ronald Hoffman, "an endeavor to discern through the lives of individuals or families the broader contours of the social and cultural landscape" (Hoffman, 1997: vii–viii). Jill Lepore (2001) offers several useful distinctions between traditional histories and microhistories. First, microhistories are founded upon the assumption that the value of examining the subject "lies not in its uniqueness, but in its exemplariness, in how that individual's life serves as an allegory for broader issues affecting the culture as a whole" (Lepore, 2001:133). In this way, microhistories converge with other disciplinary approaches, such as anthropology. As Geertz notes, "The essential task of theory building here, is not to codify abstract regularities but to make thick description possible, not to generalize across cases but to generalize within them" (1973: 26). Second, microhistories are not recapitulations of entire lives or grand sweeps of history but are, instead, limited in their scope to addressing particular questions that begin with the end of explaining the role of culture.

In organizational studies, microhistory is similar to the approach of institutional theorists who recognize the need to account for the duality of institutions and agency (Barley & Tolbert, 1997; Lawrence et al., 2009). Barley and Tolbert argue that a historical clock—that embeds actors and actions in their particular historical context—is necessary to study processes of institutionalization and change: "Unless institutions and actions are analytically as well as phenomenologically distinct, it is difficult to understand how one can be said to affect the other" (1997: 99). To capture the recursive relationship between institutions and action, researchers must study both institutions spanning periods of time and place as well as actions embedded in a particular time and place, and they must show both how existing institutions shape actions in the moment and how those actions lead, subsequently, to the maintenance or change of those institutions.

Within organization studies and related fields, such work has been built around the emergence of new institutions (e.g., Latour, 1988; Selznick, 1949) or technologies (e.g., Hargadon & Douglas, 2001; Morison, 1966; Yates, 1999) and around the founding of new organizations (e.g., DiMaggio, 1991; McKenna, 1995) or transformation of an occupation (Nelson & Irwin, 2014). The commonality in these studies is their focus on the causal links between larger social structures and individual cognition and action.[2]

History in the Making and the Making of History

As an example of the difference between microhistory and more traditional historical analysis in the study of organizational and industrial processes, compare Elting Morison's (1966) description of the U.S. Navy admiralty's interpretation of and response to the innovative and radically superior steam-powered vessel launched in 1868, the *Wampanoag*, and Sandro Mendonça's (2014) excellent history of the parallel and interdependent advances in both sail- and steam-powered ships through the 19th century. Both studies develop, rather than test, hypotheses about the emergence of steamships and the ultimate elimination of sail power. Yet, both studies do so with different theoretical and methodological perspectives that reveal what distinguishes microhistory.

Mendonça's research question is timeless: What factors affect the transition from incumbent to novel technology? This study addresses one particularly noted aspect of such transitions, called the *sailing ship effect*, which describes how incumbent technologies often make great advances when they are challenged by emerging alternatives. This research refutes this effect by showing how many of the advances in sailing technologies occurred before the threat of steam power and, rather than prolonging sail's competitive advantage, actually contributed to the development and relative value of the emerging technology. In particular, it records the evolution of a series of significant and interrelated economic, technical, and regulatory institutions and their effects on the relative and absolute population (in ships and in tonnage) of steam-powered and sailing ships from 1815 to 1911. Mendonça's research exposes the confluence of social forces shaping both an incumbent technology and the emergence of its ultimate replacement. Yet, at the same time, it does not account for the cognition and actions of individuals involved in any given moment in this historic transition.

Elting Morison similarly looks at the emergence of the steam ships and—because we know how the story ends—its ultimate displacement of the sail. His research question is the same: What factors affect the transition from incumbent to novel technologies? In his research, however, Morison is interested in capturing the perceptions and actions of the navy men sitting at—and indeed shaping—the historic transition from the sail to the steam ship. In this way, he is looking to understand the cognition and actions of individuals involved at a particular moment and, by doing so, to understand something more general about the way anyone in such a position must, in their own present, negotiate between the constraints of their past and the potential of their future.

Morison bounds his study to the particular time and place in which the steamship *Wampanoag* was built, tested, commissioned, and decommissioned by the U.S. Navy. When the *Wampanoag* completed her sea trials on February 12, 1868, a board of engineers reported that her performance could not be equaled "for speed and economy by that of any sea-going screw vessel of either the merchant or the naval service of any country." The *Wampanoag* carried out her duties effectively for a year until she and other steam vessels became the subject of a board of naval officers that reported such vessels were technically unsound and, as importantly, "not a school of seamanship for officers or men" (Morison, 1966: 114):

> Lounging through the watches of the steamer, or acting as firemen or coal heavers, will not produce in a seaman that combination of boldness, strength and skill which characterized the American sailor of an elder day; and the habitual exercise by an officer, of a command, the execution of which is not under his own eye, is a poor substitute for the school of observation, promptness and command found only on the deck of the sailing vessel. (Morison, 1966: 115)

Shortly after, the *Wampanoag* and her sister ship, the *Amonoosuc*, both of which had performed their duties well, were taken out of service and eventually sold.

Morison presents this case study not as evidence that the early steamships were technically flawed (in this case, her performance in trials and in duty, as well as that of subsequent ships, showed the *Wampanoag* was simply different from the sailing ships of the time). Nor does this case illustrate that bureaucracies, such as the U.S. Navy was, resist innovation. Rather, Morison's research shows that social structures—in this case, of the Navy and of the command of individual ships—shape the cognition and action of the individuals involved when determining the fitness of a new technology. As Morison describes:

> What these officers were saying was that the Wampanoag was a destructive energy in their society. Setting the extraordinary force of her engines against the weight of their way of life, they had a sudden insight into the nature of machinery. They perceived that a machine, any machine, if left to itself, tends to establish its own conditions, to create its own environment and draw men into it. (Morison, 1966: 119)

In this history, the focus of Morison's attention was on how these people experienced and acted within this moment, when they only had the past to guide them.

Grounded Theory Building With Historical Cases

Grounded theory building originated in Glaser and Strauss's challenge to prevalent assumptions of universal explanations of social behavior. They sought a methodological middle ground that neither presumed (nor constructed) social science as akin to the objective realities of natural sciences nor as adrift in the subjectivism of social construction. This approach provided a rationale for and method of systematic data collection that could be used to develop new theories accounting for the cognition and actions of individuals and groups in social settings (DiMaggio, 1997; Gephart, 2004; Suddaby, 2006).

This methodology is distinguished by two key precepts: *constant comparison*, the iterative process of collecting and analyzing data, and *theoretical sampling*, the unfolding determination—by the emerging theory—of what data should be collected next. The purpose of this methodology is to identify and develop new theory rather than develop and test hypotheses from prior research. Many assume this requires the researcher to begin his or her fieldwork by ignoring prior research. This is not the case. Prior theory is essential to both defining the initial research question and setting the necessary boundary conditions for what data is relevant, from which sources, and over what time periods. Without such a priori structure, the researcher faces an undistinguishable mass of potential data. "The real danger of prior knowledge in grounded theory," as Suddaby (2006: 634) notes, "is not that it will contaminate a researcher's perspective, but rather that it will force the researcher into testing hypotheses, either overtly or unconsciously, rather than directly observing." The challenge is to avoid this outcome by continually asking of the emerging theory, through constant comparison and theoretical sampling, "what about this is interesting?" On the tree of abstraction, the challenge is to move from the particulars of the data up to increasing levels of abstraction, all the while choosing which theoretical limb to climb out on, until you arrive at a view you think worthy of showing others.

Within historical case study research, grounded theory building implies a set of research questions that focus on how the cognition and actions of individuals and groups shaped and was shaped by larger social structures. It also defines what data are relevant, from which sources, and over what time periods that will enable you to capture this set of relationships. The past is, like the present, overdetermined. The researcher's task is not to search for the single set of causal forces responsible, but rather to see the variety of forces acting for and against the outcomes that ultimately prevail and, looking beyond the dominant theories, see what has been missed. Mendonça (2013) and Morison (1966), for example, provide alternative explanations for what shaped the transition from sail to steam. Mendonça shows how innovations in sailing ships were driven by a host of institutional and technological changes that predated steam vessels. Morison shows how the interpretations and actions of officers, experiencing the introduction of steam vessels, was shaped by the institutional context of the U.S. Navy.

Microhistories provide two related distinctions from qualitative studies of contemporaneous events such as ethnographies and case studies. First, while they are limited by the nature and richness of the data available relative to participant observation and interviews, microhistories are better able to move between the particulars of the moment and the larger structural, cultural, and technological milieu that unfolds over longer time periods and in which these particulars are embedded. Second, and related, microhistories know how the story ends. Van de Ven (1992: 181) notes that "real-time research may therefore be preferred to historical research because process outcomes are not known when the research commences" and yet, to historians, "'temporal distance' is a requirement for deciding which singular events are historiographically significant beyond the subjective perceptions of actors" in the moment (Rowlinson et al., 2014: 259). This enables researchers to interpret each informant's own interpretations and actions in light of their effects on history rather than their aspirations to make history, and thus to consider how actors have (or have not) contributed to institutional changes that typically unfold over longer periods.

The Microhistorical Case Study Research Approach

A microhistorical case study focuses on the dynamics between larger social and institutional forces and individual cognition and action within a single setting or event. Historical analysis enables us to understand this dynamic by studying individual behaviors in particular moments or events in relation to the institutional (the social, cultural, political, and technological) context in which they originate, and which they in turn reify or change. Table 12.1 presents examples of the microhistorical case study research approach.

Andrew Hargadon

Table 12.1 Use of Microhistorical Methods in Qualitative Research

Reference	Research Context	How Microhistorical Methods Were Used	Outcomes/Results of Innovation
Hargadon & Douglas (2001)	Edison's design and subsequent adoption of the electric light	Revisited innovation process and investigate the role of culture and cognition in adoption of new practices in established fields	Found that entrepreneurs like Edison use existing cultural elements in the design of novel technologies as a means to exploit established understandings and facilitate initial adoption and use
Latour (1988)	The emergence and rapid adoption of Pasteur's microbial theory in science and practice	Investigated how rapid cultural change precipitated around Pasteur's theories	Showed how preexisting understandings and actions within the community provided a receptive audience able to adopt and advance Pasteur's ideas as their own
Leblebici et al. (1991)	The emergence of the U.S. Radio Broadcasting Industry	Explored the organization of exchange transactions among constituents in the field	Found that three endogenous mechanisms of change were used to organize transactions: analogies, private agreements, and conventions; showed how organization of the field hinged upon institutionalized definitions of structure and content of transactions
Morison (1966)	The adoption of steamships in U.S. Navy	Studied original documents and issued reports	Found that the resistance of U.S. Navy to the novel steamships was significantly shaped by the explicit awareness, on the part of the officers involved, of the effects that such technological changes would have on the Navy's existing culture
Yates (1999)	The emergence and rapid adoption of IBM's commercial computers	Explored the fit between early computers and the extant cognition and practice within large firms	Showed that IBM's competitive success with early computers resulted from its ability to match the appearance, structure, and function of its offerings to the existing cognition and actions (and organizational structures) of its early customers

Research Question

Within microhistory, it is important to formulate an initial research question and to do so within an existing theoretical framework. The initial research question asks what happened and why. The research question plays two important roles. In the beginning, it enables the researcher to identify relevant sources of data from the mass of history and to define how those sources will be used. However, because microhistorical case studies are a research strategy for grounded theory building, the initial research question can and often does change in response to the evidence the researcher uncovers and the resulting explanations that evidence implies. As such, the research question that results—at the end of the project—plays a second role of both enabling the researcher and reader to frame the study and its contribution, as well as to evaluate the validity of the evidence and arguments it contains. As such, the research must always craft a contribution in relation to an established theory and research community.

For microhistorical case studies, research questions should consider how the cognition and actions of individuals are shaped by and in turn shape the institutional context in which a particular event takes place. Morison (1966), for example, asked what happened when U.S. Naval officers were confronted with the opportunity to adopt one of the first technically superior steam vessels into its fleet and why they responded the way they did. Latour (1988) asked what happened in the origins of the Pasteur Institute and why it so rapidly and broadly reshaped modern science and society. Leblebici, Salancik, Copay, and King (1991) asked what happened in the evolution of the U.S. Radio Broadcasting Industry and why organizations took the forms and practices they did. Yates (1999) asked what happened in the early adoption and use of computers by life insurance firms in the 1950s, and why producers and consumers made the choices they did. Hargadon and Douglas (2001) asked what technical and organizational choices Edison faced in developing his system of electric lighting and why he made the choices he did. In each of these studies, the answers were informed by the institutional context of that particular time and place.

The research question shapes the particular phenomenon—both what happened and why. It also shapes the spatial and temporal boundaries (the place and time) of the study by defining which preceding and concurrent events and conditions are relevant to understanding the particular moment and actions of interest. And finally, it shapes the choice of sources and, as importantly, the validity of those sources.

Research Setting in Time and Place

The choice of setting of microhistorical case studies is driven by the research question and, in turn, drives both the spatial and temporal bounds of the study. Researchers must decide what events and actions, and what sources of information, fall inside the scope of the study and what fall outside. This decision reflects what Glaser and Strauss (1967) and Eisenhardt (1989) call *theoretical sampling* rather than *statistical sampling*, because the case and the sources of information deemed relevant are selected for theoretical rather than statistical reasons. There are three common strategies for selecting a particular time and place. First, the particular setting may be chosen to revisit a well-known event when different sources of information suggest an alternative theoretical explanation for the outcome or a new definition of the outcome. For example, Hargadon and Douglas (2001) revisited Edison's development of his system of electric lighting to consider the role of design, rather than of technological superiority, in driving the development and subsequent adoption of Edison's system. The setting may be chosen to highlight an otherwise overlooked event for its role in reshaping institutional conditions, as when Nelson and Irwin (2014) analyzed 22 years of articles from library journals to consider how the emergence of Internet search technologies shaped the identities of professional librarians and how these responses in turn shaped the evolution of their occupational identity over time. Finally, the setting may be chosen because it provides a particularly clear window into the influences of institutional context on cognition and action in a relatively unremarkable setting, as Morison's focus on the Navy's decision regarding one ship revealed how the more general conflict between military culture and technological change shapes the interpretations and actions of Naval officers.

In all cases, the research question should determine the physical setting as well as two time frames: a smaller frame focusing on the specific event in question and the larger frame necessary to show the dominant institutional context in and through which the event plays out. The spatial and temporal bounding of the specific event may span hours, days, or even years. It should capture all of the

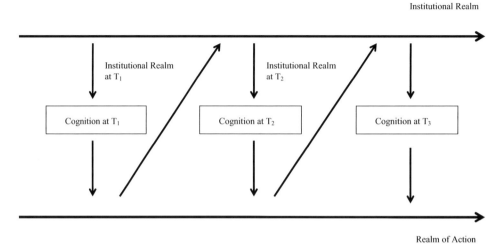

Figure 12.1 Cognition and Action Acting Within and Upon the Institutional Context
Source: Adapted from Barley and Tolbert (1997).

relevant conditions, actors, and actions that are related to the research question. For parsimony's sake, it need not and should not include more than is necessary, with the important exception of recognizing the presence of other forces shaping cognition and action within the event. The larger frame should capture the nature and structure of the institutional context that precedes and constitutes the event in question. It should also capture the resulting impact of that event—of the cognition and actions of the people involved—on the institutional context, whether that result reifies existing structures or gives rise to new ones. As Figure 12.1 shows, the context at time T_1 shapes cognition and action within event E_1, which in turn either reshapes or reifies the context at time T_2.

As Barley and Tolbert (1997) argue:

> Unless researchers use separate indicators of institutions (which span settings and time) and actions (which are localized to a specific setting), they can neither argue convincingly that the two map the same principles nor show how actions implicate structures broader than those of setting itself. (99)

For example, Hargadon and Douglas (2001) showed how Edison's design reshaped the larger institutional context by deliberately shaping the cognition and actions of early customers of Edison's electric system. Those cognitions and actions in turn shaped the larger institutional field through the uptake and subsequent evolution of electric lighting. Similarly, Morison showed how Navy leadership responded to innovative steam vessels in ways that, despite their superior performance, reflected established institutional schemas and scripts and, in turn, subsequently prolonged institutional change.

Data Gathering

There is less attention devoted in historical research texts to articulating the methods of data gathering and analysis. While the qualitative nature of historical data in many ways resembles that collected by ethnography and case study research in the management literature, as Joanne Yates (2014: 271) recognizes, qualitative organizational researchers "have developed a more conventionalized way of dealing with the issue, in the context of the scientific and social scientific article genre." Historical researchers are every bit as aware of the incomplete, subjective, multivocal nature of qualitative data; they have simply developed other means of addressing these challenges. Indeed, the lack of conventionalized ways of articulating historical methods may be what is holding back the contribution of historical research to the field of organization studies.

There are three categories of historical data: primary, secondary, and tertiary sources. Primary sources include documents, artifacts, correspondence, ledgers, records (census data, economic data), audio and video recordings, interviews, diaries, journals, peer-reviewed articles, patents, artifacts (photographs, sketches, notebooks, tools, buildings, furniture, etc.), websites, and other materials or evidence that were created in the time period under study. Secondary sources represent materials that are constructed from, comment on, or interpret primary sources such as newspaper and magazine articles, biographies, encyclopedia or other reference materials, textbooks, websites, written or oral histories, and post hoc interviews (when the outcomes of interest to your research are already known by the participants). Tertiary sources include summaries, encyclopedias, dictionaries, chronologies, almanacs, textbooks, review articles, indices, bibliographies, biographies, commentaries, criticisms, and other edited and altered accounts of primary and secondary sources.

Within a research design focused on grounded theory building, data collection reflects theoretical sampling, which thus involves moving between these different source levels to, on the one hand, recognize events and conditions that are potentially relevant to your research question and, on the other hand, to explore and gather reliable data on these events and conditions that drive the construction of novel theoretical insights. In this way, one advantage of historical case studies is that the research has more freedom to gather additional data as the theory emerges. As Eisenhardt (1989: 539) points out, "a key feature of theory-building case research is the freedom to make adjustments during the data collection process." As you get closer to understanding the cognition and actions of the individuals involved, you may find it necessary to collect further data on the context they inhabit.

Note that the distinction between primary and secondary sources will differ depending on the research frame and question and, in many ways, on the reliability of the sources.[3] What defines a primary versus secondary source depends on the focus of your research. If your question addresses how actors shape a particular sense of emerging technologies, then newspaper articles of the time serve as primary sources—as insight into the outcomes of interest. In other words, what statements they contain is not as important as the cognition and motivation that constitutes them. More important than inventorying such data sources is considering (and discussing) their reliability and credibility: what story they tell and why will determine their usefulness.

For example, in studying the emergence of the electric light, Thomas Edison's notebooks, physical artifacts, engineering drawings, financial projections, and press releases, as well those of competitors, investors, regulators, and reporters, were all fair game. But Edison's press releases and media interviews were clearly motivated by efforts to shape investor and public perceptions and thus provide more reliable and credible information if your research question regards Edison's efforts to manipulate meaning than they do if your question regards a chronology of technical development. Thus, the distinction between primary, secondary, and even tertiary sources depends upon the research question. Newspaper accounts of Edison's development of the light bulb are secondary sources to a study of the innovation process, but they could serve as primary sources to a study of public perceptions of that innovation process. Even encyclopedia entries, ordinarily considered tertiary sources, become primary sources when evidencing institutional norms. In addition, a primary source may not be more objective, independent, or reliable than a secondary source. Again, Edison's public pronouncements were often intended to attract reluctant investors or a naïve public rather than to accurately depict of his role and efforts in the innovation process. In this regard, historical sources must, like informant interviews, be interpreted within the original context and intent of the source.

Analysis and Theory Building

Data analysis is, ultimately, the central process of building grounded theory from historical cases. Separating data gathering from analysis is an artificial construct. As noted earlier, grounded theory building is distinguished by constant comparison, the iterative process of collecting and analyzing data, and theoretical sampling, the unfolding determination—by the emerging theory—of what data should be collected next. In this way, insights that emerge during initial analyses that take place in the gathering of data guide the researcher toward new data sources. As Eisenhardt (1989: 539) notes, "a key feature of theory-building case research is the freedom to make adjustments during the data collection process." Such constant comparison and theoretical sampling serves the purpose of identifying and developing new theory rather than developing and testing hypotheses from prior research.

Three challenges confront researchers undertaking grounded theory building in microhistorical case study research. The first challenge lies with the combination of overwhelmingly high volumes of data, loose temporal and geographic boundaries, and malleable research questions. This makes it difficult for researchers to know when to stop gathering data, where to draw the theoretical limits in terms of time and space, and finally when to freeze (or delimit) their research question. Constant comparison and iteration between theory building and data gathering addresses this challenge by enabling the researcher to slowly converge upon a set of constructs and confirming observations. Over time, theoretical saturation (Glaser and Strauss) emerges when incremental learning diminishes and little new confirming or disconfirming evidence results from additional data found outside the current boundaries of the study.

The second challenge lies in the shaping and testing of hypotheses that emerge from analysis. Emerging hypotheses represent opportunities for recognizing both confirming evidence in the data (or the pursuit of confirming evidence) as well as disconfirming evidence. Both serve valuable purposes. Confirming evidence provides construct validity to emerging hypotheses. At the same time, disconfirming evidence may be more valuable because it tests and refines (or refutes) the emerging construct. Moreover, disconfirming evidence can identify theoretically valuable boundary conditions regarding when emerging—as well as existing—theoretical explanations may hold.

A third challenge lies in the relationship between existing literature, the emerging theoretical constructs, and the data. Remember, the purpose of grounded theory building is to develop new and valuable explanations for how culture shapes and is shaped by cognition and action. As with disconfirming data, extant theories in the literature that conflict with emerging insights serve as a test that either refines the emerging theory or, conversely, is refined by the emerging and conflicting theory. In other words, emerging theory that provides an alternative explanation, if validated by data, offers a new and valuable explanation. In this way, the emerging theory should extend the existing literature by demonstrating its role in explaining previously unrelated phenomenon (charting new territory) or by providing a better understanding of particular aspects of the relevant literature (providing more details).

In building grounded theory from microhistorical cases, these analytical challenges often burden the researcher far more than the development of the initial research question or data gathering, and yet they are often the critical attributes of successful research efforts.

Summary

Microhistorical case studies reflect grounded theory building using historical data by focusing on how the cognition and actions of individuals and groups are shaped by and shape larger social structures. It also defines what data is relevant, from which sources, and over what time periods that will enable you to capture this set of relationships. This chapter provides an account of microhistorical case studies as well as a discussion of the roles played by the research question, the temporal and spatial bounding of the phenomenon, as well as the data gathering and analysis.

Building grounded theory is not easy. Whether in ethnographies, in case studies, or in historical case studies, many of the challenges are similar. And yet microhistories provide two related distinctions from qualitative studies of contemporaneous events such as ethnographies and case studies. First, while limited by the nature and richness of the data available relative to participant observation and interviews, microhistories enable the researcher to move between the particulars of the moment and the larger structural, cultural, and technological milieu which unfold over longer time periods and in which these particulars are embedded. Second, microhistories know how the story ends, enabling researchers to view their subjects' cognitions and actions in light of their effects on history rather than their aspirations to make history. Within organizational studies, microhistorical case study research remains a risky endeavor but, as Roy Suddaby (2006: 633) so encouragingly notes, "new discoveries are always the result of high-risk expeditions into unknown territory. Darwin, Columbus, and Freud, each in different ways, were conducting qualitative inquiries."

Notes

1 For a deeper and broader discussion of the history of historical research in organization studies, see Hansen, (2012), Kieser (1994), Leblebici and Shah (2004), Rowlinson (2004), Üsdiken and Kipping (2014), Wadhwani and Bucheli (2013), and Zald (1991).
2 It's important to note that microhistories are not measured by length but rather by approach. They range in length from Bruno Latour's elucidation of the cultural context of 19th century France within which Louis Pasteur was acting, *The Pasteurization of France*; to Elting Morison's essays in *Men, Machines, and Modern Times*; to recent articles like Paul DiMaggio's "Constructing an Organizational Field as a Professional Project: U.S. Art Museums, 1920–1940" and Chris McKenna's article on the emergence of management consulting, "The Origins of Modern Management Consulting."
3 Per Hansen (2012: 708) notes that:

> No material is useful for the historian by itself. The usefulness of, say, company minutes or ledgers depends entirely on the historian's research question, while the interpretation of these texts depends on the ontological and epistemological positions of the historian. The point is that sources are the historian's construction in the sense that they become resources to answer a specific question the historian asks.

References

Barley, Stephen R., and Pamela S. Tolbert. "Institutionalization and Structuration: Studying the Links between Action and Institution." *Organization Studies* 18, no.1 (1997): 93–117.

Clark, Peter, and Michael Rowlinson. "The Treatment of History in Organisation Studies: Towards an 'Historic Turn'?" *Business History* 46, no. 3 (2004): 331–52.

DiMaggio, Paul. "Culture and Cognition." *Annual Review of Sociology* 23 (1997): 263–87.

DiMaggio, Paul J. "Constructing an Organizational Field as a Professional Project: U.S. Art Museums, 1920–1940." In *The New Institutionalism in Organizational Analysis*, edited by W.W. Powell and P.J. DiMaggio. Chicago: University of Chicago Press, 1991.

DiMaggio, Paul. J., and Walter W. Powell. "The Iron Cage Revisited: Institutional Isomorphism and Collective Rationality in Organizational Fields." *American Sociological Review* 48 (April 1983): 148–160.

Eisenhardt, Kathleen M. "Building Theories from Case Study Research." *The Academy of Management Review* 14, no. 4 (October 1989): 532–550.

Geertz, Clifford. "Thick Description: Toward an Interpretive Theory of Culture." In *Interpretation of Cultures: Selected Essays*, New York: Basic Books, 1973.

Gephart, R.P. "Qualitative Research and the Academy of Management Journal." *Academy of Management Journal* 47, no. 4 (2004): 454–62.

Giddens, Anthony. *Central Problems in Social Theory: Action, Structure and Contradiction in Social Analysis*. Berkeley: University of California Press, 1979.

Glaser, Barney G., and Anselm L. Strauss. *The Discovery of Grounded Theory: Strategies for Qualitative Research*. Chicago: Aldine Pub. Co., 1967.

Hannan, Michael T., and John Freeman. "The Population Ecology of Organizations." *American Journal of Sociology* 82, no. 5 (1977): 929–964.

Hansen, Per H. "Business History: A Cultural and Narrative Approach." *Business History Review* 86, no. 4 (2012): 693–717.

Hargadon, Andrew B., and Yellowlees Douglas. "When Innovations Meet Institutions: Edison and the Design of the Electric Light." *Administrative Science Quarterly* 46 (2001): 476–501.

Hoffman, R. (1997). Introduction. In M. Sobel, F. J. Teute, & R. Hoffman (Eds.), *Through a glass darkly: reflections on personal identity in early America*. Chapel Hill, NC: University of North Carolina Press.

Kieser, Alfred. Why Organizational Theory Needs Historical Analysis-And How This Should Be Performed. *Organization Science* 5, no. 4 (November 1994): 608–620.

Latour, Bruno. *The Pasteurization of France*. Cambridge, MA: Harvard University Press, 1988.

Lawrence, Thomas B., Roy Suddaby, and Bernard Leca. *Institutional Work: Actors and Agency in Institutional Studies of Organizations*. New York: Cambridge University Press, 2009.

Leblebici, Huseyin. "History and Organization Theory: Potential for a Transdisciplinary Convergence." In *Organizations in Time: History, Theory, Methods*, edited by Marcelo Bucheli and Rohit Daniel Wadhwani, pp. 56–99. Oxford: Oxford University Press, 2013.

Leblebici, Huseyin, Gerald R. Salancik, Anne Copay, and Tom King. "Institutional Change and the Transformation of Interorganizational Fields: An Organizational History of the U.S. Radio Broadcasting Industry." *Administrative Science Quarterly* 36, no. 3 (1991): 333–64.

Leblebici, Huseyin, and Nina Shah. "The Birth, Transformation and Regeneration of Business Incubators as New Organisational Forms: Understanding the Interplay between Organisational History and Organisational Theory." *Business History* 46, no. 3 (2004): 353–80.

Lepore, Jill. "Historians Who Love Too Much: Reflections on Microhistory and Biography." *Journal of American History* 88 (2001): 129–44.

McKenna, Christopher. "The Origins of Modern Management Consulting." *Business and Economic History* 24, no. 1 (1995): 51–8.

Mendonça, Sandro. "The 'Sailing Ship Effect': Reassessing History as a Source of Insight on Technical Change." *RESPOL Research Policy* 42, no. 10 (2013): 1724–38.

Morison, Elting Elmore. *Men, Machines, and Modern Times*. Cambridge, MA: MIT Press, 1966.

Nelson, A. J., and J. Irwin. "'Defining What We Do—All Over Again': Occupational Identity, Technological Change, and the Librarian/Internet-Search Relationship." *Academy of Management Journal* 57, no. 3 (2014): 892–928.

Rowlinson, Michael. "Historical Analysis of Company Documents." In Essential guide to qualitative methods in organizational research, edited by Catherine Cassell and Gillian Symon, pp. 301–311. London: SAGE Publications, 2004.

Rowlinson, M., J. Hassard, and S. Decker. "Research Strategies for Organizational History: A Dialogue between Historical Theory and Organization Theory." *Academy of Management Review* 39, no. 3 (2014): 250–74.

Selznick, P. *TVA and the Grass Roots*. Berkeley: University of California Press, 1949.

Suddaby, R. "What Grounded Theory Is Not." *Academy of Management Journal* 49, no. 4 (2006): 633–42.

Üsdiken, Behlül, and Matthias Kipping. "History and Organization Studies: A Long-Term View." In *Organizations in Time: History, Theory, Methods*, edited by Marcelo Bucheli and Rohit Daniel Wadhwani, pp. 33–55. Oxford: Oxford University Press, 2014.

Van de Ven, Andrew H. "Suggestions for Studying Strategy Process: A Research Note." *Strategic Management Journal* 13, no. S1 (1992): 169–188.

Wadhwani, R. Daniel, and Marcelo Bucheli. *The Future of the Past in Management and Organizational Studies*. SSRN Scholarly Paper. Rochester, NY: Social Science Research Network, May 29, 2013. http://papers.ssrn.com/abstract=2271752

Yates, JoAnne. "The Structuring of Early Computer Use in Life Insurance." *Journal of Design History* 12, no. 1 (1999): 5–24.

Yates, JoAnne. "Understanding Historical Methods in Organization Studies." In *Organizations in Time: History, Theory, Methods*, edited by Marcelo Bucheli and Rohit Daniel Wadhwani. Oxford: Oxford University Press, 2014.

Zald, Mayer N. "Sociology as a Discipline: Quasi-Science and Quasi-Humanities." *The American Sociologist* 22, no. 3–4 (1991): 165–87. doi:10.1007/BF02691895.

13

Immersion Ethnography of Elites

Brooke Harrington

Introduction

This chapter examines an innovative form of data–gathering that brings together two of the greatest methodological challenges social scientists face: conducting classical immersion ethnography and gaining access to elites. The difficulties of accessing elites for research purposes have been well-documented (Conti and O'Neill 2007; Gilding 2010; Harrington 2003). There has been less scholarly discussion of the challenges posed by traditional ethnography, a method whose claim to scientific status is based on the length and depth of the investigator's immersion in an organization or culture.

While short-term ethnography is fairly common in organizational research, immersion is rare because it is "slow, expensive and laboriously detailed" (Neyland 2008: 90). But while the investment required to conduct traditional immersion ethnography is significant, the scholarly payoffs are commensurate. Groundbreaking insights, along with revisions of long-established theories, are frequently the results of such studies.

The method and its potential for scholarly innovation will be illustrated with examples from four recent immersion ethnographies in a variety of domains, from the fashion industry to education and finance. The projects share an ambition to demystify essential but taken-for-granted notions such as value, privilege, and beauty. Around each of these concepts, a social hierarchy has been organized, supported by elite institutions and a cadre of individual actors. These actors and institutions were the focal points of all four studies.

Elite organizations and institutions are not the only settings in which immersion ethnography may be used. Indeed, many well-known projects employing this method have examined lower ranges of the socioeconomic spectrum and have had an enormous impact on organization studies and the allied disciplines (e.g., van Maanen 1975). The research reported here stands out by overcoming the dual challenges of the method and applying it to some of the most inaccessible people and institutions in the world, shedding light on domains of activity that are as rarely glimpsed as they are powerful in shaping everyday life and organizations.

Elites and Ethnography

Organization studies have a long-standing commitment to the study of elites, as exemplified by research on the "inner circle" of leadership (McDonald and Westphal 2011; Useem 1984). Empirically, research in this domain has included corporate executives and political leaders, as well as scientists and even clergy. Across these various settings, what elites have in common is their power over others: "their actions influence the daily activities of millions of people around the globe" (Conti and O'Neil 2007: 64). They are, as Goffman (1967) put it, "where the action is."

However, elites are also notoriously difficult to engage as research participants. They are "out of reach on a number of planes" (Nader 1972: 302). Researchers wishing to gain access to corporate executives and other elites may need to navigate a gauntlet of personal assistants, secretaries, and even bodyguards (Gilding 2010). Though many researchers report finding elites surprisingly cooperative and forthcoming once engaged in a study (Kogan 1994; Smart and Higley 1977), the packed schedules of executives, political leaders, and the like mean a face-to-face meeting can take months of planning and false starts to arrange.

Paradoxically, this difficulty in gaining access may make immersion ethnography one of the most practical ways to study elites once researchers get a foot in the door. Once past the gatekeepers and the scheduling challenges, it makes sense to maximize the data-gathering opportunity by sticking around as long as possible. However, as the Hawthorne studies showed (Roethlisberger and Dickson 1939), researchers looking over the shoulders of working people can become a major source of data in its own right. Sometimes, this kind of disruption can be strategic and helpful (Harrington 2002). But often, it is less obtrusive and more conducive to naturalistic data collection for researchers simply to work side by side with the elites they are studying.

The Immersion Method

The central tool of immersion ethnography is what Wacquant (2004) called "observant participation." That is, during an extended stay in an organization or culture—Sanday (1979) defines one year as a minimum, but such projects are now almost unheard of in organization studies—researchers "subject themselves to the life contingencies of our subjects . . . [in] a kind of deliberate experiment of the self" (Mears 2013: 21). The objective is not only to see what is happening in the research site, but also to *feel* it, bodily and emotionally.

This is particularly useful in studying the cultures and practices of elites. In this social stratum, the sophistication of the participants and their organizations can pose a serious threat to the researcher's ability to gain insight (Richards 1996). For example, interview participants at the CEO level are likely quite adept at performing a role and rebuffing attempts to access information that might undermine the image they are trying to create for themselves and their firms. Indeed, many executives receive training to hone these impression management skills for media appearances, Congressional testimony, and so forth (Sims 2009). In the same way, documents may prove a disappointing source of data, since they can be created to give an intentionally superficial, if not outright misleading, record of events (Davies 2001; Glynn and Booth 1979).

Thus, while observant participation may be supplemented with interviews and archival research, those sources cannot be substituted for simply being present and working alongside the elites being studied. While it may be relatively easy for a skilled professional to mislead an interviewer or to confound an archival researcher, it is harder to fool the body. It is especially difficult over the long periods of time involved in immersion ethnography. A performance cannot be sustained indefinitely: masks slip. In this sense, immersion ethnography can access "information not . . . available (if ever) for public release" (Richards 1996: 200).

Origins of the Method and Influence on Organization Studies

For the past century, an ethnographic study's rigor, reliability, and validity have been assessed partly on the depth and duration of the researcher's immersion in the field. This is due largely to the work of Bronislaw Malinowski, whose 4 years living among the natives of the Trobriand Islands produced the classic *Argonauts of the Western Pacific* (2003 [1922]), and set the standard against which future ethnographic research would be judged. Trained in physics and chemistry, Malinowski practiced ethnography with the same discipline and analytical intentions he brought to the physical sciences. His focus was on minute observation, followed by synthesis. "The Ethnographer," he wrote, "has to construct the picture of the big institution, very much as the physicist constructs his theory from the experimental data, which always have been within reach of everybody, but needed a consistent interpretation" (2003 [1922]: 84).

While Malinowski was not the first social scientist to do fieldwork, his innovation lay in gathering and analyzing data systematically while adopting the ways of life of the people he was studying. This was in marked contrast to the "veranda ethnography" that preceded him, in which colonial-era researchers would observe natives from an authoritative distance or "have them come to the veranda of a mission station for interrogation" (Eckl 2008: 187). While these practices reinscribed the power differential between researchers and participants, Malinowski's method boldly closed that gap in the name of gaining insights that were not available in any other way:

> It is good for the Ethnographer sometimes to put aside camera, note book and pencil, and to join in himself in what is going on. He can take part in the natives' games, he can follow them on their visits and walks, sit down and listen and share in their conversations. . . . Out of such plunges into the life of the natives—and I made them frequently not only for the study's sake but because everyone needs human company—I have carried away a distinct feeling that their behaviour, their manner of being, in all sort of tribal transactions, became more transparent and easily understandable than it had been before. (2003 [1922]: 21–22)

The impact of Malinowski's work on organization studies is broad but underappreciated. For example, it is partly to him that we owe the foundational insights of the Hawthorne studies of the 1930s (Mayo 1933; Roethlisberger and Dickson 1939). The studies began as a study of ergonomics in the workforce but—under the influence of a researcher trained in Malinowski's methods—ended by creating the human relations school of organization theory (Barley and Kunda 1992).

In a later generation, van Maanen's (1975) pioneering work on occupational socialization was made possible by his adaptation of Malinowski's techniques to the study of a police department. After being refused by more than 20 police organizations when he requested to study them as an outsider looking in, van Maanen eventually broke through by immersing himself fully: entering a police academy, graduating, and going on patrol as an armed officer. The benefits of this methodological strategy included insight on informal processes that unlocked the mystery of the study's quantitative findings. When survey data showed that recruits with low motivation for police work were perceived by their superiors as better officers than highly motivated recruits, van Maanen's *in situ* observations enabled him to make sense of the results and build a new theory of how organizations socialize new members.

Contributions of Immersion Ethnography of Elites

No matter what methods they use, what researchers want is access to the "back stages" of organizations, which "are carefully protected from outsiders and . . . only known to insiders" (Mikecz 2012: 483). Immersion ethnography allows researchers to break through the superficial and misleading to access those back stages where the real work of organizations and institutions takes place. This is particularly apparent in the study by Mears (see Table 13.1), who spent two years as a runway model in order to examine the paradoxes of organizations in the fashion industry—a field dedicated to surfaces and impression management. She later summarized her contribution in Goffmanian terms as "reveal[ing] the invisible collective work it takes to construct what seems natural and effortless: *beauty*" (2013: 31).

Immersion ethnography excels at capturing the invisible, natural, and taken-for-granted aspects of organizations and institutions, then subjecting them to analytical scrutiny. Khan's (2011) study of an elite private college preparatory school achieves this by illuminating the organization's latent curriculum: In addition to teaching the usual high school subjects (English, math, science, history), the school subtly and informally trains its pupils in the bodily practices that signal privilege. This characteristic manner of being and interacting Khan terms "ease," and it becomes the defining characteristic of elite status—opening doors to those who master it, and closing doors to those who do not. This dimension of elite practice had been totally overlooked in previous research, even in work that specifically examined embodied aspects of elite status, such as Veblen's work on conspicuous consumption (1994 [1899]). And while Bourdieu's work (1998 [1989]) suggested that elites may have distinctive ways of using their bodies, Khan was the first to specify how this was expressed,

Table 13.1 Use of Immersion Ethnography in Recent Research on Elites

Publication	Context	Data-Collection Strategy	What Was Gained
Khan (2011)	Elite secondary school	Khan spent 1 year teaching at St. Paul's, where he was also an alumnus.	Discovery of unexpected features of cultural capital among elites: Khan finds that such capital is not possessed, "like money in your wallet," but rather *expressed* as "ease" in relational practices—evident to the immersed ethnographer, but inaccessible through more distanced methods.
Mears (2011)	High fashion	Mears spent 2 years modeling in New York and London, followed by interviews with models, designers, and agency staff.	Exposes the normally invisible backstage work that creates cultural capital and social institutions in the form of beauty ideals. Mears finds that these practices—largely unspoken and unconscious—are rigorously embodied in ways that can only be accessed through lived experience, rather than observation and discourse.
Ho (2009)	Investment banking	Ho worked 6 months as an analyst at Banker's Trust, followed by 1.5 years of interviews and observations.	Demystifies the taken-for-granted notion of "value"—particularly "shareholder value"—by showing how it is produced from the highly unusual working norms, beliefs, and embodied practices of Wall Street investment banks. Ho exposes these practices, which are rarely observed by outsiders and are taken for granted by insiders, to observe who makes capitalism, and how those people are made.
Zaloom (2006)	Commodities trading	Zaloom worked for nearly 1 year as a trader on the Chicago and London commodity exchanges.	Insight on the puzzle of how a coherent global market arises out of multiple trading sites. Zaloom argues that traders' shared culture and physical practices, which can only be learned by doing, serve as the coordinating mechanism linking millions of fragmented micro-transactions into a functioning whole.

representing a major contribution to the scholarly literature in sociology, organization studies, and the allied disciplines.

Khan's access to these insights stemmed from spending 1 year as an instructor at the preparatory school. He undertook this immersion after other methods, which positioned him as an outsider looking in, led to dead ends: "I found that from my attempts at an objective stance I could see almost nothing. . . . To stand outside people looking in at their lives, as if they were in some laboratory or snow globe, is not to understand them" (2011: 201–202). Insight, he found, was only possible from inside the organization. Khan argues that the benefits of taking this position, in the form of accessing what is otherwise invisible to observers, outweigh the costs in terms of undermining researcher "objectivity"—a state that he argues is unobtainable in any case.

Analytically, immersion ethnographies focus attention on meaning, embodiment, and interaction. The use of the body as a research tool often leads to analyses inspired by the work of Bourdieu (1990, 1994) on habitus and the unconscious cultural practices through which power is expressed and reproduced. The spotlight that immersion ethnography trains on embodiment and interaction is particularly useful because of the ways that contemporary organization theory sometimes privileges structural relationships—in the form of network ties among individuals or organizations (e.g., Broschak 2004)—over the negotiated encounters that make up day-to-day life in organizations.

The benefits of this approach are particularly evident in research on industries like finance, which are often subject to exclusively quantitative or structural analyses, not just in organization studies, but in economics and psychology. Zaloom's (2006) work on commodities trading, along with Ho's (2009) ethnography of investment banking, illuminate aspects of finance absent in studies relying on quantitative data or even on interviews and archival research (e.g., Hertz 1998). Zaloom, for example, spent about a year working in the commodity trading pits of Chicago and London. Her findings turn our attention away from the locus of most social studies of finance, which have centered on the calculations and devices used by traders (Knorr-Cetina and Bruegger 2002; Stark and Beunza 2003), and toward the previously unexplored realm of traders' bodily practices. In the heart of economic rationality, she finds a "cultural infrastructure" (2006: 11) linking individual trades and distributed trading sites into a coordinated global marketplace; this culture is embodied by the traders themselves, with everything from their hand gestures to signal buying and selling, to their pushing and

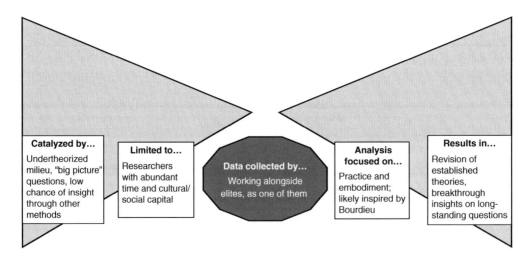

Figure 13.1 Process Characteristics of Immersion Ethnography of Elites

shoving each other on the trading floor. In that seeming chaos, she finds the seeds of a global order: "the physicality of the pit creates a direct connection between the market and the trader's body" (2006: 107).

Ho—an anthropologist, like Zaloom—spent 6 months employed as an analyst at Banker's Trust before being laid off with her entire department. Her bodily experience of investment bankers' hectic rhythms of work and serial unemployment allowed her to formulate a wholly new theory of "the cultural workings of the so-called market" and to "unpack the very process of market-making" (2009: 11). Interested in why these financial elites so often buy companies only to turn around and liquidate them (or instigate mass layoffs), Ho offers an explanation completely different from the accounts of "shareholder value" found in organizational research. Rather, she shows that investment bankers' own experience of employment flexibility leads them to generalize, erroneously, to the labor market and the economy as a whole. In other words, these elites believe that everyone can do what they do: put in 100-hour weeks, then successfully recover from sudden unemployment by rapidly retooling and retraining for a new job. Their lived experience becomes the pattern to which whole organizations are expected to conform, and their power over billions in investment capital ensures the dominance of their perspective, affecting the lives of millions of individual workers and the organizations in which they are employed.

Demands on the Researcher

This potential for making major discoveries is the main reason researchers continue to engage in immersion ethnography. However, the benefits come at a high cost, making the method impractical or unsuitable for many. Entering the field, learning the rules of participation, and cultivating relationships requires patience and time, often on a scale not compatible with the publish-or-perish rhythm of academic careers. Thus, many published studies based on immersion ethnography (including van Maanen's mentioned previously, and the four recent examples shown in Table 13.1) stem from dissertation research.

In addition, the method demands high levels of both technical skill and emotional intelligence (Salovey and Meyer 1990). The technical skills—such as record-keeping or analysis, and to can be learned in methods courses. As for the emotional skills, it is less clear whether they can be taught. Immersion ethnographers must be able to move fluidly between empathy and analysis, and to use their bodies as well as their minds as instruments of data collection (Sanday 1979). The goal of this "embodied understanding" (Crossley 2007: 87) on the part of the researcher is a specific kind of knowledge not available through other means. As Mears writes, reflecting on her years as a runway model, the result of immersion is rich insight on "what it takes to be a competent actor in the world, and . . . the situated 'knowing-how-to' that operates beneath consciousness, unreachable by interpretations of symbols, interview transcripts, or sight alone" (2013: 22). On the other hand, the intensity of the immersion experience and its combination of physical, mental, and emotional demands can result in exhaustion and disorientation for the researcher (Sanday 1979).

In addition to the demands for a lengthy time commitment to the fieldwork site and the intense physical, emotional, and intellectual engagement required of the researcher, immersion ethnographies of elites imposes a third challenge: to gather data from elites requires a high level of social and cultural capital on the part of the researcher; in the case of elite professionals, some form of expertise, or intellectual capital in the form of credentials, is also required. These forms of capital enable researchers to establish rapport with participants, which is a prerequisite for effective data-gathering (Ostrander 1993). Summoning all these forms of capital for display entails a self-presentation strategy that some find difficult to execute. It requires that researchers claim a position as the status equals of the elites they are studying, at least for the duration of an interview (Conti and O'Neil 2007; Hermanowicz 2002).

Since most academics cannot realistically claim to wield as much power, influence, or wealth as corporate executives, political leaders, or other elites, the field of expert knowledge is usually the only terrain in which they can meet as status equals. In this context, researchers' self-presentation requires projecting authority and ease (Khan 2011). This task can be particularly difficult for scholars who are young and/or female. Concerns about rejection and embarrassment abound, particularly around the challenges of "modifying dress and appearance" (Conti and O'Neil 2007: 63) or embodying appropriate manners and distinctions.

The complex, multilayered challenge this presents can make social scientists "timid" (Nader 1972: 302) about studying elites. Exceptions include a few notable scholars who were born into families of power and privilege. One of the best-known exemplars of this was E. Digby Baltzell, a scion of the Social Register who later became a sociology professor at the University of Pennsylvania. Baltzell, who coined the acronym WASP (1964) to describe the White Anglo-Saxon Protestant aristocracy that formed his milieu, would have been unlikely to feel intimidated in the presence of professional elites, many of whom might have emerged from more modest backgrounds than his own.

But unlike Baltzell, most social scientists are not brought up in the *habitus* characteristic of elites (Bourdieu 1977). They lack "the right credentials and contacts" (Odendahl and Shaw 2002: 306) necessary not only to gain access, but also to keep it. Without this background, it is particularly difficult to deploy "tone," "gestures," and "appropriate language" (Harvey 2011) when face-to-face with corporate executives, political leaders, and other elites. The resulting uncertainty and awkwardness can be fatal to establishing the rapport necessary to collecting high-quality data; they can also be very distracting for the researcher (Thomas 1993). Indeed, ethnographers working with elites often report intense anxiety and exhaustion in research encounters (Conti and O'Neil 2007; Gilding 2010).

Prospects for Future Scholarship

Immersion ethnography is most often applied to the far ends of the socioeconomic spectrum—to the most privileged or the most marginalized members of society (Venkatesh 2008). This may be because both realms are shrouded in misconceptions and ideology. To shed light on these domains requires a method that excels at piercing the veils, exposing what lies behind the conventional wisdom and the carefully managed impressions.

With inequality on the rise worldwide (Piketty 2014), both extremes of the socioeconomic spectrum are growing, increasing the need to understand what is happening within them. This amplifies the need for immersion ethnography as a method for conducting innovative, insightful research. From the domain of organization studies to that of public policy, both theory and practice would benefit from the breakthroughs that this method can provide. For that to occur, however, researchers need resources that are in short supply: abundant time, funding, and the elusive *habitus* of those they wish to study. Perhaps for that reason, immersion ethnographies may remain the province of doctoral students endowed by their backgrounds with characteristics that allow them access to domains closed to others.

Publication opportunities remain a final limitation on the dissemination of insights from such studies. As readers have no doubt noticed, this chapter departs from most others in the volume by drawing examples from research published in book form, rather than as scholarly journal articles. Long descriptive passages, which are the main way of presenting evidence used to build theory from ethnographic data, often run afoul of both the tight word counts and forms of argumentation used in such journals. It is also difficult to do justice to theoretical innovation within the discursive norms of journal articles, which rely heavily on citation and illustrations of how one's work builds on or extends recent studies. Research that really shifts paradigms doesn't easily lend itself to such narrow framing. This may be why each of the four studies described in this chapter is grounded in one of the broad disciplinary perspectives (sociology or anthropology), rather than being focused on the more applied realm of organization studies. So while this chapter makes the case that such studies are highly relevant to organizational research, they are also easy to overlook because they are unlikely to appear in the field's canonical journals.

Thus, this chapter will conclude with something rather conventional: a "call." But the call will urge organizational scholars to seek out and embrace the unconventional, in the form of research done via immersion ethnography. While rare in the pages of the *Academy of Management Journal* or *Administrative Science Quarterly*, such studies offer the kind of great leaps forward that transform disciplines. With organization theory turning into "a living museum of the 1970s" (Davis 2010: 691), increasingly composed of incremental improvements on work done 40 to 50 years ago, the discipline urgently needs such advances. To Suddaby and colleagues' (2011) question, "Where are the new theories of organization?," this chapter proposes that a partial answer lies in the work of sociologists and anthropologists who have immersed themselves in the study of organizational and institutional elites.

References

Baltzell, E.D. (1964) *The protestant establishment: Aristocracy and caste in America*. New Haven, CT: Yale University Press.

Barley, S. & Kunda, G. (1992) Design and devotion: Surges of rational and normative ideologies of control in managerial discourse. *Administrative Science Quarterly, 37*, 363–399.

Bourdieu, P. (1977) *Outline of a theory of practice*. Cambridge, UK: Cambridge University Press.

Bourdieu, P. (1990) *The logic of practice*. Cambridge, UK: Polity.

Bourdieu, P. (1994) *Distinction: A social critique of the judgment of taste*. Cambridge, MA: Harvard University Press.

Bourdieu, P. (1998 [1989]) *The state nobility: Elite schools in the field of power*. Stanford, CA: Stanford University Press.

Broschak, J. (2004) Managers' mobility and market interface: The effect of managers' career mobility on the dissolution of market ties. *Administrative Science Quarterly, 49*, 608–640.

Conti, J. & O'Neil, M. (2007) Studying power: Qualitative methods and the global elite. *Qualitative Research, 7*, 63–82.

Crossley, N. (2007) Researching embodiment by way of "body techniques." *Sociological Review, 55*, 80–94.

Davies, P. (2001) Spies as informants: Triangulation and the interpretation of elite interview data in the study of the intelligence and security services. *Politics, 21*, 73–80.

Davis, G. (2010) Do theories of organization progress? *Organizational Research Methods, 13*, 690–709.

Eckl, J. (2008) Responsible scholarship after leaving the veranda: Normative issues faced by field researchers—and armchair scientists. *International Political Sociology, 2*, 185–203.

Gilding, M. (2010) Motives of the rich and powerful in doing interviews with social scientists. *International Sociology, 25*, 755–777.

Glynn, S., & Booth, A. (1979) The public records office and recent British economic historiography. *The Economic History Review, 32*, 303–315.

Goffman, E. (1967) Where the action is. In E. Goffman (Ed.), *Interaction ritual* (pp. 149–270). New York: Doubleday.

Harrington, B. (2002) Obtrusiveness as strategy in ethnographic research. *Qualitative Sociology, 25*, 49–61.

Harrington, B. (2003) The social psychology of access in ethnographic research. *Journal of Contemporary Ethnography, 32*, 592–625.

Harvey, W. (2011) Strategies for conducting elite interviews. *Qualitative Research, 11*, 431–441.

Hermanowicz, J. (2002) The great interview: 25 strategies for interviewing people in bed. *Qualitative Sociology, 25*, 479–499.

Hertz, E. (1998) *The trading crowd: An ethnography of the shanghai stock market*. New York: Cambridge University Press.

Ho, K. (2009) *Liquidated: An ethnography of Wall Street*. Durham, NC: Duke University Press.

Khan, S. (2011) *Privilege: The making of an adolescent elite at St. Paul's School*. Princeton, NJ: Princeton University Press.

Knorr-Cetina, K. & Bruegger, U. (2002) Global microstructures: The virtual societies of financial markets. *American Journal of Sociology, 107*, 905–950.

Kogan, M. (1994) Researching the powerful in education and elsewhere. In G. Walford (Ed.), *Researching the powerful in education* (pp. 67–80). London: UCL Press.

Malinowski, B. (2003 [1922]) *Argonauts of the Western Pacific*. New York: Routledge.

Mayo, E. (1933) *The human problems of an industrial civilization*. New York: Macmillan.

McDonald, M. & Westphal, J. (2011) My brother's keeper: CEO identification with the corporate elite, social support among CEOs and leader effectiveness. *Academy of Management Journal, 54*, 661–693.

Mears, A. (2011) *Pricing beauty: The making of a fashion model*. Berkeley: University of California Press.

Mears, A. (2013) Ethnography as precarious work. *The Sociological Quarterly, 54*, 20–34.

Mikecz, R. (2012) Interviewing elites: Addressing methodological issues. *Qualitative Inquiry, 18*, 483.

Nader, L. (1972) Up the anthropologist: Perspectives gained from studying up. In D. Hynes (Ed.), *Reinventing anthropology* (pp. 284–311). New York: Pantheon.

Neyland, D. (2008) *Organizational ethnography*. London: Sage.

Odendahl, T. & Shaw, A. (2002) Interviewing elites. In J. Gubrium & J. Holstein (Eds.), *Handbook of interview research: Context and method* (pp. 299–236). Thousand Oaks, CA: Sage.

Ostrander, S. 1993. "Surely you're not in this just to be helpful:" Access, rapport, and interviews in three studies of elites. *Journal of Contemporary Ethnography, 22*, 7–27.

Piketty, T. (2014) *Capital in the twenty-first century*. Cambridge, MA: Harvard University Press.

Richards, D. (1996) Elite interviews: Approaches and pitfalls. *Politics, 16*, 200.

Roethlisberger, F. & Dickson, W. (1939). *Management and the worker*. Cambridge, MA: Harvard University Press.

Salovey, P. & Meyer, J. (1990) Emotional intelligence. *Imagination, Cognition and Personality, 9*, 185–211.

Sanday, P. (1979) The ethnographic paradigm(s). *Administrative Science Quarterly, 24*, 527–538.

Sims, R. (2009) Toward a better understanding of organizational efforts to rebuild reputation following an ethical scandal. *Journal of Business Ethics, 90*, 453–472.

Smart, D. & Higley, J. (1977) Why not ask them? Interviewing Australian elites about national power structure. *Australian and New Zealand Journal of Sociology, 13*, 248–253.

Stark, D. & Beunza, D. 2003. The organization of responsiveness: Innovation and recovery in the trading rooms of lower Manhattan. *Socio-Economic Review, 1*, 135–164.

Suddaby, R., Hardy, C. & Huy, Q. (2011) Where are the new theories of organization? *Academy of Management Review, 36*, 236–246.

Thomas, R. (1993) Interviewing important people at big companies. *Journal of Contemporary Ethnography, 22*, 80–96.

Useem, M. (1984) *The inner circle: Large corporations and the rise of business political activity in the U.S. and U.K.* New York: Oxford University Press.

van Maanen, J. (1975) Police socialization: A longitudinal examination of job attitudes in an urban police department. *Administrative Science Quarterly, 20*, 207–228.

Veblen, T. (1994 [1899]) *The theory of the leisure class: An economic study of institutions*. Mineola, NY: Dover Publications.

Venkatesh, S. (2008) *Gang leader for a day: A rogue sociologist takes to the streets*. New York: Penguin.

Wacquant, L. (2004). *Body and soul: Notebooks of an apprentice boxer*. Oxford, UK: Oxford University Press.

Zaloom, C. (2006) *Out of the pits: Traders and technology from Chicago to London*. Chicago: University of Chicago Press.

14

Accounting for Accounts
Crafting Ethnographic Validity
Through Team Ethnography

Joelle Evans, Ruthanne Huising, and Susan S. Silbey

Introduction: From Individual to Team Ethnography

A number of early "classics" in ethnographic sociology conducted research in teams (e.g., Becker, Greer, Hughes, & Strauss, 1961; Gouldner, 1954). With the recent resurgence of interest in ethnographic research, we see some projects conducted in multisited teams (e.g., Anderson, 2000; Burawoy, 1998; Cress & Snow, 2000; Heimer, 2008; Newman, 2009), although by and large, a single ethnographer still more often goes into the field alone for extended periods of time and subsequently produces an individually authored account (e.g., Blee, 2003; Duneier, 1994, 1999; Espeland, 1998; Fine, 2008, 2009; Heimer, 1989; Wacquant, 1998, 2002; Wagner-Pacifici, 2000). The solo ethnographer generally remains the most common model in organizational studies, urban sociology, and anthropology, and yet it may not always be the most appropriate model, particularly for those heading into the field for the first time or for those who wish to study large organizations or complexly coordinated distributed practices characteristic of many contemporary phenomena. In this chapter, we describe our experiences using a team model of ethnographic fieldwork, focusing on its implications for training and, more generally, for improving the validity of ethnographic fieldwork.

According to Van Maanen, fieldwork and ethnography are distinguishable:

> Fieldwork usually means living with and living like those who are studied. In its broadest, most conventional sense, fieldwork demands the full-time involvement of a researcher over a lengthy period of time (typically unspecified) and consists mostly of ongoing interaction with the human targets of study on their home ground. (1988:2)

Ethnography is the written product of the fieldwork and a standard method for those who wish to describe the culture of a group or organization—how its members "go about their everyday lives" and what sense the group members make of their activities (Emerson, Fretz, & Shaw, 2011:1). Ethnographies describe, and often explain, "the actual social context and life worlds of those being studied" in detail and with a depth not often available in other forms of research (Snow, 1999:97). As the written representation of a social system, ethnography carries quite serious intellectual and moral responsibilities, for the images of others inscribed in writing are most assuredly not neutral. Ethnographic writings can and do inform human conduct and judgment in innumerable ways by pointing to the choices and restrictions that reside at the very heart of social life. (Van Maanen, 1988:1)

In effect, as Van Maanen writes, "ethnographies join culture and fieldwork. . . . [They] are documents that pose questions at the margins between two cultures. They necessarily decode one culture while recoding it for another audience" (Barthes, 1972).

Beyond the stereotypical image of ethnography as "one anthropologist per tribe" (Van Maanen, 1988), there are two models of group ethnography. The first is the collaboration model in which researchers disperse to study a particular selected phenomenon *across sites*. Although they share their field notes and interview transcripts, discussing and analyzing them as a group, they write independent papers about different sites (Bearman, 2009), or they may pool their data to generate insights comparatively (Barley, 1996). This model of ethnography has been used successfully in several major projects in urban sociology (e.g., Anderson, Brooks, Gunn, & Jones, 2004; Newman, 2009). In the second team model, a group of ethnographers observe and interview *within the same site*, coordinating their observation and interview activities and discussing shared notes and transcripts as observation and analysis unfolds. This is the method used in the classical ethnographies by Becker, Geer, Hughes, and Strauss (1961) on medical education and by Gouldner (1954) on industrial relations in a gypsum mine. These two team models differ according to whether there is a single site or multiple sites and fields (industries, economic sectors, and organizations), either unified or distributed, creating variable implications for validity and generalizability. Both team models are often used as a means of training students.

Although writing *about* qualitative methods has proliferated in the last two decades, there has been, according to Huberman and Miles (2002: x) "no parallel proliferation of studies of the actual *process of doing* qualitative research." For example, while there are numerous texts that describe how to analyze, then theorize, and finally write up accounts from ethnographic data (Strauss & Corbin, 1990; Saldaña, 2012), collecting data is rarely specified with explicit techniques, and until very recently it was even less consistently reported in publications (but see Emerson, Fretz, & Shaw, 2011). The cause of this inattention to the process is overdetermined: a product of ethnography's own history, the epistemological debates among different approaches within qualitative methods, vociferous antagonisms between qualitative and quantitative researchers, as well as the heated culture and science "wars" following the 1980s poststructural turn in the social sciences. As a consequence, the practical skills of data collection and analysis, as well as the distinctions and connections among these, are not well understood, especially among nonpractitioners and novices. Thus, it seems important to direct more intense effort to unpacking the process and practical skills of fieldwork. This is as important for the collection of data as for the analysis, which in ethnographic fieldwork is always continuous and simultaneous with data collection (Becker, 1998; Silbey, 2004).

We unpack the processes and practical skills of fieldwork by looking through the lens of team ethnography. In the remaining text, we identify the added value that working in teams can bring to ethnographic research. Although we focus on the benefits for enhancing validity, fieldwork in teams is also an excellent method of training ethnographers. In the context of showing how validity is strengthened by (a) continuously improving accounts to create thicker description, (b) triangulating across accounts to identify subjects' interpretations, and (c) refining conceptual categories to clarify theoretical contributions, we also illustrate the range of support that group work provides for the novice fieldworker. Working in a team increases efficiency for both the supervisor and the students, while continually offering examples of more and less useful techniques. Students more quickly learn that one researcher's problems have also been experienced by others. Because skilled fieldworkers eventually develop what can be an exhausting double consciousness (observing a group while becoming part of it), working with others to develop this sensibility is especially helpful, emotionally supportive, and efficient. Sharing fieldwork stories—blunders as well as successes—helps students to develop the appropriate skills more quickly by seeing that the difficulties they are experiencing are not unique. The ethnographer is entirely dependent upon the willingness of subjects to be available for close and perhaps intrusive scrutiny; conversely, the research subjects are entirely dependent on the integrity of the researcher to protect the subjects' dignity and autonomy. Such responsibilities become more visible and tractable when fieldwork experiences are narrated, interrogated, and scrutinized among a group of similarly engaged researchers.

Seeking Ethnographic Validity

One of the most frequently voiced concerns about ethnography asks whether a different observer would have come away from the field, independent of the variations in the voice with which the account may be written, with the same basic descriptive account, interpretation, and theoretical contribution. In other words, how reliable is the description of social worlds depicted in ethnographies, and how valid is the explanation of what was observed? In ethnographic research, reliability is closely connected and perhaps best understood as a form of validity (Hammersley, 1992:79). Although these terms are conventionally discussed with respect to quantitative and positivistic research, with respect to qualitative field work we use them to refer to the ability to produce similar data from multiple observers and to produce consensually agreed upon, corroborated interpretations and theoretical explanations of a site, person, or process.

It is essential, as we will note herein, that accounts claiming to be more than personal opinions, accounts that seek the status of knowledge, be produced with methods permitting the community of observers to collectively assess its truth status. Although ethnography is a distinct model of inquiry and representation, as a social scientific enterprise it claims status as truthful knowledge. The value and truth claims of science, including social science, derive "primarily from the transparency and public representation of its methods, by displaying the grounds of [its] claims and the sources of [its] evidence" (Silbey, 2013). As such, in its most fundamental and comprehensive sense, scientific "knowledge production [is] a collaborative activity, a public civic engagement with others, other scholars and audiences" (Silbey, 2013:22–23).

With only slight modification from standard understandings of scientific reliability and validity, we can deploy these terms quite productively for ethnographic research. Maxwell (1992), for example, proposes five types of validity for qualitative researchers that offer a useful advance on the usual discussions of reliability and validity. First, *descriptive validity* refers to the factual accuracy of an account, that researchers "are not making up or distorting things they saw or heard" (Maxwell 1992:45). This is the basis for all other forms of validity and the foundation on which all subsequent interpretation and analysis builds. As Geertz (1973:17) put it, "behavior must be attended to, and with some exactness, because it is through the flow of behavior—or more precisely, social action—that cultural forms find articulation." This "reportage" function (Runciman, 1983) includes descriptions of specific events and situations, as well as of objects and spaces.

Second, *interpretive validity* refers to the meanings of the described behaviors, events, and objects for the actors observed, which is one of the central goals and most common justifications for qualitative research, especially ethnographic fieldwork. Interpretive validity seeks to capture the participants' perspectives, providing an account in emic (actors' rather than theoretical—etic) terms. Interpretive validity

> has no real counterpart in quantitative-experimental validity typologies. . . . [It] is inherently a matter of inference from the words and actions of participants in the situations studied . . . grounded in the language of the people studied, [and] relying as much as possible on their own words and concepts. (Maxwell, 1992:48)

The interpretation is the barest level of generalization across the described data: what do these activities, these things, these relationships mean to the actors? The goal of interpretation is to describe the actors' "lay sociology" (Garfinkel, 1967) or "theories-in-use" (Argyris & Schon, 1974)—their understandings of their social worlds. This criterion of interpretive validity distinguishes a form of accuracy that lies between the first form, descriptive validity, resting entirely on observable, consensually validated data and the more contestable inferences of the third type, theoretical validity. While there is "no in-principle access to data that would unequivocally address threats to [interpretive] validity" (Maxwell 1992: 290), the descriptive accounts serve as warrants. In other words, has the ethnographer/observer provided sufficient evidence to substantiate his or her claim or interpretation of what these events and actions signify to the actors? Consensus should be achievable within the relevant community of actors and/or readers that the interpretation is supported by the reported descriptive data. The terms (language and concepts) of both descriptive and interpretive validity are, to use Geertz's term, "experience-near"—the local language in use among the actors—although interpretive validity might also involve assessments of the accuracy of informants' reports (to which we will return later with an example from our fieldwork).

Third, *theoretical validity* moves the ethnographic account further from the actors' behavior, language, meanings, and interpretations to a more abstract account that proposes to explain what has been observed in the terms of the scholarly literature. No longer a matter of what the described activity means to the actors, theoretical validity asks what this activity or group signifies to the scholarly audience. What is this an example of, and to what other examples should we compare it? What conceptual label shall we affix to this setting and activity? "Theoretical validity thus refers to an account's validity as a theory of some, phenomenon" (Maxwell, 1992:51). Both the concepts used and the relationships proposed are independently assessed for what is conventionally called *construct validity* (Bernard, 2000:50–51) and *inferential* or *causal validity* (Cook & Campbell, 1979), although not all theories attempt to offer causal explanations.

The key distinction between the types of validity (descriptive, interpretive, and theoretical) in this schema lies in the "presence or absence of agreement within the community of inquirers about the descriptive or interpretive terms used. Any challenge to the meaning of the terms, or appropriateness of their application to a given phenomenon, shifts the validity issues from descriptive or interpretive to theoretical" (Maxwell, 1992:52).

Generalizability, a fourth form of validity, invokes considerations that are common across the social sciences, referring to "the extent to which the particular situation is representative of a wider population" or set (Hammersley, 1992:79). There is, however, a level of analysis issue here concerning generalizability that distinguishes internal from external validity. For generalizability (external validity) beyond the particular group or organization, the qualitative researcher must meet the same standards as any quantitative researcher: demonstrate representativeness. For most qualitative researchers, however, internal generalizability is far more important because there are strong arguments for studying outliers and unique cases as existence proofs and means for identifying variation (Small, 2009). For internal validity, however, we need to know whether the reported data (activities, statements, documents) are representative of the activities, statements, and materials of that particular group or organization, regardless of whether the group or setting is representative of some larger set. We need to avoid cherry picking examples that support a claim rather than synthesizing across all the evidence and examples.[1]

Training Ethnographers and Enhancing Ethnographic Validity Through Group Collaboration

Although some universities provide excellent training in fieldwork and ethnography, it is neither as common nor as consistent as is the preparation in quantitative data collection and various modes of statistical analyses. Thus, it is not unusual, for example, to meet a graduate student eager to begin fieldwork on a subject about which he or she has read a great deal and knows a range of scholarly positions and arguments, but who does not know how to take the first step in formulating a research design, identifying a field site, or gaining access. Or, one encounters more advanced graduate students about to write dissertations based on extensive fieldwork who have never had training in qualitative data analysis urgently seeking advice about how to make interpretive and theoretical inferences from their data. The conventional pattern of training is most often through one-on-one mentoring, although we may achieve more successful and more efficient training if we work with students in groups. In addition, training students in groups would work to challenge the fetish of ethnographic research as a personal immersion and form of creative discovery.

The Governing Green Labs project began in 2002 when Professor Susan Silbey initiated a study of the development and implementation of an environmental health and safety management (EHS) system at Eastern University, a large research university in the United States. The project included Ph.D. students from four interdisciplinary graduate programs at MIT: Urban Studies and Planning in the School of Architecture and Planning; History and Anthropology of Science, Technology and Society in the School of Humanities, Arts and Social Sciences; Behavior and Policy Studies in the Sloan School of Management; and Technology and Public Policy in the School of Engineering. The diversity of students' background knowledge, training programs, and distinct research interests was simultaneously exciting and challenging. Depending on their interests, students were assigned to collect data via participant observation and interviews within a particular group or department in the organization being studied (either Welldon University or Eastern University): senior administrators, department managers, legal-technical specialists, and laboratory researchers. Extending over 10 years, the project involved two generations of students. Beginning in the spring of 2003, the research group met every Wednesday afternoon during the summer and Friday mornings during the term to exchange information and begin to piece together a complicated field site. Students were asked to send in weekly field notes. Selections of these field notes were discussed collectively and coded during team meetings. This routine helped aspiring ethnographers develop a work discipline that, as we describe later, improved the descriptive, interpretive, and internal validity of the data. At the outset, the single most notable consequence of the group activity was its success in overcoming individual reticence about sharing one's experiences, appearing inadequate to the task, or displaying ignorance.

The general project was driven by Silbey's initial research questions, but it slowly evolved, as much fieldwork does, as more and more was learned about the organization and the problem of transforming laboratory practices to improve EHS performance. The research sought to understand how diverse institutional resources and organizational constraints influenced individual and organizational performance (and if they did)—in this case, performances mandated by law. And further, it sought to understand the relationships between law and science by looking directly within the home of science, the laboratory. Through participant observation, interviewing, and inductive analysis, Silbey intended to capture the variations in interpretation and consciousness of legal regulations that are sedimented in and through organizational cultures (Edelman & Suchman, 1997; Ewick & Silbey, 1998; Silbey, 1992). She sought, also, to understand what place law may have, or not, in routine scientific practice. By observing the invention of a new management system from day one of the commitment to create such a system, implement it, and disseminate it across the university, the research sought to unpack the black box of regulatory performance. By mapping the ways in which local organizational processes and subcultures produce environmental health and safety practices, the research hoped to discover the conditions and challenges for sustainable improvement in environmental conditions. Alternatively, the research sought to understand how good intentions may nonetheless produce unwanted or unanticipated outcomes and not actually improve environmental sustainability. As the project unfolded, many more questions arose, providing opportunities for students to follow lines of analysis fed by their disciplinary interests. Figure 14.1 provides an overview of how the process of validity enhancement unfolded through ongoing engagement among ethnographers.

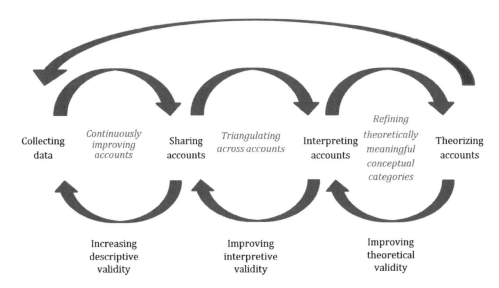

Figure 14.1 Collecting, Analyzing, and Theorizing Accounts Through Team Ethnography

Continuously Improving Accounts for Descriptive Validity

Researchers exchanged field notes, reading and discussing not only the substantive content of the notes but also critiquing the quality of the text of the notes. Was this thick description? What assumptions were embedded in particular words and concepts? What needs to be known to understand a reference? Were phenomena and actions situated locally as well as in relation to alternatives not present or possibly seen elsewhere? What was missing? Was the observer noticing silences and omissions? Was the researcher's focus too close or too distant? Most of these conversations concerned how the ethnographer could know or might have apprehended what was being described, striking out statements that were impressionistic rather than empirically observable, shifting linguistic terms to stay as close to the native categories and terms as possible, and offering local definitions where necessary.

Through these discussions, the ethnographers in training were challenged to write detailed descriptions of the scene, sometimes attending to the material conditions, the aural and aromatic sensations, and at other times focusing on language and affect. Sometimes two or more researchers attended the same meeting, learned of the same laboratory accident or injury from different sources, and heard the same gossip circulating from one group to another. Field notes were compared and discrepancies and omissions were discussed along with emerging commonalities. These discussions were opportunities to learn the discipline of constructing an empirical account and testing its descriptive validity against other empirical accounts and multiple forms of data (e.g., looking for paper records, disseminated memos, email trails). Field workers also became aware of their tendencies to report some types of data (e.g., conflict or noncompliance) and gloss over other observations (e.g., agreement or compliance) and were able to correct these tendencies, taking in the full picture over time. Descriptions generated more questions than answers, pushing the researchers in diverse directions to seek out more informants, to visit archives and organizational records, and to search the scholarly literature for comparisons and variations. This ongoing reflexive engagement about what could be known informed the practice of collecting data and continuously improved the descriptive validity of the data.

Triangulating Across Accounts for Interpretive Validity

While the accounts that our subjects gave were taken at face value, scenes were triangulated to extract a richer empirical reconstruction, often demanding that participants' divergent accounts be explained and reconciled. The data collected in one lab or one series of meetings was put in the context of other labs and meetings. For example, at different meetings with different groups, fieldworkers heard stories that the dean of science had closed a laboratory because of failures to meet environmental health and safety regulations—in other words, because the lab had consistently "failed" inspections. We collected all the different accounts heard by different researchers and assessed the ways in which they differed and collided. Together, these accounts told us about how the actors understood the authority of the dean, the limits of academic freedom, and the authority of law. However, it was also important to understand whether the dean had in fact closed a laboratory for failing an inspection. We pursued these two avenues collectively and in parallel; that is, we collected all the stories and noted in what situations they were narrated, and we also traced the story back to the actors in the stories. In doing so, we became sensitive to the differences between descriptive and interpretative validity and also to the analytical opportunities offered by our recognition of the discrepancies in the stories.

Rookie ethnographers often face an overwhelming amount of stimuli in the field. When a researcher enters the field, much is different from what was expected. We are not blank slates; we are competent mature social actors and we come with an abundance of tacit as well as explicit assumptions about how the world works. We are social scientists, after all, and we have read a great deal about the site and the phenomena we are studying. We deal simultaneously with our interpretations and our subjects' interpretations. Although our initial naïve interpretations must give way to the data and analysis process, they can be stubborn and overshadow those of our subjects. The continuous discussion about our subjects' interpretations helped to excavate and subsequently submerge our own perspectives, and we became more open to local understandings and to the need to triangulate and validate empirical observations. Every ethnographer must do this to succeed; the group process seemed to accelerate the development of this fieldwork skill.

As it turned out, the dean had shut down a laboratory some years earlier while he had been serving as a department head. It was not, however, in response to safety or environmental violations, but because the principal investigator—the professor—had overspent his research accounts and had not responded to requests to reign in his spending. Nonetheless, an apocryphal account that miscreant laboratories could be shut down was circulating as a warning to lab managers and scientists. The message was clear: This dean and these new regulations carried consequences should the lab managers and scientists become lax and inattentive to the safety requirements. At the same time as we were able to record the circulating stories and track the accurate historical event, we were discovering the hierarchy of organizational concerns. Although creating safer and cleaner laboratories was a high priority at the university, financial and scientific misconduct called forth more immediate and serious sanctions: shutting down a scientist's laboratory. This story, what is sometimes referred to as an *atrocity tale* (Best, 1990), allowed us to locate the various regulatory regimes and organizational practices within an overarching account of the university's values and enacted priorities. We could offer a more accurate interpretation of the story for the various and differentially located actors.

Refining Conceptual Categories for Theoretical Validity

Newcomers were always presented with an overview of the project: a history of what had been done to date; an opportunity to explore published and unpublished accounts; and initial questions to consider for their own work, questions posed in the form of "what is this site or activity a case of?" For instance, initial questions centered on the role of monitoring systems in organizing working relations and the effects of professional authority and autonomy on responses to regulation. The project also included a database with relevant readings on science, safety, and knowledge-sharing in organizations. This initial scoping helped individual researchers focus on theoretically relevant categories of interest. Discussions around "what is this site a case of?" provided an array of topics to investigate. The questions and associated readings allowed researchers in the team to focus observations, see data in a broader context and build on contemporary debates in sociology, legal, science, and organizational studies. While researchers eventually deviated from these orienting questions as they developed their own interests, the students were provided with an initial heuristic with which to engage conceptually meaningful categories. Theoretical validity can be challenging when members of the team are drawing from diverse literatures and are unfamiliar with the theoretical debates and advances in a field. However, exploring shared yet diverse avenues of inquiry and attempts to theorize the data together helped the research team to discard theoretical preoccupations that were valued in some disciplines and fields but were not salient in the field site. Textual coding of fieldnotes and interview transcripts was done on a continuous basis and early cohorts of fieldworkers did this collectively. However, because each team member came with different theoretical backgrounds and interests and was planning to produce a scholarly work relevant for the field in which he or she was seeking a degree, attempts to create common conceptual codes was a struggle and was eventually abandoned.

Because the team included members from diverse disciplines and professional communities, the theoretical analyses addressed multiple phenomena and theoretical questions, (e.g., organizational change and regulatory compliance; disciplinary variations in doing science; institutional and normative ordering; safety rules and routines) and produced theories of newly discovered phenomena (e.g., relational regulation [Huising & Silbey, 2011; Silbey, 2011]) and role performance (e.g., sociological citizen [Silbey, Huising, & Coslovsky, 2009]).

External and Internal Generalizability

The team project is the most effective means of dealing with questions of external and internal validity. Obviously, multisited ethnography can produce accounts that apply across a larger population, offering generalizability that one site cannot. More often than not, research teams offer more extensive and deeper multisited ethnography than can be produced by one field worker (Marcus, 1995). So, for example, Burawoy (2000) collated studies conducted by his students of the responses of individuals and organizations to processes of globalization. In our study of the development and implementation of a management system for laboratory hazards, we did not seek external generalizability through multiple organizational sites, although several students worked in laboratories in more than one university. Rather, the overall project was an in-depth case study of one university, tracing over time the processes of organizational change as enacted by participants across all levels of the organization and variations in departments and disciplines. Without question, working as a research team enhanced the internal validity because data was shared across diverse analysts and because analysis proceeded systematically by multiple researchers. There could be no purposive selection of evidence that was not corroborated across organizational locations and across observers.

Challenges of Team Ethnography

One essential, practical challenge for team ethnography is the need to balance data sharing and individual contributions. Although students were invited into the project to address questions Silbey had identified in her research proposals, students in the project were asked to write their own papers, allowing them to develop their own theoretical and empirical interests. For instance, while the project had an initial emphasis on how regulation filters through large and complex organizations, fieldworkers developed other themes, such as how professional and occupational struggles shape regulatory compliance or how experimental materials shaped laboratory practice. The theme of safety regulation functioned as a lens revealing other organizational dynamics, and this expansion of focus enabled multiple contributions.

Early writings and attempts at theorizing also functioned as a heuristic for later contributors. New observations and interpretations were compared to existing works and created an impetus to build on extant interpretations. For instance, while early works focused on the role of EHS personnel in mediating regulatory compliance (Huising, 2014, 2015; Huising & Silbey, 2011), later works explored how ground-level personnel (researchers and technicians) creatively recombined legal rules with local practice (Evans, 2014; Evans & Silbey, 2014) and struggled with moral dilemmas engendered by research strategies (Evans, 2015). Some papers pursued lines of analysis related to the use of technologies to audit regulatory compliance (Silbey & Agrawal, 2011). Others considered the place of law in the laboratory (Silbey & Cavicchi, 2005) and controversies in science (Silbey & Roosth, 2008).

Conclusion

Contemporary scholarly norms considerably limit the time frame within which researchers can collect, analyze, and publish their results. Professional expectations for a greater volume of publications as the standard of respectable accomplishment, coupled with the increasing importance of journal articles rather than book-length manuscripts, mitigate against the traditional practices of ethnographic research: one scholar totally immersed in one location for a long period of time. In this new hyperproductive scholarly universe, working in teams becomes ever more attractive, and thus group ethnography is a more interesting research option. In a sense, transforming ethnography from a personal exploration to a research collaboration mimics the evolution of scientific research practices that were the subject of this project. Contemporary experimental science is almost exclusively a collaborative group effort. Not only is team ethnography more efficiently productive, but as we indicated previously, it also offers increased validity across all dimensions—descriptive, interpretive, theoretical, and generalizable.

For those interested in studying organizational processes, especially complex processes and distributed organization characteristic of our historical time, a fieldwork team allows deep, spatially and temporally extended involvement to study not only the entire organization from top to bottom, but also often from the beginning to the end of a project of organizational change. Team work permits members to enter and exit and to be replaced or supplemented to create continuity where one or few researchers could not.

The lasting value of many ethnographic works has relied primarily on the authors' abilities to convey with clarity and nuance and make familiar the everyday experience of unfamiliar groups and cultures. As Alexander (1989) notes: "Because [social science's] object is life, it depends on the [social] scientist's own ability to understand life. It depends on idiosyncratic abilities to experience, to understand and to know." Alexander (1989) suggests two ways in which this knowledge distinguishes itself: through the interpretation of states of mind and through the reconstruction of the empirical world. Although ethnographers may bring unique sensitivities to their fieldwork, the skills needed to create detailed, subtle observation and interpretation and to carefully reconstruct the raw and disorderly empirical worlds can be made explicit and developed more effectively through collaborative strategies. Rather than being idiosyncratic, it can be a shared set of highly skilled techniques as well as developed sensibilities. Team ethnography allows for this collective construction of sociologically meaningful categories of interest, the development of more complex and complete accounts, and ultimately the transformation of a personal understanding of a field to generalizable social science.

Table 14.1 Examples of Team Ethnographies

Reference	Research Context/ Phenomena	Types of Group Allocation and Engagement With Research Context/Phenomena	Outcomes/Results of Methodological Approach
Burawoy (2000)	Globalization	Multiple industries; multiple organizations; multiple roles within and across organizations; collection of independent student projects	Diverse examples across varied sites to develop a general theory of the implications of globalization on work, communities, and organizations
Stark (2009)	Creative work	Multiple industries; multiple organizations; multiple roles within and across organizations; three ethnographies of different organizations engaging in creative work	Diverse examples across varied sites to develop a general theory of the role of competing accounts of worth on creative work
Barley (1996)	Technical work	Multiple industries; multiple organizations; same role in different industries and organizations; nine mini-ethnographies of different technicians' occupations	Large sample of same role across varied sites to develop general theory of technicians' work
Heimer (2008, ongoing)	Development and use of medical protocols in AIDS clinics	Single industry; multiple clinics; three types of medical protocols (clinical practice guidelines, rules for the conduct of research, and governance protocols); ethnographies in matched AIDS clinics in the U.S., Uganda, Africa, and Thailand	International sampling to allow for institutional comparison of the intersection of law and medicine
Bearman (2009)	Unique occupation: Doormen in New York City	Single industry (real estate); multiple organizations of same type (housing); same role in different organizations within single industry; sample of dispersed members of an occupation in a large city	Large sample of same role across similar organizations to develop in-depth, detailed account of a role, an occupation
Becker, Geer, Hughes, & Strauss (1961)	Medical education and practice	Single industry (medicine); single typical organization; same role at different stages of professional development; engaged full organizational population, no sampling	Efficiently observed 4-year process in 1 year, holding historical context constant; in-depth account of a single institution (medical education); proposed general model of a social process (professional socialization)
Gouldner (1954)	Organization of industrial production	Single industry (mining); single typical organization; multiple roles across single organization; engaged full organizational population	Able to observe entire organization over time to map change processes within limited historical frame; in-depth account of a common phenomenon (bureaucratic organization); proposed general model of the phenomenon

Reference	Research Context/ Phenomena	Types of Group Allocation and Engagement With Research Context/Phenomena	Outcomes/Results of Methodological Approach
Huising & Silbey (2011)	Risk management, regulatory compliance, scientific practices	Single industry (university research science); single typical organization; multiple roles across single organization; engaged across full organizational hierarchy, stratified sample of disciplines/departments and random sample of labs within disciplines/departments	Able to observe entire organization over time to map change processes within limited historical frame; in-depth accounts and models of multiple phenomena (organizational change, regulatory compliance, disciplinary variations in doing science); proposed model of relational regulation

Note

1 Maxwell offers a fifth form of evaluative validity, referring to the normative assessment of that which has been described or explained. This category ought not to be intrinsically different in qualitative or quantitative studies. There is, however, a large body of scholarship written from a specifically critical perspective that is designed to reveal the organization of power and interests in social organization as well as the interests served by those scholarly accounts of social practices. Such scholarship may be considered evaluative in the sense that it seeks not only to describe the interests operating in social practices—the phenomena being described as well as the descriptions, but "adds to them a superordinate benchmark . . . [and] considers a [scholarly] work more fundamentally according to the interests it serves" (Koval, 1988:127–128). From some points of view, the entire history of sociology as a critical enterprise, written from the perspective of outsiders unmasking social forms to identify what is partially hidden, categorizing what is revealed, and labeling what is sorted, does not achieve the status of critique or fidelity to its critical mission unless it adopts normative positions and attempts to shape the uses to which knowledge is put (Horkheimer, 1972). In other words, forgoing evaluative validity, ethnography cannot serve as social critique (cf. Marcus & Fischer, 1999).

References

Alexander, J.C. (1989). *Sociology and discourse: On the centrality of the classics, structure and meaning*. New York, NY: Columbia University Press.

Anderson, E. (2000). *Code of the street: Decency, violence, and the moral life of the inner city*. New York, NY: W.W. Norton & Company.

Anderson, E., Brooks, S.N., Gunn, R., & Jones, N. (2004). Being here and being there: Fieldwork encounters and ethnographic discoveries. *The Annals of the American Academy of Political and Social Science, 595*(1), 327–327.

Argyris, C., & Schon, D.A. (1974). *Organizational learning*. Reading, MA: Addison Wesley.

Barley, S.R. (1996). Technicians in the workplace: Ethnographic evidence for bringing work into organizational studies. *Administrative Science Quarterly, 41*(3), 404–441.

Barthes, R. (1972). *Mythologies*. London: Paladin.

Bearman, P. (2009). *Doormen*. Chicago, IL: University of Chicago Press.

Becker, H.S., Geer, B., Hughes, E.C., & Strauss, A.L. (1961). *Boys in white: Student culture in medical school*. New Brunswick: Transaction Pub.

Becker, H.S. (1998). *Tricks of the trade*. Chicago, IL: University of Chicago Press.

Bernard, H. R. (2000). *Social research methods: Qualitative and quantitative approaches*. Beverly Hills, CA: Sage.

Best, J. (1990). *Threatened children: Rhetoric and concern about child victims*. Chicago, IL: University of Chicago Press.

Blee, K.M. (2003). *Inside organized racism: Women in the hate movement*. Berkeley: University of California Press.

Burawoy, M. (1998). The extended case method. *Sociological Theory, 16*(1), 4–33.

Burawoy, M., Blum, J.A., George, S., Gille, Z., & Thayer, M. (2000). *Global ethnography: Forces, connections, and imaginations in a postmodern world*. Berkeley: University of California Press.

Cook, T. D., & Campbell, D.T. (1979). *Quasi-experimentation: Design and analysis issues for field settings*. Chicago, IL: Rand McNally College Publishing.

Cress, D.M., & Snow, D.A. (2000). The outcomes of homeless mobilization: The influence of organization, disruption, political mediation, and framing. *American Journal of Sociology, 105*(4), 1063–1104.

Duneier, M. (1994). *Slim's table: Race, respectability, and masculinity.* Chicago, IL: University of Chicago Press.

Duneier, M. (1999). *Sidewalk.* New York: Farrar, Straus and Giroux.

Edelman, L. B., & Suchman, M. C. (1997). The legal environments of organizations. *Annual Review of Sociology, 23*, 479–515.

Emerson, R.M., Fretz, R.I., & Shaw, L.L. (2011). *Writing ethnographic fieldnotes.* University of Chicago Press.

Espeland, W.N. (1998). *The struggle for water: Politics, rationality, and identity in the American Southwest.* Chicago, IL: The University of Chicago Press.

Evans, J. (2014). Resisting or governing risk? Professional struggles and the regulation of safe science. *Academy of Management Proceedings,* 16124.

Evans, J. (2015). Moral shifts: Ethics, legitimacy and creativity in stem cell science. *Working paper.*

Evans, J., & Silbey, S. S. (2014). Resisting or governing safety: Professional struggles and the construction of safe science. Working paper.

Ewick, P., & Silbey, S. S. (1998). *The common place of law: Stories from everyday life.* Chicago, IL: University of Chicago Press.

Fine, G.A. (2008). *Kitchens: The culture of restaurant work.* Berkeley: University of California Press.

Fine, G.A. (2009). *Morel tales: The culture of mushrooming.* Cambridge: Harvard University Press.

Garfinkel, H. (1967). Studies of the routine grounds of everyday activities. *Social Problems, 11*, 225–250.

Geertz, C. (1973). Thick description: Toward an interpretive theory of culture. In C. Geertz (Ed.), *The interpretation of cultures* (pp. 3–30). New York, NY: Basic Books.

Gouldner, A.W. (1954). *Patterns of industrial bureaucracy.* New York, NY: Free Press.

Hammersley, M. (1992). *What's wrong with ethnography?: Methodological explorations.* New York: Routledge.

Heimer, C.A. (1989). *Reactive risk and rational action: Managing moral hazard in insurance contracts* (Vol. 6). Berkeley: University of California Press.

Heimer, C. A. (2008). Thinking about how to avoid thought: Deep norms, shallow rules and the structure of attention. *Regulation & Governance, 2*(1), 30–47.

Horkheimer, M. (1972). Traditional and critical theory. In Max Horkheimer, *Critical Theory: Selected Essays* (pp. 188–243), trans M.J.O. O'Connell, et. al. New York: Herder & Herder.

Huberman, M., & Miles, M.B. (2002). *The qualitative researcher's companion.* Thousand Oaks, CA: Sage.

Huising, R. (2014). The erosion of expert control through censure episodes. *Organization Science, 25*(6), 1633–1661.

Huising, R. (2015). To hive or to hold? Producing relational authority through scut work. *Administrative Science Quarterly, 60*(2), 263–299.

Huising, R., & Silbey, S. S. (2011). Governing the gap: Forging safe science through relational regulation. *Regulation & Governance, 5*, 14–42.

Koval, J. (1988). A critique of DSM-III. *Research in Law, Deviance and Social Control, 9*, 127–128.

Marcus, G.E. (1995). Ethnography in/of the world system: The emergence of multi-sited ethnography. *Annual Review of Anthropology, 24*, 95–117.

Marcus, G. E., & Fischer, M. M. (1999). *Anthropology as cultural critique: An experimental moment in the human sciences.* Chicago: University of Chicago Press.

Maxwell, J.A. (1992). Understanding and validity in qualitative research. *Harvard Educational Review, 62*(3), 279–301.

Newman, K.S. (2009). *No shame in my game: The working poor in the inner city.* New York, NY: Random House.

Runciman, W. G. (1983). A treatise on social theory. In *The methodology of social theory* (Vol. 1). Cambridge, UK: Cambridge University Press.

Saldaña, J. (2012). *The coding manual for qualitative researchers.* Thousand Oaks, CA: Sage.

Silbey, S. S. (1992). Making a place for cultural analyses of law. *Law and Social Inquiry, 17*(1), 39–48.

Silbey, S. S. (2013). What makes a social science of law: Doubling the social in socio-legal studies? In Dermot Feenan (Ed.), *Exploring the 'socio' of socio-legal studies* (pp. 20–36). Houndmills: Palgrave Macmillan.

Silbey, S. S. (2004). Designing qualitative research projects. In C. C. Ragin, J. Nagel, and P. White (Eds.), *Workshop on scientific foundations of qualitative research* (pp. 121–126). Arlington: National Science Foundation.

Silbey, S. S. (2011). The sociological citizen: Pragmatic and relational regulation in law and organizations, editor's introduction. *Regulation & Governance, 5*, 1–13.

Silbey, S. S., & Agrawal, T. (2011). The illusion of accountability: Information management and organizational culture. *Droit et Société, 77*, 69–86.

Silbey, S. S., & Cavicchi, A. (2005). The common place of law: Transforming matters of concern into the objects of everyday life. In B. Latour & P. Weibel (Eds.), *Making things public: Atmospheres of democracy* (pp. 556–563). Cambridge, MA: MIT Press.

Silbey, S. S., Huising, R., & Coslovsky, S.V., (2009). The sociological citizen: Recognizing relational interdependence in law and organizations. *Annee Sociologique, 59*(1), 201–229.

Silbey, S. S., & Roosth, S. (2008). Science and technology studies: From controversies to post-humanist social theory. In B. S. Turner (Ed.), *Blackwell companion to social theory* (pp. 451–473). Oxford, UK: Blackwell.

Small, M. L. (2009). "How many cases do I need?" On science and the logic of case selection in field-based research. *Ethnography, 10*(1), 5–38.

Snow, D.A. (1999). Assessing the ways in which qualitative/ethnographic research contributes to social psychology: Introduction to the special issue. *Social Psychology Quarterly, 62,* 97–100.

Stark, D. (2009). *The sense of dissonance: accounts of worth in economic life.* Princeton, NJ: Princeton University Press.

Strauss, A., & Corbin, J.M. (1990). *Basics of qualitative research: Grounded theory procedures and techniques.* Thousand Oaks, CA: Sage.

Van Maanen, J. (1988). *Tales of the field: On writing ethnography.* Chicago, IL: University of Chicago Press.

Wacquant, L. (1998). Inside the zone: The social art of the hustler in the black American ghetto. *Theory, Culture & Society, 15*(2), 1–36.

Wacquant, L. (2002). Scrutinizing the street: Poverty, morality, and the pitfalls of urban ethnography. *American Journal of Sociology, 107*(6), 1468–1532.

Wagner-Pacifici, R. (2000). *Theorizing the standoff: Contingency in action.* Cambridge, UK: Cambridge University Press.

15

Qualitative Comparative Analysis
Opportunities for Case-Based Research

Reut Livne-Tarandach, Benjamin Hawbaker, Brooke Lahneman Boren,
and Candace Jones

Qualitative research is often case-based, using an array of methods (Bansal & Corley, 2011) and engaging with either theory elaboration that refines preliminary theoretical models and preexisting conceptual ideas (Lee, 1999; Lee, Mitchell, & Sabylinski, 1999) into general theories (Vaughan, 1996) or with theory abduction that seeks new insights and generates new theory (Van Maanen, Sorensen, & Mitchell, 2007). Cross-case analysis is a research method that facilitates the comparison of commonalities and differences in the events, activities, and processes that are the units of analysis in case studies (Kahn & VanWynsberghe, 2008). Researchers who use cross-case analysis are able to (a) delineate the combination of factors that may have contributed to the outcomes of a given case, (b) construct an explanation as to why one case is different from or the same as others, and (c) articulate further the concepts, hypotheses, or theories that are discovered or constructed from the original case. Cross-case analysis enhances researchers' capacities to understand how relationships may exist among discrete cases, refine and develop concepts (Ragin, 1997) and build or test theory (Eckstein, 2002). Thus, cross-case research enables researchers to provoke their imagination, prompt new questions, reveal new dimensions, produce alternative frameworks, and generate new models (Stretton, 1969).

When scholars engage with more cases, it increases exponentially the volume of information that researchers need to track and compare. Information overload threatens to overwhelm human capacity to compare cases and is likely to trigger cognitive heuristics and biases such as representation and anchoring to manage the information (Bazerman, 1994). Moreover, a significant amount of comparative case-based research is neither classic qualitative analysis that neatly fits nascent fields nor quantitative analysis that is tailored for mature fields. Fewer analytical tools are available for intermediate fields, where one or more streams of relevant research offer some but not all constructs and measures needed (Edmonson & McManus, 2007).

We introduce Qualitative Comparative Analysis (QCA) as a novel method for cross-case research that aids researchers in systematically comparing multiple cases, enriches qualitative analysis, and best fits with intermediate fields of exploration. QCA applies to a set of three closely related techniques—crisp-set (csQCA), multi-value (mvQCA), and fuzzy set (fsQCA) QCA—which are used to conduct systematic comparison of data from multiple cases. These QCA methods enable both the in-depth, information-rich study of individual cases and scientific comparison of cases to reveal complex phenomena that are typical of cross-case research (Rihoux & Ragin, 2009). Originally developed by Charles Ragin (1987), a historical sociologist, the QCA method has gained popularity across the social sciences more broadly and political science and sociology in particular. Our literature search of peer-reviewed articles published between 1988 and 2013 in the online databases Web of Science, JSTOR, and Business Source Complete reveals that 83 qualitative-based QCA articles were published in 112 journals during this time frame. Fifty-two percent of these articles were published in political science journals, 23% in sociology journals, and the remainder distributed across education, health care, and management journals. To assess the prevalence of QCA in leading management outlets, we explored the 9,262 empirical papers published in top management journals—*Administrative Science Quarterly Academy of Management Journal*, *Academy of Management Annals*, *Organization Science*, *Journal of Management Studies*, *Journal of Management*, *Strategic Management Journal*, *Organization Studies*, and *Organizational Research Method*—between 1988 and 2013 and found that qualitative QCA papers represent 0.13% of the total number of empirical papers published in these outlets. This suggests that despite the advances in QCA's methods and increases in its popularity within other fields, this innovative approach to cross-case research has yet to gain momentum in organizational studies and management research. Thus, QCA holds great promise and opportunity as a method for qualitative researchers for theory elaboration and abduction in the management field.

This chapter begins with a brief description of the key elements that make QCA a novel method. We then outline QCA's benefits to qualitative research and describe the analytic process involved in the application of QCA. The chapter concludes with a discussion of empirical exemplars that utilize QCA as method for theory elaboration and abduction.

What Is QCA?

QCA has among its foundations the canons of John Stuart Mill's *A System of Logic* (1843), in particular his methods of agreement and of difference. The method of agreement argues that a single cause present in all cases of a phenomenon is, therefore, the cause of that phenomenon; the method of difference states that where the presence or absence of a phenomenon can likewise be linked to a single difference between cases, it is thus a cause of the phenomenon. These canons are based on the idea of comparing or contrasting case data to determine causal relationships through eliminating and simplifying processes. The QCA method takes this approach and further systematizes it while also mitigating some of the logical limitations of Mill's original canons (Berg-Schlosser, De Meur, Rihoux, & Ragin, 2009).

QCA can also be viewed as a response to the limitations of conventional analyses, attempting to "incorporate the best features of the case-oriented approach with the best features of the variable-oriented approach" (Ragin, 1987: 84). Although it incorporates the formalization and consistency of statistical quantitative methods, the QCA method is rooted in deep knowledge of individual cases. It is generally conceived as being geared toward small- to intermediate-N research, in terms of the number of cases involved, and it is intended for systematic empirical assessment of similarities and differences across cases (Berg-Schlosser et al., 2009), which facilitates the aims of cross-case-based research.

The QCA method views individual cases holistically as complex combinations of case attributes, which are called *conditions* in QCA terminology. The first step for a researcher is to identify and code the conditions in each case, which demands thorough knowledge of both cases and theory. This is similar to the Gioia method in which qualitative researchers use first-order codes based on the data and then group the codes into theoretical categories, engaging in a systematic approach to qualitative data that enhances the transparency and validity of the research process (Gioia, Corley, & Hamilton, 2013). QCA identifies *configurations*, or specific combinations of case conditions, that lead to an outcome of interest and may be present in many cases, a few cases, or none at all (Rihoux &

Ragin, 2009). Given that a few conditions can generate many possible configurations (e.g., five conditions can generate 32 possible combinations), the potential set of configurations is minimized, using Boolean algebra techniques, to identify which conditions consistently combine for a given outcome and are then interpreted based on the cases and theory to gain new insights (Rihoux & De Meur, 2009). For example, Jones and Livne-Tarandach (2014) use QCA to explore how 33 architectural firms compete across 19 different client projects to win client engagements. They identified conditions from the client's projects (e.g., high vs. low budget, type of service, type of building) and used interviews and archival data to analyze how architect firms framed themselves to persuade clients: institutional logics to demonstrate conformity to key values, novel word usage to highlight their distinctiveness, experience to signal their reputation, and status to signal their quality. By employing QCA, deep knowledge of the context, and prior research, Jones and Livne-Tarandach revealed that successful architectural firms shifted their combinations of logics, distinctiveness, reputation, and status to match client projects, whereas less successful firms did not. Thus, strategy was enacted at the project level rather than at the firm level and is a form of situated action.

Advantages of QCA

QCA methods offer a number of important advantages for organizational research. First, because QCA is combinatorial and compares configurations of causal conditions, it allows researchers to examine cases as wholes and address effectively the complexity of organizational phenomena. It is specifically well suited for studies of cross-level research that address dynamic interplay between causal conditions. Second, QCA invites scholars to engage in counterfactual reasoning through the examination of all logically possible combinations of causal conditions (Ragin, 2008). Third, QCA enables the identification of multiple configurations of conditions that lead to similar outcomes and thus allows for the presence of equifinality (Fiss, 2007, 2011; Ragin, 1987). Equifinality is an assumption of much of management research, such as multiple ways to structure an organization from hierarchy to flat, networked and open, or different strategies that enact firm success (e.g., low cost, differentiation, innovation). Fourth, QCA embraces causal asymmetry, where the set of causal conditions leading to a given outcome may be very different from the set of conditions leading to the opposite outcome (Ragin, 2008). This approach extends the Eisenhardt sampling approach of comparing polar cases and focusing on different conditions (Eisenhardt, 1989; Eisenhardt & Graebner, 2007). QCA, however, explores both differences and similarities across cases of different outcomes. Fifth, QCA entails a formalized, transparent analytic process for cross-case analysis that can facilitate replication and improve the validity of results. Sixth, the QCA approach to qualitative data analysis enables dialogue and the exploration of potentially overlooked connections between qualitative and quantitative research.

QCA Analytical Process

QCA is not confined to binary conditions or outcomes. In fact, some QCA techniques enable scholars to include nonbinary conditions (e.g., mvQCA) as well as outcomes (fsQCA). Because the basic steps in performing crisp-set QCA (csQCA) apply in general to all three techniques of QCA, for simplicity, we outline the process applied in csQCA analysis. We then present a brief description of the nonbinary mvQCA and fsQCA approaches where they differ from csQCA. Figure 15.1 illustrates a step-by-step description of the fundamental QCA analytical process.

The first step in csQCA analysis is research design: identifying the outcome of interest and appropriate cases to compare. The outcome of interest should be both clearly defined and consistent across all selected cases. The specific cases are chosen on theoretical, methodological, and practical grounds, seeking both sufficient homogeneity and heterogeneity (e.g., presence/absence of outcomes) among cases. For example, in the case of Jones and Livne-Tarandach (2014) the outcome of interest is 33

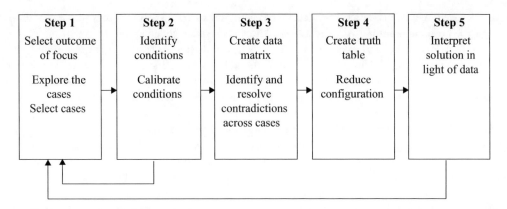

Figure 15.1 QCA Analytical Process

professional firms' ability to win one of 19 state projects. The selected cases from 33 firms include both the 19 winning firms and 118 losers of these projects, enabling a comparison of winners to losers within a project as well as winners and losers across projects. The number of cases selected is limited by the researcher's ability to gain adequate "intimacy" with each case (Berg-Schlosser & De Meur, 2009).

The second step is to identify case attributes (conditions) that may explain the outcome. Given that QCA analysis focuses on configurations of conditions of interest, the number of cases explored and the number of conditions included in the analysis are closely linked. In specifying these conditions in QCA, the researcher faces the challenge of limited diversity, where there are too few empirical instances of any configuration and the model becomes simply descriptive rather than explanatory (Fiss, 2011). For example, since QCA examines every possible combination (for the binary csQCA, 2^k, where k = number of conditions), a comparison of four attributes across cases becomes 16 configurations and a comparison of 5 attributes generates 32 comparisons. Thus, the researcher must restrict the number of attributes to only those essential to explaining differences and similarities among cases. Berg-Schlosser and De Meur (2009: 25–31) provide a detailed discussion of common strategies for selecting conditions. For example, in Jones and Livne-Tarandach (2014), the conditions of interest included shared cultural resources (professional and business-institutional logics), unique cultural resources (rare words), quality signals (status and reputation), and client project demands (budget, building type, and service type).

The third step is to calibrate conditions. Calibration into categories should be transparent and justifiable (Rihoux & De Meur, 2009), informed by relevant theory and deep knowledge of the cases. Calibration involves specifying whether a case represents the attribute fully, partially, or not at all, and different types of QCA techniques are used depending on the case representations. Crisp sets define membership in an attribute set as binary, either "fully in" (1) or "fully out" (0). At this point, research-ers should revisit case selection to ensure that the cases explored represent differing values of the con-ditions. In the Jones and Livne-Tarandach (2014) study, calibration was guided by theory when prior literature presented insights regarding meaningful anchor points. For example, prior research defined novel word usage of less than 1% in the cultural register. When theory did not offer clear guidelines, calibration was built on identified natural break(s) in the distribution (Greckhamer, Misangyi, Elms, & Lacey, 2008) while paying close attention to the sociocultural context (Basurto & Speer, 2012). For example, prior literature did not offer theoretical insights for calibration of how many professional awards signal quality. Upon examination of this condition, we noticed a single natural breakpoint in this measure's distribution around the 60th percentile. Most firms within the past 5 years had not won any awards, whereas a few had one or more. So the relevant comparison was "had won" or "had not won" an award. Thus, a crisp set was calculated: When professional awards measures were equal to or below the breaking point it was coded as 0 and those above were coded as 1.

The fourth step is to create a data table where the row indicates the case and the columns indicate conditions and outcomes. The table cells include the calibrated conditions for every case included in the sample. This table provides the input for a QCA software package. It also enables the identification and resolution of contradictions across cases, which are shown during data analysis. *Contradictions* are occasions where identical configurations of conditions are associated with different outcomes (Marx & Dusa, 2011). We discuss resolving contradictions more fully later.

The fifth step is to use a QCA software package (such as fsQCA 2.0, Kirq, Tosmana, or packages for R or Stata) to analyze the data table. This produces a "truth table" that lists all possible configurations of conditions associated with an outcome. Since QCA identifies all possible combinations from conditions, the data table will include configurations that do not occur empirically in the data. These configurations that are not associated with the sample cases can now be deleted. For example, Jones and Livne-Tarandach have 8 conditions in the truth table, generating 1,024 possible configurations. Configurations that were not associated with any of the 137 statements of qualifications of the competing firms were deleted. The truth table may also illuminate contradictory configurations where the same configurations of conditions lead to contradictory outcomes. Because each case matters equally, it is important to explore cases generating contradictory results more deeply and uncover nuanced differences that can explain the seemingly contradictory results. Such exploration can lead to the addition of conditions that can explain the difference in outcomes (thus creating a new data table). It is also possible at this point to switch to a more fine-grained QCA technique and move from csQCA to mvQCA or fsQCA. Another solution for contradictory configuration can be accomplished through theory-based deletion of cases when in-depth analysis of cases reveals that relevant boundary conditions may have been violated. Finally, in the case of theory testing using QCA, identifying contradictions could actually be the final step when the configurations elicited form the theory tested do not lead to consistent results and therefore falsify the proposed theory.

The sixth step is to specify necessary and sufficient conditions, or combinations of conditions, that explain the outcome of interest. QCA utilizes an algorithm based on Boolean minimization to generate two types of possible solutions: (1) the parsimonious solution that includes only theoretically plausible conditions, and (2) the intermediate solution that contains core and peripheral conditions (Chung & Woodside, 2012; Fiss, 2011; Ragin, 2008). The output of the software generates two indicators for solutions assessment: consistency and coverage. Solution *consistency* represents the degree to which the cases sharing a given condition or combination of conditions also display the same outcome and ranges between 0 and 1 (Ragin, 2008). In general, consistency higher than 0.75 is considered appropriate for further analysis (Ragin, 2006; Ragin & Rihoux, 2009). Consistency can also be used to further reduce the truth table. For example, in Jones and Livne-Tarandach (2014), all configurations that didn't meet 0.80 as a consistency threshold were eliminated. Solution *coverage* depicts the extent of support of the set of solutions and any given solution identified within the sample. For example, Jones and Livne-Tarandach identified four winning solutions reflecting distinct configurations of shared, unique, cultural resources and quality signals deployed in four distinct project contexts. The QCA algorithm pinpointed distinct project conditions to which architectural firms responded. The first solution identified high budget, technical buildings, which created public safety concerns and greater oversight by the legislature and media. In response, winning architectural firms crafted a strategy of using high status partners who had vast experience in technical, high budget projects for Federal and State entities.

A seventh step is to repeat this process to identify the combination of conditions that lead to the absence of the outcome, because QCA does not assume causal symmetry. Thus, two analyses are run in QCA: one to identify the combination(s) of conditions leading to the presence of the outcome, and one to identify the conditions that lead to the absence of the outcome. Jones and Livne-Tarandach (2014) simplified the solutions that they identified by comparing the parsimonious and intermediate solutions. The authors identified four winning and five losing solutions that met consistency and coverage standards.

The final step in QCA involves verification of the resultant solutions, informed by the researcher's case knowledge and theory. This step is also the most important, because the computer output alone can only falsify an outcome. It is through the researcher's validation and interpretation of this output that the links between the combinations of conditions and outcomes are explained; theories are confirmed, contradicted, or generated; and new insights are produced. The integration of QCA methods and researchers' knowledge of cases and theory generates new theoretical arguments. In practice, however, the QCA output frequently requires that researchers return to the case data for further explanation, and potentially additional rounds of analysis, before arriving at this goal (Rihoux & De Meur, 2009). In Jones and Livne-Tarandach's (2014) study, they returned to interview and archival data to understand the underlying meaning of the configurations identified and used qualitative quotes to illustrate how professional service firms deploy shared and unique cultural resources in combination with quality signals to win a client project.

Two additional QCA techniques, namely mvQCA and fsQCA, extend the process detailed previously and allow for nonbinary calibration of conditions and/or outcomes instead of the forced dichotomization of csQCA. These techniques allow the assignment of multiple values, or levels of set membership, for conditions when the case data or theory implies a need (Cronqvist & Berg-Schlosser, 2009). MvQCA limits the assignment of multiple values to conditions only, while retaining a dichotomous outcome, whereas fsQCA allows assignment of multiple values to both conditions and outcomes. The major change to the analytic process detailed previously is one of calibration. Whereas csQCA utilizes binary calibration that maps presence and absence in an attribute set, mvQCA and fsQCA allow researchers to account for the varying degrees of membership of cases, which may range, for example, from "fully in" (1), to "mostly in" (.75), "half in" (.50), "mostly out" (.25), or "fully out" (0). csQCA with binary data reflects "difference in kind"; whereas fuzzy sets define membership as having three or more values and capture "differences in degree" (Greckhamer et al., 2008: 722) and allow for the gray areas so frequently present in actual cases. With mvQCA and fsQCA, the issue of limited diversity, where the potential configurations outnumber the actual cases, is even more pronounced. As mvQCA and fsQCA yield even larger numbers of possible combinations for assessment (x^k, where x = number of values of conditions, k = number of conditions) than those identified in crisp-set analysis, it is important to focus on a few salient conditions that can be accurately depicted in the cases and analysis.

QCA Applications

To demonstrate how QCA was used, we examined in-depth five qualitative empirical articles published in peer-reviewed management and sociology journals. A summary of these papers is available in Table 15.1.

These five papers reveal two ways in which organizational researchers employ QCA in their studies: theoretical elaboration and grounded theory. We identified three papers in which QCA enables theory elaboration and QCA is used as the primary analytical tool (Bakker, Cambré, Korlaar, & Rabb, 2011; Crilly, Zollo, & Hansen, 2012; Rivard & Lapointe, 2012; for more details, see Table 15.1). In theory elaboration, researchers refine preliminary theoretical models or preexisting conceptual ideas (Lee, 1999) into general theories (Vaughan, 1992, 1996). In these exemplars, researchers focused on the complex interplay between conditions that explain the presence or absence of an outcome of interest (e.g., decoupling/implementation of CSR policy). Researchers implemented a set-theoretic approach and identified relevant conditions a priori through literature reviews. These researchers utilized content analysis to code qualitative data to measure and calibrate predefined conditions; they employed QCA to specify the combinations of conditions that led to the desired outcome or its absence.

Table 15.1 Use of QCA in Qualitative Research Methods

Reference	Research Question	Theoretical Perspective	Research Context	Number of Cases	Data	QCA Application Approach	How QCA Is a Qualitative Research Innovation	The Outcomes/Results of Using QCA as a Qualitative Innovation
Crilly, Zollo, & Hansen (2012)	Why do some firms not implement the policies they adopt?	Theories of decoupling	Multinational corporations' CSR policy	17 cases	59 interviews with internal and external actors and archival documents	Primary analytical tool, set theoretical approach	Identified the combinations of conditions that were elicited from prior theory	Firms facing identical pressure decouple policy from practice in different ways and for different reasons.
Rivard & Lapointe (2012)	What are implementers' responses to user resistance? What are the effects of these responses on user resistance?	Technology resistance	Finance, health, education, and manufacturing	89 cases	37 episodes of resistance identified from scholarly sources (secondary data)	Primary analytical tool, set theoretical approach	Content analysis to code a priori conditions and led to the identification of a taxonomy of implementer's responses. QCA was used to identify the pattern of influence of implementer's responses on user resistance.	Offers a theoretical explanation of how implementers' responses, such as inaction, during the implementation of new information technology may lead to greater user resistance and organizational disruption.
Bakker, Cambré, Korlaar, & Rabb (2011)	What factors impact the extent of knowledge transfer from project venture to project owner?	Knowledge transfer	Interorganizational project ventures in Dutch SMEs	12 cases	21 interviews and archival documents	Primary analytical tool, set theoretical approach	QCA used for cross-case analysis	No single factor is sufficient: successful project knowledge transfer is a complex process that involves the configuration of multiple factors.

Author (Year)	Research question	Literature	Setting	Cases	Data	Role of QCA	Approach	Findings
O'Neil (2008)	How do artists price their visual art?	Pricing literature	Visual artists	53 cases	53 Interviews with artists and representatives of local galleries, field work in local art world	Supplementary analytical tool, abductive approach for QCA	Inductive approach to identifying and categorizing the different conditions shaping pricing; QCA used to explore the interplay among identified conditions	Some artists take a craft whereas other artists take a fine art orientation to art production and distribution. These distinct orientations shape pricing decisions based on an artist's determination of aesthetic worth rather than market factors like demand.
Bromley, Hwang, & Powell (2012)	Why are plans enacted in different ways?	Decoupling	U.S. nonprofit sector	24 symbolic adoption; 49 symbolic implementation	200 interviews with leaders of nonprofits	Supplementary analytical tool, abductive approach for QCA	Inductive approach to identify and conditions that shape decoupling; QCA used to explore which combinations of conditions are associated with decoupling or routinization	Illuminate how multiple forms of decoupling can be used to understand micro-processes of variation.

Crilly, Zollo and Hansen's (2012) "Faking It or Muddling Through?" challenges the prior literature on decoupling as an isolated organizational event to view it as the multilevel combination of intrafirm and institutional forces. These researchers reviewed the decoupling literature and identified four relevant causal conditions: two external environment characteristics of potential for information asymmetry and stakeholder consensus and two intrafirm characteristics of organizational interest and managerial consensus. By combining 359 interviews, including both internal and external stakeholders, with archival documents, the authors presented an in-depth study of 17 multinational corporations that either decoupled or implemented corporate social responsibility (CSR) policies. They found that firms facing identical pressures decoupled policy from practice in different ways and for different reasons. When firms' responses were generated locally, without firm-wide coordination, these responses could be either intentional or emergent. When there was an information asymmetry between firms and their stakeholders, managers' responses were intentional ("faking it") and depended on how they perceived their interests. When there were competing stakeholder expectations, managers' responses were emergent ("muddling through") and depended on the degree of consensus among managers' readings of the environment.

This study illustrates two key advantages of QCA as a research method. First, QCA enables researchers to identify multiple causal mechanisms that combine to explain an outcome, such as decoupling, rather than simply treating conditions as additive or in isolation. Second, the study found two configurations that lead to decoupling and three configurations that lead to implementing CSR; these findings demonstrate equifinality and the causal asymmetry of conditions with an outcome. Equifinality illustrates multiple paths to an outcome, whereas causal asymmetry indicates that the conditions for decoupling may not be the same as those for implementing CSR.

We also identified two papers that employ QCA for grounded theory building, where QCA is the supplementary analytical tool (Bromley, Hwang, & Powell, 2012; O'Neil, 2008). These studies began with an intuitive insight into the phenomenon of interest and used abduction to identify key conditions that explained a desired outcome. In contrast to the approach detailed previously, researchers did not predefine a focus on the interplay among conditions, but rather it emerged organically during initial qualitative analysis of the data. The researchers' intuition that conditions tended to bundle together led to their use of QCA as a systematic method to examine their hunch and map differences and similarities across cases. This alternative use of QCA reflects an abductive approach (Locke, Golden-Biddle, & Feldman, 2008; Peirce, 1997), an "ampliative and conjectural mode of inquiry through which [researchers] engender and entertain hunches, explanatory propositions, ideas, and theoretical elements" (Locke et al., 2008: 908). An illustrative example of this application of QCA is evident in O'Neil's (2008) "Bringing Art to Market," which focused on pricing behaviors of organizations and explored the factors that shape individual entrepreneurs' pricing decisions. The author used 53 interviews with visual artists, 10 interviews with representatives of local galleries, and 18 months of field work to identify and categorize different styles of visual artists' pricing. O'Neil's initial qualitative analysis of the data led her to explore the similarities and differences across cases and pointed to bundles of conditions. She then used QCA to systematically reveal combinations of conditions at play. She found that some artists take a craft orientation, whereas other artists take a fine art orientation to production and distribution. Whereas the initial inductive analysis made it possible to see patterns and types of pricing styles, the QCA analysis pointed to more complex patterns, revealing connections across styles and decision types and illustrating that many artists actually make decisions that combine a craft approach and an art world approach. For example, some artists believe in pricing based on reputation or according to costs, so they increase the price when they know a work represents a major artistic accomplishment. This research not only uncovered patterns of pricing decisions, but also the complexities of actual pricing decisions, which involved artists negotiating among instrumental economic activity, creative self-expression, belief in fairness, and community norms both inside and outside the art world.

This example illuminates QCA as a fruitful tool that enables qualitative researchers to assess the coherence of their initial hunches and test working models. QCA is especially suited when an intermediate number of cases are explored because it requires in-depth knowledge of cases and restricts the number of conditions that a researcher can explore, which are problematic in large-N studies. In contrast to variable-based cross-case methods (Ayres, Kavanaugh, & Knafl, 2003), QCA does not decontextualize conditions from cases but engages in "dialogue" with cases when conditions are identified and calibrated and then solutions are interpreted (Berg-Schlosser et al., 2009).

A Word of Caution

QCA is well-suited for certain research circumstances, but it can be inappropriate for many others. A key feature of QCA is its grounding in deep knowledge of individual cases. This knowledge drives the selection of the relevant cases, outcomes, and conditions to be analyzed; it is necessary for the postanalysis interpretation based on the case data. Thus, QCA does not lend itself to situations where individual cases are not well known (e.g., survey or archival datasets in isolation from context and compiled by others) (Berg-Schlosser et al., 2009). Another essential aspect of QCA is the comparability of cases. Furthermore, if the available cases are not sufficiently homogeneous to define a clear outcome and set of conditions, then QCA methods will yield results that simply describe the cases individually, offering no additional insight for the effort. Finally, because QCA has difficulty tracking shifting configurations over time, it restricts the ability to identify temporal sequencing that is central to process studies. The static comparisons that QCA provides are insightful for discerning which combinations matter, but not for illuminating the process or processes through which these combinations came into play. Although there are initial forays into creating temporal processes in QCA (see, for example, Caren & Panofsky, 2005), researchers have not systematically incorporated temporal methods into QCA. This provides an area ripe for future contributions to QCA and how it is used in qualitative research.

Conclusions

In conclusion, QCA provides a novel and exciting methodology that enables qualitative researchers to elaborate and build theory. QCA enables scholars to hone and systematize their insights in intermediate fields of research by examining combinations where multiple theories may play a role in explaining the outcomes of interest. In addition, QCA is especially well suited for larger data comparisons because in such circumstances the sheer volume of data and number of cases overwhelm researchers' capacities to process information. When information overload is prevalent, researchers need to simplify information processing, triggering the use of cognitive heuristics. These heuristics, while simplifying cognitive processes, also engender insights that are harder to replicate and verify by other scholars. QCA demands in-depth case-based knowledge that is the hallmark of qualitative research; it complements this deep knowledge with a systematic approach that enables qualitative researchers to discern less obvious and more complex patterns in their data. By using QCA to reveal and discover these complex patterns, researchers may elaborate extant theory as well as develop new theory.

References

Note: References tagged with asterisks represent exemplars.

Ayres, L., Kavanaugh, K., & Knafl, K. A. 2003. Within-case and across-case approaches to qualitative data analysis. *Qualitative Health Research*, 13(6): 871–883.

*Bakker, R. M., Cambré, B., Korlaar, L., & Raab, J. 2011. Managing the project learning paradox: A set-theoretic approach toward project knowledge transfer. *International Journal of Project Management*, 29: 494–503.

Bansal, P. T., & Corley, K. 2011. From the editors. The coming of age for qualitative research: Embracing the diversity of qualitative methods. *Academy of Management Journal*, 54(2): 233–237.

Basurto, X., & Speer, J. 2012. Structuring the calibration of qualitative data as sets for qualitative comparative analysis (QCA). *Field Methods*, 24(2): 155–174.

Bazerman, M. H. 1994. *Judgment in managerial decision making*. New York: Wiley & Sons, Third edition.

Berg-Schlosser, D., & De Meur, G. 2009. Comparative research design: Case and variable selection. In Rihoux, B., & Ragin, C.C. (Eds.). *Configurational comparative methods: Qualitative comparative analysis (QCA) and related techniques*. Thousand Oaks, CA: Sage.

Berg-Schlosser, D., De Meur, G., Rihoux, B., & Ragin, C.C. 2009. Qualitative comparative analysis (QCA) as an approach. In Rihoux, B., & Ragin, C.C. (Eds.). *Configurational comparative methods: Qualitative comparative analysis (QCA) and related techniques*. Thousand Oaks, CA: Sage.

⋆Bromley, P., Hwang, H., & Powell, W. 2012. Decoupling revisited: Common pressures, divergent strategies in the U.S. nonprofit sector. *M@n@gement*, 15(5): 468–501.

Caren, N., & Panofsky, A. 2005. TQCA: A technique for adding temporality to qualitative comparative analysis. *Sociological Methods and Research*, 34(2): 147–172.

Chung, M., & Woodside, A. G. 2012. Causal recipes sufficient for identifying market gurus versus mavens. In A. Meier and L. Donzé (Eds.), *Fuzzy methods for customer relationship management and marketing: Applications and classifications* (pp. 312–331). Hershey, PA: Business Science Reference.

⋆Crilly, D., Zollo, M., & Hansen, M. 2012. Faking it or muddling through? Understanding decoupling in responses to stakeholder pressures. *Academy of Management Journal*, 55(6): 1483–1448.

Cronqvist, L., & Berg-Schlosser, D. 2009. Multi-value QCA (mvQCA). In Rihoux, B., & Ragin, C.C. (Eds.). *Configurational comparative methods: Qualitative comparative analysis (QCA) and related techniques*. Thousand Oaks, CA: Sage.

Eckstein, H. 2002. Case study and theory in political science. In Gomm, R., Hammersley, M., & Foster, P. (Eds.). *Case study method: Key issues, key texts* (pp. 119–163). London: Sage.

Edmonson, A.C., & McManus, S.E. 2007. Methodological fit in management field research. *Academy of Management Review*, 32(4): 1155–1179.

Eisenhardt, K., & Graebner, M., 2007. Theory building from cases: Opportunities and challenges. *Academy of Management Journal*, 40(1): 25–32.

Eisenhardt, K.M. 1989. Building theories from case study research. *Academy of Management Review*, 14(4): 532–550.

Fiss, P.C. 2007. A set-theoretic approach to organizational configurations. *Academy of Management Review*, 32(4): 1180–1198.

Fiss, P.C. 2011. Building better causal theories: A fuzzy set approach to typologies in organization research. *Academy of Management Journal*, 54(2): 393–420.

Gioia, D.A., Corley, K. G., & Hamilton, A. L. 2013. Seeking qualitative rigor in inductive research: Notes on the Gioia methodology. *Organizational Research Methods*, 16(1): 15–31.

Greckhamer, T., Misangyi, V. F., Elms, H., & Lacey, R. 2008. Using qualitative comparative analysis in strategic management research: An examination of combinations industry, corporate, and business-unit effects. *Organizational Research Methods*, 11: 695–726.

Jones, C., & Livne-Tarandach, R. 2014. *Winning strategies: Configurations of vocabularies and quality signals*. Presented at Academy of Management Conference, Philadelphia, PA.

Kahn, S., & VanWynsberghe, R. 2008. Cultivating the under-mined: Cross-case analysis as knowledge mobilization. *Qualitative Research*, 9(1): 34–40.

Lee, T.W. 1999. *Using qualitative methods in organizational research*. Thousand Oaks, CA: Sage.

Lee, T.W., Mitchell, T. R., & Sabylinski, C. J. 1999. Qualitative research in organizational and vocational psychology: 1979–1999. *Journal of Vocational Behavior*, 55: 161–187.

Locke, K., Golden-Biddle, K., & Feldman, M.S. 2008. Making doubt generative: Rethinking the role of doubt in the research process. *Organization Science*, 19: 907–918.

Marx, A., & Dusa, A. 2011. Crisp-set Qualitative Comparative Analysis (csQCA), contradictions and consistency benchmarks for model specification. *Methodological Innovations*, 6(2): 97–142.

Mill, J.S. 1843. *A system of logic, ratiocinative and inductive: Being a connected view of the principles of evidence and the methods of scientific investigation*. London: John W. Parker.

⋆O'Neil, K.M. 2008. Bringing art to market: The diversity of pricing styles in a local art market. *Poetics*, 36: 94–113.

Peirce, C.S. 1997. (First published in 1903.) In P.A. Turrisi (Ed.). *The 1903 lectures on pragmatism*. Albany: State University of New York Press.

Ragin, C.C. 1987. *The comparative method: Moving beyond qualitative and quantitative strategies*. Berkeley: University of California Press.

Ragin, C.C. 1997. Turning the tables: How case-oriented research challenges variable-oriented research. *Comparative Social Research*, 16: 27–42.

Ragin, C.C. 2006. *User's guide to fuzzy-set/Qualitative Comparative Analysis 2.0*. Tucson: Department of Sociology, University of Arizona.

Ragin, C.C. 2008. *Redesigning social inquiry: fuzzy sets and beyond*. Chicago: University of Chicago Press.

Rihoux, B., & De Meur, G. 2009. Crisp-set Qualitative Comparative Analysis (csQCA). In Rihoux, B., & Ragin, C.C. (Eds.). *Configurational comparative methods: Qualitative comparative analysis (QCA) and related techniques*. Thousand Oaks, CA: Sage.

Rihoux, B., & Ragin, C.C. (Eds.). 2009. *Configurational comparative methods: Qualitative comparative analysis (QCA) and related techniques*. Thousand Oaks, CA: Sage.

★Rivard, S., & Lapointe, L. 2012. Information technology implementers' responses to user resistance: Nature and effects. *MIS Quarterly*, 36(3): 897–920.

Stretton, H. 1969. *The political sciences: General principles of selection in social science and history*. London: Routledge & Kegan Paul.

Van Maanen J., Sorensen J.R., & Mitchell, T.R. 2007. The interplay between theory and method. *Academy of Management Review*, 32: 1145–1154.

Vaughan, D. 1992. Theory elaboration: The heuristics of case analysis. In Ragin, C.C., & Backer, H.S. (Eds.). *What is a case?* Cambridge, UK: Cambridge University Press.

Vaughan, D. 1996. Appendix C: On theory elaboration, organizations and historical ethnography In *The* Challenger *launch decision: Risky technology, culture and deviate at NASA* (pp. 456–463). Chicago: University of Chicago Press.

16

Leveraging Comparative Field Data for Theory Generation

Beth A. Bechky and Siobhan O'Mahony

Qualitative field methods are a long-standing, reliable, and generative tool in the organization theory building repertoire. They include an array of "interpretative techniques which seek to describe, decode, translate, and otherwise come to terms with the meaning, not the frequency, of certain more or less naturally occurring phenomena in the social world" (Van Maanen, 1979: 520). In 1979, Van Maanen observed "a quiet reconstruction going on in the social sciences . . . a renewed interest in and felt need for qualitative research." He argued that in response to social science methods that weakened the relationship between measures and concepts,

> there has come of age the significant realization that the people we study (and often seek to assist) have a form of life, a culture that is their own and if we wish to understand the behavior of these people and the groups and the organizations of which they are a part, we must first be able to both appreciate and describe their culture. (1979: 522)

More than 35 years later, this promise has only been partially met. The creation of this book is a sign of resurgence guided by data that show how qualitative research is uniquely able to produce "cool ideas and interesting papers," at least as analyzed by the editors at the *Academy of Management Journal* (Bartunek, Ireland, & Rynes, 2006). The unanswered question and the reason why Van Maanen's promise is only partially met is that if it is true that qualitative research is particularly apt at producing innovative research ideas, why is there still so little of it? As Ragin (2006) points out, social science remains in the methodological doldrums due to a reliance on linear, additive models that ignore causal complexity. Innovating qualitative methods to increase our understanding of when and where causes have effects can enliven our theorizing.

This volume is intended to help cultivate and foster innovation in qualitative research, and our observation is that comparative qualitative field methods are one way to gain greater purchase and leverage from the valuable field data we painstakingly collect. Our experiences with comparative qualitative field research have been very generative for us: Together, we compared contract workers' strategies for obtaining new work in the high technology and film production industries (O'Mahony & Bechky, 2006). Beth compared responses to surprises in film production and SWAT teams (Bechky & Okhuysen, 2011) and compared coordination in an equipment manufacturer with coordination on film sets (Bechky & Chung, 2014). Beth has also done a within-family analysis of technicians' work (Barley, 1996, Barley, Bechky, & Nelsen, 2014). Siobhan has compared the organizing practices of Open Source and Burning Man communities (Chen & O'Mahony, 2009). These experiences have given us some ideas for how to do the rigorous qualitative comparisons that help develop innovative theory.

There are at least three reasons why comparative field research designs are more likely to produce cool ideas and interesting papers than studies of a single setting. First, by uncovering surprising commonalities or differences across divergent field settings, comparative methods are more likely to generate novel theories. By comparing across different settings, we may be able to better explain the processes and mechanisms that contribute to outcome variance. Second, comparative qualitative theorizing enables us to enhance the generalizability of our findings to other contexts. By including well-designed contextual differences into our understanding of phenomena, comparative methods can help specify the boundary conditions of the theories we generate. Third, by comparing field data across settings or environments, we may be better able to link processes in the institutional environment to processes within organizations. Comparative designs can more precisely render the reach of institutions as organizations either respond to or ignore various institutional constraints.

Comparative Field Research: Where Is It?

While qualitative methods remain relatively rare in organization theory, studies that compare across organizations are even less common. We did an abbreviated meta-theoretical survey of the field of organizational studies to determine the prevalence and types of strategies of comparative qualitative methods. Our data collection covered a period of 23 years (1991–2013) and included five top organizational theory journals (*American Journal of Sociology, American Sociological Review, Academy of Management Journal, Administrative Science Quarterly*, and *Organization Science*). Of the 4,342 empirical articles analyzed during this time period, 81% were quantitative. Qualitative articles represented 15% of the research (648 articles). Almost half (46%) of the qualitative field research appeared in either *Administrative Science Quarterly* (23%) or *Organization Science* (23%). The rest appeared in *American Journal of Sociology* (15%), *Academy of Management Journal* (11%), and the *American Sociological Review* (9%). Hybrid research that included both qualitative and quantitative methods accounted for 2% of the total (81 articles). Of the qualitative papers, only 15% were comparative (95 papers), which was 2.2% of the total articles published from 1991 to 2013. Over time, we see a modest but promising trend—the percentage of qualitative research increased from 17% in 1991 to 20% in 2013, while comparative research increased from 0.6% in 1991 to 3.1% in 2013. While 2006 through 2009 were banner years for qualitative research, accounting for nearly 24% of journal articles as an all-time high, the percentage of comparative research articles never surpassed 5%. Thus, while qualitative research remains rare among the bulk of organizational scholarship, comparative qualitative field research is rarer still.

Of the scholars performing qualitative comparative field research, the dominant approach draws upon a replication logic to use multiple cases or sites to strengthen the robustness of findings rather than to examine differences among these settings. "In replication logic, cases which confirm emergent relationships enhance confidence in the validity of the relationships" (Eisenhardt, 1989: 542). In this regard, multiple settings are used to enhance the generalizability or external validity of the study by showing that a particular process or phenomenon occurred in more than one organization or case. Although "cases which disconfirm the relationships often can provide an opportunity to refine and extend the theory" (Eisenhardt, 1989: 542), most comparative qualitative studies in organizational theory do not compare or use differences across cases to help build theory. Often, there is not even a minimal analysis of variance, which leads one to question whether a claim of comparative research can truly be made. We argue that to be "comparative," a study should include analysis of both commonalities and variance.

There could be several reasons why analysis of variance is lacking in extant papers. It could be that qualitative field work requires more pages to present and explain the data than does quantitative research. Comparative qualitative field work, which requires exposition of multiple settings, consumes even greater real estate. Analysis of variance may simply be edited out of the process as a result. Or, it could be that analysis of variance is too distracting to the "single compelling theoretical story" researchers are trying to create to convince editors and reviewers. Then, there is the question of causality: What does the variance we uncover actually explain? Field researchers are well trained to avoid causal claims, but perhaps we need a richer repertoire to draw from in understanding how differences make a difference. The danger of the replication logic approach is that qualitative field researchers are caught in an "N" battle they cannot win. Larger sample size will simply never be a strength of qualitative field research. Instead, we would encourage scholars to spend as much time seeking variance as they do commonalities to maximize the potential for innovation and novelty. We should mine cases for the significant ways in which they vary as well as for what they have in common, because it is often those data that do not fit the paradigm that lead to new ways of thinking.

Comparative Research Designs: What Do They Look Like?

In the current body of comparative qualitative field research on organizations, many authors do not fully describe the differences in context across research sites or provide adequate justifications for their choices of settings, even when explaining their research design. However, when we analyzed the sampling choices made by authors in the papers we reviewed, we found that scholars primarily used three sampling strategies: pooled, polar, and matched.

The pooled strategy was the most common and can be applied at organizational or suborganizational levels. With this sampling strategy, data from multiple organizations are pooled to build theory on a common process. For example, Bradach (1997) analyzed five restaurant chains to explore how they managed the common tension of managing uniformity versus allowing for local adaptation. Data from across different organizations can also be pooled at the individual or team level, as in Ibarra's (1999) study of professional career transitions among consultants and investment bankers. Although in very different industries, both occupations were considered to be "junior professionals" of similar status and schooling. Ibarra compared how consultants and investment bankers experimented with provisional selves to identify an adaptation process held in common. Research in the pooled sampling tradition is typically focused on a process or practice of interest across different organizations; it is a good method to theorize about processes, provided that the researchers know a priori that such behaviors or practices exist. The benefit of these studies is a focused research question, often one that elaborates on a micro-process common to multiple settings. A danger of these studies is that they rarely examine potentially relevant aspects of differences in the organizational setting or institutional context, and therefore cannot take advantage of the variance presented in the data.

Some scholars use a polar sampling strategy in which they choose multiple cases that invite comparison based on extreme differences in performance results or outcomes. Scholars build theory to explain the different processes and mechanisms that can lead to differences in outcomes. This approach is particularly common in organizational strategy, and it is sometimes referred to as the "Eisenhardt" case method (Eisenhardt, 1989; Eisenhardt & Graebner, 2007; see also Brown & Eisenhardt, 1997, and Zott & Huy, 2007, for some empirical examples). One benefit of this design is that scholars actually use the variance in their cases and can link differences in process to differences in outcomes. For example, Seidel and O'Mahony (2014) studied six product development teams across three different industries and discovered that, counter to expectations, concept representations failed to facilitate coordination in three of the cases. They explain how concept representations created misunderstandings as well as common understandings, and they show how some teams misused concept representations and were less likely to create product integrity. The danger of a polar strategy is the risk of creating functional explanations if scholars begin with knowledge of outcome variance a priori. The result can be a distinct "best practice" process and a distinct "pathological" process. Because the polar strategy reinforces oppositions, studies using this approach leave open the question of how organizations vacillate between those two processes or how one organization might transition between the best practice process and the pathological process.

The third, and most rare, strategy is the matched pair approach. Scholars using this strategy select cases that invite comparison on the basis of some type of similarity. This match can be within-family (such as Barley's 1996 study of different types of technicians), across-family (such as Ibarra's [1999] aforementioned study of career transitions among consulting and investing professionals), or based on a key parameter of interest. For example, Bansal (2003) identified a key parameter of interest—issue selling—and examined why some issues led to organizational action and some did not in two U.S. subsidiaries. In practice, the matched pair approach has two main variants.

One approach is to match cases based on a parameter that is common across different contexts or institutional settings. For example, Vaughan notes that "forms of social organization have characteristics in common, like conflict, hierarchy, division of labor, culture, power and structured inequalities, socialization, etc., making them comparable in structure and process" (2004: 318). The objective is to show that although multiple settings appear to be very different on the surface, they actually share some common underlying mechanisms. The divergence of settings provides robustness to any commonalities identified. For example, Bechky and Okhuysen (2011) showed how, although they work in very different settings with very different goals, SWAT team workers and film crew members approach the handling of surprises using some common techniques. Similarly, O'Mahony and Bechky (2006) showed how film crew and high-technology contractors leveraged common techniques to obtain work that would enhance their skills. Even though their work was very different, both types of workers faced the same career progression paradox: the problem of finding a job without prior experience. Stretchwork that aligned with prior experience but introduced a novel element to extend their skills in a new direction helped both types of workers reconcile this paradox.

In these cases, the common element across divergent settings is a product of the findings rather than of the studies' designs. A strength of this approach is the ability to identify common processes in settings that one would expect to have little in common. This can aid in generating theory robust to contextual variation. A danger of this approach is that it can be difficult to find the key processes, constructs, or parameters of interest a priori, and the analysis runs the risk of being swamped by a large variety of contextual differences across sites.

A second type of a matched pair approach is one that matches cases based on common attributes, examining cases in very common settings where, by all appearances, the same behavior, process, or outcome should be observed but is not. For example, Barley (1986) studied the introduction of CT scanners in the radiology departments of two hospitals and found that the social structures of these departments developed very differently. In Edmondson and colleagues' study, they found that "all hospitals had top tier cardiac surgery departments with excellent reputations and patient outcomes yet exhibited striking differences in the extent to which they were able to implement a new technology" (2001: 685). Similarly, Kellogg (2009) designed a study of the surgical floors of two hospitals with similar institutional environments and discovered that one hospital allowed residents to shift their schedules to accommodate a new policy while the other hospital maintained the status quo, producing very different outcomes.

In these cases, the researcher seeks identical contexts and identifies variance in behavior to explain divergent outcomes. The cases are selected to control environmental or contextual variance rather than exploring divergent settings to develop common outcomes as in the matched parameter approach. One risk of the matched commonality approach is that cases may be too similar and not produce significant or interesting variance. The benefit of the matched commonality approach is that cases can be used to isolate select differences that help explain variation because alternative explanations shaped by macro differences in institutional environments can be largely controlled. Of course, hybrids exist. For example, Barley and Nelsen (1997) studied one occupation (emergency medical technicians) in a similar setting but matched a sample of paid EMTs with a sample of volunteer EMTs to see if this difference made a difference. With this design, Barley and Nelsen identified ways in which, when faced with the same situations, the EMTs' dress, behavior, and responses to emergency situations clearly varied in line with their conceptions of paid versus volunteer work. This type of design makes the best of both worlds: isolating only one difference, holding everything else in common, and building theory on the basis of divergent behaviors that unfold under the two conditions.

Conducting Comparative Field Research

The comparative qualitative field approach raises multiple challenges for data collection and theory building. So far, there has been little guidance on designing and conducting comparative research designs, and doing an emic analysis is a lengthy and complicated process. In our own work, we have each done several matched parameter studies and have generated some ideas as to how to approach comparative research and overcome some of the challenges of this strategy.

Research Design and Data Collection

We have discussed some of the sampling strategies chosen by scholars in the past, but the literature provides little guidance on designing comparative research and explaining how this affects data collection. Our first bit of advice: Think hard about whether you want a between- or within-family sample design and whether you are attempting to do the research independently or collaboratively; both of these decisions will dramatically affect the sampling selection process and the study's timing.

One approach is to design a comparative field research project with data collection at multiple settings conducted in parallel. Within-family analysis requires definition of what is shared at the family level as well as what is likely to differ within the family at the time of the study's design. For example, in Barley's (1996) technician project, technicians shared a family, and different types of technicians were compared within the family on emerging constructs the team identified as they conducted the research, such as identity, autonomy, and skill. This project was designed carefully prior to and during execution of the ethnographies. When comparative cases are studied in parallel, adjustments to collecting specific types of data can be made across the research team if these are identified early in the data collection process.

As an alternative, cross-family or key parameter designs can be compared and analyzed long after data collection is complete. In this case there is no common family, but a shared process or outcome that can be studied across multiple settings sequentially or in parallel. For example, Vaughan selected one parameter of interest, organizational dissent, and studied this parameter across "seemingly disparate cases as the corporate whistle-blower, the prison snitch, sexual harassment, and domestic violence" (2004: 318). This type of project could be conducted either sequentially or in parallel depending on research access and physical proximity. If the parameter of interest is less clear, then a sequential research design may be more appropriate. In that case, what is learned at one site can then help inform the research design at the next site.

For instance, when we began our stretchwork analysis, Siobhan had already uncovered some of the tactics used by high-technology contractors, and Beth had just completed field work on film sets. We compared our data after having conducted independent field research projects at different times. Siobhan and Katherine Chen were collecting data about the Burning Man and Open Source communities simultaneously and comparing notes as they met at academic conferences. In both cases, comparative analyses of ethnographic data were not a part of either study's original design, and there was no key parameter in mind. However, after independent data collection, collaborative analyses revealed commonalities worth theorizing about. What can make this approach challenging is that when data are compared across studies that were independently designed, opportunities to change or adapt the data collection strategy are limited.

Given that the comparative qualitative method starts with emic analyses of each setting, it can be time consuming. Developing thick descriptions and providing a contextual understanding requires deep investments in the data. One way to decrease the time it takes to finish a comparative project is to design a team ethnography, collecting data and writing memos in parallel, as in the Barley (1996) project. Another is to collaborate with co-authors who specialize in each setting. For example, a group of scholars funded by the European Research Council assigned every scholar in the research group to one of 22 countries in order to compare and contrast different corporate governance models (Kogut, 2012). This approach can enhance the appreciation of both deep context and variance across a group of scholars rather than having one scholar absorb all of the costs of understanding multiple settings in depth.

Comparative Analysis

When comparing the data generated from different contexts, we first start with emic analyses of each setting; this ensures that the cases have characteristics in common, provides a thick description, and offers the detailed rich context that helps build theory (Vaughan, 2004). Then, we draft memos on categories that appear across settings; for example, in the technician study we wrote a memo on autonomy, in the stretchwork study we focused on tactics our informants used to acquire their next job, and in the study of coordination we elaborated the practices used to create common ground in each setting. During the analysis, we carefully take note of similarities and differences across cases, often using tables that compare common constructs across organizational settings to foster constant comparison. We then assess how these constructs affect (rather than cause) behaviors, processes, or outcomes in each setting, with careful attention to the temporal order of the processes involved. As Katz (2001: 459) notes, "ethnographers can give a temporal structure to data collection that may put them as close to inherently elusive causal contingencies as any research can."

These grounded theoretical methods (Glaser & Strauss, 1967) encourage mining differences to build theoretical explanations. We share theoretical memos and ask questions of one another such as: Were there some processes that seemed similar but were actually different, and vice versa? Can these consequences be linked to differences in the organizations or the environments of the two settings? After many iterations, we identify theoretical constructs that apply across settings and try to understand how these constructs are instantiated in each setting. Then we begin writing our findings for each setting, which usually reveals further similarities and differences and fosters the development of a common theoretical explanation. Finally, we look for antecedents, boundary conditions, or extenuating circumstances that might affect the relevance or generalizability of any theory generated from the settings we have studied.

Because doing comparative qualitative analysis attempts to maintain some causal complexity, we can't always make our findings predictive. It can be difficult to pinpoint the causes of different outcomes across settings. Reviewers often want this, but it is important to attend to the attribution of causal differences and note that we are still engaging in theory building. Where possible, we look for primacy to understand what conditions needed to be in place before others could occur. There are a wide variety of alternatives to making causal claims and much to be explained. A question common to quantitative researchers is relevant here: How much of the variance can be explained? We worry that qualitative researchers hold themselves to the impossible bar of explaining 100% of the variance, while quantitative researchers would be happy to explain 30% of the variance they observe. Comparative field research is well suited to showing how the presence or absence of conditions contributes to a relationship or outcomes or how processes unfold. What is critical is that the researchers are clear about what phenomena they are attempting to explain.

Presenting Comparative Data

Comparative field research provides deep familiarity with each setting while maintaining causal complexity. Yet, comparative analyses require a level of abstraction to generalize across disparate research settings. Thus, data reduction and presentation can be more problematic for comparative qualitative research given the variance in research settings introduced. With the need for data reduction across multiple cases, we have encountered challenges in figuring out where to include our variance analysis in comparative manuscripts. One concern is that if you point to variance across your settings, you may cast doubt on the findings rooted in similarity. This may be why analyses of variance are missing in many of the papers we reviewed, or they are just alluded to in the discussion or implications sections. It is critical to assess how variance is related to what you are ultimately trying to explain.

Too often, scholars confuse the analysis with the writing. Despite the current trend to include data coding structures in field data manuscripts, the way the data is analyzed need not dictate the narrative structure of the manuscript. We try to interpenetrate theoretical elaboration and data presentation, which is difficult to do across multiple research settings in the length of a journal article. Authors differ in the degree to which they allow theory or narrative to drive the manuscript, but we acknowledge that it is more difficult to develop a single narrative across multiple cases. Thus, for comparative research, a theory forward framework may be the best bet. Because each context adds length, authors must isolate and select only those aspects of each setting relevant to the analysis and focus on those; otherwise, they will lose their audience in the complexity of each setting.

Tables and figures can facilitate theorizing, but, that said, data tables used for analyses often need further data reduction before reaching the publication stage. Tables that clearly present a visual pattern of where data is present or absent across settings or cases will be especially helpful to reviewers and editors. Primary data in the voice of informants should always be included and clearly distinguished from data paraphrased by authors. As reviewers and editors, we often see data tables misused—either there aren't enough tables to show the data used to support the paper's main points, or there are tables but not adequate primary data or large chunks of undigested text. We encourage authors to isolate the various elements of their theoretical argument and ensure that each claim in the argument is supported by primary data; tables that do not support a claim need not be present. Quotes included in the text need to be trimmed to illustrate the concept relevant to the argument, rather than including large chunks of interview text. It helps to sandwich quotes included in the text with some explanation and interpretation, especially in settings where the context or the work is unique or specialized.

Our focus on comparative qualitative analysis returns to the basics of the constant comparative method. There is broad agreement that comparisons enable richer, more accurate, and more generalizable theorizing, but comparative field research is still relatively rare. We encourage scholars to explicitly justify and motivate their research site selection. We need to take advantage of the explanatory power that variance can enable, and we can't do that if we aren't talking about it. We also see a strong need to put empirical findings and theories in context—driving toward explanations that can apply at the organizational level. Many comparative papers using the pooled strategy focus on individual, project, team, or business unit level processes but lack examination of the larger organizations in which these processes take place. We'd like to encourage more research that actually takes into account the organization and its environment in the analysis, as hard as that goal may be to achieve. Comparative designs that deliberately vary in their institutional parameters can push scholars in this direction. To do so, scholars need to warm up to the idea of introducing more variance into their research designs, analysis, and writing.

Table 16.1 Use of Comparative Designs in Qualitative Field Research Methods

Reference	Research Context	Type of Comparative Sampling	Outcomes/Results of Innovation
Ibarra (1999)	Investment banking and consulting professionals	Pooled	Theory about strategies for identity development
Seidel & O'Mahony (2014)	Product development teams	Polar	Theory of how concept representations affect team coordination
Barley (1996)	Technician occupations	Matched on common settings	Theory about technicians' work roles
Bechky & Okhuysen (2011)	SWAT teams and film productions	Matched on common parameter	Theory about how groups manage surprises
Nelsen & Barley (1997)	Volunteer and paid EMTs	Hybrid matched	Theory of occupational commodification

References

Bansal, P. "From Issues to Actions: The Importance of Individual Concerns and Organizational Values in Responding to Natural Environmental Issues." *Organization Science*, 2003, 14(5): 510–527.

Barley, S.R. "Technology as an Occasion for Structuring: Observations on CT Scanners and the Social Order of Radiology Departments." *Administrative Science Quarterly*, 1986, 31: 76–108.

Barley, S.R. "Technicians in the Workplace: Ethnographic Evidence for Bringing Work into Organization Studies." *Administrative Science Quarterly*, 1996, 41: 404–441.

Barley, S.R., Bechky, B.A., and Nelsen, B. "Toward an Emic Understanding of Professionalism Among Technical Workers." Stanford University, working paper, 2014.

Barley, S.B., and Nelsen, B., "For Love or Money? Commodification and the Construction of an Occupational Mandate." *Administrative Science Quarterly*, 1997, 42(4): 619–653.

Bartunek, J.M., Duane Ireland, R., and Rynes, S.L. "What Makes Management Research Interesting, and Why Does it Matter?" *Academy of Management Journal*, 2006, 49(1): 9–15.

Bechky, B.A., and Okhuysen, G. "Expecting the Unexpected? How SWAT Officers and Film Crews Handle Surprises." *Academy of Management Journal*, 2011, 54(2): 239–261.

Bechky, B.A., and Chung, D. "Integrating the Division of Labor: How Role Relations, Spatial Arenas, and Temporality Shape Coordination." Stern School of Business, working paper, 2014.

Bradach, J.L. "Using the Plural Form in the Management of Restaurant Chains." *Administrative Science Quarterly*, 1997, 42(2): 276–303.

Brown, S., and Eisenhardt, K. M. "The Art of Continuous Change: Linking Complexity Theory and Time-Paced Evolution in Relentlessly Shifting Organizations." *Administrative Science Quarterly*, 1997, 42(1): 1–34.

Chen, K., and O'Mahony, S. "Differentiating Organizational Boundaries." *Research in Sociology of Organizations*, 2009, 26: 183–220.

Edmondson, A., Bohmer, R.M., and Pisano, G.P. "Disrupted Routines: Team Learning and New Technology Implementation in Hospitals." *Administrative Science Quarterly*, 2001, 46: 685–716.

Eisenhardt, K.M., and Graebner, M. "Theory Building From Cases: Opportunities and Challenges." *Academy of Management Journal*, 2007, 50(1): 25–32.

Eisenhardt, K.M. "Building Theories from Case Study Research." *Academy of Management Review*, 1989, 14(4): 532–550.

Glaser, B., and Strauss, A. *The Discovery of Grounded Theory*. Hawthorne: Aldine Publishing Company, 1967.

Ibarra, H. "Provisional Selves: Experimenting with Image and Identity in Professional Adaptation." *Administrative Science Quarterly*, 1999, 44(4): 764–791.

Katz, J. "From How to Why: On Luminous Description and Causal Inference in Ethnography." *Ethnography*, 2001, 2: 443–473.

Kellogg, K. "Operating Room: Relational Spaces and Micro Institutional Change in Surgery." *American Journal of Sociology*, 2009, 115(3): 657–711.

Kogut, B. *The Small Worlds of Corporate Governance*. Cambridge, MA: MIT Press, 2012.

O'Mahony, S., and Bechky, B.A. "Stretchwork: Managing the Career Progression Paradox in External Labor Markets." *Academy of Management Journal*, 2006, 49(5): 918–941.

Beth A. Bechky and Siobhan O'Mahony

Seidel, V., and O'Mahony, S. "Managing the Repertoire: Stories, Metaphors, Prototypes and Concept Coherence in Product Innovation." *Organization Science*, 2014, 25(3): 691–712.
Van Maanen, J. "Reclaiming Qualitative Methods for Organizational Research: A Preface." *Administrative Science Quarterly*, 1979, 24(4): 520–526.
Vaughan, D. "Theorizing Disaster: Analogy, Historical Ethnography, and the Challenger Accident." *Ethnography*, 2004, 5(3): 315–347.
Zott, C., and Huy, Q. N. "How Entrepreneurs Use Symbolic Management to Acquire Resources." *Administrative Science Quarterly*, 2007, 52(1): 70–105.

17

Crafting and Selecting Research Questions and Contexts in Qualitative Research

Michael G. Pratt

The beginning is the most important part of the work. —Plato
All great deeds and all great thoughts have a ridiculous beginning. Great works are often born on a street corner or in a restaurant's revolving door. —Albert Camus
What we call the beginning is often the end. And to make an end is to make a beginning. The end is where we start from. —T.S. Eliot

Beginnings

Choosing a research question and context are integral to the design of a qualitative project. In fact, we often see them as the first things in design, and we typically think of them in that order: question and context. But how does one begin a research project? Before plunging into the chapter topic, I wanted to borrow a page from Michel Anteby (also in this book) who talks about the importance of telling our own stories, and perhaps to some degree John Van Maanen, who talks about "confessional tales" as a style of writing (Anteby, 2012; Van Maanen, 1988). That is, I want to begin by telling my own story about a beginning: specifically, which wellsprings I am drawing from in this chapter.

Ideas, whether in the form of research questions or ideas about context, rarely spring fully formed like Athena from the head of Zeus. So I want to be clear that even though I am writing this chapter as "my" innovation, I sincerely doubt it is just my own. First, the genesis of this book chapter came out of numerous discussions in various qualitative research classes that I have had the privilege to teach. While I very much appreciate the opportunity of moving from bullet point explicit to book chapter explicit, the bullet points themselves have been honed by dozens of students over the years who questioned, look confused, and tuned-in or tuned-out during my discussions of qualitative research design. (It is my sincere hope that I have kept the stuff that tuned people in). Second, I believe that at least some of my approach is a reflection of those who trained me, such as Anat Rafaeli, Jane Dutton, and Martha Feldman. Like many of us who do qualitative research, I learned primarily through apprenticeship. Moreover, I had graduate school classes on study design and one on qualitative methods from Raphael Ezekiel. Third, because I have had to teach qualitative methods, I have read a fair amount on the subject. In fact, before writing this chapter, I perused my growing library of qualitative research texts and I was both pleased and disturbed to find that most started with analysis, often with a cursory explanation of how to construct a research question. Few mentioned picking a context at all. However, I imagine that some of the ideas here reflect what I have read, particularly the work by Spradley (1979), Strauss and Corbin (1998), and Golden-Biddle and Locke (2007). All this is a way of saying that it would be hubris to deny that we all stand on the shoulders of giants, so if the reader finds what I wrote to be innovative, I certainly cannot take all of the credit for it.

Finally, research is often written as a "realist tale" (Van Maanen, 1988)—a dispassionate, third-person account whereby the writer knows all and dispenses wisdom to the reader (see also Geertz, 1989). I'm not going to do that. Rather, I am going to write about what I do when I choose research questions and contexts. I don't suggest that this way is right for anyone else, or even for you. I will also not promise that this will lead, as the book's first chapter suggests, to "cool ideas and interesting papers." All I can say is that it has worked for me. So to paraphrase my former, fellow distributors in Amway: "take what you like and leave the rest." You might wonder why I have used nearly a page to introduce this chapter. It is because it illustrates some important points that underlie the philosophy behind this chapter: (a) don't build an approach from scratch if you can borrow, (b) pick and choose from others to create your own voice and your own style, and (c) research, even solo research, is a group activity.

What I Was Taught (and Possibly Used to Teach)

Part of the challenge and fun in articulating a "new" approach is that it makes you think more about the status quo from which you are deviating. If I had to articulate a picture of how I was taught to design a study, and a qualitative study in particular, I would say it would look something like what I have sketched out in Figure 17.1. I will, for rhetorical purposes, refer to this view of study design as the linear model because it shows a neat progression from problem to question to method, and ultimately to context, which is a part of that method.

To provide a bit more flesh to this model, qualitative research is often problem-oriented (Pratt, 2008, 2009). Problems can be motivated by real-world issues—both personal issues, such as "how did Amway get my sister to be so positive about their business?" (Pratt, 2000a), or more impersonal sources, such as the news. For example, why did Yahoo decide to end its remote work policy, despite the fact that most organizations are going in exactly the opposite direction? Problems can also be generated from theory, either by finding gaps, looking at the "toward future research" sections of papers, or even attending research talks. Problems can even be found by relating our own work-related experiences to our theories and finding the latter to be lacking. I have found many doctoral students who have left corporate America for academia to be motivated by this comparison (and often, this misalignment) between practice and theory.

Next, this "problem" gets crafted into a more specific research question that broadly guides one's research. To ensure that one is not recreating the wheel, it is good to examine what the literature says

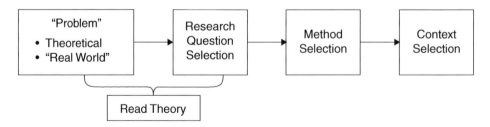

Figure 17.1 A Linear Understanding of Selecting Research Questions and Contexts in Inductive Research

about your research problem and what questions remain unanswered. To illustrate with a cautionary tale, I once worked with a doctoral student who did not like to read the literature, despite many promptings to do so. Our study was about rural doctors and their reactions to being bought out by a larger managed care organization. One day, this student came to me, very excited, and said, "Mike I have found something very interesting! It seems like people in the rural clinics see themselves as a group and treat each other well. They view people outside of their group, those in the managed care organization, quite negatively!" While the observation was spot-on, I had to let him know that he had just rediscovered a basic in-group/out-group bias that was well-known in the literature. So, theory is often involved in the crafting of research questions. While it is not used to create hypotheses, it is useful as a means of figuring out what is known and what is not yet known.

One of the first truisms taught in my doctoral research methods class is that one's method should follow from one's research question (e.g., Edmonson & McManus, 2007). That advice is still good today. However, as Strauss and Corbin (1998) note, certain people tend to be attracted to particular methodologies, which often shape the kinds of questions they ask. Inductive, qualitative research tends to ask *how* and *why* questions, while deductive, quantitative research asks *how many*. Thus, there may be a bit of blurring here between method and question in practice, likely due to a third variable: researcher interest. But, taken together, the linear method starts with a problem and ends with the method, and the context is chosen as part of one's method (e.g., sampling).

For the record, I do not see this linear approach as inherently wrong. Mostly, I see it as limiting and somewhat incomplete. Now, I realize I am creating this model as a type of "straw man" for my own arguments. However, these various steps resonate with what others have written about. Miles and Huberman (1994: 18–39), for example, outline a data collection process that starts with "building a conceptual framework," moves to "formulating research questions," and continues on to "defining the case and sampling," and ends with "instrumentation" (e.g., will you use open-ended interviews?). Similarly, Corbin and Strauss (2008) talk about choosing a research problem, then move to research question, and then jump to data collection. Finally, Creswell (1998: 19) states simply, "we begin by posing a problem, a research issue, to which we would like an answer." He then moves onto how to answer these questions. Thus, the general trend seems to be moving from problem to question to context—though, as noted, context is often enfolded into discussions of sampling or data collection.

What I Do

My evolving approach to beginning research, especially selecting research questions and contexts, is more akin to what I've sketched in Figure 17.2. As you will notice, many of the pieces are the same as those in Figure 17.1: There are problems in the world, problems in theory, and a research context. However, there are at least two main differences that reflect two main takeaways I want to leave you with in this chapter. First, I see choosing research questions and contexts as a circular, rather than a linear, process. That is, it does not matter so much where you start on the circle, as long as you get to everything. Second, I think the most impactful research looks both backward and forward. As you will see in Figure 17.2, I have included FSQ arrows in the model. As I delineate later, FSQ stands for *fundamental social question(s)*. To give away part of my punchline, I believe that interesting research questions and contexts involve fundamental social questions or problems with a modern twist.

I Follow a Circular (Nonlinear) Process

Circular is meant to describe the process, not the reasoning behind it. While *iterative* may have been more resonant with qualitative researchers—and this process is certainly iterative—its defining feature is that there are many starting points. The "classic" path is one I have already described in Figure 17.1. You can start with seeing a problem in the real world, use theory to craft a research question,

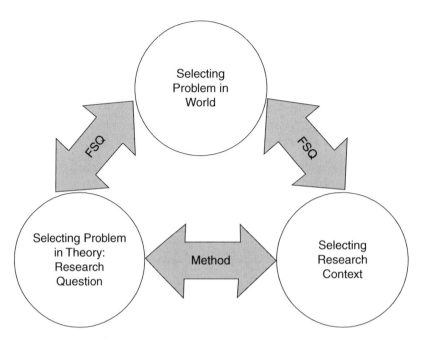

Figure 17.2   Circular Process of Selecting Research Question and Context

and finally select your research context. However, even this classic path can have some twists, as it did on a multiple-researcher study that my colleagues and I recently published. The study started with a problem that I saw in the real world. As I was working on a study with Erik Dane regarding how firefighters made decisions, the firefighters let us know that with the proliferation of fire prevention education and new building materials, there were fewer fires to fight. Thus, firefighters did not spend much time doing the very thing they were organized to do: fight fires. This made me wonder not only how firefighters dealt with this change, but also how they explained what they did all day to nonfirefighters. (Note: This conundrum also evoked a very personal question for me because my parents have—for a couple of decades now—repeatedly asked me what I did with my time when I was not teaching classes.) Voicing this question to colleagues—who were working on unrelated projects dealing with professionals—allowed them to recognize a similar problem with their informants: Professionals often dealt with clientele that had a very limited idea of what they did. Ultimately, this problem led to a common research question in contexts that already had been chosen for another purpose, and ultimately to a new theoretical problem. (And oddly enough, the final paper did not include firefighters, even though they were the initial inspiration.)

In addition to taking a usual path from a problem-in-the-world-first approach, however, I have started projects from other points in my circular model as well. These projects are discussed in Table 17.1.

Context-First Approaches

There may be times when you find a fascinating context and then need to move to find the "problem in the world" and the "theoretical" problem. One project that started out in this fashion was a 6-year study of medical residents. The context was introduced to me by a colleague and friend in strategy, Jeffrey Kaufmann. Jeffrey had been approached by the dean of a medical residency training

Table 17.1 Use of a Nonlinear Process for Selecting Research Questions and Contexts

Reference	Context	How Innovation Was Used	Outcomes/ Results of the Innovations
Vough, Cardador, Bednar, Dane, & Pratt (2013)	Multiple professions: architects, accountants, lawyers, nurse practitioners	Problem in the world approach Selecting problem in world → Contexts → Research questions	Positive: • A problem among firefighters (who don't spend much time fighting fires) allowed a group of us to see if similar problems happened among people of different professions. This made for a stronger, empirical paper. • Opened my eyes to the potential of combining different qualitative data sets. Challenge: • When looking across professions at similar problems, it is difficult to know whether to focus more on the commonalities among how these different groups address these problems or to play up their differences. The former helps with building theory, but the latter does less violence to experience.
Pratt & Rafaeli (1997)	Rehabilitation unit	Theoretical understanding-first approach Research questions → Context → Problems in the world	Positive: • One of the first empirical treatments of multiple identities in organizations • Planted seeds for future work on managing organizational identities Challenges: • Difficulties letting data "breathe" given our extensive theoretical understanding
Pratt (2000a); Pratt (2000b)	Amway	Fundamental social question-first approach Problems in the world/ FSQ → Context → Research questions	Positive: • Multiple publications (two mentioned here) • One of earliest process models of identification management • Sparked interest in other populations such as virtual workers and physicians Challenges: • Fundamental social questions are addressed in multiple disciplines and in multiple theories. Thus, the challenge here was interweaving theories from many areas and disciplines in creating a coherent story and a significant contribution.

program to figure out a way to make the socialization of physicians less brutal, but as effective. He joked with his contact, "for me, people are noise in my equations, but I do know someone who may know how to approach this." This is where I was brought into the conversation. While I had some interest in the question being asked, I was more interested in the context. My previous research was on an arguably low-status group, Amway distributors. Physicians were high status. However, distributors and physicians share a common problem: How do you socialize people to enact the collective's values when they will largely be enacting those values outside of a common location? That is, Amway distributors spend most of their time "building the business" on their own; they do not have a central business location. Yet, you always want your distributors (for legal and reputational reasons) to share a core set of values and practices. Physicians, by comparison, often spend time getting trained in one location but actually practicing in another. Moreover, you want your physician to retain the values and practices he or she was socialized with; you would not want your physician to break his or her Hippocratic oath while treating you, or to throw out his or her training and wing it in a delicate operation. Thus, what started as the introduction of a context led me to recognize a vexing problem in the world. From here, I read the literature on professionals, socialization, and medical residencies (and more) to craft a research question. It is interesting to note that our initial research question was about socialization, but it later morphed into one about professional identity construction. That metamorphosis is another story, but needless to say, the new research question led us to examine new bodies of research on identity work and careers. For the purposes of this chapter, this illustrates that the processes is indeed iterative: we moved back and forth between data, emerging research questions and problems, and the existing literature in a grounded theory fashion; however, this iterative process can begin from different starting points.

While starting with the context is plausible, the frustration and challenges I have faced and felt using this starting point is that it may take a long time—and certainly many, many iterations—of trying on theories that best align with the data. To be clear, this is always challenging (at least for me) in qualitative research, but this was the first time that it took an outsider (in particular, a reviewer) to help me step back and see the data and emerging theory that I had, and thus the type of literature that I needed to frame it.

Theoretical Understandings/First Approaches

Another starting point for research is theoretical understandings. I use *theoretical understandings* rather than just *theory* to point out that, unlike a deductive study, I did not begin with a single theory (or two) in mind from which I was going to carve out hypotheses and attempt to find answers in my qualitative study. As an aside, as an editor, I have seen this "start with a single theory" (not theoretical understandings) sequence, and it is problematic on many fronts. Perhaps most critically, this "quasi-deductive" approach makes it very difficult for the authors to fend off the critique that they found what they were looking for. But I digress. Theoretical understandings means that I started with a broad set of ideas inspired by, or adapted from, theories (kind of like how some movies are inspired by or adapted from books—but hopefully in a more satisfying fashion).

An example of this approach is illustrated with a project I had with Anat Rafaeli on the dress code of rehabilitation nurses (see Table 17.1). Anat and I had been working on a theory paper on the uses of organizational dress when we became aware of a rehabilitation unit that was struggling with its dress code. Here, our theoretical paper served as our antenna that allowed us to notice this particular unit. To be more precise, because a colleague of ours knew we were working on the issue of organizational dress, she pointed Anat—and ultimately, me—toward this organization. So here, our theoretical ideas led us to a context via a real problem they were having in the world.

The unique challenges of this approach may be many. Perhaps the most difficult one is to not be overly influenced by your theoretical frame. This can happen in two ways. To begin, theory may serve as blinders, influencing you to see largely what you thought you would see (see the previous "finding what you are looking for" critique). However, it is also possible to be tempted to do the opposite: to be so hell-bent on being different from existing theory that you miss what theory may have gotten right. In both cases, it is very easy to do violence to experience, whereby you lose sight of how your informants are experiencing their reality—a perspective that often motivates doing inductive research in the first place.

I Ground My Research in Fundamental Social Questions (FSQs)

Organizations, and social collectives more generally, have been around for a long, long time. As such, they have long been the topic of inquiry. Many questions raised about collectives and their members do not have definitive answers—or perhaps better said, they invite new answers throughout time. One of my advisors in graduate school, Lance Sandelands, often noted that the purpose of academics is to keep conversations going. This always stuck with me. And for me, to continue conversations, you have to start with the right questions. Thus, a third path for beginning research is by starting with a FSQ.

One immediate question you might ask when looking for research questions and contexts is, "what fundamental social questions interest you?" To my knowledge, there is not one comprehensive list of such questions. However, some illustrations might help. To begin, one might take some fundamental questions from philosophy such as, "who am I?" and "why am I here?" and apply them to organizational dynamics. With regard to the former, people have looked at the notion of identity as both an individual and collective phenomenon. However, this question is also echoed in Selznick's early work on organizational character, some research on organizational culture, as well as work on categorization, social comparison, image, and the like. While theoretical labels may change over time, the fundamental questions remain just that: fundamental. One very well-known scholar asked me, when he was an assistant professor, if he should continue work on organizational identity or whether it was a fad. My response then, as it is now, is that no matter what we call it, we will always be interested in how organizations define themselves. Similarly, questions about why a person or organization exists resonate in research on meaning, purpose, and vision, just to name a few.

Classic philosophical dilemmas are also good grist for the intellectual mill. For example, the "commons dilemma" is about self-interest versus the common good. The original example of this dilemma was phrased in terms of whether individuals would refrain from grazing their livestock on common land in order to not deplete the grasses and allow others to benefit, or whether they would pursue self-interest and graze as many cattle as they could on the land and deplete the resources. (Note: The bet at the time was that people would choose the latter path—hence its other name, the "tragedy of the commons.") Such dilemmas not only resonate with issues of sustainability, social justice, and corporate social responsibility, but they also point out some fundamental tensions in how individuals relate to their collectives, short-term versus long-term thinking, individualism–collectivism, and so on.

In addition to these few fundamental questions, when I teach my doctoral class, I often add a partial list of additional fundamental social questions and offer some research areas that reflect them. As an aside, it is possible for some theoretical areas to span multiple questions, so you could put some theories with a variety of questions:

- How does the individual relate to other individuals, and the individual(s) to their collectives, and collectives to other collectives (e.g., identification, impression management, commitment, exit, voice, loyalty, neglect, leadership, trust, psychological contracts, socialization, training, indoctrination, governance, justice, isomorphism, population ecology, enculturation)?
- How do individuals relate to the work they do and to the products of that work (e.g., job satisfaction, job engagement, job crafting, meaning of work, job design, careers, occupations and professions, psychological ownership, ownership)?
- How do we know social reality (e.g., sensemaking, interpretation, intuition, social perception and biases, dominant logics)?
- How do individuals, groups, and larger collectives make order out of chaos (e.g., organizing, routines, habits, institutionalization, categories, frames, scripts, stories and accounts)?
- How do individuals, groups, and larger collectives make chaos out of order (e.g., innovation, change, creativity, divergent thinking, disruptive technology, tempered radicals, constructive deviance, deviance)?

These questions may intersect each other or be cross-cutting. For example, you can look at the issue of order versus chaos in individual–organizational relationships, which can be marked by order-liness (e.g., as would be found in total institutions) or a break from the status quo (e.g., innovative cultures). Moreover, these questions may be embedded in entire fields of thought. The questions about order and chaos, for example, evoke Burrel and Morgan's (1979) dimension of radical change regulation that, along with a subjective–objective dimension, underlie four major sociological paradigms: functionalist (objective, regulation); interpretivist (subjective, regulation); radical humanist (subjective, radical change); and radical structuralist (objective, radical change). These four paradigms are another potential starting point for FSQs.

As a researcher, an understanding not only of these questions, but also which questions drive what I am most interested in, are helpful in many ways. In particular, they serve as my divining rod for noticing particular problems in the world (and likely overlooking others), choosing particular research questions and theories, and choosing contexts. For example, during graduate school, when it came the time to pick a dissertation topic, I was stuck. To help me get unstuck, I looked at all of the projects I had worked on in graduate school. Because I was in an organizational psychology program, I was not well paid and often had to work multiple teaching and research assistantships to make ends meet. The end result is that I worked on many projects, some of which I would not have chosen for myself. However, I did enjoy something about every project in which I participated. When I looked back on them all, I found I was really interested in how organizations are often governed by competing beliefs and ideas, yet they depended on the buy in of their people to function. This was true in research I did in group home workers, librarians, and visionary CEOs. Thus, this seemed like a fundamental problem that organizations had to address. With this general idea in mind, I was receptive to my sister's discussion of this new organization she joined called Amway, as it seemed to involve very contradictory beliefs, such as "put God and family before business" and "it is okay to miss your kid's birthday to build the business," yet somehow it evoked very strong and passionate attachment among its members.

Fundamental social questions can also provide some continuity or threads across projects. In my own research, I have looked at numerous theories such as identity, ambivalence, sensemaking, commitment, symbolism, and image (and more), but most of the time, they are in the service of understanding how individuals relate to the collectives with whom they belong or affiliate. In addition, I find that when my research is grounded in a fundamental social question, then it has resonance with my larger audience. Such connections with readers are particularly useful to me because my research contexts tend to be nontraditional (e.g., Amway, librarians, firefighters), and my goal is often to build rather than test theory. To unpack the connection among FSQs, nontraditional contexts, and theory building, I want to briefly segue to the challenge of inductive research in terms of being interesting (and not "too interesting"). One of Davis's (1971) core claims for interesting research is that it both affirms and denies the audience's assumptions. Theory building, by its very nature, challenges what we know. Moreover, nontraditional contexts are often viewed as weird (Bamberger & Pratt, 2010). Thus, the challenge is to also have points of affirmation with your reader, and not just have new and weird stuff that may be viewed as denying or being too different from what the audience knows. By grounding such research in fundamental social questions, new knowledge and new contexts become embedded in familiar territory (i.e., "old" questions). In sum, when asked about what makes for good qualitative research questions and contexts, I nearly always say "those that take a fundamental social question and provide a modern spin."

To Close (by Returning to Where I Started)

I want to close by returning to the three epigraphs that start the chapter and view them in light of what I have written. Plato has it right in that I don't think you can have interesting or cool research without a good start to the research project. What I have tried to show here is that research can start with a question, a problem in the world, with theoretical understanding or a context, but at some point these need to be knitted together. In other words, there are different paths that eventually travel similar territory. Camus's observation suggests that, unlike a linear understanding of research with questions leading to research contexts, sometimes we start on the street corner and move our way in. His reminder about ridiculous beginnings, if nothing else, suggests that even though the selection of research questions and contexts in a published piece looks pretty polished, the process itself was likely pretty messy and possibly even absurd at times. (And if we followed Anteby's lead, perhaps we should be more open to talk about this messiness.) Finally, Eliot's insight reminds me of what an iterative process this all is. Choosing the question or context or theory is not the end of these choices. Yes, we hopefully build from our initial choices, but we often don't end with them. If we take grounded theory seriously, we tweak our research questions and explore different places in our research contexts throughout the implementation of our study and analysis of our data. Amway distributors had a similar philosophy about not getting stuck on endings. As one distributor, Diamond, said at an Amway rally, "keep climbing, never reach your peak!" Perhaps for us, this reminds us that research is never truly done. It just gets published.

References

Anteby, M. (2012). Relaxing the taboo on telling our own stories: Upholding professional distance and personal involvement. *Organization Science* 24(4): 1277–1290.

Bamberger, P., & Pratt, M. G. (2010). From the editors: Moving forward by looking back: Reclaiming unconventional research contexts and samples in organizational scholarship. *Academy of Management Journal, 53*, 655–671.

Burrell, G., & Morgan, G. (1979). *Sociological paradigms and organisational analysis* (pp. 21–37). Corbin, J., & Strauss, A. (2008). *Basics of qualitative research* (3 ed.). Thousand Oaks, CA: Sage.

Creswell, J. W. (1998). Qualitative inquiry and research design: Choosing among five designs. Thousand Oaks, CA: Sage.

Davis, M. S. (1971). That's interesting. *Philosophy of the social sciences, 1*(2), 309.

Edmondson, A. C., & McManus, S. E. (2007). Methodological fit in management field research. *Academy of Management Review, 32*, 1155–1179.

Geertz, C. (1989). *Works and lives: The anthropologist as author.* Stanford, CA: Stanford University Press.

Golden-Biddle, K., & Locke, K. (2007). *Composing qualitative research.* Thousand Oaks, CA: Sage.

Miles, M. B., & Huberman, A. M. (1994). *Qualitative data analysis: An expanded sourcebook.* Thousand Oaks, CA: Sage.

Pratt, M. G. (2000a). The good, the bad, and the ambivalent: Managing identification among Amway distributors. *Administrative Science Quarterly, 45*(3), 456–493.

Pratt, M. G. (2000b). Building an ideological fortress: The role of spirituality, encapsulation, and sensemaking. *Studies in Cultures Organizations and Societies, 6*(1), 35–69.

Pratt, M. G. (2008). Fitting oval pegs into round holes: Tensions in evaluating and publishing qualitative research in top-tier North American journals. *Organizational Research Methods, 11*, 481–509.

Pratt, M. G. (2009). From the editors: For the lack of a boilerplate—Tips on writing up (and reviewing) qualitative research. *Academy of Management Journal, 52*, 856–862.

Pratt, M. G., & Rafaeli, A. (1997). Organizational dress as a symbol of multilayered social identities. *Academy of Management Journal, 40*(4), 862–898.

Spradley, J. (1979). *The ethnographic interview.* New York, NY: Holt, Rinehart & Winston.

Strauss, A., & Corbin, J. (1998). *Basics of qualitative research* (2nd ed.). Thousand Oaks, CA: Sage.

Van Maanen, 1988. *On writing ethnography.* Chicago: University of Chicago Press.

Vough, H., Cardador, T., Bednar, J., Dane, E., & Pratt, M. G. (2013). What clients don't get about my profession: A model of perceived role-based image discrepancies. *Academy of Management Journal, 56*(4), 1050–1080.

18

A Practice Approach to the Study of Social Networks

Maria Christina Binz-Scharf

Introduction

Work in organizations is increasingly accomplished through a complex system of formal and informal relationships. Research has emphasized the role of networks in connecting workers and spanning the occupational boundaries and different mental models that divide them (Brass, Galaskiewicz, Greve, & Tsai, 2004; Tichy, 1981). Organizations can improve creativity, innovation, and their effectiveness by establishing broader networks among their members and creating deeper ties within their work teams (e.g., Burt, 1992; Tsai, 2002). An impressive body of literature has examined organizational networks, establishing the relational view of the organization (Gittell & Douglass, 2012; Powell, 1990) as the "new normal." This research has demonstrated the important role that networks play in the workplace, for example, as a vehicle to speed up knowledge exchange, increase the efficiency of work, and foster serendipitous communication about work-related topics, adding to and interplaying with the formal communication and reporting structure (Cummings, 2004; Hansen, 1999, 2002; Knoke & Burt, 1983; Krackhardt & Stern, 1988; Tichy & Fombrun, 1979).

With few exceptions, however, extant research on social networks has focused on network structures (Ghosh & Rosenkopf, in press), treating networks as something that people *have*. The goal of this chapter is to introduce the study of networks and networking in organizations from a practice perspective that defines organizational networks as something that people *do*, rather than have. The practice view of organizations suggests that structures of meanings, rules and, norms do not have an independent effect on people's everyday work (Orlikowski, 2002). Instead, structures are produced and reproduced in practice as individuals in organizations adopt, adapt, and improvise them to address their everyday challenges at work. This promising approach to organizational phenomena has mostly been applied to prescribed processes and prescribed ties of authority and cooperation in organizations. Through the interpretation of the norms and meanings that flow through informal ties, a practice perspective of organizational networks sheds light on how individuals build, maintain, and use networks in their work practices (Binz-Scharf, Vieira da Cunha, & Vaast, 2013).

This perspective also addresses the need to understand the changed nature of contemporary work, which is shaped by technology, complexity of knowledge and organization, and globalization (Barley & Kunda, 2001; Okhuysen et al., 2013). Okhuysen and colleagues highlight the importance of including interpretations of relational practices in the study of work, as well as of adapting our analytical tools to the new nature of work. So while collaborative work has traditionally been studied through the lenses of groups and teams, whose characteristics include membership stability, boundedness, and full-time participation, we need to loosen these constraints as we focus on the actual practices of contemporary work (Okhuysen et al., 2013).

The core idea of a practice approach to the study of social networks is thus to examine through a relational lens how individuals accomplish work. This relational view of work is based on the premise that individuals are inherently social and rely on their interactions with others to validate their own assumptions and beliefs (Gittell & Douglass, 2012). Rather than following prescribed ties of authority, such as business units and teams, the researcher goes on a journey to discover the complex networks that emerge from individuals' work practices. As such, a practice approach is necessarily inductive and interpretive, at least at the outset. This approach differs substantially from traditional social network analysis, which has become a domain for quantitative research. Using interpretive methods requires a conceptual shift from focusing on structures to focusing on relations (ties) and their content. How do an individual's work practices involve others? When and why? What goes on in these relationships? Answers to these questions will provide rich data from which to theorize, giving valuable insight into emerging network structures. A practice approach can (and should!) also be the first step in quantitative network studies, where the emergent networks identified in the fieldwork provide the basis for the collection and analysis of sociometric data.[1]

The remainder of this chapter is structured as follows: I provide a brief background on social network analysis, making a case for the application of qualitative approaches in a predominantly quantitative domain. Based on a review of qualitative network studies, I then outline the practice approach for the study of networks. I conclude with suggestions for employing this approach in future research.

Background: Social Network Analysis

The study of social networks, originally grounded in sociology and anthropology, has spread across many disciplines, ranging from economics to physics and everything in between. Increasingly using the mathematically and statistically rigorous methods of social network analysis (Wasserman & Faust, 1994), social network studies have taken the academic world by storm. In the fields of organization and management, out of roughly 11,000 articles published in the leading journals over the past decade, around 1,200, or over 1 in 10, have been on social networks.[2]

It is hardly surprising that most research on social networks focuses on network structure, as structure is one of the fundamental tenets of social network analysis (Borgatti, Mehra, Brass, & Labianca, 2009). Social network analysis (SNA) operationalizes structures as networks of relationships, or ties, between actors, where patterns of interaction give rise to structures (Wasserman & Faust, 1994). As a matter of fact, one of the early contributions of SNA was the application of mathematical graph theory to the study of social networks, which allowed researchers to characterize the structure of a network in terms of actor positions and properties, as well as the distribution of ties (Borgatti et al., 2009). Based on these structural properties, social network researchers have studied the impact of network structures on actors' behaviors and outcomes, generally employing probabilistic models. The establishment of social network research as a quantitative domain has been aided by the increasing availability of massive network datasets and of ever more sophisticated mathematical and statistical solutions to the nontrivial problem of analyzing relational data (Lazer et al., 2009).

While extant social network research has provided a wealth of insight into network outcomes, and, to a lesser extent, network antecedents (Borgatti et al., 2009), it tends to neglect the malleable content that flows through network ties. Recent calls to action by organizational network researchers have advocated for a shift of attention away from broader structural views of networks and toward tie content, as well as factors that contribute to tie formation, maintenance, and dissolution (Ahuja, Soda, & Zaheer, 2012; Ghosh & Rosenkopf, in press). Qualitative approaches can add new and important dimensions to the study of networks in these domains (Hollstein, 2011). For example, they can illuminate agency behavior (Emirbayer & Mische, 1998), which in turn helps explain network dynamics (Ahuja et al., 2012). A practice approach to the study of social networks, in particular, can address the criticism of conventional SNA as seeing "the world in terms of durable relational structures in which a connection between two individuals is rendered more or less probable by the encompassing configuration of ties" (Gibson, 2005) by treating structures as fluid, produced and reproduced in practice as individuals adopt, adapt, and improvise them in their quest to accomplish work. The following section details this approach.

Using a Practice Approach to Study Social Networks

The concept of practice has a rich tradition in the social sciences and has gained substantial traction in organizational studies in recent years. Practice can be described as "what is actually done in the doing of work" (Orr, 1996: 439). A focus on practice challenges the researcher to transcend traditional levels of analysis in order to understand what it is that people do (Miettinen, Samra-Fredericks, & Yanow, 2009). Thus, practices might involve elements of individual action, organizational routines, and the institutions in which they are embedded. To study practices, the researcher needs to zoom back and forth between individual and collective levels of analysis (Ibarra, Kilduff, & Tsai, 2005) and zoom in and out of theoretical lenses (Nicolini, 2009). To illustrate how a practice approach can be applied to the study of social networks, I draw on the few purely qualitative network studies that have been conducted in the fields of management and organizations and several more mixed-methods articles.[3] Table 18.1 gives an overview of studies that have used a relational practice approach, summarizing the research context, how the approach was used, and how it affected each study's outcomes.

Based on these studies and research on work practices, I provide guidelines on formulating initial questions, exploring relational practices, understanding emergent networks, and validating and refining theories. Figure 18.1 summarizes this approach.

Table 18.1 Examples of Projects Using a Relational Practice Approach

Reference	Research Context	How Innovation Was Used	Outcomes/Results of Innovation
Binz-Scharf, Lazer, & Mergel (2012)	Knowledge sharing of in-government crime labs	Focus on problem-solving practices and analysis of interaction dynamics	Traced an emergent network of practice and mechanisms that lead to or hinder tie formation
Binz-Scharf, Kalish, & Paik (2015)	Collaborative knowledge production in biology	Collaboration practices; lab ethnographies (zoom in), informed network analysis (zoom out)	Showed influence of social structure on collaborative practices
Lingo & O'Mahony (2010)	Knowledge integration in music industry	Exploration of relational practices over time (duration of project)	Process model of collective creativity; showed how creative ideas are put into practice
Tagliaventi & Mattarelli (2006)	Knowledge transfer between professions in health care	Focus on interactions, exploration of relational practices	Knowledge sharing as organizational citizenship behavior; operational proximity promotes sharing

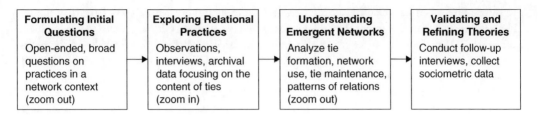

Figure 18.1 Using a Practice Approach to Study Social Networks

Formulating Initial Questions

Since the focus of this approach is on work practices from a relational view, there really are few limits to its application if we accept the premise that all practice is relational (Gergen, 2009). It is most useful in settings where network dynamics play an important role. Initial questions should combine the two elements of practice and networks. In his seminal paper on interfirm networks, Uzzi (1997) describes how he entered the field to examine management practices of garment firms, which led him to investigate the dynamics of network ties between firms. In our study of government DNA crime labs, we initially sought to understand the work practices of DNA forensic scientists, whose work is complex and subject to constant technological change (Binz-Scharf, Lazer, & Mergel, 2012). Since DNA forensic scientists are highly specialized and tend to have few peers within their lab, they reach out to peers in other labs. We therefore focused our investigation on this network among forensic scientists, asking how they search for answers to problems that arise on the job.

Sometimes the relational component is not clearly apparent at the beginning of a study. In his research on organizational caregiving, Kahn (1993) set out to study burnout of caregivers, based on the proposition that interactions with other organizational members might play a role in the primary caregivers' well-being. This proposition resulted from a review of literature on job burnout, which did not have a relational focus, and it prompted Kahn to investigate the "networks of caregiving relations among organization members" (Kahn, 1993: 541) and their effects on caregiver burnout. Similarly, Hargadon and Sutton (1997) began their investigation of technology brokering and innovation in the product design firm IDEO by asking how IDEO innovates routinely, and they came across the relational component, technology brokering, as they conducted the fieldwork.

As becomes evident from the previous examples, openness is an important characteristic of an initial question aiming at understanding relational practices, warranting an inductive approach. As neither practices nor networks have clear boundaries, the researcher should start out with a phenomenon or a context in mind from which to start the exploration of relational work practices, then let the fieldwork show the way.

Exploring Relational Practices

Departing from conventional social network analysis, the goal of a relational practice approach is to focus on dynamic practices rather than structural positions (Lingo & O'Mahony, 2010). In order to gain an in-depth understanding of relational work practices, situated field studies are the best choice. Ethnographies provide rich data from which to theorize and analyze network dynamics and tie content. However, full-fledged ethnographies are often impracticable because of the enormous time commitment. When this is the case, shorter periods of observation, combined with interviews and archival data, can be used to explore work practices through a relational lens.

While prescribed ties of authority, roles, and processes should not be the focus here, they should not be dismissed, either, because they shape work practices (Perlow, Gittell, & Katz, 2004). As such, they provide a useful context for the exploration of practices, and they can help kick off the fieldwork. A common strategy for ethnographic fieldwork among the studies reviewed here is to select a specific organizational unit, such as a department (Barley, 1990; Leonardi, 2007; Tagliaventi & Mattarelli, 2006) or a laboratory (Binz-Scharf, Kalish, & Paik, 2015), for observations and include all (formal) members in the study. Roles can also be used as an initial selection criterion for participants, and they ensure that a variety of characteristics (e.g., gender, geographical location, age, tenure) are represented. For their study on brokerage in the music industry, Lingo and O'Mahony (2010) chose participants by their professional role of independent music producers. Gersick, Bartunek, and Dutton (2000) selected female business school professors from a range of fields to study networking in professional life. However, as significant ties between workers are based on extra-role behavior, such as helping (Van Dyne & LePine, 1998), it is imperative to move beyond prescribed roles in order to fully understand relational practices. For example, Uzzi (1997) selected initial informants according to their role as CEOs of companies in the same industry and then proceeded to include other workers. In our own fieldwork, we initially focused on administrators of state DNA databases and later added participants whose prescribed role had surprisingly little to do with the task at hand, but who emerged as central players in the emergent network (Binz-Scharf et al., 2012).

As is customary in inductive research, the first interviews and observations serve to explore the field, to get a sense of how work is done, and the researcher should be as open-minded as possible in this initial phase (Glaser & Strauss, 1967). A focus on practice helps overcome a major problem in survey-based SNA: By focusing on what people do instead of what they say they do or whom they interact with, the problem of biased self-reports on interactions (Krackhardt, 1987) and perceived position (Burt, 1982) is minimized. Kahn (1993), for example, focused on the practice of caregiving, concentrating on interactions between members of the organization and the flows and content of interactions. A useful tool is to map out practices as processes or flow charts to give a general idea of how "things get done around here" (Deal & Kennedy 1982: 4) and to provide a baseline for the interpretation of network dynamics as they unfold. Nice examples can be found in Uzzi's paper on interfirm networks (1997: 40) and in Tagliaventi and Mattarelli's paper on networks of practice in healthcare (2006: 297).

Once the researcher has a general grasp of the workflows and their contexts, he or she can begin to zoom into relational practices. In our study on collaborative knowledge production in biology, we paid particular attention to instances in which individuals connected or interacted with, or repeatedly mentioned, other individuals (Binz-Scharf et al., 2015). Lingo and O'Mahony focused on observing the interactions of a subset of producers with individuals they had identified during their initial interviews as "resource gatekeepers" (2010: 53). Tagliaventi and Mattarelli (2006) recorded every interaction between doctors, nurses, radiologists, and technicians they observed during their 6-month ethnography. In each of these studies, the researchers clarified interactions with participants after each day of observation.

Interviews can also be used to explore relational practices, but the temptation to ask directly for ties should be resisted. As with observations, the focus should be on practices. In their study on the professional networks of academics, Gersick and colleagues (2000) asked participants what relationships they perceived as important, and why, instead of asking for names of individuals they go to for advice. Interviewees then were asked to tell anecdotes about the two relationships they deemed most important. Similarly, Bensaou, Galunic, and Jonczyk-Sedes (2014) anchored their interviews about professional networking strategies in concrete events, which they extracted from participants' narratives of the past year's personal and professional highlights. Finally, in our study of DNA forensic scientists, we asked participants to recall several situations where they encountered a problem at work and to describe how they solved it (Binz-Scharf et al., 2012).

Understanding Emergent Networks

As data collection progresses and themes emerge, the researcher once again zooms out to analyze relational patterns. This is a unique opportunity to understand the relational dynamics that remain generally unknown to researchers applying purely quantitative approaches: How and why do individuals create, use, maintain, and dissolve ties as they accomplish work? How are these patterns shaped by practices, and how do they change over time? Lingo and O'Mahony (2010) show how the networks of producers change as their projects move in phases from conception to production, where each phase is characterized by different sets of practices. In one of these practices, "fostering a generative network" (2010: 61), producers aim at maintaining ties with resource gatekeepers so as to have access to their resources in future projects. This is an important finding in terms of network dynamics, and it would most probably not have emerged from the analysis of sociometric data.

Qualitatively derived relational dynamics also give deeper meaning to tie properties, such as the strength of ties. In SNA, tie strength is usually measured in terms of frequency of contact, closeness (emotional intensity), or duration (Marsden & Campbell, 1984), making it a static concept. However, ties, and their strength, evolve and change over time. Jack (2005) explored the networking activities of entrepreneurs, focusing on how ties are activated and used. The author found that the strength of a tie was based on the type of information provided, the usefulness and applicability of the relationship to the entrepreneurial situation at a particular point in time, and the extent to which respondents were prepared to trust the information provided. While enterprise agencies increasingly encourage networking, this study shows that networking involves a social process that takes place over time.

Another area where conventional SNA is lacking is in explaining the absence of a tie. A relational practice approach can contribute understanding in this realm. In our study of DNA forensic scientists, we found that some participants had reputational concerns that kept them from reaching out to experts in the system who would likely be able to solve their problems. That missing tie would have misrepresented the status of the expert, as measured by in-degree centrality (the relative number of ties directed at one actor). Yet, the absence of that tie in itself is important data, and it can only be understood in the light of the background knowledge on reputational concerns.

Validating and Refining Theories

To check the validity of the theory, the researcher can either conduct follow-up interviews with participants or collect network data. Network data can also be retrieved from field notes, which has the advantage that the data are not self-reported. Tagliaventi and Mattarelli (2006) followed that procedure, recording and coding all interactions they observed. They then defined clusters of interactions according to practices they had identified and even calculated the number of hours participants had spent in the same room. In several studies, network surveys were distributed to participants to verify the consistency of the observed networks with the perceived networks (e.g., Barley, 1990; Leonardi, 2007). In our study on collaborations in biology, we collected co-authorship data from conference programs and analyzed the resulting co-author networks based on our findings from the fieldwork (Binz-Scharf et al., 2015). One observation we made by comparing the results from the network analysis with our field notes illustrates the importance of gaining an in-depth understanding of practices in the study of social networks: We had shadowed the labs of two principal investigators who had been postdoctoral fellows in the same lab several years back, during which time they co-authored a number of publications. They stayed in touch over the years, meeting at conferences and discussing ideas, and they finally co-authored a paper after almost two decades. By just looking at the network data, these two actors had a weak tie (measured in frequency of co-authorship), yet we knew from our fieldwork that they had a profound influence on each other over the years.

Conclusions

While contemporary work is increasingly network based, surprisingly few studies have examined work practices from a relational view. In this chapter, I have proposed a relational practice approach to the study of social networks, which both integrates and extends the fairly separate literatures on practices and networks. A focus on practice forces the researcher to zoom in and out of micro and macro levels of analysis in order to gain an in-depth understanding of tie content and network dynamics. Understanding people's relational practices in the workplace will lead to new theorizing about work as we continue to move toward more fluid organizational forms.

This is a chapter in a book on qualitative methods, and the approach I have outlined is inductive and interpretive. Yet, a practice approach could also be employed in quantitative network studies, ideally prior to the collection and analysis of network data, so as to be guided by the emerging relational practices identified in the fieldwork. If that is impracticable, even fieldwork following a quantitative study will prove beneficial. David Krackhardt's (1992) study on unionization is an excellent case in point. Especially with the rise in big data, it is important to zoom in and out of levels of analysis. An understanding of relational practices adds tremendous value to the study of social networks.

Notes

1 The collection and analysis of sociometric data are beyond the scope of this chapter and will not be discussed here.
2 Journals included in this count are *Academy of Management Journal*; *Academy of Management Review*; *Administrative Science Quarterly*; *American Journal of Sociology*; *American Sociological Review*; *Human Relations*; *Journal of Management*; *Journal of Management Studies*, *Management Science*, *Organization Science*, *Organization Studies*, *Organizational Behavior and Human Decision Processes*; and *Strategic Management Journal*. According to ISI Web of Science, a total of 11,068 articles were published in these journals between 2004 and 2014. Among these, 1,219 articles (11%) included the keyword "network."
3 A search for articles on networks in leading organizational journals (see footnote 2) resulted in 61 papers using some form of qualitative data. Of these, 16 were purely qualitative.

References

Ahuja, G., Soda, G., & Zaheer, A. (2012). Introduction to the special issue: The genesis and dynamics of organizational networks. *Organization Science, 23*, 434–448.

Barley, S.R. (1990). The alignment of technology and structure through roles and networks. *Administrative Science Quarterly, 35*, 61–103.

Barley, S.R., & Kunda, G. (2001). Bringing work back in. *Organization Science, 12*, 76–95.

Bensaou, B.M., Galunic, C., & Jonczyk-Sedes, C. (2014). Players and purists: Networking strategies and agency of service professionals. *Organization Science, 25*, 29–56.

Binz-Scharf, M.C., Kalish, Y., & Paik, L. (2015). Making science: New generations of collaborative knowledge production. *American Behavioral Scientist, 59*(5):531–547.

Binz-Scharf, M.C., Lazer, D., & Mergel, I. (2012). Searching for answers: Networks of practice among public administrators. *American Review of Public Administration, 41*, 202–225.

Binz-Scharf, M.C., Vieira da Cunha, J., & Vaast, E. (2013). *Living the network: Practices of connecting and bridging at work*. Introduction to Subtheme 49, 29th EGOS Colloquium, Montreal.

Borgatti, S.P., Mehra, A., Brass, D.J., & Labianca, G. (2009). Network analysis in the social sciences. *Science, 323*, 892–895.

Brass, D.J., Galaskiewicz, J., Greve, H.R., & Tsai, W. (2004). Taking stock of networks and organizations: A multilevel perspective. *Academy of Management Review, 47*, 795–817.

Burt, R.S. (1982). *Toward a structural theory of action: Network models of social structure, perception, and action*. New York, NY: Academic Press.

Burt, R.S. (1992). *Structural holes: The social structure of competition*. Cambridge, MA: Harvard University Press.

Cummings, J.N. (2004). Works groups, structural diversity, and knowledge sharing in a global organization. *Management Science, 50*, 352–364.

Deal, T. E., & Kennedy, A. A. (1982). *Corporate Cultures: The Rites and Rituals of Corporate Life*. Harmondsworth: Penguin Books.

Emirbayer, M., & Mische, A. (1998). What is agency? *American Journal of Sociology, 103*, 962–1023.

Gergen, K.J. (2009). *Relational being: Beyond self and community*. New York: Oxford University Press.

Gersick, C.J.G., Bartunek, J.M., & Dutton, J.E. (2000). Learning from academia: The importance of relationships in professional life. *Academy of Management Journal, 43*, 1026–1044.

Ghosh, A., & Rosenkopf, L. (in press). Shrouded in structure: Challenges and opportunities for a friction-based view of network research. *Organization Science*.

Gibson, D.R. (2005). Taking turns and talking ties: Networks and conversational interaction. *American Journal of Sociology, 110*, 1561–1597.

Gittell, J.H., & Douglass, A. (2012). Relational bureaucracy: Structuring reciprocal relationships into roles. *Academy of Management Review, 37*, 709–754.

Glaser, B.G., & Strauss, A.L. (1967). *The discovery of grounded theory: Strategies for qualitative research*. Piscataway, NJ: Aldine Transaction.

Hansen, M.T. (1999). The search-transfer problem: The role of weak ties in sharing knowledge across organization subunits. *Administrative Science Quarterly, 44*, 82–111.

Hansen, M.T. (2002). Knowledge networks: Explaining effective knowledge sharing in multiunit companies. *Organization Science, 13*, 232–248.

Hargadon, A., & Sutton, R.I. (1997). Technology brokering and innovation in a product development firm. *Administrative Science Quarterly, 42*, 716–749.

Hollstein, B. (2011). Qualitative approaches. In J. Scott & P.J. Carrington (Eds.), *Sage handbook of social network analysis* (pp. 404–417). London, England: Sage.

Ibarra, H., Kilduff, M., & Tsai, W. (2005). Zooming in and out: Connecting individuals and collectivities at the frontiers of organizational network research. *Organization Science, 16*, 359–371.

Jack, S.L. (2005). The role, use and activation of strong and weak network ties: A qualitative analysis. *Journal of Management Studies, 42*, 1233–1259.

Kahn, W.A. (1993). Caring for caregivers—patterns of organizational caregiving. *Administrative Science Quarterly, 38*, 539–563.

Knoke, D., & Burt, R.S. (1983). *Applied network analysis: A methodological introduction*. Los Angeles, CA: Sage.

Krackhardt, D. (1987). Cognitive social structures. *Social Networks, 9*, 109–134.

Krackhardt, D. (1992). The strength of strong ties: The importance of philos in organizations. In N. Nohria & R.G. Eccles (Eds.), *Networks and organizations: Structure, form, and action* (pp. 216–239). Boston, MA: Harvard Business School Press.

Krackhardt, D., & Stern, R. (1988). Informal networks and organizational crises: An experimental simulation. *Social Psychology Quarterly, 51*, 123–140.

Lazer, D., Pentland, A., Adamic, L., Aral, S., Barabasi, A.L., Brewer, D., et al. (2009). Computational social science. *Science, 323*, 721–723.

Leonardi, P. M. (2007). Activating the informational capabilities of information technology for organizational change. *Organization Science, 18*, 813–831.

Lingo, E.L., & O'Mahony, S. (2010). Nexus work: Brokerage on creative projects. *Administrative Science Quarterly, 55*, 47–81.

Marsden, P.V., & Campbell, K.E. (1984). Measuring tie strength. *Social Forces, 63*, 482–501.

Miettinen, R., Samra-Fredericks, D., & Yanow, D. (2009). Re-turn to practice: An introductory essay. *Organization Studies, 30*, 1309–1327.

Nicolini, D. (2009). Zooming in and out: Studying practices by switching theoretical lenses and trailing connections. *Organization Studies, 30*, 1391–1418.

Okhuysen, G.A., Lepak, D., Ashcraft, K.L., Labianca, G., Smith, V., & Steensma, K.H. (2013). Theories of work and working today. *Academy of Management Review, 38*, 491–502.

Orlikowski, W.J. (2002). Knowing in practice: Enacting a collective capability in distributed organizing. *Organization Science, 13*, 249–273.

Orr, J. (1996). *Talking about machines: An ethnography of a modern job*. Ithaca, NY: Cornell University Press.

Perlow, L.A., Gittell, J.H., & Katz, N. (2004). Contextualizing patterns of work group interaction: Toward a nested theory of structuration. *Organization Science, 15*, 520–536.

Powell, W.W. (1990). Neither market nor hierarchy—network forms of organization. *Research in Organizational Behavior, 12*, 295–336.

Tagliaventi, M.R., & Mattarelli, E. (2006). The role of networks of practice, value sharing, and operational proximity in knowledge flows between professional groups. *Human Relations, 59*, 291–319.

Tichy, N.M. (1981). Networks in organizations. In P.C. Nystrom & W.H. Starbuck (Eds.), *Handbook of organizational design* (pp. 225–249). New York, NY: Oxford University Press.

Tichy, N.M., & Fombrun, C. (1979). Network analysis in organizational settings. *Human Relations, 32*, 923–965.

Tsai, W. (2002). Social structure of "coopetition" within a multiunit organization: Coordination, competition, and intraorganizational knowledge sharing. *Organization Science, 13*, 179–190.

Uzzi, B. (1997). Social structure and competition in interfirm networks: The paradox of embeddedness. *Administrative Science Quarterly, 42*, 35–67.

Van Dyne, L., & LePine, J.A. (1998). Helping and voice extra-role behaviors: Evidence of construct and predictive validity. *Academy of Management Journal, 41*, 108–119.

Wasserman, S., & Faust, K. (1994). *Social network analysis*. Cambridge, UK: Cambridge University Press.

Part IV
Unique Forms of Qualitative Data

Denials, Obstructions, and Silences

Lessons from Repertoires of
Field Resistance (and Embrace)

Michel Anteby

Introduction

What do factory craftsmen, clinical anatomists, and business school professors have in common? Not too much, you might think, but think again. All these individuals share the ability to exhibit resistance when faced with a field inquiry into their working lives. And how can we not understand them? Few people really want to be studied—let alone by a field researcher like myself, claiming to follow an inductive research approach that might lead me to become intrigued by aspects of their lives that they do not get (ex-ante) to pick or might not want (ex-post) to discuss. Field resistance under such circumstances is understandable given that many scholars seek to "infiltrate" rather than access a field (Douglas, 1976, p. 167). By *field resistance*, I mean any reaction that field participants collectively deploy to resist a research inquiry into their social worlds. My main argument is that we can also learn a lot from capturing, analyzing, and qualifying field resistance.

Forms of field resistance teach us as much about a given field's tensions as other more traditional data sources (such as archives, interviews, observations, and surveys). For instance, moments when a field researcher is being denied access to a field call for reflexive analysis (Emerson, Fretz, & Shaw, 1995). As Gary Alan Fine reminds us when discussing the art of field research, "the limits of the art are also part of the data" (1993, p. 289). I will illustrate this point with three examples taken from field projects I conducted involving, respectively, factory craftsmen, clinical anatomists, and business school professors, and then I will broaden the scope of my argument by detailing instances of field resistance in other scholars' works (involving sex workers and couples in transition) to showcase the analytical power of such resistance. Finally, I will argue that a similar logic can apply to the "opposite" of field resistance, namely field embrace, and I will review two examples of field embrace (involving urban poor and former Ku Klux Klan members) to illustrate my point. Before doing so, however, I would like to take a small detour via the crop world to jumpstart our discussion.

Resistance is common in many of our field pursuits: Scholars trying to penetrate new social worlds or to make sense of unchartered terrains often approach field participants to gain a better understanding of the field. Not all participants welcome such an inquiry. And even if they do, they tend to resist (consciously or not) some parts of the investigation. As field scholars, we invariably encounter overt and covert resistance. Yet the term *field resistance* barely registers throughout the social sciences. (A Web of Science search conducted in 2015 on the topic of "field resistance" yielded

1,449 hits in science versus only 8 in social sciences.) Other scientific domains, by contrast, treat field resistance with much more depth and interest. Indeed, the term is widely used, for instance in physics and agronomy. I will focus here on agronomy.

In the context of agronomy, field resistance refers to a species' ability to resist threats such as pests, disease, or suboptimal environmental conditions. When faced with field intrusions, crops react in many strange, yet telling ways. An article from the *Annals of Botany* notes that crops' responses to field intrusion are "complex," but also involve "adaptive changes" that can be "modified by the superimposition of other stresses" (Chaves et al., 2002, p. 907). That last insight matters a lot for my argument. Put otherwise, the article's authors suggest that a crop's response to a given stress depends, in part, on other stress factors it faces. This has important implications for organizational scholars. Let me explain.

In the crop world, an outside stress can, for instance, be the intrusion of a new organism into a corn field. Corn can modify its shoot ratio or the accumulation of reserves in its stem in reaction to the intrusion. But corn can also grow longer husks. Also, the photosynthetic process in its leaves can be modified. In brief, the corn's responses vary widely and they all depend on other important, often evolving, "stress factors" that the crop is experiencing, such as high temperatures or insufficient water. We can translate this insight from agronomy to social sciences.

A field researcher conducting an inquiry generally constitutes an intrusion into a field and often induces some kind of disturbance. Field participants' resistance is in part conditioned by other stress factors they face. These factors, I would argue, are key field tensions: exactly the ones that inductive researchers want to uncover. Forms of resistance and their evolution therefore echo the drama of participants' daily lives. For instance, how field participants silently run you out of town or insult you to your face matters because their reactions say as much about them as about you. I learned this first-hand when studying factory craftsmen, clinical anatomists, and business school professors. The often varied and changing forms of field resistance constitute invaluable data points for field inquiries.

Evidence of Field Resistance

Factory Craftsmen's Denials

My first encounter with resistance unsurprisingly started with my first field inquiry. The research project's site was a French aeronautics plant in which craftsmen produced on the side, but on company time and with company materials, illegal artifacts (known as "homers"), such as toys for their kids, cutlery for their kitchens, or window frames for their homes (Anteby, 2008a, 2008b). As part of my research design, I conducted a survey of retirement gifts since I knew many of these artifacts were given to retirees upon their departure. The survey yielded intriguing findings, most significantly by showing that certain plant employees (namely, craftsmen) were more likely than other employees (e.g., supervisors and unskilled labor) to receive a homer as a retirement gift. One survey reply, however, froze me for days.

The anonymous respondent who identified as a craftsmen wrote directly on the survey sheet, "C'est pas beau de demander de dénoncer mes petits copains. T'es un enculé." ("It isn't nice to ask me to rat on my friends. You're a bastard."). I recall reading his reply and being quite distraught, thinking that he might be right and that I had no business meddling into their lives and affairs. (That some others had refused to meet me did not bode well.) A few weeks later, I was scheduled to interview another plant craftsman in a small-town café, sufficiently far from the main plant to give us some privacy. Upon arrival, he asked to see my ID before agreeing to talk. (All French citizens are required to carry a national identification card.) In both cases, these craftsmen's reactions were alerting me that some people might view them as thieves. They were articulating a key field tension I would only later discover, that is, the craft/theft dichotomy so central to their occupational identity.

Since homer-making was done only with scrap materials and always after completing official jobs, craftsmen never saw themselves as thieves. Yet management sometimes tried to leverage that perception to keep them in check. Thus, denying being a thief proved crucial to the craftsmen's identities. The field's main form of resistance—participants' denials that they were thieves after suggesting that I could "rat on" them to managers—embodied their key concern and provided invaluable data points into their own world.

Clinical Anatomists' Obstructions

My second encounter with field resistance occurred in a very different setting: whole-body donations programs in New York State. The clinical anatomist I met and interviewed in these programs resisted in a very different way. The project looked at the commerce in human cadavers for medical education, and clinical anatomists were often the ones entrusted with obtaining cadavers to supply anatomy classes and other medical research needs (Anteby, 2010). Increasingly, however, independent ventures were offering similar services, and the anatomists could have resisted by telling me that they were not "thieves" like the "body-brokers" (a pejorative term they used to characterize ventures) who were encroaching on their jurisdiction. That is not, however, how anatomists resisted. Instead, they tried to obstruct access to the field.

Anatomists tried to physically prevent me from accessing their field. After attending a first meeting of New York State anatomists, I was barred from returning to subsequent ones. Also, when visiting donation programs, I was often offered a small desk in a separate room—outside the program's perimeter. Interestingly, the anatomists' form of resistance against the inquiry (i.e., preventing physical intrusion) was similar to the one they deployed against independent ventures. Though anatomists mainly tried to distinguish themselves from ventures via contrasted work practices (e.g., refusing to dissect a cadaver prior to use, while ventures often did so upon receipt of the cadaver and then distributed parts to multiple users), their initial line of defense was to physically seal the state borders from out-of-state cadavers (generally procured by ventures). Again, their form of field resistance echoed the drama of their daily lives: a deeply rooted need to distinguish themselves from the "unethical" trade in cadavers promoted by independent ventures. The repeated attempts to obstruct field access ended up being a very telling data point to illuminate clinical anatomists' lives.

Business School Professors' Silences

My third encounter with field resistance occurred much closer to home, in the institution that employed me at the time. The project was an ethnography of faculty socialization at the Harvard Business School, and it was built on historical research suggesting that some elite U.S. business schools were created with an imperative to moralize business conduct (Abend, 2013; Khurana, 2007). Assuming such an imperative still existed, the project asked how it might be transmitted to new faculty members (Anteby, 2013a). The study was an (auto)ethnography of life as a rookie faculty member in a setting with traces of a moral mission in its organizational DNA. The form of field resistance here initially proved harder to pinpoint.

At first, resistance was framed in ever-shifting academic terms, such as the pushback I got from colleagues that by studying my own field I contradicted Max Weber's notion of "axiological neutrality," or the expectation that a social scientist exclude personal bias when analyzing data (Weber, 2004, p. 22).[1] With time, however, another pattern of resistance emerged: one involving silences. For instance, when quizzing a senior colleague about his views of the project, I was once told it was too risky for me to pursue. Assuming I accepted the risk, I asked him, what was the next issue I should address? None, he replied. I pressed him to explain, but he did not elaborate. At first, I did not make much of such (silent) reactions and thought they simply illustrated the "self-protective secrecy of elites" (Katz, 1997, p. 402). But another discussion with four other colleagues on the study's progress made me pause: one participant barely uttered more than a word during the hour long collective discussion. I recall thinking, why attend an hour-long meeting in silence? I should have known better.

I gradually came to understand that such silences were part of the socializing process. In fact, they proved very guiding. By not articulating what was right or wrong, the burden of moral "discovery" falls on participants. Rediscovering morals in an apparent (silent) void proved to be the organization's goal. Field participants were enacting with me what I later described as "vocal silence"—the repeated opportunities in which agents are left to make decisions ostensibly alone, but in an organizational context rich with signs that offer guidance as to what might be preferred. Their form of resistance therefore captured the field's main socialization hope and tension. Silence was not anodyne; it entailed what was primarily at stake at the school: a deeply held belief in the possibility for silent "self-discovery" within limits set by the institution. Again, the field's form of resistance was extremely suggestive of its internal functioning.

A Wide and Telling Variety of Field Resistance

The forms of field resistance that I encountered until now ranged from denials to silences via obstructions, but a wide variety of forms of resistance likely exist across social inquiries. Unfortunately, very few scholars report them or treat forms of resistance as pertinent data points. (See Table 19.1 for examples of resistance.) A careful reading of select published studies can start to expand the list of forms of resistance. I will share two alternate forms of resistance I was able to identify in other scholars' published work: field disappearance and conditional interviewing consent. Both forms of resistance proved extremely helpful to the understanding of given fields' dynamics.

When Sudhir Venkatesh started to look into sex work in New York City in 1997, he tried to find a neighborhood where he could observe changes occurring in this industry. Yet each time he tried delving deeper into a neighborhood historically associated with prostitution (e.g., Times Square, Lower East Side), local residents would tell him "everyone moved" (Venkatesh, 2013b, p. 691). Repeatedly, field participants' resistance coalesced into a narrative of disappearance: people left, they relocated, and there's basically nothing here anymore. Venkatesh looked in vain for this "new place" where all these people had moved, but the field's form of resistance was also Venkatesh's main finding: The actual geography of prostitution had migrated off the streets, moved upscale, and often online. More specifically, the elite underground economy's geography was now intertwined with the elite professionals' geography (Venkatesh, 2013a). Being repeatedly told that the field had moved away was participants' way of signaling to him the evolving and radically new geography of their industry.

As the above example suggests, forms of resistance are idiosyncratic to given fields; they capture and tell unique stories. The resistance that Diane Vaughan encountered when studying turning points in partners' intimate relations illustrates this well (Vaughan, 1990). She interviewed more than a hundred people about how their relations started, unfolded, and often ended, though also how they sometimes reconnected with their partners. In the process, she asked interviewees if she could also speak to their (often former) partners; some consented, other refused. She noticed, however, patterns of consents and refusals. The interviewees' conditional consent depended in part on "the nature of their connection to their former partner" (1990, p. 206). People's willingness to consent depended on whether they had been able to construct separate identities. As Vaughan came to understand, "coupling changes us and so does uncoupling. But in most cases relationships don't end. They change, but they don't end. When both individuals develop an identity of their own, they're free to acknowledge the ties" (1990, p. 206). In that sense, an interviewee's resistance to have her interview a former partner could also be read as a data point about the current nature of the relation—whether the partners saw themselves as having separate identities or not. Thus, the form of resistance qualified the relations she studied.

Field Embrace as Alternate and Telling Data Points

It would be a shame, however, to restrict our focus only to forms of field resistance. Indeed, if the opposite of resistance is embrace, there might be also very good reasons to try to classify forms of embrace and treat them as pertinent data points. (See Table 19.1 for examples of embrace.) While a lot can be learned from field resistance, a lot can also be learned by analyzing field participants' enthusiastic embrace of a research inquiry. Indeed, when a researcher is warmly welcomed by participants, such an embrace might similarly reflect a key tension (and sometimes its resolution) for field participants. As with resistance, a better grasp of forms of embrace can help us gain a better understanding of a given field setting. The form of embrace—for example, whether a researcher is rapidly welcomed into the population studied or gently nudged into perhaps helping participants financially—is always telling. I will illustrate this through two examples.

When the (white female) Kathleen Blee interviewed women in the 1980s who had been part of the Ku Klux Klan, she was surprised by the ease with which she established rapport with them and how little remorse they expressed about their time in the Klan (Blee, 2009). Such a welcoming embrace echoed the one Klan members used to extend to all white Protestant women who grew up and lived around them when the Klan thrived. As Blee later discovered, during the 1920s, close to a quarter million people—or almost a third of the white native-born female population in Indiana (the setting of her research)—were members of the Women of the Ku Klux Klan (p. 125). Their welcome (also a form of embrace) was therefore *typical* of Klan members trying to enroll a vast number of women into their ranks. Blee's interviewees were as welcoming as the Klan had been. Thus, the form of field embrace was a powerful early data point in this inquiry.

By contrast, when Matthew Desmond studied the urban poor, he did not initially feel welcomed and his field access proved more difficult (Desmond, 2012b). Yet, some urban poor allowed him to follow them around for some periods of time. When he quizzed a person he was following about what she was thinking about, she answered matter-of-factly, "How I gonna feed my kids tonight" (Desmond,

Table 19.1 Use of Forms of Field Resistance (and Embrace*) in Qualitative Research

Reference	Research Context	How Innovation Was Used	Outcome of Innovation
Venkatesh (2013a, 2013b)	New York City's underground economy	Tracking a "disappearing" field led to analyze the shifting geography of the underground economy	Reconsider field sites as no longer physically or geographically bound
Vaughan (1990)	Couples in transition	Tracking an interviewee's consent or refusal to agree to his or her former partner being interviewed helped qualify the degree to which partners have developed separate identities	Recognizing that former social ties with intimate partners can only be acknowledged once these partners establish distinct identities
Blee (2009)*	Women members of the Ku Ku Klan in Indiana	The warm welcome extended by former KKK members to the researcher was indicative of the Klan's broad reach	Ability to document how common it was for women in certain communities to be members of the Klan
Desmond (2012a, 2012b)*	Urban poor in the United States	Being embraced by field participants as a person who might help and then never be seen again foreshadowed the notion of disposable ties	Ability to identify and discuss a previously overlooked category of social ties ("disposable ties")

Michel Anteby

2012a, p. 1307). Her answer was also a form of field embrace and exemplified how urban poor people often need to make do in their harsh living environments. She saw the researcher as a new acquaintance from whom all kinds of resources (including maybe financial ones) could possibly flow. By voicing a financial concern, she was also telling him how he might be able to help. That genuine and fleeting embrace was characteristic of the "disposable social ties" that Desmond later identified in his field, namely ties with strangers (not kin) lasting only for short bursts of time, but ties that helped immensely in difficult times. For this field participant, Desmond (like many others around her) was a disposable tie. Again, the form of field embrace was indicative of what the field setting would later reveal.

I should add that it is important to note that field embrace and resistance are not "all or nothing" situations; embrace and resistance can be deeply intertwined, leading to much more ambivalence than the previous idealized examples suggest. Both within and across interactions between scholars and field participants, the pendulum of resistance and embrace can swing quite easily. As an illustration, during a single interaction, a field participant may exhibit resistance for fear of being "rubricized" (Maslow, 1962), namely, rapidly put into a category that only captures part of her or his experience, yet also embrace the scholarly inquiry because of the hope of finally being understood in her or his full complexity. In these instances, the pendulum will prove hard to stabilize between resistance and embrace. In a similar manner, a field participant can welcome an inquiry during a first encounter, but subsequently exhibit lots of resistance because she or he suddenly realizes that too much has been said. Thus, an ambivalent stand should be acknowledged alongside pure resistance and pure embrace.

Conclusion

By showcasing forms of embrace after discussing forms of resistance, my point is to call for closer attention to capturing and qualifying all kinds of interactions between a scholar and the field, whether these inter-actions entail resistance, embrace, ambivalence, or any other reactions. We can only learn as much as fields teach us, but fields teach us a lot even when we don't think they do—for instance, in moments when we feel frustrated at being rejected by field participants or pleased at simply being accepted by them. The field's reaction to a scholar's intrusion can be viewed as a field-level "social defense" mechanism.[2] Such a mechanism is a collective arrangement—e.g., a prevalent discourse, a typical work practice, or a common form of resistance—created or used by organizational members as a protection against a disturbing affect derived from external threats, internal conflicts, or the nature of their work (Halton, 1994). Put otherwise, the social defense tries to assuage a key tension shared by field participants. For instance, a depersonalizing method of ward rotation and task allocation can help nurses in hospitals deal with the anxiety of working too closely with dying patients (Menzies, 1960). Thus, making sense of the social defense (here, depersonalization) amounts to making sense of the field's key tension (here, dealing with death).

To return to the *Annals of Botany* article that triggered the writing of this chapter: Corn's field resistance (and possible embrace) can teach us more than botanical lessons; it can also teach us lessons for our research craft. Examining corn's subtle, slow, and recurring forms of resistance (and embrace) can seem irrelevant, yet they matter both empirically and theoretically. By better capturing and listening to evolving forms of resistance (and embrace) alongside more traditional data, we learn a lot from our fields (see Figure 19.1). In doing so, we also clarify our position in the field (Pratt, 2009). Next time graduate students approach us with field dissertation ideas, instead of focusing on whether they already have access to the field and "how long" they have been in the field (Golden-Biddle & Locke, 1993, p. 601), we should ask them how their field resisted or embraced the research pursuit and push them to try to capture and qualify their field's reaction. In the same way that Charles Tilly and Sarah Soule have drawn our attention to "repertoires" of contention (Tilly, 2006; Wang & Soule, 2012), we need to envision repertoires of field resistance (and embrace) and better understand what they mean for our inquiries. By better capturing and listening to evolving forms of resistance (and embrace) alongside more traditional data, we learn a lot from our fields.

Figure 19.1 Combining Novel and Traditional Data Sources

Moreover, by discounting repertoires of resistance, embrace or ambivalence, we are closing our-selves off from lessons from the field. As an illustration, in Elton Mayo's analysis of the Hawthorne Studies conducted at the Western Electric Plant, workers' occasional resistance to being studied was mainly seen as added evidence for managers' need to pay more attention to their employees. But Mayo's discounting of some alternate analyses, particularly the ones by William Lloyd Warner, who designed the famous "bank wiring observation room" study, led him to miss some key tensions in the field. As John Van Maanen notes, "What Mayo never reckoned with—despite Warner's insistence that there was more to employees' discontent at Hawthorne than simply the way they were treated by their bosses—is that discord in organizations arises from structural and power inequalities as well" (2013, p. 107). The Hawthorne studies are silent about such inequalities.

When ignoring field resistance or embrace, we are not only discounting important data points, but also shutting ourselves off to ways in which field participants try to tell us what matters to them in their social worlds. Assuming our goal is to analyze these worlds, we are missing a lot by ignoring the complex yet telling ways in which field participants try to speak to us and shape the nature of our field inquiries.

Acknowledgments

I am grateful to Kim Elsbach, Patrick Fabry, Rod Kramer, Gianpiero Petriglieri, Mike Pratt, Susan Silbey, and John Van Maanen for their reactions to this chapter. I also thank for their feedback the participants at the 2013 MIT Field Research Conference, the 2013 European Theory Development Workshop hosted by HEC, and the ISA 2014 annual meeting.

Notes

1 To address the issue of axiological neutrality, I wrote a piece in defense of field distance *and* involvement (Anteby, 2013b).
2 The "social defense mechanism" concept builds on the psychoanalytic theories of individual defense mechanisms (i.e., operations used by individuals to reduce or eliminate threats to their integrity and stability), but assumes they also operate at the collective level. For more details, see Jacques (1955), Laplanche and Pontalis (1973, p. 109), Petriglieri and Petriglieri (2010, pp. 47–48), and Racamier (1970).

References

Abend, G. (2013). The origins of business ethics in American universities, 1902–1936. *Business Ethics Quarterly*, *23*, 171–205.
Anteby, M. (2008a). Identity incentives as an engaging form of control: Revisiting leniencies in an aeronautic plant. *Organization Science*, *19*, 202–220.
Anteby, M. (2008b). *Moral gray zones: Side productions, identity, and regulation in an aeronautic plant*. Princeton, NJ: Princeton University Press.
Anteby, M. (2010). Markets, morals, and practices of trade: Jurisdictional disputes in the U.S. commerce in cadavers. *Administrative Science Quarterly*, *55*, 606–638.
Anteby, M. (2013a). *Manufacturing morals: The values of silence in business school education*. Chicago, IL: University of Chicago Press.
Anteby, M. (2013b). Relaxing the taboo on telling our own stories: Upholding professional distance *and* personal involvement. *Organization Science*, *24*, 1277–1290.
Blee, K.M. (2009). *Women of the Klan: Racism and gender in the 1920s*. Berkeley: University of California Press.
Chaves, M.M., Pereira, J.S., Maroco, J., Rodrigues, M.L., Ricardo, C.P.P., Osorio, M.L., et al. (2002). How plants cope with water stress in the field. Photosynthesis and growth. *Annals of Botany*, *89*, 907–916.
Desmond, M. (2012a). Disposable ties and the urban poor. *American Journal of Sociology*, *117*, 1295–1335.
Desmond, M. (2012b). Eviction and the reproduction of urban poverty. *American Journal of Sociology*, *118*, 88–133.
Douglas, J.D. (1976). *Investigative social research: Individual and team field research*. Beverly Hills, CA: Sage.
Emerson, R.M., Fretz, R.I., & Shaw, L.L. (1995). *Writing ethnographic fieldnotes*. Chicago, IL: University of Chicago Press.
Fine, G.A. (1993). Ten lies of ethnography: Moral dilemmas of field research. *Journal of Contemporary Ethnography*, *22*, 267–294.
Golden-Biddle, K., & Locke, K. (1993). Appealing work: An investigation of how ethnographic texts convince. *Organization Science*, *4*, 595–616.
Halton, W. (1994). Some unconscious aspects of organizational life: Contributions from psychoanalysis. In A. Obholzer & V.Z. Roberts (Eds.), *The unconscious at work* (pp. 11–18). London, England: Routledge.
Jaques, E. (1955). Social systems as a defence against persecutory and depressive anxiety. In M. Klein (Ed.), *New directions in psychoanalysis* (pp. 478–498). London, England: Tavistock.
Katz, J. (1997). Ethnography's warrants. *Sociological Methods & Research*, *25*, 391–423.
Khurana, R. (2007). *From higher aims to hired hands: The social transformation of American business schools and the unfulfilled promise of management as a profession*. Princeton, NJ: Princeton University Press.

Laplanche, J., & Pontalis, J.B. (1973). *The language of psychoanalysis*. London, England: Hogarth Press.

Maslow, A.H. (1962). Resistance to being rubricized. In A.H. Maslow (Ed.), *Toward a psychology of being* (pp. 119–123). Princeton, NJ: Van Nostrand.

Menzies, I.E.P. (1960). A case-study in the functioning of social systems as a defense against anxiety: A report on the study of a nursing service of a general hospital. *Human Relations, 13*, 95–121.

Petriglieri, G., & Petriglieri, J.L. (2010). Identity workspaces: The case of business schools. *Academy of Management Learning and Education, 9*, 44–60.

Pratt, M.G. (2009). For the lack of a boilerplate: Tips on writing up (and reviewing) qualitative research. *Academy of Management Journal, 52*, 856–861.

Racamier, P.C. (1970). Essais sur certains méchanismes institutionnels. In P.C. Racamier (Ed.), *Le psychanalyste sans divan* (pp. 375–415). Paris, France: Payot.

Tilly, C. (2006). *Regimes and repertoires*. Chicago, IL: University of Chicago Press.

Van Maanen, J. (2013). Hold the Mayo: Some comments on the origins of organizational ethnography. *Journal of Organizational Ethnography, 2*, 105–107.

Vaughan, D. (1990). *Uncoupling: Turning points in intimate relationships*. New York, NY: Vintage Books.

Venkatesh, S. (2013a). *Floating city: A rogue sociologist lost and found in New York's underground economy*. New York, NY: Penguin.

Venkatesh, S. (2013b). Underground markets as fields in transition: Sex work in New York City. *Sociological Forum, 28*, 682–699.

Wang, D.J., & Soule, S.A. (2012). Social movement organizational collaboration: Networks of learning and the diffusion of protest tactics, 1960–1995. *American Journal of Sociology, 117*, 1674–1722.

Weber, M. (2004). *The vocation lectures*. Indianapolis, IN: Hackett Publishing.

20

The Aesthetics of Data: Qualitative Analysis of Visual and Other Nontextual Forms of Data

Simona Giorgi and Mary Ann Glynn

The texts we read are often embedded in a plethora of visual elements, including pictures and images found in magazines, newsletters, or journals; marketing, advertising, and promotional materials, such as organizational leaflets and brochures; communication technologies, such as reports, accounts, schedules, tables, and graphs; and visual artifacts, such as dress, architecture, and office décor (Davison, McLean, & Warren, 2012). More than simply illustrating text, visual elements help to interpret text. For example, Strati (1992) shows how the discursive interaction between the chairman of an Italian firm and his assistant could be understood in light of the objects that decorated their office spaces; these artifacts revealed the implicit hierarchical, social, and cultural differences that were difficult to express (Glynn, Giorgi, & Lockwood, 2012). Similarly, Elsbach (2003) found that the display of photos, awards, and mementos in the office helped organizational members express their workplace identities. Research in marketing suggests that consumers are influenced by visual elements in evaluating products (Hagtvedt & Patrick, 2008). In sum, these studies point to how textual messages are encoded in a "language of images" (Davison, 2007, p. 135).

We conceptualize visual elements as the *aesthetic context* in which text (e.g., Phillips, Lawrence, & Hardy, 2004), the traditional object of qualitative research, is embedded. We use the term *aesthetic* (from the Greek *aesthesis*, to perceive or feel with the senses) to refer to all types of sensory experiences of visual forms, not necessarily simply a "feeling of beauty" (Strati, 1992, p. 568) associated with artistic expression and consumption. More specifically, we focus on the aesthetic (visual) context and seek to detail its relationship to organizational texts and to draw out implications for qualitative research. With rare exceptions, the wealth of images, visuals, plans, figures, and graphs that embed text is often overlooked or simply taken to be an adjunct to textual data (Davison et al., 2012). Meyer, Hollerer, Jancsary, and Van Leeuwen (2013, p. 490) point to the gap in the literature: "surprisingly enough, and despite a prominent line of research that addresses discourse . . . the *visual* mode of meaning construction has remained largely unexplored in organization and management research." We seek to address this gap.

Understanding the aesthetic context in which text is embedded is important to qualitative analyses because it more closely approximates how people actually process information. Two-thirds of all stimuli reach the brain through individuals' visual systems (Kosslyn, Seger, Pani, & Hillger, 1990) and, although human thought consists of neither words nor visual images, it seems closer to the latter (Pinker, 2003; Zaltman, 1997). Indeed, there is general consensus that most human meaning is understood and shared nonverbally, with less than 10% of the meaning in any message expressed through verbal language (Zaltman, 1997).

Given the "complexity, ambiguity, subtlety, and pervasiveness" (Strati, 1992, p. 569) that can characterize an aesthetic context, we focus on one aspect: the visual context in which discourse is embedded. We explore this dimension in its own right as well as in relationship to the text it envelopes. For illustration, we draw on examples from two of our own research projects: one examining cultural entrepreneurship, with data from Martha Stewart's *Living* magazine, and another examining the logics of worth (Boltanski & Thevenot, 2006) behind the appreciation of nature (Fourcade, 2011) in an environmental nonprofit that publishes a magazine, *Chicago Wilderness*.

We propose that visual analyses can enrich textual analyses in three ways: first, by offering a visual representation that enriches the meaning of the text; second, by conveying an emotional dimension that is less easily expressed through words; and finally, by offering a peek at a deeper dimension of organizational culture that is often not consciously or openly acknowledged. Explicitly incorporating aesthetic context makes both theoretical and empirical contributions to qualitative research in particular. Despite some attempts to quantify and content-analyze images (e.g., Benschop & Meihuizen, 2002), visual forms such as pictures and photographs are especially resistant to translation into quantitative terms (Davison et al., 2012) because of a lack of "dictionaries" that can unequivocally assign meanings to certain images. Thus, we see qualitative analyses to be particularly fitting to the study of the visual.

We explore how the aesthetic context can relate to the text it embeds in three distinct ways that reflect varying degrees of coupling between the two: (1) *tight coupling*, when the aesthetic context is a visual representation of the associated text; (2) *loose coupling*, when the aesthetic context is somewhat related to the text but may reinforce (or even contradict) the text, often by providing a repertoire of emotions not reflected in the text; and (3) *decoupling*, when the aesthetic context is only marginally related to the text and tells its own story that can complement textual elements or even create contrast, irony, dissonance, or ambivalence with its associated text. We see our work as an initial step in advancing the study of the visual dimension in qualitative research. We begin by discussing existing approaches to the aesthetic context and the organization and its texts.

The Aesthetic Context and the Organization

Evidence abounds on the vital role of the visual in organizations, but it is all but absent in organization research (e.g., Taylor & Hansen, 2005). Visual images are sometimes dismissed as trivial, or at best, only partially reliable information (Davison & Warren, 2009). This may be due to the inherent ambiguity of the aesthetic context, which tends to resist clear definition and theory (Mitchell, 1995, 2005), or our lack of an established methodological toolbox with which to analyze visual elements.

Philosophers and social theorists have long pointed out that the sphere of aesthetics, that is, the sphere of appreciation of the visual, cannot be decoupled from cognition. The human experience is filtered not only through cognitive schemas, but also through sensual perception (Merleau-Ponty, 1962), comprising two inseparable parts of people's experiences. Interestingly, early organization theorists like Chester Barnard (1938, p. 235) pointed out that management was "aesthetic rather than logical" and better described by terms such as "feeling, judgment, and sense."

Organizational disciplines, it seems, come endowed with a particular aesthetic. Guillen (1997) has argued that Taylorization and scientific management present an aesthetic that equates beauty with efficiency, which is represented in texts like "it's working beautifully," meaning that it is working smoothly, efficiently, and exactly as planned—the realization of modern management ideals. The visual images of whirring machinery and stopwatches would now strike us as out of place when we see leaders such as Steve Jobs, Sergey Brin, or Larry Page represented in relaxed, minimalistic settings that help us visualize not a particular product, but the power of their ideas (Hansen, Ropo, & Sauer, 2007).

An interest in the visual is evident in a number of fields that focus on organizations, including management (Barry & Rerup, 2006; Gagliardi, 1999; Sandelands & Buckner, 1989; Sorensen, 2014; Strati, 1992), accounting (Davison & Warren, 2009; Quattrone, 2009), advertising (Schroeder, 2002), and marketing (Patrick & Hagtvedt, 2011; Scott, 1994). Visual forms, such as pictures, tables, or décor, have a demonstrated influence on brand evaluations (DeRosia, 2008) so much so that their comprehension seems relatively effortless and unproblematic (e.g., Hagtvedt & Patrick, 2008). Now we turn to examine the interrelationship between the visual and the textual, and the possibilities for qualitative research.

Relating Aesthetic Context to Organizational Text

We use the term "aesthetic context" to refer to the visual elements that embed or surround a focal text and recognize two key dimensions of that context: the *content of the image* and the *mode by which it is represented*. There are a variety of ways in which these two dimensions can be related; understanding how they are can be revealing for qualitative researchers. Take, for instance, the November issue of Martha Stewart's magazine, *Living*, which perennially features articles on how to properly set the table for a Thanksgiving feast. Over the years, the visuals embedding Stewart's "how-to" text have ranged from the richly, autumnally hued "natural Thanksgiving table," to the monochromatic "yellow Thanksgiving table," to the opulently gilded "Midas Touches: Flocking Together" (www.marthastewart.com). In all these, the photos, images, and colors visualize the "technical" aspects of arranging a table, often superseding the message in the accompanying text. Here, there is a tight coupling between the visual and the textual to the point where they can be substitutes for the instruction of setting a Thanksgiving table. However, the visual is more evocative and functions as a touchstone of emotional appeal, making the "how-to" a "beautiful how-to" (Stewart, 2001).

More than simply representing text, the aesthetic context can communicate an organization's worldview and ideology, thereby offering a complementary story to that in the text. For instance, in a report on orchids as an endangered species in the Midwest in the *Chicago Wilderness* magazine, visual elements are woven into the written narrative, with displays of photos and paintings. They are meant not only to help the reader visualize the orchids described in the text—white lady slippers, rose pogonia, and prairie white fringed orchids—but also to highlight two key values of the organization: biodiversity and restoration of nature to its pre-Colombian times. The first is conveyed by photographs that attest to the variety of forms and colors of the orchids native to the area; the second, more subtly communicated through the choice of two Audubon-inspired paintings of orchids, points to the importance of harkening back in time. The inspired language used in the narrative resonates with, and tells a broader story, not only with its content, but also the mode of representation (photos and paintings, rather than graphs and tables):

> If a time machine could take us back to the swales, prairies and woodlands surrounding the southern shore of Lake Michigan, early 1800s, we would see biodiversity paralleled only by the tropics. Thousands of species made this area their home, and of those, few were more exotic than the orchids. (Garness, 2009)

Advertising research on visual images supports the idea that both content, or what is depicted in the visual image (e.g., Childers & Houston, 1984; Edell & Staelin, 1983; Mitchell, 1986), and its mode of representation, that is, the choice of depicting an image in the form of a painting, photograph, or watercolor drawing, for example, matter in interpretations (Bloch, Brunel, & Arnold, 2003; Hagtvedt & Patrick, 2008). In her call for a theory of visual rhetoric, Scott (1994) emphasizes the need to distinguish content from representation so as not to misinterpret images as "copies" of reality. Even rather mundane visual elements such as the choice of fonts can influence the manner of picturing certain content and define a visual style. Returning to the previous examples, Martha Stewart's magazine tightly couples the manner and content of visual images to the message in the text: a gold-edged metallic turkey accompanies the "Midas Touches," and there's not another color but yellow in the "yellow Thanksgiving table." Stewart's focus on the right color of the tablecloth or the gilding on the golden turkey signals the importance of paying attention to even the smallest of details so as to legitimate a lifestyle. Similarly, portions of text in the *Chicago Wilderness* magazine are presented through hyperlinks, allowing the reader freedom to dig deeper into a particular topic and creatively control their own aesthetic experience. In a 2008 article, "Learn how you can enjoy a prairie, woodland, and wetland," the phrase "plant communities" is hyperlinked; with a click, the reader discovers over 300 prairie wildflowers represented through a vivid choice of colors, fonts, and other visual elements. These opportunities for discovery suggest thoroughness, a scientific approach, and a deep love and curiosity for nature and ecosystem biodiversity.

The distinction between the two visual dimensions—content and representation mode—is critical to understanding the meaning of a visual form. Consider an example from the art world. In his analysis of Caravaggio's two versions of St. Paul's conversion on the way to Damascus, Sorensen (2010, p. 307) shows that while the "content" of the two paintings is the same, the way such content is represented communicates two different meanings of spiritual conversion: In one painting, St. Paul is in a realistic setting with human semblances, and in the other, he is represented as a "pure transcendent spirit" isolated from his surroundings. A less high-brow, but equally telling, example emerges from the *Chicago Wilderness* magazine's choice of representing the Midwest landscape through watercolor paintings, drawings, and close-up pictures of its magnificent flowers; these artistic modes of representation all emphasize the sacred and aesthetic value of the land, unlike merely descriptive snapshots of its different locales.

Analyzing Content and Mode of Representation

Understanding the two dimensions of the aesthetic context—content and mode of representation—can equip qualitative researchers with needed tools for analyzing visual data. Examining each independently, and in concert with the other, can reveal not only *what* is being communicated (content), but also *how* it is being communicated (mode of representation) and with what degree of consistency or reinforcement. Beyond examining these dimensions of the aesthetic context, researchers have an opportunity to examine the correspondence between the visual of the aesthetic context and the textual of the verbal language; doing so should yield a more nuanced understanding of the meaning of the communication. We focus on three possibilities of relating the aesthetic context to the verbal text: (1) tight coupling, where the visual represents the associated text; (2) loose coupling, when the visual supplements the text, perhaps enriching it with emotional appeal, and (3) decoupling, when the visual seems unrelated to the text, potentially offering an alternative story. These different degrees of coupling between the text and its aesthetic context are depicted in Figure 20.1 and discussed next.

Tight Coupling: Aesthetic Context as Visual Representation of Text

Building on Latour (1990), we can say that ideas and things, thoughts and actions, words and images are not separate, noncommunicating worlds. On the contrary, images can represent the materialization of ideas (Czarniawska-Joerges & Joerges, 1996). For example, Catholic nuns who wear habits in their everyday lives use this dress to visually represent their conservative orientation to the church (Giorgi, Guider, & Bartunek, 2014). Similarly, employees use workplace dress as portable identity markers (Rafaeli & Pratt, 1993) in various occupations from medical professionals (Pratt & Rafaeli,

Text and Aesthetic Context

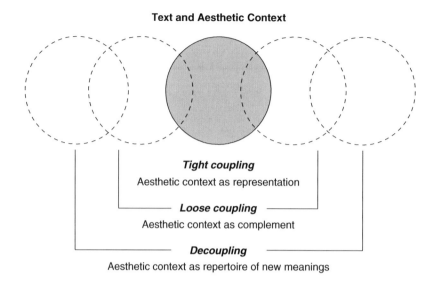

Tight coupling

Aesthetic context as representation

Loose coupling

Aesthetic context as complement

Decoupling

Aesthetic context as repertoire of new meanings

Figure 20.1   The Coupling Between the Visual and the Textual

1997) to administrative assistants (Rafaeli, Dutton, Harquail, & Mackie-Lewis, 1997). And, the choice of a large, expensive abstract painting in the chairman's office might suggest not only his refined, avant-garde taste, but also the hierarchical difference in power from others who decorate their offices with posters (Strati, 1992).

In these instances, text and aesthetic context are tightly coupled, with the aesthetic context visualizing and explicating the text. In this case, "images and visual artifacts are not just add-ons to verbal texts, mere transmitters of information or means of communication: They have become an elementary *mode* for the construction, maintenance, and transformation of meaning" (Meyer et al., 2013, p. 491). In the *Chicago Wilderness* magazine, the aesthetic context of "11 Fresh Ways to See Nature" consists of childlike drawings that emphasize a sense of wonder in appreciating nature, along with a quote by Walt Whitman. Together, these visual elements tell us that the drawings are not meant for children, but for a highly educated public that dreams of a state of innocence through contact with nature.

Tight coupling is not limited to "technical" texts. For example, Gagliardi (1999, p. 317) examines the relation between Italian futurism and fascism and observed: "the conception source of fascism is to be found in Futurism and its trumpeted values of determination, thirst for the new, the rejection of tradition, youth, modernity and forces." The leaders of the movement themselves (Gentile, 1975; Marinetti, 1924) stressed the links between futurist ideology and aesthetic codes and fascist ideology, especially in its original revolutionary elements. As fascist ideologues chose futuristic art as their preferred aesthetic context, this context also becomes an illustration of what this political movement was about. In sum, the aesthetic context in these instances is a tool to embellish, support, and visualize text.

Loose Coupling: The Aesthetic Context as an Enlarged Repertoire of the Visual

The aesthetic context can be loosely coupled to the embedded text. Semiotic analysis makes the distinction between "signified," which refers to a particular object or concept (e.g., a product), and its "signifiers," which include forms that are used to convey an object or concept, such as photographs or drawings that can physically resemble the object or abstract representations that can be only symbolically connected by arbitrary convention without an obvious, physical connection.

Visual representations can compensate for, or evoke, emotions that are sometimes difficult to convey with text (Gagliardi, 1999, p. 320). A visual image can evoke pleasure or disgust, elevate our feelings, and associate nature with art; conversely, it can repulse us and show us a side of reality that we do not expect (Davison et al., 2012). For example, environmental nonprofits with a focus on wetland restoration published articles on hypoxia (oxygen deficiency in a biotic environment) accompanied by evocative pictures of dead fish in the Gulf of Mexico, which conveyed shock value and urgency in a way that a diagram or data table could not. Visual forms can also elicit emotions that are strong and unexpected. Elsbach (2003) reports that when the chief executive officer of a New York City advertising agency introduced a hotel-style work space with depersonalized offices, employees' reactions were quite negative because they could no longer visually make their office spaces their own; without a familiar visual context, employees felt that their workplace identities and self-concepts were compromised.

Organizations often aim at managing and controlling the aesthetic context to elicit a desired set of emotions. Sandelands and Buckner (1989) demonstrated that visual representations of "excellence" had uplifting and motivating qualities, without the need for an explicit message. Similarly, according to Hansen et al. (2007), Wal-Mart may ask, "What aesthetics are associated with our company? How do people feel about us?" and answer with images of frugality, patriotism, and family fun. Beyond such positive emotions, visuals can also elicit ugly, sublime, comic, or grotesque feelings (Strati, 1992). The aesthetic context can be rich in evoking multiple or complex felt meanings (Hansen et al., 2007).

In sum, the aesthetic context can be loosely coupled to a text and carry forth its own message, acting like a repertoire of emotions. Organizations can be strategic in the choice of such visual elements to exert some control on how people feel about them (Hansen et al., 2007); in other instances, however, relatively unconscious choices—the physical reorganization of an office (Elsbach, 2003) or the choice of paintings (Strati, 1992)—can reveal deeper-seated commitments and values.

Decoupling: The Aesthetic Context as an Alternative Story

The aesthetic context can open significant "windows in the walls of the organization" (Strati, 1992, p. 569) by offering "clues" to ways of seeing and feeling different from those given by actors in surveys or interviews (Gagliardi, 1999, p. 314). Although the analysis of words may be an entrée for investigating meanings, words do not capture ideas or feelings not expressed or discussed openly (Maanen, 1979; Meyerson, 1991).

Caravaggio's two versions of St. Paul's conversion (described earlier) met with very different fates. Sorensen (2010, p. 307) shows that, despite the similarity of content, the first version of the painting was rejected because the portrayal of the saint as human represented a subversive break from the dogmatic hegemony of the church in the 17th century. Similarly, for the 10-year anniversary of *Chicago Wilderness*, the magazine published an essay entitled "Chicago Wilderness 2030: Visions for the Future" (Packard, 2006). Despite the forward-looking content of the piece and its emphasis on developing an ambitious vision for the future, the choice of a watercolor painting with buffalos and herons against a lusciously green background with just a hint of the Chicago skyline in the background revealed an alternative story: that of an organization looking backward, returning the area to its pre-Colombian times. Although the tagline of the painting reads, "Imagine a region transformed—for people and nature," the visual uncovers the core interest of the organization: the health of natural ecosystems.

An analysis of the aesthetic context—and a potential assessment of decoupling with the text—could lead to a more nuanced and potentially critical way of analyzing organizations (Sorensen, 2010).

Benschop and Meihuizen (2002) offer a telling example: If in annual reports corporations state their intent to embrace and promote women's careers, these statements can be contradicted by a choice of images of women engaged in stereotypical occupations.

Finally, although we have made a clear distinction among these three different types of coupling the aesthetic with the textual, we do not mean to imply that they are necessarily mutually exclusive. An image can faithfully represent the accompanying text (tight coupling) but, at the same time, convey or evoke emotions that go beyond the text (loose coupling). Often, the feelings expressed are derived from an underlying dimension of identity or culture. For example, Davison (2007) analyzed the cover photographs of Oxfam's annual reviews and found that these images represented the organization's dual engagement with the developed and the developing world, aroused sentiment and compassion, and hinted at the organization's charitable and commercial orientations. Thus, the coupling between the visual and textual can be complex and multifaceted.

Discussion

To date, qualitative researchers in the field of management have devoted the majority of their attention to the study of verbal text to the relative neglect of visual data, in spite of their omnipresence in organizational life. The reasons for this "absent presence" of the visual dimension (Meyer et al., 2013, p. 490) are complex and diverse. It may be due, in part, to the scholarly attitude of "inveterate doubt" about the scientific validity of studying the visual (Sandelands & Buckner, 1989, p. 107) and, in part, to the nature of visual data and the methodologies needed for their investigation. Somewhat similar to words, images are polysemic and open to various interpretations but, unlike words, there are not dictionaries of meanings, expert analysts, or agreed-upon conventions to interpret visual data.

In this chapter, we have argued for the importance of studying the aesthetic context in which text is embedded and suggested what we believe are fruitful avenues for future research and especially qualitative analyses. One avenue examines the nature of the aesthetic context itself. We unpacked the aesthetic in terms of two key dimensions—content and mode of representation—and proposed that examining these dimensions independently and in concert may reveal a more nuanced understanding of organizational meanings.

One site we have suggested—and used—for studying the aesthetic context is that of magazines, for what they reveal about the organizations that produce them or the readers who consume them. For example, an examination of the covers of Stewart's *Living* magazine over time affords insight about the organization's relationship with its founder through its emergence (when Stewart's image was on every cover), the crises precipitated by Stewart's imprisonment (when Stewart's image was absent and the font size used for her name decreased and receded), and her energetic return (when she was again on the cover). Moreover, the varied representations of Stewart—in photographic images and in lettering—could be examined with regard to organizational changes. Related to this point is what the aesthetic context reveals about the audience that consumes a particular text; it is in this relationship with the audience that meanings come alive and evolve over time. For example, while the 19th-century art world rejected impressionist paintings because they did not conform to existing aesthetic standards, over time a new audience of critics and consumers developed a new appreciation for impressionism as an emotional and contemplative experience (Podolny & Hill-Popper, 2004; White & White, 1965).

A second avenue of research might pursue the ideas we advanced on the different and multiple ways in which the visual and the textual may relate to each other (see Figure 20.1). We conceptualized three variants of the coupling between the visual and the textual: tight coupling, when visuals represent the text; loose coupling, when visuals complement and enlarge the meanings in the text, potentially by offering a repertoire of emotions; and finally, decoupling, when visuals offers cues to an alternate story that participants do not want to or cannot tell.

Although we feel that the pathways we have identified for studying the aesthetic context offer qualitative researchers a useful toolbox, we acknowledge that mere "aesthetic awareness" (Strati, 1992) does not resolve issues of research design, measurement, and analysis. However, three options offer potential solutions. The first option is to take a focus on the natives' views. Rather than imposing our own interpretations on visuals, we might use visuals as part of our interviews, keep track of the emotions and thoughts they elicit, and include these elaborations in our data analysis. The second option is to take a greater recognition of the subjectivity of research. Researchers might leverage their in-depth knowledge of an organizational setting to interpret what the visuals stand for in that particular context. Finally, an imperfect but still important source of data on visuals could result from the development of a codebook for images that classifies certain modes of representations, such as graphs and tables as a form of "logical/mathematical" aesthetic or watercolors and paintings as an "inspired" aesthetic, along the lines of existing categorizations of multiple orders of worth (Boltanski & Thevenot, 2006). In conclusion, we have argued for ways to examine text as embedded in its aesthetic context; after all, pictures are worth a thousand words.

References

Barnard, C.I. (1938). *The Functions of the Executive.* Cambridge, MA: Harvard University Press.

Barry, D., & Rerup, C. (2006). Going mobile: Aesthetic design considerations from Calder and the constructivists. *Organization Science, 17*(2), 262–276.

Benschop, Y., & Meihuizen, H.E. (2002). Keeping up gendered appearances: Representations of gender in financial annual reports. *Accounting, Organizations and Society, 27*(7), 611–636.

Bloch, P.H., Brunel, F.F., & Arnold, T.J. (2003). Individual differences in the centrality of visual product aesthetics: Concept and measurement. *Journal of Consumer Research, 29*(4), 551–565.

Boltanski, L., & Thevenot, L. (2006). *On justification: Economies of worth.* Princeton, NJ: Princeton University Press.

Childers, T.L., & Houston, M.J. (1984). Conditions for a picture-superiority effect on consumer memory. *Journal of Consumer Research,* 11(2), 643–654.

Czarniawska-Joerges, B., & Joerges, B. (1996). Travel of ideas. In B. Czamiawska & G. Sevon (Eds.), *Translating the organizational change.* New York, NY: Walter De Gruyter.

Davison, J. (2007). Photographs and accountability: Cracking the codes of an NGO. *Accounting, Auditing & Accountability Journal, 20*(1), 133–158.

Davison, J., McLean, C., & Warren, S. (2012). Exploring the visual in organizations and management. *Qualitative Research in Organizations and Management: An International Journal,* 7(1), 5–15.

Davison, J., & Warren, S. (2009). Imag[in]ing accounting and accountability. *Accounting, Auditing & Accountability Journal, 22*(6), 845–857.

DeRosia, E.D. (2008). The effectiveness of nonverbal symbolic signs and metaphors in advertisements: An experimental inquiry. *Psychology & Marketing, 25*(3), 298–316.

Edell, J.A., & Staelin, R. (1983). The information processing of pictures in print advertisements. *Journal of Consumer Research,* 10(1), 45–61.

Elsbach, K.D. (2003). Relating physical environment to self-categorizations: Identity threat and affirmation in a non-territorial office space. *Administrative Science Quarterly, 48,* 622–654.

Fourcade, M. (2011). Cents and sensibility: Economic valuation and the nature of "nature." *American Journal of Sociology, 116*(6), 1721–77. doi:10.1086/659640

Gagliardi, P. (1999). Exploring the aesthetic side of organizational life. In S.R. Clegg & C. Hardy (Eds.), *Studying organization: Theory and method.* Thousand Oaks, CA: Sage.

Garness, K.M. (2009). Orchids of the Chicago wilderness. A passion for saving paradise. *Chicago Wilderness Magazine.* Retrieved from www.chicagowilderness.org/CW_Archives/issues/summer2009/paradise.html

Gentile, E. (1975). *Le origini dell'ideologia fascista (1918–1925).* Rome, Italy: Laterza.

Giorgi, S., Guider, M.E., & Bartunek, J.M. (2014). Productive resistance: A study of change, emotions, and identity in the context of the Apostolic Visitation of U.S. Women Religious, 2008–2012. In N. Phillips, M. Lounsbury, & P. Tracey (Eds.), *Research in the sociology of organizations* (Vol. 41, pp. 259–300). Bingley, UK: Emerald.

Glynn, M.A., Giorgi, S., & Lockwood, C. (2012). Organizational culture. In R. Griffin (Ed.) *Oxford Bibliographies in Management.* New York, NY: Oxford University Press. www.oxfordbibliographies.com/view/document/obo-9780199846740/obo-9780199846740-0059.xml

Guillen, M. (1997). Scientific management's lost aesthetic: Architecture, organization, and the taylorized beauty of the mechanical. *Administrative Science Quarterly*, *12*(4), 682–715.

Hagtvedt, H., & Patrick, V.M. (2008). Art infusion: The influence of visual art on the perception and evaluation of consumer products. *Journal of Marketing Research*, *45*(3), 379–389.

Hansen, H., Ropo, A., & Sauer, E. (2007). Aesthetic leadership. *The Leadership Quarterly*, *18*(6), 544–560.

Kosslyn, S.M., Seger, C., Pani, J.R., & Hillger, L.A. (1990). When is imagery used in everyday life? A diary study. *Journal of Mental Imagery*, *14*(3), 131–152.

Latour, B. (1990). Technology is society made durable. *The Sociological Review*, *38*(S1), 103–131.

Maanen, J. Van. (1979). Reclaiming qualitative methods for organizational research: A preface. *Administrative Science Quarterly*, *24*(4), 520–526.

Marinetti, F.T. (1924). *Futurismo e fascismo*. Foligno, Italy: F. Campitelli.

Merleau-Ponty, M. (1962). *Phenomenology of perception*. London, England: Routledge.

Meyer, R.E., Höllerer, M.A., Jancsary, D., & van Leeuwen, T. (2013). The visual dimension in organizing, organization, and organization research: Core ideas, current developments, and promising avenues. *The Academy of Management Annals*, *7*(1), 489–555.

Meyerson, D.E. (1991). Acknowledging and uncovering ambiguities in cultures. In P.J. Frost, L.F. Moore, M.R. Louis, C.C. Lundberg, & J. Martin (Eds.), *Reframing organizational culture* (pp. 254–270). Thousand Oaks, CA: Sage.

Mitchell, A.A. (1986). The effect of verbal and visual components of advertisements on brand attitudes and attitude toward the advertisement. *Journal of Consumer Research*, 13(1), 12–24.

Mitchell, W.J.T. (1995). *Picture theory: Essays on verbal and visual representation*. Chicago, IL: University of Chicago Press.

Mitchell, W.J.T. (2005). *What do pictures want?: The lives and loves of images*. Chicago, IL: University of Chicago Press.

Packard, S. (2006). Chicago Wilderness 2030: Visions for the future. *The Chicago Wilderness Magazine*, Spring. www.chicagowildernessmag.org/CW_Archives/issues/spring2006/cw2030.html

Patrick, V.M., & Hagtvedt, H. (2011). Aesthetic incongruity resolution. *Journal of Marketing Research*, *48*(2), 393–402.

Phillips, N., Lawrence, T.B., & Hardy, C. (2004). Discourse and institutions. *Academy of Management Review*, *29*(4), 635–652.

Pinker, S. (2003). *The blank slate: The modern denial of human nature*. New York, NY: Penguin.

Podolny, J.M., & Hill-Popper, M. (2004). Hedonic and transcendent conceptions of value. *Industrial and Corporate Change*, *13*(1), 91–116.

Pratt, M.G., & Rafaeli, A. (1997). Organizational dress as a symbol of multilayered social identities. *Academy of Management Journal*, *40*(4), 862–898.

Quattrone, P. (2009). Books to be practiced: Memory, the power of the visual, and the success of accounting. *Accounting, Organizations and Society*, *34*(1), 85–118.

Rafaeli, A., Dutton, J., Harquail, C.V., & Mackie-Lewis, S. (1997). Navigating by attire: The use of dress by female administrative employees. *Academy of Management Journal*, *40*(1), 9–45.

Rafaeli, A., & Pratt, M.G. (1993). Tailored meanings: On the meaning and impact of organizational dress. *Academy of Management Review*, *18*(1), 32–55.

Sandelands, L.E., & Buckner, G.C. (1989). Of art and work: Aesthetic experience and the psychology of work feelings. *Research in Organizational Behavior*, *11*, 105–131.

Schroeder, J.E. (2002). *Visual consumption* (Vol. 4). Psychology Press. New York, NY: Routledge.

Scott, L.M. (1994). Images in advertising: The need for a theory of visual rhetoric. *Journal of Consumer Research*, *21*(2), 252–273.

Sorensen, B.M. (2010). St Paul's conversion: The aesthetic organization of labour. *Organization Studies*, *31*(3), 307–326.

Sorensen, B.M. (2014). Changing the memory of suffering: An organizational aesthetics of the dark side. *Organization Studies*, *35*(2), 279–302.

Stewart, M. (2001). Remembering: Living, working, dreaming. *Martha Stewart Living*, January 2001, issue 86, 196.

Strati, A. (1992). Aesthetic understanding of organizational life. *Academy of Management Review*, *17*(3), 568–581.

Taylor, S.S., & Hansen, H. (2005). Finding form: Looking at the field of organizational aesthetics. *Journal of Management Studies*, *42*(6), 1211–1231.

White, H.C., & White, C.A. (1965). *Canvases and careers: Institutional change in the French painting world*. Chicago, IL: University of Chicago Press.

Zaltman, G. (1997). Rethinking market research: Putting people back in. *Journal of Marketing Research*, *34*, 424–437.

21

Leveraging Archival Data from Online Communities for Grounded Process Theorizing

Natalia Levina and Emmanuelle Vaast

Motivation and Background

Process theorizing—theorizing that focuses on how social events unfold over time—has been a stronghold for qualitative research for many years (Hernes, 2014; Langley, 1999; Langley et al., 2013; Markus & Robey, 1988; Pentland, 1999). Whereas there are many flavors of process theorizing (Van de ven & Poole, 1995), there is a shared concern among process theorists to observe and explain how social life unfolds over time. Process theorizing thus depends on accessing longitudinal data, either through direct observations of events unfolding over time, archival records, or narratives of people who took part in these events.

Most seminal process theories have been developed on the basis of in-depth, longitudinal qualitative field studies, including the work of Weick, Latour, March, Barley, Feldman, Orlikowski, and Pentland to name just a few (Hernes, 2008; Langley et al., 2013). However, there are some aspects of organizing that take many years to unfold and are widely dispersed in space, which makes it difficult to collect data through ethnographic methods. Pettigrew (1990) and Van de Ven and Poole (1995) have proposed methods for studying such phenomena on an organizational level of analysis by designing multiyear research studies. Such studies, however, are not only difficult to execute with limited research time and budget, but are also often subject to biases associated with human recollection as the researcher tends to access only a few people or events in organizations, directly relying on them to narrate events from the past.

The challenges are even more pronounced for phenomena that are on individual or group levels of analysis, which are often harder to access through available archival data (e.g., there is no equivalent of company reports for these levels). The challenges abound for building process theories of human judgment and interpretation (e.g., sense making, judgment, identity) if such phenomena take a long time to unfold since there is little substitute for direct observation of organizational discourse and events.

These limitations of traditional research approaches for the purpose of building process theories can be partially addressed in modern times by using online data sources, both private (e.g., organizational electronic mail exchanges) and public (e.g., interactions taking place on the World Wide Web on social media platforms) (Urquhart & Vaast, 2012). There are a number of significant advantages in using online data: (a) the longitudinal data, often spanning years and decades, can be obtained;

(b) the data is "always there," so that the researcher can go "back in the past" as new categories of analysis emerge; (c) the data is not subject to the traditional response biases, such as recollection bias and social desirability bias; and (d) the discourse among participants can be observed directly in the natural setting of their interaction.

While there are certain advantages in using such data, there are also challenges. Indeed, the data sets are often vast, and it is very hard to attack them with standard tools of qualitative research such as coding entire data archives by hand. The other challenge is that the data is often rich within the context of online interaction, but data is generally missing the wider sociocultural contexts shaping interactions such as the backgrounds of participants, their organizational histories, events in the institutional environment in which the interaction takes place, and so forth. Also, while the participants are not trying to please the researcher, they are usually concerned about presenting a certain image to their peers. This can make a difference for certain research questions. Finally, researchers also face a number of new ethical concerns associated with using public data sources that may reveal private, sensitive information without explicit consent.

In this chapter we outline some approaches for how to manage these challenges while also building strong process theories by focusing on two papers, of which at least one used large online discourse archives to build theory: online bankers dealing with the new occupational identity threat associated with the 2008 financial crisis (henceforth, the "bankers study") and tech bloggers promoting their blogs to other users (the "tech bloggers study"). We also discuss other published examples of using online data for grounded theory building that use more advanced quantitative techniques to deal with "big data" sets in process theorizing.

Bankers Study

In this research, Vaast and Levina (2015) investigated how members of an online community of retail bankers reacted as the banking profession faced a new threat to their identity following the financial and economic crises of 2007 and 2008.

They theoretically sampled entire discussion threads from an online community of retail bankers that had been in operation since before the crisis. In their examination of discussions, they were able to assess whether and how members of the community experienced the identity threats and how they reacted to them within the online community. Following a highly recursive data collection and analysis process, they contextualized their observations with what was happening within the community as well as beyond it (e.g., banks defaulting, new regulations, professional association mobilizing).

Findings revealed that members of the online community protected their occupational identity but did not attempt to repair their external image. The dynamics of an occupational online community revealed that protecting the existing identity of its members superseded taking a more proactive stance to address the identity threat. The research yielded a process theory through which reactions progressed from rejecting the taint to establishing distance from it, and then, finally, resigning oneself to it.

Tech Bloggers Study

In this research, Vaast et al. (2013) examined how tech bloggers (i.e., people who use weblogs to publish their discourse about technology and innovation) emerged over time as a new actor category in the field of innovation discourse.

They relied upon extensive archives collected mostly from a web aggregator that gathered publicly available links related to technology discourse and that focused especially on tech blogs. They systematically collected 3 years of archives of discourse from tech bloggers, from September 2005 to September 2008, that is, toward the beginning of the emergence process.

Through an iterative interpretive analysis of these archives, they identified major themes that characterized what tech bloggers talked about (e.g., new product launch, start-up funding or acquisition) as well as key intracommunity dynamics (e.g., how tech bloggers addressed one another and what they said to each other) as well as intercommunity relationships (e.g., how tech bloggers positioned themselves with regard to established categories such as tech journalists or venture capitalists).

The iterative data analysis led the researchers to theorize a process of emergence of the new actor category that was deeply related to the new media used by the category and that was marked by three tendencies of coalescence, fragmentation, and dispersion, which were in tension with one another.

Process Theorizing from Online Discourse

Process theory is about identifying how the phenomenon of interest changes over time and explaining the nature of this change. The approach that can be used with online community data can be broken down into the steps depicted in Figure 21.1. Next, we will describe these major steps in more detail.

Much writing on process theory building (Hernes, 2008; Langley, 1999) emphasizes the importance of getting a qualitative understanding of the context of the study to form a notion of what the key concepts are that describe the phenomenon of interest. For example, in the tech bloggers study, the researchers first became acquainted with the overall field of technology innovation discourse (including, among others, mainstream media, trade press, and tech blogs) and with the more specific

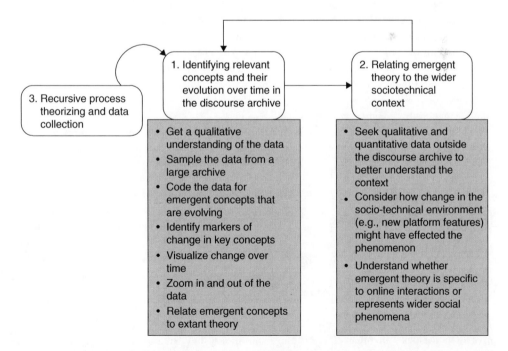

Figure 21.1   Identifying Key Concepts and Their Evolution Over Time in the Discourse Archive (DA)

world of tech blogs. This first interpretive and holistic step led them to gain an appreciation of the discourse of various actors on technology and innovation, as well as become acquainted with how similar yet distinct the discourse of tech bloggers was in this field.

The next phase of the process involves sampling the data, usually from a very large (sometimes exceeding many thousands of entries) DA. This is a big challenge as the researcher has to understand the data to identify the right theoretical sampling strategy. In the case of the bankers study, the qualitative interpretation of the data allowed the researchers to understand which key terms to search for in the larger DA (e.g., subprime landing, financial crisis, regulators) so as to pull out the threads that had to do with the discourse pertaining to the identity threat. One also needs to decide how much "surrounding dialogue" to analyze. In the case of the bankers study, the whole discussion thread was analyzed if at least one utterance had to do with the identity threat.

The next phase involves coding the data to identify key themes, concepts, and categories using standard grounded theory building approaches (Glaser and Strauss, 1967; Strauss and Corbin, 1998). For instance, in the tech bloggers study, as first-level analysis, the researchers identified the main topics that tech bloggers talked about in their discourse. As they became more familiar with the context, they were able to refine their coding scheme to include grounded discursive practices that seemed especially prevalent among tech bloggers during the investigated periods (e.g., assuming common interests, directing attention, stimulating debate). Finally, they grouped these codes into key themes of relevance during the emergence process (e.g., engaging with new media technologies, positioning relative to other actor categories).

The *critical difference* in using online DA and more traditional sources of data for process theory building is how to identify critical events, patterns, and rhythms in data—a key part of process theorizing (Langley, 1999; Pentland, 1999). Accessing data from online communities does not provide researchers with obvious and definite events and trends. Researchers need to find ways to make sense of these data without informants pointing out in interviews what was important given specific question asked or, in the case of ethnographic work, researchers directly observing ongoing key changes in their environments.

Online community data, however, offer markers of interest and importance for identifying specific events for members of the community under investigation. These markers come from technical features (e.g., automated number of page views, indicators of comments or rating of entries) as well as from the actions of community members (e.g., length of online discussions and frequency of a topic or event discussed online). The other advantage of having access to full sets of discursive interactions is that unlike interview data, where frequency counts of particular utterances may be misleading and driven by questions asked, here frequency counts may indeed serve as a good proxy for the change in the salience of this concept over time.

Because the data sets that researchers deal with are usually very large, employing some quantitative analysis tools may be very useful for good process theory building. The simplest approach is to visualize how critical markers change over time, which can be a very useful tool for researchers looking for key events and patterns in the data. For instance, in the bankers study, the frequency counts of coping tactics (total X) was used as a key marker of the process under study. Visualizing evolution of these key markers over time showed some significantly noticeable changes, with some tactics' use subsiding and other tactics only starting toward the end of the time period studied. Noticing these shifts in frequency counts among many tactics in unison also suggested to the researchers that it would be useful to see correlations in the tactics' use. This led to further theorizing and realization that the nature of some of the tactics was theoretically related, and the researchers grouped them into more general categories: rejecting tactics, distancing tactics, and accepting tactics.

Process theory strength often comes from combining the macro-level examination of the entire data set with a more minute attention to specific conversations in the so-called zooming in and out of their data set (Nicolini, 2009). Online community DA has unique advantages in that the researcher can truly zoom out of the whole data set, reducing the risk of missing important events.

In the research on tech bloggers, the authors systematically collected all tech blog entries published at 12:00 p.m. ET on the web-aggregator Techmeme during its first 3 years of observations, which yielded about 17,500 blog posts on a variety of events that marked the tech blog community during this period. The authors then relied upon this data set in order to pinpoint the key events that marked the tech blogging community. The visualization of the data helped researchers recognize that the tech blogging community did not grow through a linear evolution from birth to establishment and/or decay. Rather, the tech blogging community exhibited three key patterns in tension with one another: coalescence, fragmentation, and dispersion. If the authors had only focused on specific events and not on the holistic evolution, it is very likely that they would not have been able to identify and make sense of these three tendencies in tension with one another. Identifying only one or two of these tendencies (e.g., coalescence and fragmentation) would have led to an incomplete and biased grounded theorizing of the emergence of the tech blogging community.

Similarly, as researchers engage in relating emergent concepts to extant theories in the academic field, they will formulate novel or modified explanations for the data they have collected. These alternative theories have to earn their place in the grounded theorizing effort in a way that is supported by the data. Often, such incorporation of extant theories leads to the need for new data collection. The advantage of an online archive is that it is often possible to get data that is necessary to support or rule out these alternative explanations even though the events already took place.

Relating to the Outside World

While online community DA is a great source of discursive accounts of the phenomenon of investigation, it is generally missing details of the wider context that exists outside the community. These missing pieces are particularly important for process theory building, as major events in the industry may be critical in understanding why online discourse suddenly changes. As an illustration, in the tech bloggers research, the authors often had to know what was happening in the technology and innovation industry and in the Silicon Valley social and economic scene in order to make sense of some particular topical blog posts that seemed to gather much attention online. As they became more familiar with the online and offline community of actors involved in web-based technologies, they could grasp more completely the nuances and shifts in the discourse that tech bloggers produced over time.

In order to capture these missing pieces of the puzzle, it is important for researchers to relate DA with external sources such as public press releases, company documents, and so forth. Usually, this can only be done by having an interpretive feel for the data that comes from the narratives relayed in the text (e.g., mentions of new regulation, industry changes).

Another critical piece missing in the online community DA is participants' private (unshared) interpretations of the phenomenon. It is well established that participants present a certain face online that is socially desirable to fit into a particular culture of an online community (Yee et al., 2007). Sometimes, it is only important to capture this "face," but other times it is important to get access to more private thoughts and feelings of the participants. Thus, in the study of bankers, it was important to establish whether the discourse in the online community actually reflected how bankers privately felt about the crisis and the associated taint that it inflicted on the banking profession. To address this issue, the researchers conducted interviews with participants. The interviews revealed that bankers indeed felt the identity threat and that their coping tactics were similar to the ones expressed through discourse online.

Recursive Process Theorizing and Data Collection

Recursively iterating between theory and data is a key principle of grounded theorizing (Glaser & Strauss, 1967). Online archives constitute historical documents that researchers may conveniently get back to as dictated by the needs of their theorizing (Vaast & Walsham, 2013). Such recursiveness can be especially useful for process theory building. Researchers may adjust their investigated period(s) (e.g., by extending them or looking more deeply into specific subperiods) as they run into new and intriguing aspects of their analysis. They can also go back to their archives if they identify gaps in the theorized process or are willing to test their theory in the making by looking for counterfactuals (Morgan & Winship, 2007).

To illustrate, in the research on the online communities of bankers, the authors originally only considered investigating in-depth the online discussions that happened after the bankers perceived an identity threat. Yet, they realized that to be able to theorize more fully the process through which members of the community reacted to the threat, they also needed to be able to establish a baseline and compare discussion before and after the identity threat was experienced. They also often went back to the DA as they wanted to check for possible alternative interpretations. For instance, an emerging element of theorizing in this research was that online community participants, unlike members of a typical professional association, do not engage with external constituents (e.g., regulators) to fix their tainted image. The researchers needed to check whether this emerging element was indeed corroborated by empirical evidence. They searched the data on new key terms having to do with regulation response. Indeed, the data corroborated that even when the community was asked to comment on the proposed regulation, it did not engage. This kind of opportunity to recode the data for alternative theoretical explanations in a full historical archive of online discourse is a unique advantage of such a data set.

Challenges of Developing Process Theory With Online Communities

So far, this chapter has discussed the benefits for researchers willing to build process theory by relying upon archives from online communities. Researchers, however, also need to appreciate new challenges associated with such research. Here we highlight ethical and practical challenges.

Complicated and Evolving Ethical Matters

Researchers who dig into online archives navigate delicate and changing ethical dilemmas. Social scientists have highlighted, for instance, how online data can be considered simultaneously "public" and "private" (Buchanan & Ess, 2008), and such research may qualify both as human subject- and discourse-based (Lawson, 2004). Researchers may then, wittingly or not, use the data in a way that was not intended by participants and potentially hurt them in the process (Bruckman, 2002).

Ethical challenges are obviously not to be underestimated, and any responsible scholar should take them very seriously. These challenges have already attracted a lot of attention within academia and beyond (Stanton, 2010). Therefore, there are guidelines available to researchers who are unsure about how to proceed on some issues (e.g., seeking informed consent, determining the appropriate volume of data collection, and deciding whether to try to anonymize the data) (Schultze & Mason, 2012). These guidelines are undeniably useful, but they come with two key caveats. First, these recommendations cannot be considered fixed once and for all because of technology changes and the addition of new features that transform (and often expand) the traceability of online data. Second, and even more important, it is researchers' responsibility to assess whether and how their specific research may cause harm. Researchers should thus not consider ethical recommendations as definitive standards that may release them from carefully and compassionately considering their research setting. For instance, in the research on the online community of bankers who had experienced new identity threats, the authors thought to protect the anonymity of the participants in the public discussions they analyzed by concealing the name of the online community as well as identifying information (user names, workplaces, etc.) of its participants. The authors considered these steps important to protect the participants of the online community, and they were aware that such anonymity came at the cost of a lower transparency of their research, since other scientists would not be able to fully retrace their analytical steps.

Overwhelming Volume of Data

We have so far presented the ability of traditionally qualitative researchers to access and make sense of large data sets as promising access to everything, potential for mixed methods, introduction of innovative approaches, and so forth. However, there are challenges associated with this as the volume of data can be overwhelming and not at all amenable to basic qualitative analysis techniques. Researchers who do not wish to deploy quantitative analysis may need to go for a very selective sampling strategy by which the data can still be handled through reading and coding. However, some researchers will opt for getting further analytical insights through the use of quantitative data analysis methods.

Beyond descriptive statistics and frequency counts, researchers can use statistical techniques to analyze changes in patterns over time, such as the Markov Chain analysis. They may also use methods for analyzing changes in network patterns. For example, Angelopoulos studied an online community of cigar smokers to understand online–offline interaction (e.g., where cigar smokers sent each other offline free gifts of cigars). He used social network analysis techniques focused on network evolution to explain changes in patterns of interaction over time, noting that the social status of participants lead to different behaviors (Angelopoulos & Merali, 2012).

Uncertainty Regarding Data Durability

Another important but less recognized challenge that researchers of online communities face has to do with the durability of their data. Due to the traceability and huge data storage capabilities of today's computers, as well as to the popularity of cases involving web-search engines and the "right to be forgotten" (Rosen, 2012), researchers may be misled in thinking that their focal data are and will remain available to them online.

There are multiple social and technical causes that may negatively affect the durability of the data. Examples of such causes include changes in rules of access of the online community, technical crashes and servers breaking down, Internet domains becoming abandoned, or posts, comments, or content being taken down by their authors or censored by online community administrators. The tech bloggers research illustrates this challenge. Over time, some blog posts seemed to simply "disappear" and only exist as broken links. Facing the risk of holes in their collected data, the researchers responded in two main ways. First, they strove to collect data upfront systematically and as exhaustively as possible early on. Second, when they at times identified expired and inaccessible blog entries, they examined the context and events that these blog entries were likely to refer to and used their interpretation as part of their theorizing. In other words, the links that had become nonfunctional did not seem to appear randomly in the data set, but often seemed related to some of the most heated discussions among tech bloggers. They thus represented an opportune, and unexpected, occasion to further theorize.

Overall, recognizing the challenge of data durability is of the utmost importance for researchers willing to develop process theory because some of the key benefits of leveraging online community data come from the potential to collect all relevant data and to go back to collecting new data to better theorize the process. It is thus advisable that researchers assess early on in their project the risk of not being able to continuously access data or to maintain safely their data set. It is also important for researchers to try to understand the source(s) of the impermanence of their data, as these sources could turn out to be fortuitous opportunities for further theorizing.

Conclusion

To conclude, the online community DA offers a valuable opportunity for process theory building research as illustrated by several process theory papers published on the basis of such data in recent years (see Table 21.1). The availability of long-term historical accounts of the interactions among participants in a natural setting allows researchers to build stronger theory. Some of the unique aspects of such data include the ability to vary the time window, to collect data on new concepts and theoretical propositions by going back to the archive, and to analyze the data in a natural setting "unperturbed by researchers." However, some of the more traditional research tools for process theorizing, such as identifying key events through an informant's narrative emphasis and ethnographic observations of the changing setting, are not available in this case. We have articulated how one can hone in on such key events and understand rhythms and patterns of interaction in the online DA. We have also noted how to address challenges that have to do with the lack of contextual information that is often critical for good theory building. We caution researchers about challenges associated with ethical issues, size of the data set, and potential overreliance on public sources of data that may disappear one day. Finally, we believe that as the size of the data grows, the distinction between qualitative and quantitative methods may become vaguer as researchers may use all tools available to them to generate stronger theoretical insights grounded in data. "All is data," after all (Glaser, 1998, p. 42)!

Table 21.1 Use of Online Community Discourse for Process Theory Building

Reference	Research Context	Collected Data	Resulting Process Model
Vaast and Levina (2015)	Online community of retail bankers experiencing new identity threat	Theoretical sample of more than 100 discussion threads produced within an online community of retail bankers since before the threat to when the occupational identity was experienced. Additional data from semidirected interviews with retail bankers were collected to complement observations from the DA of the online community of bankers. Other banking industry–related contextual data were also collected in order to build more reliable theory.	Process model of reaction to new threat to occupational identity in online community that reveals temporal progression from rejecting to distancing from and, finally, resigning to changes in the image of the occupation.
Vaast et al. (2013)	Online community of tech bloggers	Researchers systematically collected daily sample of discourse from tech bloggers during a 3-year period from web aggregator. They complemented these data with theoretical sampling as their analytical and grounded theorizing process revealed the need to look more deeply into certain events and topics and to contrast tech bloggers' discourse with other actors' discourse and to situate this discourse within a broader context.	Process model of emergence of new actor category that reveals not a linear progression over time of the category but rather persistent tensions in emergence between coalescence, fragmentation, and dispersion.

Reference	Research Context	Collected Data	Resulting Process Model
Da Cunha & Orlikowski (2008)	Online forum in organization undergoing change	Researchers looked through an archive of more than 3,000 messages during the 22-month lifespan of the forum to identify and analyze messages that specifically addressed the change program. They complemented these data with six semidirected interviews with key informants.	Employees used the online forum to express their resentment toward the change. This cathartic expression had ironic implications in that the dynamics of the online forum facilitated the eventual changes that employees perceived as problematic.
Kane et al. (2014)	Online community of Wikipedia contributors resolving controversial issues while producing the article on autism	The researchers analyzed 250 deliberation threads for the autism Wikipedia article. The authors mapped the process for each issue that was deliberated, coding each move in the discourse. The authors then coded 10 threads in great detail, focusing on their key interest in knowledge change retention. The examination of coded data revealed three generative response patterns: chaotic generating, joint shaping, and defensive filtering. Finally, the patterns were plotted over time to reveal significant difference in which response patterns were used in different time periods.	A novel process theory of knowledge coproduction in an online community that conceptualizes knowledge co-production in terms of resolving tension between knowledge retention or change.

References

Angelopoulos, S., & Merali, Y. 2012. *Online-to-offline interactions: Exploring social processes on online communities.* Paper presented at the 8th UK Social Networks Conference, Bristol, UK.

Bruckman, A. 2002. Studying the amateur artist, a perspective on disguising data collecting in human subjects research on the Internet. *Ethics and Information Technology 4(3): 217–231.*

Buchanan, E.A., & Ess, C. 2008. Internet research ethics: The field and its critical issues. In K.E. Himma, & H.T. Tavani (Eds.), *The handbook of information and computer ethics*: 273–292. New York, NY: Wiley.

Da Cunha, J.V., & Orlikowski, W.J. 2008. Performing catharsis: The use of online discussion forums in organizational change. *Information and Organization*, 18: 132–156.

Glaser, B., & Strauss, A.L. 1967. *The discovery of the grounded theory: Strategies for qualitative research.* Chicago, IL: Aldine Pub. Co.

Glaser, B.G. 1998. *Doing grounded theory: Issues and discussions.* Mill Valley, CA: Sociology Press.

Hernes, T. 2008. *Understanding organization as process : Theory for a tangled world.* London: Routledge.

Hernes, T. 2014. *A process theory of organization.* New York, NY: Oxford University Press.

Kane, G.C., Johnson, J., & Majchrzak, A. 2014. Emergent life cycle: The tension between knowledge change and knowledge retention in open online coproduction communities. *Management Science.*

Langley, A. 1999. Strategies for theorizing from process data. *Academy of Management Review*, 24(4): 691–710.

Langley, A., Smallman, C., Tsoukas, H., & Van de Ven, A.H. 2013. Process studies of change in organization and management: Unveiling temporality, activity, and flow. *Academy of Management Journal*, 56(1): 1–13.

Lawson, D. 2004. Blurring the boundaries: Ethical considerations for online research using synchronous CMC forums. In E.A. Buchanan (Ed.), *Readings in virtual ethics: Issues and controversies*: 80–100. Hershey, PA: Idea Group.

Markus, M.L., & Robey, D. 1988. Information technology and organizational change: Causal structure in theory and research. *Management Science*, 34(5): 583–598.

Morgan, S.L., & Winship, C. 2007. *Counterfactuals and causal inference: Methods and principles for social research*. Cambridge: Cambridge University Press.

Nicolini, D. 2009. Zooming in and out: Studying practices by switching theoretical lenses and trailing connections. *Organization Studies*, 30(12): 1391–1418.

Pentland, B.T. 1999. Building process theory with narrative: From description to explanation. *Academy of Management Review*, 24(4): 711–724.

Pettigrew, A. M. 1990. Longitudinal field research on change: Theory and practice. *Organization Science*, 1(3): 267–292.

Rosen, J. 2012. The right to be forgotten. *Stanford Law Review Online*, 64: 88.

Schultze, U., & Mason, R.O. 2012. Studying cyborgs: Re-examining Internet studies as human subjects research. *Journal of Information Technology*, 27(4): 301–312.

Stanton, J.M. 2010. Virtual worlds, the IRB and a user's bill of rights. *Journal of Virtual Worlds Research*, 3(1): 3–15.

Strauss, A.L., & Corbin, J. (1998). *Basics of qualitative research—Techniques and procedures for developing grounded theory*. London: Sage.

Urquhart, C., & Vaast, E. 2012. *Building social media theory from case studies: A new frontier for IS research*. Paper presented at the International Conference of Information Systems, Orlando, FL.

Vaast, E., Davidson, E.J., & Mattson, T. 2013. Talking about technology: The emergence of new actors with new media. *MIS Quarterly*, 37(4): 1069–1092.

Vaast, E. & Levina, N. 2015. Speaking as one, but not speaking up: Dealing with new moral taint in an occupational online community. *Information and Organization* 25(2): 73–98.

Vaast, E., & Walsham, G. 2013. Grounded theorizing for electronically-mediated social contexts. *European Journal of Information Systems*, 22(1): 9–25.

Van de Ven, A.H., & Poole, M.S. 1995. Explaining development and change in organizations. *Academy of Management Review*, 20(3): 510–540.

Yee, N., Bailenson, J.N., Urbanek, M., Chang, F., & Merget, D. 2007. The unbearable likeness of being digital: The persistence of nonverbal social norms in online virtual environments. *CyberPsychology & Behavior*, 10(1): 115–121.

22

Analyzing Visual Rhetoric in Organizational Research

Lianne Lefsrud, Heather Graves, and Nelson Phillips

The claim that "a picture is worth a thousand words" has become a commonplace in modern culture. Yet, despite this general recognition of the importance of images, organizational research has focused almost exclusively on words (Meyer, Höllerer, Jancsary, & van Leeuwen, 2013). In this chapter, we will argue that we need to do much more to include images in our analysis and present a novel approach for doing so.

By advocating for the importance of images, we do not mean to dismiss words as unimportant. Rather, we simply wish to highlight that organizational messages (e.g., advertisements, PowerPoint presentations, annual reports, prospectuses, strategic plans, web pages, tweets, and blogs) are often complex texts that combine images *and* words. Therefore, to adequately analyze many of the texts that occur in organizations, we need to concern ourselves with both the images and the words that make them up.

One useful approach to analyzing these complex organizational texts is to incorporate theory from visual rhetoric. Visual rhetoric captures persuasion as (a) a *dialogic* phenomenon among diverse sets of stakeholders who are in conversation, (b) a *semiotic* phenomenon that depends fundamentally on symbolic texts produced and interpreted by these stakeholders, and (c) an *affective* process evoked through not only the connotations of words but also the images.

This last point is an important one. One of the primary reasons for combining words with images is to increase the emotional impact of the resulting message. Actors use images in the construction of text precisely because they affect readers' emotions. Given the increasing interest among organizational scholars in emotion, it becomes critical to understand how texts produce emotion. Therefore, our discussion here of images and their use in complex texts both responds to the increasing interest in emotion among some organization studies researchers and continues to sensitize organizational researchers more generally to the importance of emotion.

Although there is increasing attention to methods for analyzing the visual (Drori, Delmestri, & Oberg, in press; Meyer et al., 2013) and emotional (Creed, Hudson, Okhuysen, & Smith-Crowe, 2014), the means of examining the relative impact and persuasiveness of these modes are not well developed. In this chapter, we discuss an approach to understanding the rhetorical appeal of images and words assembled into texts. The approach we will discuss also allows us to examine the rhetorical struggles that occur among actors through texts. Drawing from social semiotics and rhetoric, we analyze the persuasive elements present in the text and images and in the complex interaction among and between them. Our goal is to show researchers the significant potential of this method to inform organizational research.

We begin by summarizing methods of examining images and emotion. Next, we discuss the applications and implications of this method of organizational research. To provide an example of the application of the method we have described, we analyze an advertisement drawn from the controversy around the Canadian oil sands. We conclude with a summary of the process of analyzing visual rhetoric and provide examples from the literature.

The Analysis of Visual Rhetoric

Our discussion of the analysis of visual rhetoric in management research grows out of three recent turns. First, there has been a broad increase in interest in the symbolic across the social sciences including an appreciation of the importance of images: the visual turn. Second, there has been a more recent, but rapidly increasing, interest in emotion in management research: the emotional turn. And, third, there has been a more modest yet still significant increase in interest in the application of linguistic methods more broadly, and rhetoric more specifically, in organization studies: the rhetorical turn. These three turns create the conditions of possibility for visual rhetoric by providing the necessary theoretical and philosophical underpinnings for this approach, and we will discuss each in turn.

The Visual Turn

Management research is undergoing an interesting "visual turn," with more research focusing on the visual and more being written on how important it is to consider this aspect of the symbolic. As Meyer et al. (2013: 490) argue, "other disciplines have more readily recognized the omnipresence of visual artifacts in modern societies that goes hand in hand with new information and communication technologies [in] the usage of 'visual language' (e.g. Kress & van Leeuwen, 1996; Mitchell, 1994)."

This interest in the visual grows out of a broader interest in the symbolic that followed the linguistic turn in social science. The idea that language is not a simple mirror of nature but rather is a tool through which the social is constructed has reverberated through the humanities and social sciences, and it has created fundamental change in how the social world comes to be and the role of meaningfulness in its construction. As a result, there has been an increased awareness and attention to the symbolic, and even a cursory examination of organizational life shows that the symbolic world of the organization is not just about words; in fact, visual artifacts of all kinds populate the modern organization. These visual artifacts, and their impact, are therefore of fundamental interest to organizational scholars. Yet, as Meyer et al. (2013: 490) argue, "due to a lack of integrative efforts we are in danger of constantly reinventing our knowledge about the visual."

The Affective Turn

In addition to their recent interest in the symbolic, organizational researchers have also become more interested in emotion (Ashkanasy, Humphrey, & Huy, 2014; Zietsma, 2013). Of course, organizational behaviour scholars working at an individual level (Hochschild, 2003) and on social movements have long had an interest in emotion (Goodwin, Jasper, & Poletta, 2001; Jasper, 1997), but the subject of emotion at an organizational or field level has received little attention. Recently, however, researchers interested in organizations have started to consider the nature and role of emotion in assessing potential partners and creating identification with others (see Briscoe, Gupta, & Anner, 2013; Gray, Purdy, & Ansari, 2015; Haack, Pfarrer, & Scherer, 2014). Institutional theorists are also beginning to include emotion (Creed et al. 2014; Creed, Hudson, Okhuysen, & Smith-Crowe, 2014; Friedland,

Mohr, Roose, & Gardinali, 2014; Grodal & Granqvist, 2014; Gutierrez, Scully, & Howard-Grenville, 2010; Hallett & Ventresca, 2006; Voronov & Vince, 2012).

The Rhetorical Turn

Rhetoric remains an essential tool for understanding the interaction between the visual and the emotional in the process of developing and using persuasive messages. Historically, rhetoric was conceptualized as embodied language, with speakers delivering affective arguments to a living and responsive audience. More recently, scholars have theorized the relationship between words and image in persuasive contexts, giving rise to a visual rhetoric (Birdsell & Groarke, 2007; Fleckenstein, Hu, & Calendrillo, 2007; Foss, 2004; Hope, 2006; McQuarrie & Mick, 1996; Scott, 1994; Scott & Batra, 2003; Smith, Moriarty, Barbatsis, & Kenney, 2004; van Eermeren & Garssen, 2012).

Visual rhetoric enables the systematic analysis of how words and images interact to enhance the impact of a persuasive message by heightening emotional appeals through visual elements. Visual rhetoric is a method of analysis useful in identifying and accounting for the ways in which they present persuasive content (i.e., argument). Visuals are rarely neutral; they are nearly always composed by an actor with details selected to communicate a particular and intended meaning. Graphs, charts, and tables all present data with the intent of making a point.

Images also shape viewer response to the subject matter. That is, visual representation has a communicative function and very often a persuasive function, aiming to convince viewers of some truth or point about the subject. A neo-Aristotelian view argues that persuasion consists of three interdependent and relational parts (Grimaldi, 1980): the *logic* or internal consistency of the point or message; the *ethos* or credibility of the source of the message; and the *pathos* or emotional impact of the delivery of the message. Of these parts, the appeal to credibility is fundamental: Audiences must trust the speaker for logic or emotion to have an impact (Aristotle, 1984). Once audiences trust the source, they are willing to hear evidence (logic) that supports the argument. However, emotion can shape the audience's response to the logic (Walker, 2000), including inducing them to ignore it completely.

The Use of Visual Rhetoric in Organizational Research

As a result of these three important shifts, management researchers have turned their attention to the organizational role and impact of texts made up of complex systems of words and images. As we mentioned, these texts can be advertisements, annual reports, PowerPoint presentations, pitches, posters, Facebook pages, tweets, TED talks, or any of the multitude of texts of this type that flow through organizations. But we are left with an important question: How do we actually analyze these sorts of texts?

For rhetorical analysis, researchers must determine (Conrad & Malphurs, 2008): Who is "speaking"? What motivates their message? Who is the target audience? How do speakers try to motivate the audience? These questions guide which texts to analyze and how to analyze them. Depending upon the research question, the first step is often determining which persuasive texts are most representative of particular speakers' positions created to address various audiences. Second, depending upon the volume of messages, these may have to be theoretically sampled to capture the range of speakers, persuasion tactics, and audiences. Third, these texts are then analyzed for the rhetorical strategies used. Last, the interaction between texts is analyzed. We illustrate each of these methodological steps (see Figure 22.1) with a sample analysis.

Visual Rhetoric in Action

We draw on a larger study that we are currently conducting to examine the ongoing legitimacy struggle over the Canadian oil sands. The oil sands are a strategic energy resource with large and

Lianne Lefsrud et al.

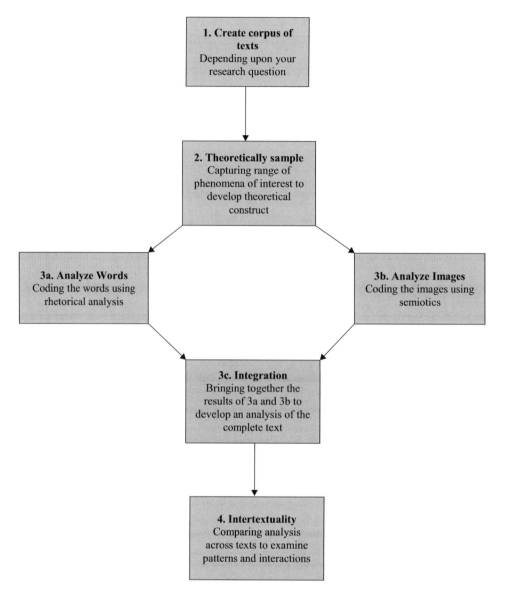

Figure 22.1 Analyzing Visual Rhetoric

visible environmental effects; consequently, they are becoming increasingly controversial and emotional. Challengers to the institutional order (Fligstein, 1996) reframe a once-legitimate energy source as illegitimate, while incumbents attempt to reframe it as legitimate by defining its opponents as themselves illegitimate. This discursive contest provides the opportunity to examine their interactive processes of delegitimation and relegitimation as these unfold in real time.

Identify the Appropriate Corpus of Texts

The first step is to identify the appropriate texts to gather. For example, to examine the relative persuasiveness of entrepreneurs' pitches to a venture capitalist, the most appropriate texts might be their PowerPoint presentations and prospectuses. To determine whether corporations are green washing, a sample of their marketing campaigns, annual reports, product labeling, and websites might be compared to internal documents to reveal any inconsistencies in how they present themselves to customers, shareholders, and the public versus their employees.

In the past 6 years, the oil sands have gone from being taken for granted to becoming increasingly contested, visual, and emotional. In our case, we were interested in how organizational actors contest the legitimacy of the oil sands through imagery. So, we searched electronic and print media for multimodal messages about the oil sands. In this case, we defined "multimodal" as messages that combined words and images. Video messages (containing music and voiceover as well as words and image) are, of course, also multimodal but beyond the scope of this discussion. A majority of the texts that we found were created by opponents to oil sands development and were posted on billboards, run as print advertisements in magazines and newspapers, and posted on websites. Supporters of development countered with their own messages in similar venues. In our study, this process yielded a database of 200 unique multimodal texts relating to the struggle over the legitimacy of the oil sands.

Theoretically Sample These Texts

If the corpus is small, it is possible for the researcher to analyze all the texts. If the volume is greater, however, the corpus may have to be theoretically sampled to capture the range of the phenomenon of interest (i.e., speakers, persuasion tactics, and audiences). Glaser defines theoretical sampling as "the process of data collection for further generating theory whereby the analyst jointly collects, codes, and analyses his data and decides which data to collect next and where to find them, in order to develop his theory as it emerges" (1978: 36). Thus, as theoretical concepts emerge from the data, researchers would sample those texts that further elaborate and test these conceptual lines.

In our study, we selected a small sample of advertisements related to the debate over the legitimacy and illegitimacy of the oil sands. Our criteria for sampling these stakeholders' advertisements were as follows: (a) they meaningfully linked to each other (visually and/or argumentatively), (b) they contained both words and images, and (c) the example reframed the grounds for argument about the oil sands. The various sponsors for the categorizations presented were not consistent: one organization sponsored a perspective, briefly engaged the debate, then vanished, and a different organization stepped in and reinvented the grounds for argument.

We also chose these advertisements because they present complex moral arguments using relatively simple combinations of words and image. Finally, these advertisements were selected because they engaged in overt strategies of category creation to attack their opponents' moral grounds for arguments, explicitly delegitimating not only the antagonists' positions but also their organizations.

Analyze the Visual Rhetoric and Social Semiotics Embedded in the Texts

Next, the researcher must use appropriate tools to code the texts. In our case, we coded the advertisements using visual rhetoric and social semiotics to identify and categorize the persuasive elements used in the words and in the images of the advertisement (see Table 22.1). More specifically, we analyzed the text using two conceptual frameworks from rhetoric: Aristotelian/classical and Burkean rhetoric. We used Aristotle's (1984) modes of proof: ethos (appeals to credibility), pathos (appeals to emotion), and logos (appeals to logic). These categories were assigned based on standard criteria for establishing each appeal. For example, ethos—textual credibility—arises out of phrases that demonstrate the advertisement sponsor understands the problem (is competent to speak on the issue) or that establish common ground with viewers (the sponsor and viewer share similar values). Pathos—an appeal to emotion—arises from effective word choice (negative/positive connotations) and figurative language (metaphors). Logos—the internal consistency of the message—arises out of series of

Lianne Lefsrud et al.

claims, both formal (syllogisms) and informal (enthymemes). Words, phrases, and sentences in the advertisements were analyzed to determine which label(s) best explained their function (or multiple functions) in the argument.

From classical rhetoric, we analyzed the use of tropes (metaphor, irony, metonymy, parallelism/isocolon, paronomasia, and antithesis) (Crawley & Hawhee, 1999) and figures (phrasing that results in a change of word order) in the linguistic structures (Corbett, 1990). The text was analyzed to identify patterns that correspond to traditional definitions for the trope or figure. We also used Burke's (1969) concept of identification (the sense of shared sameness between sponsor and viewer) as arising through five tactics: (1) establish shared values between sponsor and viewer (similar to Aristotle's credibility); (2) demonstrate how interests align between sponsor and viewer; (3) illustrate that sponsor and viewer belong to a privileged group; (4) create a dichotomy between "them" (the enemy) and "us" (allies); and (5) invite viewers to join sponsor in acting against the enemy. Word phrases or image details that employed these tactics were coded as instances of identification.

Table 22.1 Coding Scheme for Analyzing Words and Images in Multimodal Messages

Coding	Example
Type of visual representation: isomorphic	Photograph: traditional news media shot of a person observing a fire
Image framing: composed	Cropped view, chest upward (traditional photo portrait)
Relationship between words and image: complementary, supplementary, juxtaposition	Supplementary (image is dominant; words supplement)
	People can be helpless observers in the face of devastation or taking action for restoration
Gaze of figures: object/subject	Indirect; people are objects to be observed
Viewer distance: intimate, mid, estranged	Mid-range, creates distance
Vantage point of viewer: subordinate, level, superordinate	Level: equal relationship with figure on the left
	Subordinate: trees and reforestation person are held up
Framing of argument: environmental, economic, morality/ethics, political/human rights	Environmental: degradation versus reforestation
Identification: creating "us versus them," creating shared vision, invoking mythologies	Creates shared purpose: We want a society that values reforestation and rejuvenation, not degradation and destruction
Modes of argument: ethos, pathos, logos	Ethos: sponsor revitalization; viewer should too
	Pathos: Pride in healthy forests, Canadians for protecting the environment versus destroying it
	Logos: What kind of person do you want to be? The gas you buy reflects your values.
Method of argument: isocolon, anastrophe, anaphora, epistrophe, analogy, simile, etc.	Isocolon "conflict oil, ethical oil", anastrophe " . . . OIL, . . . OIL". Ethical oil is presented as antithesis to conflict oil: thesis/**antithesis**
Positioning: old/familiar, centered/emphasized, new/unfamiliar	Canada's reforestation placed as "new/surprising" information (i.e., the antithesis of how conflict oil countries destroy the environment)
Tropes—irony, metonymy, pun, metaphor	Metonymy: forester stands for all company employees in Canada; oil sands stands in for Canada; "valuing environment" represents kind of person viewer wants to be

230

We coded the images using Kress and van Leeuwen's (1996) visual grammar, which included figure/gaze, viewer distance and vantage point, image framing, and image positioning (see Table 22.1 for coding scheme). First, we identified details in the images and coded them separately; then we assessed the function of the detail (as a part of the argument, the whole argument, or both).

The final area of analysis—how words and image interact—required multiple coding. We also drew on three of Schriver's (1997) categories to label this relationship: (1) supplementary (one mode dominates, the other elaborates), (2) complementary (each mode presents different information, combined they give the whole story), and (3) juxtapositioning (each mode seems unrelated, combined they reveal a new meaning).

First the advertisements were coded by hand using the rhetorical and semiotic frameworks discussed previously. The labels were entered into a table under a set of headings: topic or advertisement title; code or label; words; image; and analysis. The topic was selected from the topmost or most prominent words on the message. Codes were applied in this order: relationship between words and image; the type of representation; semiotic codes (for visual elements) of gaze, viewer distance, vantage point, image frame; rhetorical codes (for textual/argumentative features) of tactics of identification; argument frame, methods of argument; modes (ethos, pathos, logos); positioning (left/right; old/new; familiar/strange); and figuration (e.g., metaphor, metonymy, irony). The third column identified the word passage being analyzed, and the fourth identified the visual feature. The fifth column summarized the analysis of the code and verbal or visual detail from columns three or four.

To ensure systematic analysis of the message features, the coder first identified the relationship between the words and image (using Schriver's categories), and second, the visual elements. Each message features a central image that arrests viewer attention. We assume that viewers start at the left and then move to the right image, following conventional eye movements of readers of the English language (cf. Gutenberg diagram, Lidwell, Holden, & Butler, 2010). The third stage, analyzing the text, also followed a conventional pattern, from the top left systematically right and downward, left panel first then right. Finally, the whole advertisement was analyzed, combining the panels into a unit and considering first the images, then the textual/argumentative features. If a particular code was not relevant, it was omitted.

One researcher hand-coded the messages. These labels were checked and validated by a second researcher as the information was entered into MaxQDA software and attached to the relevant features of the messages. Each feature was checked, labeled, and cross-labelled to capture the multiple layers of meaningful relationships among the multimodal elements (see Table 22.2). The labels were assigned based on the codes in columns three and four of the table.

Analyze the Interaction Between Texts

The final stage of this process required analyzing the coded material to identify patterns across the texts. From these patterns, we developed three mid-level theoretical concepts that provided the basis for categorizing legitimacy: argument framing, identification, and rhetorical tropes. We then linked the theoretical concepts to the process by which the message sponsors created the categories that designated particular organizations as legitimate or illegitimate. In this way we were able to catalogue the processes of legitimation and delegitimation to develop a representative model.

An Example of Visual Rhetoric in Action: Conflict Oil, Ethical Oil

To make this more concrete, we will provide a short analysis of one of the advertisements from our study. Prior to 2011, arguments about the oil sands centered on its legitimacy from an environmental perspective. In 2011, the Ethical Oil Institute published a series of advertisements (static web-based advertisements appeared at ethicaloil.org, video versions appeared on television and on youtube.

Table 22.2 Analysis of Conflict Oil, Ethical Oil Advertisement

Code	Words	Image	Analysis	Theoretical Concepts
Vantage point: God's eye view and worm's eye view		P1 level; P2 worm's eye	P1 viewer has equal relationship with figure: we are him if we buy oil from his country. P2 viewer is subordinate to majestic trees: these trees look after viewer, keep the planet livable.	Framing: Environmental concern: conflict oil countries degrade the environment through abusive practices, political unrest; ethical oil countries reclaim land (reforest it), foster growth of vegetation, and enable the environment to flourish again.
Argument frame: environmental	Conflict Oil: degradation Ethical Oil: reforestation	P1 nature being destroyed by fire/ human violence; P2 Tranquil park where vegetation flourishes, human supports	Some oil producers destroy the environment through poor extraction practices, some through political unrest (where environment is collateral damage). Ethical oil countries preserve the environment and reclaim it following extraction.	Creates explicit categories of conflict oil (members include tropical areas with poor extraction practices or political unrest) and ethical oil (members include North American countries that reclaim the land by reforesting it [racist implications]). Also creates categories of environmental steward versus environmental degrader.
Argument method: syllogisms, parallel, epistrophe, isocolon, thesis/ antithesis	Parallel phrases (same structure, different length) Epistrophe (same ending) Thesis: degrade Antithesis: reforest	Human figure in both pictures, set in natural environment: P1 on fire, P2 being cared for. Trees minute in background in P1; god-like depiction of trees in P2.	Three point syllogistic argument (only conclusion explicitly stated) (see Table 22.3 for syllogisms). Visual and verbal parallelism: similarity highlights the differences: P1 is old, P2 is new; together the panels ask viewers to choose who they will use to source their oil.	Identification: "Us" is the good guys who reforest (ethical oil) and "them" the bad guys who degrade the environment and burn vegetation. Scapegoats tropical/African countries that harm the environment.
Modes of proof: pathos	"Degradation" versus "reforestation"	Color: P1 black and orange flame, citizen engaging in mayhem (throwing something?); P2 green, sunshine, peaceful forestry employee.	P1 colors and scene evoke emotional appeal of environmental destruction; P2 colors and scene evoke feelings of peace and tranquility	Metonymy: African/black-skinned countries all degrade the environment, while all (White) Western countries "save" the environment by planting and overseeing forests.
Trope: metonymy	Conflict oil Ethical oil	African country, palm trees, Black man clad in street clothes; deciduous forest, Caucasian forestry worker	Conflict oil: stands in for all African/ tropical oil-producing countries; ethical oil: (stands in for North America, Western countries)	Implications: Ethical oil creates two categories to separate itself from "other" oil producers who don't care about the environment. Asks viewers to choose which side they are on.
Metaphor			Degradation: refers to both environment and human	

com) that reframed the discussion about oil sands extraction from its effects on the environment to its implications for political and human rights globally. Here, we examine Ethical Oil's advertisement "Conflict Oil, Ethical Oil" (see Figure 22.2 and Table 22.2).

The advertisement features two panels. In the left panel, viewers see the text "Conflict Oil" and "Degradation" before their eyes drop down to see the photograph of an orange inferno toward the left and the dark-skinned man dressed in civilian clothes in the center while a black cloud of smoke blows to the right behind him. Viewers are then likely to see the right panel text, "Ethical Oil" and "Reforestation," before noticing the towering young deciduous forest with a distant figure of a (white-skinned) forestry worker in the center background. The color of the reverse text boxes also communicates visually: in Western culture, red signals "danger" and "stop," here associated with "conflict oil" and "degradation"; green signals "environmentally friendly" and "go," here associated with "ethical oil" and "reforestation." Finally, viewers read the argument conclusion: "Ethical Oil. A choice we have to make". The dark-skinned figure is level with viewers, indicating an equal relationship: we could be him. The right figure, the forestry worker, is distant, and viewers look up to him and the trees that surround him; this positioning demotes viewers to a subordinate position. Both men are presented as visually parallel: they face left, pictured in profile as objects for contemplation. These illustrations position viewers as partners to the man in the tropical setting and subordinate to the distant, god-like man in the deciduous forest. The panel text is also parallel, the phrasing identical in structure (adjective modifying noun in conflict/ethical oil; nominalization in degradation/reforestation), similar but not identical in length (three beats in "conflict oil" versus four beats in "ethical oil," four beats in "degradation" and five beats in "reforestation"), and both use epistrophe (clauses or phrases that end in the same word or lexeme, i.e., "oil" and "-ation"). This advertisement uses syllogisms (logic) (key premises are outlined, but only the conclusion is explicitly stated) (see Table 22.3).

Figure 22.2 Ethical Oil Institute's Conflict Oil, Ethical Oil Advertisement

Table 22.3 Syllogistic Argument Presented in Ethical Oil Advertisement

	First Step	*Second Step*	*Final Step*
Major premise	Conflict oil causes degradation [of the environment].	Ethical oil causes reforestation [improves the environment].	We must make moral choices.
Minor premise	Degradation [of the environment] is morally wrong.	Reforestation is morally responsible.	The moral choice is ethical oil.
Conclusion	Conflict oil is morally wrong.	Ethical oil is morally responsible.	We must choose ethical oil.

The logic of this advertisement creates an emotional appeal (i.e., it morally pressures viewers to choose "ethical" oil), as do the images. The red text boxes and the burning landscape create painful emotions in viewers (fear, guilt), while the green text boxes and tranquil forest scene evoke feelings of peace and pride. The advertisement also employs the rhetorical trope of metonymy (an attribute stands for the concept) to create emotion: The Black man and the burning tropical landscape represent all countries with dark-skinned inhabitants, who are characterized as "degrading" the environment, while the forestry worker and deciduous trees signify all (White) Western countries, who are characterized as planting and nurturing forests. This representation is racist but it also creates identification: the bad (Black) guys who degrade the environment are "them" (conflict oil, the illegitimate category) and the good (White) guys who reforest are "us" (ethical oil, the legitimate category). This dichotomy (ironically) scapegoats all countries with dark-skinned populations as evil groups that degrade the environment and elevates countries with white-skinned inhabitants as environmental stewards.

The analysis presented here by no means exhausts the possibilities of this method applied to this advertisement, but it does illustrate how meaning can be extracted from it to understand how the categories are created and how viewers are pressured to make different choices when they buy fuel.

Conclusions: Visual Rhetoric in Organizational Research

This method of visual rhetoric enables researchers to document and explain how visuals can contribute to and significantly strengthen a textual argument. In our study, it allowed us to trace the dynamic process of category creation as the various proponents for and against the oil sands aimed to demonstrate why the organizations associated with this oil source were legitimate or illegitimate. In the context of the debate about the oil sands, legitimacy and illegitimacy are emotion-based designations. Participants focus their arguments primarily on the moral legitimacy of this energy source: that is, they accord or rescind legitimacy based on moral principles.

To trace the role of argument in the legitimation struggle around the oil sands, we had to move from the visual rhetorical analysis of the advertisements to a model of legitimation. We identified three general theoretical concepts that provided a foundation for legitimacy claims: argument framing, identification, and rhetorical tropes. Regarding framing, before 2011, arguments about the legitimacy of the oil sands were framed mainly in terms of the environment (that is, the oil sands negatively impact the local/global environment). When the Ethical Oil Institute entered the discussion, it reframed the argument from perspectives based on degrading the environment and on politics. The second theoretical concept, identification, embodies the emotional appeal in these advertisements. The advertisement designers set up an "us versus them" dichotomy and invites viewers to decide who they support. In the case of ethicaloil.org, viewers must choose between the good guys who reforest (ethical oil) or the bad guys who degrade the environment ([political] conflict oil). Each side is framed in such a skewed and emotionally freighted way so viewers will identify with the "good guy." The third theoretical concept, tropes (in this case, of metonymy), also contributes to the emotional appeal of the arguments. In our advertisement, the evil is located in a specific site (the dark-skinned man) that then represents others (metonymy) who also degrade the environment and then to all other people associated with production of "conflict oil."

These theoretical concepts enable us to connect the details in the words and image to the emotional appeals that shape viewer response to the advertisement's message. These enhance viewers' emotional responses to the legitimacy or illegitimacy of the industry. The fact that the legitimacy can be established or compromised through arguments based on moral judgments with various framings suggests that legitimation can be a dynamic process.

Our analysis method for multimodal messages is an extension and consolidation of others' research into visually persuasive texts, with broader applications for organizational research (see Table 22.4). Phillips and Brown (1993) developed a critical hermeneutic approach, based on social semiotics, to examine how a corporation used signs as an attempt to restructure its image and the publics' attitudes toward it. They demonstrate that knowledge is never value-neutral, but is a function of the context's culture, communication, and power. Munir and Phillips (2005) illustrate how institutional

Table 22.4 Use of Visual Rhetoric in Qualitative Research Methods

Reference	Research Context	How Innovation Was Used	Outcomes/Results of Innovation
Phillips & Brown (1993)	Advertising	Critically examines a corporation's use of signs as an attempt to restructure its image and attitudes toward it	Develop a critical hermeneutic approach, based on social semiotics, to examine connotations and denotations evoked by imagery to demonstrate (a) relationship between culture, communication, and power; (b) creative interpretation requirements; (c) underused interpretivist methods to extend quantitative method; (d) "conversational" relationship between object and subject; and (e) all knowledge is value laden.
Munir & Phillips (2005)	Advertising	Explore the role of institutional entrepreneurs in the adoption of a radically new technology	Institutional entrepreneurs engage in discursive work to shape the social context around a new technology—photography—from being a specialist product used by professionals to a general product for anyone "keeping the story" of their life.
Lefsrud, Graves, & Phillips (2014)	Advertising	Examine how multimodal texts are used to construct cultural classifications in a legitimacy struggle	Examine how competing classifications rhetorically leverage symbolic meaning systems; show that legitimacy struggles may not be linear or lifecycle, but can be both, resulting in a helical model; and demonstrate how images and words are used to evoke emotion to "win" an audience.

entrepreneurs use imagery, such that the public identifies with a radically new technology, changes their conception of it, and adopts it into their everyday lives. Lefsrud, Graves, and Phillips (2014) also demonstrate how symbolic meaning systems are leveraged (per Phillips & Brown, 1993) to create identification and a persuasive alternative to the status quo (per Munir & Phillips, 2005) to examine alternative classifications of an industry, as means of legitimation and delegitimation.

By codifying an approach to analyzing multimodal messages, we hope to seed further research into the persuasiveness of multimodal messages, beyond discursive processes. Research into the legitimacy struggles around other controversial (and possibly highly visual) practices and products—like the conflict minerals, sweatshop labor, or blood diamonds—could benefit from understanding the rhetorical use of imagery. Additionally, this method could be used to examine how entrepreneurs use imagery to legitimate new products to venture capitalists, potential customers, and regulators. Indeed, a picture *and* a thousand words might prove to be the most persuasive of all.

References

Aristotle. (1984). *The Rhetoric and Poetics of Aristotle* (Modern College Library Ed.). New York: Random House.

Ashkanasy, N. M., Humphrey, R. H., & Huy, Q. N. (2014). Integrating affect and emotion in management theories. Special topic forum, call for papers. *Academy of Management Review.*

Birdsell, D. S., & Groarke, L. (2007). Outlines of a theory of visual argument. *Argumentation and advocacy,* *43*(3–4), 103.

Briscoe, F., Gupta, A., & Anner, M. (2013, June). The humanizing tactic: The effects of victim testimonials on target and non-target organizations during a successful campaign of the collegiate anti-sweatshop movement. In *Connecting Rigor and Relevance in Institutional Analysis conference at Harvard Business School.*

Burke, K. (1969). *A Rhetoric of Motives.* Berkeley: University of California Press.

Conrad, C., & Malphurs, R. (2008). Are we there yet? Are we there yet?. *Management Communication Quarterly,* *22*(1), 123–146.

Corbett, E. P. J. (1990). *Classical Rhetoric for the Modern Student.* New York: Oxford University Press.

Creed, W. E. D., Hudson, B., Okhuysen, G., & Smith-Crowe, K. (2014). Swimming in a sea of shame: Incorporating emotion into explanations of institutional reproduction and change. *Academy of Management Review,* *39*, 275–301.

Crowley, S., & Hawhee, D. (1999). *Ancient rhetorics for contemporary students.* Boston: Allyn and Bacon.

Drori, G.S., Delmestri, G., & Oberg, A. (in press). In P. Scott and L. Engwall (Eds.), *Branding the university: Relational strategy of identity construction in a competitive field.* Portland, WA: Portland Press.

Fleckenstein, K., Hu, S., & Calendrillo, L.T. (2007). *Ways of Seeing, Ways of Speaking: The Integration of Rhetoric and Vision in Constructing the Real.* West Lafayette, IN: Parlor Press.

Fligstein, N. (1996). Markets as politics: A political–cultural approach to market institutions. *American Sociological Review,* 61, 656–673.

Foss, S. K. (Ed.). (2004). *Rhetorical criticism: Exploration and practice.* Long Grove, IL: Waveland Press.

Friedland, R., Mohr, J. Roose, H., & Gardinali, P. (2014). The institutional logics of love: Measuring intimate life. *Theory and Society,* *43*(3–4), 333–370.

Glaser, B. G. (1978) *Theoretical Sensitivity.* Mill Valley, CA: Sociology Press.

Goodwin, J., Jasper, J.M., & Polletta, F. (2001). *Passionate Politics: Emotions and Social Movements.* Chicago: University of Chicago Press.

Gray, B., Purdy, J. M., & Ansari, S. S. (2015). From interactions to institutions: Microprocesses of framing and mechanisms for the structuring of institutional fields. *Academy of Management Review,* *40*(1), 115–143.

Grimaldi, W. (1980). *Aristotle, "Rhetoric" I: A Commentary.* New York: Fordham University Press.

Grodal, S., & Granqvist, N. (2014). Great expectations: Discourse and affect during field emergence. *Emotions and the Organizational Fabric, Research on Emotion in Organizations,* *10*, 139–166.

Gutierrez, B., Howard-Grenville, J., & Scully, M. A. (2010). The faithful rise up: Split identification and an unlikely change effort. *Academy of Management Journal,* *53*(4), 673–699.

Haack, P., Pfarrer, M. D., & Scherer, A. G. (2014). Legitimacy-as-feeling: How affect leads to vertical legitimacy spillovers in transnational governance. *Journal of Management Studies,* *51*(4), 634–666.

Hallett, T., & Ventresca, M. J. (2006). Inhabited institutions: Social interactions and organizational forms in Gouldner's Patterns of Industrial Bureaucracy. *Theory and Society,* *35*(2), 213–236.

Hochschild, A. R. (2003). *The managed heart: Commercialization of human feeling, With a new afterword*. Oakland: University of California Press.

Hope, D. S. (2006). *Visual Communication: Perception, Rhetoric, and Technology*. Cresskill, NJ: Hampton Press.

Jasper, J. M. (1997). *The Art of Moral Protest: Affective and Reactive Emotions in and Around Social Movements*. Chicago: University of Chicago Press.

Kress, G., & van Leeuwen, T. (1996). *Reading Images: The Grammar of Visual Design*. New York: Routledge.

Lefsrud, L., Graves, H., & Phillips, N. (2014). *Dirty Oil, Ethical Oil: Legitimate or Illegitimate? The Struggle to Categorize the Alberta Oil Sands*. Working paper.

Lidwell, W., Holden, K., & Butler, J. (2010). *Universal Principles of Design* (second edition). Minneapolis, MN: Rockport Publishers.

McQuarrie, E. F., & Mick, G. D. (1996). Figures of rhetoric in advertising language. *The Journal of Consumer Research*, 22, 424–438.

Meyer, R. E., Höllerer, M. A., Jancsary, D., & Van Leeuwen, T. (2013). The visual dimension in organizing, organization, and organization research: Core ideas, current developments, and promising avenues. *The Academy of Management Annals*, 7(1), 489–555.

Mitchell, W. J. (1994). *The reconfigured eye: Visual truth in the post-photographic era*. Boston: MIT Press.

Munir, K. A., & Phillips, N. (2005). The birth of the "Kodak Moment": Institutional entrepreneurship and the adoption of new technologies. *Organization Studies*, 26, 1665–1687.

Phillips, N., & Brown, J. (1993). Analyzing communications in and around organizations: A critical hermeneutic approach. *Academy of Management Journal*, 36, 1547–1576.

Schriver, K. A. (1997). *Dynamics in Document Design: Creating Texts for Readers*. New York: Wiley.

Scott, L. M. (1994). Images in advertising: The need for a theory of visual rhetoric. *Journal of Consumer Research*, 21, 252–273.

Scott, L. M., & Batra, R. (2003). *Persuasive Imagery: A Consumer Response Perspective*. Mahwah, NJ: Lawrence Erlbaum Associates.

Smith, K. L., Moriarty, S., Kenney, K., & Barbatsis, G. (Eds.). (2004). *Handbook of visual communication: Theory, methods, and media*. New York: Routledge.

Van Eemeren, F. H., & Garssen, B. (Eds.). (2012). *Exploring argumentative contexts* (Vol. 4). Amsterdam: John Benjamins Publishing.

Voronov, M., & Vince, R. (2012). Integrating emotions into the analysis of institutional work. *Academy of Management Review*, 37(1), 58–81.

Walker, J. (2000). *Pathos* and *katharsis* in "Aristotelian" rhetoric: Some implications. In A. Gross & A. E. Walzer (Eds.), *Rereading Aristotle's Rhetoric* (pp. 74–92). Carbondale: Southern Illinois University Press.

Zietsma, C. (2013). Emotions and Institutions Workshop, call for papers.

23

Markers, Metaphors, and Meaning

Drawings as a Visual and Creative Qualitative Research Methodology in Organizations

Sarah J. Tracy and Shawna Malvini Redden

Visual methods including drawing have historically been neglected in organizational and management research, often dismissed as "trivial, constituting decoration, insubstantial rhetoric, illusion, or at best, partially reliable information" (Davison, McClean, & Warren, 2012, p. 6). However, the use of drawing is quite common in arts-based approaches (Leavy, 2009) and research with children (Backett-Milburn & McKie, 1999; Davis, 2013; Myers, Saunders, & Garret, 2003; Sewell, 2011; Tay-Lim & Lim, 2013). Visual methods are burgeoning across disciplines (Barnhurst, Vari, & Rodriquez, 2004; Guillemin, 2004; Pain, 2012; Singhal & Rattine-Flaherty, 2006), with increasing momentum in management and organizational studies (Meyer, 1991), and with arguments that the arts are critically important for developing complex aspects of the mind (Eisner, 2002). Specifically, visual methods prove to be particularly powerful tools for examining implicit assumptions (Schyns, Tymon, Kiefer, & Kerschreiter, 2013), exploring emotionally turbulent topics (Kearney & Siegman, 2004), and understanding organizational change (Barner, 2008; Vince & Broussine, 1996).

In this chapter, we outline an innovative qualitative data collection and analytic approach that makes use of visual drawings and metaphor analysis. Metaphors—words that compare one thing (e.g., an organization) to another (e.g., a party, a competition, a prison)—provide insight into how people experience and frame their worlds. Metaphors are abundant in almost all types of textual data such as interviews, documents, and fieldnotes, yet they can be difficult for participants to identify on demand via traditional "forced metaphor" approaches. The data collection and analysis approach we outline in this chapter explains a method that asks participants in group or individual interviews to craft artistic drawings in response to researcher questions, such as "What does a leader look like?" or "What does this interagency collaboration seem like?" or "What does workplace bullying feel like?" After participants draw, they write descriptors of their drawings and, together, use those words and images to share workplace experiences.

Depending on the research goals, participants can also consider implications and groupings of other participants' metaphors and discuss the complex interpretations that emerge (e.g., how responses might differ depending on whether participants view the bully as a "king" or a "demon"). This innovative approach provides unique empirical value and an avenue for co-creation of knowledge through participant collaboration. Furthermore, as a result of this approach, participants become engaged in the research process and are better equipped to speak about difficult and vague experiences.

Importantly, they are able to analyze how their metaphorical framings enable or constrain actions for possibility and transformation. Meanwhile, the approach lends itself to rich pedagogical activity by creating space for transformative thinking as well as a vehicle for learning inductive qualitative interpretation. Finally, researchers and readers are provided with a vivid visualization of workplace experience, which adds vibrancy to written reports.

The chapter unfolds as follows: First, we provide some background on metaphor analysis and list several examples of studies that use drawing as an innovative method of data collection and analysis. Then we offer explanations of four primary functions of this unique approach: (1) empirical value, (2) power-sharing and collaboration, (3) pedagogy, and (4) memorable representation process (as illustrated in Figure 23.1).

The Value of Metaphors

When people describe the unique value of qualitative research methodology, they often point to the ability to develop insight into how people interpret and make sense of their worlds (Tracy, 2013). However, meaning in fieldwork is frequently tacit (Altheide & Johnson, 1994). People often cannot say what is important to them or why they acted in a certain way. This is especially true when people are in the midst of change, disruption, or trauma. In such cases, participants may be unable to narrate coherent plots, scripts, scenarios, recipes, and morals. Metaphor analysis provides a valuable approach for accessing meaning in such situations.

Metaphors—words that compare one thing to another—are embedded in the way we think, communicate, and act, which impacts the way we make sense of the world (Lakoff & Johnson, 1980). Qualitative scholars are perfectly situated to take note of and analyze metaphors for what they say about why participants act the way they do. Metaphors are not just rhetorical, analytical, or conceptual devices, but rather are embodied and serve as embedded framing and orienting devices. In other words, metaphor *is* the cake and not just the icing—providing a linguistic link to reality and giving birth to meaning in a "world in which subjectivity and objectivity remain an indivisible whole . . . beneath the everyday linguistic patina of human interaction" (Hogler, Gross, Hartman, & Cunliffe, 2008, p. 400).

Let us illustrate by discussing a focus group study in which we were interested in understanding how people made sense of managing medicated-assisted treatment (MAT) for opiate addiction—a treatment that includes medications such as methadone to relieve dependency (Malvini Redden, Tracy, & Shafer, 2013). When we asked participants directly about their challenges, many found it difficult to articulate why they found MAT helpful or hurtful. However, we were able to assess

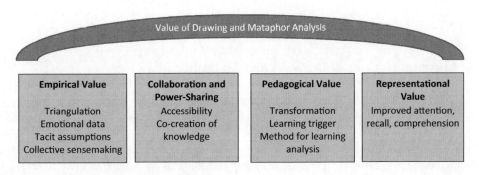

Figure 23.1   Value of Drawing and Metaphor Analysis

MAT-related challenges by analyzing the metaphors participants used to speak about their dependence. One commonly cited metaphor was that MAT was a "crutch." The crutch metaphor illustrates that the participants viewed MAT as helping them to get by, but that it did not allow them to practice standing on their own feet. Furthermore, MAT essentially served as a symbol of sickness and weakness. Identifying and interpreting the crutch metaphor efficiently explained why our participants had mixed feelings about MAT and led us to explore linkages among language, agency, and expectations of future sobriety success. So, how do we encourage people to articulate metaphors, and what does drawing have to do with it?

Methodologies for Metaphors and Drawing

Just knowing that metaphors are valuable qualitative data is not enough to use them effectively in organizational research. Specific methods are necessary for accessing metaphors during data collection. We will review three approaches: the forced metaphor approach, the idiographic approach, and the drawing approach.

In a forced metaphor approach, the researcher directly asks participants to provide a metaphor (e.g., what does your workplace feel like?). Although efficient, this approach can be limited in its success (Sheenan, Barker, & McCarthy, 2004). Even though metaphors are ubiquitous, most people cannot spontaneously name them or tend to come up with something that is obvious or trite (e.g., this workplace is like a prison).

In contrast, an idiographic approach to metaphor collection can provide richer data because it identifies and analyzes metaphors that emerge naturally in people's talk (Grant & Oswick, 1996). In an idiographic approach, researchers avoid specifically asking participants for metaphors, but rather review the data with an eye toward metaphors in use. We used this approach in the MAT study discussed previously.

Third, drawings can serve as wonderfully rich sources of metaphorical data. For example, in a study on workplace bullying, the first author and two colleagues (Tracy, Lutgen-Sandvik, & Alberts, 2006) asked participants who self-identified as targets of workplace bullying to draw a picture in response to the question "what does workplace bullying feel like?" Participants drew pictures of fist fights, dark clouds, pointing fingers, demons, and more (see Figure 23.2). Coupled with their narratives, these drawings provided insight into the emotive and tacit nature of bullying—that bullying felt like a nightmare in which their boss was akin to a "little Hitler," and they felt like "abused children" and "slaves." Identifying and teasing out the implications of these metaphors helped to reveal the deep pain and shame associated with bullying and explain why it was difficult for participants to effectively deal with the situation.

This article about workplace bullying is among a growing number in the field of organizational studies that make use of drawing analysis. In Table 23.1, we provide the context and outcomes of four empirical studies published in the last 10 years that effectively use drawings as a method of data collection, analysis, and representation in relation to organizational research. We then discuss the four ways drawings lend value to organizational research in the areas of empirical value, power-sharing and collaboration, pedagogy, and enhanced representation.

Four Important Values of Drawing and Metaphor Analysis

The Unique Empirical Value

The first overall value of drawings in organizational research is that they provide unique empirical insight. At their most basic, when supplemented with other methods of data collection, drawings increase trustworthiness or credibility of analysis via triangulation (Copeland & Agosto, 2012) or crystallization (Tracy, 2010). For example, in a study of organizational change, Kearney and Siegman (2004) asked participants to come to the interview with a drawing about their experiences and then

Figure 23.2 Drawing from Target of Workplace Bullying Responding to the Question "What Does Workplace Bullying Feel Like?"

Source: Tracy et al. (2006).

interpret it. Methodologically, the authors argued that drawing served as a triangulation tool, especially as drawings require interpretation from participants, and researchers can test their assumptions.

However, drawings are more than just one more layer of data collection. They are also especially valuable for accessing data on topics that are linked to emotion, identity, change, disruptions, or complex issues that are difficult to articulate (Barner, 2008). Describing experience is especially difficult during trauma. Language alone is often inadequate when trying to discuss extreme betrayal and pain (Emery & Lloyd, 1994). Survivors frequently experience significant gaps in memory, and as individuals remember missing fragments, stories morph and change (Herman, 1992).

> Some people are not ready to narrate their story. They are approached by social scientists and invited, even required to narrate. . . . Death, divorce and disease stories are hard to narrate. One can only trace the edges of the wounds. There are experiences that are just too shattering to put into words, too fantastic to narrate. (Boje, 2001, p. 7)

Drawings are very helpful in emotionally difficult situations. For instance, in the first author's workplace bullying research, drawings provided a summing up and interpretive mechanism (Tracy et al., 2006). Participants who had been faltering and hesitant before the drawing portion of the focus group were suddenly able to narrate their workplace bullying situation in a coherent manner as they reflected on their drawings.

This benefit of drawing lends itself to a range of studies associated with emotion, change, shame, disruption, or abuse (Kearney & Siegman, 2004; Palmberg & Kuru, 2000; Sewell, 2011). As noted by Barner (2008), "the construction of drawings as visual metaphors can help work groups 'give voice' to their emotional reactions to organizational change events, and provide groups with a vehicle for interpreting and framing their experience of organizational change" (p. 120). This allows researchers

Table 23.1 Empirical Studies Featuring Drawing Analysis in Organizational Studies

Reference	Research Context and How Drawing Was Used	Outcomes/Results of Innovation
Bell & Clark (2014)	Students from four UK business schools were asked in groups of 2–5 to visualize and draw "a management researcher," with the prompt: "If a management researcher were an animal, what kind of animal would they be?" (p. 253). After drawing, students discussed their findings in focus groups.	Through visual metaphors, symbolism and mythology can be made "practically intelligible" (p. 262). "The use of visual methods facilitates expression of ideas, feelings and concerns that may be difficult or threatening to articulate using words alone, in a situation founded on unequal power relations, in terms of both pedagogical and research processes. This enables analysis of the beliefs and values associated with management research practice, and provides insight into how it is lived, not as a rational, technical enterprise but as an embodied, socially enacted and emotional enterprise" (p. 14).
Kearney & Siegman (2004)	Employees at a technology training school experiencing organizational change were asked to draw their experiences of the change. Subsequently, they interpreted and discussed the drawings during individual interviews.	In addition to allowing researchers to quickly assess connections between experiences and emotions, drawing enabled participants to succinctly communicate about their experiences. Methodologically, the authors argue that drawing can be a tool for triangulation, especially as drawings require interpretation from participants, and researchers can test their assumptions.
Schyns, Tymon, Kiefer, & Kerschreiter (2013)	Students in groups of 2–5 were asked to think about leadership characteristics and then "draw a leader." Drawings were coded for "people versus metaphors," gender, bodies, symbols, followers, and size of followers in relation to leaders.	Researchers used the analysis of drawings to explore theories of leadership and advocate for adjustments to leadership development practices. In particular, drawings revealed implicit but unarticulated images of leadership. The findings suggest that drawing is a valuable learning intervention for students to acknowledge, question, and potentially transform their implicit theories and beliefs.
Tracy, Lutgen-Sandvik, & Alberts (2006)	Focus group interviews with targets of workplace bullying. Participants drew how workplace bullying made them feel, labeled their drawings with keywords, and then interpreted the drawings for the group.	Analysis revealed vivid metaphors participants used to refer to workplace bullying, to bullying victims, and to bullies themselves. "Whether empowering or disempowering, the metaphors pinpointed through this analysis provide targets with words to explain their situation to others—an important move considering that one of the main problems targeted employees face is that their plight is largely invisible" (p. 178).

to quickly assess connections between events and emotions, and enables participants to succinctly communicate their experiences (Nossiter & Biberman, 1990).

Another empirical strength of drawings is accessing and revealing tacit and potentially non-politically–correct assumptions. On the one hand, this is because drawing makes the familiar strange. It forces participants and researchers alike to suspend preconceptions of familiar territory and create anew mundane topics, issues, places, or ideas (Mannay, 2010). For example, when people are asked to "draw a leader," it suddenly becomes evident how leaders are usually imagined as male and solitary (Schyns et al., 2013). Indeed, drawings allow people to express unconscious aspects of their situation or identify what they would otherwise be unable to explicitly discuss, similar to the way metaphor works (Marshak, 1996). Drawings "act as a catalyst for members of teams to 'say the unsaid' both on an emotional/psychological and on a political level" (Vince & Broussine, 1996, p. 9).

For example, Bell and Clark (2014) used visual approaches to access often unspoken assumptions about management researchers by asking UK business students: "If a management researcher were an animal, what kind of animal would they be?" (p. 253). The most consistent genre of drawing to emerge from the analysis was the "great wild beast." The drawings revealed that students view the management researcher as "a powerful, high-status, masculine hero, supported by a cadre of young, junior academics. The consequences of this symbolism are exclusionary and marginalizing of those who cannot or choose not to conform to it" (p. 262). Asking participants to draw puts them in a space of child-like vulnerability, where tacit assumptions may be revealed, providing insight on how management practice "is lived, not as a rational, technical enterprise but as an embodied, socially enacted and emotional enterprise" (p. 14).

Metaphor and drawing analysis also provides access to larger collective narratives. Indeed, "metaphor drives creativity, leading to a communal recognition of the 'way things are' in the world" (Hogler et al., 2008, p. 394). In a study of organizational change by Barner (2008), participants created together a visual metaphor that described their collective reaction to the organization's ongoing changes. Participants discussed and subsequently modified their drawings several times. In doing so, the results of the analysis literally provided a picture of the collective discussion. Drawings in a group setting enable researchers to assess individual-level and collective-level sense-making and compare participant interpretations to their own (Donnelly & Hogan, 2013; Vince & Broussine, 1996).

How Drawing Facilitates Power-Sharing, Collaboration, and Co-Creation of Knowledge

A second primary value of drawings in organizational research is the way they enable researchers to share power with participants, collaborate, and co-create knowledge. This contributes not only to empirical rigor, but also ties to ethical commitments of fairness and equity.

Especially for historically low-power or inarticulate populations, such as children (Mutonyi & Kendrick, 2011); those speaking about trauma, abuse, or stigmatized experiences; front-line or low status employees; and those speaking in a second language, drawings can aid with expressing complex emotions and experiences. For some, whether due to cognitive ability, age, or language, speaking and writing can be inaccessible, difficult, and threatening (Sewell, 2011). Drawing provides a more accessible and face-saving way to share. In a study with women and children in the Amazon, for instance, Singhal and Rattine-Flaherty (2006) claimed that their participants took "the pencil—a symbol of text, literacy and elitism . . . and turn[ed] it on its head to privilege the creative expression of the unlettered, silenced and the marginalized" (p. 315). On the opposite end of the spectrum, drawing can also destabilize power when researching with very high power individuals such as executives. For those for whom texts and eloquent talking are second nature, introducing a drawing activity reminiscent of childhood may help shake off and disrupt comfortable routines of text centrism and conversational dominance.

By incorporating drawing, researchers open up a space for collaboration with participants as they are asked to help generate material for analysis and consideration (Papa & Singhal, 2007). Drawings can be more complex or ambiguous than verbal answers and encourage dialogical engagement in ways that situate participants as powerful experts and equal players (Tay-Lim & Lim, 2013). Thus, in sharing conversational authority, researchers also enable participants to co-create knowledge in ways that are less common in social science research. As such, drawing provides an important method of conducting participatory action research (Kemmis & McTaggart, 2000) where researchers and organizational members work together to address local issues or problems. With drawing, researchers vividly learn what the participants, themselves, believe is important.

Finally, when coupled with interviews, drawing encourages shared analysis. By explaining their drawings, participants provide first-order or basic interpretations that can themselves be important data for researchers. Subsequently, participant-led interpretations can generate further conversation and subsequent analytic insights. In a group setting, shared interpretations can be a critical analytical tool for collective meaning making and also basic analysis as participants identify themes and ask questions of the drawing data (Bell & Clark, 2014; Vince & Broussine, 1996). A nice consequence of tapping into this group-level interpretation is data reduction (Copeland & Agosto, 2012) that still captures contextual information (Schyns et al., 2013).

Pedagogical Value of Drawing

Third, drawing activities and metaphor analysis provide significant pedagogical value for teaching theoretical concepts and data analysis techniques in accessible, creative, and accelerated ways. Utilizing drawings in the classroom enables students to literally see theoretical concepts and, in turn, make sense of otherwise unarticulated assumptions. For instance, in the second author's organizational communication classroom, students are asked to draw an "ideal leader" in whatever way that makes sense to them based upon experience and course readings. Not only do students see through the drawings how they imagine leadership, but they can also quickly compare and contrast their thinking with others (Schyns et al., 2013).

Critically, drawing and discussing enable students to identify and analyze certain assumptions; in the case of leadership, for instance, leaders are commonly drawn as heroic (larger than life), separate from followers, and male. By comparing drawings, students can see and discuss theoretical concepts, identify themes and commonalities, and also challenge stereotypes or problematic assumptions. Additionally, drawing activities are a fun, engaging, short, and nonthreatening way to engage in critical self-reflection (Donnelly & Hogan, 2013). Using drawing activities as a mechanism for course evaluation also enables students to have a more substantial voice in the classroom than provided for in traditional course satisfaction evaluations (Ward & Shortt, 2013).

For qualitative methodology students, drawing and metaphor analysis are important tools for learning how to analyze and interpret data. Qualitative methodology students can learn how to identify themes, group them together, compare and contrast differences in data and interpretations, choose exemplars, and ask important analytic questions (Donnelly & Hogan, 2013). In the first author's advanced qualitative methods course, she regularly asks students to "draw what graduate school feels like." This leads to a class discussion whereby students ask questions such as: "If a student sees graduate school as a roller coaster, what might that suggest?" Interpretations might include the following: that graduate school has ups and downs; that it can be exhilarating, disorienting, and scream-inducing; that it is finite; and that it can make people throw up (see Figure 23.3).

Participants not only find drawing activities fun and energy producing (Davis, 2013), but they also learn how interpretations lead to important analytic claims. For instance, students who view graduate school as a terrifying, seemingly out of control experience might also view themselves as less agentic in their program than do students who view graduate school as an exhilarating ride with ups and

Figure 23.3 Drawing from a Student in Response to the Question "What Does Graduate School Feel Like?"

downs as a matter of course. By practicing with drawings, students can also helpfully understand the difference between interpretation and analysis, learn how to make analytic claims, and note useful areas for collecting more data to support claims (Tracy, 2013).

Drawings as Valuable Representation Practice

Fourth, drawings provide an interesting, vibrant, and easy-to-remember representation practice that is useful in today's increasingly technologically mediated world. People process visuals 60,000 times faster than text, and while they remember only 10% of what they hear and 20% of what they read, they remember 80% of what they see and do (Byrom, 2014). We have found that audiences and students perk up during research presentations that include drawings and other visual elements. They ask more questions. They "get" the research findings more quickly and remember them longer. Consider, for instance, the impact of the following hypothetical description of a leader: A good leader is like an energetic bunny, surrounded by knowledge and performing leadership not only for others, but for himself. Now, compare the impact of those words to the impact of the drawing in Figure 23.4. If you are like most audiences, the visual drawing is more quickly communicated, impactful, and memorable than the textual description.

Visual data has been linked to increased information processing, comprehension, and decision making (Meyer, 1991). It enriches and enhances textual representations as people find visuals interesting and memorable. As Pain (2012) notes: "At a cognitive level, because visuals use different parts

Figure 23.4   Drawing from a Student in Response to the Prompt "Draw an Ideal Leader"

of the brain than language, the two in combination . . . provide additional cues for understanding and encourage new connections between the two patterns of thought, thus facilitating insights" (p. 7). Indeed, we as authors found it quite enjoyable to "read" and review the literature for this chapter in large part because so many of the pieces included drawings.

Conclusion

As discussed, drawing activities coupled with metaphor analysis have a number of distinct empirical, power-sharing, pedagogical, and representational benefits. As a creative approach to research, these methods generate vivid and compelling data that can lead to insightful, memorable analyses. They are also a lot of fun, especially in a group setting, as organizational issues come to life in vivid, impactful, and playful ways.

Of course, drawing can also have some potential downsides. We have found that some people say they are uncomfortable sharing drawings because of their supposed lack of artistic talent. Furthermore, because drawings reveal tacit assumptions, sometimes participants can be surprised or disturbed when they draw something that reveals an otherwise unknown bias or way of being. That said, these downsides can be mitigated with some good humor and coaching. For example, we recommend that researchers reassure participants, saying, for instance, "Stick figures are totally cool!" (It also helps if researchers with little artistic talent, like both authors of this chapter, draw along with participants.)

Providing extra paper with reassurances that it is okay to start over as many times as necessary is also helpful. Furthermore, during the sharing and debrief, the researcher might offer the following advice: "If you or others find something surprising in your drawing, try not to resist it, but rather be open to what you can learn about yourself through this alternative form of representation."

We encourage organizational researchers to consider incorporating drawing and metaphor analysis into their research and classroom activities, whether as a standalone data collection method or in conjunction with interviews or focus groups. These approaches are especially well-suited for qualitative researchers, as illustrated in an entire special issue of visual approaches in organizational studies published by *Qualitative Research in Management and Organization* (Davison et al., 2012). The value gained from a few markers and some creative energy has the potential to energize participants, surprise researchers, and delight readers.

References

Altheide, D.L., & Johnson, J.M. (1994). Criteria for assessing interpretive validity in qualitative research. In N.K. Denzin & Y.S. Lincoln (Eds.), *Handbook of qualitative research* (2nd ed., pp. 485–499). Newbury Park, CA: Sage.

Backett-Milburn, K., & McKie, L. (1999). A critical appraisal of the draw and write technique. *Health Education Research, 14*, 387–398.

Barner, R. (2008). The dark tower: Using visual metaphors to facilitate emotional expression during organizational change. *Journal of Organizational Change Management, 21*, 120–137.

Barnhurst, K., Vari, M., & Rodriguez, I. (2004). Mapping visual studies in communication. *Journal of Communication, 54*, 616–644.

Bell, E., & Clark, D. W. (2014). "Beasts, burrowers, and birds": The enactment of researcher identities in UK business schools. *Management Learning, 45*, 249–266.

Boje, D.M. (2001). *Narrative methods for organizational and communication research*. London, England: Sage.

Byrom, M. (2014, March). The power of visual communication infographic. Retrieved from www.wyzowl. com/blog/power-visual-communication-infographic

Copeland, A.J., & Agosto, D.E. (2012). Diagrams and relational maps: The use of graphic elicitation techniques with interviewing for data collection, analysis, and display. *International Journal of Qualitative Methods, 11*, 513–533.

Davis, C.S. (2013). *Communicating hope: An ethnography of a children's mental health care team*. Walnut Creek, CA: Left Coast Press.

Davison, J., McClean, C., & Warren, S. (2012). Exploring the visual in organizations and management. *Qualitative Research in Organizations and Management, 7*, 5–15.

Donnelly, P., & Hogan, J. (2013) Engaging students in the classroom: "How can I know what I think until I see what I draw?" *European Political Science, 12*, 365–383.

Eisner, E.W. (2002). *The arts and the creation of mind*. New Haven, CT: Yale University Press.

Emery, C., & Lloyd, S.A. (1994). A feminist perspective on the study of women who use aggression in close relationships. In D.L. Sollie & L.A. Leslie (Eds.), *Gender, families and close relationships: Feminist research journeys* (pp. 237–262). Newbury Park, CA: Sage.

Grant, D., & Oswick, C. (1996). The organization of metaphors and the metaphors of organization: Where are we and where do we go from here? In D. Grant & C. Oswick (Eds.), *Metaphor and organizations* (pp. 213–226). London, England: Sage.

Guillemin, M. (2004). Understanding illness: Using drawings as a research method. *Qualitative Health Research, 14*, 272–289.

Herman, J.L. (1992). *Trauma and recovery*. New York, NY: Basic Books.

Hogler, R., Gross, M.A., Hartman, J.L., & Cunliffe, A.L. (2008). Meaning in organizational communication: Why metaphor is the cake, not the icing. *Management Communication Quarterly, 21*, 393–412.

Kearney, K.S., & Siegman, K.D. (2004). Drawing out emotions: The use of participant-produced drawings in qualitative inquiry. *Qualitative Research, 4*, 361–382.

Kemmis, S., & McTaggart, R. (2000). Participatory action research. In N.K. Denzin & Y.S. Lincoln (Eds.), *Handbook of qualitative research* (2nd ed., pp. 567–605). Thousand Oaks, CA: Sage.

Lakoff, G., & Johnson, M. (1980). *Metaphors to live by*. Chicago, IL: University of Chicago Press.

Leavy, P. (2009). *Method meets art: Arts-based research practice*. New York, NY: Guilford Press.

Malvini Redden, S., Tracy, S.J., & Shafer, M. (2013). A metaphor analysis of recovering substance abusers' sensemaking of medication assisted treatment. *Qualitative Health Research, 23*, 951–962.

Mannay, D. (2010). Making the familiar strange: Can visual research methods render the familiar setting more perceptible? *Qualitative Research, 10,* 91–111.

Marshak, R.J. (1996). Metaphors, metaphoric fields and organizational change. In D. Grant & C. Oswick (Eds.), *Metaphor and organizations* (pp. 147–165). London, England: Sage.

Meyer, A. (1991). Visual data in organizational research. *Organization Science, 2,* 218–236.

Mutonyi, H., & Kendrick, M.E. (2011). Cartoon drawing as a means of accessing what students know about HIV/AIDS: An alternative method. *Visual Communication, 10,* 231–249.

Myers, O.S., Saunders, C., & Garret, E. (2003). What do children think animals need? Aesthetic and psycho-social conceptions. *Environmental Education Research, 9,* 305–325.

Nossiter, V., & Biberman, G. (1990). Project drawings and metaphor: Analysis of organizational culture. *Journal of Managerial Psychology, 5,* 13–16.

Pain, H. (2012). A literature review to evaluate the choice and use of visual methods. *International Journal of Qualitative Methods, 11,* 303–319.

Palmberg, I., & Kuru, J. (2000). Outdoor activities as a basis for environmental responsibility. *The Journal of Environmental Education, 31,* 32–36.

Papa, M.J., & Singhal, A. (2007). Intellectuals searching for publics: Who is out there? *Management Communication Quarterly, 21,* 126–136.

Schyns, B., Tymon, A., Kiefer, T., & Kerschreiter, R. (2013). New ways to leadership development: A picture paints a thousand words. *Management Learning, 14,* 11–24.

Sheenan, K.H., Barker, M., & McCarthy, P. (2004). Analysing metaphors used by victims of workplace bullying. *International Journal of Management and Decision Making, 5,* 21–31.

Sewell, K. (2011). Researching sensitive issues: A critical appraisal of "draw-and-write" as a data collection technique in eliciting children's perceptions. *International Journal of Research & Method in Education, 34,* 175–191.

Singhal, A., & Rattine-Flaherty, E. (2006). Pencils and photos as tools of communicative research and praxis analyzing Minga Perú's quest for social justice in the Amazon. *International Communication Gazette, 68,* 313–330.

Tay-Lim, J., & Lim, S. (2013). Privileging younger children's voices in research: Use of drawings and a co-construction process. *International Journal of Qualitative Methods, 12,* 65–83.

Tracy, S.J. (2010). Qualitative quality: Eight "big-tent" criteria for excellent qualitative research. *Qualitative Inquiry, 16,* 837–851.

Tracy, S.J. (2013). *Qualitative research methods: Collecting evidence, crafting analysis, communicating impact.* Hoboken, NJ: Wiley-Blackwell.

Tracy, S.J., Lutgen-Sandvik, P., & Alberts, J.K. (2006). Nightmares, demons and slaves: Exploring the painful metaphors of workplace bullying. *Management Communication Quarterly, 20,* 148–185.

Vince, R., & Broussine, M. (1996). Paradox, defense, and attachment: Accessing and working with emotions and relations underlying organizational change. *Organization Studies, 17,* 1–21.

Ward, J., & Shortt, H. (2013). Evaluation in management education: A visual approach to drawing out emotion in student learning. *Management Learning, 44,* 435–452.

Part V
Unique Data Collection Methods

24

Structural Sampling
A Technique for Illuminating Social Systems

Sonali K. Shah and Andreea D. Gorbatai

Introduction

Qualitative research has been heralded for contributing novel insights and theoretical perspectives to the management and organization literature (Eisenhardt, 1989; Pratt, 2009; Van Maanen, 1979, 1998; Whetten, 1989). The processes used by qualitative researchers to achieve these outcomes are often invisible to the reader, yet a set of principled, systematic approaches underlies the practices followed by qualitative researchers. In this chapter we illuminate a sampling technique that has been employed in recent works but has yet to be delineated as a methodology: structural sampling.

Structural sampling is a technique designed to uncover the inner workings of a social system. Social systems are comprised of various sets of actors, each occupying different roles and potentially engaging in different practices. As a result, social systems can be complex and multifaceted, and the full set of roles, as well as the norms and behaviors present in the system, may not be known at the start of a study. Structural sampling employs an open, emergent, and systematic sampling approach to meet this challenge. As a result, the practice of structural sampling departs from traditional sampling methodologies in two primary ways. Structural sampling guides a researcher to identify the full set of roles in a social system and thoroughly investigate each of these roles. These roles may be uncovered over time, as more data are collected and informants' perspectives are synthesized. In contrast, traditional qualitative sampling methods instruct the researcher to prespecify the roles to be studied. Structural sampling also encourages researchers to gather data on the social system from people who participate in the system *and* people who interact with the system or are affected by it in some way. In contrast, traditional qualitative sampling methods often focus on gathering data from the focal actors of interest.

Structural sampling can be used to investigate a wide range of social systems, such as an organization, a segment of an organization, or the relationships among multiple organizations, markets, or fields. In addition, a wide array of theories and research questions can be examined through structural sampling. To illustrate this point, we present a number of examples of structural sampling. Our foray into the literature to identify examples is not intended to be exhaustive, but rather illustrate the range of scholarly work that can be conducted using this approach. The examples presented also provide interested scholars with materials to further support and inspire their own studies by providing examples of published descriptions of methods, by showing how large volumes of data collected using structural sampling have been synthesized to build new theory, and by providing examples that illustrate how the details of complex social systems can be concisely communicated.

Our goal is to make this sampling technique explicit, characterize appropriate situations for its use, and help make its application increasingly accessible and attractive to senior and budding scholars alike. We begin by describing the purpose and technique of structural sampling, and we then provide examples of structural sampling, delineate several potential uses for structural sampling, contrast it to other qualitative research methodologies, and highlight its advantages and challenges.

The Purpose of Structural Sampling

We envision structural sampling being most useful when researchers are interested in one or more of three objectives: (1) to identify and understand the actors who shape and are shaped by a particular social system (Coleman, 1994); (2) to uncover the relationships, and the content of those relationships, between actors occupying different roles; and/or (3) to understand how the norms, rules, or other aspects of the social system's governance structure shape individual behavior and relationships (see Figure 24.1).

The Technique of Structural Sampling

Structural sampling is a data collection technique for illuminating how social systems are structured and how they function. Structural sampling seeks to uncover the inner workings of a complex social system composed of actors in heterogeneous roles or positions. Doing so often requires the identification of roles within a social system and/or of the relationships among those roles. Because the sets of actors and/or their relationships may not be clear at the outset of a study, structural sampling is, by necessity, an open and emergent sampling technique. By *open* we mean that, in contrast to traditional

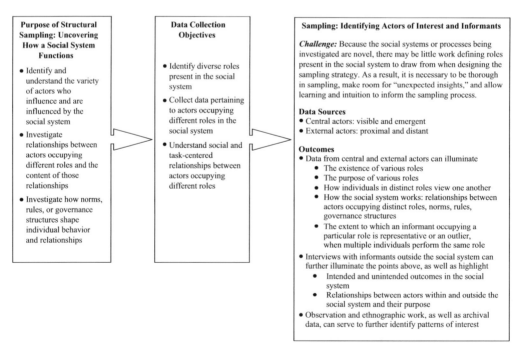

Figure 24.1 Structural Sampling: Purpose, Benefits, and Technique

qualitative sampling methods that tend to prespecify the characteristics of the sample population to be studied, structural sampling requires the researcher to identify the roles played by multiple sets of actors in a social system. By *emergent* we mean that these roles may be uncovered over time, as more data are collected and more informants' perspectives are synthesized.

In some cases, the researcher may understand the salient roles within a social system at the outset of the study and be interested in collecting information from people occupying these roles. In others, the identification of roles may be a wholly emergent component of the research process. In such cases, the process of data collection is often simultaneous with the process of role identification. As a result, role identification does not necessarily precede the onset of data collection or necessarily even occur as a "first stage" of data collection. Most cases are likely somewhere in between these two extremes, with the researcher being able to identify some roles at the outset of the study while being unaware of others. The researcher should also be open to new understandings and be willing to revisit preconceived notions of how the social system functions in light of new data.

The process of identifying roles will often require iteration and a deep understanding of the social system that often begins to coalesce in the later stages of data collection and analysis. Roles can be especially tricky to identify because salient roles are often different from formal titles, and there are also situations where no or few organizational titles exist (e.g., open source software communities or Wikipedia). We encourage researchers to refrain from blindly using formal structures and titles to guide their sampling or analysis.

There is no magic formula for identifying various roles. This process requires analysis, observation, insight, and dedicated effort. There are, however, practices one can engage in to ensure that data are collected to support identification of roles and an understanding of the social system. These are the practices that we seek to illuminate and refer to as *structural sampling*.

Scholars employing this method should be open to using learning and intuition as they gather data on the social system. Following a hunch may uncover knowledge that dramatically alters the researcher's understanding of how or why a social system functions. The cost of engaging in learning is relatively low—an additional handful of interviews or observations—while the potential benefits are high. And the costs of *not* being open to new insights during the data collection process are high because this may result in a skewed understanding of the system.

Truly understanding a social system requires being sensitive to its broader social context, to the rationale behind a system's organizational design, and to the perspectives of actors both in and affected by the social system. To this end, we identify two categories of actors whose perspectives might be collected in the course of structural sampling: central participants and external participants. Central participants represent the focus of the analysis; these are the actors who make up the social system of interest. External participants are actors located at or beyond the boundaries of the focal social system who can provide detailed perspectives on the system.

Investigating the Social System from Within

Structural sampling seeks to assist the scholar in identifying the positions that various actors occupy in a social system and the relationships among these positions. Doing so involves identifying and speaking to participants in the social system, as well as those connected to it. A researcher may define the boundary of a social system in various ways; often this boundary will echo the system's formal boundaries, but it may also contract or recede as necessary to allow the researcher to communicate how a system's underpinnings pertain to the phenomena of interest.

One of the outcomes of structural sampling should be the identification of the role types that comprise the *core* of the social system. Central participants are actors who comprise the core of the social system. Understanding their actions, interactions, and beliefs and the outcomes they create is critical to the study. We differentiate between two types of central participants: visible and emergent participants. Visible participants are particularly easy for the researcher to identify; they are likely to be well known outside or within the social system. Despite their visibility, these individuals are not the only relevant actors in the social system. Emergent actors may take longer to identify and or approach. They may be instrumental to the functioning of the social system, but less visible—perhaps they operate "behind the scenes" or they are less vocal about their actions and contributions. Both visible and emergent participants are critical for a nuanced interpretation and analysis of the data. Researchers should take care not to give more weight to the views of one set of actors/system participants over another. In fact, it is in reconciling the perspectives of different actors that a nuanced view of a social system can emerge.

Data collection and analysis for studies employing structural sampling may be particularly time consuming because social systems are often, although not always, composed of multiple sets of actors. Identifying the roles played by each set of actors and understanding the interconnections among sets of actors is a crucial component of the researcher's work. Adding complexity to this task is the fact that even actors who occupy the same or similar roles may provide varying perspectives on the social system. Thus, to arrive at a satisfying conclusion, the researcher will need to gather data from multiple individuals occupying each role and make sense of the similarities and differences amongst their accounts.

Putting the Social System in Context

Data from such external actors enables researchers to paint a more comprehensive picture of the phenomenon of interest and to account for systematic "blind spots" of central actors. The perspectives of external actors benefit research by allowing for better understanding of agency, path dependence, or system interdependencies.

We classify external actors into two types: proximal and distant actors. Proximal actors are often in a position to provide the researcher with a broad and potentially deep understanding of all or components of the social system. For example, a researcher interested in understanding an industry might contact a well-established attorney or consultant catering to that industry, an industry analyst, the author of a book documenting the history of a particular industry, or the editor of an industry trade journal. Pragmatically, researchers may find it useful to contact at least some proximal actors while planning or in the early stages of a study. Distant actors are further from the social system, but they may also have useful insights on the system and may shape and be shaped by the system.

Differentiating between proximal and distant external actors allows the researcher to contextualize a social system by seeing the effects of the social system on various actors, as well as analyzing the factors and actors that shape and influence the social system. We believe it is necessary for a researcher to develop these understandings because it is only by possessing these understandings that the researcher can decipher the function and purpose of the social system and its constituent elements.

When Is Sampling Complete?

The focal social system is both nested in and connected to other social systems. Therefore, each scholar must draw bounds around his or her phenomenon of interest: "Not everything can be examined at once and limitations of scope and depth abound" (Van Maanen, 1998, p. xiii). Scholars employing structural sampling must be cognizant of the boundaries of the social system they are studying, while being aware of system dependencies and contributions to adjoining social systems.[1]

Social systems are complex and inhabited by a variety of actors in heterogeneous roles. No single type of actor is inherently more important than others. Yet, the nature of the research question and of the phenomenon of interest may result in focusing the analytical lens on a particular role or set of roles. For example, researchers interested in understanding how financial analysts evaluate firm strategies may focus their sampling on analysts across several market research firms and interview a smaller number of company CEOs. Conversely, a researcher interested in how firms develop strategies might interview a large number of CEOs and other executives and interview a smaller number of analysts.

Benefits of Structural Sampling

Structural sampling provides researchers with three distinct benefits that cannot be attained using prespecified sampling techniques: it allows the researcher to recognize and take into account the complexity of a social system; to capture the different voices present in the social system; and to understand the forces shaping everyday life within the social system. Social systems are complex and composed of different, interdependent sets of actors. This complexity is difficult to account for when collecting data only about one type of actor. So even in cases when scholars are primarily interested in theorizing about a social system's visible central actors, we advocate gathering data on and from emergent central actors and external actors to provide a more nuanced image of the phenomenon of interest.

Different actors within the social system may possess different perspectives on the phenomenon of interest. Understanding these perspectives is a critical component of a researcher's work. The term *polyvocality* refers to the idea that organizations are "discursive spaces where heterogeneous and multiple voices engage in a contest for audibility and power" (Belova, King, & Sliwa, 2008). Gathering data on a variety of central actors is crucial for adequately representing the polyvocality in the social system, including the competing frameworks and heterogeneous perspectives that coexist in it. Gathering data from external actors will benefit a research project in this regard, as external actors may have a broader set of perspectives—both laudatory and critical—on the outcomes achieved within the social system. Moreover, they may, in some cases, be more willing to share knowledge pertaining to rifts or disagreements occurring within the social system than central actors. Obtaining such knowledge from external participants prepares a researcher to open dialogues with system participants on these issues; direct the conversation such that relevant issues are discussed, explored, and ultimately understood by the researcher; and/or develop more nuanced interpretations of what system participants are saying (or are hinting at).

Structural sampling also allows the researcher to depict the nuances of life within a social system. Structural sampling affords researchers at least two avenues for capturing these nuances. Researchers can use structural sampling to uncover the forces affecting everyday life within the social system. These forces span rules, norms, culture, beliefs, power, and so forth.[2] Such forces can be best identified and understood in context—by understanding the objectives of those creating and supporting the forces, as well as the effects of the force on the perspectives and behaviors of others. By collecting data from and on actors occupying a variety of roles in the social system, structural sampling also opens the door to inclusion of data on or from "unexpected" actors whose roles and insights may change scholars' understanding of the phenomenon analyzed. This may allow the researcher to discount alternative social mechanisms or better account for the particularities of the context examined. Data on the forces shaping everyday life can be combined with unexpected insights to arrive at depictions of everyday life within the social system from the perspectives of different actors.

Challenges of Structural Sampling

Structural sampling also presents some challenges. Chief amongst these are challenges related to access to actors and presentation of data in limited space. Similar to other qualitative data collection methods, access may represent an inherent problem in structural sampling approaches. Access to actors situated in high-power roles, corporate employees, or parties engaged in conflict, for example, may be limited or precluded. Even when access is granted, scholars must take care to differentiate between open responses and "canned" public relations or legal responses that lack informative value for the research project. In such cases, researchers may need to seek out respondents who are willing to share their views openly, collect data over time in the hopes that actors will become more transparent as situations change, and/or carefully annotate the source and potential informant biases within the manuscript.

From a presentation perspective, scholars employing structural sampling may struggle to abide by the page limits being imposed with increasing stringency by journals. Methods and findings sections may be lengthy in order to describe and explain the rationale for using particular sampling and analysis methods. Despite this challenge, we join other researchers in advocating clear description of data collection methodologies employed, particularly in light of the variety of qualitative data collection, sampling, and analysis currently in use (Bettis, Gambardella, Helfat, & Mitchell, 2014). Additionally, the complexity captured by structural sampling methods, whereby researchers account for the roles of informants and the network of relationships connecting actors, can also make it difficult to present findings in a limited number of pages. We suggest that scholars in such situations begin by sharply separating data that was used largely for sense-making purposes from data that illustrate the core findings. While both sets of data feed the analysis and should be described in the methods section of the manuscript, only those data that illustrate the core findings should be included in the manuscript.

Examples of Structural Sampling

Table 24.1 summarizes several examples of structural sampling that we have encountered in management and social science research. The list includes published qualitative research studies that employ a data collection method similar to structural sampling. Several of these papers serve as inspiration for our approach, and more broadly, as inspiration for our own research investigating social structures. This list is by no means exhaustive. We use each of these works to illustrate the key advantages to be gained by structural sampling: the opportunity to account for social system complexity, polyvocality, and rich description of the phenomenon of interest. For each key benefit, we describe one example in depth and briefly mention one or two other examples that illustrate the benefit.

Structural sampling allows scholars to map the complexity of a social system. We see this illustrated in Kellogg's (2009) work on organizational change in hospital settings. Kellogg conducted interviews with central and proximal actors to gauge prechange support for the new regulation at different levels in the social structure of two hospitals. This enabled her to account for the complexity of the social system by being sensitized to particular actor types and preexisting relationships and to power dynamics in relation to organizational change. Barley (1986) illustrated social system complexity and power dynamics as a result of organizational change engendered by the introduction of a new medical imaging technology used within hospitals. Turco (2010) examined the importance of cultural schemas in reproducing social structures of occupational inequality in the leveraged buyout industry.

Structural sampling highlights polyvocality in the social system by documenting heterogeneous frameworks employed by actors. This benefit can be observed in Turco's (2012: 388) work on an organization providing motherhood services. For this study, Turco combined participant observation with formal interviews, including 55 interviews with central actors and 16 with external actors including "investors engaged in [evaluating the organization], consultants to the company, local hospital administrators and doctors who refer clients to [the organization], and directors of local nonprofits" and hundreds of informal conversations with customers and employees. She used these data to investigate various elements of organizational life, finding that each type of participant viewed the organization differently. From the managers' perspectives, the business model of the organization relied on providing support for new mothers, for a price; executives felt that the stress experienced by new mothers lowered their inhibitions to spend. From the customers' perspectives, new moms

Table 24.1 Examples of Structural Sampling in Management and Social Science Research

Reference	Title	Phenomenon of Interest and Setting	Details of Sample	Insights Generated	Benefits of Method: 1. System complexity 2. Polyvocality 3. Nuances of everyday life
Barley (1986)	Technology as an Occasion for Structuring: Evidence from Observations of CT Scanners and the Social Order of Radiology Departments	Effects of technology on organization; two hospitals adopting CT scanners	Central actors (radiologists and technologists at two community hospitals) and distant external actors (senior radiologists at large medical centers)	Link between social system, introduction of new technology, and change in the institutionalized roles and patterns of interaction; structures are dynamic	System complexity, nuances of everyday life
DeSoucey (2010)	Gastronationalism Food Traditions and Authenticity Politics in the European Union	Case study of the link between nationalist sentiment and food: foie gras in France	Central and external actors: producers, industry representatives, activists, consumers, employees, chefs, government officials	Highlighted the power of national attachment in the context of production and marketing of specific foods	System complexity, nuances of everyday life
Kellogg (2009)	Operating Room: Relational Spaces and Microinstitutional Change in Surgery	Response to organizational change; two hospitals	Central and proximal actors in the hospital setting	Allowed the researcher to identify the role that relational spaces—areas of isolation, interaction, and inclusion—play in a successful change process	System complexity, nuances of everyday life
Kunda (2006)	Engineering Culture: Control and Commitment in a High-Tech Corporation	Culture as a mechanism for control in a technology company	Central actors (engineers) and proximal external actors: staff, managers, and executives of the firm	Culture is not only about rules in the workplace, but is also about a vehicle for influencing experience and behavior of employees	System complexity, polyvocality, nuances of everyday life
Shah (2006)	Motivation, Governance, and the Viability of Hybrid Forms in Open Source Software Development	Community-based innovation; two open source software development communities	Visible and emergent central actors; proximal external actors	Uncovered relationships between roles and individuals and the differential motivations and contributions of individuals; documented how structural differences due to governance structures affected the roles individuals chose to adopt	System complexity, nuances of everyday life

(Continued)

Table 24.1 Continued

Reference	Title	Phenomenon of Interest and Setting	Details of Sample	Insights Generated	Benefits of Method: 1. System complexity 2. Polyvocality 3. Nuances of everyday life
Taylor (2010)	The Next Generation: Technology Adoption and Integration Through Internal Competition in New Product Development	New product development	Interviewed actors in all levels of the organization, from CEO to engineer, with emphasis on the project level (central actors) and also top executives of each firm (external actors)	Showed how competition among projects in the organization can lead to integrating new technology into incremental innovation for existing products	System complexity, nuances of everyday life
Turco (2010)	Cultural Foundations of Tokenism: Evidence from the Leveraged Buyout Industry	Tokenism; leveraged buyout industry	Central actors (employees) and external proximal and distant actors (recruiters, investors in LBO funds, executives of LBO-owned companies, investment bankers and consultants to the industry, and trade journalists)	Explored the importance of cultural schemas in reproducing occupational inequality	System complexity
Turco (2012)	Difficult Decoupling: Employee Resistance to the Commercialization of Personal Settings	Commercialization of personal settings; organization offering support and services for new mothers	Central actors (founders, employees, customers) and external actors (evaluators, consultants, directors of nonprofits)	Outlined the conflicting logics at play in commercializing personal settings; exposed the tension between customer and investor evaluation of the business model and employee resistance to commercialization	System complexity, polyvocality, nuances of everyday life

were drawn to the organization's framing of itself as a "safe, warm environment." From the employees' perspectives, Turco unexpectedly found significant resistance to the *commercialization* of motherhood services. Such resistance is illustrated by the following quote: "It's hard to support moms by upselling." Ultimately, the actions of employees led to the failure of the organization. By examining multiple voices, the researcher was able to highlight the origins and motivation behind the framing of the organizational mission and the extent to which various sets of actors facilitated or impeded the commercialization of personal settings that the organization attempted to achieve.

Taylor's (2010) research on new technology projects in the networking and database industry also illustrated how structural sampling can be used to capture polyvocality. This study sampled central actors involved in innovation projects and examined the perspectives of external proximal actors—executives of the technology firms studied—to understand how new projects were viewed from an executive perspective, in light of the overall firm identity and strategy. By attending to polyvocality, this study highlights the resource allocation concerns and priorities of different actors (innovation team members versus executives) and their long-term consequences for organizational innovation.

Structural sampling can also be used to richly depict the nuances of life with a social system, as illustrated by DeSoucey's (2010) work on the French foie gras food industry. DeSoucey used structural sampling to provide a rich description of how "food production, distribution, and consumption can demarcate and sustain the emotive power of national attachment" (p. 432) and of the effect of nationalism on the production and marketing of specific foods. Her data include extensive archival analysis and 40 interviews with a wide array of actors participating in the social and economic system of food production: French foie gras producers, high-level industry representatives, social movement activists, consumers, chefs, tourism employees, and local government officials. By employing a structural sampling approach, DeSoucey richly documented the "salient roles played by history and tradition in supporting contemporary cultural identity and uniqueness" (p. 448) as layers in the creation of cultural markets and institutionalized protections in the European Union. Shah (2006) used structural sampling to richly depict the "organizational life" of participants in open source communities, showing how different governance structures shaped individuals' decisions to contribute to the community and their adoption of new roles over time. Kunda (2006) also used structural sampling to portray life inside a high-technology organization, showing how culture can be used a vehicle for influencing employee behavior and perception of work experiences.

Structural Sampling in the Context of Qualitative Sampling Methodologies

Many qualitative researchers have built their samples through purposive sampling or one of its variant forms, quota and snowball sampling. All of these sampling methods seek to identify actors based on specific criteria. Purposive sampling groups actors according to preselected criteria relevant to a particular research question. Quota sampling involves specifying how many people with particular characteristics to interview at the onset of the study; the key distinction between purposive and quota sampling is that in quota sampling the number of individuals interviewed in various subgroups of the population reflects their proportions in the population. Snowball sampling is used to identify interviewees in hidden or hard-to-reach populations that are not readily accessible to researchers. Snowball sampling allows a researcher to identify relatively homogenous members of a population by requesting that informants provide introductions to their peers.

Each of these sampling techniques focuses on assembling samples of actors who occupy similar roles within a social system and involves prespecification of the criteria used to select actors. These sampling methodologies are thus best suited for understanding a particular practice or behavior, aspects of relationships between actors in a relatively well-understood social context, or the perspectives of a single type of actor. We advocate the use of structural sampling when a researcher seeks to unveil the inner workings of a relatively unknown social system or complex, little-understood social processes occurring within social systems.[3]

Structural sampling can be used in conjunction with various data collection methods, such as interviews, ethnography, and observation. Qualitative data may be supplemented with archival data. Data collected using a structural sampling methodology may be analyzed using grounded theory or other qualitative data analysis methods.

Concluding Thoughts

In this chapter we present structural sampling as a method for unveiling social structures and positions. Structural sampling advocates observing single roles in social systems from multiple perspectives, as well as identifying the full spectrum of roles in a social system. As a result, structural sampling can provide novel insights that may not be known or fully understood by actors within the social system (and hence not observable to researchers choosing to interview only those individuals occupying a particular role); uncover the polyvocality of actors in a social system; and account for complex dependencies in social systems. We believe that this data collection approach can be used to illuminate a wide variety of theoretical questions. We suggest a method for implementation; review a series of studies that have employed similar data collection methods in order to demonstrate the wide range of potential applications for structural sampling and its benefits; and situate structural sampling within the wider field of qualitative research methodologies.

Notes

1 Practically speaking, we observe that researchers often focus on a large sample of central actors while interviewing several external actors to learn more about the context.
2 In this way, the system characteristics that can be captured by structural sampling go well beyond structural interdependencies.
3 Structural sampling may make use of a snowball-type methodology. Similar to snowball sampling, informants can identify additional informants. As opposed to snowball sampling, however, researchers engaged in structural sampling might request informants to assist them in identifying important roles to be examined and informants occupying those roles. (Note that they may also engage in traditional snowball sampling as well in order to enlarge the group of informants of a particular type.)

References

Barley, S.R. (1986). Technology as an occasion for structuring: Evidence from observations of CT scanners and the social order of radiology departments. *Administrative Science Quarterly*, *31*(1), 78–108.

Belova, O., King, I., & Sliwa, M. (2008). Introduction: Polyphony and organization studies: Mikhail Bakhtin and beyond. *Organization Studies*, *29*(4), 493–500.

Bettis, R.A., Gambardella, A., Helfat, C., & Mitchell, W. (2014). Editorial: Qualitative empirical research in strategic management. *Strategic Management Journal*, *35*(7), 949–953. doi:10.1002/smj.2317

Coleman, J.S. (1994). *Foundations of social theory*. Cambridge, MA: Harvard University Press.

DeSoucey, M. (2010). Gastronationalism food traditions and authenticity politics in the European Union. *American Sociological Review*, *75*(3), 432–455.

Eisenhardt, K.M. (1989). Building theories from case study research. *Academy of Management Review*, *14*(4), 532–550.

Kellogg, K.C. (2009). Operating room: Relational spaces and microinstitutional change in surgery. *American Journal of Sociology*, *115*(3), 657–711.

Kunda, G. (2006). *Engineering culture: Control and commitment in a high-tech corporation*. Philadelphia, PA: Temple University Press.

Pratt, M.G. (2009). From the editors: For the lack of a boilerplate: Tips on writing up (and reviewing) qualitative research. *Academy of Management Journal*, *52*(5), 856–862.

Shah, S.K. (2006). Motivation, governance, and the viability of hybrid forms in open source software development. *Management Science*, *52*(7), 1000–1014.

Taylor, A. (2010). The next generation: Technology adoption and integration through internal competition in new product development. *Organization Science*, *21*(1), 23–41.

Turco, C. (2012). Difficult decoupling: Employee resistance to the commercialization of personal settings. *American Journal of Sociology*, *118*(2), 380–419.

Turco, C.J. (2010). Cultural foundations of tokenism evidence from the leveraged buyout industry. *American Sociological Review*, *75*(6), 894–913.

Van Maanen, J. (1979). Reclaiming qualitative methods for organizational research: A preface. *Administrative Science Quarterly*, *1(24)*, 520–526.

Van Maanen, J. (1998). Different strokes: Qualitative research in the Administrative Science Quarterly from 1956 to 1996. *Qualitative Studies of Organizations*, *1*, ix–xxxii.

Whetten, D.A. (1989). What constitutes a theoretical contribution? *Academy of Management Review*, *14*(4), 490–495.

25

Ethnography Across the Work Boundary

Benefits and Considerations for Organizational Studies

Melissa Mazmanian, Christine M. Beckman, and Ellie Harmon

Multisited Ethnography: An Overview

Ethnographic data is always indebted to the people we study—the people who let us in to their spaces, share their stories, and allow us to observe their everyday practices. Thus, every piece of ethnographic data is the result of a specific relationship between ethnographers and the people they study. While the importance of the relationship exists in all ethnographic research, the significance and intimacies of the link are particularly salient when people agree to be studied in multiple (public and private) spaces. In this chapter we explore these intricacies of engagement with individuals across multiple spaces through our own research studying technology use by busy professionals at work, at home, and in the various locations of their daily lives (including church, restaurants, sporting events, and grocery stores).

We describe a method for conducting a multisited ethnographic study (Marcus, 1998) that focuses on following participants across the "work boundary" as they transition between the multiple roles of worker, colleague, friend, spouse, and parent. Ethnographers in anthropology have a long history of studying the lives of their participants across such multiple aspects of daily life (e.g., Malinowski, 1922). Here, we argue for the importance of this method for organizational scholars and show how studying people at home can provide new insights into the workplace and vice versa.

Organizational scholars have made clear the powerful relationships between people and the organizations that provide them security, identity, and social relations. A subset of this work examines the intersection of work with individuals' other roles, such as "boundary theory" research focused on the work/nonwork relationship (Kreiner, Hollensbe, & Sheep, 2009; Nippert-Eng, 1996; Perlow, 1998; Rothbard, Phillips, & Dumas, 2005; Trefalt, 2013). In this realm, there is an ongoing conversation in the field about whether a blurring of roles between work and home enables flexibility and autonomy with positive implications for individuals or is draining and cognitively fracturing with negative implications for individuals (Ashforth, Kreiner, & Fugate, 2000; Clark, 2000; Desrochers & Sargent, 2003; Shumate & Fulk, 2004). This work has become especially relevant with the proliferation of technologies that enable constant connectivity to the workplace (Chesley, 2005; Mazmanian, 2012; Mazmanian, Orlikowski, & Yates, 2013; Stanko & Beckman, in press).

Yet, there is a dearth of research in management scholarship that focuses directly on everyday experiences outside of the workplace and the impact of work on those experiences. Although there are intensive ethnographies of work detailing the personal costs of work life (Kunda, 1992; Michel, 2011; Perlow, 1997), comparably intensive ethnographies of home life (Lareau, 2011; Ochs & Kremer–Sadlik, 2013; Stacey, 1990) conducted by scholars in other disciplines are not positioned to contribute to this debate. While some organizational ethnographers conduct interviews in people's domestic settings (Anteby, 2008; Perlow, 1997), rare are those researchers who engage with the family as well as the workplace as a locus of study. We highlight in Table 25.1 those scholars who have tackled multisited ethnographic research from a variety of disciplines. For example, in anthropology, Darrah et al. (2007) detail the multitude of ways that families are busy by observing families in all aspects of their daily lives (including school and work). In sociology, Hochschild (2001) begins within a company and follows six families to understand how work can become a respite from the

Table 25.1 Ethnographies of Work and Private Space

Reference	Research Context	Physical Spaces	Disciplinary Space	Outcomes/Results of Innovation
Mazmanian, Beckman, & Harmon	Silver Lake Hospitality in Southern California; interviewed 91 individuals and conducted 6 months of workplace observations; observed 9 families at home, 60–80 hours per home, interviewed every family member	Home, work, other activities	Organizational theory	Understanding how mobile communication technology shapes work and home lives
Hochschild (1997/2001)	Americo in Spotted Deer, a Midwestern town; interviewed 130 workers and observed six families at work and at home	Work, home, day care center	Sociology	Understanding how time pressures and the amenities of the workplace make home life challenging and encourage more time at work
Darrah, Freeman, & English-Lueck (2007)	14 American families, following each family member for 4 full days, observing family time; 140–170 hours per family	Home, school, work, other activities	Anthropology	Understanding the impact of work on home life and how people experience and manage busyness
Desmond (2007)	Woodlands of northern Arizona; member of the firecrew, worked for four seasons; last season formally observed (4 months): "worked, ate, slept, traveled, socialized and fought fire" with 14 other men In-depth interviews with all 14.	Living with fire crew, total institution	Sociology	Show how firefighters understand risk and death and how they are socialized to risk; insights into how high-risk organizations motivate workers to undertake life-threatening jobs

ambiguity and stress of family life. We have yet to find scholarship in the management field that uses ethnographic methods to deeply engage with participants in all aspects of daily life.

In our current work, we conducted 6 months of fieldwork with employees at a hospitality company, followed by intensive fieldwork engagements with the families of nine employees. These engagements with families included an initial 6-week in-home engagement in which researchers spent between 60 and 80 hours with each family. Then, over the period of the following year, researchers returned for three to four follow-up visits, including 2-day visits to observe life changes and interview family members about these changes (some of these follow-ups are still ongoing). We began our study of the workplace in early 2012. We concluded the initial engagement with our ninth family in the summer of 2014 and conducted follow up visits through 2015.

By substantially engaging with participants across the work/nonwork boundary, we are able to better understand individual outcomes typically associated with work and nonwork, such as engagement and spillover (e.g., Rothbard, 2001), or stress, burnout, and family strain (e.g., Meyerson, 1994) as they play into both work and nonwork experiences. We gain insight into micro practices through which people negotiate professional and personal relationships (both through virtual and face-to-face modes of communication) and ways that family decisions and interpersonal relationships affect organizational practices and the daily experience of work.

In this chapter, we highlight the research benefits of gaining a richer understanding of the whole person who is navigating and responding to both work and nonwork pressures and obligations in the course of life. We give concrete examples from our own work of the insights for organizational studies that we can gain from taking this kind of multisited approach. We provide suggestions about how to go about organizing such a multisited study for researchers who would like to adopt a similar approach. Alongside this more pragmatic methodological direction, we also present a set of challenges and considerations with which ethnographers entering personal spaces must grapple.

Multisited Ethnography: Benefits for Organizational Studies

A multisited ethnography gives researchers a nuanced perspective on the whole self of the research participant. We see how personal relationships come to matter in the workplace and how workplace relationships come to matter at home. We witness firsthand how people navigate multiple and different types of vulnerability (e.g., identity as parent, reputation as an employee) in the course of negotiating obligation and responsibility in multiple spaces. As in any ethnography, we glean insight into how meaning is constructed in the moment. Because many organizational scholars are familiar with the value of qualitative and ethnographic research in the context of the workplace, in this section we focus primarily on what we learn about work by seeing nonwork spaces.

In particular, we gain insight into four key areas of knowledge. First, we are able to understand more deeply how self and work relate. For example, when a father comes home late at the end of a long day excited to share how successful a particular meeting went at work, we gain insight into the ways that work outcomes can generate feelings of competency and triumph that spillover into the home. When a single mother comes home too exhausted by a long day at work to engage with her children, we witness both the guilt and the practicality associated with letting them watch cartoons. Or when a working mother and primary breadwinner shares with her husband the triumph of being included in a meeting with executives, we are privy to the ways in which her identity as a successful employee plays into broader family decisions about careers and child care. In addition, knowing that someone carries certain values derived from their cultural heritage and is striving to make enough money so their spouse can stay home with the kids provides insight into behaviors witnessed in the workplace—such as frustration with a superior after being overlooked for a promotion or willingness to work extensive hours. Overall, by seeing work through the lens of family life, we gain a better sense of the intensity of what is at stake for people at work and home.

Second, we gain firsthand insight into the multifaceted nature of relationships that cross the work/nonwork boundary. When people are taking care of work emails late at night on the couch, we can observe the ways that similar emails on similar topics generate different emotional reactions. For example, when an employee gets a late-night email from someone they like, we see them laugh good naturedly, while an email from a different person engenders resentment and feelings of intrusion. We witness how work colleagues share funny texts outside of work, meet for dinner with their families, or spread gossip. It becomes clear who has each other's backs when challenges arise at work, and why that is the case. We learn how these implicit emotional ties play into broader organizational patterns of promotion and hierarchy. For example, we see managers express intensely negative feelings about their bosses that are suppressed in the workplace and the advantages of mentorship that emerge from personal friendships. In particular, we observed two supervisor–subordinate relationships as they were experienced outside of work by the subordinate and supervisor.

Third, we can see how nonwork relationships influence how individuals engage with their work. When workplace questions or problems are topics of conversation at home, employees often gain new insights into their own work practices. One spouse might relish the everyday work gossip her husband brings home, asking numerous questions and brainstorming solutions to everyday challenges and personnel issues. Another spouse offers emotional support through text messages during the workday as a deadline approaches. We also learn about what kinds of workplace encroachments on the home are acceptable and legitimate. For example, a husband might not notice his wife checking her phone in the kitchen while making dinner, but he rolls his eyes when she picks up her phone in the backyard while they sit drinking a glass of wine.

Finally, the relationships we develop over these long engagements provide an opportunity to contextualize what we are witnessing. Crossing the boundaries between work and home with our participants enables us to see how they are making sense of and accounting for various activities. When a mother tells us that she has "snuck away" to answer a few emails while doing laundry, we get firsthand knowledge of multiple conflicting motives: her desire to physically separate work activity from time with her children; her need to respond to a colleague; and the ongoing pressure to find time for the daily necessities of housework. By sitting with a manager as she sends an email, we are able to gain insight into what *type* of email someone is reading and how the email makes that person *feel*. Thus, we are able to "see" technology use with a nuance unavailable to other forms of data gathering.

Altogether, the insights gained from such a multisited approach are nontrivial. Certain moments at work (or even entire jobs) during which crises or ethical dilemmas have to be dealt with may be particularly affected by the work/nonwork relationship. However, all workers, regardless of position, are continually navigating demands, social norms, identities, and desires in multiple arenas. Thus, attending to the work/nonwork interplay broadly is illuminating for management scholars and practitioners alike.

Multisited Ethnography: Pragmatics

We now offer reflections on how to design and conduct such a study. Given the plethora of quality organizational ethnographies available to organization scholars, we focus on the pragmatics of our nonwork ethnographic engagements. See Figure 25.1 for an outline of our research process.

Access and Recruitment

We decided to build our ethnographic engagement from a single organization to facilitate trust and access. This research design also served to ground our participants in a shared organizational context. In the course of a 6-month organizational engagement, we formally interviewed 75 firm employees and 16 spouses. These interviews provided us with various family demographics and gave the

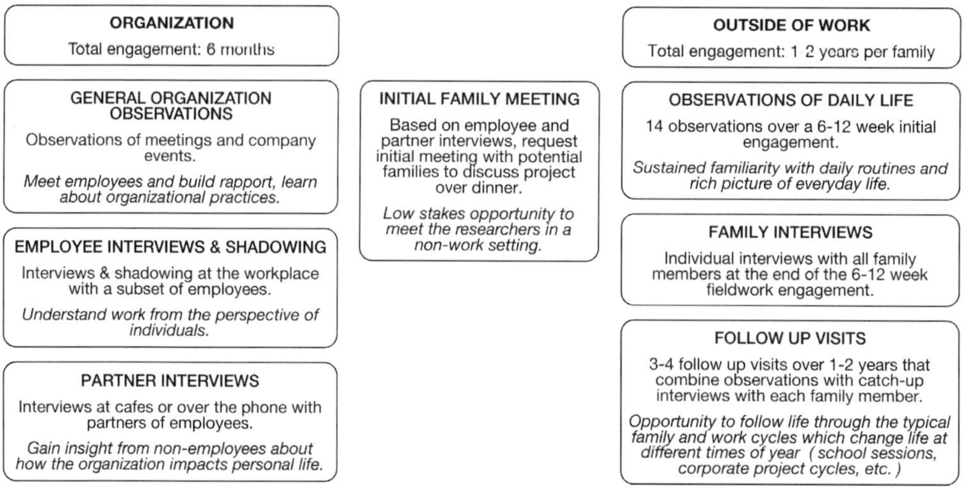

Figure 25.1 Ethnography Across the Work Boundary

potential participants a sense of who we were and what we were interested in (mobile technology use). It also provided us a legitimacy that stemmed from our presence in their workplace.

At the end of our organizational engagement, we made a list of potential families that met our initial criteria: at least one child under the age of 12 and a variety of family situations (one- and two-parent families, one and two working parents). We then emailed the adults of each potential family thanking them for their participation in the prior organizational study and describing the follow-up study. We stressed privacy and ensured potential participants that we would not share with anyone whether or not they chose to participate in the nonwork study. We emphasized that nothing about the home study would be shared with the company. We also offered financial compensation for the significant time commitment associated with this research. Although it was clear that families appreciated the compensation, no one in our study was in a position that the amount could be considered coercive.

We also benefited from word of mouth as the study progressed. Although we ensured confidentiality to our families, we asked employees if they had colleagues interested in participating in the study. If they offered to put in a good word about us, we encouraged this assistance. Thus, we know that some families shared with each other that they were participating in our research. Although we were not part of these conversations and do not know what was said, relationships between our families created moments we had to navigate carefully. Of the 15 families we initially emailed, 9 agreed to participate.

Aside from the pragmatics of entry and legitimacy, the characteristics of the ethnographer (gender, race, nationality, etc.) affect his/her ability to gain access into a space and engage in that space as an insider. We are very aware that families invited three Caucasian women (aged early 30s to mid-40s) into their homes.[1] Sitting on an 8-year-old girl's bed and doing homework with her may not be as easy for a male researcher of any age. The number of times we sat on different beds in different homes, braiding hair, watching Netflix, and reading goodnight stories was not insubstantial. Parents trusted us entirely with their children, rarely checking in when we were in a room with them alone. Children showered us with affection (and occasionally dislike), offering hugs, sitting on our laps, and sharing their secrets. As we strove to honor this trust, we realized that cultural gender norms played a significant role in our ability to conduct this kind of research.

Research Design

In designing this study, we hoped to satisfy three research aims: spend enough time with families so that we could develop deep relationships and become somewhat "invisible"; observe a representative cross-section of daily life across days and weekends; and spend time with various family members. Thus, we suggested to families that we visit 14 times and observe every day of the week twice (two Mondays, two Tuesdays, etc.). We found this to be a generative study design for scheduling visits and negotiating when to come and who to follow.

On weeknights we would come whenever the children came home from school/day care (generally 3–5 p.m.) and follow whoever was around regardless of activity until after the children (or the entire family) went to bed (generally 9–11 p.m.). Before leaving, we would check in with the parents as to whether they were going to be doing any work for the remainder of their evenings and asked them to quickly review any emails/texts that came in during the visit. On weekends, we would spend a half a day with the family, alternating between the first and second half depending on activities of day. Visits generally lasted between 4 and 6 hours each. The entire engagement lasted 6 to 12 weeks depending on the schedule of the researcher and the family. After this, we conducted reflective interviews with each family member. We decided to dedicate one researcher to a family in order to facilitate comfort level over time. We did, however, make sure that two researchers came to the initial meeting and interviews. This way we each had someone else in the research team who had met the participants, seen their home, and could conduct follow-up visits if necessary.

Conducting Oneself in the Home

With every family we found ourselves negotiating how to blend into their personal space (where to sit, how much to engage in conversation). We generally found that these patterns fell into place after the first few visits. We would wear clothes that matched their basic level of formality, notice norms of where people moved and sat, and tried to find a central but innocuous place to settle (the couch, a bar stool, kitchen table). We found that we would engage with the family more in the first few visits. While we never became silent observers, we slowly slipped into the background, moving around the house freely as time went on. In this way, the 14 visits were crucial. We needed a long enough engagement for such patterns to emerge organically.

The longer engagement also helped in our relationship with children. Young children generally expected and asked for attention and one-on-one play early in the study (and parents reported appreciating someone who could interact positively with their children). However, young children quickly moved on and often ignored the researcher after the first few visits (or after the first few minutes of any visit). Older children (11–18), however, were generally more reserved earlier in the study and opened up slowly over time.

One important lesson we learned early on was that we needed to find a way to enter all rooms of the house as soon as possible because if we did not venture upstairs or into bedrooms within the first few visits, it became awkward to attempt to do so and felt like a violation of personal space. Thus, we soon began asking for a tour of all of the technology in the house on our first visit. This allowed us to see each room early on and develop a norm of entering all areas of the house.

Field Notes

Just as our presence in the house mirrored those in the household, so did our techniques for capturing field notes. If, for instance, the family was regularly on their computers watching TV in the evening, we would bring a laptop, join them, and type field notes directly into a Word document. If people were constantly on their phones, we would use our phones to type in field notes in their presence. And if technology was not so present in the home, we would bring a small notebook and jot down key words, times, and reminders of events as inconspicuously as possible. Regardless of the form of capture, we dictated our field notes soon after leaving the house. This preserved memory for detail as much as possible.

Multisited Ethnography: Considerations

In engaging in a multisited ethnography of this scale, we have stumbled into multiple challenges, quandaries, and considerations that we could not have anticipated. By sharing these considerations, we hope to provide future researchers with the insight into the practical, ethical, and moral considerations of engaging in this type of research.

Complexity of Researcher–Participant Relationship

After engagements with nine different families, we are struck by the intensity and complexity of the relationships we developed with our participants. We are not "friends" in the traditional sense, yet we are also not "scientists" who take on an antiseptic or distant role of observer.[2] In witnessing everyday activities, we became privy to joys, fears, mundane frustrations, and vulnerabilities. And in developing a human relationship that respected this access, we found ourselves actively crafting relationships with participants that included both personal engagement and self-revelation.

We strove to be both authentic and neutral. However, in order to project an open attitude toward whatever we were observing, we were conscious not to reveal too many of our personal opinions, tastes, and experiences. As ethnographers, our goal is not to appear critical or judgmental when engaging in everyday activities. For example, when asked about religion, we all strove to project openness and not suggest our private beliefs. We expressed more interest in sports, guns, country music, mystical teachings, health food, fast food, cooking, and video games (just to name a few) than we actually feel. In addition, when our personal preferences did come out (accidentally or otherwise) we found that it could compromise the ethnographic relationship. For example, a family accidentally discovered that one of our children is in a school that discourages media use, and we worried it reflected on their choices for their own children in a negative light.

Another way in which we discovered we could not be authentically friends with our participants is our obligation to research ethics (which are not entirely aligned with ethics of friendship). We are committed to confidentiality even when the research participants are not. For example, when teenage girls "hacked" one of our phones and posted pictures of themselves on Instagram, it was a sign of affection and intimacy. To us, it was a violation of confidentiality and, even when their mother said it was "no big deal," the pictures were deleted—at the risk of offending the participants. Further, we didn't share the intimate details we learned about individuals that would normally be a source of conversation between friends. For example, if we learned about one person's misbehavior or deception, we would not share that with anyone else in the family.

Yet, we strove to provide emotional validation and point out genuine and positive observations of the family (especially toward the end of the engagement) while withholding our own advice and judgment. In spite of, or in parallel with, these examples of crafted relationships, we found ourselves developing meaningful and deep connections with the people we studied. The degree of authenticity felt by the researcher depended, to some extent, on how similar the participants felt to our own families, values, and tastes. However, we became invested in each and every family.

Nature of Ethnographic Data

The ethnographer is a pawn in the game of social life. We enter into a social environment that is infused with politics, histories, relationships, and insecurities. In this study we found that our presence legitimated certain topics and often inspired articulations of motives and desires. The conversations we sparked figured into family dynamics in complex ways, and we became players in relationships between parent and child as well as between husband and wife.

Thus, we found ourselves in a position of being told by a grandmother (in front of her son) that she did not approve of the way the children were being raised. Spouses occasionally registered discontent with each other in front of us or turned to us for support in discipline decisions. And children tested limits—asking for exceptions to family rules or grabbing researcher notebooks and phones. Children will also say things that parents do not expect—inviting the ethnographer to spend the night, asking if they could visit the ethnographer's house and meet their children (requests that we did, in fact, honor whenever possible), and even wanting the researcher to be a second mother. Children also revealed what parents might not—that a parent was uncomfortable being observed, that a sibling was caught using the computer in the middle of the night, or any number of embarrassing stories.

These exchanges illuminated the ways in which an ethnographer subtly affects interpersonal dynamics. While they could be awkward, they also provided insight into points of tension and issues to explore. Further, we found that the duration of the study tended to mitigate these exchanges and allow everyone a chance to recover, save face, and develop a more seamless relationship.

Ethical and Moral Questions

Although we had prior experience with ethnographic research in the context of the workplace, we discovered that being in people's homes engendered more complex issues of privacy and confidentiality. Although it is not unheard of to witness ethical lapses or deceptive behavior in the context of work, in the home we became privy to numerous thoughts, practices, and insights that we will choose not to report when writing about these data. We have been forced to articulate to ourselves what is outside the ethical bounds and implicit contract we established with participants and question whether marital conflict, parenting struggles, work gossip, and personal issues and foibles are within the bounds of this research and relevant to our findings.

We also found that issues of privacy and confidentiality were more complex than we initially anticipated because some participants knew each other and had shared that they participated in the study. We avoided curious questions by participants about other families in the study. Our silence about our time with other families was essential to demonstrate that details of participants' own daily lives were confidential. These issues were accentuated in four families—families of two supervisors and two of their subordinates. It is possible that frustrations about the other individuals in our study were muted and not shared as a result of their participation in the study. However, the advantages of knowing the personalities and details of organizational members was incredibly useful to better understand the work that was conducted at home—emails responded to, presentations prepared, or budgets sorted out. These relationships also have implications for how we report our data, an issue that we are still debating and discussing in our research team.

Benefits of Multiple Researchers

We found that each of the quandaries and considerations previously outlined benefited from engaging in this research collaboratively. Our research is indebted to the various personalities, academic backgrounds, and life stages we bring to this study. Our regular discussions and brainstorming sessions have proven invaluable throughout the study: we often challenge each other, question implicit assumptions, and help brainstorm potentially difficult engagements.

Further, this work is time intensive and emotionally exhausting. Engaging with families and upholding the multiple roles of ethnographer as outlined is simply draining. It would be impossible for any one of us to spend the time required to conduct such a study given our other obligations, and we regularly left our own families and partners during the exact hours we would generally be spending with them. Having each other as cheerleaders, emotional supporters, and confidants has been invaluable.

Despite the challenges and ethical considerations of this work, we believe the advantages of "following the person" far outweigh the costs. When engaged in an organizational ethnography, we know intellectually that employees are shaped by what occurs outside of work. By observing those nonwork moments alongside the many moments when work and nonwork intersect, we develop an appreciation for what is at stake for individuals both at work and at home, an understanding of the complexities of daily life, and new insights into the reciprocal relationship between work and our personal lives.

Notes

1 Families were Caucasian, Asian, and Latino.
2 For a hilarious take on ethnographic research in intimate spaces that strives for distance and neutrality, we recommend the Norwegian film *Kitchen Stories*: www.imdb.com/title/tt0323872/

References

Anteby, M. (2008). *Moral gray zones: Side productions, identity, and regulation in an aeronautic plant*. Princeton, NJ: Princeton University Press.
Ashforth, B.E., Kreiner, G.E., & Fugate, M. (2000). All in a day's work: Boundaries and micro-role transitions. *Academy of Management Review, 25*(3), 472–491.
Chesley, N. (2005). Blurring boundaries? Linking technology use, spillover, family distress and job satisfaction. *Journal of Marriage and Family, 67*, 1237–1248.
Clark, S.C. (2000). Work/family border theory: A new theory of work/family balance. *Human Relations, 53*, 747–770.
Darrah, C. N., Freeman, J. M., & English-Lueck, J. A. (2007). *Busier than ever: Why American families can't slow down*. Stanford, CA: Stanford University Press.
Desmond, M. (2007). *On the Fireline: Living and dying with Wildland firefighters*. Chicago, IL: The University of Chicago Press.
Desrochers, S., & Sargent, L. D. (2003). Work-family boundary ambiguity, gender and stress in dual-earner couples. In *From 9-to-5 to 24/7: How Workplace Changes Impact Families, Work, and Communities*, BPW/Brandeis University Conference, Orlando, Florida.
Hochschild, A. R. (1997/2001). *The time bind: When work becomes home and home becomes work* (Holt Paperback ed.). New York, NY: Metropolitan Books.
Kreiner, G.E., Hollenbse, E.C., & Sheep, M.L. (2009). Balancing border and bridges: Negotiating the work-home interface via boundary-work tactics. *Academy of Management Journal, 52*, 704–730.
Kunda, G. (1992). *Engineering culture: Control and commitment in high-tech corporation*. Philadelphia, PA: Temple University Press.
Lareau, A. (2011). *Unequal childhoods: Class, race, and family life* (2nd ed.). Berkeley: University of California Press.
Malinowski, B. (1922/2014). *Argonauts of the Western Pacific: An account of native enterprise and adventure in the archipelagoes of Melanesian New Guinea*. New York, NY: Routledge Classic.
Marcus, G. (1998). *Ethnography through thick and thin*. Princeton, NJ: Princeton University Press.
Mazmanian, M. (2012). Avoiding the trap of constant connectivity: When congruent frames allow for heterogeneous practices. *Academy of Management Journal, 56*(5), 1337–1357.
Mazmanian, M., Orlikowski, W.J., & Yates, J. (2013). The autonomy paradox: The implications of mobile email devices for knowledge professionals. *Organization Science, 24*(5), 1337–1357.
Meyerson, D.E. (1994). Interpretations of stress in institutions: The cultural production of ambiguity and burnout. *Administrative Science Quarterly, 39*(4), 628–653.
Michel, A. (2011). Transcending socialization: A nine-year ethnography of the body's role in organizational control and knowledge workers' transformation. *Administrative Science Quarterly, 56*(3), 325–368.
Nippert-Eng, C.E. (1996). *Home and work: Negotiating boundaries through everyday life*. Chicago, IL: The University of Chicago Press.
Ochs, E., & Kremer-Sadlik, T. (Eds.). (2013). *Fast-forward family: Home, work and relationships in middle-class America*. Berkeley: University of California Press.

Perlow, L.A. (1997). *Finding time: How corporations, individuals, and families can benefit from new work practices.* Ithaca, NY: Cornell University Press

Perlow, L.A. (1998). Boundary control: The social ordering of work and family time in a high-tech corporation. *Administrative Science Quarterly, 43*(2), 328–357.

Rothbard, N.P. (2001). Enriching or depleting? The dynamics of engagement in work and family roles. *Administrative Science Quarterly, 46*(4), 655–684.

Rothbard, N. P., Phillips, K. W., & Dumas, T. L. (2005). Managing multiple roles: Work-family policies and individuals' desires for segmentation. *Organization Science, 16*(3), 243–258.

Shumate, M., & Fulk, J. (2004). Boundaries and role conflict when work and family are colocated: A communication network and symbolic interaction approach. *Human Relations, 57*(1), 55–74.

Stacey, J. (1990). *Brave new families: Stories of domestic upheaval in late-twentieth-century America.* Berkley: University of California Press.

Stanko, T. E., & Beckman, C. M. (in press). Watching you watching me: Boundary control and capturing attention in the context of ubiquitous technology use. *Academy of Management Journal.*

Trefalt, S. (2013). Between you and me: Setting work-nonwork boundaries in the context of workplace relationships. *Academy of Management Journal, 86,* 1802–1829.

26

Strategic Conversations
Methods for Data Collection and Analysis

Christina Kyprianou, Melissa E. Graebner, and Violina Rindova

Introduction

Conversations—verbal interactions between two or more people—are fundamental to the study of both language and human action, and they represent an important source of data in social sciences such as anthropology and sociology. Anthropologists have observed real-time conversations to understand a group's social, cultural, and institutional practices (e.g., Bosk, 1979; Malinowski, 1922; Mead, 1928), and sociologists have examined conversations to reveal the linguistic processes underlying power relations (e.g., Fishman, 1978). Management scholars have also examined conversations, typically focusing on mundane, day-to-day interactions, to understand individual and group-level cognitive and interpretive processes in organizational settings. For example, scholars have used conversation data to explore how employees acquire job skills (O'Mahony & Bechky, 2006), how team members' shared beliefs influence team learning outcomes (Edmondson, 1999), how individuals' actions during brainstorming sessions increase team effectiveness (Sutton & Hargadon, 1996), and how evolution in individuals' interpretive schemas impacts organizational change (Bartunek, 1984).

Until recently, however, conversation data have rarely been examined by strategy researchers. Instead, strategy scholarship has relied primarily on archival data, and to a much lesser extent, on interview-based case studies. Nonetheless, a handful of scholars have recently pioneered the use of conversation data to understand strategy processes and practices. Our focus in this chapter is on describing this innovative use of *strategic conversations*, defined as any naturally occurring, as opposed to scripted or interview-based, interactions (including talk and nonverbal cues) among executives, managers, and various stakeholders, the content of which is of strategic importance. Strategic conversations may occur frequently and regularly during the course of top management team (TMT), board of directors, project, and client meetings, or in less frequent occasions such as workshops, strategic planning retreats, or executive training sessions. These conversations may be concerned with developing, changing, and implementing firm strategy; evaluating past strategic decisions; and vetting strategic alternatives. In this chapter, we explore the use of strategic conversation data, reviewing the research questions scholars have examined as well as the data collection procedures and analytical techniques they have employed. Our review suggests the study of strategic conversations can unravel the links among micro-level actions, cognition, and strategy.

Studying Strategic Conversations

Research Questions and Insights

Strategic conversation data are distinct from archival and interview data, and they are likely to generate insights into otherwise unobservable (and neglected) aspects of strategy (Godfrey & Hill, 1995) because of two sets of characteristics. First, strategic conversations are unscripted, naturally occurring, and fluid. Archival documents such as shareholder letters and press releases are static documents and reflect careful composition and editing. Interview responses may be shaped and filtered to some degree by the logic of researchers' questions or self-presentational or impression management concerns. In contrast, the emergent character of conversations preserves the instantaneous meaning participants bring to phenomena (Creswell, 2007), rendering processes of meaning construction more readily observable. As a result, conversation data have proven valuable in understanding sensemaking and other fluid cognitive processes in strategic contexts (e.g., Henfridsson & Yoo, 2013; Jay, 2013). For example, Jay (2013) draws on strategic conversations to identify the cognitive processes that enable members of a newly formed public–private energy alliance to synthesize paradoxical institutional logics over time. Conversation data can be particularly insightful for understanding how cognition evolves during periods of strategic change when sensemaking processes and cognitive schemas are likely to surface during discussions (Elsbach, Barr, & Hargadon, 2005). For instance, Zbaracki and Bergen (2010) found that uncertainty about how to implement an unusual change in prices induced overt discussions of organizational members' previously implicit assumptions about organizational strategy.

Second, conversation data include multiple voices and perspectives. Conversations occur when two or more participants (excluding the researcher) communicate, meet, argue, discuss, and socialize. Their inherently interactive and polyphonic nature has the potential to reveal how social structures influence strategy processes (Balogun, Jacobs, Jarzabkowski, Mantere, & Vaara, 2014; Samra-Fredericks, 2005; Whittle, Housley, Gilchrist, Lenney, & Mueller, 2014). Strategic conversations have been especially useful for illuminating the links between individual and collective sensemaking processes (e.g., Jay, 2013; Maitlis, 2005; Maitlis & Lawrence, 2007; Stigliani & Ravasi, 2012). For example, Stigliani and Ravasi (2012) identify four phases—noticing and bracketing, articulation, elaboration, and influence—and their associated cognitive processes in the transition from individual to collective sensemaking.

In addition, the interaction of multiple voices in strategic conversations enables scholars to explicate the role of power and politics in strategy, including how managers gather support for their own views and preferred courses of action (Kaplan, 2008; Liu & Maitlis, 2014; Samra-Fredericks, 2003, 2004); how they discursively resist or gain control of other managers during strategy development (Laine & Vaara, 2007); and how organizational actors not directly involved in strategy intensify certain strategy discourses and eventually constrain or enable strategy development (Hardy & Thomas, 2014). The underlying idea in these papers is that strategy is primarily a process through which discourse is used to gain or resist power (Balogun et al., 2014; Mantere, 2013).

A final advantage of conversation data is that they may provide insights into the interaction of material and linguistic practices. Researchers may observe not only what is said, but also what gestures, emotional expressions, and physical actions occur during strategic discussions. For example, Liu and Maitlis's (2014) analysis of individuals' linguistic and physical expressions of emotion during strategy meetings reveals that positive emotion induces more collaborative strategizing, while conflict between intense positive and negative emotions maintains divergence in views. Stigliani and Ravasi's (2012) study emphasizes the enabling role that participants' conversational and material practices (e.g., assembling artifacts, sketching on whiteboards) play in the development of future-oriented collective sensemaking.

In summary, strategic conversations render processes of meaning construction and power more readily observable, thus providing opportunities to unravel the complex interactions of managerial cognition and action that shape strategy work.

Data Collection

While strategic conversation data offer unique possibilities for understanding organizational processes, they also create special challenges in data collection and analysis. We next review the decisions that researchers have made regarding empirical settings, observation techniques and analytical procedures (see Tables 26.1 and 26.2). We also discuss how scholars have supplemented conversation data with additional types of information.

Empirical Settings

Strategic conversations are usually observed in the contexts of TMT meetings (Jarzabkowski & Seidl, 2008; Jay, 2013; Liu & Maitlis, 2014; Maitlis, 2005; Maitlis & Lawrence, 2007), board meetings (Jay, 2013; Kwon, Clarke, & Wodak, 2014; Maitlis, 2005; Maitlis & Lawrence, 2007; Tuggle, Sirmon, Reutzel, & Bierman, 2010), strategy workshops (Heracleous & Jacobs, 2008; Johnson, Prashantham, Floyd, & Bourque, 2010), executive retreats (Heracleous, & Jacobs, 2008), or in project, gate review, or steering committee meetings (Henfridsson & Yoo, 2013; Kaplan, 2008). Although many studies focus exclusively on executives and board members (e.g., Kwon, Clarke, & Wodak, 2014; Samra & Fredericks, 2003, 2004), others observe a wider range of organizational members, including both executives and nonexecutives (e.g., Jay, 2013; Maitlis, 2005; Maitlis & Lawrence, 2007; Stigliani & Ravasi, 2012).

The sensitivity and importance of strategic conversations may make gaining access to field sites difficult. Some authors have addressed this issue by trading their expertise for site access, for example by facilitating management training or strategy workshops in return for observing TMTs' conversations and interactions (Heracleous & Jacobs, 2008; Laine & Vaara, 2007). Other scholars sidestep the challenges of gaining the trust of a large group of executives by approaching either a subsidiary or a single department within a larger organization (e.g., Hardy & Thomas, 2014; Henfridsson & Yoo, 2013; Kaplan, 2008). Tuggle and colleagues (2010) offer another innovative solution. In studying the factors that affect board members' allocation of attention, the authors had to convince publicly traded firms to provide access to transcripts of private board meetings. The researchers overcame companies' resistance by ensuring confidentiality; by choosing to study older transcripts, the content of which was not likely to impact future stock performance; and most ingeniously, by hiring the firms' auditors (who already had access to the transcripts) to carry out the coding process. In this case, auditors served as important conduits of trust because they had preexisting relationships with the firms and because auditors' professional code of conduct prohibited disclosure of any client information (Tuggle et al., 2010).

Data Recording and Observation Mode

Studying strategic conversations also involves choices about whether researchers will observe conversations in real time or solely through recordings and/or written transcripts. In-person observation may present logistical challenges, but it has the benefit of enabling researchers to seek immediate clarification as well as to observe elements that would not be adequately captured by audio recordings or transcripts, such as the physical setting or informants' use of artifacts (Patton, 2001). A middle path is to attend meetings in real time but virtually, through electronic media. For example, Kaplan (2008) joined the meetings of an R&D group electronically. Virtual, real-time observation of strategic conversations overcomes the geographical barriers of visiting field sites and limits researchers' obtrusiveness. However, it also limits researchers' abilities to capture the physical environment.

Whether researchers attend in real time or examine conversations after the fact, they often rely on audio recordings that can be transcribed verbatim. Audio recordings and transcripts offer relative precision and allow researchers to review strategic conversations multiple times, an option absent from traditional ethnographic observation methods (Whittle et al., 2014). Video recordings have

Table 26.1 Use of Strategic Conversations in Strategy Research

Reference	Research Context (setting, # of cases, study period)	Research Focus	How Innovation Was Used		Conversation Participants	Outcome of Innovation
			Conversations Observed (#)	Conversation Topics		
Henfridsson & Yoo (2013)	Subsidiary of a major car manufacturer (1); 9 years	The process through which institutional entrepreneurs pursue new innovation trajectories in the face of ambiguity	Project meetings (53) Gate review meetings (2) Steering committee meetings (2) Workshops (22)	Disruptive technology development: creating and marketing new products that connect customer devices to cars (car infotainment)	TMT Steering committee members Project managers Project team engineers Consultants	Identification of cognitive processes that enable institutional entrepreneurs to complete innovation trajectories such as processes of reflective dissension, imaginative projection, and eliminatory exploration
Jay (2013)	Public–private energy alliance (1); 2 years	The impact of change processes on hybrid organizations' innovative potential	Strategy meetings (9) Board of directors meetings (9) Core group meetings (27) In-office observation (80 days at 2–5 hours each)	Strategy development and evaluation: developing an organizational identity, discussing changes in organizational structure and their challenges, defining success and failure, and selecting a client strategy	TMT Board members Consultants Alliance members: city officials and partner organizations	An interpretive process model that shows how hybrid organizations are able to combine paradoxical institutional logics: initially organizational members oscillate between paradoxical logics and ultimately synthesize them with the help of outsiders' interpretations. Synthesis of logics is linked to more innovative outcomes.
Kaplan (2008)	R&D group in a communication technologies manufacturer (1); 8 months	Interpretive and cognitive processes by which certain cognitive frames predominate during strategy making under uncertainty	Project and steering committee meetings (33) In-office observation (7 one-day site visits)	Strategy development and implementation: making decisions about resource allocations and investments in projects	TMT Professional staff in R&D and marketing departments	A cognitive process model that links political processes of cognitive frame dominance with strategic decision-making processes: convergence of conflicting frames facilitates decision making whereas divergence postpones decisions

(Continued)

Table 26.1 Continued

Reference	Research Context (setting, # of cases, study period)	How Innovation Was Used				Outcome of Innovation
		Research Focus	Conversations Observed (#)	Conversation Topics	Conversation Participants	
Kwon et al. (2014)	Aerospace engineering firm (1); 6 months	Managers' use of linguistic devices in sensemaking processes	Board of directors meetings (6)	Strategy evaluation and strategic change: evaluating the potential of future projects and identifying external conditions as opportunities or threats	Board members	Evidence of how particular linguistic devices (e.g., use of narratives, scenarios, metaphors, analogies) form five different discursive practices (equalizing, defining/ redefining, simplifying, legitimating, reconciling), which in turn influence strategists' construction of shared meaning
Laine & Vaara (2007)	Engineering consulting firm (1); 6 years	The role of subjectivity, that is, the discursively constructed sense of identity and social agency, in strategy making	Management training/strategy development program (8)	Strategic plan evaluation: reflecting on and evaluating divisional strategic plans and discussing challenges of strategy implementation	Middle-level managers Professional staff	Evidence of the ways in which three features of strategy discourse (recurrent concepts, metaphorical expressions, and modality shifts) are used by corporate managers and middle-level managers to gain or resist control and by project engineers to distance themselves from managers' strategy discourse so as to protect their identity
Liu & Maitlis (2014)	Computer gaming firm (1); 3 months	The role of managers' display of emotion in strategy development	Strategy meetings (7)	Strategy development and implementation: discussing possible changes to organizational structure, allocating resources, and evaluating products'	TMT	Evidence of the role of emotion and its valence on how strategic issues are proposed, discussed, and evaluated: positive emotions are related to collaborative strategizing processes, whereas conflict

Author (year)	Context/sample	Aim/focus	Data collection	Issues	Informants	Findings
				development and competitor strategies		between intense positive and negative emotions is related to "unreconciled" strategizing.
Maitlis (2005)	Symphony orchestras (3); 2 years	Sensemaking processes of diverse stakeholders around typical organizational issues	TMT meetings (11) Board of directors meetings (15) Board subcommittee meetings (10) Senior management and board retreats (3) Various meetings, e.g., orchestra meetings and tours (67) Team-building workshop (1)	Operational issues: programming, renewing staff contracts, inviting guest players, dealing with low-performing staff, appointing key players Strategic change: identifying areas for cost cutting, and increasing income generation	TMT Board members and trustees Orchestra committee members, conductors, and musicians External stakeholders (customers, funders, guest artists, and musicians' union)	A model of the social processes of organizational sensemaking: the interaction of high/low leader and stakeholder sensegiving produces four different forms of organizational sensemaking—guided, fragmented, restricted, and minimal. Each form has different process characteristics and outcomes, e.g., different levels of animation and control.
Samra-Fredericks (2003)	Manufacturing firm (1); 1 year	The linguistic manifestation of strategists' behaviors and actions and its role in influencing managerial attention and decision making	Strategy meetings In-office observation (half-day to 3-day field visits)	Strategy implementation: addressing technical staff shortage, enforcing company policies, and evaluating strategic investments	TMT	Evidence of six features of strategists' speech that influence others' opinions: speaking forms of knowledge, mitigating and observing the protocols of human interaction (the moral order), questioning and querying, displaying appropriate emotion, deploying metaphors, and putting history "to work"

been employed occasionally, particularly when researchers are interested in participants' physical cues (Liu & Maitlis, 2014) or use of physical objects (Heracleous, & Jacobs, 2008). However, participants may perceive video recording to be intrusive.

In some cases, researchers will not be able to gain consent for either audio or video recording of sensitive content. As a result, they will have no choice but to observe strategic conversations in real time and take copious notes, capturing direct quotes whenever possible. In limited cases, conversation data can be collected through preexisting archives such as transcripts of public firms' board meetings (Tuggle et al., 2010). However, as with virtual participation, this approach is not well suited for capturing the physical environment and will obscure tone and other cues to the speaker's emotional state.

If a researcher observes conversations in real time, whether in person or virtually, he or she may take the role of either observer or participant-observer. Regardless of the researcher's intent, informants may enlist the researcher's input because of his or her expertise or merely because he or she happens to be present. In the case of participant observation, a good practice is to document one's own inputs to the conversations. In this way, the researcher's impact can, to some extent, be separated from the natural evolution of the strategic process under study. For example, when Jay (2013) was asked to share his insights with the group he was observing, he wrote up his contributions and audio-recorded both his response and the group's subsequent discussion.

Additional Data

Finally, researchers need to make decisions regarding supplementing strategic conversations with other types of data. Most studies combine conversations with interviews and archival data (see Table 26.2). Collecting meeting-specific documents such as agendas and presentation slides can be useful for retracing the logic of conversations during data analysis. The collection of multiple types of data may also aid in identifying and interpreting what is *not* said in strategy meetings. Researchers may gain insights by comparing comments gathered from interviews or informal "water-cooler" conversations with statements made during "official" strategic conversations. Understanding what individuals choose *not* to say in the context of formal strategic conversations may be as revealing as analyzing what is actually said. Moreover, conversations that seem stilted may come alive after meetings end, or when people meet in hallways.[1] Getting clarity on participants' perceptions of a meeting and its outcomes and clarifying one's own impressions can be facilitated by lingering after meetings to observe interactions and postmeeting discussions (Jarzabkowski & Seidl, 2008).

An innovative approach to collecting complementary data was developed by Balogun and Johnson (2004), who provided managers with a set of structured questions and asked them to log their views about an ongoing organizational change every few weeks. These logs served as diaries through which researchers were able to observe, without being present, changes in managers' cognitive schemas. The authors compensated for their absence from the field by organizing focus groups with the same managers. In this case, field notes were produced by informants, and conversations were observed in events organized by researchers.

In sum, research examining strategic conversations presents some unusual issues related to field site access and data collection, but existing studies point to a number of innovative means of overcoming these challenges. Next, we identify challenges and potential solutions in the analysis of strategic conversation data.

Analytical Approaches

Strategic conversations can be analyzed in a variety of ways, depending on researchers' specific goals. Given the large volume of data produced by observing conversations, researchers often begin with preliminary

Table 26.2 Data Collection and Analysis of Strategic Conversations

Study	Data Collection			Data Analysis				
	Researcher Participation	Conversation Recording Mode	Additional Data Sources	Grounded Theory	Discourse Analysis	Conversation Analysis	Concept Mapping	Other
Henfridsson & Yoo (2013)	Observer	Audio Note-taking	Interviews and archives	☐				
Heracleous & Jacobs (2008)	Participant-observer	Video	None	☐				
Huisman (2001)	Observer	Video	Interviews			☐		
Jay (2013)	Participant-observer	Note-taking	Interviews and archives	☐			☐	
Johnson et al. (2010)	Observer	Video	Interviews	☐				
Kaplan (2008)	Observer	Note-taking	Interviews and archives	☐				
Kwon et al. (2014)	Observer	Audio	Interviews and archives		☐			
Laine & Vaara (2007)	Participant-observer	Audio	Interviews and archives		☐			
Liu & Maitlis (2014)	Observer	Audio Video	None		☐			
Maitlis (2005)	Observer	Note-taking	Interviews and archives	☐				
Maitlis & Lawrence (2007)	Observer	Note-taking	Interviews and archives	☐				
Samra-Fredericks (2003)	Observer	Audio	None			☐		
Samra-Fredericks (2004)	Observer	Note-taking of nonverbal cues	None			☐		
Stigliani & Ravasi (2012)	Participant-observer	Audio Note-taking	Interviews and archives	☐				
Tuggle et al. (2010)	Absent from field site	Preexisting board of director meeting transcripts	Corporate filings and Compustat database					☐
Whittle et al. (2014)	Participant-observer	Audio Note-taking	Interviews and archives			☐		
Zbaracki & Bergen (2010)	Observer	Note-taking	Interviews and archives	☐				

Christina Kyprianou et al.

analyses designed to summarize one or more aspects of the data (e.g., the events that occurred, the types of language used, or the issues discussed). These initial analyses guide the direction of subsequent, more detailed techniques such as discourse analysis, conversation analysis, and grounded theory-building.

Early-Stage Analyses

Initial analyses may include building chronological case histories (Eisenhardt, 1989) to describe the organization and outline key events (e.g., Heracleous and Jacobs, 2008; Kaplan, 2008). They may also involve coding a manageable subset of transcripts to reveal preliminary themes that can later be explored in the full data set (e.g., Kwon et al, 2014). Researchers may also generate initial descriptions of conversation data using linguistic analyses such as concept mapping. Concept mapping is a form of content analysis that identifies closely related words in a particular text; groups them into categories, or concepts; identifies links, or relations, among concepts; and then maps them visually. The result is a visual representation of general and more specific concepts found in the text and the relationships between them (Novak & Cañas, 2008; Novak & Musonda, 1991). Hardy and Thomas (2014) implemented concept mapping by using Fowler's (1991) concept of the "lexical register" to identify clusters of terms that participants used to describe distinct components of their firm's strategy. Jay (2013) employed concept mapping by carrying out a visual network analysis to consolidate and clarify initial data codes. A number of software packages can easily, quickly, and inexpensively carry out concept mapping and other types of content analysis to generate descriptions of large volumes of data. These descriptions are not likely to generate deep theoretical insights, but they provide guidance and ideas for subsequent analysis. However, it is advisable for researchers to understand the software packages' underlying algorithms before interpreting the results.

In-Depth Analyses

While chronologies and concept maps can provide initial insights into conversation data, scholars turn to more in-depth analytical techniques to confirm, disconfirm, or elaborate these preliminary results. In-depth analytical approaches that have been applied to strategic conversation data include discourse analysis, conversation analysis, and grounded theory-building.

Discourse Analysis

Discourse analysis emphasizes the role of language in the construction of reality. Analyzing discourse involves studying how participants interact through writing or speech; how they represent the world, its social practices, and their own views in their language; and the ways their physical behaviors facilitate or hinder communication (Fairclough, 2003). Discourse is an umbrella term for "any body of language based communications, however organized, whether or not these are concretized as texts" (Hendry, 2000: 964). The goal of discourse analysis is to understand how all of these forms of communication construct social order (Phillips & Hardy, 2002).

In the context of studying strategic conversations, discourse analysis begins with coding texts to identify either general types of discourses (e.g., corporate management vs. business unit management discourse) (Laine & Vaara, 2007), or specific issues being discussed (Liu & Maitlis, 2014). Discourse analysis involves looking for themes in the content of strategists' talk such as "be first, be best" or "be cost-effective" (Hardy & Thomas, 2014). Once main themes are identified, in-depth analysis of discourses involves searching for related themes, or subdiscourses, that appear close to the main discourses. For instance, Hardy and Thomas (2014) find that one of the main components of strategy discourse in a firm undergoing organizational restructuring, the "be cost-effective" discourse, appeared when broader discourses, such as "fast growing market" and "competitive market," were invoked.

Discourse theorists often emphasize the role of power and politics and may analyze how strategic discourses vary by organizational role, that is, corporate managers versus middle managers (Laine & Vaara, 2007; Liu & Maitlis, 2014). They delve deeper into each group's discourse by exploring not only recurrent concepts in the content of its talk but also its use of particular discursive and linguistic practices, such as metaphorical expressions and modality shifts (Laine & Vaara, 2007).

Conversation Analysis

A less common but growing approach to analyzing the role of language in strategy is conversation analysis. Rooted in ethnomethodology, which is interested in the processes and knowledge people use to make sense of their worlds (Garfinkel, 1967), conversation analysis is concerned with the ways that social order and meaning are constructed through individuals' talk and actions. Primarily applied to the analysis of naturally occurring talk, conversation analysis assumes that conversations have a different structure from that of interviews or debates (Goodwin & Heritage, 1990; Sacks, Schegloff, & Jefferson, 1974) and are more complex than any written interaction (Peräkylä, 2005).

Conversation analysts examine how meaning is constructed conversationally by examining both the structure and content of talk. To do so, they look for patterns in turn taking, that is how individuals take turns in responding to each other, how adjacent utterances are linked (e.g., a question produces another question), or how individuals use particular conversation practices such as agreements or disagreements or telling and receiving news (Peräkylä, 2005). More generally, conversation analysis treats both the structure and content of talk as "a basic form of organization" that generates social reality in that particular setting (Sacks et al., 1974). It also assumes that "talk is action" (Peräkylä, 2005: 875) because, "when people converse, they are not merely talking, not merely describing. . . . They do things in their talk. They are constructing their turns to perform an action or be part of the management of some activity" (Drew, 2005: 86). In sum, conversation analysis attempts to explicate the connections between linguistic phenomena and the resulting construction of social order. Thus, the goal of conversation analysis is to render "the 'tacit' procedures of talk for reality construction . . . more explicit" (Samra-Fredericks, 2003: 147).

To do so, conversation analysts utilize precise transcripts that preserve, among other details, exact pronunciations, pauses, pitch, and prolongation of sounds (see Jefferson, 2004, for one type of notation system used in conversation analysis). Moermann (1988), however, suggests moving beyond the transcript and gathering information about the context, history, or culture of a setting so as to understand more broadly what may influence participants' processes of meaning construction.

More recent work seems to subscribe to this more inclusive approach for incorporating data gathered through ethnography into conversation analysis. For example, Samra-Fredericks (2003), combined conversation analysis with her observations from field site visits to understand how strategists created shared understandings of the future. During field site visits, she first observed that one strategist was particularly effective in influencing his colleagues' opinions. She then identified moments in the course of strategy meetings that were pivotal in deciding how the group would address two organizational weaknesses (also observed during her field work). She further examined these pivotal conversation moments through a conversation analysis lens to understand how this one strategist generated support for his views. Her analysis revealed the use of six linguistic devices (e.g., the use of queries or references to the past) that influenced others' opinions. It is implied, albeit not described in much detail, that the six linguistic devices emerged from a meticulous application of the conversation analysis method.

The limited number of studies that either use conversation analysis or explain the specific analytical steps involved in applying the method to strategy research suggests the application of the method is still at a nascent stage. However, efforts to outline more clearly conversation analysis' specific methodological steps will be necessary for encouraging the method's wider adoption by strategy scholars.

It is worth noting that both connections and gaps exist between discourse analysis and conversation analysis. Both have an interest in how language is used to exercise power and construct meaning. However, discourse and conversation analyses differ in their scope and process. Discourse analysis draws on a variety of texts, the types of which depend on whether a study focuses on a narrower topic, such as displays of emotion and their role during strategy development (e.g., Liu & Maitlis, 2014), or a broader one, such as how different management groups resist or gain control through strategy discourses (Laine & Vaara, 2007). Moreover, the discourse analytic process looks for shared themes across texts (Foucault, 1980; Heracleous, 2006), such as similarities between written and verbal communication or between interviews and conversations (Abdallah & Langley, 2014; Hardy & Thomas, 2014). Connections between texts are also known as *intertextuality* (Wodak, 2008). Lastly, discourse analysis of strategic conversations takes into account the broader discourses that bear upon strategic processes (Hardy & Thomas, 2014).

In contrast, conversation analysts take a narrower approach; they focus on studying interactions within a conversation episode (e.g., a meeting) to understand how social order is constructed in that particular episode and thus use little additional data (e.g., Huisman, 2001; one already mentioned exception is Samra-Fredericks, 2003). In the context of strategy research, conversation analysis has primarily been adopted by strategy-as-practice scholars who study the actions of strategists and the implications of those actions for strategy-making (Jarzabkowski, Balogun, & Seidl, 2007; Samra-Fredericks, 2005; Whittington, 2003). Lastly, conversation analysis has been used to explore power relations specifically among those who directly influence strategy, such as TMT members and other senior managers (Samra-Fredericks, 2003, 2004; Kwon et al., 2014).

Grounded Theory

The third and last group of papers analyzes strategic conversations using grounded theory-generation techniques (e.g., Jay, 2013; Stigliani & Ravasi, 2012). Broadly speaking, generating grounded theory involves iterative analysis of data and prior literature to develop inductively new constructs and relationships (Eisenhardt, 1989). In its original, more-specific formulation (Glaser & Strauss, 1967), grounded theory-building begins with identifying initial themes by associating sections of text with codes that are close to informants' language. These *in vivo* codes are progressively clustered into more abstract ones until the majority of observations are categorized into theoretically relevant themes (Boyatzis, 1998; Headland, Pike, & Harris, 1990). While studies of conversations using grounded theory techniques draw from and contribute to a variety of theories, their common goal is to explicate complex organizational processes that are poorly understood (e.g., Stigliani & Ravasi, 2012). Likely due to the complexity of the processes observed, authors tend to analyze data from multiple sources and at both the individual and collective levels.

Further innovation in the analysis of strategic conversations may emerge from adopting additional tools from other disciplines. One example is the Linguistic Inquiry Word Count (LIWC), a text analysis tool that examines the style, as opposed to the content, of language. LIWC identifies patterns in a text by counting pronouns, prepositions, negations, quantifiers, and other categories of words that have been found to relate to social, affective, cognitive, perceptual, and biological processes (Pennebaker & King, 1999; Tausczik & Pennebaker, 2010). LIWC has been used sparingly in strategy research to analyze archival data such as press releases and letters to shareholders (e.g., Pfarrer, Pollock, & Rindova, 2010). It is, however, also well suited for naturally occurring language (Pennebaker & King, 1999) and could aid in studying conversations.

Conclusion

We have reviewed the innovative use of conversation data in strategy research, focusing on the insights that strategic conversations may reveal, as well as the challenges involved in data collection

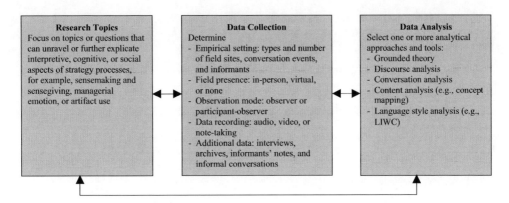

Figure 26.1 Research Topics and Methods Suitable for Strategic Conversation Data

and analysis of strategic conversations. We argue that this distinct and unique type of data advances our understanding of otherwise unobservable aspects of strategy, especially its micro-foundations, that is "the underlying individual-level and group level actions that shape strategy" (Eisenhardt, Furr, & Bingham, 2010: 1263). We hope our discussion provides insights into strategic conversations' value and usefulness, offers guidance for overcoming the challenges of working with conversation data, and stimulates further research and methodological innovation in this area.

Note

1 We thank our editor, Roderick Kramer, for highlighting yet another use of strategic conversation data.

References

Abdallah, C., & Langley, A. (2014). The double edge of ambiguity in strategic planning. *Journal of Management Studies, 51(2)*, 235–264.

Balogun, J., Jacobs, C., Jarzabkowski, P., Mantere, S., & Vaara, E. (2014). Placing strategy discourse in context: Sociomateriality, sensemaking, and power. *Journal of Management Studies, 51(2)*, 175–201.

Balogun, J., & Johnson, G. (2004). Organizational restructuring and middle manager sensemaking. *Academy of Management Journal, 47(4)*, 523–549.

Bartunek, J.M. (1984). Changing interpretive schemes and organizational restructuring: The example of a religious order. *Administrative Science Quarterly, 29(3)*, 355–372.

Bosk, C.L. (1979). *Forgive and remember: Managing medical failure*. Chicago, IL: University of Chicago Press.

Boyatzis, R.E. (1998). *Transforming qualitative information: Thematic analysis and code development*. Thousand Oaks, CA: Sage.

Creswell, J.W. (2007). *Qualitative inquiry and research design: Choosing among five approaches*. Thousand Oaks, CA: Sage.

Drew, P. (2005). Conversation analysis. In K.L. Fitch & R.E. Sanders (Eds.), *Handbook of language and social interaction* (2nd ed., pp. 71–102). Mahwah, NJ: Lawrence Erlbaum.

Edmondson, A. (1999). Psychological safety and learning behavior in work teams. *Administrative Science Quarterly, 44(2)*, 350–383.

Eisenhardt, K.M. (1989). Building theories from case study research. *Academy of Management Review, 14(4)*, 532–550.

Eisenhardt, K.M., Furr, N.R., & Bingham, C.B. (2010). Crossroads—Microfoundations of performance: Balancing efficiency and flexibility in dynamic environments. *Organization Science, 21(6)*, 1263–1273.

Elsbach, K.D., Barr, P.S., & Hargadon, A.B. (2005). Identifying situated cognition in organizations. *Organization Science, 16(4)*, 422–433.

Fairclough, N. (2003). *Analysing discourse: Textual analysis for social research*. London, England: Routledge.

Fishman, P. M. (1978). Interaction: The work women do. *Social Problems, 25(4)*, 397–406.

Foucault, M. (1980). *Power/knowledge: Selected interviews and other writings, 1972–1977*. New York, NY: Random House.

Fowler, R. (1991). *Language in the news: Discourse and ideology in the press*. London, England: Routledge.

Garfinkel, H. (1967). *Studies in ethnomethodology*. Englewood Cliffs, NJ: Prentice-Hall.

Glaser, B.G., & Strauss, A.L. (1967). *The discovery of grounded theory: Strategies for qualitative research*. New York, NY: Sociology Press.

Godfrey, P.C., & Hill, C.W.L. (1995). The problem of unobservables in strategic management research. *Strategic Management Journal, 16(7)*, 519–533.

Goodwin, C., & Heritage, J. (1990). Conversation analysis. *Annual Review of Anthropology, 19*, 283–307.

Hardy, C., & Thomas, R. (2014). Strategy, discourse and practice: The intensification of power. *Journal of Management Studies, 51(2)*, 320–348.

Headland, T.N., Pike, K.L., & Harris, M. (1990). *Emics and etics: The insider/outsider debate*. Thousand Oaks, CA: Sage.

Hendry, J. (2000). Strategic decision making, discourse, and strategy as social practice. *Journal of Management Studies, 37(7)*, 955–978.

Henfridsson, O., & Yoo, Y. (2013). The liminality of trajectory shifts in institutional entrepreneurship. *Organization Science, 25(3)*, 932–950.

Heracleous, L. (2006). *Discourse, interpretation, organization*. Cambridge, England: Cambridge University Press.

Heracleous, L., & Jacobs, C.D. (2008). Understanding organizations through embodied metaphors. *Organization Studies, 29(1)*, 45–78.

Huisman, M. (2001). Decision-making in meetings as talk-in-interaction. *International Studies of Management and Organization, 31(3)*, 69–90.

Jarzabkowski, P., Balogun, J., & Seidl, D. (2007). Strategizing: The challenges of a practice perspective. *Human Relations, 60(1)*, 5–27.

Jarzabkowski, P., & Seidl, D. (2008). The role of meetings in the social practice of strategy. *Organization Studies, 29(11)*, 1391–1426.

Jay, J. (2013). Navigating paradox as a mechanism of change and innovation in hybrid organizations. *Academy of Management Journal, 56(1)*, 137–159.

Jefferson, G. (2004). Glossary of transcript symbols with an introduction. In G.H. Lerner (Ed.), *Conversation analysis: Studies from the first generation* (pp. 13–31). Philadelphia, PA: John Benjamins.

Johnson, G., Prashantham, S., Floyd, S.W., & Bourque, N. (2010). The ritualization of strategy workshops. *Organization Studies, 31(12)*, 1589–1618.

Kaplan, S. (2008). Framing contests: Strategy making under uncertainty. *Organization Science, 19(5)*, 729–752.

Kwon, W., Clarke, I., & Wodak, R. (2014). Micro-level discursive strategies for constructing shared views around strategic issues in team meetings. *Journal of Management Studies, 51(2)*, 265–290.

Laine, P.-M., & Vaara, E. (2007). Struggling over subjectivity: A discursive analysis of strategic development in an engineering group. *Human Relations, 60(1)*, 29–58.

Liu, F., & Maitlis, S. (2014). Emotional dynamics and strategizing processes: A study of strategic conversations in top team meetings. *Journal of Management Studies, 51(2)*, 202–234.

Maitlis, S. (2005). The social processes of organizational sensemaking. *Academy of Management Journal, 48(1)*, 21–49.

Maitlis, S., & Lawrence, T.B. (2007). Triggers and enablers of sensegiving in organizations. *Academy of Management Journal, 50(1)*, 57–84.

Malinowski, B. (1922). *Argonauts of the western Pacific: An account of native enterprise and adventure in the archipelagoes of Melanesian New Guinea*. London, England: Routledge.

Mantere, S. (2013). What is organizational strategy? A language-based view. *Journal of Management Studies, 50(8)*, 1408–1426.

Mead, M. (1928). *Coming of age in Samoa*. New York, NY: William Morrow.

Moerman, M. (1988). *Talking culture: Ethnography and conversation analysis*. Philadelphia: University of Pennsylvania Press.

Novak, J.D., & Cañas, A.J. (2008). *The theory underlying concept maps and how to construct and use them*. Pensacola: Florida Institute for Human and Machine Cognition.

Novak, J.D., & Musonda, D. (1991). A twelve-year longitudinal study of science concept learning. *American Educational Research Journal, 28(1)*, 117–153.

O'Mahony, S., & Bechky, B.A. (2006). Stretchwork: Managing the career progression paradox in external labor markets. *Academy of Management Journal, 49(5)*, 918–941.

Patton, M. (2001). Fieldwork strategies and observation methods. In M. Patton (Ed.), *Qualitative research and evaluation methods* (3rd ed., pp. 259–332). Thousand Oaks, CA: Sage.

Pennebaker, J.W., & King, L.A. (1999). Linguistic styles: Language use as an individual difference. *Journal of Personality and Social Psychology, 77(6)*, 1296–1312.

Peräkylä, A. (2005). Analyzing talk and text. In N.K. Denzin & Y.S. Lincoln (Eds.), *The Sage handbook of qualitative research* (3rd ed., pp. 869–886). Thousand Oaks, CA: Sage.

Pfarrer, M.D., Pollock, T.G., & Rindova, V.P. (2010). A tale of two assets: The effects of firm reputation and celebrity on earnings surprises and investors' reactions. *Academy of Management Journal, 53(5)*, 1131–1152.

Phillips, N., & Hardy, C. (2002). *Discourse analysis: Investigating processes of social construction.* Thousand Oaks, CA: Sage.

Sacks, H., Schegloff, E.A., & Jefferson, G. (1974). A simplest systematics for the organization of turn-taking for conversation. *Language, 50(4)*, 696–735.

Samra-Fredericks, D. (2003). Strategizing as lived experience and strategists' everyday efforts to shape strategic direction. *Journal of Management Studies, 40(1)*, 141–174.

Samra-Fredericks, D. (2004). Managerial elites making rhetorical and linguistic "moves" for a moving (emotional) display. *Human Relations, 57(9)*, 1103–1143.

Samra-Fredericks, D. (2005). Strategic practice, "discourse" and the everyday interactional constitution of "power effects". *Organization, 12(6)*, 803–841.

Stigliani, I., & Ravasi, D. (2012). Organizing thoughts and connecting brains: Material practices and the transition from individual to group-level prospective sensemaking. *Academy of Management Journal, 55(5)*, 1232–1259.

Sutton, R.I., & Hargadon, A. (1996). Brainstorming groups in context: Effectiveness in a product design firm. *Administrative Science Quarterly, 41(4)*, 685–718.

Tausczik, Y.R., & Pennebaker, J. (2010). The psychological meaning of words: LIWC and computerized text analysis methods. *Journal of Language and Social Psychology, 29*, 24–54.

Tuggle, C.S., Sirmon, D.G., Reutzel, C.R., & Bierman, L. (2010). Commanding board of director attention: Investigating how organizational performance and CEO duality affect board members' attention to monitoring. *Strategic Management Journal, 31(9)*, 946–968.

Whittington, R. (2003). The work of strategizing and organizing: For a practice perspective. *Strategic Organization, 1*, 117–126.

Whittle, A., Housley, W., Gilchrist, A., Lenney, P., & Mueller, F. (2014). Power, politics, and organizational communication. In F. Cooren, E. Vaara, A. Langley, & H. Tsoukas (Eds.), *Language and communication at work* (pp. 71–94). Oxford, England: Oxford University Press.

Wodak, R. (2008). Introduction: Discourse studies—Important concepts and terms. In R. Wodak & M. Krzyzanowski (Eds.), *Qualitative discourse analysis in the social sciences* (pp. 1–29). Basingstoke, NH: Palgrave Macmillan.

Zbaracki, M.J., & Bergen, M. (2010). When truces collapse: A longitudinal study of price-adjustment routines. *Organization Science, 21(5)*, 955–972.

27

Triangulate and Expand

Using Multiple Sources of Data for Convergence and Expansion to Enrich Inductive Theorizing

Elizabeth D. Rouse and Spencer H. Harrison

Introduction

In this chapter we focus on the use of multiple sources of data in inductive, qualitative data collection and analysis, and we present a four-step process for data triangulation and expansion, as illustrated in Figure 27.1. We have two goals in this chapter:

1. We want to encourage scholars to provide evidence of data triangulation by showing, in their findings sections, examples from the multiple data sources they describe in their methods sections, thereby providing a wider window for their data "to speak."
2. We embolden scholars to use multiple sources of data to triangulate and expand their theorizing by combining data sources to account for differences in temporal stance (retrospective, real time, or prospective) and differences in researchers' influence on the data source (co-construction, observation, or interpretation).

Multiple Data Sources in Theory and Practice: A Review of the Current State of the Field

Miles and Huberman's (1994) influential "sourcebook," *Qualitative Data Analysis*, suggests that qualitative analysis consists of data reduction, data display, and conclusion drawing. The result of these activities is like boiling sugar in water to create a syrup or a *reduction*: data reduction is described as "simplifying," data display is described as "compressing," and conclusion drawing is described as "noting regularities" (1994: 10–11). While it is true that all analytical strategies, quantitative or qualitative, require reducing data, qualitative data provides researchers a unique and important opportunity for finding paradoxes, contrasts, and complexities that can enrich theorizing. To help leverage these opportunities, we want to call attention to an important tool in the qualitative researchers' quiver of techniques: triangulation.

While triangulation speaks broadly to the concept of using multiple perspectives to understand a single phenomenon, given our concern with the use of multiple data types, we focus our discussion on a particular type of triangulation—data triangulation. The notion of triangulation, or "the

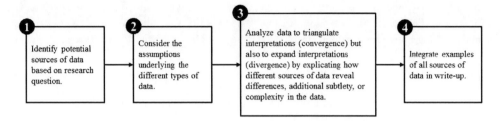

Figure 27.1   Four-Step Process for Data Triangulation and Expansion

combination of different methods, study groups, local and temporal setting, and different theoretical perspectives in dealing with a phenomenon" (Flick, 2014: 183), is often presented as one of the dominant reasons for designing a study with multiple sources or types of data. Denzin (1978) first described data triangulation as the use of multiple data sources to collect diverse views about a phenomenon. He described three forms of data triangulation: (1) time, in which data is collected at different points in time; (2) space, in which data is collected at different sites; and (3) person, in which data is collected at more than one level, such as individual and group levels. In focusing on case studies, Yin (2009) described primary categories of evidence, or potential data sources—documentation, archival records, interviews, direct observations, participant observation, and physical artifacts—that can be used in combination with one another.

Often, an underlying assumption of the use of data triangulation is that the purpose of using multiple data sources is convergence or corroboration among the sources. For example, Patton (2002) suggested that triangulation provides a test for consistency, and Yin (2009: 115–116) argued that "the most important advantage presented by using multiple sources of evidence is the development of *converging lines of inquiry*, a process of triangulation and corroboration." In other words, in finding agreement or convergence between different data sources, researchers can be more certain that they are accurately describing the phenomenon; convergence among data sources helps reduce threats to construct validity (Yin 2009). A secondary assumption of data triangulation is that all data sources have their weaknesses, and by including multiple sources of data, scholars can offset these weaknesses (Yin 2009). For example, interviews can be problematic because they are tainted by retrospective bias; by incorporating direct observation, the study can capture events in real time. By comparing the findings from these data sources, researchers might be able to determine the accuracy of statements made during interviews.

Existing guidance on data triangulation also hints at a potentially paradoxical purpose of the use of multiple sources of data—that contradictions between data sources can improve a researcher's understanding of the focal phenomenon (Denzin & Lincoln, 2011; Flick, 2014; Miles & Huberman, 1994). Mathison argued that:

> Because of the predominance of the assumption that triangulation will result in a single valid proposition we look for the convergence of evidence and miss what I see as the greater value in triangulating. . . . The value of triangulation is not as a technological solution to a data collection and analysis problem, it is as a technique which provides more and better evidence from which researchers can construct *meaningful propositions* about the social world. (1988: 15)

In other words, the ultimate goal is to understand the phenomenon as deeply as possible, and multiple sources of evidence allow us to better capture and describe the phenomenon regardless of whether the data sources confirm, complement, or contradict one another. Contradictions offer opportunities to elaborate findings, explore new lines of thinking, and develop new theoretical explanations (Flick, 2014; Miles & Huberman, 1994). Arnould and Wallendorf made a similar argument, describing how ethnographers in the marketing discipline look for "disjunctures":

> Comparisons indicate some convergences as well as some disjunctures. Rather than just noting disjunctures, or (worse) assimilating them to one convergent interpretation, market-oriented ethnographers question why convergences and disjunctures between methods occur. *The interpretive meanings of codes are "thickened" into constructs in light of these additional data.* (1994: 498, emphasis added)

To date, however, there has been little guidance on how scholars might leverage differences between types of data to expand and enrich their theorizing efforts.

In writing up their research, scholars often acknowledge the importance of using multiple data sources; nonetheless our impression was that, in practice, scholars often rely on one dominant source of data for their analysis, even though they collect multiple sources of evidence. As Gioia, Corley, and Hamilton acknowledge in reflecting on qualitative research:

> Like all good qualitative research, we employ multiple data sources (archives, field observation, media documentation, etc.), but the heart of these studies is the semi-structured interview—to obtain both retrospective and real-time accounts by those people experiencing the phenomenon of theoretical interest. (2013: 19)

In other words, interviews are at the center of a great deal of inductive, qualitative research, and while other sources are important to understanding the phenomenon, they are often not fully incorporated into the analysis and the full potential of data triangulation is unrealized.

To test and build on our initial suspicions, we conducted an analysis of the recent use of multiple data sources in inductive, qualitative research. We searched for articles in four of the top empirical management journals—*Academy of Management Journal, Administrative Science Quarterly, Organization Science*, and *Strategic Management Journal*—using the key words "qualitative" and "inductive." We limited our search to articles published between 2007 and 2013 to capture the most recent trends. From this search, we then eliminated articles in which the primary analysis was deductive hypotheses testing and/or where the qualitative data was not formally analyzed. Our analysis revealed that of the 92 studies in our sample, 34 studies (37%) claimed to use two sources of data in the methods sections and 44 (48%) claimed to use three. However, when examining the data tables and figures in the findings sections only, 22 (24%) provided evidence of using two sources and only six (7%) provided evidence of using three sources. This suggests that while scholars often collect multiple sources of data, they might not be fully harnessing the potential of the sources of data to enrich their understanding of the phenomenon of interest.

A New Framework for Using Multiple Data Sources: Leveraging Data Expansion

While we believe that data triangulation is important, we argue that *data expansion*, which we define as the use of multiple data sources to reveal divergence in order to gain new insights about a phenomenon, offers an innovative way of looking at the use of multiple data sources in inductive, qualitative research. Rather than focusing on how multiple sources provide evidence of convergence, we assume that each data source offers a unique lens on the focal phenomenon. Given this assumption, we expect that conflict or divergence among data sources is relatively common and something that should be embraced rather than explained away. As Denzin and Lincoln (2011: 5) wrote, "Objective reality can never be captured. We know a thing only through its representations." We view data expansion as an "alternative to validation . . . that adds rigor, breadth, complexity, richness, and depth" (Denzin & Lincoln, 2011: 5). In this section, we develop a framework for thinking about data expansion in data collection.

Starting with the assumption that interviews will likely remain a foundational data source,[1] we examine the key characteristics of interviews and attempt to create a framework that presents the contrasting characteristics in order to generate meaningful divergence. In other words, if interviews continue to be the dominant method in qualitative, inductive research, what sources of data provide the most divergent perspectives so that we can build on interview data to add to our complex understanding of phenomena?

Dimension 1: Temporal Stance—Retrospective, Real-Time, and Prospective Accounts

One of the key criticisms of interviews is that they may be biased given that events are reported retrospectively. In particular, participants may not accurately *recall* the past and they may not *report* the past given a desire to construct events in a positive light (Miller, Cardinal, & Glick, 1997). Therefore, in most research, the retrospective nature of interviews is viewed as a limitation that must be overcome. Rather than viewing this as a limitation, we believe that retrospection offers answers to specific types of questions. In other words, rather than viewing retrospective reports as fiction or retrospective bias as something to guard or protect against, we view interviews, and other retrospective accounts, as conveying a specific type of information that may be the most appropriate type of data to answer certain types of research questions.

While scholars often disparage retrospection, within the management literature there has been a growing interest in the use of narratives and narrative methods, especially to answer questions related to sensemaking and identity (e.g., Ashforth, Harrison, & Corley, 2008; Ibarra & Barbulescu, 2010; Sonenshein, 2010). Boje (2001) suggests that in narrating events, sensemaking occurs in which events which were once unorganized or chaotic are given a narrative order. If we view interviews as constructed narratives, the questions that can be answered are less about specific facts or events and more about how people make sense of those events and potentially about how different people make sense of the same events; each interview offers a "situated retelling" in which individuals craft a story of who they are, often with the aim of generating a sense of coherence (Mishler, 1999: 51). We argue here, then, that interviews, and other retrospective accounts, offer unique information about how people make sense of and generate coherence around events and themselves in organizations.

Real-time accounts are often described as a solution to retrospection. Observations, archival materials, and, more recently, diary entries present ways of gathering data that are less colored by retrospection. For example, Hargadon and Bechky (2006) argued that observations of problem-solving and technological artifacts provided important counters to informant narratives of the problem-solving process that were colored by rationalizations. Diary data offers a means of reducing the time difference between experiences and the retelling of those experiences, which might be most appropriate for considering within-person changes over time as well how individual differences change over time (Bolger, Davis, & Rafaeli, 2003). For example, Amabile and colleagues (described in Amabile, Barsade, Mueller, & Staw, 2005) used daily diaries that included both quantitative and more open-ended questions for the collection of qualitative data to study creativity (Amabile et al., 2005), leader behaviors (Amabile, Schatzel, Moneta, & Kramer, 2004) and "inner work life" more generally (Amabile & Kramer, 2011). Unsworth (2001) suggested that diary studies might provide a way of tracking ideas as they occur and change.

In the first author's dissertation (Rouse, 2013), Bess used both interviews and weekly diary entries. In some of her interviews, she asked participants questions about events they described in their diary entries. It was not uncommon for participants to forget what they wrote even after they reread their own diary entries. Some commented that so much had happened in the last couple of weeks that it was hard for them to remember any more details about the event, or that while an event seemed really important in the moment, in hindsight the event was inconsequential. One way to describe this phenomenon is that rather than a retrospective bias, these more real-time accounts have a momentary bias. Another interpretation is that these retrospective accounts and real-time accounts offer very different perspectives that should not be compared for consistency, but rather offer a window into different interpretations of events that offer meaningful information. As Kahneman and Riis (2005) suggest, much of our data collection focuses on understanding the *remembered* evaluative self, rather than the *experiencing* self. Comparing these perspectives opens up new questions around why some events are important in the moment and others are important over time, and these perspectives inform one another.

Pushing this dimension of temporal stance even further, we consider how the use of prospective or future-oriented accounts might provide new insights. In considering prospective sensemaking (Gioia & Mehra, 1996) specifically, Stigliani and Ravasi (2012: 1234) claimed that, "despite the fact that prospective sensemaking underpins fundamental organizational processes, such as [strategy making, entrepreneurship, and innovation], this process is underresearched and undertheorized." Part of the reason this might be so is that we lack the methods, and particularly the data sources, to capture this future-focused perspective. Artifacts such as PowerPoint presentations, models, prototypes (Stigliani & Ravasi, 2012), and business plans, are often produced within organizations to convey this type of future-focused information. Interviews, too, might also be used to capture participants' perspectives on the future. Like comparing findings from retrospective and real-time accounts, comparing future accounts to real-time accounts might offer a deeper understanding of how visioning and narratives of the future influence how events transpire and how stories of "who I might become" (Ashforth et al., 2008: 340) inform identity narratives and construction in the future.

While Denzin (1978) suggested time as one form of data triangulation, he articulated this as collecting data at multiple time points to corroborate (which is different from the intention of longitudinal data collection). We take a different viewpoint on this time dimension to focus on the temporal stance of the source itself—does the source look back, look forward, or describe real-time events and experiences? Instead of trying to corroborate at different time points or offset weaknesses, we argue that each of these temporal stances offers unique information that, when combined, can generate a fuller, more nuanced perspective of a phenomenon.

Dimension 2: Researcher Influence on the Data Source—Co-Construction, Observation, Interpretation

Scholars acknowledge reflexivity in the sense that researchers' theoretical assumptions, beliefs, and interests shape and impact the research produced (King & Horrocks, 2010); they have also focused on the researcher's relationship to the data collection site to articulate approaches in which the researcher is an insider versus an outsider (Evered & Louis, 1981). In focusing on ethnography, a fundamental insider approach, Van Mannen also suggested that the first-order, "facts" of data come in two primary forms—operational data, which include the conversations and activities observed, and presentational data, which include the "appearances that informants strive to maintain (or enhance)" (1979: 542). These distinctions hint that both the person producing the data and the audience for that production matter. In this dimension, we focus on the role of the researcher in shaping the data source itself. Researchers can influence the source in interpreting data, as an audience member of events that serve as data, and in co-constructing the data through specific collection probes. We propose that different sources, which are more or less shaped and guided by researchers, can be combined to offer different perspectives in service of data expansion.

With interviews, researchers might have the most influence on the data source itself. In fact, the ability to influence the source offers one of the most important benefits of interviews, particularly semistructured interviews, since researchers have the freedom to choose particular questions, follow particular promising leads that emerge within the interview, and interact with the participant to follow up and probe further on specific points. The source is tailored toward specific research questions and objectives (Yin, 2009). We must acknowledge, then, that many times interviews are co-constructions between the interviewer and the participant in which the participant's audience is the researcher. At its extreme, in interviews, researchers aid participants in constructing a coherent narrative or story of events that serves the specific purpose of the researcher. If we take this as co-construction as the dominant pole, we begin to consider data sources that remove researcher influence.

In observations, the participants generate the action which researchers observe and the role of the researcher is slightly more complicated. Initially, the researcher will likely be considered an outsider, influencing the data collection with his or her presence. However, over time, the researcher might become an insider, in which he or she influences the events as an insider/participant. We became acutely aware of this distinction in our own research on modern dance companies. For our paper (Harrison & Rouse, 2014), each of us observed a different set of groups. Spencer was unable to attend one of the final rehearsals for one of his groups and asked Bess to observe. The rehearsal process that day grew rather intense since the final performance was approaching and one dancer was struggling to keep up with the rest of the group members. Bess quickly recognized that she was being perceived as an outside, audience member. In a follow-up email to Spencer, the choreographer described how Spencer had become an insider and Bess's presence as an outsider had heightened the tense dynamic within the room. From this set of interactions, we learned that even in nonparticipant observation there can be distinctions in how research participants view researchers and that this distinction might influence the data being generated. Rather than the participants intending to mislead the research process (Van Maanen, 1979), participants' perceptions of audience influence the data source. There-fore, when researchers are perceived as outsiders, observations may offer a window into ideal or intended behaviors (presentational data), rather than behaviors in reality (operational data).

Video observation provides a means to begin to remove the researcher further from the data collection process. We have used video observation in two settings—in modern dance, as a supplement to our in-person observations, and in product design, as our primary source of data. In both contexts, video allowed us to capture processes over time without us needing to be present in the room, and, in both cases, research participants claimed that they forgot the camera and conducted rehearsals and meetings without being affected by the "audience." One dancer described, for instance, "We acted just the same as we would if there was no camera or researcher. Most of the time we would forget the camera was even there" (Harrison & Rouse, 2014). Nonetheless, the use of the phrase "most of the time" suggests that the presence of the camera was not entirely neutral, but likely less influential than the physical presence of a researcher (or two) in the room. Therefore, video observation provides a data source that is relatively uninfluenced by researcher presence, but it still allows researchers to interpret and theorize from the data, much like they would from archival data. However, video data has the added benefit of being able to capture ongoing processes and actions over time.

We propose that by combining these different data sources, researchers are able to use data expansion to build new insights. For example, in our study on creative feedback (Harrison & Rouse, 2015), we used in-person observation, video observation, and interviews. The observations were primarily generated by the participants and we primarily served as *interpreters* and *observers* of the events; this information allowed us to theorize how the feedback process occurred over time. Interviews allowed us to unpack why certain events took place after observations occurred; we actively sought to guide the participants to explore their own feedback interactions, *co-constructing* the data to meet our specific research aims. This provided our understanding of the "arrows" between the "boxes" in our theoretical model. In other words, rather than focusing on how observations and interviews might simply verify one another, we leveraged the fact that each of the sources offered a different perspective that allowed us to understand the phenomenon of feedback in a more nuanced and layered way. Figure 27.2 provides a schematic that arrays potential data sources along the dimensions we have proposed—temporal stance and researcher influence. Given the various ways each type of data collection can be executed, this is meant more as a rough approximation of the assumptions behind each type of data rather than a definitive taxonomy.

Implications

Tracy (2010) suggested eight criteria for evaluating qualitative research. "Rigor" was one of these criteria, and she made an interesting observation about the positive spillovers of focusing on rigor; since we opened the chapter with a metaphorical cooking pun about "reductions" we found her insight apropos:

> Just like following a recipe does not guarantee perfect presentation, or completing a vigorous training plan does not guarantee race-day success, rigor does not guarantee a brilliant final product. That being said, rigor does increase the odds for high quality, and the methodological craft skills developed through rigorous practice transcend any single research project, providing a base of qualitative fitness that may enrich future projects. (2010: 841)

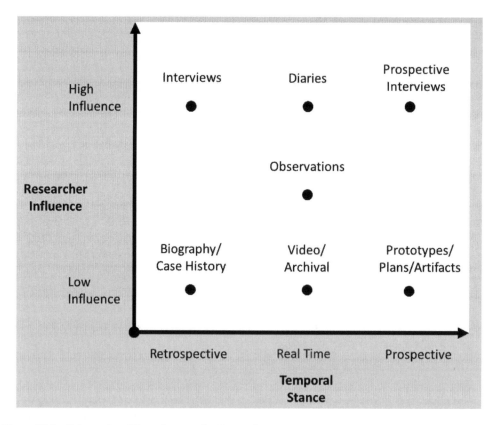

Figure 27.2   Schematic of Data Sources for Expansion

We agree with this sentiment: Even if triangulation and expansion do not benefit one project, the practice of using multiple sources of data to accomplish both will have a tendency toward increasing rigor and will likely have payoffs over the course of a career. That said, in considering the implications, and more explicitly, the benefits of triangulation and expansion, we want to highlight two trends that could enhance rigor in future research: (1) encouraging researchers to more transparently provide evidence of triangulation in their findings and (2) persuading researchers to embrace expansion as a necessary and enriching compliment to the goal of convergence in using multiple sources of data.

Providing Evidence of Triangulation

To begin, it is worth reconsidering the data we reviewed at the start of this chapter because it seems to indicate several obvious areas for enhancing qualitative research. First, of the 92 we identified as "qualitative studies" in top management journals, only 78 used two or more sources of data, which means 15% of qualitative studies relied on one source of data. It is difficult to imagine situations where only one source of data would be an improvement over having several sources. For example, Thanning, Vendelo, and Rerup (2012) have compelling archival data about a tragedy at a rock concert in which several audience members were killed. They used this data to construct a very precise, to the second, timeline of events, interpretations, and actions. However, they enhanced their understanding of the situation by the first author working as a safety guard at concerts to better empathize with the actions of the individuals they were studying. It was not a necessary step per se, but it is difficult to argue that the paper is not better as a result of this addition.

Another implication from our analysis, and one that is more pervasive and likely more important, was that few (only 31%) of the papers reporting to have multiple sources of data actually presented data from multiple sources in their findings. If we need qualitative research, in part because it provides thick, rich descriptions that potentially anchor the thin abstractions of theorizing (Folger & Turillo, 1999; Weick, 1989), then we are losing an important supply of these thick descriptions by claiming triangulation without showing triangulation. One robust way of emphasizing how and why multiple sources of data are important is through data displays. For example, Heaphy (2013) provides a table that outlines how and why each type of data was used and then goes on to provide quotes and examples from each type in the findings. The result is richer, more coherent set of evidence.

Enriching Theorizing Through Expansion

Our arguments about types of data carrying different assumptions about temporal stance and researcher influence might be simplified by stating that each type of data offers a slightly different way of telling a story. By showing data from different sources, in effect, researchers are allowing these different ways of telling a story to come through, allowing the reader to better understand the nuances of the phenomena being studied. We are also urging researchers to go one step further and to embrace these different ways of telling a story (embedded in different data source types) as opportunities to expand their theorizing about emerging concepts, thereby producing richer theory. Richardson (1998: 358) suggests an important outcome of this sort of expansion, suggesting that it creates a sort of multifaceted crystalline way of understanding data:

> Crystallization, without losing structure, deconstructs the traditional idea of "validity" (we feel how there is no single truth, we see how texts validate themselves), and crystallization provides us with a deepened, complex, thoroughly partial understanding of the topic. Paradoxically, we know more and doubt what we know. Ingeniously, we know there is always more to know.

Table 27.1 Use of Data Expansion in Qualitative Research Methods

Reference	Research Context	How Innovation Was Used	Outcomes/Results of Innovation
Bresman (2013)	Pharmaceutical firm	Semistructured interviews and real-time observations of teams to capture retrospective and real-time accounts (temporal stance)	"The design allowed me to both trace phenomena backwards and follow them forward as they occurred. The combination of retrospective and real-time data is helpful because the former promote collection of multiple observations of routine change (improving external validity), and the latter enable understanding of how events unfold (leading to better internal validity) (Bingham & Eisenhardt, 2011; Leonard-Barton, 1990)." (42)
Schultz & Hernes (2013)	LEGO Group	Multiple data sources (participant observation, semistructured interviews, and archival materials) used to capture retrospective, real-time, and prospective accounts (temporal stance)	"Of particular relevance to this study is that the past was deliberately evoked during both occasions, but each occasion drew upon its own memory of evoked historical periods. It is important to note that differences in the time horizon of the past were echoed in the time horizons of the identity claims for the future." (12)
Sonenshein (2010)	*Fortune* 500 entertainment and leisure products retailer	Multiple data sources (interviews, documents, archival records, observations, and surveys) to capture retrospective and real-time accounts (temporal stance)	"Unlike most research on change, which only uses retrospective data (Van de Ven, 1992), this study includes both retrospective and real-time data." (482)
Stigliani & Ravasi (2012)	Continuum	Multiple data sources (archival data, observations, and interviews) to generate a model of retrospective and prospective sensemaking (temporal stance)	"Our model describes prospective collective sensemaking as based on three interrelated cycles of retrospective cognitive work occurring as members of groups go back and forth between the tentative organization of selected material cues and the refinement of corresponding categories, embody provisional interpretations in material form, and engage in retrospective reflection to establish the plausibility of emerging accounts." (1233)
Thanning Vendelø & Rerup (2012)	Rosklide rock music festival	Multiple data sources (semistructured interviews, archival data, direct observations, and field notes) to collect different temporal stances on the events with different levels of researcher influence	"The use of four data collection mechanisms (semi-structured interviews, archival data, direct observations, and fieldnotes) helped us to capture how: a) slow realization across the crowd about the unfolding of the accident caused a delay in giving space for the crowd safety personnel to rescue victims, and b) the OSO reworked the crowd safety set-up in order to achieve crowd sensegiving during concerts." (7)

Reference	Research Context	How Innovation Was Used	Outcomes/Results of Innovation
Harrison & Rouse (2014)	Modern dance	Video data to capture real-time (temporal stance) process with minimal researcher influence	"To strengthen the trustworthiness (Lincoln & Guba, 1985) of our findings, we used video to document the majority of the groups' rehearsals, so that we could review their interactions later. This proved invaluable during our analysis and during the review process, allowing us to enrich our theoretical memos and enlarge our understanding of the phenomena as we were challenged by reviewers." (1263)
Gersick (1989)	Lab study of teams with qualitative analysis	Video data and interviews to combine data sources with different levels of researcher influence	"By videotaping meetings and replaying those key events (among others) for the groups, participants could be asked to observe their own specific behaviors and to discuss their own understanding of what those behaviors meant, independent of researcher conjecture. Data from meetings and interviews could then be combined to refine and enrich the model of group development and to explore some questions about it through grounded theory (Glaser & Strauss, 1967)." (277)
Ashforth & Reingen (2014)	Natural foods co-op	Multiple data sources (participant observation, archival materials, and semistructured interviews) to use data expansion.	"We triangulated emerging insights across the multiple data sources (was the insight/phenomenon evident in, say, the interviews and archival data?) . . . Triangulation revealed not only convergences but 'disjunctures' (Arnould and Wallendorf, 1994) that provided important insights." (482)
Harrison & Rouse (2015)	Modern dance and product design	Multiple data sources (video observation, in-person observation, interviews) for data expansion	Observations provided the primary evidence for understanding feedback provider, creative worker, and response moves, while data from interviews with creative workers helped inform our understanding of how and why creative workers responded to particular feedback moves.

This description is strikingly similar to Weick's (1993) description of the relationship between humility and wisdom—the ambivalence about existing knowledge that enables a willingness to doubt what is "known." Since much of qualitative research is meant to either build or extend theory, this attitude of wisdom is a necessity, since it presumes that the new theory is necessarily incomplete and contingent. This attitude of wisdom can be evoked by consciously using multiple sources of data for expansion (and not just triangulation) in analysis, writing, and data displays. In doing so, researchers make the contingencies of their theorizing more explicit and thereby provide a stronger foundation for future researchers to extend the theory and for practitioners to begin to use the theory.

One technique that might be adopted to help signal and improve the use of triangulation and expansion as a complimentary dyad of analytic techniques would be to provide data collection/analysis process maps (Harrison & Rouse, 2014) or data collection timelines (Nag, Corley, & Gioia, 2007) that explicitly highlight when triangulation and expansion occurred and how they influenced subsequent data collection. Graphically illustrating this convergence and divergence and how it drives new, more focused rounds of data collection—focused both in terms of chasing down the phenomena and in terms of honing on the types of data that provide the most insight—might help readers better appreciate both the "grounded" nature of the process and the necessary sensitivity of the researcher guiding the process.

Taken together, in this chapter, we encourage scholars to more explicitly consider the data sources they choose to collect and how they use these sources in their analysis and theorizing, as summarized in Figure 27.1. We have outlined two dimensions, temporal stance and researcher influence, that we believe can help frame researchers' thinking around the concept of data expansion; however, these dimensions are merely a starting point to begin thinking about the unique lenses that each data source offers. Table 27.1 provides examples of published and working papers that we think implicitly embrace the notion of data expansion that we make explicit in this chapter. The use of data expansion, in tandem with data triangulation, promises to enrich and deepen our understanding of phenomenon within organizations.

Note

1 We acknowledge that we are entering an age where, given the use of social media, there are new and emerging opportunities to access qualitative data beyond interviews. Indeed, even more "classic" methods like ethnography and varieties of observation or archival work do not require interviewing per se. That said, because interviews are easy to count and because they allow for so much flexibility in chasing down phenomena that are theoretically interesting, we assume that interviews will remain a dominant and legitimate core of rigorous qualitative research (Tracy, 2010).

References

Amabile, T.M., Barsade, S.G., Mueller, J.S., & Staw, B.M. (2005). Affect and creativity at work. *Administrative Science Quarterly, 50*, 367–403.

Amabile, T.M., & Kramer, S.J. (2011). *The progress principle: Using small wins to ignite joy, engagement, and creativity at work.* Cambridge, MA: Harvard University Press.

Amabile, T.M., Schatzel, E.A., Moneta, G.B., & Kramer, S.J. (2004). Leader behaviors and the work environment for creativity: Perceived leader support. *The Leadership Quarterly, 15*, 5–32.

Arnould, E.J., & Wallendorf, M. (1994). Market-oriented ethnography: interpretation building and marketing strategy formulation. *Journal of Marketing Research, 31*, 484–504.

Ashforth, B., & Reingen, P. (2014). Functions of dysfunction: Managing the dynamics of an organizational duality in a natural food cooperative. *Administrative Science Quarterly, 59*, 474–516.

Ashforth, B.E., Harrison, S.H., & Corley, K.G. (2008). Identification in organizations: An examination of four fundamental questions. *Journal of Management, 34*, 325–374.

Boje, D.M. (2001). *Narrative methods for organizational and communication research.* London, England: Sage.

Bolger, N., Davis, A., & Rafaeli, E. (2003). Diary methods: Capturing life as it is lived. *Annual Review of Psychology, 54*, 579–616.

Bresman, H. (2013). Changing routines: A process model of vicarious group learning in pharmaceutical R&D. *Academy of Management Journal, 56*, 35–61.

Denzin, N. (1978). *The research act* (2nd ed.). New York, NY: McGraw-Hill.

Denzin, N., & Lincoln, Y. (2011). Introduction: The discipline and practice of qualitative research. In N. Denzin & Y. Lincoln (Eds.), *The SAGE handbook of qualitative research* (4th ed., pp. 1–20). Thousand Oaks, CA: Sage.

Evered, R., & Louis, M.R. (1981). Alternative perspectives in the organizational sciences: "Inquiry from the inside" and "inquiry from the outside." *Academy of Management Review, 6*, 385–395.

Flick, U. (2014). *An introduction to qualitative research.* Los Angeles, CA: Sage.

Folger, R., & Turillo, C.J. (1999). Theorizing as the thickness of thin abstraction. *Academy of Management Review, 24*, 742–758.

Gersick, C.J. (1989). Marking time: Predictable transitions in task groups. *Academy of Management Journal, 32,* 274–309.

Gioia, D.A., Corley, K.G., & Hamilton, A.L. (2013). Seeking qualitative rigor in inductive research notes on the Gioia methodology. *Organizational Research Methods, 16,* 15–31.

Gioia, D.A., & Mehra, A. (1996). Sensemaking in organization—Weick, KE. *Academy of Management Review, 21,* 1226–1230.

Hargadon, A., & Bechky, B. (2006). When collections of creatives become creative collectives: A field study of problem solving at work. *Organization Science, 17,* 484–500.

Harrison, S.H. &, Rouse, E.D. (2014). Let's Dance! Elastic coordination in creative group work: A qualitative study of modern dancers. *Academy of Management Journal, 57,* 1256–1283.

Harrison, S.H., & Rouse, E.D. (2015). An inductive study of feedback interactions over the course of creative projects. *Academy of Management Journal, 58,* 375–404.

Heaphy, E.D. (2013). Repairing breaches with rules: Maintaining institutions in the face of everyday disruptions. *Organization Science, 24,* 1291–1315.

Ibarra, H., & Barbulescu, R. (2010). Identity as narrative: Prevalence, effectiveness, and consequences of narrative identity work in macro work role transitions. *Academy of Management Review, 35,* 135–154.

Kahneman, D., & Riis, J. (2005). Living, and thinking about it: Two perspectives on life. In F.A. Huppert, N. Baylis, & B. Keverne (Eds.), *The science of well-being* (pp. 285–304). New York, NY: Oxford University Press.

King, N., & Horrocks, C. (2010). *Interviews in qualitative research.* Thousand Oaks, CA: Sage.

Mathison, S. (1988). Why triangulate? *Educational Researcher, 17,* 13–17.

Miles, M.B., & Huberman, A. M. (1994). *Qualitative data analysis: An expanded sourcebook.* Thousand Oaks, CA: Sage.

Miller, C.C., Cardinal, L.B., & Glick, W.H. (1997). Retrospective reports in organizational research: A reexamination of recent evidence. *Academy of Management Journal, 40,* 189–204.

Mishler, E.G. (1999). *Storylines: Craftartists' narratives of identity.* Cambridge, MA: Harvard University Press.

Nag, R., Corley, K.G., & Gioia, D.A. (2007). The intersection of organizational identity, knowledge, and practice: Attempting strategic change via knowledge grafting. *Academy of Management Journal, 50,* 821–847.

Patton, M.Q. (2002). *Qualitative research and evaluation methods* (3rd ed.). Thousand Oaks, CA: Sage.

Richardson, L. (1998). Writing as a method of inquiry. In N. Denzin & Y. Lincoln (Eds.), *Collecting and interpreting qualitative materials* (4th ed., pp. 345–371). Thousand Oaks, CA: Sage.

Rouse, E. (2013). *Kill your darlings? Experiencing, maintaining, and changing psychological ownership in creative work.* Chestnut Hill, MA: Boston College.

Schultz, M., & Hernes, T. (2013). A temporal perspective on organizational identity. *Organization Science, 24,* 1–21.

Sonenshein, S. (2010). We're changing—or are we? Untangling the role of progressive, regressive, and stability narratives during strategic change implementation. *Academy of Management Journal, 53,* 477–512.

Stigliani, I., & Ravasi, D. (2012). Organizing thoughts and connecting brains: Material practices and the transition from individual to group-level prospective sensemaking. *Academy of Management Journal, 55,* 1232-1259.

Thanning Vendelø, M., & Rerup, C. (2012). Crowd sensegiving and the Pearl Jam concert accident. *Proceedings of the New Frontiers in Management and Organizational Cognition Conference,* Maynooth, Ireland.

Tracy, S.J. (2010). Qualitative quality: Eight "big-tent" criteria for excellent qualitative research. *Qualitative Inquiry, 16,* 837–851.

Unsworth, K. (2001). Unpacking creativity. *Academy of Management Review, 26,* 289–297.

Van Maanen, J. (1979). The fact of fiction in organizational ethnography. *Administrative Science Quarterly, 24,* 539–550.

Weick, K.E. (1989). Theory construction as disciplined imagination. *Academy of Management Review, 14,* 516–531.

Weick, K.E. (1993). The collapse of sensemaking in organizations: The Mann Gulch disaster. *Administrative Science Quarterly, 38,* 628–652.

Yin, R.K. (2009). *Case study research: Design and methods* (4th ed.). Thousand Oaks, CA: Sage.

28

"What's Cooking?"
Serendipitous Opportunities and Creative Action in Data Collection

Silviya Svejenova

"What's cooking?" is old-fashioned slang for asking about what is happening or what someone is planning. In this chapter, it denotes an approach to prospective data collection in qualitative research and captures the gist of a case study from the field of haute cuisine that inspired the saying. The approach involves seeking proactively, noticing, and acting creatively upon serendipitous opportunities that are associated with the case's future. These opportunities may bring researchers into contact with social worlds other than those in which the studied case is grounded and may require that they negotiate and play diverse roles for data collection, yielding novel insights and offering possibilities for building interesting stories and theories. Next I describe the background of and inspiration for the approach, introduce its elements and workings, and highlight potential benefits and caveats.

Background and Inspiration

From 2005 to 2011 I was involved in a case study research project that evolved into an exploration into how the innovative chef Ferran Adrià and his collaborators in the famed Spanish restaurant elBulli organized their activities in the pursuit of creative freedom and a new culinary language, initiating change in haute cuisine (Svejenova et al., 2007, 2010, 2015). When I entered the field, it was already a highly regarded case that attracted a great deal of media and other attention. An "unanticipated, anomalous and strategic datum" (Merton, 1948, p. 506), of which I became aware and inquired about during my first interview with the chef concerning his debut interaction with art in a sculptor's studio in the early 1990s, unlocked the conversation and permitted my return for further exploration. The research project concluded in July 2011 with the restaurant closing to become a foundation dedicated to culinary experimentation and innovation. My interest in it persisted, however, and I continued following "what's cooking," though from a distance.

In the span of the research I "lived" the case intensely, having the feeling that it unfolded much faster than my ability to follow it and to account for the numerous potentially interesting and relevant occurrences. I investigated it retrospectively, through a deep, multimodal and multimedia immersion in the past, including press archives, books, documentaries, interviews, as well as photographs and names of dishes. I also followed aspects of the case in the present as they took place in diverse locations, for example, some daily activities of the team; presentations of the chef at varied forums and to distinct audiences (managers, students, scholars, general public, etc.); the creation of an exhibition on him, in which I got involved in a consulting capacity; and, not least, two meals at the renowned restaurant. All that allowed me to savor the case's different flavors and provided a richer taste of it.

What kept me engaged with the case over time was the ongoing curiosity for and fascination with its future. I was continuously asking about "what's cooking," being attentive to clues in order to get a glimpse of potentially important twists and turns. Unusual or anomalous data spotted during observations, interviews, or informal encounters with informants was noted and explored for its potential to yield further insights, both empirically and theoretically, and for the feasibility of gaining access to it. As a result, I took initiative and acted upon some of the serendipitous opportunities encountered, that is, those that were not only anomalous but also strategic, offering possibilities for story-building (Fine & Deegan, 1996).

Box 28.1 briefly relates two such "episodes" that I encountered fortuitously and during which I gathered data using different roles: (1) in 2007, accredited as a journalist at the contemporary art exhibition documenta 12 in Kassel Germany, which for the first time featured a chef—Ferran Adrià—among the artists; (2) in 2010, as a sponsor's representative at the Science and Cooking public lectures, a pioneering series in Cambridge, Massachusetts, organized by Harvard SEAS together with the chef and the Spanish Alicia Foundation. These two episodes provided inspiration for and insights into the data collection approach detailed in this chapter.

Box 28.1 Two Episodes of Using the "What's Cooking?" Approach

Episode 1: A journalist at a contemporary art exhibition featuring the chef

The event that unlocked my access to the case involved the chef taking time off from the restaurant kitchen in the early 1990s to work in a sculptor's studio in Barcelona, cooking and discussing art with him. It stood out amidst other more conventional occurrences, such as visiting or staging briefly with renowned French chefs. While explaining why and how he did that, the chef mentioned in passing that he had been invited to take part in a major art exhibition (documenta 12) in Kassel, Germany. I took note of this future event (and of a potential art-related theme to the case), yet had no idea of its significance. In the coming months, I investigated the exhibition and discovered that it was a major event for contemporary art that took place every 5 years, and this was the first time a chef participated alongside the artists. Closer to the event, the media attention became overwhelming and a polemic unleashed, flared by the art establishment, about the relationship between art and cooking, and whether the latter could be considered a form of artistic expression. I thought it would be interesting to observe what happened at the opening of documenta 12 and looked into ways to follow that.

In 2007, I travelled to Kassel accredited as a journalist representing my business school's alumni magazine and experienced the chef's introduction to the media as one of the artists. Claiming this role involved ingenuity and mobilization of support by a number of organizations and individuals. It was the only way available to be present at the event. It allowed me to get a unique view of the case and the way in which the interaction of cuisine and art was argued and presented to the media. Furthermore, it permitted me to experience the surprise of the media present, as it happened to be the only time the chef was going to be in Kassel. The elBulli contribution could not be decontextualized, so for the 100 days of the exhibition, some artists and randomly selected guests of documenta 12 were flown to the restaurant to have a meal and experience the chef's culinary creations. These guests were requested to write briefly about it upon their return. Their contributions, as well as writings on the evolution of the cooking–art relationship in general and at elBulli, were depicted in the book *Food for Thought, Thought for Food*, written by Ferran

Adrià and his team in collaboration with the late pop artist Richard Hamilton and the then-director of Tate Modern, Vicente Todolí. I attended the media introduction of that book, thus completing the cycle. This episode provided a window into the chef's trespassing into and dialogue with the art world.

Episode 2: A sponsor's representative at science and cooking public lectures

In 2010, while a visiting scholar at Harvard Business School (HBS), I met informally for lunch with a key informant from the case who was in town for what he described as collaboration between scientists and chefs. The collaboration appeared to be for the preparation and delivery of a pioneering Harvard College General Education course "Science and Cooking: From Haute Cuisine to the Science of Soft Matter" and a series of public lectures by renowned Spanish and U.S. chefs, food experts, and Harvard scientists. The course and lecture series, created by The Harvard School of Engineering and Applied Sciences (SEAS) together with Ferran Adrià and the Spanish Alícia Foundation, used food and cooking to explain applied physics and engineering's fundamentals. I managed to gain access to it as representative of one of the course's sponsoring organizations and my then employer, ESADE Business School, which was collaborating with Adrià and the Alícia Foundation.

This role allowed me to interview or talk informally to most of the participating chefs, some of the scientists and staff involved, as well as journalists and representatives of sponsoring organizations. It also permitted me not only to observe the course and lecture series unfolding, but also to get proactively involved in tasks ranging from carrying materials, to translating for a chef during a lab visit and a lunch meeting with scholars, or introducing two of the chefs to the audience at their public lectures. I also had the opportunity for observations of the fair with student projects that connected cooking and science, as well as the subsequent evaluation and decision on winners by the committee of Spanish and U.S. chefs and Harvard scientists. The experience allowed for discoveries related to the chef's trespassing into and dialogue with the world of science.

The two episodes were serendipitous (unusual, anomalous, and strategic), required creative action for trespassing into the social worlds they represented (art and science), and involved negotiating and playing new roles for data collection (journalist and sponsor's representative). My involvement in them represented an entrepreneurial venture of sorts, as I had to enlist cooperation and secure resources from a number of individuals within and outside the organizations and events studied in order to pursue the opportunities arising.

After gathering data on each of them, I "returned" to the case with an enhanced understanding as well as additional questions and puzzles ripe for untangling. Further, having completed data collection during the second episode, new patterns of insight emerged from juxtaposing it with the first episode. That permitted expanding the theorizing in a new direction, that is, the creation and institutionalization of a new (modern) language for haute cuisine through a dialogue with other, higher status domains, such as art and science (Svejenova, 2014). This new direction would not have been possible had I not used what in this chapter I denote a "what's cooking?" approach.

Introduction to the "What's Cooking?" Approach to Data Collection

"What's cooking?" is a *bisociation* of sorts, a term coined by Koestler in his 1964 book *The Act of Creation* to denote something pertaining to two mental planes and perceived from two perspectives. Bisociation has been found useful in arriving at creative acts, scientific discoveries, and metaphors depicting our research (Czarniawska, 2011; Meyers, 2007). As used in this chapter, the two planes and perspectives involved are those of the research process in general and the studied case in particular. In case-specific terms, "What's cooking?" inquires into what practice and skill in preparing food are about. As such, it captures the essence of the case that I had followed—one of innovation that redefines what cooking is (about). In research process terms, the question draws on its meaning in general parlance, as old-fashioned slang used to inquire about what is happening or what someone is planning. It reveals curiosity, invites discoveries, and welcomes surprises.

"What's cooking?" is an approach to prospective data collection that shares an orientation to future events with prospective case study design (Bitektine, 2008), yet differs from it in that it is not preceded by hypotheses formulation. Rather, it involves noticing and acting creatively upon seren-dipitous opportunities associated with some of the case's twists and turns that may connect it with other social worlds and, thus, have the potential to open up new avenues for investigation and insight that would otherwise be foregone.

I suggest that such an approach is driven by curiosity about the case's future. When coupled with one's previous theoretical and empirical experience, curiosity helps the researcher recognize seren-dipitous opportunities that can expand his or her understanding of the case. Several qualities, such as imagination, social skill, and entrepreneurial capabilities, permit to act creatively toward and seize such opportunities, initiating data gathering on them. The data collection process involves exploring the relevance of the fortuitous event; negotiating (and playing) new roles for accessing it; trespassing into other social worlds, that is, areas external to the case's core; and returning to the case to enrich and challenge it with passionate humility (Yanow, 2009).

Overall, the approach is yet another window to those generative moments (Carlson & Dutton, 2011) that reveal and revitalize (Glynn, 2011) and, overall, to the discovery and creativity involved in qualitative research (Klag & Langley, 2013; Locke, 2011). However, its serendipitous nature also makes it part of those "sizeable swaths of the methodological approach [that] remain largely invisible, obscured in part by reporting practices inimical to it" (Locke, 2011, p. 639). Hence, examples of it are usually underreported and subject to rare admissions, mainly in award acceptance speeches, autobi-ographies, or personal interviews (Meyers, 2007).

Next I define the main elements and workings of the approach and highlight some of its benefits and caveats.

Elements and Workings of the Approach

Figure 28.1 reveals the main elements of and steps in using this approach. I have distinguished between preconditions and process of data collection. *Preconditions* refer to the background in which the prospective data collection unfolds, both the spadework and skills required. The spadework allows recognizing a serendipitous opportunity, while the skills shape the capacity to act creatively toward exploring and seizing this opportunity. This entails several steps, from exploring the relevance and feasibility of the serendipitous event, to negotiating roles for accessing it and trespassing into the social worlds in which it unfolds, to "returning" to the case with new insights and further questions.

Preconditions

Serendipity-driven data is gathered on the basis of spadework and skills.

Spadework

In order to notice serendipitous patterns during an ongoing case study, the research requires ground-work, both in empirical and theoretical terms. Empirically, it is essential to have a deep immersion

Silviya Svejenova

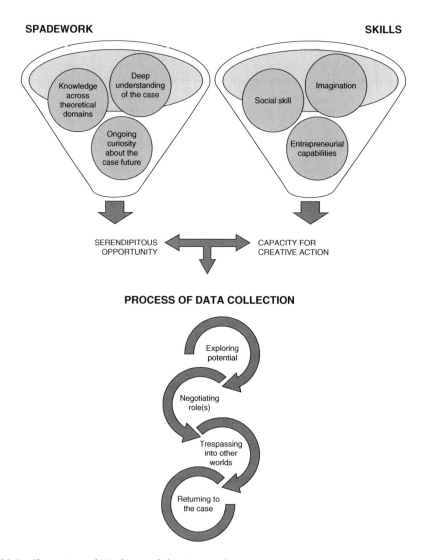

Figure 28.1   Elements and Workings of the Approach

in the case so that unexpected, unusual, and strategic events are recognized and their potential value appreciated. Theoretically, it is advantageous for the researcher to have an exposure to a broader scholarly domain and to playfully tap into it when exploring the relevance of the serendipitous pattern for the advancement of theoretical insights. The empirical and theoretical preparedness allow for serendipity to meet a "prepared" or "ripe" researcher's mind. For that to happen, an additional ingredient is his or her insatiable curiosity toward the case.

Curiosity, as depicted in the psychological literature, is a critical motive that influences one's behavior. It reveals an appetite for learning and is a major impetus behind discoveries, transforming mere observations into "findings" (Akerström, 2013; Loewenstein, 1994; Nowotny, 2008). Curiosity energizes exploration, drives playful behaviors, enables proactivity and adaptation, and provides new ways for understanding the world and of seeing a situation (Harrison, Sluss, & Ashforth, 2011). It "likes interstices where it can move unchecked" and "prepares for the new without already knowing what form the new will take (Nowotny, 2008, p. 64). In the context of a case study, curiosity entails a genuine interest in the case's margins and footnotes, as well as a willingness to talk and listen to the informants beyond one's guiding focus and research questions. Further, it requires ability to inquire into a case's future by asking questions in a way that is noninvasive, generative, and leads to discoveries. It is a prerequisite for serendipitous opportunity recognition and a driver for its realization, particularly in scientific breakthroughs (Jacobsson, Göransson, & Wästerfors, 2013; Meyers, 2007).

Serendipity is a notion with a long history and a wide-ranging significance (Merton & Barber, 2004). Its meaning for sociology was first captured in a footnote by Merton (1945) and defined subsequently as "an unanticipated, anomalous and strategic datum which becomes the occasion for developing a new theory or for extending an existing theory" (Merton, 1948, p. 506). According to Merton (1948), a fact is strategic if it has implications for a generalized theory. Fine and Deegan (1996) extended the meaning of serendipity to ethnography, defining it "as the unique and contingent mix of insight coupled with chance" (p. 436) and suggesting that it helps generate plausible stories rather than a generalized theory. They identified different serendipity components, one of which—serendipity relations that refer to the alliances or partnerships a researcher makes in the early stages of a project and that can be capitalized on later—is of particular relevance for keeping pace with a case and identifying serendipitous opportunities. These opportunities constitute specific instances of emergence that characterize any inductive research. What distinguishes them from other instances of emergence is that they are set in motion by the researcher's proactively inquiring his or her relations about "what's cooking", i.e. what is about to take place, in reference to the case future. Further, serendipitous opportunities are options (to be exercised or forgone) for advancement of a case study in new and unexpected directions, with expected higher magnitude of significance for the case's unfolding. They bring the researcher (temporarily) in contact with social worlds that are outside the case's scope, as defined by the study's research questions, helping "to inject novelty" (Klag & Langley, 2013, p. 150).

Skills

To recognize and act upon serendipitous opportunities, the researcher needs awareness and possession of certain skills and abilities. First, imagination is essential for approaching a serendipitous pattern in an ingenuous and playful way, envisioning potential courses of action to ensure data collection. Imagination is about seeing, which is essential for making conceptual leaps, and "implies uncovering new ways of making sense of some aspects of existing social worlds" (Klag & Langley, 2013, p. 150). It needs to go hand in hand with sagacity, understood as the "penetrating intelligence, keen perception and sound judgment" (Meyers, 2007, p. 6). It is necessary not only to envision how the prospective event, which has not yet taken place, could be of potential significance for the research under way, but also in what capacity (i.e., through what roles) one can gain access to and research it. In that, one may have to recur to stretchwork, i.e. "work that largely fits with an individual's previous work experience but introduces a small novel element that extends his or her skills in a new direction" (O'Mahony & Bechky, 2006, p. 919), especially if these are new for the researcher's roles.

Second, social skill, that is, "the ability to induce cooperation in others" through different tactics and by creating meanings of appeal to them (Fligstein, 2001), facilitates the researcher's mobilizing support for accessing and examining a serendipitous event and benefitting from the access. Social skill facilitates establishing and sustaining a social connection with key informants in order to get an insight into serendipitous events. It also helps in leveraging one's embeddedness for the making of conceptual leaps (Klag & Langley, 2013).

Finally, one's capacity for creative action toward serendipitous opportunities calls for entrepreneurial capabilities (Svejenova, Slavich, & AbdelGawad, 2015). These are abilities that permit the sensing, selecting, and shaping of research opportunities and the synchronizing of a number of necessary activities for their realization. In collecting data about these social worlds, sensing is about noticing the seeds of future events of potential significance for the case's trajectory and theorizing, as well as about selecting which ones to approach and how. It calls for researchers to be(come) "amphibious" entrepreneurs—trespassers or boundary crossers with positions of some influence in disparate social worlds—who are able to transport (and transpose) practices and assumptions across them (Powell & Sandholtz, 2012).

Taken together, imagination, social skill, and entrepreneurial capabilities shape the researcher's capacity for creative action and, through it, for action-anchored thinking (Glynn, 2011). Creative action is about daring to engage, for example, "handling uncertainty, entering new worlds" (Dutton & Carlsen, 2011). It is particularly generative when recognizing and realizing serendipitous opportunities in the process of data collection.

Process of Data Collection

Gathering data based on fortuitous opportunities requires a number of specific steps and stages, such as exploring their potential for adding insight, negotiating role(s) for engagement with them, trespassing into the "foreign" (outside the case study's scope) social worlds by playing the negotiated roles, and returning to the case with discoveries and further questions.

Exploring Potential

Complex and dynamic cases followed over a lengthy period of time may present the researcher with several serendipitous opportunities, some of which may not necessarily be relevant for the researcher's domain of interest and/or not feasible to access. Hence, an important step before seeking access and immersion is to explore the potential of these opportunities to bring surprises and yield novel insights. Exploring the potential involves gathering data that permits speculating about the opportunity's significance for the trajectory of the case and its participants. It also entails using one's imagination and sagacity to "see" how the opportunity can be accessed and researched and to envision interesting potential connections for story development and theorizing.

Negotiating Roles

The researcher's roles are vantage points for engagement with a field, and they have to be culturally meaningful to, negotiated with, and approved by those studied (Harrington, 2003). The literature on qualitative research, particularly on ethnography, has recognized the multiplicity of roles a researcher can play as an insider or an outsider to a research setting. However, it has been less vocal (particularly in relation to case studies) about roles as research resources and the creative possibilities and limitations arising from taking on and playing different roles for data collection, story-building, and theorizing. Following Baker and Faulkner (1991, p. 279):

> [a] role is a resource in two senses: it is a means to claim, bargain for, and gain membership and acceptance in a social community, and it grants access to social, cultural, and material capital that incumbents and claimants exploit in order to pursue their interests.

The acceptance of one's playing a role, however, is not automatic, as claims of roles and their use as resources could be challenged and even rejected by those studied.

Role negotiation is about identifying legitimate modes of engagement with "foreign" domains and establishing degrees of freedom and constraint for data gathering through the specific role. It involves attentiveness to the unexpected, imagination for action, and resourcefulness of what one could become for doors to open to the research process, as well as certain restraint—acting with authenticity to the role. Each new role within a "foreign" domain brings a new angle and a set of relationships that enrich the case and allow the understanding of it to evolve. That requires learning about and using the languages and norms of these foreign domains in order to be accepted in that role. It also requires having a valued and plausible identity that fits the claimed roles and the participants' interpretations of the researcher's traits, as well as "enhance[s] or do[es] not threaten participants' group identity" (Harrington, 2003, p. 609).

Trespassing Into Other Social Worlds

As acknowledged by Albert Hirschman in a 1993 interview with Carmine Donzelli, "the idea of trespassing is basic to my thinking. . . . When it seems that an idea can be verified in another field, then I am happy to venture in this direction." Trespassing is about the researcher's access and entry into foreign (for the case under consideration and for the expertise and experience of the researcher who studies it) territories or social worlds after the serendipitous pattern has been found potentially worthy of and feasible for investigation. It involves gathering background data on these foreign social worlds and claiming credible roles for accessing them.

Returning to the Case

For trespassing to inform the case and provide theoretical openings, it needs to be followed by constant returning to the core case and the research questions guiding the serendipity-driven event's exploration. This returning allows for identification of other unexpected, anomalous, and strategic patterns as well as needs for additional data collection. Further, in order for its potential to be realized, the "what's cooking?" question needs to be addressed continuously alongside two other core questions—"what's going on?" and "what is this a case of?" The former aims at situational specificity and calls for descriptive mastery, and the latter requires theoretical craftsmanship and imagination for expanding the application of the conceptual understandings at which one has arrived (Tsoukas, 2009).

Benefits and Caveats

The suggested approach has several benefits for those working in qualitative research, particularly with complex, longitudinal case studies. First, it allows one to stay current, keep pace with a case, and unravel new avenues for its exploration. As such, it is particularly relevant when following a complex and dynamic case over a longer period of time that requires decisions to be made about what (or what not) to follow. Further, it stimulates a variety of insight because it may lead to branching out into different domains and involve spatial and temporal shifting—that is, changing the context or temporality of one's thinking (Klag and Langley, 2013, p. 153). As suggested by Fine and Deegan (1996, p. 439), "serendipitous insight provides the opportunity for constructing a plausible story." Identifying anomalous, strategic events, either serendipitously or through a systematic curiosity, allows the researcher to create plausible stories that "attack" the deep-seated assumptions of the audiences to which these stories are directed (Davis, 1971), potentially leading to more interesting theories. Last but not least, unraveling and following such prospective episodes can keep one's excitement about the case high and the creative juices from it flowing.

Several challenges and limitations are worth acknowledging. First, one cannot plan a serendipitous discovery but, rather, can only recognize one (the famous reference to the "prepared mind") when exposed to it. Second, even if such an odd and strategic datum is recognized, the researcher may not be able to activate support and gain access to it. Further, the role negotiated may not be a sufficient resource for gathering data that allows arriving at meaningful theorizing. It may also require additional time for the researcher to get familiarized with its workings, especially if it involves accessing foreign social worlds. Also, as with other aspects of case study research, the prospective episodes—while seemingly interesting *a priori*—may not lead to conceptual leaps and impactful theoretical insights. Finally, as these episodes will likely take place in different spaces and at different time periods and be experienced through different roles by the researcher, comparisons of such episodes toward cumulative understanding may be difficult to achieve.

Despite these caveats, the "what's cooking?" approach to data collection detailed in this chapter has the potential to reinvigorate the researcher's engagement with the case and to enhance the richness and depth of his or her understanding of it. When curiosity drives the discovery and serendipity meets the researcher's capacity for creative action, data gathering could pave the way to cool ideas, provide the groundwork for conceptual leaps, and plant the seeds for interesting work.

References

Åkerström, M. (2013). Curiosity and serendipity in qualitative research. *Qualitative Sociology Review, 9*, 10–18. Retrieved from www.qualitativesociologyreview.org/ENG/archive_eng.php

Baker, W.E., & Faulkner, R.R. (1991). Role as resource in the Hollywood film industry. *American Journal of Sociology, 97*, 279–309.

Bitektine, A. (2008). Prospective case study design: Qualitative method for deductive theory testing. *Organizational Research Methods, 11*, 160–180.

Carlsen, A., & Dutton, J.E. (2011). Research alive: The call for generativity. In A. Carlsen & J.E. Dutton (Eds.), *Research alive: Exploring generative moments in doing qualitative research* (pp. 12–25). Malmö/Copenhagen/Oslo: Liber/CBS Press/Universitetsförlaget.

Czarniawska, B. (2011). What comes first, the egg or the chicken? Or: Where do the metaphors we use in our research come from? In A. Carlsen & J.E. Dutton (Eds.), *Research alive: Exploring generative moments in doing qualitative research* (pp. 50–58). Malmö/Copenhagen/Oslo: Liber/CBS Press/Universitetsförlaget.

Davis, M.S. (1971). That's interesting! Towards a phenomenology of sociology and a sociology of phenomenology. *Philosophy of the Social Sciences, 1*, 309–344.

Dutton, J.E., & Carlsen, A. (2011). Seeing, feeling, daring, interrelating and playing: Exploring themes in generative moments. In A. Carlsen & J.E. Dutton (Eds.), *Research alive: Exploring generative moments in doing qualitative research* (pp. 214–235). Malmö/Copenhagen/Oslo: Liber/CBS Press/Universitetsförlaget.

Fine, G.A., & Deegan, J.G. (1996). Three principles of Serendip: Insight, chance, and discovery in qualitative research. *Qualitative Studies in Education, 9*, 434–447.

Fligstein, N. (2001). Social skill and the theory of fields. *Sociological Theory, 19*, 105–125.

Glynn, M. A. (2011). The "Martha" moment: Wading into others' worlds. In A. Carlsen & J.E. Dutton (Eds.), *Research alive: Exploring generative moments in doing qualitative research* (pp. 63–66). Malmö/Copenhagen/Oslo: Liber/CBS Press/Universitetsförlaget.

Harrington, B. (2003). The social psychology of access in ethnographic research. *Journal of Contemporary Ethnography, 32*, 592–625.

Harrison, S.H., Sluss, D.M., & Ashforth, B.E. (2011). Curiosity adapted the cat: The role of trait curiosity in newcomer adaptation. *Journal of Applied Psychology, 96*, 211–220.

Jacobsson, K., Göransson, K., & Wästerfors, D. (2013). Introduction to the special issue Curiosity and serendipity in qualitative research. *Qualitative Sociology Review, 9*, 6–8. Retrieved from www.qualitativesociologyreview.org/ENG/archive_eng.php

Klag, M., & Langley, A. (2013). Approaching the conceptual leap in qualitative research. *International Journal of Management Reviews, 15*, 149–166.

Locke, K. (2011). Field research practice in management and organization studies: Reclaiming its tradition of discovery. *Academy of Management Annals, 5*, 613–652.

Loewenstein, G. (1994). The psychology of curiosity: A review and reinterpretation. *Psychological Bulletin, 116*, 75–98.

Merton, R.K., & Barber, E. (2004). *The travels and adventures of serendipity: A study in sociological semantics and the sociology of science*. Princeton, NJ: Princeton University Press.

Merton, R.K. (1945). Sociological theory. *American Journal of Sociology, 50*, 462–473.

Merton, R.K. (1948). The bearing of empirical research upon the development of social theory. *American Sociological Review, 13*, 505–515.

Meyers, M. (2007). *Happy accidents—serendipity in modern medical breakthroughs. When scientists find what they're NOT looking for.* New York, NY: Arcade.

Nowotny, H. (2008). *Insatiable curiosity: Innovation in a fragile future.* Cambridge, MA: MIT Press.

O'Mahony, S., & Bechky, B. (2006). Stretchwork: Managing the career progression paradox in external labour markets. *Academy of Management Journal, 49,* 918–941.

Powell, W.W., & Sandholtz, K.W. (2012). Amphibious entrepreneurs and the emergence of organizational forms. *Strategic Entrepreneurship Journal, 6,* 94–115.

Svejenova, S. (2014). Grammar to grunts: Emergence and evolution of a new language for haute cuisine. Working paper. Imagine Creative Industries Research center, Copenhagen Business School, Denmark.

Svejenova, S., Mazza, C., & Planellas, M. (2007). Cooking up change in haute cuisine: Ferran Adrià as institutional entrepreneur. *Journal of Organizational Behavior, 28,* 539–561.

Svejenova, S., Planellas, M., & Vives, L. (2010). An individual business model in the making: A chef's quest for creative freedom. *Long Range Planning, 43,* 408–430.

Svejenova, S., Slavich, B., & AbdelGawad, S. (2015). Creative entrepreneurs: The business models of haute cuisine chefs. In C. Jones, M. Lorenzen, & J. Sapsed (Eds.). *The Oxford handbook of creative industries* (pp. 184–199). Oxford, UK: Oxford University Press.

Tsoukas, H. (2009). Craving for generality and small-N studies: A Wittgensteinian approach towards the epistemology of the particular in organization and management studies. In D. Buchana & A. Bryman (Eds.), *Sage handbook of organizational research* (pp. 285–301). London, UK: Sage.

Yanow, D. (2009). Ways of knowing: Passionate humility and reflective practice in research and management. *The American Review of Public Administration, 39,* 579–601.

Part VI
Innovative Forms of Analysis

29

Adventures in Qualitative Research

Connie J. G. Gersick

There are at least three compelling reasons for using established methods to analyze qualitative data. First, it is good science. We want our advances to be cumulative. Second, it is efficient. Qualitative data can be messy and overwhelmingly complex. Proven methods may save enormous amounts of time, effort, and anxiety. Finally, it helps legitimize our work. Qualitative research lacks the objective precision of numbers and the persuasiveness of large samples and small p-values. Drawing on well-respected methodological precedent can increase confidence in our findings—and help us survive the combative culture of academic colloquia and journal reviews.

Alongside powerful benefits, there is a risk in using tried-and-true methodology, particularly in theory-generating research: It may sabotage the work at hand. Thanks to scholars like Eisenhardt (1989), we understand the importance of launching exploratory research with minimal received theory in mind, to keep our eyes open to new discoveries. To the extent that method implicitly embodies theory, it may also restrict our vision. As essential as it is to learn and use the best available methods, it is a mistake to be intimidated by precedent. Sometimes we need to (get to!) create new methods in order to do our best work.

My goals in this chapter are to encourage adventurousness and invention in data analysis and to present a new tool that I hope may be helpful to others—an approach I devised to sort out a tangle of long-term pathways. I offer two stories that show my own trials and errors and ups and downs in working this way, and I make no claim to represent the state of the literature.

Story One: Time and Transition in Work Teams

In my third year of graduate school, Richard Hackman hired me to help him generate an "observers' guide" for an upcoming field test of his theory of group effectiveness (Hackman, 1982). Having read about group development in college, I decided to prepare by studying the entire life spans of a few teams, to see if his variables operated differently as projects moved forward. Being in a management school, I had access to lots of excellent subjects—student groups assigned to create original reports on real-life cases over the course of several weeks between clear start and deadline dates. I promised to provide four MBA teams with personal "biographies" of their work in exchange for letting me observe and tape all their meetings.

At that time, group development was widely conceptualized as a predictable series of behaviors, indelibly exemplified by Tuckman (1965) as "forming, storming, norming and performing." Methods for analyzing group development, honed through decades of research, were designed to rise above the idiosyncratic content of groups' talk to get to the universal stages underneath. It was assumed that researchers would code members' speech into a few categories of behavior, count frequencies of each category at several points, and plot and compare broad changes in the frequencies over time. That was the way to study group development.

Partly because of the promises I made to the student teams and partly because I wanted to contribute special value to the research, I did not use the accepted analytical tools. The meetings I observed were dramatic and colorful. How could a good biography be depersonalized? More importantly, I really wanted to know what each team did to create their unique products and when they did it. My goal was to dive into the content of teams' meetings, not rise above it.

I had worked as a secretary in the past, and it occurred to me that a good way to analyze the transcripts of my tape recordings—to capture the action—would be to create detailed minutes of every meeting. I could then trace specific features of each group's finished product back to the time they were first mentioned and see how the pieces came together. Then, by condensing each team's minutes and looking over the set, I could describe their overall plot line and pick out milestones within it. There were hundreds of transcript pages, and the minutes took a long time to construct. But they tamed my data into displays that showed the big pictures and also helped pinpoint crucial moments to examine in detail. (For a complete description of this method, including examples, see Gersick, 1988.)

I delivered my presentations to the teams one by one, over a few months. Their histories didn't seem to have much in common. Not only were the groups' clients very different (ranging from a recycling plant to an international data management company), but their interaction patterns also refuted Tuckman's model and the notion of universal sequences. They varied from harmonious to contentious to clueless, right from the start. It was not until I had presented all four teams with their biographies that I was able to see beyond their differences and notice some astonishing similarities.

Each group's first few minutes together encapsulated the topics, themes, and approaches that dominated the entire first half of its time. Each group experienced a clear turning-point meeting when they stepped back, evaluated and revised their work, and restarted themselves. The second half of each group's work took its direction from that routine-breaking meeting, which always happened exactly mid-way between their first meeting and the deadline. Moreover, the turning-point was highlighted by at least one team member in every group noting (usually in a single quick sentence) that they were halfway through their time.

All these discoveries were completely unexpected. I did find some useful applications for Hackman's model, but after my work for him was finished, I decided to observe four more teams and see if my own results held up. I had found a dissertation topic.

Much later, after I turned the dissertation into a journal submission, a skeptical reviewer asked how I could have come up with findings that three decades of group researchers did not see. The answer was not that I had better eyesight. It was that I had not looked through the traditional methodological lens. My "meeting minutes" were not at all revolutionary, but they fit my particular question wonderfully well. They let me examine groups' work directly, yet comprehend it without having to hold entire meetings in my head. They delayed my leap from the specific to the general long enough to perceive certain patterns and let me move back and forth easily between ideas and raw data.

The traditional analytic approach would have (intentionally) precluded any examination of how groups' individual projects took shape. The preview-power of the first few minutes, along with teams' midpoint content revisions, would have stayed hidden. The traditional approach would also have missed the lone statements about being "half-way through" that signaled the critical role of temporal pacing in these groups' development. While the questions I asked of my data were highly important in shaping the discoveries I was able to make, so were my homemade methods of analysis.

Story Two: Women's Career Development Through Adulthood

Many years after I had learned from my own research that universal stage theory was not the perfect paradigm for groups, I dug myself into a deep hole by searching for universal stages in women's adult development. To climb out, I had to let go of an analytical approach I had considered sacrosanct and, once again, invent a new way to tackle my data.

This adventure in qualitative research played out through a study designed to build upon Daniel Levinson's path-breaking work on adult development in men (Levinson et al., 1978) and women (Levinson, 1996). Among other findings, Levinson's empirical research had led him to a stage theory. He saw an elegant series of themes and dilemmas—a necessary sequence of developmental tasks—that unfolds as people construct their lives through early adulthood. Moreover, he found that this sequence progressed by decades. The twenties, thirties, and transition to the forties each brought their own distinctive sets of challenges, aligned with age-linked social norms and biological constraints around career and status, marriage and family. I wanted to extend his findings by looking at women in a more recent cohort than he had studied and by catching them 10 years later in their lives.

My first foray into the research was a pilot study, with Kathy Kram, of 10 women executives in a global financial services corporation. With Levinson's work as a platform, we set out "to clarify the central [developmental] tasks that high achieving women at mid-life have faced, as they have moved into increasingly responsible leadership roles in complex organizations" (Gersick & Kram, 2002).

We conducted multiple biographical interviews with every study participant and then cut and pasted each woman's transcripts into a detailed life history, akin to my meeting minutes. We expected the content of their stories to differ significantly from those of Levinson's interviewees, but we did not question that our analytical task was to find a linear, universal, decade-by-decade string of stages.

Accordingly, we divided participants' biographies into 10-year segments and searched everyone's twenties, then everyone's thirties, forties, and fifties, in turn, to see what shared themes would emerge for each decade. We did find a sequence of tasks, though it was untidy enough to require some equivocation. We described each of our stages as "characteristic of (though not limited to)" its decade (Gersick & Kram, 2002). The fact that the pilot sample sloshed outside the lines did not shake our attachment to the decade-by-decade approach.

At the conclusion of the pilot study, Kathy Kram turned to other work, while I slowly expanded the research. I added 30 more participants from settings chosen for contrast with the heavily male world of banking: 10 social service agency executives, 10 family business owner-managers, and 10 artists. These women had faced plenty of obstacles, but in occupations that I assumed would allow more flexibility than high finance. Their histories, many of which were complex and tangled, varied wildly from person to person. Some knew as little girls what they wanted to be when they grew up; others found their callings much later, at 40 or even 50. Among the 31 women in the total sample with children, the age of first motherhood ranged from the teen years to the early forties. These are not superficial differences. Our pilot stage theory was creaking under the load of variability.

The contrast with the orderly journeys of Levinson's men was significant. Summarizing very roughly, he had identified the twenties as a time for exploration and provisional choices. In their thirties, having "*completed the allotted time* for . . . getting established in the adult world" (Levinson et al., 1978: 139, emphasis added), his men wrestled with the tasks of establishing families and climbing career ladders. Those who fell behind experienced consequences. A deep homogenizing force for the men was the strong pull they felt to achieve their youthful goals by age 40.

Levinson's women posed a different kind of contrast with my sample, but one which I attributed to their coming of age too soon to benefit much from the women's movement. Their stories were

313

fraught with disappointment, while nearly all 40 women in my sample were thriving. Chronicling the frustrations and halting pace of their careers, Levinson saw the women he studied as struggling to master the same schedule as the men, and coming up short.

In retrospect, the inappropriateness of Levinson's analytic template for my diverse and ebullient sample should have been obvious. But I persevered for months, separating participants' biographies into the 10-year segments that had worked in the pilot study and searching for an age-linked series of underlying themes. I was sure there was order to be found, and I was much more confident in the method than I was in my own powers of insight. If my search wasn't working, the problem must be with me, not my analytic tools. This sort of impasse can also occur with quantitative data, but it takes much less time to try out different statistical tests.

I do not remember the trigger for conceding that nothing was jelling, and it was time to try something else. I do recall that, to break through my sense of having exhausted the options, I had to go back to my original question. What did I want to know? I realized that I had been looking for abstract stages instead of focusing directly on my research goal. What had the women actually said about the developmental tasks they faced?

Given all the groundwork I had done, it did not take quite so long to identify a small and robust set of answers. Four key tasks emerged that women work and rework through adulthood. They deal with: (1) vocation: the task of developing my passions and gifts; (2) money and power: the task of securing my lifestyle; (3) love: the task of forming and nurturing relationships; and (4) priorities: the task of managing trade-offs (Gersick, 2013, 2014). In particular, understanding the task of vocation involved me in an exasperating and ultimately exhilarating slog of methodological trial, error, and discovery. Findings about that task, along with illustrated analyses, are available in Gersick (2014). The following paragraphs explicate the slog and the new tool it produced.

Having accepted that it was not productive to analyze study participants' stories by decade, I decided to organize my search by developmental task. The next several steps were demanding but mostly familiar for me. For the vocation task, I combed through all the detailed biographies I had already made, excerpting statements about occupational goals, ambitions, progress, setbacks, milestones, turning points, internal and external hurdles, and supports—anything that illustrated, characterized, or clearly affected the women's occupational journeys. I marked every excerpt's location in the raw transcript and gave each one a boldface summary/headline to help me see the forest as well as the trees. The result was a vocational chronology for each study participant.

Working from those comparatively manageable sets of headlines, I extracted a large number of themes and then consolidated them, first by occupational group and then across the whole sample. Each theme was anchored by a clutch of exemplary headlines, easily traced back to the original excerpts behind it. In addition to the themes, I had one-page chronologies summarizing every participant's biography. I had made almost every kind of data display I could think of. As a new step, I made a notecard for each participant that listed the highlights of her career journey. I used these as a deck that I could arrange and rearrange on the floor to try out different ways of sorting participants into categories. I knew every one of the 40 women very well, and it was time to see what I had.

The first harvest of all this work was rewarding. In brief, I could see that "developing my passions and gifts" actually involved two distinct and orthogonal tasks: the internal job of finding a vocational identity ("What do I want to be?") and the external job of navigating a career ("How am I going to make my way through a given occupational world?"). A woman could know what she wanted to be and have no idea how to get there, or know how to get ahead in a given job even with little sense of whether she actually wanted to do it. My analysis was finally on a productive track. The women fanned out into four empirically based levels of vocational identity, ranging from low (unformed) to high (clear), and three levels of control over career navigation, ranging from low to high. The resulting four-by-three matrix worked well. It was a breeze to place each participant in one cell of the matrix based on where she stood on the two dimensions as she embarked upon adulthood.

At that point I stalled again. I knew where women started out, but when I delved into the groups that clustered in each cell, they did not hang together well. Some of the women stayed through middle age in the cells where they began, but most had moved over the years. Many clarified and raised their sense of vocational identity or increased their navigational control over their careers; some moved in the opposite directions. Women who seemingly started in the same place progressed to different destinations. Women who ended up in the same place got there without having started together.

Pinning women down in a static display of their starting points did not reveal any satisfying patterns. My simple decade-by-decade approach had failed as well, but I was not ready to concede that every woman's life is just different, with nothing more to be said. I still needed to look for coherent patterns in the way participants' lives changed over time. I had to find an organized way to accommodate the reality of their complex, disparate pathways.

In what felt like a last-ditch effort, I decided to try using my matrix as if it were a map and treated the cells as geographical locations through which women moved. I taped a matrix/map to the back of every woman's notecard and started recording their career histories as dynamic journeys. The two dimensions held up extremely well. It was easy to plot the major steps each one took as she became more or less clear about her vocational identity (or stayed at the same level) and as she exerted more, less, or the same degree of control to navigate her career. The examples in Figure 29.1 show how it worked.

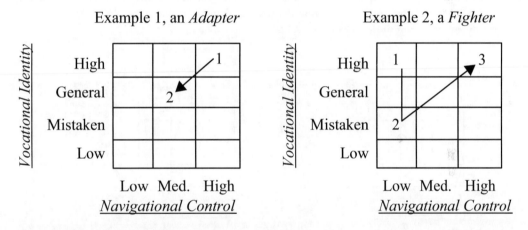

Example 1, an *Adapter* began with a clear, high vocational identity and high navigational control: she had a specific career in mind and a plan for achieving it (1). When her choice was blocked, she broadened her vocational identity and also loosened her navigational plan (2). Her shift from (1) to (2) opened her eyes to new possibilities and made her career more adaptable.

Example 2, a *Fighter* started out with a strong vocational identity, but with little sense of how to make it into a career (1). When rejected from the college program she wanted, she dropped into a stereotyped role that was wrong for her (2). Later, with help learning to navigate, she increased her navigational control over her career and reclaimed her original vocational identity (3).

Figure 29.1 Two Examples Showing How to Read the Career Trajectories

Source: Gersick (2014).

I had little idea what to expect, but when everyone was mapped, I laid out the cards. To my delight and surprise, I did not have 40 unrelated scribbles. Mapping was flexible enough to reveal journeys that were *shaped* the same, even though they were not identical. This was an epiphany. The patterns here lay in a limited set of cogent trajectories, not in one universal string of stages. Six distinctive trajectories emerged, and they were easy to group and easy to tell apart. But the value of my new data display was not yet confirmed. I had a basis for clustering the women; the test lay in whether the clusters were meaningful.

I went back to women's histories, one subgroup at a time. The more closely I looked, the more I was able to clarify and deepen what I had learned about women's career paths. Not only did women within each "shape" of trajectory share fundamental characteristics, but the essence of each was also importantly different from the others. The map provided a way to construct dynamic visual representations, showing different challenges and solutions to the tasks of finding vocation and navigating a career over long periods of time. Figure 29.2 helps illustrate how the mapping data display worked. It shows similarities within and differences between four of the six clusters of mapped journeys.

My sense is that the map itself has broader value than the particular trajectories I found, since it can be used to plot any number of undiscovered pathways. Beyond that, I hope that other scholars may be able to adapt this analytical method for their own research. The idea of displaying findings in a multicelled matrix is well accepted, and such displays can encompass a great deal of richness and complexity. Even so, they may still be too simple for the task at hand because they are static. The mapping idea offers the opportunity to capture dynamic, evolving phenomena as coherent trajectories, while streamlining their presentation.

Trajectory 1, *Drifters:* Catching Fire in the Dark. N = 8

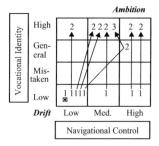

Core Challenge: Having felt little choice and given little thought to career, Drifters' core challenge was to take up the task of finding a vocation suitable for the self. Seven of eight participants found occupations they loved, suddenly and by chance. This pattern occurred across levels of navigational control.

Trajectory 2, *Mistaken Identities:* Homing In. N = 6

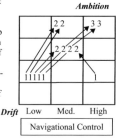

Core Challenge: Having been pigeonholed into stereotyped vocations, the core challenge was to discover they did not fit the stereotype / mistaken identity, find authentic vocational identities and take more active navigational control. Typically, participants addressed this by homing in on their talents through trial and error.

Trajectory 3, *Generalists:* Finding the Right Vehicle. N = 7

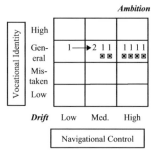

Core Challenge: Generalists wanted vocations to serve broad missions or achievement needs: helping people or solving problems. Their vocational identities didn't change, because they were so accommodating. Their challenge was to find specific occupational vehicles for their general goals, and to find new vehicles as particular missions were met or problems solved. Six women's navigational control levels were ample for the challenge; one increased from low to moderate.

Trajectory 4, *Adapters:* Reframing the Dream. N = 4

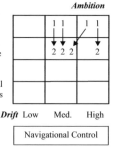

Core Challenge: Finding the way blocked to their crystallized vocational choices, adapters needed to broaden their definition of their interests and reframe their dreams in more general terms so they could express their ambitions in accessible occupations. Three of the four had appropriate levels of navigational control; one needed to become more opportunistic, i.e. loosen her navigational control.

Figure 29.2   Illustration of Four Career Trajectories

Source: Adapted from Gersick (2014).

Conclusion

My two stories are largely about trial-and-error tinkering, the main message being: Yes, get all the help you can from existing methods, but be willing to try making up something new. The point does not lend itself directly to a schematic for how to proceed. However, I can make two observations about what I have found helpful in doing qualitative research.

First, I like to put off coding my data long enough to get to know it directly and well before trying to translate it into great insights. I transcribe my own recordings (granted, I am a fast typist). I try to create data displays in slow steps, starting by arranging raw materials into stories, chronologies, and sets of themes through simple cutting and pasting, with minimal editing. Only then do I start reducing voluminous material by making fairly literal summaries (e.g., headlines), bit by bit. These steps help me to start learning the material on its own terms, organizing it enough to make it easier to work with before I start to search in earnest for patterns.

Second, I have found that the most important guide to analyzing qualitative work is to understand your research question. The question must come first, the methods must follow. What do you really want to know?

Acknowledgments

I am grateful to Roderick Kramer, Kimberly Elsbach, Michael Haedicke, and Kelin Gersick for their helpful comments on this chapter.

References

Eisenhardt, K.M. (1989). Building theories from case study research. *Academy of Management Review, 14*, 532–550.

Gersick, C. J., & Kram, K. E. (2002). High-achieving women at midlife: An exploratory study. *Journal of Management Inquiry 11(2)*, 104–127.

Gersick, C.J.G. (1988). Time and transition in work teams: Toward a new model of group development. *Academy of Management Journal, 31*, 9–41.

Gersick, C. J. G. (2013). Having it all, having too much, having too little: How women manage trade-offs through adulthood. *SSRN Yale School of Management Working Paper*. http://papers.ssrn.com/sol3/JELJOUR_Results.cfm?form_name=journalbrowse&journal_id=222968

Gersick, C. J. G. (2014). Getting from "Keep Out" to "Lean In": A new roadmap for women's careers. *SSRN Yale School of Management Working Paper*. http://papers.ssrn.com/sol3/JELJOUR_Results.cfm?form_name=journalbrowse&journal_id=222968

Hackman, J. R. (1982). *A set of methods for research on work teams*. Office of Naval Research. www.dtic.mil/dtic/tr/fulltext/u2/a123123.pdf

Levinson, D. (1996). *The seasons of a woman's life*. New York, NY: Knopf.

Levinson, D., Darrow, C., Klein, E., Levinson, M., & McKee, B. (1978). *The seasons of a man's life*. New York, NY: Ballantine.

Tuckman, B. (1965). Developmental sequence in small groups. *Psychological Bulletin, 63*, 384-389.

30

Concept Mapping as a Methodical and Transparent Data Analysis Process

Peter Balan, Eva Balan-Vnuk, Mike Metcalfe, and Noel Lindsay

Introduction

In this chapter, the results of two different methods of analysis of the same set of qualitative data are directly compared. The research aim for this case study was to identify the dimensions of the innovation capability construct using a grounded approach. For this research, innovation capability was explored in a homogenous industry sector (viz., small general hotels in Australia). The qualitative data used in this research was obtained from relatively unstructured in-depth interviews with 36 hotel owner/managers. Two researchers independently analyzed interview transcripts using two different grounded approaches. Researcher 1 used the rigorous matrix method (Charmaz, 2006) using NVivo, and Researcher 2 implemented the concept mapping network method (Borgatti, Everett, & Johnson, 2013; Trochim & Kane, 2007).

The independently conducted analyses yielded similar findings. This case study demonstrates that concept mapping has certain advantages over the more traditional matrix analysis in that it does not depend on the researcher identifying nodes or categories *a priori*, the visual output allows a quick assessment of the results and the possibility to evaluate construct validity and interdimensional relationships between clusters or coding categories, it provides a clear audit trail, and it takes less time.

The Research Question, the Innovation Capability Construct, and the Research Methodology

The research question in this case study was: "What are the dimensions of the innovation capability construct for small service businesses?" The innovation capability (IC) literature describes this construct as the capacity of a firm to develop new products, processes, and systems (Lawson & Samson, 2001; Prahalad & Hamel, 1990) in order to compete in dynamic competitive markets. It has been proposed that firms with "good" levels of IC have a sustained competitive advantage and use it to achieve higher levels of performance (Alvarez & Barney, 2001). Thus, it is important to understand IC to assist firms in improving their ability to innovate and hence their abilities to survive, compete, and grow.

The relatively small number of empirical IC studies undertaken to date are primarily in the manufacturing sector (Guan & Ma, 2003; Yam, Guan, Pun, & Tang, 2004), although one study has been undertaken across a variety of professional service firms (Hogan, Soutar, McColl-Kennedy, & Sweeney, 2011)). These studies are characterized by researchers developing scales from different theoretical starting points that result in measures with significant differences in the number and nature of dimensions and scale items (Balan, 2013; Balan & Lindsay, 2009). For example, one measure consists of eight dimensions with 101 scale items (Terziovski & Samson, 2007), another comprises seven dimensions and 70 scale items (Guan & Ma, 2003), a further study includes two dimensions with 10 scale items (Tuominen & Hyvönen, 2004), and another comprises one dimension with five scale items (Grawe, Chen, & Daugherty, 2009). The variation in dimensions and number of scale items used by researchers supports the proposition that "there is no clear agreement of what the real variables of innovation capability might be" (Lawson & Samson, 2001, p. 389) and that the nature of innovation capability may depend on the industry sector (Lawson & Samson, 2001). For these reasons, this research adopted a "grounded" approach consistent with the philosophy of pragmatism to investigate the dimensions of IC for the particular sector being investigated (small service businesses). This is similar to the approach adopted by Rosas and Camphausen (2007) to develop a scale to evaluate a particular type of family support program.

The Sample and Data Collection

The hotel sector is a good example of the services sector (Lovelock, 2001; Sundbo, 1997). It is prevalent in communities across most developed countries, has a relatively high profile, contributes to the economic development of communities, is a significant employer, is subject to rapid and continuing change, and is highly competitive. This research focused on independent hotels in Australia that are classified in the industry as "general hotels" or "pubs." These constitute the majority of Australian hotels, and they are typically independently owned or members of small groups, with fewer than 10 full-time employees (ABS, 2006). Most general hotels are local businesses and draw their clientele from the surrounding localities. About 50% of these hotels provide accommodations and their facilities are either ungraded or range between one and three stars (ABS, 2006). A major feature of general hotels is that they are small service businesses managed by people with a direct day-to-day involvement with the business and who are frequently the owners as well as being the CEOs. This research excluded four- and five-star hotel chains and two large groups of general hotels because innovation decisions in these businesses are largely made in corporate head offices.

A first stage of exploratory qualitative research showed that the "richest" interview data were obtained from hotels in suburban areas with higher levels of competition and operated by owner/managers who were known to their industry association to be innovators. In the subsequent stage of research that is reported in this case, Researcher 1 interviewed six "innovator" owner/managers as key respondents in each of six Australian capital cities—Brisbane, Sydney, Melbourne, Hobart, Perth, and Darwin—to provide a theoretical sample. A relatively unstructured interview questionnaire was used in line with the "grounded" approach to encourage participants to describe innovation initiatives in their particular business. The aim was to identify from their narratives as many different factors as possible that might be relevant in supporting such innovation activities, whether these concerned innovation in products or services or in operating systems or methods used in the business. Interviews were carried out in the premises of each of the participants; the duration of each was approximately one hour. The researcher took notes, interview recordings were transcribed by a professional agency, and the researcher checked the transcriptions against the recordings. Transcriptions were used in each of the two methods of analysis described next, as shown in Figure 30.1.

The matrix method of analyzing qualitative data (using NVivo) is the one most familiar to qualitative researchers (Lewis, 2004; MacMillan & Koenig, 2004; Miles & Huberman, 1994). Researcher 1 analyzed the interview data using an inductive method borrowed from the "grounded" approach (Bringer, Johnston, & Brackenridge, 2006; Charmaz, 2006; Glaser & Strauss, 1967) and carried this out using NVivo (QSR International Pty Ltd, 2010).

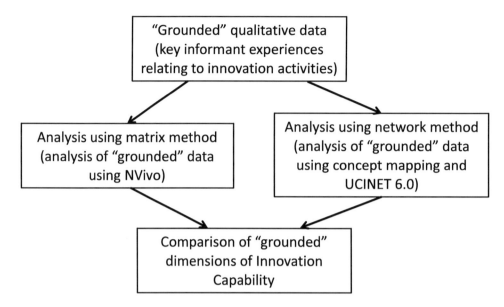

"Grounded" qualitative data (key informant experiences relating to innovation activities)

Analysis using matrix method (analysis of "grounded" data using NVivo)

Analysis using network method (analysis of "grounded" data using concept mapping and UCINET 6.0)

Comparison of "grounded" dimensions of Innovation Capability

Figure 30.1   Research Overview

Drawing from Charmaz (2006), the analysis started with incident to incident coding (p. 53) because the purpose was to discover patterns and contrasts (p. 55), as well as fit and relevance (p. 54) of the categories that were identified. In this way, components of innovation capability were created as categories or NVivo nodes. The analysis started with the Sydney interviews, as these were judged by Researcher 1 to be the richest in terms of providing the greatest number of innovation examples.

During the process of coding data, Researcher 1 named the nodes or categories and recorded reflections on the incidents and on the meaning of the categories and their relationships to other categories in memos, as suggested by Charmaz (2006, p. 72). This used the NVivo facility for creating a memo for each individual category and allowed aspects of manager perceptions of innovation and innovation capability to emerge in an unprompted way, thus providing rich results.

Researcher 1 then carried out focused coding (Charmaz, 2006, p. 57). This used the categories identified by coding the Sydney interviews as the basis for coding the other regions using the same incident to incident coding approach. The purpose was to identify similarities and differences in those regions, compared with Sydney. In practice, this meant that further categories (NVivo nodes) were created as needed, whereas some other categories were not used (to the same extent) in coding interviews for the other locations. In effect, this process involved comparing data for the city being analyzed with the Sydney codes to refine them (Charmaz, 2006, p. 60). The analysis was facilitated by using the memos for each category and taking into account the observations and reflections that had been recorded during the activity of coding data into the individual categories. This approach resulted in the creation of 38 different and a further eight nodes derived from participant statements relating to barriers to innovation, resulting in a total of 46 NVivo nodes or categories.

During the focused coding process, an exercise was carried out to assess the feasibility of using two coders to encode this type of data using a grounded approach. Researcher 1 briefed a third researcher (MacQueen, McLellan, Kay, & Milstein, 1998), and they independently coded the same two interviews and reviewed and discussed the results. A further six interviews were coded separately by the two researchers. The average intercoder reliability, however, was 61%, which fell far below the 70% minimum (Miles & Huberman, 1994, p. 64), with significant variability in concurrence at the individual category level. In addition, it was found to be very time-consuming to compare the two outcomes of coding using NVivo to try to resolve coding differences. As a result, the attempt to use two coders was abandoned, and Researcher 1 coded all the interviews.

The 46 categories were then grouped using "axial coding" (Strauss & Corbin, 1998) to identify themes or dimensions of innovation capability, and this was done in two stages:

1. Researcher 1 prepared descriptors of each category, and verbatim examples of each were provided to two other experienced researchers in the field of innovation and entrepreneurship. These two independent researchers used this information, as well as comments relating to barriers to innovation, to develop nine separate dimensions that included the 34 categories.
2. Guided by the NVivo coding stripes as described by Bringer et al. (2006, p. 255), Researcher 1 checked this classification based on a detailed examination of the extensive content of each category and adjusted the classification after discussion with the other researchers.

This constituted an abductive (Reichertz, 2010) or "grounded" approach for identifying the dimensions and components of innovation capability for this sector *ab initio* (Charmaz, 2006; Glaser & Strauss, 1967; Strauss & Corbin, 1998), and it resulted in the dimensions of innovation capability shown in Table 30.1.

Rigor was achieved in this matrix analysis by ensuring that the data selected were adequate and appropriate and that there was a documented audit trail consisting of "raw data, data reduction and analysis products, data reconstruction and synthesis products, process notes, materials relating to intentions and dispositions, and instrument development information," with the intention that others "can reconstruct the process by which the investigators reached their conclusions" (Morse, 1998, p. 77). The audit trail was embedded in the nodes and memos in the NVivo software (Bringer, Johnston, & Brackenridge, 2004).

Table 30.1 IC Dimensions Identified from the Matrix Analysis

IC Dimensions	NVivo Categories/Nodes
Alliances	Alliances with organizations such as external agencies, other hotels, and suppliers
Customer intelligence	Customer feedback, customer knowledge
Business environment awareness	Awareness of constant change and awareness of competition, regulations, business trends, market position, technology changes, foresight
Manager characteristics	The manager's personal knowledge, knowledge about the business, leadership and lifestyle
Experimentation	Including proactiveness
Human resources and human capital	Having good staff, job design, staff incentives and motivation, team culture, team knowledge, formal education, formal skills training, in-house training, and organizational structure
Operations	Having good operations, management systems, and quality control
Resource awareness	Financial investment and resource management
Strategy and planning	Planning, vision, strategic view of the business and portfolio management

Data Analysis Using Concept Mapping

Concept mapping, as used here represents ideas in network form (Metcalfe 2007; 2014). It is an integration of qualitative and quantitative methods, where qualitative information can be represented quantitatively, and quantitative analysis is enhanced by qualitative judgment (Alvarez & Barney, 2013; Greene, Caracelli, & Graham, 1989). Concept mapping is useful as it helps qualitative researchers capture and discover meaning in social reality through words and pictures, allowing concepts and ideas to emerge (Rappa, 2001). UCINET 6.0 social network analysis software (Borgatti, Everett, & Freeman, 2002) is used to generate maps and data displays to represent the relationships between the ideas and illustrate a conceptual framework, presented as a concept map (Kane & Trochim, 2007). Other software that performs concept mapping includes Pajek, NodeXL, and NetMiner for PCs, as well as Gephi, which is suitable for Apple computers.

The concept mapping method was carried out by Researcher 2, who was not involved in the original interview process or in the matrix analysis (using NVivo) described previously. Researcher 2 reviewed the 36 transcripts to extract statements provided by participants that described what was required to be innovative in their businesses or referred to barriers to innovation. This process resulted in a total of 377 individual verbatim statements that were entered into an Excel spreadsheet. After careful review, however, Researcher 2 averaged out 129 duplicate statements (Borgatti et al., 2013, p. 258) to result in item reduction, leaving a total of 248 statements to be analyzed. Researcher 2 then went through a linking process to identify which of the 248 statements were most similar to each other. This was done by identifying keywords from each phrase and matching these based on the context of the statement. Concept mapping requires that this linking process be done as parsimoniously as possible to ensure the number of linkages of each individual statement is kept to a minimum (e.g., less than five or six linkages); otherwise, the map produced by the software will be too dense and difficult to interpret. Researcher 2 identified 361 one-way linkages based on perceived similarity of statements.

These linkages were entered into an Excel spreadsheet and uploaded to the UCINET 6.0 social network analysis software (Borgatti et al., 2002). Using the NetDraw function, a three-dimensional concept map was created, with each statement represented by a numbered node on the map. This allows the researcher to return to the original data spreadsheet and identify exactly where each statement is located on the map and its relationship to other statements. Researcher 2 then analyzed the resulting concept map using Girvan-Newman subgroup analysis (Girvan & Newman, 2002). This analysis presumes that within a community there will be subgroups, and it uses statistics to measure the "betweenness" of the clusters within the map. This analysis allows the number of clusters to be varied as required by the researcher, and Researcher 2 evaluated each set of clusters. This subgroup analysis identified 12 clusters; the researcher merged two clusters to reduce these to 11 meaningful clusters. Fewer clusters did not yield enough variation in the statements, and more clusters did not provide significant insights. As this method makes it possible for the researcher to track where each individual piece of data is at any one time within the process, the researcher made some adjustments to the links where statements did not appear to "fit" within their cluster. Notes pertaining to the amended links were recorded. Figure 30.2 shows how the 248 qualitative comments extracted from the 36 in-depth interview data were grouped into 11 clusters or themes to form a concept map.

Researcher 2 referred to the original statements grouped together in each cluster to arrive at names or labels for each theme. The 11 clusters are named and described in Table 30.2.

Comparing the Results of the Two Methods of Analysis

At this point, both researchers carefully reviewed the statements in each cluster to ascertain the appropriateness of the name for each cluster, and they compared the findings from the grounded matrix approach using NVivo and the concept network approach. The goal was to identify whether

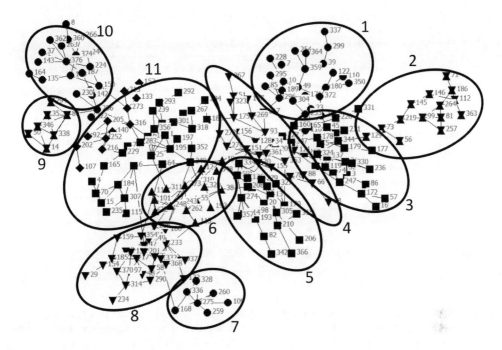

Figure 30.2 IC Dimensions Concept Map

Table 30.2 IC Dimension Concept Map Clusters

Cluster Number in Figure 30.2	Node Shape	Cluster Name
1	Circle	Multiskilled and trained staff
2	Hourglass	Partnerships and alliances
3	Square	Systems and management procedures
4	Down triangle	Planning and resources
5	Square	Facilities and infrastructure
6	Up triangle	Compliance and regulations
7	Circle	Customer engagement
8	Down triangle	Community engagement
9	Hourglass	Market scanning
10	Circle	Objective data and research
11	Diamond (and cluster 12, square)	Experimentation

it was possible to align the IC dimensions revealed by each data analysis method drawn from the same sample of 36 in-depth interview transcripts. As shown in Table 30.3, as a collaborative exercise, the researchers were able to match the nine matrix analysis dimensions with the 11 concept map dimensions.

The comparability of the dimensions in Table 30.3 indicates that the outcomes of the two separate analyses were quite similar at this broader level, thus indicating that they could be used interchangeably for the purpose of further research, such as for the development of items that could be included in a scale for innovation capability.

Table 30.3 Comparison of IC Dimensions Generated From Both Methods

#	*Matrix (NVivo) Analysis Dimensions of IC*	*Concept Mapping Dimensions of IC*
1	Environmental awareness	Objective data and research, compliance and regulations, market scanning
2	Alliances	Partnerships and alliances
3	Customer intelligence	Customer engagement, community engagement
4	Experimentation	Experimentation
5	Strategy and planning	Planning and resources
6	Manager attributes	Multiskilled and trained staff
7	Human resources and human capital	Multiskilled and trained staff
8	Resource awareness	Facilities and infrastructure
9	Operations	Systems and management procedures

Discussion

The research question addressed in this case study required an exploratory "grounded" approach to analyze qualitative in-depth interview data. Although the relevant literature was reviewed and formed a context for the research, the dimensions of IC in this research emerged through a comprehensive "grounded" analysis of in-depth interviews with hotel owner/managers using a matrix method. The same qualitative data set was also used to generate a concept map using a network method, and similar findings emerged. Concept mapping has been used in a number of different situations (Table 30.4), such as evaluating entrepreneurship policies (Balan-Vnuk, Dissanyake, & O'Connor, 2014), identifying business model strategies for non-profit social enterprises (Balan-Vnuk, 2013), identifying dimensions of innovative business models of hotels (Reynolds, Balan, Metcalfe, & Balan-Vnuk, 2014), identifying dimensions of student engagement with a particular teaching method (Balan & Balan-Vnuk, 2013), and exploring the dimensions of student learning motivations (Balan, Balan-Vnuk, Lindsay & Lindsay, 2014). In particular, this exploratory research identified factors not previously identified in IC scales developed for other industry sectors or for other types of service businesses (Balan, 2013).

With regard to the two methods presented, the analysis of qualitative data can be described in terms of the stages of coding data into nodes or categories, integrating categories, developing theoretical insights, and continuing the analysis until saturation is reached (Shah & Corley, 2006, p. 1828), and these stages provide a framework for comparing matrix analysis using NVivo and concept mapping.

Coding Data Into Nodes or Categories and Naming Categories

Matrix analysis (NVivo) requires the researcher to devise and name nodes, to allocate similar data elements to appropriate nodes, and to write memos that capture the researcher's reflections on the data during this analysis (Bringer et al., 2006; Hutchison, Johnston, & Breckon, 2010). This is a process that requires clear judgement and consistency, and some researchers have identified problems in accuracy of data assignment and incorrect labelling of codes (Davis & Meyer, 2009). In a like manner, concept mapping requires the researcher to identify similarities between data elements in as objective a manner as possible. The researcher, however, is not required to name categories or nodes during coding, as this interpretive step is taken only after the concept mapping software has revealed clusters and the researcher has examined data elements in those clusters. Similarly, reflection on the data groupings (categories) takes place at this later stage when the researcher has the benefit of examining the data arrangements; this replaces the writing of memos.

Integrating Categories

Axial coding involves making comparisons at the category and subcategory levels (Strauss & Corbin, 1998) and is carried out in matrix analysis with the assistance of facilities such as NVivo coding stripes (Bringer et al., 2006). Concept mapping software generates cluster maps that directly display the integration of categories for conceptual development (Figure 30.2). In particular, the researcher has the ability to select the number of clusters generated by the software and examine the data elements contained in clusters of different sizes to identify possible integrative relationships.

Developing Theoretical Insights and Providing a Visual Representation

NVivo provides matrix coding query functions that can be used to explore relationships between categories at different levels, and relationship nodes can be created to identify possible relationships between categories. Theoretical development can be further supported by the modeling tool in NVivo that allows the researcher to manually move nodes into related clusters and then interrogate nodes to identify the data behind them (Bringer et al., 2006; Hutchison et al., 2010).

In comparison, concept mapping generates a visual output drawn directly from all of the data elements (Figure 30.2). The software enables two- and three-dimensional views; this provides the qualitative researcher with an efficient, yet very clear and rich, illustration of the analyzed statements, the constructs that emerge from the analysis, and their interrelationships (Corley, 2011). This gives the researcher (visual) insights into the structure of the data and possible theoretical development and allows the reader to "connect the raw data with the analyzed data, and the analyzed data with the emergent theorizing" (Bansal & Corley, 2012, p. 511). For example, in the concept map developed in this research, the cluster "location and physical assets" is located next to the cluster "community engagement and relevance." This provides additional insights into the data that can be used for theory development.

The Girvan–Newman (2002) analysis in UCINET 6.0 provides an additional benefit, as this makes it possible for the researcher to select the number of clusters to be revealed. For example, the software can be set to display two clusters, or three, or any number. The researcher can examine the structure of each of the resulting clusters to assess the nature and homogeneity of the data elements in each. This allows the researcher to determine when an optimum number of themes (clusters) has been reached by observing if the addition of a further cluster does not add further understanding or insight. For example, in this case the researchers considered that 11 clusters were optimal, as when the software was set to identify 12 or more clusters, each additional cluster consisted of only two or three individual but linked data elements or statements. This provided a visual indication suggesting that setting the software to display 12 (or more) clusters did not add insights into the analysis. In a different qualitative research project, the researchers determined that only three clusters provided the most useful theoretical insights into the problem being investigated (Reynolds, Balan, Metcalfe, & Balan-Vnuk, 2014).

Achieving Saturation or Theoretical Density

In the analysis described in this chapter, data analysis using NVivo was carried out location by location, and this made it possible to identify when saturation was reached (Charmaz, 2006, p. 299). The same approach can be applied when analyzing data using concept mapping. In particular, the manual coding process allows additional data to be added to an existing data set for cluster analysis. The cluster maps for each increment in data grouping can be compared, and this will reveal if any new clusters emerge. Saturation is achieved when the cluster structure does not change, but existing clusters become denser. The same approach can be used to carry out "coding-on" to develop dense categories and explore links to other categories (Bringer et al., 2006, p. 255).

Other key differences identified between the two methods included the audit trail, intercoder reliability, and the time required for analysis.

Audit Trail

A central consideration in qualitative analysis is the trustworthiness or conceptual soundness of the analysis. In particular, trustworthiness has been described as being made up of the following criteria: credibility, transferability, dependability, and conformability. This is supported by the provision of a systematic audit trail (Lincoln & Guba, 1985). The need to have a sound audit trail has been emphasized in the literature (Bowen, 2009; Shah & Corley, 2006). For analyses using NVivo, an audit trail is made up of records of analysis and project journals including descriptions of analytical procedures (Bringer et al., 2004; Hutchison et al., 2010). Nonetheless, it is time consuming to read and follow the audit trail for the generation of nodes and categories using the matrix approach. This makes it challenging for other researchers to "replicate" a given analysis or identify possible coding errors (Davis & Meyer, 2009).

In comparison, the concept mapping process provides a clear and straightforward audit trail consisting of a limited set of documents: the raw data records, a spreadsheet displaying individual comments or data elements with similarity codings, and a spreadsheet with data elements grouped by clusters. This means that one researcher may collect the statements, make the links between similar statements on a spreadsheet, generate the map, and group the data elements in another spreadsheet. Another researcher, by virtue of the visual output and the spreadsheets, can then examine and question the link between each statement in the map. The transparency of the method allows other scholars to use the limited number of documents described previously to rigorously examine the steps taken to arrive at a result, which is a desirable attribute for any research.

An additional benefit of concept mapping is the qualitative evaluation of construct validity. This is a challenge in qualitative data analysis because it is not always clear whether statements placed in the same node or category in fact belong together. In concept mapping, the items most similar to each other are clustered together, and this allows construct validity to be more readily assessed, both visually and in reference to the Excel spreadsheet displaying the grouped data elements. These audit trail documents provide a sound basis for researcher collaboration.

Intercoder Reliability and Researcher Collaboration

The experiment carried out in this research that used two researchers to independently analyze the same data using matrix analysis (NVivo) showed that intercoder reliability when using a grounded research approach was unreliable, falling below the recommended 70% concurrence (Miles & Huberman, 1994, p. 64). In addition, it was found to be time consuming to compare the NVivo coding outcomes for the two researchers. This means that, in practice, it may not be practical for others to "reconstruct the process by which the investigators reached their conclusions" (Morse, 1998, p. 77). In the case of concept mapping, collaboration is facilitated by the existence of the clear audit trail for each step in the process. The list of statements, ordered by cluster, can be checked against the visual output and examined carefully to identify any possible anomalies, and these can be quickly remedied. In this research, Researchers 1 and 2 were able to subsequently review Researcher 2's coding and to agree quickly on the optimum coding of statements using the Excel spreadsheet records. This demonstrates the value of concept mapping in supporting researcher collaboration.

Time Required for Analysis

There was a significant difference in the amount of time required by each method to analyze the same data set. The 36 interview transcripts ranged from 7,000 to 22,000 words each. Implementing the matrix approach using NVivo, many hours were required to go through each line of each transcript and identify nodes and categories while becoming familiar with the data. This was an ongoing process, and Researcher 1 had to constantly evaluate whether new nodes were required based on new statements or whether statements could fit into an existing node or category. When using the concept mapping method, Researcher 2 identified statements that helped to answer the research question and pasted these into an Excel spreadsheet. The statement linking process, where each statement was carefully examined in relation to the remaining statements in the spreadsheet, was time consuming, although the researcher was not required to identify themes, even though some could be observed. Categories were identified as clusters in the concept map generated by the UCINET 6.0 software. Researcher 2 used the map to qualitatively evaluate the homogeneity of the statements in each cluster. The researchers estimated that the concept mapping process took considerably less time to execute than the matrix approach using NVivo.

Due to these aspects, it is suggested that concept mapping, a network method, is a valid and credible approach for analyzing this type of qualitative data. It does not depend on the researcher identifying nodes or categories a priori, it provides a visual output to assist in theory development, and it provides a clear audit trail, while saving time.

Summary

The purpose of this research was to make a direct comparison between two different research methods to determine whether one may have advantages over the other. The concept mapping method has been used in a number of situations. In this section, a "grounded" investigation of the innovation capability construct was used as a case example. Data was collected using relatively unstructured in-depth interviews with the owner/managers of small general hotels in Australia. Interview transcripts were analyzed independently, first using traditional matrix analysis and NVivo software, and second by implementing concept mapping using UCINET6.0 software. It was found that concept mapping, a network method, is a valid and credible approach for analysing this type of qualitative data using a grounded approach (Figure 30.3). It takes less time, it does not depend on the researcher identifying nodes or categories, and the visual output provides several key benefits

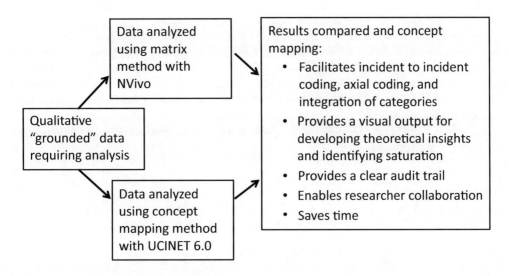

Figure 30.3 Textbox summarizing the innovation

Table 30.4 Use of Concept Mapping for Grounded Data Analysis in Qualitative Research

Reference	Research Context	How Innovation Was used	Outcomes/Results
Balan-Vnuk, Dissanyake, & O'Connor (2014)	Evaluating entrepreneurship policies for the Sri Lankan government	Summarize secondary data to identify themes in publicly available data	Identify eight clusters of development strategies to support entrepreneurship education and new venture formation
Balan-Vnuk (2013)	Identify business model strategies for nonprofit social enterprises	Analyze in-depth interview data to identify business model strategy types	Development of a typology of five business model strategies adopted by nonprofit social enterprises in Australia
Reynolds et al. (2014)	Identify the dimensions of innovative business models of general hotels	Analyze qualitative data from the websites of a sample of hotels	Identified three major themes of business model innovation that can be used by hotel managers to improve their business
Balan & Balan-Vnuk (2013)	Identify the dimensions of student engagement with a particular teaching method	Analyze student engagement with the team-based learning method of teaching with data obtained from minute paper evaluations	Identified common dimensions of student engagement with the team-based learning method
Balan, Balan-Vnuk, Lindsay, & Lindsay (2014)	Identify the dimensions of student learning motivations	Analyze student learning motivations with data obtained from minute paper evaluations	Identified common dimensions of student learning motivations for six classes

in helping to visualise the relationships between themes. In addition, concept mapping provides a detailed audit trail that facilitates both collaboration and verification, and an opportunity to evaluate construct validity and inter-dimensional relationships between the clusters.

Many researchers have found matrix analysis using NVivo (for example) to be a valuable research tool. This case study suggests that qualitative researchers might consider adding concept mapping to their repertoires as a valid and credible approach for analyzing this type of qualitative data when using a grounded approach. This exercise found that concept mapping does not depend on the researcher identifying nodes or categories ahead of time, so the data interpretation can be left to a later stage of analysis when it is facilitated by a visual output that helps to identify relationships between categories or nodes. In addition, concept mapping provides a clear and detailed audit trail that facilitates collaboration and verification.

References

Alvarez, S.A., & Barney, J.B. (2001). How entrepreneurial firms can benefit from alliances with large partners. *Academy of Management Executive, 15*(1), 139–148.

Alvarez, S.A., & Barney, J.B. (2013). Epistemology, opportunities, and entrepreneurship: Comments on Venkataraman et al. (2012) and Shane (2012). *Academy of Management Review, 38*(1), 154–157.

Australian Bureau of Statistics (ABS). (2006). 8687.0 — Clubs, Pubs, Tavern and Bars, Australia, 2004–05. Canberra: Author.

Balan, P. (2013). *Innovation capability in small service businesses*. Ph.D. Thesis, University of South Australia, Adelaide.

Balan, P., & Balan-Vnuk, E. (2013). Student engagement with team-based learning in undergraduate entrepreneurship courses: An exploratory study. In P. Davidsson (Ed.), *Proceedings of the ACERE International Entrepreneurship Research Conference, Brisbane* (pp. 1–15). Brisbane, Qld, Australia: Queensland University of Technology.

Balan, P., Balan-Vnuk, E., Lindsay, N., & Lindsay, W. (2014). Identifying the motivations of students in undergraduate entrepreneurship classes. In P. Davidsson (Ed.), *Proceedings of the ACERE International Entrepreneurship Research Conference, Sydney* (pp. 1–15). Brisbane, Qld, Australia: Queensland University of Technology.

Balan, P., & Lindsay, N.J. (2009). *Innovation capability and entrepreneurial orientation dimensions for Australian hotels*. Gold Coast, Queensland: Cooperative Research Centre for Sustainable Tourism.

Balan-Vnuk, E. (2013). *Social enterprise business models: Identifying the trading concepts that inform them*. Ph.D., The University of Adelaide.

Balan-Vnuk, E., Dissanyake, M., & O'Connor, A. (2014). Policy analysis for entrepreneurship education in necessity-based contexts: a Sri Lankan case study. In J. Brewer & S.W. Gibson (Eds.), *Necessity entrepreneurs: Microenterprise education and economic development* (pp. 160–182). Cheltenham, UK: Edward Elgar.

Bansal, P., & Corley, K. (2012). Publishing in AMJ-part 7: What's different about qualitative research? Editorial. *Academy of Management Journal*, 55(3), 509–513.

Borgatti, S.P., Everett, M.G., & Freeman, L.C. (2002). *Ucinet for Windows: Software for social network analysis*. Harvard, MA: Analytic Technologies.

Borgatti, S.P., Everett, M.G., & Johnson, J.C. (2013). *Analyzing social networks*. London, England: Sage.

Bowen, G.A. (2009). Supporting a grounded theory with an audit trail: An illustration. *International Journal of Social Research Methodology*, 12(4), 305–316.

Bringer, J.D., Johnston, L.H., & Brackenridge, C.H. (2004). Maximizing transparency in a doctoral thesis: The complexities of writing about the use of QSR★NVIVO within a grounded theory study. *Qualitative Research*, 4(2), 247–265.

Bringer, J.D., Johnston, L.H., & Brackenridge, C.H. (2006). Using computer-assisted qualitative data analysis software to develop a grounded theory project. *Field Methods*, 18(3), 245–266.

Charmaz, K. (2006). *Constructing grounded theory*. London, England: Sage.

Corley, K. (2011). The coming of age for qualitative research: Embracing the diversity of qualitative methods. *Academy of Management Journal*, 54(2), 233–237.

Davis, N.W., & Meyer, B.B. (2009). Qualitative data analysis: A procedural comparison. *Journal of Applied Sport Psychology*, 21(1), 116–124.

Girvan, M., & Newman, M.E.J. (2002). Community structure in social and biological networks. *Proceedings of the National Academy of Sciences of the United States of America*, 99(12), 7821–7826.

Glaser, B.G., & Strauss, A.L. (1967). *The discovery of grounded theory: Strategies for qualitative research*. New York, NY: Aldine de Gruyter.

Grawe, S.J., Chen, H., & Daugherty, P.J. (2009). The relationship between strategic orientation, service innovation, and performance. *International Journal of Physical Distribution & Logistics Management*, 39(4), 282–300.

Greene, J.C., Caracelli, V.J., & Graham, W.F. (1989). Toward a conceptual framework for mixed-method evaluation designs. *Educational Evaluation and Policy Analysis*, 11(3), 255–274.

Guan, J.C., & Ma, N. (2003). Innovative capability and export performance of Chinese firms. *Technovation*, 23(9), 737–747.

Hutchison, A.J., Johnston, L.H., & Breckon, J.D. (2010). Using QSR-NVivo to facilitate the development of a grounded theory project: An account of a worked example. *International Journal of Social Research Methodology*, 13(4), 283–302.

Hogan, S.J., Soutar, G.N., McColl-Kennedy, J.R., & Sweeney, J.C. (2011). Reconceptualizing professional service firm innovation capability: Scale development. *Industrial Marketing Management*, 40(8), 1264–1273.

Kane, M., & Trochim, W.M.K. (2007). *Concept mapping for planning and evaluation*. Thousand Oaks, CA: Sage.

Lawson, B., & Samson, D. (2001). Developing innovation capability in organisations: A dynamic capabilities approach. *International Journal of Innovation Management*, 5(3), 377–400.

Lewis, R.B. (2004). NVivo 2.0 and ATLAS.ti 5.0: A comparative review of two popular qualitative data-analysis programs. *Field Methods*, 16(4), 439–464.

Lincoln, Y.S., & Guba, E.G. (1985). *Naturalistic inquiry*. London: Sage.

Lovelock, C. (2001). *Services marketing: People, technology, strategy* (4th ed.). Upper Saddle River, NJ: Prentice Hall.

MacMillan, K., & Koenig, T. (2004). The wow factor: Preconceptions and expectations for data analysis software in qualitative research. *Social Science Computer Review*, 22(2), 179–186.

MacQueen, K.M., McLellan, E., Kay, K., & Milstein, B. (1998). Codebook development for team-based qualitative analysis. *Cultural Anthropology Methods*, 10(2), 31–36.

Miles, M.B., & Huberman, A. M. (1994). *Qualitative data analysis.* Thousand Oaks, CA: Sage.

Metcalfe, M. (2007). Problem Conceptualisation Using Idea Networks. *Systemic Practice and Action Research,* *20*(2), 141–150.

Metcalfe, M. (2014). *How Concepts Solve Management Problems.* Cheltenham, UK: Edward Elgar Publishing.

Morse, J.M. (1998). Designing funded qualitative research. In N.K. Denzin & Y.S. Lincoln (Eds.), *Strategies of qualitative enquiry* (pp. 56–85). Thousand Oaks, CA: Sage.

Prahalad, C.K., & Hamel, G. (1990). The core competence of the corporation. *Harvard Business Review, 68*(3), 79–91.

QSR International Pty Ltd. (2010). NVivo qualitative data analysis software (Version 9).

Rappa, M. (2001). Business models on the web: Managing the digital enterprise. Retrieved from http://digital-enterprise.org/models/models.html

Reichertz, J. (2010). Abduction: The logic of discovery of grounded theory. *Forum: Qualitative Social Research, 11*(1), article 13.

Reynolds, P., Balan, P., Metcalfe, M., & Balan-Vnuk, E. (2014). *Investigating innovative business models of general hotels in South Australia.* Refereed working paper presented at the CAUTHE Conference, 10–13 February 2014. Brisbane, Queensland. Available from peter.balan@unisa.edu.au

Rosas, S.R., & Camphausen, L.C. (2007). The use of concept mapping for scale development and validation in evaluation. *Evaluation and Program Planning, 30*(2), 125–135.

Shah, S.K., & Corley, K.G. (2006). Building better theory by bridging the quantitative–qualitative divide. *Journal of Management Studies, 43*(8), 1821–1835.

Strauss, A.L., & Corbin, J. (1998). *Basics of qualitative research: Grounded theory procedures and techniques.* Newbury Park, CA: Sage.

Sundbo, J. (1997). Management of innovation in services. *The Service Industries Journal, 17*(3), 432–455.

Terziovski, M., & Samson, D. (2007). *Innovation capability and its impact on firm performance.* Paper presented at the Regional Frontiers of Entrepreneurial Research, Brisbane, Australia.

Trochim, W.M.K., & Kane, M. (2007). *Concept mapping for planning and evaluation.* Thousand Oaks, CA: Sage.

Tuominen, M., & Hyvönen, S. (2004). Organizational innovation capability: A driver for competitive superiority in marketing channels. *International Review of Retail, Distribution & Consumer Research, 14*(3), 277–293.

Yam, R.C.M., Guan, J.C., Pun, K.F., & Tang, E.P.Y. (2004). An audit of technological innovation capabilities in Chinese firms: Some empirical findings in Beijing, China. *Research Policy, 33*(8), 1123–1140.

31

Innovation Through Collaboration

Working Together on Data Analysis and Interpretation

Kevin G. Corley, Courtney R. Masterson, and Beth S. Schinoff

The quality of connections that researchers form with each other and with others . . . is key to developing and sustaining interesting research. (Dutton & Dukerich, 2006, p. 21)

Qualitative research is an inherently social process. When conducting qualitative research, scholars engage with the social world through participants, settings, and, oftentimes, co-authors. While the relationships qualitative researchers form with their subjects have received a good deal of attention (e.g., Barley, 1990; Charmaz, 2006), connections made within research teams (i.e., between co-authors) remains largely underexplored. Yet ties between team members are likely critical to the overall impact of the research (Hackman, 2011). For example, collaborations enable researchers to engage in dialogue and debate over the phenomenon and the methodological approach. Importantly, when working together, partnerships also serve as a lens through which the data are interpreted and shared with the field. To help advance our understanding of how connections within research teams influence qualitative research outcomes, this chapter explores how working with others bolsters the innovativeness of the research process—in particular during the data analysis and interpretation phase.

Examining the potential value of research collaboration during the analysis and interpretation phase of qualitative research is especially appropriate because it is during this time that researchers seek social cues to make sense of and reveal the meaning behind a phenomenon. Regardless of the qualitative analysis techniques scholars draw upon, individuals have to make sense of a large amount of data, coding relatively discrete sections to look for patterns within or across samples to develop or support theories at a higher level of abstraction (e.g., Charmaz, 2006; Glaser & Strauss, 1967; Yin, 2014). Unfortunately, discussion of the potential for collaboration in this process is largely absent from our literatures (see Dutton & Dukerich, 2006, for an exception). Research in other fields, however, has broached the topic. Most illustrative, in the field of education, Wasser and Bresler introduced the concept of "the interpretive zone," defined as "the place where multiple viewpoints are held in dynamic tension as a group seeks to make sense of fieldwork issues and meanings" (1996, p. 6). The authors examined this concept from a procedural perspective—how do multiple individuals come together to form a single interpretation of qualitative data? Through the analysis of one of their own qualitative collaborations, they tackled issues such as how the group negotiated the researchers' diverse perspectives and feelings of ownership and territoriality, the important role of the "leader" in facilitating and shaping the collaboration, and how the group itself became an interpretive tool for the researchers. However, deeper insight into *how* collaboration positively influences the individuals involved in making sense of the data—beyond the obvious benefit of diffusion of effort—remains relatively uncodified.

Drawing from a sensemaking perspective, we argue "two [or more] heads are better than one" (Bahrami, Olsen, Latham, Roepstorff, Rees, & Frith, 2010, p. 1081)—that collaboration allows for fresh perspectives, the challenging of old ways/habits, and a more robust analysis and interpretation of the data. We offer support for such arguments with a discussion of the cognitive (i.e., diversity of perspectives and creative self-efficacy), emotional (i.e., positive affect), and physiological (i.e., energy) paths to innovation that collaboration generates during the analysis phase of qualitative research. After grounding our chapter in a sensemaking perspective, we discuss how these paths surface and exert influence on the data analysis and interpretation phase. We briefly bring our theorizing to life with illustrations of what these paths to innovativeness look like in two particular types of collaborations: the professor–student relationship during a doctoral program and the academic–practitioner relationship (Bartunek, 2007; Rynes, Bartunek, & Daft, 2001).

Sensemaking in the Qualitative Research Process

If we stop for a moment and consider what researchers do when analyzing and interpreting qualitative data, the closest theoretical analog we have is organizational sensemaking. Consider Weick's (1995, p. 2) description of what makes something an instance of sensemaking:

> First, someone notices something, in an ongoing flow of events, something in the form of a surprise, a discrepant set of cues, something that does not fit. Second, the discrepant cues are spotted when someone looks back over elapsed experience. The act of looking is retrospective. Third, plausible speculations . . . are offered to explain the cues.

Weick was describing the emergence of Battered Child Syndrome within the Pediatric community, but he similarly could have explained what it is like for a qualitative scholar during an inductive field study. We go out, observe, conduct interviews, and read contextual archives. Throughout these data collection efforts, we look for things that don't fit our expectations or that current theory would not predict. We reflect on our growing experiences with that phenomenon, in that context, and try to assemble the noticed set of cues (our data) into plausible explanations for what is happening, why it is happening, and how it is happening. We then develop theories about what we now think we understand and write papers to share those understandings with the scholarly communities in which we are embedded, with the hope of affecting the next set of researchers interested in the same phenomenon. In essence, we are "placing stimuli into some kind of framework" (Weick, 1995, p. 4) and participating in the "reciprocal interaction of information seeking, meaning ascription, and action" (Thomas, Clark & Gioia, 1993, p. 240). In a very real sense, then, the analysis and interpretation of qualitative research is the practice of sensemaking as we are "authoring as well as interpret[ing], creat[ing] as well as discover[ing]" (Weick, 1995, p. 8).

Scholars have approached sensemaking from two ontological perspectives (Maitlis & Christenson, 2014; Weick, 1995), both of which pertain to collaboration during qualitative research. Those who ground the process in the social cognition literature argue that collective meaning making takes place as individuals make sense of what's going on a priori and then advocate for their position, thereby influencing others' views of the world (e.g., Starbuck & Milliken, 1988). Alternatively, scholars in the social construction camp argue that individuals make sense of their environment together, co-creating their world views (e.g., Gephart, 1993). These two perspectives prove useful in diving deeper into the role of collaboration in qualitative data analysis as they provide foundations to understand not only what scholars are doing as they collaborate, but also how that collaboration provides empirical and theoretical benefits beyond that which a sole researcher can produce alone.

Collaboration as a Path to Thinking, Feeling, and Being More Innovative

We acknowledge that all projects that involve multiple researchers or co-authors are not necessarily collaborative, nor are all experiences of collaboration similar in nature (Katz & Martin, 1997). For the purposes of this chapter, we define *collaboration* as two or more individuals who actively engage together in a research project and possess a sense of shared accountability for the product of that project. Further, we focus our attention on *high-quality collaborations*, defined as collaborations associated with shared positive subjective experiences (cf. Stephens, Heaphy, & Dutton, 2011). Building on these foundations, we outline three distinct pathways—cognitive, affective, and physiological—by which these partnerships can generate greater resources to help foster innovativeness in the data analysis and interpretation stage of qualitative research (see Figure 31.1).

In this section, we illustrate how these pathways can emerge and help foster resources in a particular relational context by drawing upon the example of professor–student collaborations. The relationships that doctoral students form with faculty members are of the utmost importance to their career success (Johnson, 2007; Kramer & Martin, 1996). Faculty members, including but not limited to dissertation advisors, profoundly shape the way emerging scholars view and make sense of the world around them. From the student's perspective, a faculty member's past experience and expertise in conducting a high-quality inductive project is invaluable as scholars have noted that qualitative research cannot be learned exclusively in a classroom (Cassell, Bishop, Symon, Johnson, & Buehring,

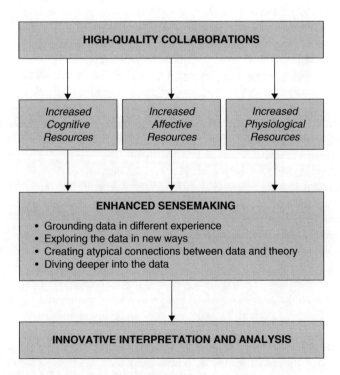

Figure 31.1 Innovative Analysis Through Collaboration

2009). At the same time, students can positively transform faculty members' research experiences when they actively engage in the co-creation of knowledge together. Students may bring a fresh set of ideas and a sense of eagerness to the data analysis. As described later, the potential for enhanced data analysis and interpretation grows out of the positive interactions between faculty members and students in several ways.

Cognitive: Innovation Through Thought

The first and seemingly most obvious way a high-quality collaboration enhances the process of analyzing and interpreting data is by enabling cognitive diversity—that is, allowing individuals to share and leverage their different experiences, perspectives, and expertise (Miller, Burke, & Glick, 1998) to the interpretation of the data. Depending on the ontological assumption through which one views the sensemaking process, diversity of perspectives plays a different role in how it affects sensemaking. In the social cognition tradition, individuals draw upon their mental models or schemas which arise from past, relevant experiences when making sense of the data (Fiske & Taylor, 1984; Lord & Foti, 1986). The data is then interpreted through these experiences, opening the door for different ways of interpreting the data through schemas before sharing with others how that sense has been made. In the social construction camp, scholars see diversity of perspectives playing a role in the social processes (e.g., use of language; Sonenshein, 2006; Taylor & Robichaud, 2004) through which sense is made. In this tradition, individuals' backgrounds influence how data is made sense of collectively. Regardless of how including multiple individuals' knowledge influences the sensemaking process, seeing the data from different perspectives likely leads to more innovative interpretations and a richer understanding of the phenomenon of interest. Indeed, though the empirical relationship between diversity and team performance has been somewhat elusive and equivocal (see Jackson & Joshi, 2010, for a review), the notion that diversity can lead to more creative outcomes (Amabile, Conti, Coon, Lazenby, & Herron, 1996; Milliken, Bartel, & Kurtzberg, 2003) as well as more creative processes (Woodman, Sawyer, & Griffin, 1993) is well-known.

In the professor–student collaboration, both parties enter the research effort with varying levels of knowledge or previous exposure to the research context, methods, and phenomenon under investigation (Kramer & Martin, 1996). It is this diversity of perspectives that allows the research team to examine the data through not only a microscope (i.e., a singular, in-depth focus) but through a kaleidoscope of perspectives—one that enables the research to team to examine the data in myriad ways. The kaleidoscope can be seen as a tool for challenging the professor and student to look at the data through each other's lenses and through the similarities and dissimilarities of viewpoints. For example, diverse perspectives may prove particularly useful when developing conceptual categories or naming data (Locke, 2001), as individuals may see the data as conceptually distinct or similar. Furthermore, depending upon a professor's or student's background (e.g., undergraduate field, work experience), each individual may turn to vastly different areas of literature to enrich their understanding of the data.

Beyond potential for greater innovativeness in seeing the data from different vantage points, faculty and students who work together may see shifts in how they understand the analysis and interpretation process. For instance, a student working with a more experienced professor is able to learn the nuances of qualitative research, such as how to ensure credibility or rigor (see Tracy, 2010), from an experienced scholar. At the same time, that student may question the faculty member's ways of doing research, disrupting potentially "stale" routines. In addition, both parties may experience a heightened sense of creative self-efficacy, defined as "the belief one has the ability to produce creative outcomes" (Tierney & Farmer, 2002, p. 1138). To be sure, a key antecedent of creative self-efficacy is supportive cues from the social environment, as individuals look to others to help them make sense of creative acts and how capable they are of being creative (Amabile & Gryskiewicz, 1987; Tierney &

Farmer, 2002). As students and faculty may experience feelings of self-doubt and uncertainty while venturing into an abyss of data, a high-quality collaboration may provide the opportunity for both to bolster their own perceptions of how they can analyze and interpret the data in original ways by fostering a research environment comprised of socially supportive cues (Tierney & Farmer, 2002).

Affective: Innovation Through Positive Feeling

Even those who possess the greatest passion for their work can fall prey to feelings of frustration, fear, or anxiety, particularly during the data analysis and interpretation phase of research. While one may begin a research project bright-eyed and enthusiastic about the promise of making a significant contribution to the field, such sentiments may begin to linger and even take a turn for the worse while pouring over reams of data. Questions such as, "Is this work even going to matter to others?" or "Is this data revealing anything new and interesting?" can quickly escalate into a downward emotional spiral of self-doubt. In addition to the personal discomfort experienced as a result of such feelings, the potential for the research to make a significant impact may also be at risk.

Here is where collaborations—in particular, high-quality collaborations—have the power to help guide researchers through the data analysis process. High-quality collaborations can serve as a buffer to negative emotions and also increase the meaning found in the work itself by serving as a means of social support (Cohen & Wills, 1985; Wrzesniewski, Dutton, & Debebe, 2003). Further, positive social interactions can create positive affective experiences for researchers, including broader state positive affect, as well as momentary discrete emotions including pride, happiness, and joy (Elfenbein, 2007). These positive affective experiences are not only pleasant for the researcher but can also foster the creation of interesting and meaningful research insights. According to Fredrickson's (2001) broaden and build theory, positive affective experiences motivate individuals to engage with the social environment, produce greater intellectual resources, and generate acceptance of a wider range of thoughts and ideas. In contrast to the impulse to escape when faced with negative feelings, positive emotions can trigger an urge to explore (Fredrickson, 2001, 2004). Thus, researchers involved in high-quality collaborations may be more attune to social cues, open to new ways to interpret the data, or make atypical connections (Schilling & Green, 2011) in an effort to make sense of the data.

Returning to our example of the faculty–student collaboration, the benefits of positive affective experiences do not just flow from professor to student. Rather, students can also bring a sense of excitement and enthusiasm to the research project that encourages professors to reconsider their routines and to explore the data in a new manner. For example, positive emotional experiences originating from students' excitement may spark a more discovery-oriented approach to the data analysis, thus enabling greater openness to serendipitous moments when traveling between the data and theory (Charmaz, 2006; Glaser & Strauss, 1967). Additionally, a creative mindset fuelled by positive affect and emotions is likely valuable when engaging in analytical memoing as it involves the interplay of data and theory, making connections between the two while also developing rich, original insight into how the data informs our understanding of the phenomenon beyond extant theory (Charmaz, 2006; Locke, 2001).

Physiological: Innovation Through Physical Energy

In addition to *feeling* more positive from working with others, individuals may be strengthened physiologically as a result of working with others. As noted, researchers in the analysis and interpretation phase simultaneously code data, make sense of the emergent codes, grapple with the possibility of additional rounds of data collection, and strive to understand how the emergent theory fits into existing literature. In short, this phase of a project is complex, possibly overwhelming, and likely energy depleting. That is why scholars' physical energy—the energy that "enables individuals to

335

move, to do, and to think" (Quinn, Spreitzer, & Lam, 2012, p. 341)—can be a particularly valuable and critical resource during analysis and interpretation.

Though physical energy may wane as scholars dive deeper and deeper into analysis and interpretation, a high-quality research collaboration has the potential to buttress energy. As Dutton and Heaphy (2003) noted, high-quality connections are "life-giving," they provide "vital nutrients," and have been proven to positively influence the amount of effort individuals allocate to an activity (Baker, Cross, & Wooten, 2003; Quinn & Dutton, 2005). Indeed, research has shown that individuals in high-quality relationships experience an increase in physical energy or the ability to do work (Quinn, 2007; Quinn, Spreitzer, & Lam, 2012). Positive social interactions can provide researchers with a stronger physiological base from which they can draw resources and become more highly engaged in their work (Heaphy & Dutton, 2008). For instance, as professor and student make sense of large amounts of data together, the physical resources they garner from the subjective experience of the connection (i.e., feelings of vitality and aliveness, positive regard, and mutuality; Dutton & Heaphy, 2003) may be applied to making sense of the phenomenon and data in novel ways. It is easy to imagine a virtuous cycle of positive physical energy that emerges from an otherwise depleting scenario when one member of the team (e.g., the advisor) supports the other member (e.g., the student) when he/she is "stuck" in the data (cf. Lilius, 2012).

An Additional Illustration: The Academic–Practitioner Collaboration

While we have utilized the example of professor–student collaborations to illustrate our ideas above, perhaps a more novel (and increasingly more relevant) example is found in collaborations between academics and practitioners. This form of collaboration is seen as an effective way to answer calls for increasing the relevance of our research for those practicing management (cf. Bartunek, 2007; Gulati, 2007; Porter, 2008; Rynes, Bartunek & Daft, 2001). Despite its popularity in discussion, however, there are few examples of academic–practitioner (A-P) research (also referred to as *insider/outsider collaborations;* see Bartunek & Louis, 1996) published in our top journals (see Amabile et al., 2001, and Gioia, Price, Hamilton, & Thomas, 2010, as notable exceptions). Nonetheless, A-P research is trending upward, and we believe this is due to the benefits available to both sides.

By bringing together a team with diverse backgrounds and schemas (in particular at least one member of the partnership is a practitioner and one a scholar), data analysis and interpretation can be taken to new levels as team members interact and share their varied thoughts on what is happening and why. A-P collaborations can provide an additional basis for increased capacity to "generate more heterogeneous thought trials—to cover more interpretive as well as observational bases" (Louis & Bartunek, 1992, p. 103). This unique partnership benefits the academic side by increasing the likelihood of developing novel, ground-breaking theoretical insights rooted in the phenomenon of interest that can help advance scholarly understanding of how it is lived in organizations (Bansal & Corley, 2011; Corley & Gioia, 2011). Likewise, on the practitioner side, developing novel practice insights increases the likelihood that the research will serve as the basis for effective organizational change (Bartunek & Louis, 1996). Additionally, the trustworthiness of the findings (Lincoln & Guba, 1985) is enhanced as "such heterogeneity increases the soundness and richness of interpretations and conceptual analysis" (Thomas, Blacksmith, & Reno, 2000, p. 827) for both sides as the practitioner can ensure that the emerging theory is grounded in the actual participants of the phenomenon and the scholar can ensure the phenomenon's theoretical basis.

The cognitive bases of these benefits (e.g., improved sensemaking via increased capacity to capture and process more diverse cues) are well complemented by the affective and physiological pathways discussed previously. But what makes A-P collaborations unique is the way in which the collaboration can produce emotional and physiological benefits. Consider that as field researchers (even experienced ones), one of the most anxious times for us is when we first enter a new organization, most likely as an outsider (Cunliffe & Karaunanayake, 2013; Sherif, 2001) and often with only a very basic understanding of the context (and perhaps of the phenomenon, too). Those initial observations, interviews, and interpretations are often filled with doubt and uncertainty (and the accompanying physiological manifestations of these feelings) about what we are seeing (and should be seeing) and how we are (or should be) interacting with informants. And just as that initial anxiety begins to subside, new anxieties arise about what we are seeing and how well it matches with what we might expect (from theory or our own preconceptions). Equally, the anxiety of having an outsider "snooping around" is one of the drawbacks of field research for practitioners and often results in decreased productivity and increased suspicions of management. A-P collaborations help minimize these anxieties by (a) affording academics not only improved access to the organization, but also prior knowledge of the context and the sociopolitical climate (thus facilitating the initial period of interpretation) and (b) providing practitioners the basis for legitimately bringing in outsiders and provoking less concern among other insiders, thus establishing a more positive environment for joint interpretation to occur. Minimizing anxiety in these ways allows for enhanced sensemaking to occur earlier and with fewer "start-up costs" than non-A-P collaborative efforts, thus fostering a more engaged analysis process that can uncover novel and helpful insights into the phenomenon.

Overall, the positive social connection associated with a high-quality collaboration can be leveraged as a resource that not only buffers against the demands of inductive field research, but also generates stronger engagement in the team's work. These additional resources can then strengthen the individual and collective sensemaking processes that typify the data analysis and interpretation phase of qualitative research.

Discussion

In considering the potential value of collaborations, it is especially surprising that there exists a dearth of theoretical and empirical insight into our own scholarly experiences. We believe a primary contribution of this chapter lies in bringing awareness to how working together on inductive, qualitative research changes the nature of making sense of and applying meaning to the data (see Table 31.1 for published examples). We shed light on this subject by focusing on high-quality collaborations and highlighting how a research partnership creates value through three distinct pathways (i.e., cognitive, affective, and physiological). Though each collaboration we discussed (i.e., professor–student and academic–practitioner) brings with it unique benefits, we posit that high-quality collaborations can lead to an increased ability to look at data from different perspectives, a greater sense of creative self-efficacy, a surge of positive affect, and an increase of physical energy amongst the collaborators.

While drawing from a sensemaking perspective, this chapter also contributes back to the sensemaking literature. Though much is known about how individuals and collectives make sense of the social world (see Maitlis & Christenson, 2014), far less is understood about how the process of sensemaking can be enhanced by the context in which sensemaking occurs. We believe that collaborative data analysis and interpretation represents a unique situation that bridges the social cognition and social construction approaches to sensemaking. In the case of a sole author who analyzes and interprets the data on his/her own, collective meaning making likely begins after the author has already ascribed meaning to the data, either in informal conversations with others or in the review process. In contrast, when multiple researchers make sense of the data concurrently, sensemaking is likely to occur both intra- and interindividually. Consequently, the ascription of meaning to the data is more likely to be co-authored, or an individual's interpretations are more likely to be malleable, so that the final construal is less reflective of one individual's interpretation of the data and more reflective of the collective's. And as our pathways discussed previously illustrate, the benefits of connecting with others throughout the entirety of the inductive research process may ultimately lead to more innovative and interesting contributions to our collective knowledge.

Table 31.1 Examples of Collaboration in Qualitative Research Methods

Reference	Research Context	Example of How Innovation Was Used	Outcomes / Results of Innovation
Amabile, Patterson, Mueller, Wojcik, Odomirok, Marsh, & Kramer (2001)	Innovation Research Group, an A-P team examining long-term corporate projects requiring creativity	To gain access to an A-P team during its collaborations and capture (in real time) how the collaboration worked	Deep insight into how A-P teams work and the value of combining academic and practitioner perspectives
Cunliffe, & Karaunanayake (2013)	Sri Lankan tea plantation	To gain legitimacy as an outsider and thus collect data not accessible to other researchers	Unique narratives and perspectives from inside an organizational context otherwise inaccessible to research
Gioia, Price, Hamilton, & Thomas (2010)	Identity formation at College of Interdisciplinary Technology Studies	To gain access to parts of the organization and data sources not available to outsiders	Unique perspective on organizational history from founder; deeper insight into organizational processes
Harrison & Rouse (2014)	Modern dance groups	Student and faculty member were able to collectively gather and analyze a larger quantity of data than the faculty originally planned	Detailed insights into the micro and macro processes of elastic coordination in creative work
Stigliani & Ravasi (2012)	Continuum—an internationaldesign consulting firm	The student was able to spend large amounts of ethnographic time in the research context (providing the faculty member access to previously unavailable data) and the faculty was able to mentor the student on how to analyze the data effectively	Inimitable insights into prospective sensemaking that would not have been possible without the student's access to the data and the faculty's knowledge and experience analyzing sensemaking data

Beyond the theoretical contributions of our arguments, however, lie the contributions to practice in how we accomplish our craft (Sennett, 2008). Inductive research is challenging (Charmaz, 2006), yet the rewards for both our field and individual scholars can be tremendous. At the foundation of both those challenges and rewards lies the process of encountering the unknown—or at least the "not well understood"—intimately engaging with it through intense data collection and methodically developing meaning as to what is happening, how it is happening, and (perhaps most importantly) why it is happening. As we have described, engaging in this process with others has the potential not only to enhance the end product (i.e., emergent understanding of the phenomenon) but also to enrich us as scholars as we socially accomplish that practice. Our hope is that this chapter not only provides the foundation for realizing that enrichment, but spurs more qualitative scholars to consider engaging in some of the collaborations we have detailed above. If so, we believe that innovativeness (in both method and theoretical insight) will continue to flourish amongst qualitative researchers for the betterment of both our scholarly community and the communities we study.

References

Amabile, T.M., Conti, R., Coon, H., Lazenby, J., & Herron, M. (1996). Assessing the work environment for creativity. *Academy of Management Journal, 39*, 1154–1184.

Amabile, T., & Gryskiewicz, S.S. (1987). *Creativity in the R&D laboratory*. Greensboro, NC: Center for Creative Leadership.

Amabile, T.M., Patterson, C., Mueller, J., Wojcik, T., Odomirok, P.W., Marsh, M., & Kramer, S.J. (2001). Academic-practitioner collaboration in management research: A case of cross-profession collaboration. *Academy of Management Journal, 44*, 418–431.

Bahrami, B., Olsen, K., Latham, P.E., Roepstorff, A., Rees, G., & Frith, C.D. (2010). Optimally interacting minds. *Science, 329*, 1081–1085.

Baker, W., Cross, R., & Wooten, M. (2003). Positive organizational network analysis and energizing relationships. In K. Cameron & J. Dutton (Eds.), *Positive organizational scholarship: Foundations of a new discipline* (pp. 328–342). San Francisco, CA: Berrett-Koehler Publishers.

Bansal, P., & Corley, K. G. (2011). From the editors—The coming of age for qualitative research: Embracing the diversity of qualitative methods. *Academy of Management Journal, 54*, 233–237.

Barley, S.R. (1990). Images of imaging: Notes on doing longitudinal field work. *Organization Science, 1*, 220–247.

Bartunek, J. M. (2007). Academic-practitioner collaboration need not require joint or relevant research: Toward a relational scholarship of integration. *Academy of Management Journal, 50*, 1323–1333.

Bartunek, J. M., & Louis, M. R. (1996). *Insider/outsider team research*. Thousand Oaks, CA: Sage.

Cassell, C., Bishop, V., Symon, G., Johnson, P., & Buehring, A. (2009). Learning to be a qualitative management researcher. *Management Learning, 40*, 513–533.

Charmaz, K. (2006). *Constructing grounded theory: A practical guide through qualitative analysis*. London, England: Sage.

Cohen, S., & Wills, T.A. (1985). Stress, social support, and the buffering hypothesis. *Psychological Bulletin, 98*, 310–357.

Corley, K.G., & Gioia, D.A. (2011). Building theory about theory building: What constitutes a theoretical contribution? *Academy of Management Review, 36*, 12–32.

Cunliffe, A. L., & Karaunanayake, G. (2013). Working within hyphen-spaces in ethnographic research: Implications for research identities and practice. *Organizational Research Methods, 16*, 364–392.

Dutton, J.E., & Dukerich, J.M. (2006). The relational foundation of research: An underappreciated dimension of interesting research. *Academy of Management Journal, 49*, 21–26.

Dutton, J.E., & Heaphy, E.D. (2003). The power of high-quality connections. In K. Cameron, J. Dutton, & E. Quinn (Eds.), *Positive organizational scholarship: Foundations of a new discipline* (pp. 263–278). San Francisco, CA: Berrett-Koehler Publishers.

Elfenbein, H.A. (2007). Emotion in organizations. *Academy of Management Annals, 1*, 315–386.

Fiske, S.T., & Taylor, S.E. (1984). *Social cognition*. New York, NY: Random House.

Fredrickson, B.L. (2001). The role of positive emotions in positive psychology: The broaden-and-build theory of positive emotions. *American Psychologist, 56*, 218–226.

Fredrickson, B.L. (2004). The broaden-and-build theory of positive emotions. *Philosophical Transactions of the Royal Society of London. Series B, Biological Sciences, 359*, 1367–1377.

Gephart, R.P. (1993). The textual approach: Risk and blame in disaster sensemaking. *Academy of Management Journal, 36*, 1465–1514.

Gioia, D.A., Price, K.N., Hamilton, A.L., & Thomas, J.B. (2010). Forging an identity: An insider-outsider study of processes involved in the formation of organizational identity. *Administrative Science Quarterly*, 55, 1–46.

Glaser, B., & Strauss, A. (1967). *The discovery of grounded theory: Strategies for qualitative research*. Chicago, IL: Aldine.

Gulati, R. (2007). Tent poles, tribalism, and boundary spanning: The rigor–relevance debate in management research. *Academy of Management Journal*, 50, 775–782.

Hackman, J.R. (2011). *Collaborative intelligence: Using teams to solve hard problems*. San Francisco, CA: Berrett-Koehler Publishers.

Harrison, S. H., & Rouse, E. D. (2014). Let's Dance! Elastic coordination in creative group work: A qualitative study of modern dancers. *Academy of Management Journal, 57*(5), 1256–1283.

Heaphy, E.D., & Dutton, J.E. (2008). Positive social interactions and the human body at work: Linking organizations and physiology. *Academy of Management Review, 33*, 137–162.

Jackson, S.E., & Joshi, A. (2010). Work team diversity. In S. Zedeck (Ed.), *APA handbook of industrial and organizational psychology* (pp. 651–686). Washington, DC: American Psychological Association.

Johnson, B. (2007). Student-faculty mentorship outcomes. In T. Allen & L. Eby (Eds.), *The Blackwell handbook of mentoring: A multiple perspectives approach* (pp. 189–210). Malden, MA: Blackwell.

Katz, J.S., & Martin, B.R. (1997). What is research collaboration? *Research Policy, 26*, 1–18.

Kramer, R.M., & Martin, J. (1996). Transitions and turning points in faculty-student research relationships. In P. Frost & S. Taylor (Eds.), *Rhythms of academic life* (pp. 165–180). Thousand Oaks, CA: Sage.

Lilius, J.M. (2012). Recovery at work: Understanding the restorative side of "depleting" client interactions. *Academy of Management Review, 37,* 569–588.

Lincoln, Y.S., & Guba, E.G. (1985). *Naturalistic Inquiry.* Newbury Park, CA: Sage.

Locke, K. (2001). *Grounded theory in management research.* Thousand Oaks, CA: Sage.

Lord, R.G., & Foti, R.J. (1986). Schema theories, information processing, and organizational behavior. In H.P. Sims & D.A. Gioia (Eds.), *The thinking organization* (pp. 20–49). San Francisco, CA: Jossey-Bass.

Louis, M.R., & Bartunek, J.M. (1992). Insider/outsider research teams: Collaboration across diverse perspectives. *Journal of Management Inquiry, 1,* 101–110.

Maitlis, S., & Christianson, M. (2014). Sensemaking in organizations: Taking stock and moving forward. *The academy of management annals, 8,* 57–125.

Miller, C.C., Burke, L.M., & Glick, W.H. (1998). Cognitive diversity among upper-echelon executives: Implications for strategic decision processes. *Strategic Management Journal, 19,* 39–58.

Milliken, F.J., Bartel, C.A., & Kurtzberg, T.R. (2003). Diversity and creativity in work groups: A dynamic perspective on the affective and cognitive processes that link diversity and performance. In P. Paulus & B. Nijstad (Eds.), *Group creativity: Innovation through collaboration* (pp. 32–62). New York, NY: Oxford University Press.

Porter, L.W. (2008). Organizational psychology: A look backward, outward, and forward. *Journal of Organizational Behavior, 29,* 519–526.

Quinn, R.W. (2007). Energizing others in work connections. In J. Dutton & B.R. Ragins (Eds.), *Exploring positive relationships at work: Building a theoretical and research foundation* (pp. 73–90). Mahwah, NJ: Lawrence Erlbaum.

Quinn, R.W., & Dutton, J.E. (2005). Coordination as energy-in-conversation. *Academy of Management Review, 30,* 36–57.

Quinn, R.W., Spreitzer, G.M., & Lam, C.F. (2012). Building a sustainable model of human energy in organizations: Exploring the critical role of resources. *The Academy of Management Annals, 6,* 337–396.

Rynes, S. L., Bartunek, J. M., & Daft, R. L. (2001). Across the great divide: Knowledge creation and transfer between practitioners and academics. *Academy of Management Journal, 44,* 340–355.

Schilling, M.A., & Green, E. (2011). Recombinant search and breakthrough idea generation: An analysis of high impact papers in the social sciences. *Research Policy, 40,* 1321–1331.

Sennett, R. (2008). *The craftsman.* New Haven, CT: Yale University Press.

Sherif, B. (2001). The ambiguity of boundaries in the fieldwork experience: Establishing rapport and negotiating insider/outsider status. *Qualitative Inquiry, 7,* 436–447.

Sonenshein, S. (2006). Crafting social issues at work. *Academy of Management Journal, 49,* 1158–1172.

Starbuck, W.H., & Milliken, F.J. (1988). Executives' perceptual filters: What they notice and how they make sense. In D. C. Hambrick (Ed.), *The executive effect: Concepts and methods for studying top managers* (pp. 35–65). Greenwich, CT: JAI Press.

Stephens, J., Heaphy, E., & Dutton, J.E. (2011). High quality connections. In K. Cameron & G. Spreitzer (Eds.), *Oxford handbook of positive organizational scholarship* (pp. 385–399). New York, NY: Oxford University Press.

Stigliani, I., & Ravasi, D. (2012). Organizing thoughts and connecting brains: Material practices and the transition from individual to group-level prospective sensemaking. *Academy of Management Journal, 55,* 1232–1259.

Taylor, J.R., & Robichaud, D. (2004). Finding the organization in the communication: Discourse as action and sensemaking. *Organization, 11,* 395–413.

Thomas, J.B., Clark, S.M., & Gioia, D.A. (1993). Strategic sensemaking and organizational performance: Linkages among scanning, interpretation, action, and outcomes. *Academy of Management Journal, 36,* 239–270.

Thomas, M. D., Blacksmith, J., & Reno, J. (2000). Utilizing insider-outsider research teams in qualitative research. *Qualitative Health Research,* 10, 819–828.

Tierney, P., & Farmer, S.M. (2002). Creative self-efficacy: Its potential antecedents and relationship to creative performance. *Academy of Management Journal, 45,* 1137–1148.

Tracy, S.J. (2010). Qualitative quality: Eight "big-tent" criteria for excellent qualitative research. *Qualitative Inquiry, 16,* 837–851.

Wasser, J.D., & Bresler, L. (1996). Working in the interpretive zone: Conceptualizing collaboration in qualitative research teams. *Educational researcher, 25,* 5–15.

Weick, K.E. (1995). *Sensemaking in organizations.* London, England: Sage.

Woodman, R.W., Sawyer, J.E., & Griffin, R.W. (1993). Toward a theory of organizational creativity. *Academy of Management Review, 18,* 293–321.

Wrzesniewski, A., Dutton, J.E., & Debebe, G. (2003). Interpersonal sensemaking and the meaning of work. *Research in Organizational Behavior, 25,* 93–135.

Yin, R.K. (2014). *Case study research: Design and methods* (5th ed.). Thousand Oaks, CA: Sage.

32

Multilevel Discourse Analysis

A Structured Approach to Analyzing Longitudinal Data

Steven J. Kahl and Stine Grodal

Introduction

In order to address the growing theoretical interest in temporally unfolding organizational phenomena like the emergence of new organizational forms, the practice and process of organizing, formation of occupational identities, and organizational change, we need better methods for studying longitudinal data. Qualitative analysis of organizational phenomena has historically relied on analysis of interviews and ethnographic observations. Due to the necessity of the researcher to be present during the time of data collection, the temporal periods studied using these methods are restricted.

Recently, a theoretical push to understand how events unfold over time, coupled with the availability of large online repositories of texts and images, has made qualitative analysis of longitudinal data more prevalent (Ventresca and Mohr, 2002). These data sources include documents that people in and around organizations produce as part of their tasks and communication, such as meeting notes, email exchanges, formalized reports, interviews, and verbal exchanges.

Collectively, data from interviews, ethnographic observations, and archival data is called *discourse*. Discourse is part of the social fabric within and around organizations in which individuals sense-make, organizations act, processes evolve, concepts develop, and identities form. Discourse can be produced with intervention by the researcher (as in interviews and ethnographic observations) or without such intervention (as in archival research). The primary unit of analysis for analyzing discourse is texts. Within discourse analysis, the term *texts* is used broadly to refer "not just to written transcriptions but to any kind of symbolic expression requiring a physical medium and permitting of permanent storage" like objects and images (Phillip, Lawrence, and Hardy, 2004, p. 636).

However, analyzing large quantities of longitudinal data sources challenges our existing methods regarding both data selection and data analysis. First, studying longitudinal data often necessitates drawing on diverse data sources, which challenges our traditional approaches to data analysis that have tended to rely on linguistic texts only. Second, when analyzing texts longitudinally, it becomes important not just to understand the meaning of the text itself, but also the temporal relationship among texts. For example, Heracleous and Barrett (2001) analyze the relationship between different enthymemes (that is arguments in use) in order to study how the implementation of a new trading platform in the London Insurance Market enabled organizational change. Third, because the institutional context in which texts are produced is likely to change over time, it also becomes more pertinent to have a theory that is able to capture such contextual changes. Last, when tracking discourse over time we need a method that allows us to record even subtle changes in meaning between texts.

To measure changes in meaning over time requires a structured approach to coding texts and images. This is a challenge because traditionally textual coding has used interpretive approaches that lack precision (Franzosi, 2010). Indeed, if we are not able to address these challenges, the analysis that we engage in is likely to be distorted because it does not account for the temporal patterns that are at the core of conducting longitudinal analysis.

In this chapter, we argue that to address the mentioned challenges, we need a structured contextualized approach to analyzing longitudinal data. In particular, we advocate for the use of multilevel discourse analysis, which decomposes text into its semantic relationship and uncovers textual relationships.[1] At its core, discourse analysis

> involves analysis of collections of texts, the ways they are made meaningful through their links to other texts, the ways in which they draw on different discourses, how and to whom they are disseminated, the methods of their production, and the manner in which they are received and consumed. (Phillips, Lawrence, and Hardy, 2004, p. 636)

Discourse analysis treats text as a communicative act such that language does not just express what people say, but also helps create their understandings, beliefs, and processes (Phillips and Hardy, 2002; Phillips and Oswick, 2012). Discourse scholars use the term *texts* broadly as communicative expressions that come in different forms, including written documents, verbal expressions, visual representation, and physical design (Hargadon and Douglas, 2001; Phillips and Hardy, 2002).

The first (and often challenging) step in doing multilevel discourse analysis of longitudinal data is to generate a nonbiased sample. To develop such a sample, we advocate using the historical method (see Kipping, Wadhwani, and Bucheli, 2014) to select texts, organize them temporally, and develop an initial understanding of the domain area. We call this first step *historical reconstruction*. The next steps include a structured contextualized approach to analyze the texts in the sample. We build upon Fairclough (1992; 1995) and argue that texts ought to be analyzed at three different levels: intratextual, intertextual, and contextual. At the *intratextual level*, researchers code both the content and linguistic structure of the text, such as not only the noun phrases of the text, but also linguistic structures like semantic clauses (subject/verb/object combinations) and sentence types. For example, Bingham and Kahl (2013) coded noun/verb combinations within insurance texts to analyze the evolution of different analogies used for the computer. To bring structure to the intratextual coding—which helps in detailed tracking of meaning over time in longitudinal data—we build upon Franzosi (2010) and advocate a coding process based upon grammatical and semantic rules. This approach contrasts to traditional coding methods, which rely on interpretive techniques, such as grounded theory (see Glaser and Strauss, 1967).

Whereas the intratextual level of analysis focuses on the language used within the text, the *intertextual level* addresses the purpose and process of producing the text, the relationship between texts, as well as the audiences' interpretations and understandings of the text. This analysis examines how the languages of producers and audiences mutually react to each other and the context of the exchange that influences its production and reception (Fairclough, 1992). Intertextual relations include both the content that links texts together and how those relations between texts are created. The intertextual level stresses the importance of understanding the social processes that created these linguistic expressions in the first place by capturing the production and consumption of texts. These processes can be traced through the direct dialogue or references between texts.

Last, discourse itself takes place within a broader institutional and cultural context that may extend beyond the organization. The *contextual level*, therefore, investigates how discourse is embedded within the institutional and social practices. Part of this analysis entails measuring the uptake of conventional norms within the focal discourse (see Khaire and Wadhwani, 2010). This level entails understanding the significance of the discourse in terms of the patterns of exchange within the broader institutional and cultural context.

Instead of coding all levels simultaneously (see Alvesson and Karreman, 2000; Phillips and Oswick, 2012), we propose to follow Barry, Carroll, and Hansen (2006), who emphasize that each level should initially be coded separately and then be integrated as a last step in the analysis, which we call *iteration and theory development*. This allows researchers to use the different levels to triangulate between the data, identify inconsistencies and use the process to link the analysis back to the original theoretical question.

Figure 32.1 provides an overview of the five steps in what we term *multilevel discourse analysis*: (1) historical reconstruction; (2) intratextual analysis, (3) intertextual analysis, (4) contextual analysis, and (5) iteration and theory development (see Kahl and Grodal, forthcoming) for more detail). We elaborate each step next.

Step 1: Historical Reconstruction

We propose that the first step in the multilevel discourse analysis should use historical methods to reconstruct the broader discourse in which the phenomenon of interest exists (see Wodak, 2001; Khaire and Wadhwani, 2010; and Kipping, Wadhwani, and Bucheli, 2014, for similar approaches). Because many organizational phenomena take place in heterogeneous environments, historical reconstruction facilitates capturing texts from different participants, organizing them in the proper temporal order, and addresses potential biases.

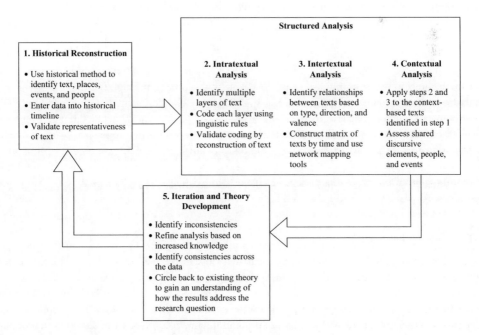

Figure 32.1 The Five Steps in Multilevel Discourse Analysis

Based on the researcher's general theoretical question, they should use the historical method to identify texts, who produced them, the location of production and consumption, as well as the contemporaneous cultural themes that were occurring at the time that the texts were produced. These nontextual factors help develop the broader context in which each text is embedded. Moreover, the historical method yields a more comprehensive data set because it does not privilege a single point of view. For example, if a report has several authors, the historical method encourages tracing prior texts from each of the authors as a means to understand the focal text. Last, the historical method guards against potential sample bias by questioning whether the gathered text is representative (Golder, 2000). That is not to say that unique texts are not included in the sample, but this method encourages identifying other texts to corroborate the focal text. In fact, validating representativeness helps identify those texts and points of view that are less prevalent and developed.

This process culminates with a historical timeline of the texts, people involved, events, and locations. Finally, as a last element in historical reconstruction, researchers should read through the texts as they unfolded. This open-ended reading helps develop a sense of how the discourse progressed over time, as well as identify aspects of the discourse that warrant more structured coding. This last part of structural coding, thus, bears resemblance to the "open coding" used in grounded theory building (see Glaser and Strauss, 1967).

Steps 2 Through 4: Structured Analyses at Multiple Levels

Whereas historical reconstruction focuses on organizing the data by participants, audiences, time, and interactions, structured analysis focuses on the detailed and systematic coding of the collected texts. The goal of these analyses is thus to track the phenomena of interest over time with a great degree of precision.

A general issue identified with textual coding is to systematically capture the same kind of data across different modes of text. For example, data may be comprised of an image as well as written text (see Chapter 22 in this volume regarding the use of visual data). Because an adequate identification of the phenomena of interest necessitates understanding the relation between different forms of text, the researcher must take care in making sure that images and text are coded in such a way that allows comparability. Consider an image of the organization chart in a text. We may treat this image holistically and code its broad image. Features of the image—in this case reporting relationships—can be captured at different levels of coding. Finally, structured analysis requires detailed analysis of texts, which can be cumbersome; however, computers can help automate this process through the use of sophisticated linguistic analysis algorithms (Phillips and Hardy, 2002). For example, Kennedy, Chok, and Liu (2012) use automated linguistic analysis to track the evolution of what it means to be "green" over time. The advantage of structured analysis of texts at the multiple levels is three-fold: (1) to generate tables, graphs, and other visuals, which can help communicate and illustrate the phenomena of interest to the reader; (2) accountability in the form of a precise tool to understand the temporal unfolding; and (3) the generation of new insights and challenges to existing understandings. As we detail below, structured analysis requires coding at each intratextual, intertextual, and contextual level of analysis.

Step 2: Intratextual Analysis

At the intratextual level, researchers code each text's discursive elements (e.g., analogies, imperative sentences, or certain semantic relationships between nouns and verbs) in a systematic way. Currently, researchers have used a wide variety of discursive approaches to code text (Van Dijk, 1997), including rhetoric (Heracleous, 2006; Sillince, Jarzabkowski, and Shaw, 2012; Suddaby and Greenwood, 2005), narrative analysis (Lounsbury and Glynn, 2001; Wry et al., 2011), hermeneutics (Heracleous, 2006; Khaire and Wadhwani, 2010; Phillips and Brown, 1993), and metaphorical analysis

(Bingham and Kahl, 2013; Etzion and Ferraro, 2010). Some studies combine discursive approaches, like Heracleous's (2006) combination of hermeneutics with rhetorical analysis. Other studies use more grounded theory approaches to broadly coding the content of text (Glaser and Strauss, 1967). One issue with selecting a specific discursive approach is that it only codes one element of the text's discursive structure. For example, while Bingham and Kahl's (2013) metaphorical analysis identified noun/verb combinations, it did not capture the text's rhetoric, such as the use of tropes or argument structures. However, many research questions often require using multiple textual analysis techniques. For example, studies of how an organization's identity evolves over time necessitate analyzing texts using multiple different discursive approaches because organizational members might use a variety of ways of expressing their views on the organization's identity whether in objects, images, or different discursive forms.

Another issue is that texts are comprised of different layers (e.g., clauses, sentences, paragraphs) and that these discursive elements occur at different layers within the text. For instance, think of a management journal article. It includes clauses, sentences, paragraphs, and sections. Argument structures often occur at higher levels of the text, which involve combinations of sentences and paragraphs, whereas others, such as metaphors, operate within sentence clauses. Therefore, a more systematic coding of the texts requires addressing how different discursive expressions occur at these multiple layers.

To address this problem, we advocate for a more flexible and structured coding approach based on grammatical and semantic coding. At the clause level, Franzosi (2010) suggests coding semantic triplets or, put more generally, the subject/verb/object combinations. For example, take the previous sentence. *Franzosi* is the subject; *suggests* and *put* are the verbs; and *coding semantic triplets* and *the subject/ verb/object combinations* are the objects. In addition, the researcher can code aspects of the triplet, such as the modality of the verb or its type (see Halliday, 1994, for one kind of classification of verbs), pronouns and their referents, and modifiers. At the sentence level, researchers can code its type, such as declarative versus imperative, as well as the complexity (clause combinations). At the paragraph level, the sequence of sentences and their relations, for example, the use of conjunctions such as *therefore* or *however* can be coded.

It is important to recognize the differences between this grammatical/semantic approach and the discursive approaches like rhetorical or hermeneutic analysis that are currently in use within organizational research. As Franzosi (2010) points out, starting with a particular discursive approach requires interpretation of the text on behalf on the researcher. In contrast, our structured approach requires an understanding of the grammatical and semantic rules. As such, it is much easier to validate coding procedures and minimize error. As an additional validation step, one should be able to reconstruct higher level textual layers based on the coding of the lower layers; for example, the coding of clauses at a lower level can be recombined to identify the argument structure at a higher level. In addition, this coding approach captures the core semantic structure of the texts and is flexible enough to provide data for the more specific discursive approaches. For example, coding the semantic relations of a sentence's core clauses also isolates words and phrases, which could be used in hermeneutical analysis. Or, the coding pronouns, types of verbs, their modality, types of sentences, and their sequence can all be used in rhetorical analysis. While we recognize that coding schemes cannot be exhaustive and may vary depending upon the research question, we believe that coding texts following grammatical rules and semantic relations provides a more structured way to code the texts that is also more flexible for analysis.

Step 3: Intertextual Analysis

As mentioned earlier, one of the core challenges when engaging in longitudinal analysis is to understand how different texts are related in their production and consumption. Intertextual analysis involves capturing these relations between texts. Texts can related to each other in at least three ways: (1) conceptually, (2) personally, or (3) spatially.

Analyzing conceptual relations entails identifying whether texts share the same language and structure (Khaire and Wadhwani, 2010). These relations can be studied by comparing the intratextual coding of each text and identifying the occurrence of similar themes across texts. However, links between texts can also be created because the same people produced or consumed them. For example, if two texts are authored by the same person, these two texts will have an intertextual tie. Texts can also be linked because they were produced in the same location. For example, several texts might be produced at the same team meeting, so these texts have a spatial link. Moreover, since we are measuring the discourse over time, the directionality of relationships is important. Finally, not all texts agree with each other; some may respond negatively or even reject the points of previously made texts. Therefore, it is also important to capture the valence of the relationship.

We have found that network-mapping tools greatly facilitate developing and analyzing the intertextual relations. This requires formulating what constitutes a tie between texts and building out the relational matrix that assists in analyzing the structure and relations between the texts.

Step 4: Contextual Analysis

Contextual analysis involves identifying the presences of broader cultural themes within the text. Empirically, this first requires identifying themes that are present in the broader culture at the time that the texts were produced. Sometimes this will entail collecting an additional data set from which these broader themes can be identified. Second, after cultural themes have been identified, intertextual analysis can be used to identify connections (conceptual, personal, or spatial) between the broader corpus of texts from the general culture and the corpus of texts of interest. Recognizing that cultural themes can enter through the mode of production and consumption of the texts aids in identifying dissident and less dominant viewpoints. Situating the texts of interest within the broader culture is important when conducting longitudinal analysis because the cultural context differs in various historical periods and thus exerts differentiated influences at different points in time.

Step 5: Iteration and Theory Development

The last step in multilevel discourse analysis is iteration and juxtaposition between the various steps in the analysis, which culminates in new theory development. An important part of this process is to identify inconsistencies in the coding at all the different levels. For example, by engaging in intertextual analysis, researchers might realize that they have overlooked some important texts during historical reconstruction. Or contextual analysis might reveal the importance of coding for other linguistic elements during the intratextual coding. This comparative process can also resolve coding errors because it helps triangulate coding between the different levels. Consequently, iteration between the different levels can reopen analysis at each of the steps and serve to resolve inconsistencies in the coding between the levels.

Another important part of iteration is to begin the process of theory development. During the iterative process, researchers should circle back to their original research question to use the empirical material to develop new insights about the phenomena in question. Iteration also serves to test alternative explanations to the emerging theory. Indeed, during steps 1 through 4, researchers ought to create alternative explanations to emerging interpretations that can be compared to other parts of the data. Consequently, the structured contextualized approach to multilevel discourse analysis is an iterative process meant to manage potential interpretive bias, deepen the analysis, and develop novel theory.

Application of Multilevel Discourse Analysis

Few current studies go through all of the five steps outlined in Figure 32.1. However, each of the studies listed in Table 32.1 incorporate some of the elements of the process and serve as examples

Table 32.1 Examples of Articles Using Elements of Multilevel Discourse Analysis

Reference	Research Context	How the Innovation Was Used	Outcomes/Results of Innovation
Barley (1986)	The introduction of CT scanners into two hospitals	Detailed structural coding of ethnographic data collected from June 1982 to June 1983	Ability to track the interaction between structure and agency over time
Bingham & Kahl (2013)	The emergence of the computer; used archival historical data	Tracked the emergence of the schema for the computer from 1945–1975	Ability to identify the specific mechanisms through which the schema emerges over time
Khaire & Wadhwani (2010)	Creating a market for modern Indian art	Used discourse analysis to track the changing meaning of modern Indian art from 1995 to 2007	Allowed the authors to compare the relationship between the creation of meaning around modern Indian art and the evaluation of this work
Navis & Glynn (2010)	The emerging satellite radio industry	Tracked the change in reference categories from mid-1990s to 2005	Allowed the authors to identify a shift during industry emergence from focusing on legitimating the category to differentiating among competitors
Dunn & Jones (2010)	Medical education	Used a structured approach to identify changes in the care and science logic from 1910–2005	Authors were able to associate changes in the care and science logic to the interest of different communities
Maguire & Hardy (2009)	Environmentalism and the use of DDT	Tracked discourses related to DDT from 1962–1972	Identified how participants engaged in defensive institutional work by authoring texts
Nelson & Irwin (forthcoming)	Librarians occupational identity and relationship to Internet search	Investigated the role of librarians' attitude toward search in their professional journal over the 22-year period 1980 through 2010	Show how occupational identity conditions the interpretations of technology, while also showing how these interpretations might change over time

of how multilevel discourse analysis might be carried out in practice. For example, Khaire and Wadhwani (2010) used historically informed processes to identify the distinct stages of the institutionalization of Indian art, hermeneutics to examine the influence of the context and broader themes on this process, and tracked the development of key concepts through intra- and intertextual analysis.

Conclusion

In this chapter, we highlight a structured contextualized approach to multilevel discourse analysis as a novel method for analyzing large volumes of temporally unfolding data. In particular, we suggest that such data need to be analyzed through a five-step process: (1) historical reconstruction, (2) intratextual analysis, (3) intertextual analysis, (4) contextual analysis, and (5) iteration and theory development. Multilevel discourse analysis improves upon existing research methods in its ability to both ground the analysis within an evolving context and systematically track the phenomenon of interest over time. In so doing, multilevel discourse analysis allows for the creation of graphs and visuals, which illustrates the progression of the phenomenon of interest over time. It also strikes a balance between the rich contextualization of traditional qualitative research and quantitative analysis.

Note

1 This method is based on work done in Kahl and Grodal forthcoming.

References

Alvesson M., Karreman D. 2000. Varieties of discourse: On the study of organizations through discourse analysis. *Human Relations* 53(9): 1125–1149.

Barley S.R. 1986. Technology as an occasion for structuring: Evidence from observations of CT scanners and the social order of radiology departments. *Administrative Science Quarterly*, 31(1): 78–108.

Barry D., Carroll B., Hansen H. 2006. To text or context? Endotextual, exotextual, and multi-textual approaches to narrative and discursive organizational studies. *Organization Studies*, 27(8): 1091–1110.

Bingham C.B., Kahl S.J. 2013. The process of schema emergence: Assimilation, deconstruction, unitization and the plurality of analogies. *Academy of Management Journal*, 56(1): 14–34.

Dunn M.B., Jones C. 2010. Institutional logics and institutional pluralism: The contestation of care and science logics in medical education 1967–2005. *Administrative Science Quarterly*, 55(1): 114–150.

Etzion D., Ferraro F. 2010. The role of analogy in the institutionalization of sustainability reporting. *Organization Science*, 21(5): 1092–1107.

Fairclough N. 1992. *Discourse and social change*. Cambridge: Polity.

Fairclough N. 1995. *Critical discourse analysis: The critical study of language*. London: Longman.

Franzosi R. 2010. *Quantitative narrative analysis*. Thousand Oaks, CA: Sage.

Glaser, B.G., & Strauss, A.L. 1967. *The discovery of grounded theory: Strategies for qualitative research*. Chicago: Aldine Publishing Company.

Golder P.N. 2000. Historical method in marketing research with new evidence on long-term market share stability. *Journal of Marketing Research*, 37(2): 156–172.

Halliday M.A.K. 1994. *An introduction to functional grammar*, 2nd ed. London: Edward Arnold.

Heracleous L. 2006. A tale of three discourses: The dominant, the strategic and the marginalized. *Journal of Management Studies*, 43(5): 1059–1087.

Heracleous L., Barrett M. 2001. Organizational change as discourse: Communicative actions and deep structures in the context of information technology Implementation. *Academy of Management Journal*, 44(4): 755–778.

Kahl S.J., Grodal, S. forthcoming. Discursive strategies and radical technological change: Multi-level discourse analysis of the early computer (1947–1958). *Strategic Management Journal*.

Kennedy M.T., Chok J.I., Liu J. 2012. What does it mean to be green? The emergence of new criteria for assessing corporate reputation. In *Oxford Handbook of Corporate Reputation*, Barnett M.L., Pollock T.G. (eds). New York: Oxford University Press.

Khaire M., Wadhwani R.D. 2010. Changing landscapes: The construction of meaning and value in a new market category—modern Indian art. *Academy of Management Journal*, 53(6): 1281–1304.

Kipping M.R., Wadhwani R.D., Bucheli M. 2014. Analyzing and interpreting sources: A basic methodology. In *Organizations in time: History, theory, and method*, Bucheli M., Wadhwani R.D. (eds). Oxford: Oxford University Press.

Lounsbury M, Glynn M.A. 2001. Cultural entrepreneurship: Stories, legitimacy, and the acquisition of resources. *Strategic Management Journal*, 22(6–7): 545–564.

Maguire S., Hardy C. 2009. Discourse and deinstitutionalization: The decline of DDT. *Academy of Management Journal*, 52(1): 148–178.

Navis C., Glynn M.A. 2010. How new market categories emerge: Temporal dynamics of legitimacy, identity, and entrepreneurship in satellite radio, 1990–2005. *Administrative Science Quarterly*, 55: 439–471.

Nelson A., Irwin J. forthcoming. "Defining what we do—all over again": Occupational identity, technological change, and the librarian/internet-search relationship. *Academy of Management Journal*.

Phillips N., Brown J.L. 1993. Analyzing communication in and around organizations: A critical hermeneutic approach. *Academy of Management Journal*, 36(6): 1547–1576.

Phillips N., Hardy C. 2002. *Discourse analysis*. Thousand Oaks, CA: Sage.

Phillips N., Lawrence T., Hardy C. 2004. Discourse and Institutions. *The Academy of Management Review*, 29(4): 635–652.

Phillips N., Oswick C. 2012. Organizational discourse: Domains, debates, and directions. The *Academy of Management Annals*, 6(1): 435–481.

Sillince J., Jarzabkowski P., Shaw D. 2012. Shaping strategic action through the rhetorical construction and exploitation of ambiguity. *Organization Science*, 23(3): 630–650.

Suddaby R., Greenwood R. 2005. Rhetorical strategies of legitimacy. *Administrative Science Quarterly*, 50: 35–67.

Van Dijk T.A. (Ed.). 1997. *Discourse as social interaction* Vol. II. London: Sage.

Ventresca M.J., Mohr J.W. 2002. Archival research methods. In *The Blackwell companion to organizations*, Baum J.A.C. (ed.). Oxford: Blackwell.

Wodak R. 2001. The discourse-historical approach. *Methods of Critical Discourse Analysis*, R. Wodak and M. Meyer, (eds). London: Sage.

Wry T., Lounsbury M., Glynn M.A. 2011. Legitimating nascent collective identities: Coordinating cultural entrepreneurship. *Organization Science*, 22(2): 449–463.

33

Tabula Geminus

A "Both/And" Approach to Coding and Theorizing

Glen E. Kreiner[1]

For newcomers to qualitative research, one of the more mysterious aspects of the work is the coding process. In teaching graduate students and faculty peers who are learning qualitative methods, I have found that they are typically at a loss as to *how* to code, even after reading the seminal texts in the field. I suspect that we as qualitative researchers haven't done a sufficient job in being transparent about this process. Whether this is because of the limited journal space for each article (which constrains a thorough explanation of coding procedures) or because we fail to notice and reveal our own taken-for-granted data analysis routines, the result is the same: Newcomers often experience a great deal of frustration, anxiety, and surprise when learning how to code. In this chapter I attempt to "part the curtain" a bit to explain *one* way of coding that I have used with 20 co-authors thus far on varying projects—a coding approach I call *tabula geminus*, or twin slate.

An element that perhaps sets this coding process apart from many others is that we *overtly* invite theory into the coding from the very beginning and continue to overtly draw on existing theory throughout the coding and theorizing process. (Another element is that we always have two sets of eyes scrutinize the data sources and overtly co-construct our interpretations, a point of elaboration later.) One of the early tenets of coding in traditional grounded theory and related abductive/inductive methods was that the researcher should not impose codes onto the data that are derived from existing theory, or at least refrain from doing so during the early phases of coding and analysis. Rather, *in vivo* and other codes that emanate more directly from the primary data sources were typically privileged. (Indeed, while discussing this chapter recently with a graduate of a well-known management Ph.D. program, she noted that her advisor had forbidden her from looking at the literature "for a whole year" while she collected and analyzed her dissertation data.) In this chapter, I explain why many of us have reconsidered this stance. Specifically, I advocate an overtly hybrid approach to coding in which two types of codes are used throughout the analysis—code labels emerging from the language of the data *and* code labels based on existing theory (hence the *tabula geminus* term). Note that both kinds of codes derive from what the researchers see in the data, but the labeling process allows us to draw both on the rich language of those we study as well as the rich vernacular of our academic peers. This "both/and" approach has proven to be tremendously valuable for my colleagues and me and has clear advantages compared to eschewing or delaying the use of codes based on existing theory: (a) it offers analytic flexibility, allowing the researcher to use two sources of information for labeling codes throughout analysis (phrases/ideas in the raw data and in extant theory); (b) it does not create artificial "blinders" for the researcher (who too often has been encouraged to suppress knowledge of theory); and (c) it results in fewer "silo-style" grounded theories that emerge as too disconnected from the broader research conversations.

Perhaps an apt metaphor for the *tabula geminus* approach is the relationship between the right and left sides of the human brain. While each side has its strengths (e.g., left side logic, linguistic, and literal; right side emotional, verbal, and experiential), the greatest potential is when both sides work in tandem and in routine interplay with one another. Commenting on how such a synergy might exist between theory and data, Van Maanen, Sorensen, and Mitchell (2007: 1146) noted:

> There is a back-and-forth character in which concepts, conjectures, and data are in continuous interplay. . . . Flexibility in the connections within and between the conceptual (ideas) and empirical (data) planes and allowing for a logic of discovery rather than only a logic of validation is seemingly a prerequisite if research is seen as a cognitive process. Yet rarely are such matters discussed—at least in print.

This chapter is but a small attempt to put these matters of the theory–data interplay into print.

The Role of Theory in the Coding Process

The struggle of how to balance attention to theory versus data is a longstanding one in qualitative research. For example, after Pratt (2008: 498) surveyed qualitative researchers in management, he found that one of the key tensions they experienced was "the need to both be embedded in and break from extant theory . . . qualitative research has to recognize and draw on existing theory while simultaneously distancing itself from it in an attempt to generate something new." Similarly, Suddaby (2006: 635) noted that "between a theory-laden view of the world and an unfettered empiricism is to . . . constantly remind yourself that you are only human and that what you observe is a function of both who you are and what you hope to see."

This theory versus data struggle manifests itself perhaps most strikingly during the coding process. Coding is at the heart of many qualitative methods and is an established method of "meaning condensation" (Lee, 1999: 89) in which the researcher identifies and keeps track of the most relevant themes or "codes" from the data. *Theory codes* use terminology from extant theory (such as "institutional logics" or "work-family conflict"), whereas *grounded codes* use terminology and ideas directly flowing from the data (e.g., emergent phenomena observed by the researcher, in vivo codes, words/phrases uttered in interviews or texts).

Many researchers, including early pioneers of grounded theory, have advocated a very deliberate delay in using codes that are based on existing theory (e.g., Charmaz, 2014; Gioia, Corley, & Hamilton, 2013; Glaser & Strauss, 1967; Strauss, 1987; Strauss & Corbin, 1998). The logic to this approach is that we, as researchers, should not contaminate the voices of our informants with the baggage of our theories. By deliberately delaying the use of theory codes, the goal is for ideas to be grounded in the data rather than come from the researchers. This delay was an admonition of classical grounded theory; early writers advocated delaying infusing the literature until after the new grounded theory had emerged (e.g., Glaser & Strauss, 1967). The stance was strongest in Glaser and Strauss' (1967) original work on grounded theory, and it was clearly reinforced by Glaser's later writings (1992). Glaser continued to argue that theory should be left out until the end of the analysis—when writing up the new grounded theory begins. Strauss and Corbin (1990, 2008) softened that stance in their writings, but still gave primacy to informant-based themes. Overall, all of these pioneers "advocated delaying comprehensive use of the literature until after the analytical story emerged and stabilized" (Lempert, 2007: 254). Their concern was valid—that new theories could be hindered if we clung too closely to existing ones. Their goal was "a delicate balance between using pre-existing, theoretical disciplinary knowledge as a sensitizing tool for comparative analysis and remaining unaffected, virtual research *tabulae rasae* or clean slates from the same existing theories" (Lempert, 2007: 254).

Some early grounded theory writers suggested the use of a "sensitizing construct" to orient the research in broad brushstrokes, but they discouraged theory-based codes during analysis. In the organizational sciences, the "Gioia methodology" (described thoroughly in Gioia, Corley, & Hamilton, 2013) also takes a similar stance by suggesting the use of a sensitizing construct but otherwise minimizing the role of existing theories until later stages of data analysis. Referring to the early phases of data analysis, they note that

> there is value in semi-ignorance or enforced ignorance of the literature, if you will. Up to this stage in the research, we make a point of not knowing the literature in great detail, because knowing the literature intimately too early puts blinders on and leads to prior hypothesis bias (confirmation bias). (21)

Hence, the Gioia and colleagues stance softens the initial admonitions from the pioneers of grounded theory by allowing incorporation of the literature during data analysis, but suggests doing so primarily during later phases.

Tabula Geminus—*An Abductive Approach to the Theory and Data Interplay*

The approach I use with my co-authors formally, consciously, and reflexively brings existing theory into the coding process, even into the earliest stages of data analysis. It is an approach that I have come to call—somewhat tongue-in-cheek, mind you—*tabula geminus*, or "twin slate." Geminus was a Greek philosopher, astronomer, and mathematician, and in today's parlance the term *geminus* refers to something that is a twin or pair. Notably, and appropriate to both his name and the analytic method described herein, Geminus separated the world of mathematics into two halves—the "mental" half of pure, theoretical mathematics and the "observable" half of applied, experiential mathematics. This bifurcation corresponds nicely to the longstanding separation between the role of theory and the role of data in qualitative methods. Our approach keeps both worlds in mind throughout the coding process. I use the *tabula geminus* term to conjure up the well-known concept in qualitative methods of *tabula rasa* (or blank slate) and yet to also connote that theory and data are each used throughout. Hence, rather than a blank slate, this approach perpetually draws on *two* slates—theory and data. This addresses the balancing act articulated by Van Maanen, Sorensen, and Mitchell (2007: 1147) who argued:

> If we pay too much attention to available or potentially available data, we are trapped by operations, and theorizing is stifled. If we pay no attention to data, our theorizing will be rather too remote and will occur all on the conceptual plane. In either case, the potential interplay between method and theory is limited. The key, then, is to find a way to serve two masters at once.

My co-authors and I have found that drawing on existing theory early, often, and overtly serves the two masters of theory and data, and it has greatly enriched our grounded theorizing. On the practical side, as well, we have found it much more *efficient* to code on both the theory and in vivo fronts simultaneously. It simply saves time to avoid weeks (or months!) of work on a potential path that seems new to the researcher but is actually an area already well covered by the literature. To ignore theory early on also runs the risk of creating new theory that is either too disconnected from or too similar to existing theory. I have found that involving the literature throughout the process helps my co-authors and I know what truly is a new idea versus erroneously believing that

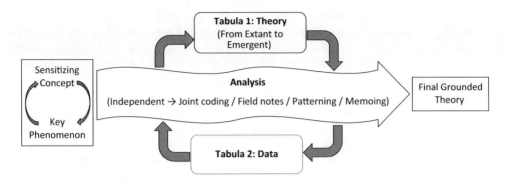

Figure 33.1 The *Tabula Geminus* Process

something which is new to us from our data is new to the wider research community. Without such knowledge, valuable time can be lost by pursuing paths that have already been explored by others.

Mischel (2008) lamented that theories have become like toothbrushes—nobody wants to use someone else's, and therefore everyone creates a new theory. And while the need to create a new theory is reinforced at the individual level (by scholars getting their qualitative work accepted at top journals), at the collective level it results in the proliferation of constructs such that we are no longer using a common language for similar phenomena. Too many idiosyncratic silo-like theories are not good for the field's development. Indeed, too much qualitative work fails to connect meaningfully to extant theory, sometimes getting relegated to the "conceptual ghetto." By contrast, keeping theory on the proverbial radar throughout analysis helps the scholar to find ways to bridge and incorporate existing theories rather than artificially be divorced from them. Hence, our belief is that if you see an existing construct in your data, why not code it that? But *also* ask yourself (a) what *else* is here beyond existing theory and (b) how can I categorize this phenomenon using the interviewee's terms and vantage point? Perhaps an apt turn-of-phrase would be "If you see something, *code* something." In our experience, by simultaneously searching the data for both theory-based and grounded codes, we can best live up to the iterative goals of grounded theory.

Approaches that overtly delay the integration of theory-based codes into their coding procedures have yielded a tremendous wealth of knowledge for organizational scholars. For us, however, the *tabula geminus* process is simply what works, and we have found in sharing this approach that it's the way many researchers' minds work. (Indeed, I have found it comes as a relief to many newcomers that they don't have to pretend to not know about the literature!) The key, it seems to me, is to be very conscious—indeed, *conscientious*—about allowing both types of codes in so that we neither suffocate the voices of those we study *nor* ignore the voices of our fellow researchers.

Sensitizing Concepts

Few scholars—especially in management and organization—would advocate that we should begin a study *tabula rasa*, with no orientation toward existing theory. Many traditions in the qualitative arena (e.g., grounded theory, ethnography) advocate beginning with a "sensitizing concept"—a theory or literature or construct that is of initial interest to the researcher. Blumer (1954: 7) originated the notion of sensitizing concepts and notes that they "merely suggest directions along which to look. The hundreds of our concepts—like culture, institutions, social structure, mores and personality—are not definitive concepts but sensitizing in nature." Researchers choose a sensitizing concept that they believe would be a useful lens through which to study the phenomenon of interest. But it is just that—a lens. And lenses can be changed. As (Charmaz, 2003: 259) noted:

> Sensitizing concepts offer ways of seeing, organizing, and understanding experience; they are embedded in our disciplinary emphases and perspectival proclivities. Although sensitizing concepts may deepen perception, they provide starting points for building analysis, not ending points for evading it. We may use sensitizing concepts only as points of departure from which to study the data.

One of the benefits of the *tabula geminus* approach is that because we overtly incorporate theory throughout the analysis, we are holding ourselves accountable to whether the original sensitizing concept remains an appropriate lens once we immerse in the phenomena at hand. Further, by keeping one eye on the literature, we can be attuned to *which* theories and constructs might be appropriate to incorporate. A metaphor I have used when teaching qualitative data analysis is to liken grounded theorizing to a boat ride—you might not know exactly where you're going on the journey, but you have some idea of what you'd like to see, and you can't leave on your trip until you know which boat you're taking! Hence a sensitizing concept at the start of a grounded theory study is the "vessel" you choose for your exploration. And just as conditions and information might change along your aquatic journey (weather updates, new and interesting sights to see along the way), so too might emerging data and insights from pertinent literatures lead you in new directions for grounded theory.

Coding Process

Since the coding process is at the heart of the *tabula geminus* approach, I'll now describe how we typically undertake it. First, each transcript is read word-for-word and independently coded by two or more authors. A code is assigned to sections of text when we identify the phenomenon present in an interviewee's transcript (or blog entry or speech—whatever the data source might be). The length of a coded block of text varies dramatically—from a few words to several pages—but is typically a few sentences or paragraphs. The short block of coded text might be a phrase we want to track, whereas the multipage coded text might be a compelling story. (We code these stories "NQ" for *narrative quote*; it is useful to keep track of these as we go so that we can analyze them separately using narrative analysis.) The main goal in deciding the length of the passage to be coded is to capture the essence of the speaker's/writer's stance to a degree that it can be appropriately interpreted later on in the analysis. (Note that if you use NVivo or similar qualitative data software, it's fairly easy to click and see the paragraphs preceding and/or following a quote, making access to some contextual information rather straightforward.) We have also always used a code called "DQ" or *demonstrative quote*. We use it to capture a block of text that is (a) an outstanding example of a particular phenomenon and/or (b) a vivid, compelling way to express a phenomenon. This handy code is always double coded along with the code(s) it exemplifies. (That is, no passage is ever coded *only* DQ since at least one other code must be represented/exemplified.) An important note: Multiple codes may be overlaid onto any given passage of text when multiple phenomena are found. Note that both theory-based and in vivo style codes could be put onto the same passage. Indeed, it is a core tenet of our coding approach to *re-read passages multiple times* in order to be open to both theory-based and in vivo codes. This not only guards against the confirmation bias that other researchers have warned about (i.e., only seeing theory rather than phenomena), but also encourages the both/and thinking that has helped us to stimulate theorizing.

Second, we analyze transcripts in joint coding meetings, wherein the authors who coded that transcript compare the independently coded transcripts. (I describe this process in more detail later.) Insights from early data drive decisions about the next wave of data collection (theoretical sampling) and/or analysis. Our method also compares emerging ideas from the data with existing literatures and vice versa, such that each is used to inform interpretation of the other. See Appendix A for a portion of a transcript with coding labels placed on it.

We place codes in a hierarchy to log their relationships and keep the codes in a dictionary format (to document their precise meanings) that builds during data analysis. For the first interview, there is no dictionary until the authors code the transcript; the initial dictionary gets built from the first interview. The dictionary grows and changes throughout the coding process as we discover more codes and condense others. For example, we will merge codes when we perceive the phenomena are similar enough to one another. In other instances, we will add or subdivide codes when important differences among pieces of coded data become evident. Specifically, we create "children" codes that are more specific than their "parent" codes, and "grandchildren" codes that are more specific than children codes. This nesting helps us to articulate relationships among codes and invites conversations about the precise meanings—both absolute and relative—of each code.

The evolution of the dictionary is purposefully an iterative process of comparing newly analyzed data, previously coded data, *and* existing literature. How does the coding dictionary develop if the researcher uses both in vivo and extant-theory style codes? We place both types of codes into the coding dictionary, which includes detailed definitions and parameters of each code. For example, in our study on ethics officers, we had an in vivo parent code called "human nature" that derived from interviewees discussing their vantage points on whether people were inherently good or bad. In contrast, we also had theory-based codes such as "sensegiving." Note that unlike many other coding processes, we do not imply that the "parent" codes are necessarily second-order codes, nor are "children" codes necessarily first-order codes. Rather, parent and children codes might use either theory-based or interviewee-based language. Hence, instead of structuring the dictionary strictly by first- and second-order themes, we structure in a way that theory-based and in vivo style codes might be a parent, child, or grandchild in the structure; that is, a theory code might be equal to, above, or below an in vivo style code. This process allows us to create some structure early on, which facilitates the coding process, but also allows us flexibility since the dictionary can be changed at any time during data analysis. We have found this to be a "not too hot, not too cold" way to balance structure and flexibility in the coding process. Further, the approach allows for maximal analytic flexibility and provides a way to interweave existing literature with the emergent themes throughout analysis (as opposed to only creating higher-order abstracted terms later in the process). At the end of the dictionary, we keep track of all deletions and merges, and include the date of each change. This helps us to know exactly how and when we made changes to the dictionary.

Note that our approach of creating a hierarchical dictionary is in contrast to the traditional approaches in which codes are created as freestanding at first (open coding) and their relationships explored only in later phases of the analysis (axial coding) (e.g., Corbin & Strauss, 2008). Our approach essentially merges open and axial coding throughout the analysis. This has the benefit of helping us refine our codes and determine next steps throughout the research process. (In fact, with most of our studies, we only gather a small amount of data [e.g., 3 to 7 interviews] at first, code all of it, then revise our protocols based on our early analysis.) Further, it helps us to think early and often about the interplay between theory and data. See Appendix B for an example of a portion of a coding dictionary.

Two or More Coders

Continuing the *tabula geminus* theme of the synergy between "twin slates," we have found that there is tremendous benefit to having two or more authors code each interview (or whatever other source of data). In the joint coding meetings (described earlier), we each bring our marked-up transcript on which we have independently placed codes prior to the meeting. This independence is key, for it helps us to bring two lenses to the data. We have found it useful to use multiple colors of pens to demarcate the beginning and ending of codes. The particular color used does not matter (that is, a given color is not associated with any particular code in the dictionary); rather, they are just used for easy reference during the meeting (e.g., "my blue block ends here"). During the meeting, we go page by page, coded passage by coded passage. I typically use two typing stands to hold up the two coded transcripts so that we can see the two pages side-by-side (e.g., my coded page five right next to my co-author's coded page five). Through comparison and discussion, we determine the final codes to be used on each transcript. (We bring a blank copy of the interview to these joint coding sessions. That copy becomes the "master" which is then input into NVivo for future analysis.) Having two sets of eyes on all data further helps the both/and approach philosophy of *tabula geminus* that we take because we are increasing our chances to see both in vivo and theory codes. Further, the joint discussions take place at both the in vivo and theory levels *as well as between them*. Indeed, many discussions in these joint coding sessions are typically about the connections between the two types of codes, the dictionary structure, and so forth. We have found these joint coding meetings to be an essential part of the grounded theorizing process. In the meetings, we are reflexive both individually and interpersonally, pushing and challenging each other's observations and inferences. While some time is spent on the more mundane issues of coded passage length, for example, the most important conversations are ones in which we (a) are reflexive about our stances on the data, (b) debate the structure of the dictionary (e.g., which codes to create, which codes to make parents versus children, how to define each code), and (c) develop theoretical memos to bridge the data and the theory. (See Charmaz, 2014, and Lempert, 2007, for excellent chapters on memo writing.)

Transparency of the Process

Van Maanen et al. (2007: 1149) lamented, "It is an irony of scholarly practice in organizational research that the process of abduction, which likely goes on in most if not all promising research projects, is largely hidden from view." I concur wholeheartedly and encourage newcomers to grounded theory and qualitative methods to be more transparent about the coding and analytic processes in their writing. One way we can be more transparent is to tell our readers the degree to which existing theory played a role in our coding processes. As an interesting anecdote, in preparation for this chapter, I was curious to see how often this occurred. In perusing qualitative articles in several top management journals, I found it very rare for authors (myself included sometimes!) to overtly discuss this issue. Much more typical was a brief description of coding without explicitly mentioning whether and when codes based on existing theory were used. In addition to explanations in methods sections, information can also be provided visually through a figure that outlines the data collection and analysis process for a given study. For example, Harrison and Rouse (2014) provided a figure with three planes (theory, data collection, and data analysis) showing the role that each played during their study of dancers.

Another way to increase transparency is to explain how the research question changed through the abduction process. For example, I now explain in the front end of the paper how that happened. Earlier in my career as a scholar, I was too afraid to do this. Reviewers clearly wanted a more traditional, linear—and ultimately unrealistic—story about how the research proceeded. Now, we aim for more transparency in how things changed. We do this by first explaining what our original interest or intent was with the project, which usually includes the original research question; second, explaining how the data analysis process unearthed new themes that were more promising and/or nuanced than our original intentions; and third, by offering revised research questions that emerged after the initial data analysis.

Let me offer a concrete example of how we reported the process of change that resulted from the *tabula geminus* approach. In our paper on identity elasticity, in which we studied changes in the

Episcopal Church over a 10-year period, we wrote the following at the end of our introduction to the paper (Kreiner, Hollensbe, Sheep, Smith, & Kataria, 2015):

> We did not begin the project with an eye toward the elasticity construct, but it emerged as part of our inductive approach detailed below. Rather, we began with this fairly broad research question: *How do organizational leaders and members negotiate organizational identity in the context of a controversial event?* As is often the case with qualitative research, our initial research question became refined (Charmaz, 2014). As we dug deeper into the naturally unfolding case, following a process of iteratively comparing our existing and emerging data, the conceptual importance of elasticity became increasingly apparent to us. As events in the Episcopal Church unfolded over time, and as we fine-tuned our data collection and analyses to follow those events. . . . [Herein we described details of the data, extant literature, and how those shaped our theorizing; deleted for space considerations.] Their processes were more complex than existing theories and interpretations of organizational identity theory would adequately explain; thus, we sought to understand better those processes as we observed them in our data. Hence, our refined research question became:
>
> Refined Research Question: (a) How do organizational leaders and members expand and contract their constructions of organizational identity? (b) What challenges are experienced in this process? (c) What are the consequences of this process?

The above example shows the transparency of our process—the original research question (which illuminates our sensitizing concept), the way we engaged with the data and existing theory, and then the revised research questions. Writing in a transparent way serves two main purposes. First, it honors the integrity of research practices by explaining our *actual* process. Too often, authors are forced into writing a false account of their process by having to conform to the traditional research question-methods-findings model. They feel compelled to write as if their research questions stayed the same throughout the process, as if their interview protocols never morphed during data collection, or as if their knowledge of the literature never changed nor influenced the process. Second, it provides a window into the process through which other researchers can both critique and learn from our processes. By openly acknowledging that our research questions changed because of the emerging themes in the data and our (re)visiting the literature, we normalize the process for emerging scholars or those new to qualitative methods.

Before closing, I want to make an important point about this iterative process. I think it is incredibly important that—whenever possible—researchers doing grounded theory collect their data in waves rather than all at once. (Sometimes, of course, this isn't possible because of the parameters of the study, such as limited time window for access to data, so researchers just make the best of it.) When I first started doing qualitative research, I didn't realize how important this was, but experience, as they say, is the best teacher. Now, I too often review manuscripts for which the authors apparently collected all the data, *then* began data analysis. I have found that iterating among data collection and analysis many times for a given project tremendously helps the theorizing process. With each wave of data collection, the analysis can generate insights into the most (and least) promising themes emerging from the data. These early insights then help the researcher to adapt the protocol and/or sources of data. Gathering and analyzing iteratively also has the practical benefit of saving the researcher from collecting massive amounts of data that are later discovered to be unusable.

In conclusion, the *tabula geminus* approach to coding and data analysis has provided my co-authors and me with a structured yet flexible way to capitalize on the interplay among existing theory, our data, and our emerging theory.

Table 33.1 Use of *Tabula Geminus* in Qualitative Research Methods

Reference	Research Context	How Tabula Geminus Was Used	Outcomes/Results of Tabula Geminus Approach
Kreiner, Hollensbe, & Sheep (2006, 2009)	Episcopal priests—how they manage identity challenges, work–home balance	Coding of interview transcripts by multiple authors to create grounded theory	(2006) Linked existing construct of identity work to emerging themes of identity tensions, challenges, and tactics (2009) Linked existing construct of work–family conflict to emerging themes of boundary violations and boundary work tactics
Smith et al. (2010)	Social enterprises and the identity challenges they experience at start-up and beyond	Coding of interview transcripts and archival data by multiple authors to create grounded theory	Linked existing construct of identity tensions (as documented in Kreiner et al. [2006] listed above) to emergent themes found in social enterprises
Hollensbe, Khazanchi, & Masterson, (2008)	Fairness perceptions at work	Coding of interview transcripts by multiple authors to create grounded theory	Linked existing construct of fairness to the emerging construct of rules that underlie justice perceptions
Knapp et al. (2013)	Family businesses—their tactics for negotiating boundaries between "family" and "business"	Coding of interview transcripts, on-site observations, archival data by multiple authors to create grounded theory	Linked existing construct of "boundary work" to (a) the emergent theme of "social boundaries" experienced by people in family businesses and (b) the tactics they employ
Treviño et al. (2014)	Chief ethics and compliance officers—how they work to create and maintain legitimacy in their organizations	Coding of interview transcripts, secondary data (e.g., newsletters, white papers) by multiple authors to create grounded theory	Linked existing literature on legitimacy to emerging theme of "legitimacy work" undertaken by ethics officers and the tactics they use
Kreiner et al. (2015)	Episcopal Church—how identity "elasticity" helped the organization navigate identity change	Coding of interview transcripts, media sources, site visits, organizational presentations by multiple authors to create grounded theory	Linked existing literature on organizational identity to the emerging theme of "elasticity," which shows how organizations can simultaneously expand conceptions of who they are and stay the same
Ashforth, Kreiner, Clark, & Fugate (2007)	Managers of dirty work occupations	Coding of interview transcripts by multiple authors to create grounded theory	Linked existing literature on dirty work to emerging themes of how *managers* deal with the stigma

Appendix A: Sample Transcript Page Showing Codes

This is a page of an interview transcript with codes overlaid; it comes from a research project on ethics and compliance officers (Treviño et al., 2014).

P.I
- be yourself
• infuse self

figure out what the right approach to this stuff is. So I start by believing everybody wants to move in a positive direction, everybody wants to be part of an organization that is well-respected and operating with integrity, and if we can help people do that, we're all going to be in a much better place. So training. And then the other place is clearly in helping people address and solve issues. That's another place where – I'm not pretending that it's easy and I'm not pretending that I always got it right. I didn't. But for the most part, if you try to put yourself in that person's chair and how would you want to be treated, and how would you want the solution to be communicated to you, and how often would you want to be contacted if you had raised an issue and somebody else was investigating it, understanding that you can't just view people as inputs, right? Oh, you gave me an issue. Great. Thank you very much. Bye, bye now. You have to connect with people repeatedly and that gives credibility to your program and to your process and to your organization.

human nature.

Tactics
- connections

Interviewer: To what extent do you think – this sort of builds on the last question. To what extent do you think that you could really be yourself in this job, but what I'm also curious about is whether you have to oppress parts of yourself to be an effective person who has this job?

Resp:
- be yourself • infuse self

Interviewee: This job fit very well with who I am, so that part was great. I think the hardest part of the job was understanding that not every senior leader is going to see things the way you do, and not every employee who brings you an issue is going to understand there are many ways to resolve an issue and they may not like the one that's been selected as the business solution to the problem. So being an advocate for a different solution if you're providing information to senior management, having promoted something other than what they ultimately choose to do is very difficult to get over because at some point you want to say, really? No. This is the way to do this? You need to terminate this person? You can't keep them on? Or you need to reduce this person's salary? If a different solution is chosen than the one you've advocated, I think that's hard. And then trying to talk to employees to explain why the person that they think is the most evil person known to mankind and has done all these terrible things is still going to be an employee at the company when everybody knows they should have been fired, that's hard to do, too.

challenge
- control.
DQ
tactics
- fairness

Interviewer: So how did you do it? How did you manage to sort of cope with these parts of the job even though it was difficult?

Respondents
- past roles
• legal

Interviewee: I guess the legal training helped a lot in that. You mentioned that earlier. One of the things that you understand as a lawyer is that even criminals deserve a defense, right? Murderers get defended by somebody who takes their side. So you need to understand, and I certainly did understand, and I think people who've gone through legal training understand that there

Appendix B: Sample Portions of a Coding Dictionary

Sample from research project on chief ethics and compliance officers (Treviño et al., 2014). Sample codes (not exhaustive) to show structure and how we use a dictionary to keep track of codes and their meanings.

Challenges (and tensions; what keeps them "up all night")

- Always on defense (always worried ~ possible problems; anti-terrorism mindset; when they discuss sheer volume of risks/challenges; *not* workload issue)
- Big picture vs. individuals (e.g., lawyers look at need of individual client, whereas ECOs need to see the system)
- Business pressures (bumping up against them, e.g., need for profit vs. ethics)
- Control (lack of) (e.g., outsourcing contractors, suppliers, etc.—lack of control over them/ their practices, yet company held accountable for them)

Note

1 I thank Chad Murphy, Kim Elsbach, and Rod Kramer for their helpful comments on an earlier draft of this chapter. I express deep appreciation to each of my co-authors on qualitative projects with whom I have used variations of this *Tabula Geminus* method over the years—Blake Ashforth (who initially taught me qualitative coding procedures), Elaine Hollensbe and Mathew Sheep (with whom I adapted much of this approach early on), Chad Murphy, Linda Trevino, Derron Bishop, Niki den Nieuwenboer, Aparna Joshi, Tiffany Johnson, Vilmos Misangyi, Gary Weaver, Heather Vough, David Sluss, Niyati Kataria, Joshua Knapp, Brett Smith, Chamu Sundaramurthy, Sid Barton, Mark Clark, and Mel Fugate. With each project, I have gained from my co-authors both content and process insights that have helped me improve as a scholar.

References

Ashforth, B.E., Kreiner, G.E., Clark, M.A., & Fugate, M. (2007). Normalizing dirty work: Managerial tactics for countering occupational taint. *Academy of Management Journal, 50,* 149–174.

Blumer, H. (1954). What is wrong with Social Theory? *American Sociological Review, 19,* 3–10.

Charmaz, K. (2014). *Constructing Grounded Theory* (second edition). Thousand Oaks, CA: Sage.

Corbin, J. & Strauss, A.L., (2008). *Basics of Qualitative Research: Techniques and Procedures for Developing Grounded Theory* (third edition). Newbury Park, CA: Sage.

Glaser, B. G. (1992). *Emergence vs. Forcing: Basics of Grounded Theory.* Mill Valley, CA: Sociology Press.

Glaser, B. G. & Strauss, A. L. (1967). *The Discovery of Grounded Theory.* New York: de Gruyter.

Harrison, S. H. & Rouse, E. D. (2014). Let's dance! Elastic coordination in creative group work: A qualitative study of modern dancers. *Academy of Management Journal, 57,* 1256–1283.

Hollensbe, E., Khazanchi, S., & Masterson, S.S. (2008). How do I assess if my supervisor and organization are fair? Identifying the rules underlying entity-based justice perceptions. *Academy of Management Journal, 51,* 1099–1116.

Knapp, J. R., Smith, B. R., Kreiner, G. E., Sundaramurthy, C., & Barton, S. L. (2013). Managing boundaries through identity work: The role of individual and organizational identity tactics. *Family Business Review, 26,* 333–355.

Kreiner, G. E., Hollensbe, E. C., & Sheep, M. L. (2006). Where is the "me" among the "we"? Identity work and the search for optimal balance. *Academy of Management Journal, 49,* 1031–1057.

Kreiner, G. E., Hollensbe, E. C., & Sheep, M. L. (2009). Balancing borders and bridges: Negotiating the work-home interface via boundary work tactics. *Academy of Management Journal, 52,* 704–730.

Kreiner, G. E., Hollensbe, E. C., Sheep, M. L., Smith, B. R., & Kataria, N. (2015). Elasticity and the dialectic tensions of organizational identity: How can we hold together while we're pulling apart? *Academy of Management Journal, 58,* 981–1011.

Lee, T.W. (1998). *Using Qualitative Methods in Organizational Research.* Thousand Oaks, CA: Sage.

Lempert, L.B. (2007). Asking questions of the data: Memo writing in the grounded theory tradition. In A. Bryant & K. Charmaz (Eds.), *The SAGE Handbook of Grounded Theory* (pp. 245–264). Thousand Oaks, CA: Sage.

Mischel, W. (2008). The toothbrush problem. *Observer, 21*(11). Retrieved from www.psychologicalscience.org/index.php/publications/observer/2008/december-08

Peirce, C.S. (1995. First published in 1903.) *The 1903 lectures on pragmatism.* (Edited by P.A. Turrisi.) Albany: State University of New York Press.

Pratt, M.G. (2007). Fitting oval pegs into round holes: Tensions in evaluating and publishing qualitative research in top North American journals. *Organizational Research Methods, 11,* 481–509.

Smith, B.R.; Knapp, J.; Barr, T. F.; Stevens, C. E., & Cannatelli, B. L. (2010). Social enterprises and the timing of conception: Organizational identity tension, management, and marketing. *Journal of Nonprofit & Public Sector Marketing, 22,* 108–134.

Strauss, A. L. (1987). *Qualitative Analysis for Social Scientists.* New York: Cambridge University Press.

Strauss, A. L. & Corbin, J. (1990). *Basics of Qualitative Research: Grounded Theory Procedures and Techniques.* London: Sage.

Strauss, A. L. & Corbin, J. (1994). Grounded theory methodology: An overview. In N. K. Denzin (Ed.), *Handbook of Qualitative Research* (pp. 273–285). London: Sage.

Strauss, A. L. & Corbin, J. (2008). *Basics of Qualitative Research: Grounded Theory Procedures and Techniques* (third edition). London: Sage.

Suddaby, R. (2006). From the editors: What grounded theory is not. *Academy of Management Journal, 49,* 633–642.

Treviño, L. K., den Nieuwenboer, N., Kreiner, G. E., & Bishop, D. (2014). Legitimating the legitimate: A grounded theory study of legitimacy work among ethics and compliance officers. *Organizational Behavior and Human Decision Processes, 123,* 186–205.

Van Maanen, J., Sorensen, J. B., & Mitchell, T. R. (2007). The interplay between theory and method. *Academy of Management Review, 32,* 1145–1154.

34

Using Qualitative Comparative Analysis (QCA) as a Descriptive Numerical Method in Support of Narrative Methods

Rodney Lacey and Lisa Cohen

Contest and Complement in Narrative and Quantitative Methods

An important reason that qualitative research has had such an impact on the field of organization studies is that it uses narrative methods to cull coherent stories from complex realities that still manage to explain what really goes on in organizations. It might seem tautological to equate qualitative research with narrative methods, but it is only in practice that they have become all but synonymous among organizational scholars. Relatively few qualitative organizational scholars include detailed quantitative analyses in their studies. Indeed, looking through a sample of exemplar qualitative papers can easily lead to the conclusion that these scholars are number averse. One reason for this is that the philosophical foundations of the quantitative methods that currently predominate in organizational studies are generally in direct conflict with those of qualitative research. As a result, qualitative researchers have had few numerical methods available as potential options to include in their work. Additionally, qualitative researchers who use narrative methods are often subtly (and not so subtly) under pressure to convert their research to fit the "general linear reality" (Abbott, 1988) of dominant quantitative methods and thus displace the logic of qualitative research (see Goertz & Mahoney, 2012, for an example of this division). Any inclusion of numerical analysis within narrative analysis can become an opportunity for requests for its expansion at the expense of the narrative methods. Qualitative researchers who have sufficient cases in their studies are invariably asked by reviewers (friendly and not) to run a regression or a similar type of analysis. This tendency drives some qualitative researchers to bury their numbers even when they have numbers to support their findings.

Yet while avoiding quantitative analyses has helped maintain the integrity of qualitative research to its theoretical commitments, it has left the qualitative researcher without the power of numerical analysis to produce descriptions of data, both for the researcher's own use in the process of developing narrative and for presenting descriptions of the data in support of the final narrative. The strength of narrative is that it identifies the coherent stories in complex data, not that it provides parsimonious pictures of the full complexity of that data. The cliché that a "picture is worth a thousand words" holds true in data description, and numbers are themselves pictures, or abstractions, of a great deal of underlying features and should not be entirely avoided in qualitative research. In many cases, a few numbers can parsimoniously describe what in a narrative form would require thousands of words.

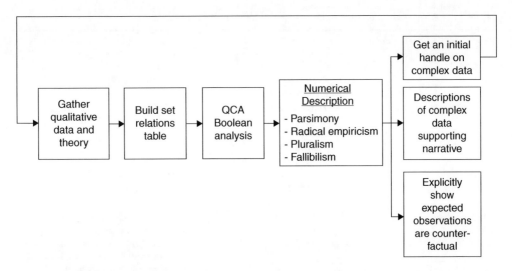

Figure 34.1   Using QCA as Descriptive Numerical Analysis to Support Narrative Qualitative Research

Further, seeing those numbers may aid the researcher in gaining initial insights into the data as well as in communicating these to their audiences.

Qualitative researchers using narrative methods have an opportunity to make it easier to engage in the process of research and to communicate their findings by using Qualitative Comparative Analysis (QCA) as a numerical method for description of data as a supportive complement, and not a displacement, of narrative methods. While QCA has been almost entirely used as a method for causal analysis, it has great potential for standalone descriptive analysis.

Figure 34.1 illustrates the process of using QCA to take raw data through fresh insight for both researchers and readers. In the particular case of researchers using narrative methods, using QCA as a descriptive numerical method can aid in three ways. First, it can help the researcher get a handle on the data in initial stages of analyses. Second, it can help the researcher to describe the full plurality of data that will not be included in the main narrative. And finally, it can be used to show explicitly that theoretically expected but counter-factual conclusions were not ignored or over-looked, but rather were not supported by the data.

Philosophical Foundations of Narrative Methods Versus Dominant Quantitative Methods

QCA is a method that is equally complex and has as many subtleties as any other general numerical methods, so it is beyond the scope of this chapter to fully explain it (see Ragin, 2008, for full descriptions of the method; Table 34.1 gives excellent sources for examples of how it has been used).

In short, QCA is a Boolean-based method for the analysis of configurations of set memberships of cases across theoretically defined dimensions of analysis. It uncovers whether and how frequently cases share similar groupings of theoretical dimensions. It is best illustrated by example (found later in this chapter), but it is important to start with the philosophical foundations that it shares with most narrative qualitative methods that differ from the dominant numerical methods in organization studies.

Most narrative qualitative research is based on a pragmatist epistemology and ontology (see Platt, 1995; see also Stuhr, 2000, for a summary of pragmatism in social theory). There are three foundations

Table 34.1 QCA Research of Interest to Researchers Using Narrative Methods

Source	Description	Value
Ragin (2008)	Theoretical, philosophical, and methodological introduction to QCA and comparative methods	Comprehensive explanation of QCA method by its creator
www.compasss. org	COMPASSS (COMPArative Methods for Systematic cross-caSe analySis) is a worldwide network for common interest in advancements in a systematic comparative case approach	Free QCA software and bibliography of nearly all QCA research
www.u.arizona. edu/~cragin/ fsQCA/	Home page of the fuzzy-set QCA (fsQCA) software and method	Free QCA software and other reference material
Lacey & Fiss (2009)	Theoretical framework for multilevel comparisons using comparative methods such as QCA	How QCA departs from common assumptions in multilevel quantitative research, e.g., perfect nesting of levels and usefulness of controlling for level effects
Glaesser & Cooper (2011)	Demonstrates how QCA can be used to select cases for interview from a large-N population in a systematic and theoretically informed manner	Example of using QCA to "get a handle" on a huge quantitative dataset to simplify it for purposes of selecting key cases for narrative study
Paul, Clarke, Grill, & Savitsky (2013)	Multimethod study of 30 cases shows similarities and differences of narrative, bivariate comparison, comparative qualitative analysis, and K-medoids clustering	Empirical example of differences in QCA and narrative qualitative methods on the same data

of pragmatism that are common to most qualitative research and QCA but are completely at odds with dominant numerical methods: radical empiricism, pluralism, and fallibilism.

Radical empiricism holds that perception is an "active, ongoing affair in which experienc*ing* subject and experienc*ed* object constitute a primal, integral, relational unity" (Stuhr, 2000, p. 100). For our purposes, a central implication of this view is that the world as we know it is constituted by our transaction with it, as we give it meaning through our creative effort to organize, catalog, interpret, and the like the experiences we have of that world and in relation to our past and ongoing experiences. Experience is not neatly bounded by time or sensed by individuals on their own from outside of the social world. Rather, it is an ongoing flow that is created in interaction with the world. Dominant quantitative methods, however, violate radical empiricism in several ways, the most direct of which is that the researcher disappears as data and observations are represented as objective facts discovered independent of the process of discovery. Even the specification of what constitutes a population or a case—that is, the subject of study—is a separate, usually unquestioned act prior to analysis so that the statistical representations are treated as objective definitions of a world that is itself exterior to the theorist's conceptions of that world.

Pluralism refers to the diversity of experiences of individuals, groups, and organizations. It suggests that "our transactions with the natural environment are individual and qualitatively unique" (Stuhr, 2000) because of our unique subjectivity and social structural location. Pluralism is an essential implication of a rejection of the duality of subjectivity and objectivity in epistemology. If there was an objectivity to be known, then experience would be universal of that objectivity, varying only by quality and position of interpretation. When there is no objective referent for knowing, then there can be no assumption of universality of experience, and thus there can only be multiple—a plurality of—experiences and interpretations. Qualitative researchers using narrative methods give primacy to lived experience of observed individuals precisely because they expect no single uniform experience.

Dominant numerical methods violate pluralism because they assume homogeneity across cases in a population such that the entire population's experience can be summarized in a single number or equation. This aggregation and abstraction from the diversity of the population can easily, and often does, produce theories that do not correspond to the actual experience of any single member of the population. Complete homogeneity is presented as objectively real.

Fallibilism is defined by the pragmatist philosopher Charles Sanders Pierce as the "the doctrine that our knowledge is never absolute but always swims, as it were, in a continuum of uncertainty and indeterminacy" (Hartshorne & Weiss, 1931, p. 70). The epistemological implication of fallibilism is that theorists abandon the "quest for certainty" and instead engage in the process of "piecemeal, multi-directional efforts to verify and warrant beliefs" (Stuhr, 1987, p. 6). One must assume that all truth claims are only as stable as the actions and action outcomes that produced them and thus are open to constant, expected revisions.

Dominant numerical methods, however, are based on assumptions of falsifiability rather than fallibilism. Falsifiability assumes that a theory must have internal consistency and external measures that can be tested by correlation with the objectivity of the outside world. Falsifiability depends upon an outside, objective referent to be used to determine whether a theory is falsified or not yet falsified. Fallibilism treats theories as processes of accumulation, sedimentation, and exfoliation over time. Dominant numerical methods obscure even the hint of fallibilism in a theory. The estimates of the analysis are either statistically confirmed or not; they are not open to any incremental change.

Getting a Handle on Data with QCA

Given this gulf between dominant numerical methods and qualitative research with respect to assumptions about the world and our knowledge of it, the reliance on narrative in qualitative research and avoidance of numerical methods is entirely understandable. Yet it leaves narrative researchers with at least one practical problem: getting a handle on all the data and theory they generate in the early, less structured stages of research. What we mean by "get a handle on it" is create a parsimonious representation of the data for purposes of sensemaking and theory development. The problem of how to make sense of all the data in early stages of a study—when frames and concepts are still tentative and yet to emerge from the analysis and repeated collection of data—is known to all qualitative researchers because neither their data nor theory are well-bounded by initial considerations of data availability or experimental design. There comes a time in the process when a researcher would like a complete view of the data that is sufficiently parsimonious to be interpretable, but simultaneously does not obscure or lose relatively rare or unusual data that may be very important to the overall project (thus maintaining the pluralism of the data in its representation). This is the point in time when a researcher is asking, "What have I got?" from a global perspective and is not sure what is important enough to stay in the analysis and what is not. This is a problem for every qualitative researcher because even a very small organization (e.g., a work group) will generate an enormous number of observations of behavior, interactions, documents, and other artifacts, and with those the potential for many theoretical concepts that could be descriptive or explanatory.

Using QCA as a purely descriptive numerical method is a systematic, inclusive, and mechanically easy way to take these early steps. Take, for example, a QCA analysis used in an unpublished paper (Cohen & Spataro, 2009) to make sense of complicated data presented in Table 34.1. The context was a study of fact checkers at high status magazines (see Cohen & Staw, 1998, for a description of the data collection methods). The fact checking job is an entry level one usually filled by recent graduates of prestigious universities who hope to step into better jobs in publishing later. The study was on the coping strategies—both actions and rhetorical presentations—for these people who are asked to perform relatively menial work but have high status college degrees and high career aspirations. The researchers examined how fact checkers acted at work, how they described their work, and the ways that they reconciled the low demands (and pay) of the job with their own identities and self-worth. The data for the research came from interviews and observations of 12 fact checkers, most of whom worked in one magazine's fact checking department.

Analysis of the data generated a long list of actions or rhetorical devices used to make sensible their situation. Two of these involved actually doing things in the workplace: performing tasks that were beyond the scope of their jobs, and gathering and exercising power in their relationships with writers and editors. Several involved describing the job in its better light. They did this by focusing on some of the tasks and qualities of the job that were less central to it, on the fact that they were working in journalism and for a prestigious magazine, that their work was important to the magazine, that they worked with celebrity writers and editors, and that it was in some ways much better than it seemed. When talking to people outside of the magazine world, they invoked other roles that they had beyond their job. They also made frequent claims that they intended to leave the job very soon.

This was a lot of data to make sense of. Altogether there were 12 categories of coping tactics and 12 fact checkers interviewed. The natural next questions for this research was whether there were any patterns across these practices and people: were there any sets of activities that were more common; did any of the activities group together; did practices vary by fact checker age, gender, and experience; or did each fact checker have a distinctive way of coping?

The data, when summarized as they are in Table 34.2, seem relatively simple, and they are—until you need to systematically and comprehensively analyze the data to answer this set of questions. Then it is too much to keep in one's head at one time.

The relatively simple question of whether there are common configurations of strategies used by multiple fact checkers is quite a hard task to do by hand. A QCA analysis of this table, however, can quickly and easily identify the common configurations and the percentage of cases in each and produce a logical expression using Boolean algebra that is the parsimonious description of all the configurations in the data. This Boolean reduction analysis is given in Table 34.3.

In this particular case, there are 10 unique configurations of strategies among the 12 people (see the Boolean simplification in Table 34.3), with only two configurations having two people using the same configuration, which suggests that coping in this context is a very individualized activity.

Table 34.2 Truth Table for QCA Analysis of Fact Checker Coping Strategies

Coping Tactic	Fact Checker											
	1	*2*	*3*	*4*	*5*	*6*	*7*	*8*	*9*	*10*	*11*	*12*
Doing more (mo)	0	1	1	0	1	0	1	0	1	0	1	1
Exercising power (xp)	1	1	1	1	1	1	1	1	1	1	1	1
Focus on tangential tasks (tk)	1	1	1	0	1	1	1	1	0	1	0	1
Describing self as a journalist (ij)	0	0	0	0	1	0	0	1	1	1	0	0
Describing self as working for the magazine (wi)	0	0	0	0	1	0	0	1	1	0	1	1
Explaining job's importance for the magazine (im)	1	1	1	1	1	1	1	1	1	1	1	0
Saying that the job is better than it seems (bs)	1	1	1	1	1	1	1	1	1	1	1	0
Saying that being in the job is not intentional (ni)	0	1	1	0	1	0	0	1	1	1	1	1
Saying that being in the job is for the money (dm)	1	1	0	1	1	1	1	1	1	1	1	1
Saying that being in the job is for developing skills (sk)	0	0	1	0	1	1	1	1	1	0	1	1
Saying that on way out (zz)	1	1	0	0	1	1	1	1	1	1	1	1
Defining self by other roles (ot)	1	0	0	0	1	0	1	1	1	1	1	1

Table 34.3 QCA Truth Table Reduction of Fact Checker Coping Strategies

Unique Configurations	Simplified Boolean Expression
1	mo*xp*tk*ni*bs*dm*sk*zz*wi*im*ot
2	mo*xp*ni*bs*dm*sk*zz*wi*ij*im*ot
3	xp*tk*ni*bs*dm*sk*zz*wi*ij*im*ot
4	mo*xp*tk*ni*bs*~dm*sk*~zz*wi*~ij*~im*~ot
5	~mo*xp*tk*~ni*bs*dm*sk*zz*wi*~ij*~im*~ot
6	~mo*xp*tk*~ni*bs*dm*~sk*zz*wi*~ij*~im*ot
7	mo*xp*tk*ni*bs*dm*~sk*zz*wi*~ij*~im*~ot
8	~mo*xp*~tk*ni*bs*dm*~sk*zz*wi*ij*~im*ot
9	mo*xp*tk*~ni*bs*dm*sk*zz*wi*~ij*~im*ot
10	mo*xp*tk*ni*~bs*dm*sk*zz*~wi*~ij*im*ot

Note: * = True or present, ~ = False or not present

The parsimonious Boolean algebraic simplification of the table also has the nice feature that it represents all the pluralism (or diversity) of the data. None of the strategies, or fact checkers, are dropped from the analysis or obscured by it, even as it becomes a much simpler representation. Consider the case of the strategy "work as a journalist" in Table 34.2. It refers to fact checkers representing themselves as doing the work of a journalist, even though that is an aspiration rather than a reality. It is the least frequent strategy used, with only 4 of the 12 fact checkers using it. If the same data were analyzed using clustering methods based on linear methods, this infrequent strategy would likely be treated as error and dropped from the final results.

Yet the importance of that strategy, and its inclusion in continued analysis, should be a theoretically and analytically driven decision, not driven by a statistical algorithm. The QCA analysis, despite providing a more parsimonious depiction of the data, would maintain the full plurality of the data in its description and thus avoid unintentionally shaping causal interpretations at early stages of analysis.

With a dozen subjects or cases, it is possible to do this analysis just by looking at the data, but this is cumbersome. It is much faster (and less prone to error) to use QCA even with small numbers of cases. It is necessary to use QCA (or some systematic method) if the number of cases was to be more than a couple dozen. Given that qualitative researchers make lists and tables that are similar to the data input for a QCA analysis (especially at the beginning of a project), it is possible to perform a QCA analysis with little additional effort, and the benefits would likely outweigh the small initial investment.

Other benefits of using a QCA analysis are easier iteration and making it easier to communicate about the research with informants or other scholars. It is a fundamental theoretical commitment of the QCA method that theory is not a separate object tested against data, but rather, reflexively (and easily) developed in iteration with the data, data collection, analysis, and theory development (Ragin, 2008). In the example of fact checkers, for instance, it could be plausible if a rhetorical device is used by nearly everyone that the dimension is too abstract and should be broken into multiple underlying strategies. For fact checkers, all but one made claims about the job being important to the magazine. A closer examination of this apparent homogeneity, however, revealed that some said that this was because it protected the magazine from expensive lawsuits and some said it was because it helped maintain the journalistic integrity of the magazine. QCA is designed specifically for the easy adding or removing of dimensions as part of the iteration between theory and data.

The QCA analysis may also serve as a powerful communication device by acting as a boundary object between different communities (Bechky, 2003). For example, QCA analysis can be a bridge between a researcher and informants. If the researcher wants to check these patterns with informants, a QCA simplification into configurations is much easier to understand than the full complexity of all the data.

Using QCA Analyses as Descriptives

A QCA analysis could also be useful in helping support a narrative directly and formally in the final research findings, not just as a support to the research process. It is most likely to be helpful because providing descriptions of the data as a whole in a pluralistic way that cannot be achieved by narrative alone. Narrative focuses on a main story, or maybe a handful of stories, but it cannot tell all the stories. Otherwise the narrative would lack coherence. There are individuals or events or occasions that they encounter that are not part of the general narrative but nonetheless are important and may have been influential in the formation of the main narrative as well, but they cannot be included in the narratives. QCA provides a way to note and describe the greater pluralism in the data than is found in the narrative alone.

The QCA analysis can also be a superior substitute for descriptions of data using central tendency statistics such as the mean. These statistics remove all plurality in a data description. For example, a mean is a single number used to represent all of the cases in a population as if they were fully homogeneous. The cases that are far removed from the mean disappear in this description of the data. In contrast, using tabular data from a QCA analysis, or a Boolean simplification of that data, will provide a description of data in all of its plurality. No datum is more important than any other, nor is any of it treated as an error term or outlier and thus obscured and ignored. In addition, any measure of distribution of the existent cases is based on an underlying theoretical framework developed by the researcher that is used to frame and display the data.

Another advantage of using QCA rather than other descriptive statistics is that it is effective with a small population of cases. Qualitative researchers may generate a great deal of data, but they do so as a complex picture of only a handful of cases or settings. So even if a qualitative researcher was willing to try to use typical quantitative tools for analysis, they might not have a sufficiently large amount of cases necessary to create a statistical sample large enough for most numerical methods to work. The original purpose of the QCA method was to specifically investigate small-n populations common in comparative analysis (Ragin, 1987), so it does not depend on a lot of cases to produce meaningful results.

Using QCA Descriptives to Address the Expected Counterfactual

One of the great strengths of narrative qualitative research—and why it has had such an impact on the field of organization studies—is that the researcher can be confronted with data that run counter to widely held assumptions in the field, and thus advances (or corrects) theory in a way that has a very powerful effect (Davis, 1971). The qualitative researcher becomes so immersed as to see past initial frames of analysis that the data does not fit and can adjust his or her data gathering and analysis to further pursue potentially very interesting insights that emerge in early stages.

The obstacle for narrative research that challenges common assumptions is that it must address the expected, but counterfactual, finding based on those assumptions. The researcher must both convince the audience to let go of their assumptions and accept the findings from his or her research. Anecdotally, overcoming assumptions is harder when studying fields of interest to everyone in the audience (e.g., higher education), or when there are many fictionalized accounts of that industry (e.g., policing, armed forces, artistic endeavors), or when many are keenly interested consumers in that field (e.g., automotive industry, consumer electronics, fashion). All of these make it even harder for the narrative researcher to build authority for his or her account that runs counter to the "knowledge" of the audience.

The use of QCA as a descriptive framework has the advantage that it is equally easy to describe counterfactuals as it is to describe existing cases —meaning it can formally present and analyze theoretically plausible options that represent no (or very few) empirical cases as easily as those that are descriptive of empirically observed cases. A QCA analysis can be easily done on all the plausible but nonexistent configurations of theoretical concepts, thus specifically describing what was not found, even if the counterfactuals are more likely to be more complex than existing configurations of data. For example, with 12 theoretical concepts of interest (as in Table 34.1), there are 2^{12} or 4,096 plausible combinations (although only 10 are empirically observable).

A narrative description is not very appropriate for describing all that complexity, but a QCA analysis can explicitly describe what was considered and yet was not found. Such a description points out that the researcher considered as a possibility any widely held counterfactual assumptions. It helps bolster the authority of the narrative by pointing out (without necessarily needing to note it so in the narrative) that the researcher had not missed or ignored the counterfactual through oversight or lack of theoretical consideration. In the example of the fact checkers, the researchers found that coping strategies were used simultaneously that were contradictory in effect by expressing loyalty, voice, and exit (Hirschman, 1970) at the same time. The researchers found that even the fact checkers who made efforts to expand the task boundaries of their job all used rhetorical devices to distance themselves from the job. There are no cases where there is a 1 in the row for adding tasks and zeros in all of the rows for the rhetorical devices. This runs counter to the expectation that expressing this kind of voice to try to improve things would preclude the desire to create distance to at least emotionally exit. The QCA analysis makes it clear to the audience that the researchers were examining the strategies in a way that would allow for detecting consistency in the strategies as would be expected even as such consistency was not empirically evident.

Conclusion

The use of QCA as a numerical method for description by qualitative narrative researchers is one that so far has not been explored explicitly. While some narrative researchers have used it to get a handle on their data, it has not made it into their final narratives. The QCA method has been expanding mostly by those who use it as their causal and descriptive method simultaneously, and not as a complement to narrative analysis. Table 34.1 provides references of interest to those wanting to use QCA as a complement to narrative analysis, even though none of the publications specifically used QCA in that way. Instead, the publications are either important background readings to learn about the QCA method or examples of where QCA was used as an adjunct to other methods rather than a primary method for study, and thus they would be helpful for analogous learning by narrative researchers.

References

Abbott, A. (1988). Transcending general linear reality. *Sociological Theory*, 6, 169–186.

Bechky, B.A. (2003). Sharing meaning across occupational communities: The transformation of understanding on a production floor. *Organization Science, 14(3)*, 312–330.

Cohen, L. E., & Spataro, S. (2009). *Fashioning provisional jobs: Methods for coping with low status positions*. Paper presented at Academy of Management, Chicago.

Cohen, L.E., & Staw, B.M. (1998). Fun's over, fact checkers are here: A case study of institutionalized dissent in the magazine publishing industry. *Advances in Qualitative Organization Research*, 1, 105–135.

Davis, M.S. (1971). That's interesting! *Philosophy of the Social Sciences, 1*(2), 309–344.

Glaesser, J., & Cooper, B. (2011). Selecting cases for in–depth study from a survey dataset: An application of Ragin's configurational methods. *Methodological Innovations Online, 6*(2), 52–70.

Goertz, G., & Mahoney, J. (2012). *A tale of two cultures: Qualitative and quantitative research in the social sciences*. Princeton, NJ: Princeton University Press.

Hartshone, C., & Weiss, P. (Eds.). (1931). *Collected papers of Charles Sanders Peirce*. Cambridge, MA: Harvard University Press.

Hirschman, A.O. (1970). *Exit, voice, and loyalty: Responses to decline in firms, organizations, and states*. Cambridge, MA: Harvard University Press.

Lacey, R., & Fiss, P. (2009). Comparative organizational analysis across multiple levels: A set theoretic approach. *Research in Sociology of Organizations, 26*, 119–116.

Paul, C., Clarke, C. P., Grill, B., & Savitsky, T. (2013). Between large-n and small-n analyses: Historical comparison of thirty insurgency case studies. *Historical Methods, 46*(4), 220–239.

Platt, J. (1995). Research methods and the second Chicago school. In G.A. Fine (Ed.), *A second Chicago school?: The development of a postwar American sociology* (pp. 82–107). Chicago: University of Chicago Press.

Ragin, C. (1987). *The comparative method: Moving beyond qualitative and quantitative strategies*. Berkeley: University of California Press.

Ragin, C. (2008). *Redesigning social inquiry: Fuzzy sets and beyond*. Chicago: University of Chicago Press.

Stuhr, J. (2000). *Pragmatism and classical American philosophy*. Oxford: Oxford University Press.

Stuhr, J. J. (1987). *Classical American philosophy: Essential readings and interpretive essays*. Oxford: Oxford University Press.

35

Discovery, Validation, and Live Coding[1]

Karen Locke, Martha S. Feldman, and Karen Golden-Biddle

Some time ago, Weick (1989) argued that elaboration of the theorizing process in organization studies and management requires us to move away from a singular preoccupation with validation because it provides a narrow and incomplete perspective on how new theoretical insights are developed. In the meantime, committed to broadening understanding of method and supporting the development of theorizing capability, a number of scholars have focused attention on discovery (e.g. Alvesson & Skoldberg, 2007; Czarniawska, 1999; Locke, Golden-Biddle, & Feldman, 2008; Swedberg, 2012; Weick 2005), underscoring the importance in the theorizing process of breakdowns and anomalies (Alvesson & Skoldberg, 2007; Van de Ven, 2007), ongoing speculation and conjecture (Weick, 2005), and the living continuing experience of doubt (Locke, Golden-Biddle, & Feldman, 2008). In this chapter, we further elaborate the theorizing process by reconnecting validation and discovery. We use coding as an example and show how the process of coding is different when researchers engage validation and discovery as mutually constituted rather than independent approaches to research.

In the logical empiricist account of theorizing, discovery and validation are separate and incommensurate; discovery is concerned with origination and genesis, while validation is contrasted as interested in evaluation and warrant (Kordig, 1978; Siegel, 1980). Methods sections tend to focus on validation, bringing forward the systematic and procedural nature of research as they leave out its untidy emergent aspect. Although some methods sections do allude to this more open-ended, imaginative dimension, even these accounts have had much more to say about the steps researchers follow to facilitate systematic interaction with their data than about the activities researchers employ and stances they assume to generate and form new interpretations and theoretical sightlines.

This separation means that discovery and validation are typically conceived as either different ways of dealing with data or as different moments in the research process. Glaser and Strauss (1967) famously divided research into two categories: studies that verify theory and studies that generate theory. Similar distinctions have been made between inductive and deductive studies, between interpretive studies that propose relations and positivist studies that test hypotheses (Lin, 1998; Roth & Mehta, 2002), and between contexts of discovery and justification (Swedberg, 2012). This separation is further represented in the injunction to test your hypothesis on a different set of data than was used to develop it (King, Keohane, & Verba, 1994) and in proposals for combining types of theorizing sequentially, for instance, generating theory with qualitative, interpretive research and validating it with quantitative, positivist research (Eisenhardt, 1989; Lin, 1998).

We argue here that this is an artificial separation that conveys a misleading picture of how research actually evolves, and in so doing, it hinders theorizing efforts. In overemphasizing validation, researchers render invisible discovery and perpetuate its continuing absence from our understanding and practice of research. By contrast, research in its fullness is orderly and systematic as well as messy and iterative (Law, 2006). It is tentative and certain, and it involves both conjecture and proof making. Research brings forth new ideas while assuring their patterned representation in the data. Thus, rather than conceiving discovery and validation as independent processes enacted sequentially in our analytic work, we conceive them here as a mutually constituted duality working together within an open-ended, forward-looking, trial-and-error theorizing process. This conception builds on the American pragmatist, Peirce, who treated scientific inquiry as an ongoing lived activity in which discovery and validation are inseparable, not distinct (Peirce, 1934; Timmermans & Tavory, 2013). They work together—discovery and validation—rather than through a periodic emergence of discovery within a context of validation.

This mutuality is observed in Diane Vaughan's work on the *Challenger* disaster: A faltering analysis centered on coding for rule violations as an expression of misconduct was instrumental in bringing about a shift in focus to rule-following behavior and the insight that NASA engineers understood their decision making as conforming to engineering and organizational principles. This behavior was eventually theorized as normalized deviance (Vaughan, 2008). Vaughan's inability to validate her original analytic focus in coding "transformed [her] research immediately", making it "infinitely more complex and interesting" (Vaughan, 2004, p. 320), and it energized the shift that resulted in her eventual discovery—itself, of course, validated as such.

Coding is central to the shift in Vaughan's work and to the way that researchers engage validation and discovery. In this chapter, we illustrate the mutual constitution of validation and discovery by focusing on coding. Specifically we identify a process of "live" coding that we contrast with "inert" coding, and we show how live coding uses the connection between validation and discovery to produce shifts that support insightful and rigorous theorizing.

Live Coding

Coding is a methodological activity researchers follow in which they "symbolically assign a summative, salient, essence-capturing and/ or evocative attribute" to a portion of data (Saldana, 2009, p. 3), which applies to other portions or segments as well (Fielding, 2002). A code is a result that follows from the work of scrutinizing, pondering, and organizing observations to shape names that abstract particular features and possible relationships that are expressed in data (Locke, 2007). Naming constitutes an object by synthesizing what this work leads researchers to believe they "see" in their data. To illuminate how discovery and validation work together as a mutually constituted duality in coding, we distinguish "live" coding and its counterpart "inert" coding. Table 35.1 provides an explicit comparison and summarizes these two kinds of coding.

Coding is often described in a context of validation, in which there is little or no room for discovery. In this inert coding, the activity of coding is viewed procedurally, directed toward generating a list of code objects—named groupings of observations and relationships—that is complete when we have the list. As an analytic practice, it treats those code objects as expressing aspects of social life that are singular, definite, and independent (Law, 2006). Researcher satisfaction that the developed codes capture and represent what is happening in observations limits curiosity and the development of further understanding of phenomena by prompting disconnection from the data (Seidel & Kelle, 1995). In separating out discovery from coding, the practice of inert coding not only prevents researchers from learning, but also promotes replication of what we already know; it is too easy to fall into self-confirming bias[2] because whatever codes we start with (even if not very applicable or helpful) are not changeable because we don't "go back" in the coding process.

As Table 35.1 highlights, live coding enacts the mutual constitution of the discovery–validation duality. The activity of coding is organic in which coding, codes, and data shape each other; they are interdependent and inseparable. Thus, on an ongoing basis, the process of coding alters the list of codes by creating codes and by changing the meaning of any specific code. It is not at all unusual for researchers to start out thinking they know what they are looking for, but the more they code, the more they find that the object of their research isn't an object at all—or at least does not have the qualities of singularity, definiteness, or independence. This experience is captured by Emerson, Fretz, and Shaw (1995) when they talk about the student who "lost her paper"—her original research focus—the more she coded (p. 158). Rather than being "satisfied" and static, the meaning of live codes expands, contracts, and mutates as the ideas they generate and observations they bring into focus direct further observations and comparisons that transform their meaning, as relationships with other codes and observations change them into different inclusive codes or cause them to fall away in relevance, and so on. Live codes then are not understood as representations but as dynamically created lenses through which to consider and interact with further observations and ideas.

The process of naming and materializing observations into objects renders them potentially consequential, producing clearly articulated pathways for our thinking. At the same time, it also does several other things. Coding abridges and condenses so that any given code a researcher articulates is incomplete; it cannot exhaust the meaning possibilities in the data. Accordingly, coding creates possibilities and simultaneously represents bounded choices carved out of possibility. In live coding possibility is kept open, and the choices represented by the code will be repeatedly revisited as codes are pressed against more observations, against extant theory, and against the researcher's developing understanding of what is happening in his or her field sites.

Table 35.1 Comparing Live and Inert Coding

Features of Codes and Coding	Inert Coding	Live Coding
Orientation	Validation	Validated discovery
Nature of codes	Static: List of codes is complete and definitions of codes are final and transferable (e.g., would have same meaning to any coder). Codes are inert.	Mutable: The process of coding alters the list of codes and the meaning of any specific code. Codes talk back.
Nature of the process	Procedural: Coding systematizes data according to predefined rules. Coding and data are independent.	Organic: Coding and data shape each other. Coding and data are interdependent and inseparable.
Learning and theorizing	Learning is an outcome of having completed coding. Categorizing data into fixed codes provides a picture of the data. The data become a fixed object that can be described and compared to support or falsify theory.	Coder learns by seeing how codes change. Coder engages multiple possible meanings of codes as well as the multiple potentialities in data to produce shifts in theorizing.
Dualities	Strives to identify data as orderly, definite, singular, and independent.	Seeks to use codes to encompass orderliness and messiness, definiteness and tentativeness, singularity and multiplicity, independence and interdependence.

In addition, the patterns of social action we characterize, designate, and gather together through coding are not perfectly bounded; they run into each other—especially as a project develops—and exactly what it is that particular codes relate to can keep going out of focus as everything appears to be related. Yet, the engagement of these sources of "messiness" with coding objects that are provisionally stable is potentially productive as it allows for codes to be both generative and recursively reshaped as part of the researcher's developing understanding of and theorizing about what her data explains. Returning to Vaughan, her analyses would not have permitted the discovery of normalized deviance if she had ignored how her initial analysis on rule breaking was faltering and if she had not been open to a shift toward new ideas that emerged on how rule following was implicated in the launch decision. In other words, she would have stopped the discovery process prematurely and prevented her ongoing observations from being developed into a theory that both offered new insights and was credible to others.

Accordingly, the emergence of new ways of understanding what our observations may instantiate is only possible by embracing their fluidity through a struggle to articulate and fix them that plays out in successive cycles over time. We suggest live coding involves organizing, ordering, and naming particular features and possible relationships—materializing the named features and relationships and the observations that support them (whether in software or on index cards in shoe boxes) so that they are available to us as objects to think with that are capable of "talking back" about what we see and understand, thereby providing a way to take us beyond the "observations" and understandings with which we began. Created by the researcher, coding thus involves generating thinking "objects" that become intermediaries between the researcher's perceiving, her developing understanding, and her observations. We emphasize live coding as a dynamic and improvisational activity that uses the friction of working discovery and validation to create legitimate new insights. From this view, productive theorizing occurs *through* coding's dynamism rather than as a follow up to finished codes (Dey, 2004).

Live Coding of Gersick's Live Coding

What does this live coding look like? We have earlier noted that Diane Vaughan's path breaking work on the *Challenger* launch decision could not have emerged without the fluid approach she took to coding her data. In this section we take another example—Connie Gersick's research resulting in a punctuated equilibrium model of group development. In developing this example, we rely on her own account of this research in three publications: a technical report titled "Life Cycles of Ad Hoc Task Groups" (1983); the article "Time and Transition in Work Teams: Toward a New Model of Group Development" the *Academy of Management Journal* (1988); and a commentary on that research, "Time and Transition in My Work on Teams: Looking Back on a New Model of Group Development," *Doing Exemplary Research* (Frost & Stablein, 1992). We also read her dissertation supervisor's commentary (Hackman, 1992).

Live coding entails creating objects through naming, pressing the named object against the data causing friction, and using the friction to create shifts in the researcher's questions, perspectives, analysis, and so forth. In our discussion of Gersick's work, we focus on two shifts. The first is the shift from a focus on group effectiveness to a focus on group development—a shift in the research question. The second is a shift from a broadly defined notion of temporality to the specific concept of midpoint transition—a shift in the analytic perspective.

This analysis of Gersick's research does not just repeat what Gersick said about her research, but rather interprets it to bring forward the process of live coding. In doing this, we are also engaged in live coding, learning about our own observational objects as we press them against the descriptions of her research available to us.

Shift I: From Team Effectiveness to Life Cycle Model

Gersick began work on what came to be this project in the winter of 1980 as a research assistant for Richard Hackman, who asked her to "develop a field guide for observing groups that could be used to test Hackman's team effectiveness model . . . [by] watching some real live groups and develop anchored rating scales based on how they actually got work done" (Gersick, 1992, p. 53). The focus on "real live groups" promoted an orientation to group life cycles thinking that "people might work differently depending on where they were in their development as a group" (Gersick, 1992, p. 53). She describes her method as not using existing categorization schemes, but using "descriptions and quotations from transcripts and interviews . . . to document for the reader what is going on in the team, and what kind of progress the team has made at given points in its history" (Gersick, 1983, p. 9).

She further identifies the following observational objects: the ease or "difficulty reaching a res-olution," whether the team stuck "with a particular design (with minor revisions)" or made "major substantive changes in the work" as it went along, and whether "a group's product does (or does not) conform to outside requirements as it develops" (Gersick, 1983, p. 8). The following questions provided the basis for additional summarizing and interpretive codes: What were the major topics of discussion? What were the major arguments, questions, and decisions of the meeting? What kind of planning did the group do? Were agendas made for the meeting itself, and was any long-term plan-ning done? Was discussion logical and structured, or free-flowing and meandering? Over the entire course of a group's meetings, what were the milestones—decisions, disagreements, or major revisions in the work itself? How were members relating to each other and to relevant stakeholders outside the group? When were there major changes in these relationships? (Gersick, 1983, p. 10). In addition to these linguistic codes, she also developed visual objects in the form of "a series of sketches of products taking shape, which looked a little like a stop-action film of toast popping out of a toaster" (Gersick, 1992, p. 4).

As is typical, these coded observations point to a broad range of features, in this case of the groups' behaviors, but they do not make self-evident what might become theoretically focal. It is certainly not obvious that time will emerge as focal from, for example, whether the team is sticking with a design for its product, what major arguments arose, the disagreements that arose, how members related to each other—to repeat just a few of the observational objects or codes she created in interaction with her data. At the same time, her efforts to generate a grounded basis for validating a group effective-ness model—creating objects that captured concrete features of the groups' behavior—disrupted her focus on group effectiveness and invited discovery. For instance, one avenue of discovery work she pursued was to visualize the sense of what she believed was happening through the toaster image, which highlighted the groups making progress at different points in time.

As she pressed these observational objects/codes against the data (observations of ad hoc task groups), thinking about what it was that she was observing, her project shifted away from an explo-ration of group effectiveness to such an extent that when she presented preliminary findings to Hackman, he "wondered what this had to do with his model" (Gersick, 1992, p. 54). While the cod-ing she had done did not speak to the effectiveness model, it did provide the basis for "a search for general pattern" that would culminate in the life cycle model (Gersick, 1983, p. 10). As she compared similarities and differences using the case histories of the four groups, she identified generalizations, which she rechecked against the original data. As she noted, the shift from the effectiveness model to the "life cycle model did not emerge until then" (Gersick, 1983, p. 10).

Shift II: From Life Cycle to Midpoint

Live coding in this research created a second shift involving the refining and shaping of a gen-eral notion of temporality in the form of a life cycle model, moving away from the prevailing literature-based temporal representation of stages and toward a more specific idea of midpoint.

As part of her research, Gersick had committed to the teams she studied to develop a "history of how they made their product" (Gersick, 1992, p. 53). Consistent with her methodology described previously, she tried to "identify exactly what the team did, at what times, to make its product come out as it did," an approach focused on the particulars of "teams' outputs and actions" that departed from the dominant approach to studying teams. She reflected on her approach, "had I been trying to abstract team's behavior into categories at that point, I would have missed these things" (Gersick, 1992, p. 54). In developing presentations for each of the teams, she "thought it would be most helpful . . . to show them the patterns and decisive actions I had observed, picking out quotations from their meeting transcripts to illustrate." She remembers "explaining to the first team . . . how they had begun a new era" at a certain meeting, and to the second team how they had "turned a corner" in their work (Gersick, 1992, p. 54) and recollects, "I think it was not until I had studied and presented feedback to four teams that I realized all of them had turned a corner" in the middle of their projects (Gersick, 1992, p. 55).

The idea and implications of "turning a corner" and starting anew had clearly become more salient in this analysis for Gersick. Whereas in the first shift it was an expansion to a larger set of codes than initially considered around effectiveness, the second shift was toward condensing and narrowing around temporal dynamics. Gersick took a systematic approach (1988, p. 15) as she "condensed each team's transcripts in three successive steps" of (1) numbering "every turn members took to speak" and condensing content to "retain the literal meaning in a streamlined form"; (2) condensing documents "by abstracting members' exchanges, a few statements at a time, into a detailed topic-by-topic record of the meeting"; and (3) condensing events of the meetings by producing "a concise list of the events—the discussions, decisions, arguments, and questions—of each meeting."

These "condensations" not only helped present insights to the groups, but they also created a friction in the process that drove her focus more to the phenomenon of the midpoint shift by providing observational objects for comparison and generalization across the teams as well as for use in pressing against her emergent theoretical ideas about group development. As Gersick put it (1988, p. 18), "further comparisons, across meetings within groups and across groups, revealed five empirical earmarks of the transition, a set of events uniquely characteristic of midpoint meetings."

The cross-team comparisons also provided objects for involvement of others in the live coding process. In Gersick's case, the initial codes provided a way for her supervisor, Richard Hackman, to ask probing questions that caused additional friction, pushing her deeper into her analyses:

> He would ask me why some group behaved as it had, and I would start describing the specifics of what happened, for example, between Sandra and Bernard at the first meeting. "But you've got to go beyond that!" he would say. I didn't know what he was getting at, and he, meanwhile, expressed doubts about pushing me to do something I hadn't automatically chosen myself. After a while, I finally understood, and it was an invaluable lesson in how to build abstract theory—not just interesting stories—from qualitative data. (Gersick, 1992, p. 58)

Through refusing to validate the initial, lower-level explanations, Hackman's queries produced friction, prompting her to shift her perspective to a higher abstraction of what her phenomenon was and how she might develop it theoretically.

In addition to the data condensations aiding interactions with her supervisor, the live nature of her codes also allowed her to bring to bear on her process analogous theories that would otherwise have seemed unrelated or unhelpful. Gersick shared that:

> Dan Levinson's work on adult development (which I had been following avidly for years, for entirely nonacademic reasons) both helped me appreciate important patterns in my own data

and showed me ways to understand them. My "midpoint transition" is an explicit analogy to Levinson's (1978) concept of the midlife transition. (1992, p. 55)

Finally, Gersick's live coding allowed for a powerful, fundamental shift by changing the meaning of a term she used initially as descriptive coding into one of an abstracted theoretical concept. The specific shift was from using the code *mid-point* initially to indicate a marker in a timeline to using *midpoint*, which became the focus of her theorizing efforts. The aliveness of her coding can be seen in comparing her original 105-page technical report with her later 29-page *AMJ* article on the subject. In the former, "mid-point" appears only six times. In the latter, it appears 26 times as "midpoint."[3] The *midpoint transition* had been named, crystallized, and moved from the periphery of her analysis to center stage as the focus of her theorizing efforts.

Further Glimpses of Live Coding

As we have noted, the norms for writing methods sections in research journals are to describe validation and obscure the discovery that is necessary to live coding. So even when live coding is central to inventive qualitative work (including in our own), it is not reported, and therefore it is difficult to find explicit published examples of the process other than in explicitly reflective accounts of methods work such as the aforementioned Gersick and Vaughan descriptions. Despite the barriers of formal writing, however, glimpses of live coding do appear in other studies, as shown in Table 35.2.

Barry Turner's work on disaster and how accidents happen due to technological, social, and organizational factors shows evidence of live coding in his methodological expositions of the grounded theory approach. For example, he points to fluidity in his coding as he pressed it against further observations and other codes. He notes how he developed the idea of susceptibility to accumulating distractions when managing risk (Turner, 1978 pp. 234–235):

> I have one card which was initially labeled: "Acceptance of partial view of problem obscuring sider view. Or/confusion of one factor with another (synecdoche?)." To this, later in the analysis, I added: "Ignoring the beam because of concentrating on the mote." Later still, this category card was combined with two others, which I felt dealt with essentially the same phenomenon: "Acceptance of partial view of problem obscuring wider view of problem" and "Chain phenomena." Finally the term "Decoy phenomena" was felt to embody the crucial features of concern.

Martha Feldman gives a live coding glimpse in her methods section in her work challenging the prevailing understanding of resources as stable entities independent of the actions needed to bring potential resources into practice. She points to messiness, interrelationships, and multiplicity in the relationship between evolving understanding and observations as she shapes the phenomenon that becomes focal in her theorizing efforts. For example, she notes of her analytic process (Feldman, 2004, p. 298):

> As I attempt to pull out and follow one strand, I must make decisions about what constitutes a strand, and about what surrounding fabric needs to be explained in order to make sense of the strand. During this process I find that questions arise that did not arise from any of the previous analytical efforts. I interpret this as a function of the richness of the data rather than a failing of any of the earlier analytical efforts.

Live coding is evident in the idea that even as researchers identify the strands they focus on for a particular research project, new questions arise, opening new possibilities for exploration.

Table 35.2 Illustrations of Live Coding

Result	Shifts Brought About With Aid of Live Coding	Research Context	Intermediary Works and Reflections That Provide Glimpses Into Live Coding	Reference
Punctuated equilibrium theory of ad hoc group process	Team effectiveness *to* life cycles of teams; temporality *to* midpoint	Ad hoc project teams	Gersick (1983, 1992, this volume)	Gersick (1988)
Theory of normalized deviance theory	Decision to launch was violation of rules due to time pressure *to* controversial and risky decisions were the norm at NASA	Explaining causes of flawed decisions behind space shuttle *Challenger* disaster	Vaughan (2004, 2008)	Vaughan (1996)
Theory that resources need resourcing actions to bring them into practice	Action constrained by resource availability *to* resources are input to value-creating actions *to* actions as resources	Organizational processes in university residence halls	Feldman (1995)	Feldman (2004)
Theory of liminality as symbolic apparatus for cultural change	Difficult for embedded actors to create change *to* some actors crafted symbolic spaces that fostered change *to* how actors craft liminal spaces that introduce new cultural resources for change	Cultural innovations in sportswear firm; health care mergers; and adult beverage firm	Golden-Biddle & Locke (2007); Locke, Golden-Biddle, & Feldman (2008)	Howard-Grenville, Golden-Biddle, Irwin, & Mao (2011)
Theory of "incubation periods" that precede disaster when risks accumulate unnoticed	Perception *to* information difficulties *to* incubation periods	Three disasters: colliery tip onto a school, railroad crossing collision, nightclub fire	Turner (1981)	Turner (1978), man-made disasters; Turner (1976)

The work of Jennifer Howard-Grenville, Karen Golden-Biddle, Jennifer Irwin, and Jina Mao (2011) provides the most explicit account of live coding we have yet found in a published methods section in their work demonstrating the limits of accepted change models. They note:

> We summarized our conversations and early coding efforts in memos that we circulated and used in subsequent discussion. . . . During this process, we began to see that our actors were often using normally occurring venues such as meetings, workshops, or encounters in a way that helped others to entertain new ideas, experiment with new ways of doing things, and reflect on their actions. . . . As we conducted more focused coding . . . considered reviewer comments, and engaged in further reading, we came to see the work these people do as crafting symbolic spaces

for others to engage new ideas for change. In reading the work of Turner (1967,1987) we came to consider these symbolic spaces as liminal, connected to the organization's prevailing cultural repertoire yet also introducing new cultural resources for change. (p. 527)

They demonstrate live coding in the way in which coding and data shape each other and the phenomenon they come to theorize.

Conclusion

Live coding suggests some principles about the practice of coding and the teaching of coding practices. First, live coding is dynamic and fluid; provisionally stable live codes take on meaning and also change as they are pressed against collected data and theorizing efforts. Second, live coding permits a shift from what we already know to that which is entirely new or counterintuitive to our initial theoretical frames—as in the profiled cases of Vaughan and Gersick. This fluidity then provides opportunities for reconceptualization and the generation of new theory. Third, live coding highlights coding as a starting point rather than an ending point in analysis. As we create and shape observational objects that produce friction when put to work, we enable our potential to see and access different understandings of our phenomenon.

This chapter illustrated the mutual constitution of discovery and validation by developing the idea of "live coding." Live coding is differentiated from inert coding which, in privileging validation, leaves little room for discovery. Live coding does not represent an analytic invention; rather, it brings forward and encourages researchers to use the coding process more fully to engage with discovery and validation as mutually constituted.

Notes

1 We are grateful to Rod Kramer and Rodney Lacey for their constructive and insightful comments.
2 We are grateful to Rodney Lacey for this insight.
3 According to Gersick, the change from *mid-point* (hyphenated) to *midpoint* may have been an editorial change.

References

Alvesson, M., & Skoldberg, K. (2000). *Reflexive methodology: New vistas for qualitative research*. London, England: Sage.

Czarniawska, B. (1999) *Writing management: Organization theory as a literary genre*. New York, NY: Oxford University Press.

Dey, I. (2004). Grounded theory. In C. Seale, G. Gobo, J. Gubrium, & D. Silverman (Eds.), *Qualitative research practice* (pp. 80–93). Thousand Oaks, CA: Sage.

Eisenhardt, K. M. (1989). Building theories from case study research. *Academy of Management Review*, 14, 532–550.

Emerson, R.M., Fretz, R.I., & Shaw, L.L. (1995). *Writing ethnographic fieldnotes*. Chicago, IL: University of Chicago Press.

Feldman, M.S. (1995). *Strategies for interpreting qualitative data*. Thousand Oaks, CA: Sage.

Feldman, M.S. (2004). Resources in emerging structures and processes of change. *Organization Science*, 15, 295–309.

Fielding, N. (2002). Automating the ineffable: Qualitative software and the meaning of qualitative research. In T. May (Ed.), *Qualitative research: An international guide to issues in practice* (pp. 161–178). London, England: Sage.

Gersick, C.J.G. (1983). *Life cycles of ad hoc task groups* (Technical Report No. 4). Research program on group effectiveness, Yale School of Organization and Management.

Gersick, C.J.G. (1988). Time and transition in work teams: Toward a new model of group development. *Academy of Management Journal*, 31, 9–41.

Gersick, C.J.G. (1992). Time and transition in my work on teams. In P. Frost & R. Stablein (Eds.), *Doing exemplary research* (pp. 52–64). Thousand Oaks, CA: Sage.

Gersick, C.J.G. (2016). Adventures in qualitative research. In K. D. Elsbach & R. M. Kramer (Eds.), *Handbook of Qualitative Organizational Research: Innovative Pathways and Methods*. New York: Routledge.

Glaser, B., & Strauss, A. (1967). *The discovery of grounded theory*. Chicago, IL: Aldine.

Golden-Biddle, K., & Locke, K. (2007). *Composing qualitative research*. Thousand Oaks, CA: Sage.

Hackman, R. (1992) Time and transitions. In P. Frost & R. Stablein (Eds.), *Doing exemplary research* (pp. 73–76) Thousand Oaks, CA: Sage.

Howard-Grenville, J., Golden-Biddle, K., Irwin, J., & Mao, J. (2011). Liminality as cultural process for cultural change. *Organization Science*, 22, 522–539.

King, G., Keohane, R., & Verba, S. (1994) *Designing social inquiry*. Princeton, NJ: Princeton University Press.

Kordig, C.R. (1978). Discovery and justification. *Philosophy of Science*, 45, 110–117.

Law, J. (2006). Making a mess with method. Retrieved from www.heterogeneities.net/publications/Law2006MakingaMesswithMethod.pdf

Lin, A.C. (1998). Bridging positivist and interpretive approaches to qualitative methods. *Policy Studies Journal*, 26, 162–180.

Locke, K. (2007). Rational control and irrational free play: Dual-thinking modes as necessary tension in grounded theorizing. In A. Bryant & K. Charmaz (Eds.), *The Sage handbook of grounded theory* (pp. 565–579). London, England: Sage.

Locke, K., Golden-Biddle, K., & Feldman, M. (2008). Making doubt generative: Rethinking the role of doubt in the research process. *Organization Science*, 19, 907–918.

Peirce, C.S. (1934). *Collected papers of Charles Sanders Peirce. Vol. 5, Pragmatism and pragmaticism*. Cambridge, MA: Harvard University Press.

Roth, W., & Mehta, J.D. (2002). The rashomon effect: Combining positivist and interpretivist approaches in the analysis of contested events. *Sociological Research Methods and Research*, 31, 131–173.

Saldaña, J. (2009). *The coding manual for qualitative researchers*. London, England: Sage.

Seidel, J., & Kelle, U. (1995). Different functions of coding in the analysis of textual data. In U. Kelle (Ed.), *Computer-aided qualitative data analysis: Theory, method and practice* (pp. 52–61). London, England: Sage.

Siegel, H. (1980). Justification, discovery, and the naturalizing of epistemology. *Philosophy of Science*, 47, 297–310.

Swedberg, R. (2012). Theorizing in sociology and social science: Turning to the context of discovery. *Theoretical Sociology*, 41, 1–40.

Timmermans, S., & Tavory, I. (2013). Theory construction in qualitative research: From grounded theory to abductive analysis. *Sociological Theory*, 30, 167–186.

Turner, B. A. (1976). The organizational and interorganizational development of disasters. *Administrative Science Quarterly*, 21, 379–397.

Turner, B.A. (1978). *Man made disasters*. London, England: Wykeham Press.

Turner, B.A. (1981). Some practical aspects of qualitative data analysis. *Quality and Quantity*, 15, 225–247.

Van de Ven, A.H. (2007). *Engaged scholarship: A guide for organizational and social research*. New York, NY: Oxford University Press.

Vaughan, D. (1996). *The Challenger launch decision: Risky technology, culture, and deviance at NASA*. Chicago, IL: University of Chicago Press.

Vaughan, D. (2004). Theorizing disaster: Analogy, historical ethnography, and the Challenger accident. *Ethnography*, 5, 315–347.

Vaughan, D. (2008). Interview: Diane Vaughan, sociologist, Columbia University. Retrieved from www.consultingnewsline.com/Info/Vie%20du%20Conseil/Le%20Consultant%20du%20mois/Diane%20Vaughan%20%28English%29.htl

Weick, K.E. (1989). Theory construction as disciplined imagination. *Academy of Management Review*, 14, 516–531.

Weick, K.E. (2005). Organizing and failures of imagination. *International Public Management Journal*, 8, 425–438.

36

Between Text and Context

Innovative Approaches to the Qualitative Analysis of Online Data

Anca Metiu and Anne-Laure Fayard

Introduction

In the age of Web 2.0 and social media of all forms—blogs, online social networks, online forums, tweets, and the list goes on—studies relying heavily on online data have multiplied (Fayard and DeSanctis 2005, 2008, 2010; Nardi 2004; O'Mahony and Ferraro 2007; Orlikowski and Scott in press; Schulze in press; Vaast 2007, 2013). Who would not want to use online data, which are publicly available and easy to access? No need to go negotiate access to an organization, you can just open your browser and, at most, create an account. However, ease of access is not synonymous with ease of analysis and interpretation. Indeed, having access to a large amount of data does not necessarily mean that we have access to "rich data" in the sense anthropologists talk about "thick descriptions" (Geertz 1973), that is, descriptions that specify many details, conceptual structures, and meanings and put them *in context*. In that sense, context is at the core of ethnography and qualitative research, broadly speaking. In order to produce thick descriptions of social practices, qualitative researchers rely heavily on an understanding of the settings and circumstances in which the practices take place (Geertz 1973; Van Maanen 2011).

Such an understanding is what we miss while analyzing online data, which are mostly text based and for which we often lack context. While we can read all the posts on a forum, and while we can access them "forever," we are at the same time missing a lot of important elements regarding the posters' identities, moods, and environments, as the famous *New Yorker* cartoon "On the Internet, nobody knows you're a dog"[1] reminds us. This lack of information is what we call the *contextual challenge*. The question for researchers studying online phenomena then becomes: How can one provide thick descriptions of the social world by studying text-based online interactions?

This is the question we will explore in this chapter by borrowing from literary criticism and building on the distinction between text and context[2] that is at the core of that field. Indeed, as qualitative researchers studying online phenomena, our endeavor seems very close to those of literary critics because of the textual nature of online phenomena: Whether you are studying online forums, email exchanges, tweets, or interactions in virtual worlds like Second Life or World of Warcraft, interactions and practices are mainly textual. Despite the immense amount of text to study (for example, O'Mahony and Ferraro [2007] examined over 17,000 mailing list postings in an open-source project), we are regularly faced with the question as to how much of the context relevant to the understanding of the interactions is captured in these texts. For example, have authors discussed the same issues in face-to-face meetings as they have in online postings? And if so, how can we interpret the positions expressed in the postings? To what extent can the exchanges of text gathered through online observation constitute a foundation for studying topics such as work coordination, conflict, power relations, or identity?

The challenge of providing "sufficient" and "relevant" context is not specific to online qualitative research; it is also present in traditional qualitative studies in which the researcher is breathing and moving in the same physical world as the people he or she studies. Yet, it takes particular forms when the practices we examine are performed online because we have limited, if any, interactions with the people we study, and thus less familiarity with their social worlds and little understanding of what happens offline. Because of this limited access, it becomes difficult to determine the *relevant* context to interpret these multifaceted social phenomena and to give a sense of immediacy for the practices and behaviors observed in situ. In this chapter, we suggest that a fruitful way to study online data is by rethinking our conception of the relationship between text and context and by recognizing that online phenomena text may sometimes become context. Based on this distinction between text and context, we present three innovative strategies that have been used by qualitative researchers—including ourselves—in order to address these context-related challenges and provide meaningful, rich interpretations of online practices.

The Relationship Between Text and Context in Traditional Qualitative Research

Qualitative research aims to develop rich accounts of practices that provide an understanding of the meanings participants in particular social worlds attach to themselves, their worlds, and the events around them (Elsbach and Bechky 2009; Geertz 1973; van Maanen 2011). To develop such rich accounts, qualitative researchers have immersed themselves in the cultures of the "natives"—that is, their everyday contexts in faraway islands, slums, manufacturing plants, hospitals, police departments, or banks. For example, Bechky (2003) unveiled the complex and subtle knowledge exchanges and transformations taking place between engineers, technicians, and assemblers in a manufacturing plant by developing a deep understanding of the occupational communities involved in the work. Similarly, Fayard and Weeks (2007) illuminated the variations in how different organizational spaces trigger informal interactions by paying attention not only to the physical dimensions of the space, but also by developing an understanding of what was socially recognized as work and appropriate interactions in the different organizations they studied. Also, Metiu (2006) was able to grasp the dynamics among members of a distributed software development team by uncovering the underlying tensions existing between established centers of innovation (in this case, Silicon Valley) and new centers (in this case, Bangalore). These studies derive their explanatory power from their rich descriptions of the links between what has been deemed as context and the focal behavior, from the immediacy of the account, and from the authors' ability to say, "I was there" (Van Maanen, 2011). People's utterances and actions became meaningful thanks to the knowledge acquired by researchers deeply familiar with the context.

Thus, the discovery, the surprise that is at the heart of qualitative methods, come from the writing of a meaningful account of one's deep immersion in a context; through attention to the minutia of everyday life and through attending to the natives' idiosyncrasies and their interactions, the qualitative researcher focuses on particular aspects of the context that he or she explores deeper (Bartunek et al. 2006; Elsbach and Bechky 2009). It is this immersion that draws the researcher's attention to various issues (Elsbach and Bechky 2009). For example, from the myriad contextual factors that could have influenced the dynamics in a virtual team, Anca's presence in the field helped her determine that it was the status relations among the two subgroups (as opposed to the history of the organization, the national culture, or some other factor) that had the greatest traction in terms of explaining what was going on (Metiu 2006).

In qualitative research, context never lives without its textual counterpart; text and context are deeply intermingled. The written text that we call ethnography (Van Maanen 2011) emerges from the researchers' ongoing interpretations of multiple types of texts, some of which are produced by the researcher (e.g., field notes, transcripts, analytical memos) and others produced by the members of the organization studied (e.g., archival documents, meeting minutes, strategy statements). In a sense, qualitative research, and especially ethnography, does not exist in the absence of text. Ethnography, a written representation grounded in the interpretations we researchers developed, is produced through the constant dialogue between the "context" experienced during field work and the multiple textual forms—field notes, transcripts, memos—through which we captured the context. The context is never captured "objectively," of course, but on the basis of the field researcher's often spontaneous decisions on what is important, meaningful, or relevant.

While context is crucial for developing rich and insightful qualitative accounts (hence the articles chosen as most impactful by AMJ editors [Bartunek, Rynes, and Ireland 2006] were lauded for their fit between the data and the theory), it is also important to remember that what is defined as context in an ethnography is largely a choice made by authors as they shape their final accounts (Van Maanen, 2011). During fieldwork, what is the figure and what is the background is never clearly cut. Only later, and due to the constraints involved in writing ethnography, the context is presented as something separate from the practices, as a background or a pretext that influences or shapes the focal practices. Thus, the distinction between the foreground and the contextual background is not an objective reality, but rather emerges from the interpretative act of the researcher. In qualitative studies of online phenomena, because context seems less available,[3] the interpretative act is even more salient, with the distinction between text and context at its core.

The Relationship Between Text and Context in Online Qualitative Research

Qualitative research based on online data seems to be the poor cousin of more traditional qualitative research due to our limited access to context: You don't see people nor their nontextual interactions, and you often know very little about their surroundings. Hence, when it comes to online data, our role becomes one of a literary critic whose analysis focuses on the text, because the author's intention or background experience is rarely accessible, or of a historian, who makes sense of a certain historical period using prominently textual data with no direct access to context (except for contemporary historians). In the analysis of online data, context seems minimal and reliance on text is maximal. Table 36.1 summarizes the main challenges associated with capturing the context in both traditional and online qualitative research.

In online studies, the main corpus of data consists in textually enacted interactions. The interactions thus become objectified, made visible and thus indefinitely accessible and traceable; one can follow the thread of a conversation, go back to previous posts, read through the comments. In that sense, online data might seem richer than field observations because they provide us with an objective image of what is going on—conversations and interactions—without the subjective bias of the researcher taking notes, which always involves some degree of interpretation. For example, in traditional qualitative fieldwork, we might notice a sign between two participants but miss the sign made by a third one that led to the conflict, or we might misinterpret a tone of voice or a nod as friendly or aggressive. While in our fieldwork we try to catch every instant, we always "miss" something and we cannot replay the scene. In contrast, in online data, we can just go back to the evidence of the text, which now seems to have the power of the proof. This is what often makes online data so attractive to researchers: You can observe the online world in a nonobtrusive way (of course this poses particular ethical challenges, which we won't be able to address here; see, for example, Hine [2000] for an overview of these issues); moreover, these posts are potentially available forever.

Table 36.1 The Contextual Challenge in Qualitative Research

Aspects of the Qualitative Research Process	Traditional Settings	Online Settings
Data collection	Accessing the data can be difficult, and building the corpus of data usually takes a long time. The researcher interacts with the people she is studying. The researcher becomes familiar with the studied people's social and material world. *Lengthy process but rich and deep context.*	Accessing and building the corpus of data can be easy, and data collection may be done in a short time. There may be no interaction whatsoever with the people studied. The researcher may not access at all the participants' sociomaterial worlds. There are no nonverbal cues. *Easy access and large amount of data, but limited context.*
The producer of the main corpus of texts	The field researcher. May include texts produced by people studied.	The people studied. The field researcher may also produce some texts.
Nature of text	Real-time collection of observational data. Recollection and transcription of observations and experiences in the field. Transcripts of interviews. Interpretations of the field researchers. Various documents such as white papers, meeting minutes, design documents, etc. produced by people being studied.	Posts, threads, interactions of people being studied. Their interactions are textual and hence the online text becomes an important part of their context. Field researcher's notes on the (textual) interactions they observe and on their interpretations of the observed online interactions.
Data analysis and interpretation	Emerging themes, theoretical memos, case studies. Back and forth between the different types of data; using context to interpret and make sense of events and specific practices. *Interpretation by researcher is at the core.*	Emerging themes, theoretical memos, case studies. Difficult sometimes to interpret a situation, an interaction without knowing the specific context of the actors or if they also interact offline. *Interpretation by researcher is at the core.*

This stands in stark contrast with the time and effort involved in negotiating entry, observing and interacting with the "natives" before getting one's bearings, and writing rich texts in an attempt to capture as much of the context as possible in traditional qualitative research. These efforts are offset by the advantages of daily immersion in people's lives and environments and of frequent interaction with the people we study, which in turn contrast with the lack of context for online data (i.e., the lack of offline interaction—or of any kind of interaction—with the members of online communities, participants of virtual worlds or games, authors on blogs, etc., and the lack of familiarity with the nontextual aspects of their lives) that can be a major stumbling block for constructing a meaningful account of online posts.

Whether context comes first or text comes first and whether text is produced mostly by us or by those we study, qualitative research remains grounded in the same interpretative act aiming to provide meaningful accounts of social practices. Still, the challenge of context posed starkly by the use of online data demands a clear understanding of the relationship between text and context. In the next section, we will use some of the ideas advanced by literary criticism to provide such a conceptualization.

Innovative Approaches for Addressing the Contextual Challenge in Online Qualitative Research

Qualitative researchers examining online settings have addressed the contextual challenge and managed to develop thick descriptions and rich understandings of online practices by developing innovative approaches to collecting and analyzing online data. On the basis of the extent of their reliance on online text, we identify three such analytical strategies—the structuralist, the explanatory, and the "virtual" ethnography (see Table 36.2 for a summary of the different approaches).

Table 36.2 Innovative Strategies for Analyzing Online Data and Exemplars

Analytical Strategy and Exemplar Papers	Reliance on Online Text	Use of Other Data Sources	Focus of Analysis/ Phenomenon Studied
Structuralist			
Vaast (2007, 2013)	Exclusive	None	Online self-presentation and emergence of a new online actor category
Fayard and DeSanctis (2005, 2008, 2010)	Exclusive	None	The emergence of language games in online forums and construction of a shared identity through discursive practices
Explanatory			
Fayard and Metiu (chapters 7 and 8, 2012)	Heavy	Archival (blog posts, interviews posted online, etc.)	How online written exchanges enable knowledge creation and the development of trust among distributed collaborators
O'Mahony and Ferraro (2007)	Moderate to heavy (over 17,000 postings)	Interviews with project contributors; archival (project constitution, manual, charter, etc.)	The blending of bureaucratic and democratic governance mechanisms in an open source community
Virtual Ethnography			
Rheingold (1993)	Heavy	Long-term participant observation, some interviews with community members	How people use online text and interactions to engage in the full range of social activities
Nardi (2010)	Moderate to heavy	Long-term participant observation, interviews and visits with community members	Rich account of the culture of World of Warcraft players in the U.S. and China

Anca Metiu and Anne-Laure Fayard

The "structuralist"[4] approach relies exclusively on text, with no additional data from other sources. The analysis consists of looking for patterns within the text and considering the text as the sole context for the interactions. This approach has been often used to illuminate phenomena where additional context does not seem needed to develop thick descriptions and rich understandings. For instance, Fayard and DeSanctis (2005, 2008, 2010) did a qualitative discourse analysis of the messages posted by participants in several public online forums on knowledge management. In particular, they examined the emergence and development of specific discursive practices enacted by forum members. Their analysis was grounded solely on the textual analysis of the posts and exchanges that they considered as the main context for the interactions between online forum members; looking at the evolution and structure of the threads and the content and styles of the posts allowed them to unveil the construction of specific language games in each forum.

In one specific study, for example, Fayard and DeSanctis (2010) provided a grounded understanding of the construction of collective identity and culture in two online forums, KM Forum and KM Chapter (pseudonyms) based on their qualitative analysis of 782 messages posted by participants in the two forums over 9 months. Analysis consisted of multiple readings of all the messages with regular discussions between the authors to adjust and refine the emerging analytical dimensions. In these first phases of the analysis, they were surprised by the frequent references to a collective, which created a sense of we-ness. This surprise led them to explore how this sense of we-ness was enacted by the participants—beyond the expressions of collective identity (e.g., use of the collective *we*, references to the group). They then compared and contrasted specific messages and built theoretical categories that served as the basis for the language-game analysis. The focus here was on understanding the emergence of practices within the online forum and thus the text was seen as the main context.

Messages posted online were also the main focus of Vaast et al.'s (2013) examination of the emergence of a new actor category, that of technology bloggers. Analyzing over 1,100 entries of numerous bloggers, the researchers identified the identity claims made and how they were enabled by the Internet medium. They showed how the discursive practices were built in response to continuous evolutions in the media and thus were able to distinguish both identity-enabling and identity-unsettling effects of new media. The analysis proceeded in a grounded fashion by coding the entries and identifying main themes and practices. Throughout the analysis, the researchers interpreted the themes by contextualizing them: They paid attention to how bloggers interrelated with one another, how they reacted to new media developments, and how other actors constructed technology discourses. The blog posts constituted both the text and the context of the analyses, and no complementary data was invoked in the interpretation.

Such studies assume that text provides enough context, or even that text has become the context. This perspective resonates with Sherry Turkle's claim (2011), in her book *Life on the Screen*, that some people playing multiuser dungeon games developed a specific online identity and that their online life "counts" as much or even more than their offline life. In such cases, the "online life" of participating in or online communities becomes the context for the offline interactions.

The explanatory approach[5] still involves a heavy reliance on online text. Yet, to analyze online texts and interpret online practices and interactions, researchers rely on complementary data, understood as the context to which qualitative researchers usually turn when developing their interpretation of practices. Researchers using this approach use a variety of complementary data sources to the online texts posted by the participants: interviews with participants, archival data such as historical monographs and biographies, or participants' own writings. These complementary sources of information are deemed important in explaining online practices by giving researchers some access to the contexts in which these practices occurred.

This is the approach we took in our study of two online communities—openIDEO and open source software development (Fayard and Metiu 2013, chapters 7 and 8). Our aim in these studies was to investigate the mechanisms at play within the text: how community members either produced knowledge or developed a sense of community through writing. In both cases, we relied heavily on online posts by community members. However, to make sure we understood the particularities of the two online communities while developing our interpretation of the participants' interactions, we resorted to additional knowledge about these settings. For example, Anne-Laure has been a participant observer on openIDEO and has done multiple interviews with community members. While we did not rely specifically on these data in our analyses of the role of writing in developing new ideas and solutions to social challenges by openIDEO members, Anne-Laure's contextual knowledge, observations, and interviews helped us understand better the collaborative process among participants while doing textual analysis of the posts and comments. Similarly, Anca's extensive knowledge of the open source community through her previous work (Kogut and Metiu 2001) and her readings of participants' blogs and books about the community (such as Raymond's [2001] *The Cathedral and the Bazar*) helped us while analyzing the interactions of open source members. We were also helped by a research assistant whose technical knowledge was invaluable in allowing us to grasp some of the technical issues passionately debated in the threads we were analyzing. We also did some research on the key participants involved, as some of them seemed to have a certain status among the community. In both studies, complementary data permitted us to develop a fine-grained understanding of some of the tensions and disagreements we observed in the messages posted by community members.

The need for complementary data usually arises when one realizes that the research question requires more than an exclusive reliance on online data—for example, a surprise emerges from the analysis of the online data, but multiple readings still don't provide any insights or possible interpretation, and complementary data seem needed to develop a deeper understanding of the phenomenon studied. Thus, O'Mahony and Ferraro (2007) examined a wealth of complementary data sources to examine the evolution of governance in an open source software community: 17,317 mailing list postings, 48 interviews with project contributors and users, archival data. Through this triangulation approach, they identified several phases in the project's governance and explained the relationship between this process and the community members' evolving views and interpretations of various concepts of authority.

The virtual ethnography approach consists of deep, long-term immersion in an online environment in order to understand it from the point of view of the natives. Akin to traditional ethnography, this strategy aims to give a rich account of a particular online world. The difference here is that the "context" is not a sociomaterial, collocated world, but a web platform like the WELL or openIDEO or virtual environments where people can create avatars like World of Warcraft or Second Life. Similar to ethnographies of offline environments, this approach relies on a vast array of data sources in order to understand the online practices and environments, including online text, interviews, observation of online and offline interactions and practices, and archival data. The extent to which the researchers rely on online data in their virtual ethnography varies from heavy reliance (e.g., Rheingold in his virtual ethnography of the WELL community) to moderate and light (e.g., Nardi [2010] and Lindtner et al. [2004] who started their examinations of World of Warcraft players by focusing on online text, but then shifted to collecting more and more offline data). As in traditional ethnography, when the researcher finds intriguing, interesting aspects, he or she pursues them by looking for appropriate data sources.

Rheingold's (1993) well-known qualitative study of the WELL is a great example of a virtual ethnography that provided a nuanced, sensitive, and path-breaking account of an online community. Through long-term immersion as a participant observer in the community, Rheingold produced an insightful and in many ways surprising account of the emotional support provided by online community members. Another recent and compelling virtual ethnography is Nardi's (2010) study of the World of Warcraft. For more than three years, Nardi was a participant observer of World of Warcraft games in both the United States and China. She systematically observed players' behaviors both online and offline and provided a rich account of their culture, motivation, beliefs, and cooperative and addictive conduct.

In virtual ethnographies—similarly to what happens with structuralist and explanatory approaches—text, as produced and interpreted by the participants, is central. The messages posted and commented upon are one of the main data sources used by virtual ethnographers in their effort to develop an understanding of the interactions, emergent meanings, values, and practices enacted by members of an online environment. In virtual ethnographies, the "field" is textual, it is the online environment in which text-based interactions take place and practices are enacted and in which the virtual ethnographer becomes a participant. To this corpus of texts produced by members of the online communities, the researcher adds his or her own texts produced through note-taking and interpreting the natives' texts. Texts and contexts again are deeply intertwined, just as they are in traditional ethnography.

In all three approaches—structuralist, explanatory, and virtual ethnography—the data analysis, as in any forms of qualitative research, is an interpretative act and involves various activities that have been well described in previous methodological work (Becker 2008, Corbin and Strauss 2008, Glaser and Strauss 2009), such as writing notes describing practices observed in the online interactions (i.e., producing researcher-written texts), reading the texts (produced by the members of the community as well as notes produced by the researcher) numerous times, multiplying perspectives to achieve triangulation, and writing theoretical memos during the research. When possible, or perceived as needed (in explanatory and virtual ethnography approaches), researchers might rely on key informants. Informants might in some cases take on the role of "tutors," as was done in the virtual ethnography of an online musical community where Lysloff (2003) relied heavily, in the early stages, on a young composer who taught him a lot about using some of the software used by community members to compose electronic music. The tutor's guidance enabled Lysloff to gain a deep contextual immersion and an understanding of community members' views on creativity and ripping. Here the loop between online and offline seems to close as we find ourselves again interacting with the natives, who teach us the intricacies and routines of their online everyday lives.

When the Frontiers Between Offline and Online Become Blurred

The three innovative strategies identified previously make clear that while text and context vary in their nature and relationships, they are always interweaved and at the center of qualitative research, regardless of whether our data are collected offline or online. Such an intertwinement reflects the important similarities existing between qualitative studies of collocated interactions and online interactions: They provide a meaningful, contextually informed account of social practices; they rely on inductive reasoning; and they are always a written account built on the basis of other texts. In both cases, the interpretative act central to any qualitative approach doesn't change no matter the balance between native- and researcher-produced texts.

The text/context intertwinement central to all qualitative work is particularly important for qualitative researchers to reflect upon as the blurring between online and collocated interactions increases; today, many studies of organizations, even those with no focus on online phenomena, might involve some type of online data in the mundane form of email exchanges or chat messages. As Osterlund et al. (see chapter 37 in this volume) shows, the context often consists of a multitude of documenting practices aimed at tracing otherwise invisible distributed work. Thus, the relationship between text and context, and the innovative approaches developed to address the contextual challenge in online studies, are of interest even to researchers whose focus might not be specifically on online phenomena.

Notes

1 Cartoon by Peter Steiner published by *The New Yorker* on July 5, 1993.
2 Text and context as used by literary criticism are intimately related and their relations have been investigated and debated at length in literary studies. How much of the "context"—in particular its historical context, unpublished materials, correspondence, the life of the author—does one needs to know to analyze and understand a text? Various types of literary critics have emerged depending on their positions on the relations between text and context, ranging from the stance that the text cannot be understood without heavily relying on the context (whether biographical contexts or pretexts like in hermeneutic approach, e.g., Eco 1992; Poulet 1971) to the notion that the text can and should be understood as "stand alone" as suggested by structuralist approaches (e.g., Barthes 1973, 1976; Genette 1976).
3 However, even in traditional ethnographies, full access to the context of the people we study is a myth: No matter how long we stay in the field, we never have access to the "whole" context.
4 Structuralism in literary studies, as its name suggests, focuses on how the structures of the single text emerge and evolve or examines the structure of a large number of texts to discover the underlying principles that govern their composition (e.g., Barthes 1973, 1976; Genette 1976).
5 Explanatory, or contextual, approaches to literary criticism ground their analysis of text on extratextual elements, such as the life of the author, correspondence, and the general historical context.

References

Barthes, R. (1973). *Le plaisir du texte*. Paris: Seuil.
Barthes, R. (1976). *S/Z*. Paris: Seuil.
Bartunek, J.M., Rynes, S.L., & Ireland, R.D. (2006). What makes management research interesting, and why does it matter? *Academy of Management Journal 49(1)*, 9–15.
Bechky, B.A. (2003). Sharing meaning across occupational communities: The transformation of understanding on a production floor. *Organization Science 14(3)*, 312–330.
Becker, H.S. (2008). *Tricks of the trade: How to think about your research while you're doing it*. Chicago: University of Chicago Press.
Corbin, J. & Strauss, A. (Eds.) (2008). *Basics of qualitative research: Techniques and procedures for developing grounded theory*. Thousand Oaks, CA: Sage.
Eco, U. (1992). *Les limites de l'interprétation*. (trad. Myriem Bouzaher). Paris: Grasset.
Elsbach, K. & Bechky, B.A. (2009). Introduction: Research context and attention of the qualitative researcher. In K. D. Elsbach and B. A. Bechky (eds.), *Qualitative organizational research 2: Best papers from the Davis Conference on Organizational Research*, 1–10. Greenwich, CT: Information Age Publishing.
Fayard, A. L. & DeSanctis, G. (2005). Evolution of an online forum for knowledge management professionals: A language game analysis. *Journal of Computer-Mediated Communication 10(4)*, http://onlinelibrary.wiley.com/doi/10.1111/j.1083-6101.2005.tb00265.x/full
Fayard, A. L. & DeSanctis, G. (2010). Enacting language games: The development of a sense of "we-ness" in online forums. *Information Systems Journal 20(4)*, 383–416.
Fayard, A. L. & Metiu, A. (2012). *The power of writing in organizations: From letters to online interactions*. New York: Routledge.
Fayard, A. L. & Metiu, A. (2013). The role of writing in distributed collaboration. *Organization Science 25(5)*, 1391–1413.
Fayard, A. L. & Weeks, J. (2007). Photocopiers and water-coolers: The affordances of informal interaction. *Organization Studies 28(5)*, 605–634.
Geertz, C. (1973). *The interpretation of cultures: Selected essays* (Vol. 5019). New York: Basic Books.
Genette, G. (1976). *Figures I*. Paris: Seuil.
Glaser, B.G. & Strauss, A. (2009). *The discovery of grounded theory: Strategies for qualitative research*. New Brunswick, NJ: Aldine Transaction.
Hine, C. (2000). *Virtual ethnography*. London: Sage.
Kogut, B. & Metiu, A. (2001). Open-source software development and distributed innovation. *Oxford Review of Economic Policy 17(2)*, 248–264.
Lindtner, S., Nardi, B., Wang, Y., Mainwaring, S., Jing, H., & Liang, W. (2008, November). A hybrid cultural ecology: World of Warcraft in China. *Proceedings of the 2008 ACM conference on computer supported cooperative work*, 371–382.
Lysloff, R.T. (2003). Musical community on the Internet: An on-line ethnography. *Cultural Anthropology 18(2)*, 233–263.
Metiu, A. (2006). Owning the code: Status closure in distributed groups. *Organization Science 17(4)*, 418–435.

Nardi, B. (2010). *My life as a night elf priest: An anthropological account of World or Warcraft*. Ann Arbor: University of Michigan Press.

Nardi, B.A., Schiano, D.J., Gumbrecht, M., & Swartz, L. (2004). Why we blog. *Communications of the ACM 47(12)*, 41–46.

O'Mahony, S. & Ferraro, F. (2007). The emergence of governance in an open source community. *Academy of Management Journal 50(5)*, 1079–1106.

Orlikowski, W. & Scott, S. (in press). Entanglements in practice: Performing anonymity through social media. *Management of Information Systems Quarterly*.

Poulet, G. (1971). *La conscience critique*. Paris: Jos. Corti.

Raymond, E.S. (2001). *The cathedral & the bazaar: Musings on Linux and open source by an accidental revolutionary*. Sebastapol, CA: O'Reilly Media.

Rheingold, H. (1993). *The virtual community: Homesteading on the electronic frontier*. Reading, Massachusetts: Addison–Wesley. Schultze, U. (in press). Performing embodied identity in virtual worlds. *European Journal of Information Systems*.

Turkle, S. (2011). *Life on the screen*. New York: Simon and Schuster.

Vaast, E. (2007). Playing with masks: Fragmentation and continuity in the presentation of self in an occupational online forum. *Information Technology & People 20(4)*, 334–351.

Vaast, E., Davidson, E., & Mattson, T. (2013). Talking about technology: The emergence of a new actor category through new media. *Management of Information Systems Quarterly 37(4)*, 1069–92.

Van Maanen, J. (2011). *Tales of the field: On writing ethnography*. Chicago: University of Chicago Press.

37

Documenting Work

From Participant Observation
to Participant Tracing

*Carsten Østerlund, Jaime Snyder, Steve Sawyer,
Sarika Sharma, and Matt Willis*

Introduction

Distributed work is hard to observe. A focus on the more tangible aspects of this work, namely documents, provides a useful lens into the work practices of organizational members in general, and those working in heterogeneous and distributed environments in particular. Imagine the distributed collaboration going into the production of this book involving many research teams distributed across the globe, the publishers, and the editors. The individual chapters have taken form first by circulating among co-authors and then reviewers and editors to finally end up at the publisher. Multiple databases, organizing schemes, email servers, and cloud-based systems have been part of this process as documents have flowed among distributed participants.

Conceptually, a document can serve as a lens into the sociomaterial nature of what organizational members do, day in and day out. We view documents as artifacts that reflect social, material, temporal, and spatially structured communicative practices invoked in response to recurrent situations (Briet 2006; Buckland 1997; Frohmann 2004; Lund 2009; Østerlund 2008; Østerlund and Boland 2009; Zacklad 2006). Analytically, one can approach documents not only as standalone artifacts characterized by specific content, form, participants, time, and place, but also traces of ongoing work practices. By tracking documents over time, following their changes, movements, and uses, we can depict the unfolding of work. As in a time-lapse photo document, traces make organizational behaviors come alive. Studying documents in work allows us to position people's immediate activities and situated routines in their larger social and organizational contexts. Because documents carry institutional structures and point to both past and future activities, they open a window to larger organizational practices.

Recently, scholars have argued that "documents are not simply instruments of bureaucratic organizations, but rather are constitutive of bureaucratic rules, ideologies, knowledge, practices, subjectivities, objects, outcomes, and even the organizations themselves" (Hull 2012, p. 253). The focus of many current approaches to document studies is not solely on texts as semiotic constructions abstracted from their material vessels (i.e., concentrating primarily on the content of documents) but has expanded to examine dynamic processes and activities in which documents play a role. For example, scholars have examined the relations among documenting *practices* (Brown and Duguid

1994; Harper 1998; Knorr Cetina 1999; Latour 1987; Latour and Woolgar 1986; Randall et al. 2007; Van Maanen and Pentland 1994), document materiality (Barad 2003; Orlikowski 2007; Suchman 2007), infrastructures (Hine 2006; Ribes 2014; Star and Ruhelder 1996), genres (Bazerman 1995; Orlikowski and Yates 1994; Østerlund 2007; Swales 1990; Yates and Orlikowski 2007), the physical organization of the document (Feldman 2008), and documents as *boundary objects* (Bechky 2006; Carlile 2004; Star and Griesemer 1989). This requires us to look at, rather than through, documents as things that translate, transform, modify, or distort the meanings or things they are supposed to convey (Latour 2005).

Studying Documenting Work

Recognizing the conceptual relationship between documenting work and distributed organizational work practices gives rise to a methodological question: How do we best study documenting work? The answer may seem tantalizingly straightforward. You collect the artifacts left behind as organizational members go about their work and then begin to dig through your stack to look for evidence of work practices. But if you consult your qualitative methods books for guidance as you undertake this task, you will be reminded that documents subsist as a lower caste in field research as "the most despised of ethnographic objects" (Latour 1990, p. 54). Method texts (not counting history and political science) often devote significant attention to helping the reader refine their interview and participant observation skills, while documents and other artifacts are often addressed in passing under headlines such as "secondary sources" or "unobtrusive techniques," if at all.

Many an ethnographer has gathered piles and piles of documents in the field with the best of intentions, yet without a robust understanding of the larger body of documents from which they are drawn or the technical infrastructure supporting them. More importantly, this type of gathering obscures the traces documents leave of organizational members' unfolding work practices, their documenting work. In other words, focusing not only on documents but also the traces that are left by documenting practices, especially in digital environments, provides an opportunity for new integrative strategies to track work practices in distributed environments. The studies summarized in Table 37.1 illustrate how such traces lead to innovative approaches for understanding phenomena such as distributed science collaborations, conflict handling in crowdsourced environments, and the unruly life of electronic medical records in modern health care.

As seen in these studies, examining document traces challenges the ways in which we think about the location or field of action for an ethnographic study. Traditionally, ethnographers seek a physical site that is shared by actors and can provide a rich interactional environment for participant observation (Ribes 2014). A reliance on co-location is not viable in distributed organizations. Many interactions are neither co-located nor synchronous. There is not a single site from which to conduct observations.

Anne Beaulieu (2010) advances the concept of co-presence as an alternative to co-location. For workers, co-presence might be established in numerous ways, co-location being just one among others such as email exchanges, phone conferences, activity logs for repositories such as Dropbox, threaded exchanges on discussion boards, or changes in folder structures in a shared database. These traces also serve as data for researchers interested in coordination and collaboration activities (see Table 37.1). While such traces of organizational behaviors might be regarded as thin data compared to the thick descriptions produced by classic ethnographers (Geertz 1973), they reflect the same types of co-presence many actors themselves live in their distributed and online organizations. In this sense, the researcher and the actors are in symmetrical positions. In Ribes's words: "actors and ethnographers both relied on thin data to go about their 'thick activities'—though for different

Table 37.1 Use of Document-centric Participant Tracing in Qualitative Research Methods

Reference	Research Context	How Innovation Was Used	Outcomes/Results of Innovation
Sawyer, Kazianus and Østerlund (2012)	Science collaborations	Combines document tracking, participant observation, and interviews to study distributed collaborations among social scientists	Demonstrates the shortcomings of contemporary cyberinfrastructure in the support of distributed social science collaborations
Østerlund, Sawyer and Kazianus (2011)	Science collaborations	Combines document tracking, participant observation, and interviews to study distributed collaborations among social scientists	Details the method and evaluates how best to combine document tracking with interviews and participant observation, and discusses the challenges and benefits associated with digital instrumentation, practicality, privacy, verifiability, and reliability
Geiger and Ribes (2011)	Wikipedia	Combines the richness of participant observation with the wealth of data in logs to reconstruct patterns and practices in a distributed organization	Details the blocking of a vandal in Wikipedia involving many different editors with many different software tools and mechanisms to coordinate their work
Østerlund (2008)	Health care	Traces medical record production and use through document tracking, participant observation, and interviews	Illustrates how doctors carefully craft their medical histories in various electronic record systems to demarcate specific places for coordination with specific collaborators; such documents serve as portable places, allowing doctors to navigate a constantly changing landscape of relevant patients, participants, times, and spaces

purposes" (2014, p. 2). Similarly, Metiu and Fayard (2015) ask in this volume how we can produce thick descriptions based on thin online texts. In their rich discussion, the problem is framed as one between text and context. Co-located researchers and participants often have immediate access to the context of their activities. Without co-location, online participants and researchers have to discern context from texts left behind.

In this chapter, we present our own approach to working with document traces as evidence of organizational practices in distributed collaborations. Our approach to data collection builds on the basic assumption that documents are central elements of organizational infrastructure and provides evidence of unfolding coordination over time. Figure 37.1 summarizes our document-centric data gathering strategy. The two white boxes represent mapping activities, and the gray boxes show tracking activities.

Carsten Østerlund et al.

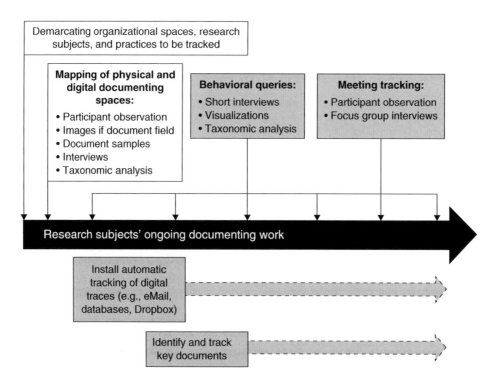

Figure 37.1 Document-centric Data Gathering Strategy

Mapping the Field of Documents

Document mapping is framed by two overarching questions: Where do your documents live? How do they support your work practices? Pursuing these questions is done in a phased approach. We begin with initial interviews with key informants to help bound the study by determining, for instance, the number of relevant participants, organizational goals and structure, spaces, temporal rhythm, and tools. At this time, we ask them to complete a brief survey to gather details about tools used for document production, sharing, or storing. Second, we spend a day or two with key informants to detail their document arrangements across both physical and digital spaces. We ask the informants to guide us through their physical and electronic document spaces, which may take the researcher from unwieldy piles of papers stacked on an office floor to neatly structured desktop file folders and bulky email inboxes. This phase of data collection includes participant observation, interviews, document sampling, and taxonomic probes. Photos of the physical space and screenshots of file directories and other aspects of the informant's digital environment serve as helpful tools for capturing data.

We follow these broad questions with focused inquiries into specific documents associated with particular work practices of interest. For example, lists constitute the oldest form of records (Goody 1986) and the foundation for the most advanced forms of documentation in the form of databases (Hull 2012, p. 262). Together with taxonomies, they also serve as particularly helpful data in the mapping phase of this methodology. Lists of pending tasks found on a whiteboard or carefully maintained folders and subfolders in an email program or repository speak volumes about participants' core activities and how those are organized into subsets and the way they are related to the whole. This allows us to map the relationships among the various subrepositories and their relationship to the larger whole (Spradley 1979, 1980). These analyses are central to an emergent qualitative understanding of the participants' distributed work, but more importantly, they are a necessary step in setting up the technical infrastructure that will allow us to track traces of unfolding documenting practices.

For instance, mapping distributed collaboration among scientists has revealed that most project teams created a shared repository, yet participants rarely synchronized their personal classification and storage schemes for paper or electronic documents (Østerlund et al. 2011; Sawyer et al. 2012). Taxonomies vary greatly across collaborators. On one science project, graduate student Liz had 12 subfolders in her electronic project file. Senior faculty member Caroline had only two. Email folders seemed to be less organized than file folders and came with fewer subfolders, if any. To complicate matters, some participants used email folders as prime storage devices for documents. One senior faculty member consistently went to his deleted mail or sent mail folders to retrieve old documents associated with distributed collaborations. Similarly, several other scientists we have spoken with reported slowly giving up on folders to organize documents, relying more and more on search functions to retrieve project documents on their desktop, email, and shared repositories.

Tracking the Process of Documenting Work

After initial interviews and exploratory observations of participants' work environments, tracking the process of documenting work revolves around four data gathering techniques. First, we set up a system for automated gathering of digital traces. Software tools provide a range of choices from simply tracking changes in specific folders (e.g., www.dropbox.com) to using screen recording software such as Camtasia Studio (Ignatova and Brinkman 2007; Tang, Liu, Muller, and Drews 2006). For shared repositories, change logs permit us to follow the flow of documents and to see who contributes to what documents, when, and where. Individual electronic desktops and email offer more of a challenge due to heterogeneous technologies, organization schemes applied by each participant, and privacy concerns. Depending on an individual scholar's organizational habits and setup, we can install an email tracking application and/or file tracking software on an informant's primary computer, with logs saved to a secure online repository. We analyze these digital traces for process cycles and other major events. For instance, when do people tend to work on the project? How does content flow among collaborators? How quickly do they respond to other's inquires or postings? What division of labor do we find among the participants?

Tracking scientists' documenting work revealed that, in many cases, shared repositories quickly become dead zones (Østerlund et al. 2011; Sawyer et al. 2012). Documents go in, occasionally, but they rarely come back out. In most cases, no clear taxonomy emerges in these shared repositories and nobody takes responsibility for keeping up an organizing scheme. Instead, participants maintained their own filing systems and shared documents via email. One senior faculty member provides a notable exception to this pattern. She tends to be the driver for many of her distributed projects, which she conducts via email and a blackboard learning management site. She maintains a clear file structure for project documents, and collaborators rely on her to push the project forward and keep documents organized.

Second, through the ongoing analysis of digital and behavioral traces, we identify a small number of key documents that play a central role in the scholars' coordination activities. These could be heavily distributed email attachments, frequently edited PowerPoint decks, or documents highlighted by informants in interviews. We track these documents in detail and analyze how they evolve through different iterations. Content and document-level analyses reveal how key documents relate to other artifacts and events.

For example, to-do lists emerged as a key document in science collaborations (Østerlund et al. 2011; Sawyer et al. 2012). Often merely lists outlining activities to be accomplished by the group or specific members, these summaries represent both the discussions and reflections that have gone into their production and they outline pending future activities. The materiality of these lists often repeatedly changes. They might start out on a whiteboard, be captured on a cell phone photo, shared via email, be transferred to word documents, or end up on project tools like Omnifocus or Basecamp.

Third, we track the participants' activities through behavioral inquiries. Short phone calls to individual participants become targeted interviews around key documents or project events. Specific documents or visualizations of document flows serve as interview prompts. For instance, automated tracking of email allows us to visualize the rhythm of email exchanges among collaborators. Such visualizations may lead to interesting conversations about project management, division of labor, temporal rhythms of work, and so forth.

Tracking and inquiring about to-do lists, for instance, reveal that operational leadership appears to be closely tied to the person producing those documents. For many collaborations, one or more graduate students would produce and circulate to-do lists following email discussions or teleconferences. These correspondences prompt the rest of the team to engage in specific activities. However, close to major deadlines, the production and circulation of to-do lists tend to shift to senior faculty members, only to return to the graduate student after the article or proposal had been submitted.

Our fourth and last data collection strategy is more closely related to traditional participant observation. Collaborators tend to organize teleconferences or face-to-face meetings to discuss the progress of their distributed collaboration. These regular gatherings offer excellent opportunities to build rapport through informal interaction and focus group interviews. Participating in these meetings can, to some extent, substitute for the individual focused behavioral inquires and enable us to contextualize the use of particular documents or triangulate insights gained from the document tracking or individual behavioral inquiries.

Methodological Implications

Placing documents and the practices associated with them at the center of our qualitative methodology comes with clear benefits, but also new challenges. Table 37.2 summarizes insights gleaned from our study of distributed work among science teams.

Table 37.2 Methodological Implications

Implications	Comments
From participant observation to participant tracing	Participant tracing allows researchers to study documents as processes or practices with temporal, spatial, and material manifestations that change over time.
Digital instrumentation	Software tools allow researchers to track a range of document activities, if carefully selected and implemented.
Commitment	Many document-tracking strategies require the research subjects' active engagement.
Privacy	Monitoring people's physical and electronic documents brings the researcher in proximity with highly private information. Enabling the subjects to control monitoring parameters and review data before they are released to the researcher protects subjects' privacy.
Heightened awareness	A document-centric methodology increases the research subjects' awareness of their own documenting work and can influence practices, if only temporarily.

From Participant Observation to Participant Tracking

Traditional participant observation involves co-located observing and interviewing, with rich ethnographic descriptions emerging from deep immersion. Studying the flow of documents requires the collection and intermediate analysis of larger bodies of documents before a complete picture of work practices can begin to emerge. We refer to this as *participant tracking*. Through this tracking, information gathered during interviews and observations becomes helpful in elaborating the dynamics of how documents reflect work practices and are linked to situated contexts. A hermeneutic approach supports the tracking of documents by organizing observations into short repeated cycles of data gathering and analysis. The researcher performs an initial mapping of the document field followed by automated tracking and repeated behavioral queries (i.e., iterative mappings). Analyzing the change logs along with collected and tracked documents in preparation for each behavioral query and participant meeting becomes necessary if one wants to illuminate the ongoing flow. Not only does this allow the researchers to refine their tracking techniques and time their mapping to important events and places for collaboration, but it also makes it possible to triangulate document-based observations through interviews, participant observation, and new document analysis.

Participant tracking positions documents not as stable artifacts but rather as dynamic processes with temporal, spatial, and material manifestations. For instance, tracking the specific location of documents in a physical pile or whether a document could be found in the office or workbag offers insights to the unfolding coordination of the group. Does an informant bother to print and file a document received as an email attachment, or is it digitally shuttled into an email folder to be forgotten? Does another informant insist on printing out all documents only to lug them around in a briefcase or allow them to be buried on a cluttered desktop? Participant tracking of this nature can be captured by a document-centric methodology and serves as snapshots of unfolding organizational practices.

Digital Instrumentation

Given the ever-expanding range of programs available to collect digital traces, it becomes a significant task to determine the appropriate software and configuration needed to capture data with the desired level of granularity to address research questions. Distributed collaborators often use different email clients, servers, and operating systems, which limits the types of tracking software that can be installed on participant computers. Differences in email clients and institutional difficulties in accessing mail servers curb, to different degrees, how one can catalog documents. Unsurprisingly, the blurring of work and personal documents is prevalent. Isolating those messages and attachments that are pertinent to a particular work practice, thereby avoiding announcements about the childrens' soccer practice, requires us to explore how participants use their tools to partition different activities within their digital and physical environments. However, decisions about tracking tools do not need to be cast in stone as they would need to be for a laboratory setup. Ethnographers regularly adjust their participation and interview techniques to particular contexts and the evolving relations to informants. Similarly, a document-centric study calls for a flexible approach to data gathering where the researcher continuously adjusts and refines data gathering techniques based on what has been learned to date. Filters are adjusted, added, or deleted as work habits evolve, new collaborators come on board, or changes to infrastructure require reconfigurations of tools. Responsiveness to the sociomaterial infrastructure of our field of inquiry gives "voice" to the technology (Latour 1990) and its role in distributed organizational practices.

Commitment

Many documenting tracking techniques require the active involvement of the research subjects. For example, at times we have asked participants to add our team's research email account to the recipient list for project relevant emails; to participate in behavioral inquires; to save project documents in folders accessible to the researchers; and to regularly scan collections for sensitive emails before they are analyzed by the research team. All of these activities consume the subjects' time and attention, as documented by the many computer science studies of document provenance that call for subjects to log changes to documents and applications over time (Dragunov, Dietterich, Johnsrude, McLaughlin, Li, and Herlocker 2005; Lonsdale, Jensen, Wynn, and Dedual 2010). From the research subjects' perspectives, these tasks quickly become a burden, or the tracking activities simply fall to the wayside as more pressing concerns crowd out people's attention and they simply forget to "cc" the project account on an important email. Document-centric studies that exploit digital traces require a set of data collection tools that balance comprehensive coverage against the commitment required of research subjects.

Privacy

Over the years, qualitative researchers have developed a series of techniques to afford confidentiality to their research participants and to keep private participants' identities and behaviors. However, dwelling in somebody's document universe raises a number of additional privacy issues. Most people use their computers for multiple purposes, many reaching deep into their private sphere. It can be difficult to set up a system that only monitors specific documenting practices, and overly restrictive filters can mask important behaviors related to work practices of interest. As mentioned earlier, Dropbox and other file-sharing systems allow researchers to track designated folders, but they leave many other activities invisible, such as applications and documents use during the production, classification, storage, and retrieval of relevant documents. Further complicating matters, having access to a participant's communication also means having access to information about the individuals with whom he or she corresponds. Care needs to be taken in designing an informed consent protocol that adequately addresses the privacy concerns of all parties. As a safeguard for maintaining adequate privacy for participants, we recommend giving informants control of their own trace data and/or the opportunity to delete undesired documents before the researchers gain access to the data.

Heightened Awareness

All qualitative research methods face a Heisenberg-style challenge where the process of observing can influence the observed. Document-centric data gathering is not different. When people are asked about their documenting work, they often develop a heightened awareness of their own habits and "digital hygiene," inevitably tidying and reorganizing files, sometimes right in the midst of an interview. This can include straightening piles of documents around the office, deleting files on a cluttered computer desktop, or finally taking the time to clean out a bulging email inbox.

Instead of seeing this as a threat to reliability, we see these actions as offering important insights into how research subjects perceive and work with their document infrastructure. Expressions of embarrassment about a desktop cluttered with digital files or a prideful boast about a "zero-inbox" policy reflect expectations, assumptions, and intentions. It is also informative to see just how malleable documenting practices can be and understand tensions between documenting policies and the reality of unfolding documenting practices. Although a conversation with a researcher may motivate a participant to perform an email inbox purge, such enthusiasm is often short-lived, lasting only for a few days. Returning to the subject repeatedly through behavioral inquiries will allow the researcher to verify such observations. Thus, having research subjects react to the process of observation and the insights it gives them into their own documenting practices need not reduce the reliability of a document-centric methodology, but it may enhance it.

Conclusion

The document-centered methodology developed in this chapter offers a new perspective on work in technology dense environments and a call for revised research strategies. Traces accessible through digital environments present valuable opportunities to examine not only the content of documents, but also the rich contexts and processes that surround the creation, modification, and dissemination of documents within and across organizations. We argue that this perspective has the potential to make important contributions to the study of organizational behaviors. The document-centered approach described here complements traditional ethnographic techniques, such as participant observation and interviews, by providing insights into important sociomaterial elements of organizational members' work practices. Additionally, these techniques for working with digital traces provide a bridge to quantitative methods such as social network analysis and automated text analysis, introducing new opportunities for mixed method studies grounded in a document-centric perspective.

References

Barad, K. 2003. "Posthumanist performativity: Toward an understanding of how matter comes to matter." *Signs: Journal of Women in Culture and Society* 28: 801–831.

Bazerman, C. 1995. "System of genres and the enactment of social intentions." Pp. 79–104 in *Genre and the New Rhetoric*, edited by A. Freedman and P. Medway. London: Taylor & Francis.

Beaulieu, A. 2010. "From co-location to co-presence: Shifts in the use of ethnography for the study of knowledge." *Social Studies of Science* 40(3): 453–470.

Bechky, B. 2006. "Talking about machines, thick description, and knowledge work." Organization Studies 27(12): 1757–1768.

Briet, S. 2006 [1951]. *What Is Documentation?* Translated and edited by R.E. Day, L. Martinet, and H. Anghelescu. Lanham, MD: Scarecrow.

Brown, J.S. and P. Duguid. 1994. "Borderline issues." *Human-Computer Interaction* 9: 3–36.

Buckland, M. K. 1997. "What is a document?" *Journal of the Association for Information Science and Technology* 48: 804–809.

Carlile, P. R. 2004. "Transferring, translating and transforming: An integrative framework for managing knowledge across boundaries." *Organization Science* 15: 555–568.

Dragunov, A. N., T. G. Dietterich, K. Johnsrude, M. McLaughlin, L. Li, and J. Herlocker. 2005. "TaskTracer: A desktop environment to support multi-tasking knowledge workers." Pp. 75–82 in *IUI'05*. New York: ACM Press.

Feldman, I. 2008. *Governing Gaza: Bureaucracy, Authority, and the Work of Rule, 1917–1967*. Durham, NC: Duke University Press.

Frohmann, B. 2004. *Deflating Information: From Science Studies to Documentation*. Toronto: University of Toronto Press.

Geertz, C. 1973. *The Interpretation of Cultures*. New York: Basic Books.

Geiger, S. and D. Ribes. 2011. "Trace ethnography: Following coordination through documentary practices." In *The 44nd Annual Hawaii International Conference on System Science (HICSS-44)*. Kauai, HI: IEEE Computer Society Press.

Goody, J. 1986. *The Logic of Writing and the Organization of Society*. Cambridge, UK: Cambridge University Press.

Harper, R. 1998. *Inside the IMF: An Ethnography of Documents, Technology, and Organizational Action*. San Diego: Academic Press.

Hine, C. 2006. *New Infrastructures for Science Knowledge Production: Understanding E-Science*. Hershey, PA: Idea Group.

Hull, M. S. 2012. "Documents and bureaucracy." *Annual Review of Anthropology* 41: 251–267.

Ignatova, E. and W. Brinkman. 2007. "Clever Tracking User Behavior Over the Web: Enabling Researchers to Respect the User." In *21st British Computer Society HCI Group Conference*, vol. 2. Lancaster University, UK.

Knorr Cetina, K. 1999. *Epistemic Cultures: How the Sciences Make Knowledge*. Cambridge, MA: Harvard University Press.

Latour, B. 1987. *Science in Action: How to Follow Scientists and Engineers Through Society*. Cambridge, MA: Harvard University Press.

Latour, B. 1990. "Drawing things together." Pp. 19–68 in *Representation in Scientific Practice*, edited by M. Lynch and S. Woolgar. Cambridge, MA: MIT Press

Latour, B. 2005. *Reassembling the Social*. Oxford: Oxford University Press.

Latour, B. and S. Woolgar. 1986. *Laboratory Life: The Construction of Scientific Facts*. Princeton, NJ: Princeton University Press.

Lonsdale, H., C. Jensen, E. Wynn, and N. J. Dedual. 2010. "Cutting and pasting up: 'Documents' and provenance in a complex work environment." In *The 43nd Annual Hawaii International Conference on System Science (HICSS-43)*. Kauai, HI: IEEE Computer Society Press.

Lund, N.W. 2009. "Document theory." *Annual Review of Information Science and Technology* 43: 399–432.

Metiu, A. & A.-L. Fayard (2015). "Between text and context: Innovative approaches to the qualitative analysis of online data." In *Handbook of Innovative Qualitative Research Methods: Pathways to Cool Ideas and Interesting Papers*, edited by K.D. Elsbach and R.M. Kramer. London: Taylor and Francis Group.

Orlikowski, W.J. 2007. "Sociomaterial practices: Exploring technology at work." *Organization Studies* 28: 1435–1448.

Orlikowski, W. J. and J. Yates. 1994. "Genre repertoire: The structuring of communicative practices in organizations." *Administrative Science Quarterly* 39: 541–574.

Østerlund, C. 2007. "Genre combinations: A window into dynamic communication practices." *Journal of Management of Information Systems* 23: 81–108.

Østerlund, C. 2008. "Documents in place: Demarcating places for collaboration in healthcare settings." *Computer Supported Cooperative Work (CSCW)* 17: 195–225.

Østerlund, C. and D. Boland. 2009. "Document cycles: Knowledge flows in heterogeneous healthcare information system environments." In *The 42nd Annual Hawaii International Conference on System Science (HICSS-42)*, edited by J.F. Nunamaker, Jr. and R.H. Sprague, Jr. Big Island, HI: IEEE Computer Society Press.

Østerlund, C., S. Sawyer, and E. Kazianus. 2011. "Studying technologically dense environments through documentary practices." 27th Conference of the European Group for Organizational Studies, 6–9 July, Gotenborg, Sweden.

Randall, D., R. Harper, and M. Rouncefield. 2007. *Fieldwork for Design: Theory and Practice*. London: Springer.

Ribes, D. (2014). "Ethnography of scaling: Or, how to fit a national research infrastructure in the room." In *The 17th ACM conference on Computer supported cooperative work and social computing (CSCW '14)*. New York: ACM, (pp. 1–11).

Sawyer, S., E. Kazianus, and C. Østerlund. 2012. "Social Scientists and Cyberinfrastructure: Insights from a Document Perspective." CSCW 2012, 11–15 February, Seattle, Washington.

Spradley, J.P. (1979). *The Ethnographic Interview*. New York: Holt, Rinehart & Winston.

Spradley, J.P. (1980). *Participant Observation*. New York: Holt, Rinehart & Winston.

Star, S.L. and J.R. Griesemer. 1989. "Institutional ecology, 'translations' and boundary objects: Amateurs and professionals in Berkeley's museum of vertebrate zoology 1907–39." *Social Studies of Science* 19: 387–420.

Star, S. L. and K. Ruhdeler. 1996. "Steps toward an ecology infrastructure: Design and access for large information spaces." *Information Systems Research* 7: 111–134.

Suchman, L.A. 2007. *Human-Machine Reconfigurations: Plans and Situated Actions*. Cambridge, UK: Cambridge University Press.

Swales, J. 1990. *Genre Analysis*. Cambridge, UK: Cambridge University Press.

Tang, J., S. Liu, M. Muller, and C. Drews. 2006. "Unobtrusive but invasive: Using screen recording to collect field data on computer-mediated interactionscreen recording to collect field data on computer-mediated interaction." In *The 20th conference on computer supported cooperative work (CSCW '2006)*. Alberta, Canada. (pp. 479–482).

Yates, J. and W. Orlikowski. 2007. "The PowerPoint presentation and its corollaries: How genres shape communicative action in organizations." In *Communicative Practices in Workplaces and the Professions: Cultural Perspectives on the Regulation of Discourse and Organizations*, edited by M. Zachry and C. Thralls. Amityville, NY: Baywood Publishing.

Van Maanen, J. and B. Pentland. 1994. "Cops and auditors: The rhetoric of records." Pp. 53–90 in The Legalistic Organization, edited by S.B. Sitkin R.J. Bies. Thousand Oaks, CA: Sage.

Zacklad, M. 2006. "Documentarisation processes in documents for action (DofA): The status of annotations and associated cooperation technologies." *Computer Supported Cooperative Work* 15: 205–228.

38

The Journey From Data to Qualitative Inductive Paper

Who Helps and How?

Špela Trefalt and Marya L. Besharov

When a qualitative inductive researcher leaves the field, he or she faces mountains of data and a blank computer screen. Recognizing that the road to producing a paper is often long and difficult, scholars have written a number of texts aimed at helping new and seasoned researchers navigate the journey from data collection to publication. Most of this work focuses on collecting better data, analyzing it more deeply and comprehensively, and writing it up in ways that articulate compelling theoretical contributions (e.g., Becker, 1998; Carlson & Dutton, 2011; Given, 2008; Glaser & Strauss, 1967; Golden-Biddle & Locke, 2007; Locke, Golden-Biddle, & Feldman, 2008; Lofland & Lofland, 1995; Pratt, 2009; Strauss & Corbin, 1998; Van Maanen, 1988; Weiss, 1995). Yet it is well known that we do not travel alone on the road from data to paper, even when we are single authors of our work. To produce exemplary papers, we enlist others to help us make sense of our data and write up our work for publication. We engage trusted colleagues in conversations and consultations, and we organize ourselves into groups and communities to provide venues for social support.

Despite their importance, these forms of help have received little systematic attention in previous work. Scholarly resources for analyzing and writing up qualitative inductive research may acknowledge that even sole authors do not work entirely on their own, but critical questions about where to look for such help and who to engage, for what purpose, and at what time remain unanswered. As authors, moreover, qualitative inductive scholars often recognize in acknowledgment sections any help and support received, but we rarely share in full what really happened. How do others help us get from raw data through analysis, theorizing, framing, more analysis, more theorizing, and reframing to a paper and then to a published article? Through what venues do others amplify our excitement, alleviate our anxiety, end our despair, and cheer us on to keep going?

Our chapter addresses these questions. We offer a comprehensive overview of the types of help qualitative inductive researchers receive, the people to whom they turn for help, and the process through which authors engage these individuals. Our motivation in doing so stems in part from our own experiences taking single-authored qualitative inductive papers from data to publication. In graduate school together at Harvard, both of us were working on qualitative, inductive dissertations (Marya also included quantitative methods). To help one another with challenges we were facing in analyzing our data, we initiated regular research meetings to talk through our questions about the research process (often with a heavy dose of concerns and doubts). After graduating and moving on to separate institutions, we continued this practice, holding research calls every 3 weeks. Today, as mid-career scholars, we still hold these calls. They have been pivotal in the development of our own single-authored qualitative studies, in addition to helping to advance our co-authored works.

Over the years, Špela has helped Marya devise new approaches to analyzing her data when her existing approaches were producing dead ends, she has been a partner in redesigning figures and tables and in thinking through the structure of findings sections, and she has been a careful and detailed critical reader in the later stages of paper development. Marya has helped Špela to stay on course by being an enthusiastic supporter, to reframe a research question that led her down a dead-end road, and to design additional analyses that would persuade reviewers of her findings' credibility. She also pointed her to published articles that served as models of a suitable structure for her manuscript, and she was a responsive and thorough friendly reviewer as the manuscript began to take its final shape.

The ideas in this chapter draw on our experiences with one another and with other helpers, as well as on detailed accounts from three other qualitative inductive researchers—Michel Anteby, Emily Heaphy, and Tammar Zilber—who described the journey of one of their papers and the process by which they develop qualitative inductive papers more generally. We also incorporate insights from a focus group we convened with expert and novice qualitative inductive researchers who shared their experiences about the help they look for and receive on their journeys from data to paper. Drawing out common themes from these varied accounts, we illuminate the broad range of helpers that authors engage—from "travel companions" who accompany the author on the entire journey to "concierges" who serve as process facilitators with very specific and clearly defined tasks that move the process along. We further provide insight into specific practices for effectively engaging each type of helper.

The Journey

In working through the process of data analysis and writing, qualitative inductive researchers engage travel companions and other helpers in a variety of different tasks. First, we sometimes work with others as we analyze our data, getting help condensing raw data into more abstract chunks through coding or other mechanisms. Second, we engage others to help us uncover what ethnographer Leslie Perlow (personal communication) calls "the little t"—the story in the data that explains what happened and why. Third, we seek help in developing "the big T"—a theoretical framing and narrative that explains the conceptual implications of the story from the data. In doing so, we construct a "theorized storyline" (Golden-Biddle & Locke, 2007), in which we articulate our study's theoretical significance by establishing a gap in the existing literature that our study helps to fill. Fourth, we seek advice in establishing the structure of our paper, deciding what goes where to convincingly and credibly convey our story and our theoretical contribution. Several additional tasks are required in order to accomplish these things, and qualitative researchers seek help here as well. We need to hold ourselves accountable to ensure that we are making progress. We need to be emotionally supported, because developing a qualitative paper can feel very lonely and emotionally taxing (Hoepfl, 1997; Wolcott, 2001). We need to make appropriate process choices, such as when to look for model papers, where and when to present our paper, and who to talk to regarding framing. And finally, we need to effectively respond to journal reviewers and editors by making sure we understand what they are asking from us and then addressing these issues not only in the paper but also in the response letter.

Qualitative inductive researchers engage several types of helpers as they navigate these different components of the journey from data to paper. Some are true "travel companions," the fellow qualitative inductive researchers who constitute our community of practice and are with us from beginning to end. Others are "friends we are trying to make"—members of the wider academic audience we are seeking to engage with our paper. Still others serve as "customs officers"; these are the journal editors and reviewers who offer valuable guidance in helping us move from submitted to published manuscript, even as they serve as gatekeepers who get to decide whether we can bring our findings "home." We also engage "natives"—informants from the field and experts in our empirical context who help us stay true to the phenomenon we are studying. Finally, we may seek help from one or more "concierges"—writing coaches, copy editors, and others who facilitate the analysis and writing process, often by holding us accountable or providing motivation. In the sections that follow, we elaborate on these different types of helpers and identify exemplary practices authors use to engage them. Figure 38.1 provides a summary.

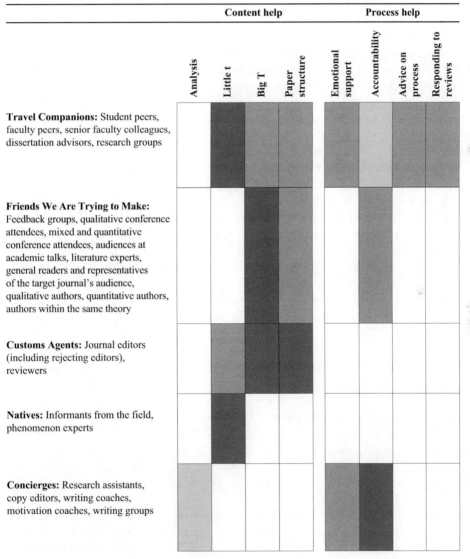

* Darker cells indicate more help received.

Figure 38.1 Types of Helpers and the Help They Provide*

Špela Trefalt and Marya L. Besharov

Travel Companions (a Community of Practice of Qualitative Researchers)

Even though we focus on sole authors, they rarely travel alone. Each has a set of travel companions—fellow qualitative inductive researchers that accompany the author on the journey from raw data to a published article with an interesting story and a theoretical contribution. Experienced authors tend to have one or more individuals with whom they talk regularly—some daily, others biweekly or every three weeks—about their progress and their developing theory. These travel companions may be peer students or faculty, dissertation advisors, or trusted senior faculty colleagues. They may also include members of formal or informal qualitative inductive research groups in which authors participate, with the group splitting its time and focus among members' dilemmas and questions. Taken together, travel companions form an "inner circle" or "community of practice" on whom authors rely throughout the analysis and writing process.

Authors engage their travel companions for the length of the journey. They start early, when they have developed only the kernels of the emerging story or "little t" in the data. To engage others in this process, the author often provides a quick representation of the data or of data fragments—a picture, a table, a set of bullet points, a quotation—that serves as fodder for a conversation about interesting pieces of the data and possible storylines to draw out. These exchanges are helpful in part because they create an opportunity for the author to articulate early ideas emerging from the data. In addition, they help the author learn what others think is interesting and new in the data and what could be further explored (cf. Locke et al., 2008).

The travel companions who provide help developing the "little t" differ from the "peer debriefers" described by Given (2008) in that they need not be familiar with the phenomenon under study. It is critical, however, that these travel companions are intimately familiar with qualitative inductive research methods, particularly at this early stage in the analysis process. Until framing solidifies, feedback from quantitative scholars, while well intentioned, can derail qualitative researchers. Because quantitative researchers tend to focus on explaining variance, their reactions and suggestions may steer qualitative researchers away from the types of research questions for which the method is best suited: deep explorations of phenomena and the processes and mechanisms that connect them. Suggestions from quantitative researchers sometimes prompt analyses that are counterproductive because they aim to explain variation rather than unpack processes. They can also introduce literatures in which it is difficult to make a contribution using qualitative inductive methods because the phenomenon is already well understood. Such feedback can sometimes raise paralyzing doubts, particularly for junior scholars. In contrast, qualitative inductive travel companions help build a safe space in which theory can be induced from the data.

In addition to engaging travel companions to help identify and refine the "little t," authors also turn to these individuals later in the process to help them find an appropriate framing for the paper. They do so by having frequent and regular in-depth conversations as well as obtaining feedback on full drafts of a paper. Even as travel companions offer guidance on framing, though, they need not be experts in the literature in which the research will eventually be situated, just as they are often not experts in the phenomenon. Finding someone who understands and is engaged in qualitative inductive research is most important. Trust is also essential: The author must feel comfortable revealing doubts and weaknesses in the emerging storyline, as surfacing and working through these issues is critical to strengthening the manuscript. Authors want their travel companions to be tough but constructive critics who are willing to expose flaws and help the author figure out how to address them. Those who read full drafts may also address questions about the structure of the paper, such as what material belongs in the methods versus the findings section, how much of the findings to foreshadow in the introduction and framing of the paper, and in what order to present the findings.

404

Finally, authors turn to travel companions, particularly those who are more experienced, when they receive journal editors' letters and formal reviews. At this stage, authors seek help interpreting what reviewers are saying, understanding what needs to be done and how to do it, as well as thinking through how to craft a response letter. Just as many authors share snippets of data with travel companions earlier in the process, some also share discrete paragraphs from an editorial decision or review as a precursor to a conversation about how to address the particular issue raised. In contrast, other authors seek guidance on their overall approach to a revision and share the full editor's letter and all reviews.

Across all these stages of analysis and writing, travel companions are particularly well suited to provide emotional support. Because they are intimately familiar with the process, they understand the challenges and are well positioned to empathize and encourage. Indeed, several qualitative authors we spoke with described their travel companions as not only intellectual partners but also true friends who had the author's best interests at heart. Travel companions are also well positioned to provide process suggestions, something especially important for more junior qualitative inductive scholars. Suggestions might include advice about whether to write up a draft of findings first (to focus the analysis) or to start with tables and figures (to focus the writing), as well as ideas about how to keep track of insights, where to turn for good model papers, when in the process to present the paper to a particular audience, and who could serve as an effective friendly reviewer.

Friends We Are Trying to Make (Wider Academic Audience)

Writing qualitative inductive papers represents an imperative to befriend the wider academic audience. We must convince other researchers that our work is credible, relevant, and valuable. To do so, qualitative inductive authors engage individuals from multiple, increasingly broad circles of the wider academic audience with whom their research is in conversation. First, as they are developing their "big T" theoretical framing (and continuing to refine the "little t" story in the data), authors engage other qualitative researchers. They present their work at conferences attended primarily by other qualitative researchers and in departments with a qualitative research orientation. Through informal conversations and feedback on presentations, these audience members help the author continue to refine the "little t," and, more critically, contribute to shaping the framing or "big T" of a paper. For one author, we spoke with the framing and ultimate title of a paper emerged in large part from comments made by two fellow qualitative inductive researchers at an informal feedback session during a conference. Authors also use these conferences and seminar presentations as deadlines that prompt them to articulate and focus their ideas within a particular time frame, even if full papers are not required.

In a related practice, some authors establish or join existing groups of qualitative inductive researchers who read and comment on one another's papers. We call these "feedback groups" to distinguish them from the "research groups" described earlier, which focus on sharing ideas and fragments of data much earlier in the process. Feedback groups represent one of the most intense and in-depth forms of help authors receive. Comments are often critical, even "harsh," but members couple these with suggestions for how to improve the paper. The feedback received ranges from ideas about the "little t" to suggestions on the "big T," from comments on paper structure to help interpreting and responding to journal reviews. Authors often enter these meetings confused or ambivalent about the direction in which to take their papers, but they leave with a clear sense of next steps and the desired final destination. Self-organized groups of this nature tend to comprise qualitative researchers at similar stages of their careers, often—but not always—geographically co-located. Some authors also get help from feedback groups of which they are not regular members. For example, some senior colleagues we know have generously offered up their own feedback groups after one-on-one conversations in which a junior author sought their guidance.

Once the framing of the paper starts taking shape and the literature(s) in which the study will be framed and to which it will contribute become clearer, authors reach out to experts in those literatures for feedback and ideas. Their goal in doing so is to further refine the "big T" and craft a paper that will appeal to the desired audience. At this stage, authors tend to engage quantitative as well as qualitative scholars, with expertise in the literature being more important than expertise in the method. In order to not overburden these individuals, some authors choose to approach them with specific questions instead of asking them to read full drafts. Others seek out informal interactions with experts on particular literatures at conferences or in research groups instead of or in addition to asking for feedback on written text. Even seemingly cursory conversations can sometimes enable substantive progress, pointing authors to particularly relevant papers or helping them to more clearly articulate the gap in the literature.

As authors get ready to submit their work to journals, some engage an even broader audience by circulating well-developed full drafts to colleagues from their departments and to other academics with whom they are friendly, with the aim of getting general feedback about how compelling and interesting the paper is and identifying any major flaws or "reviewer landmines"—issues that could aggravate or confuse reviewers and prompt a negative evaluation. This practice differs in important ways from the practice of asking "travel companions" to provide feedback on well-developed drafts. When circulating drafts to representatives of the wider academic audience, authors tend not to expose flaws and point out weaknesses, whereas they actively do so when engaging travel companions. The deep trust that exists with travel companions is not essential for this kind of help. Any active academic, preferably someone familiar with the targeted journal and willing to devote the time to reviewing a draft, can serve as a helper at this stage and for this purpose.

Finally, qualitative inductive researchers also get help from individuals with whom they never directly engage, a group one author described as an "imagined community." They spend time thinking about the audience to whom they are trying to speak and the conversation they are trying to enter, to decide how best to appeal to them. They also study published qualitative inductive papers for ideas about structure, data representation, analysis, and even specific wording. In addition, they sometimes examine papers published by their handling editors in an attempt to decipher which types of paper structures appeal to that editor. Some authors also review published quantitative papers and general guidance on how to write those in order to more effectively appeal to the quantitative researchers in their audience.

Customs Officers (Editors and Reviewers)

To return home from our travels, we need to clear customs. Customs officers check the goods that we are bringing along and decide whether we can enter with them or not. Similarly, there are gatekeepers in publishing our research: journal editors and reviewers. Perhaps surprisingly, authors are often effusive in describing how extraordinarily helpful these people can be in the development of their papers. Experienced qualitative inductive researchers view themselves as working in collaboration with their reviewers and editor to co-create a paper, and they find this process to be extremely generative. As a result, for their initial submission they aim to craft a paper that is "good enough" to receive an invitation to revise and resubmit, but they fully expect the editor and reviewers' help in working through their ideas. As one author put it, "you dance with the reviewers who see promise" in order to get the paper into a publishable form.

Even editors and reviewers who reject a paper can sometimes be extremely helpful. Once authors get past the initial sting of a rejection, they are often able to strengthen their paper significantly based on the suggestions of those who did not see enough promise in the paper to invite a revision. Authors may also talk to the editor who rejected their paper, to seek clarification about what needs to change for the paper to be more convincing.

Natives (Field Informants and Phenomenon Experts)

A journey is much more memorable, and the story of the journey more compelling, if the traveler establishes meaningful relationships with those who live at the destination. Similarly, qualitative inductive researchers often go back to field informants from whom they collected data to gather reactions on their emerging findings and check for factual accuracy. Some also ask informants for feedback on framing and conclusions. Many authors feel deeply indebted to these individuals, whose help is usually invisible to a paper's final audience but often quite significant for the author. In addition to seeking feedback from informants in the field, authors engage experts on the phenomenon under study, including personal connections who are familiar with the setting as well as scholars from other disciplines, to gauge their reactions to the story and to check technical language. However, to avoid becoming co-opted and to maintain the required critical distance from their phenomenon, authors must balance the perspective of natives, particularly field informants, with help from other sources.

Concierge (Process Facilitators)

On a trip, a good concierge can sometimes help more than all the well-intentioned friends combined. Similarly, experienced qualitative inductive researchers recognize that for some kinds of tasks, engaging process facilitators is the most effective way to go. In the early stages of the analysis process, authors sometimes engage research assistants (RAs) to help them work through the often tedious process of coding raw data. One author we spoke with uses RAs as a source of diversity, seeking out individuals who will become familiar with the data but who can offer a different point of view. Other authors, particularly those with a strong interpretive focus, feel strongly about doing the analysis themselves. They find it counterproductive to outsource coding to RAs because doing so prevents the author from fully engaging with and "feeling" the data. Even authors who do use RAs for help with coding distinguish this from the help they seek in developing an emerging storyline or "little t," relying primarily on themselves and fellow qualitative inductive "travel companions" for the latter.

Further along in the journey from data to paper, process facilitators include copy editors, writing coaches, motivation coaches, and writing groups. Copy editors can serve two purposes. First, they improve one's writing and provide suggestions on how to improve the structure of the paper to clarify the message. To be able to provide this kind of help, it is important that the copy editor be familiar with academic writing. Second, copy editors can sometimes serve as a source of accountability and pacing. One experienced qualitative inductive author we spoke with prepays a copy editor and commits to a deadline for submitting a draft for editing. In this way, working with a copy editor can help an author make steady progress and complete work by a chosen deadline. Some authors also use writing coaches who are either hired directly or, more fortunately, provided by a publisher. These individuals advise authors on how to "chunk up" their work to prevent them from becoming overwhelmed, they hold authors accountable for their progress, and they help fine-tune their writing, offering advice on finding the right words and clarifying meaning, paragraph by paragraph. In addition to writing coaches, authors sometimes engage motivation coaches who provide structure and accountability and prevent feelings of being overwhelmed, thereby contributing to forward progress on a manuscript.

Writing groups constitute still another kind of process facilitator. Members of these groups often simply sit together at a specified time and location to provide social support for one another's writing. To hold one another accountable, some groups use "carrots" such as celebratory parties when a member submits a paper or finishes a draft; others use "sticks" such as donating to a cause the author abhors if the agreed upon writing is not completed. (This may raise ethical dilemmas if a contribution is actually made, but none of our informants knew of examples where the author did not complete the writing on time.) Some authors use online writing communities for the same purpose—to provide accountability and pacing and to offer company in the often lonely process of writing up a sole-authored paper. Given the nature of this support, the expertise of the other writers is not important, in contrast to the research groups and feedback groups discussed earlier.

Crafting Your Own Journey

Sole authors of qualitative inductive articles are not alone on their journeys from data to published papers. To the contrary, they rely on a number of helpers, ranging from close friends and spouses who happen to be fellow qualitative inductive researchers to hired professionals whom authors did not know until they were hired. In this chapter, we sought to illuminate this broad range of helpers, the means by which authors engage them, and the forms of help they provide.

In closing, we want to draw out a few key considerations for readers planning their own research journeys. First, the helpers we described differ in how critical and how supportive they are. It is up to the author to create a balance between people who help him or her move forward by highlighting the strengths of the work and those who point out its weaknesses and ways to improve it further. (Some excellent helpers can do both.) Supportive, friendly helpers are particularly essential early on, while more critical helpers are often engaged later in the process. Second, each author also has to figure out how many helpers to engage. Too many and the author can be pulled in too many different directions; too few, especially if they are powerful ones such as former advisors or esteemed senior researchers, and the author may struggle to find his or her own voice and direction. Third, authors adopt different approaches to engaging their helpers. Some make deliberate choices about who they ask and what they request, actively choosing some forms of help and rejecting others. Others, particularly more junior ones, do not know where to turn for help in the long and arduous journey from data to paper and often reactively accept whatever help comes their way.

To illustrate the variety of paths individual authors take, we summarize in Table 38.1 how the five authors we studied in depth engaged others in their journeys from data to paper. Our intention is that readers will draw from these ideas to chart their own journeys, engaging travel companions and other helpers on their unique paths toward publication of exemplary qualitative inductive research.

Table 38.1 Use of "Travel Companions" and Other Helpers in Qualitative, Inductive Research

Reference	Research Context	Main Three Sources of Help	Outcomes/Results
Anteby (2010)	U.S. commerce in cadavers	• Journal editor and reviewers	• Suggested a new framing
		• Qualitative researcher expert in literature used to frame paper	• Asked probing questions that the author then answered by further analysis
		• Spouse who is a writer	• Provided inspiration—seeing his spouse write tirelessly without immediate reward, the author is constantly inspired to keep moving forward
Besharov (2014)	Socially responsible retail company	• Regular conversations with trusted qualitative researchers	• Provided help with "little t" and structure of the paper; offered feedback on emerging model and full manuscript drafts
		• Feedback groups	• Helped craft strategy for responding to each round of reviews
		• Journal editor and reviewers	• Conversations with the editor confirmed and clarified approach to revisions; reviewer comments illuminated key insights from the "little t"

Reference	Research Context	Main Three Sources of Help	Outcomes/Results
Heaphy (2013)	Patient advocates in a hospital	• Dissertation advisor/senior faculty colleague • Writing coach • Journal editor and reviewers	• Provided emotional support and process advice about how to make progress; helped with response letter • Provided emotional support and pacing with writing; helped to identify what writing needed clarification • Offered developmental feedback, including specific suggestions for reframing and a list of citations
Trefalt (2013)	Attorneys at a large law firm	• Regular conversations with trusted qualitative researchers • Journal editor and reviewers • Research group	• Provided accountability, helped with "little t" and structure of the paper, helped to articulate the final framing • Helped with theoretical contribution and structure; helped focus the "little t" • Quantitative researcher proposed a literature that ended up being part of the framing
Zilber (2011)	High technology conferences in Israel	• Regular conversations with trusted qualitative researcher • Conference presentations • Journal editor and reviewers	• Helped identify "little t," "Big T," and structure of paper; provided emotional support, advice on process; helped interpret feedback, respond to reviewers • Crafting presentations helped clarify and focus the theoretical contribution, conference deadlines provided accountability for developing a full paper • Suggested more transparent means of explaining data analysis process; proposed theoretical hook for framing "little t"

In planning their journeys, readers should keep in mind that much of the help we describe in this chapter is mutual: qualitative inductive researchers who help others create goodwill, so that they can count on others' help when they need it. In addition, the process of helping others affords a unique opportunity to hone the craft of research and writing. In the words of Tammar Zilber (personal communication), when examining others' work "our emotional investment does not stand in the way of learning, as it might when it is our own work." That makes it easier to notice patterns, errors, and opportunities for improvement, and to learn from them. It is therefore important not only to seek out help but also to seize opportunities to help others. We hope our chapter provides a foundation for doing so in a more thoughtful manner.

References

Anteby, M. (2010). Markets, morals, and practices of trade: Jurisdictional disputes in the U.S. commerce in cadavers. *Administrative Science Quarterly, 55,* 606–638.

Becker, H.S. (1998). *Tricks of the trade: How to think about your research while you're doing it.* Chicago, IL.: University of Chicago Press.

Besharov, M.L. (2014). The relational ecology of identification: How organizational identification emerges when individuals hold divergent values. *Academy of Management Journal, 57,* 1485–1512.

Carlson, A., & Dutton, J.E. (Eds.). (2011). *Research alive: Exploring generative moments in doing qualitative research.* Copenhagen, Denmark: Copenhagen Business School Press.

Given, L.M. (Ed.). (2008). *The Sage encyclopedia of qualitative research methods* (Vol. 2). Thousand Oaks, CA: Sage.

Glaser, B.G., & Strauss, A.L. (1967). *The discovery of grounded theory: Strategies for qualitative research*. Hawthorne, NY: Aldine de Gruyter.

Golden-Biddle, K., & Locke, K. (2007). *Composing qualitative research* (2nd ed.). Thousand Oaks, CA: Sage.

Heaphy, E.D. (2013). Repairing breaches with rules: Maintaining institutions in the face of everyday disruptions. *Organization Science, 24*, 1291–1315.

Hoepfl, M.C. (1997). Choosing qualitative research: A primer for technology education researchers. *Journal of Technology Education, 9*, 1–16.

Locke, K., Golden-Biddle, K., & Feldman, M.S. (2008). Making doubt generative: Rethinking the role of doubt in the research process. *Organization Science, 19*, 907–918.

Lofland, J., & Lofland, L.H. (1995). *Analyzing social settings: A guide to qualtiative observation and analysis*. Belmont, CA: Wadsworth.

Pratt, M.G. (2009). For the lack of a boilerplate: Tips on writing up (and reviewing) qualitative research. *Academy of Management Journal, 52*, 856–862.

Strauss, A.L., & Corbin, J.M. (1998). *Basics of qualitative research: Techniques and procedures for developing grounded theory* (2nd ed.). Thousand Oaks, CA: Sage.

Trefalt, Š. (2013). Between you and me: Setting work-nonwork boundaries in the context of workplace relationships. *Academy of Management Journal, 56*, 1802–1829.

Van Maanen, J. (1988). *Tales of the field: On writing ethnography*. Chicago, IL: University of Chicago Press.

Weiss, R.S. (1995). *Learning from strangers: the art and method of qualitative interview studies*. New York, NY: Free Press.

Wolcott, H.F. (2001). *Writing up qualitative research* (2nd ed.). Thousand Oaks, CA: Sage.

Zilber, T.B. (2011). Institutional multiplicity in practice: A tale of two high-tech conferences in Israel. *Organization Science, 22*, 1539–1559.

39

Worth a Second Look?

Exploring the Power of Post-Mortems on Post-Mortems

Roderick M. Kramer

In a reflective moment during his brief but crisis-prone presidency, the late President John F. Kennedy once observed:

> The essence of ultimate decision remains impenetrable to the observer—often, indeed, to the decider himself. . . . There will always be the dark and tangled stretches in the decision-making process—mysterious even to those who may be most intimately involved. (quoted in Allison & Zelikow, 1999, p. i)

Kennedy's observation notwithstanding, organizational scholars have afforded considerable attention to explicating the antecedents of organizational decisions, especially those that have proven particularly catastrophic or costly (Janis, 1982). The aim of such research is to shed light on precisely those dark and tangled stretches where consequential decisions are evaluated and executed—with sometimes disastrous effects.

As a result of such research, our understanding of the determinants of decision-making fiascoes has grown enormously. This research has benefited, moreover, from the use of a variety of methodological approaches, ranging from laboratory experiments on escalatory decision dynamics (e.g., Staw, 1976) to computer simulations of "garbage can" decision processes (e.g., Cohen, March, & Olsen, 1972). One particularly fruitful approach to the study of decision-making fiascoes has been the qualitative *post-mortem* or *decision autopsy*. As these labels suggest, the purpose of a post-mortem or decision autopsy is to identify, to the extent possible, all of the causal factors implicated in a given fiasco.

The logic and justification for such post-mortems is straightforward. By probing the origins of extreme failures of judgment and choice, it has been argued, researchers and practitioners alike can learn something new and hopefully useful about how such decisions happen—as well as how they might be averted in the future (Janis, 1982). On the basis of this rationale, a large number of major decision-making fiascoes have been subjected to such post-mortems, including the U.S. government's failure to anticipate the surprise attack on Pearl Harbor, the failure by the Secret Service and the FBI to prevent the assassination of President John F. Kennedy, the disastrous space shuttle *Challenger* launch decision, the decisions leading up to the Three-Mile Island nuclear meltdown, the flawed Iran-Contra arms-for-hostages crisis, the failed Iranian rescue mission during the Carter presidency, the BP oil spill, and, most recently, the failure to anticipate the 2008 global financial meltdown.

Interestingly, once a particular fiasco has been studied empirically, and cogent theory has been generated from it, qualitative researchers have generally shown little interest in revisiting that case. In part, the aversion to reexamining "cold cases" may reflect two considerations. The first is a perception that the "evidentiary bones" have been pretty much picked over, and thus the theoretical yield from further scrutiny is likely to be slight. Second, in much the same way that experimental scientists tend to perceive few career incentives in replicating someone else's experiments, qualitative researchers may discern little personal gain to be had in revisiting the scene of someone else's research. Given the value placed on originality and uniqueness in science, most researchers do not want to be seen using someone else's toothbrush, as Walter Mischel (2008) colorfully put it.

In this chapter, however, I wish to suggest that there may very well be significant value in conducting post-mortems on post-mortems, especially as (a) additional and potentially probative data become available to researchers and (b) the theoretical "arsenal" that can be brought to bear on the understanding of that new data accumulates. In short, I will argue that it is often the case that new lessons can be gleaned by revisiting even the "coldest" of cases. The benefits from exhuming a long-buried body of data and theory might be particularly important with respect to those case studies that have been especially influential in the organizational sciences. In this chapter, therefore, I wish to advocate for the value of sometimes taking a second look at cases that have been put to rest, using a methodology that I characterize as *second-look decision autopsies* (or, for short, *second looks)*. Second looks, I suggest, give researchers a valuable opportunity to (re)assess the adequacy and completeness of the original data analyses pertaining to major fiascoes, as well as the validity of the theoretical inferences that emerged from them.

I further argue that the value of such second looks lies not only in the opportunity they provide to reevaluate the status of extant theory (i.e., how well the originally induced theory has stood the test of time), but equally, the validity or adequacy of the prescriptions that emerged from those original studies. One significant thread that runs through all of the post-mortems of major decision-making fiascoes mentioned earlier is the list of recommendations that emerged from them, including prescriptions regarding how organizational leaders and their advisors might avoid such disasters in the future (see Janis, 1982, and Neustadt & May, 1986, for particularly thoughtful and thorough examples).

Finally, I argue that second-look decision autopsies provide an opportunity for qualitative researchers who study decision making to "re-mine" a given case, no matter how exhausted the original vein might seem, with the aim of producing a fresh and fruitful wave of theory generation. Such theory generation is, after all, one of the major rationales for inductive case studies.

In keeping with the spirit of a qualitative inquiry, I endeavor to advance these arguments by working backward from a well-established and much celebrated post-mortem—indeed, one of the earliest and most influential decision post-mortems in the social sciences. Specifically, I revisit here Irving Janis's analysis of the fateful decision by President Kennedy to approve a plan to invade Cuba in the early 1960s in the hope of toppling the Castro regime and establishing a democratic government in its place. I will argue, in particular, that a sustained second look at this case—with the advantages of a treasure trove of newly available data, as well as a considerably enhanced repertoire of explanatory constructs from the decision sciences—significantly calls into question some of the most seemingly well-established inferences from Janis's original study and leads as well to fundamentally different conclusions and prescriptions.

Before examining this particular case in detail, however, it may be helpful first to describe in more detail the protocol for the typical second-look decision autopsy.

Exhuming the Body: Conducting Second-Look Decision Autopsies

Most broadly construed, the ultimate aim of second-look decision autopsies is to enable organizational scholars to reconstruct as fully and as faithfully as possible the psychological, social, and organizational processes that resulted in a given fiasco. In this respect, the rationale for taking a second look mirrors perfectly the aim of the original post-mortem. Recall that, in an initial post-mortem, researchers endeavor to assemble all of the available data in order to identify the discernible antecedents of the original decision(s). Thus, researchers endeavor, among other things, to identify the primary decision maker(s) responsible for a given decision or sequence of decisions and elaborate on the organizational context in which those decisions took place. They hope further to assess the state of information available to decision makers and determine the role, if any, that advisors played in the decision-making process. Finally, they endeavor to determine what psychological stresses and strains might have been operating on the primary decision makers and/or their advisors, including time pressures and other factors that might have adversely influenced the quality of decision making. In short, a second-look decision autopsy involves revisiting the scene of the crime (figuratively speaking) in the hope of learning something new and different.

As indicated schematically in Figure 39.1, researchers conducting a second-look study first make every effort to review all of the data that were available to the researchers in the original case study. Doing so provides a reference point or empirical anchor that can help them appraise the accuracy and completeness with which the then-extant data were originally construed. Two qualitative researchers, independently looking at the same data set may, after all, form entirely different interpretations of the theoretical insights to which those data lead.

The next step is for the researcher to collect and analyze all new pertinent data that have become available subsequent to the original study. In the post-mortem research I've done on three major fiascoes (viz., the Vietnam decisions by the Johnson administration beginning in the fall of 1963, the Bay of Pigs decisions by the Kennedy administration in the early months of his administration, and the pre-9/11 threat-assessment decisions by the White House, FBI, and U.S. intelligence agencies), these additional sources of data were quite substantial and included routinely declassified information, as well as information released under specific Freedom of Information requests by journalists and other researchers (e.g., Prados, 2003; White, 1999). With the passage of time, moreover, key decision makers (often nearing the ends of their careers) write revealing memoirs or consent to interviews that provide candid assessments of their decisions (e.g., Kennedy, 1988; Schlesinger, 2007). Moreover, errors in the original factual record are often corrected by journalists, political scientists, historians, and biographers who have themselves scrutinized emerging evidence pertaining to such celebrated fiascoes.

Importantly, in taking this second look, researchers can also take advantage of theoretical advances in their disciplines that have accumulated subsequent to the original case study. For example, extensive theoretical developments in decision theory have taken place since Janis's original case studies, including (to offer just a few) research on the impact of decision framing, the impact of various judgmental biases such as availability and representativeness, and the impact of various positive illusions on decision makers (Farnham, 1994; Gilovich, Griffin, & Kahneman, 2002; Kahneman, 2011; Kramer, 1989; Kramer, Meyerson, & Davis, 1990). As a result, the analytic or (in keeping with our prevailing metaphor) "dissective" tools available for forensic decision analysis are substantially greater than those available to the original researchers.

In the fourth stage, the researcher attempts to formulate a revised model of the decision-making process that reflects all of the new data integrated with the contemporarily available relevant theory. As a final stage, the prescriptions that emerged from the original analysis can be reappraised in accord

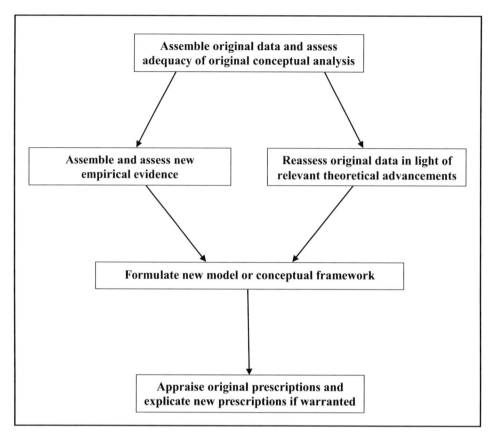

Figure 39.1 Conducting Second-Look Decision Analyses

with the evidence afforded by this second look. If the evidence mandates it, an attempt should be made to reformulate those original prescriptions or, if warranted, replace them altogether. Arguably, this final stage is not a formal obligation or responsibility of the qualitative researcher. The primary role of the organizational scientist is to marshal new evidence and advance new theory. However, researchers have often been motivated to draw out useful managerial or leadership lessons from their findings (e.g., Janis, 1982; Neustadt & May, 1986).

With this brief methodological overview in hand, I turn now to illustrating more concretely the power of a second look when it comes to understanding the origins of a given decision-making fiasco. To do so, I turn to a reexamination of Irving Janis's well-known study of the decision-making process engaged in by President Kennedy as he wrestled with the wisdom of proceeding with a plan to invade the island of Cuba—a plan originally hatched by the CIA during the final years of the Eisenhower presidency.

Revisiting the Bay of Pigs: Why It's Worth the Second Look

Within the substantial academic literature dealing with post-mortems of major organizational decision fiascoes, Janis's (1972, 1983) groupthink remains by far the most cited and influential framework. Google Scholar reports more than 18,000 citations to academic studies on the groupthink hypothesis. Even five decades after its conception, the groupthink framework remains an enduring fixture in the social psychological and organizational literatures on decision-making fiascoes (Hart, 1990; Turner, Pratkanis, & Struckman, 2007). Among all of the fiascoes he examined, it should be noted, Janis himself regarded President Kennedy's decision to approve the CIA's plan to land a contingent of Cuban exiles on the shores of Cuba in 1961 as *the* prototypic example of groupthink. In his eyes, it constituted a "perfect failure."

From the standpoint of the present analysis—which aims to show the value in taking a second look at even such seemingly well-established and influential post-mortems—there are several reasons why revisiting this particular case study might prove especially fruitful at this time. First, with the passage of time, a considerable amount of fresh archival material bearing on this fiasco has become available to scholars. This material includes a substantial trove of declassified records, such as presidential logs, memos, and transcripts of crucial meetings (Kornbluh, 1998; Prados, 2003; Reeves, 1993; Widmer, 2012). Further, comprehensive oral histories are also available for the Kennedy presidency (e.g., Strober & Strober, 1993). Additionally, there are new reassessments by journalists, historians, and political scientists, as well as detailed memoirs from principal participants in the Kennedy years (Benson, 2003; Burns, 2006; Fursenko & Naftali, 1997; Jones, 2010; Kornbluh, 1998; Leogrande & Kornbluh, 2014; Naftali, 2001; Rasenberger, 2014). These substantial and highly relevant sources of data were not available when Janis originally conceived his groupthink hypothesis.

Second, and equally important, the scholarly literature on group and organizational decision making has made substantial theoretical strides in the decades since Janis originally articulated the groupthink hypothesis (see, e.g., Edmondson, 2012; Hackman, 2011; March, 1995; Tetlock, 1991; Turner, Pratkanis, Probasco, & Leve, 1992; Turner, Pratkanis, & Struckman, 2007; Whyte, 1989). Thus, qualitative researchers today have a much richer set of theoretical perspectives from which to assess the validity of the groupthink hypothesis and evaluate the evidence for it. For these reasons, it seems prudent to select this particular case to revisit in order to illustrate the potential value in taking second looks at seemingly secure and established qualitative findings in order to generate fresh insights and revised conclusions.

Just how well *has* Janis's original construal of the Bay of Pigs decision-making process held up to more than five decades of emerging empirical evidence and theoretical strides in the decision-making literature? In answering this question, it is important to recall that Janis's characterization of the Bay of Pigs decision-making process attached considerable importance to a specific series of meetings involving President Kennedy and several of his advisors during which the Bay of Pigs was explicitly discussed. Janis implied that the planning for the invasion occurred *primarily* within the context of these deliberations and that they could be characterized, in turn, as discussions by a small, cohesive, and relatively isolated group that consisted, moreover, of a fixed cast of characters.

In recent years, the release of classified records has provided scholars with new information regarding the actual scale, scope, duration, and content of the planning sessions leading up to the Bay of Pigs. These records also reveal the magnitude of Kennedy's efforts to decide what to do about the Cuban operation *outside* the context of the few meetings on which Janis focused particular attention (see, e.g., Higgins, 1987; Neustadt & May, 1986; Reeves, 1993; Strober & Strober, 1993). Viewed in aggregate, these new sources provide a detailed chronicle of the decision-making process, including not only *with whom* Kennedy explicitly discussed the Bay of Pigs, but *how often* and *for how long*, as well as the specific content of those discussions.

This recently available material reveals that President Kennedy did not rely exclusively, or even predominantly, on a fixed, tightly knit group of advisors in making his decisions regarding the Bay of Pigs operation. Instead, he employed a broad and complex—even if also somewhat idiosyncratic and unsystematic—advisory process. This new evidence shows that Kennedy prudently sought advice from a wide corridor of diverse opinion, including secretly soliciting the views of President Eisenhower, quietly seeking the views of a number of prominent journalists and magazine editors he respected, consultations with various senators he trusted, and even close friends and colleagues whose intelligence and political acumen he valued (Dallek, 2003; George, 1980; Reeves, 1993). This new evidence shows that the comparatively few group planning sessions devoted specifically to the Bay of Pigs are better characterized as a "series of *ad hoc* meetings" involving a "small but shifting set of advisers" (Neustadt & May, 1986, p. 142).

In making his case for groupthink, Janis faulted Kennedy and his advisors for not attending more diligently to the details of the CIA plan and uncovering its prospective flaws. However, with the release of classified documents over the past decades, scholars are now in a much better position to appreciate that the planning for this operation occurred during a period of what Reeves (1993) has aptly characterized as "an astonishing density of [simultaneous or co-occurring] events" (pp. 74–75). As a consequence of this very packed agenda, Kennedy's advisors had to make difficult—but necessary—discriminations as to how best to allocate their limited and strained attentional resources.

To begin, Janis made much of Kennedy's tendency to ignore expert advice that questioned the wisdom of the operation. Janis afforded particular attention to the fact that Kennedy gave little weight to Chester Bowles's reservations regarding the logistics of the operation—concerns which in retrospect turned out to be quite prescient. However, recently available documents indicate that President Kennedy had little confidence in Bowles's judgment or his strategic acumen with respect to such matters. Bowles had acquired a reputation within the Kennedy administration and the State Department for gloomy, fatalistic analyses. "Chet was just telling me there are four revolutions [going on around the world] that we need to worry about," Kennedy once humorously quipped after one encounter with Bowles (Reeves, 1993, p. 53).

In contrast, Kennedy had a great deal of confidence in Richard Bissell's operational abilities and his strategic acumen regarding covert operations. By all accounts, Bissell (the primary architect of the Cuban operation) was a brilliant and compelling thinker and speaker. He displayed a deft grasp of strategic issues and a confident command of operational details. Whenever doubts were expressed about the wisdom or feasibility of some aspect of the Bay of Pigs operation or the logic of its assumptions, Bissell was able to provide convincing and reassuring answers.

In trying to further assess why President Kennedy proceeded with what seemed such an obviously flawed plan, Janis also afforded considerable attention to the role that overconfidence and unrealistic optimism played in the deliberation process. There was, as Janis aptly noted, some evidence of buoyant optimism in the early months of the Kennedy administration. However, much of the evidence Janis cites refers to what might be better characterized as a general mood of optimistic "can do-ism" in the White House about what might be accomplished in the four years that lay ahead. Significantly, the new evidence indicates that this uncritical or unrealistic optimism did *not* extend to Kennedy's deliberations about the Bay of Pigs operation in particular. Indeed, as soon as the operation had been presented to him, Kennedy immediately appreciated the serious political risks it posed and discerned the need to "turn down the noise" level on the operation (Reeves, 1993, p. 70). He called for a change to a remote landing and informed the CIA to make it a "quieter" landing, preferably even conducting the operation at night.

Janis also suggests that Kennedy and his advisors displayed symptoms of an "illusion of invulnerability" when ultimately deciding to proceed with the operation. This critique was predicated on his assumption that available evidence was sufficient to indicate serious problems with the proposed CIA operation. In his view, therefore, the decision to continue with the invasion plans reflected an *avoidable* decision error of precisely the sort that defined groupthink. As evidence of this, Janis invoked Kennedy's spontaneous exclamation to speechwriter Ted Sorensen shortly after the failure: "How could I have been so stupid to let this thing go forward?" When Kennedy's complete statement is examined, however, it is clear he was referring specifically to his stupidity over uncritically accepting and trusting the specific recommendations of his military and CIA experts on the feasibility of the operation and its odds for success. As Neustadt and May (1986) noted, Kennedy was "scarcely stupid to think Castro a problem. *Most Americans thought so too, not least Eisenhower and Nixon*" (p. 270, emphases added). As Neustadt and May (1986) further noted, Kennedy was hardly stupid for trying to "hold firm against the overt use of American Force [during the invasion itself]. [International and U.S.] law and morality were buttressed by military considerations" (p. 270). Thus, they concluded, "The stupidity for which [Kennedy] blamed himself comes down to a small handful of judgments and presumptions on a handful of particulars" (p. 270).

New evidence indicates that Kennedy's evaluation of the prospects for success of this operation was influenced not only by the CIA's deliberately misleading intelligence assessments, but also by the fact that the plan had been developed under the leadership of President Eisenhower. It was inconceivable to Kennedy that a plan developed under Eisenhower's watchful eye—and which the former president now seemed to endorse unconditionally during their two top-secret briefings together—could be so inherently flawed.

New evidence also reinforces the conclusion that President Kennedy's assessment of the merits of the CIA plan was more heavily influenced by political considerations than its military prospects alone. As Reeves (1993) concluded in a recent assessment of this new evidence, Kennedy was "concerned about the politics of the invasion—he wanted the least possible political risks—even though that meant military risks would be greatest" (p. 134).

Implications and Conclusions

This chapter has argued that a second-look study reveals rather clearly that Janis's original analysis of the Bay of Pigs decisions overstates the causal importance of small group dynamics, while underestimating the significance of other important factors, including political pressures that influenced President Kennedy's judgment and choice. In reaching this conclusion, I have revisited Janis's original inferences and arguments in the context of substantial new and pertinent data now available to scholars.

Having covered a fair bit of ground in advancing toward this argument, it may be useful at this point to attempt to align the strands of conceptual argument and empirical evidence more closely. What does this analysis suggest about the nature of President Kennedy's decision making? First, there is no doubt that group deliberations did play a role in Kennedy's appraisal of the alternatives available to him, just as Janis argued. However, it is also clear that Kennedy's ultimate decision was not determined exclusively by this group process. Rather, Kennedy reached far and wide beyond his small, inner circle for advice. Second, it is clear that although Kennedy trusted his advisors and relied on their assessments, the evidence also shows his level of trust in specific advisors varied. Moreover, it is also clear when the evidence is viewed in aggregate that he deeply trusted his own political instincts and judgment, especially when it came to protecting his power and prestige as president and his image in history.

Although the evidence documents that Kennedy made a concerted effort to be the author of his own decisions, this is not to claim that his decision-making process was systematic, thorough, or optimal. As Burns (2006) aptly noted,

> Crisis followed crisis [in the Kennedy administration]. . . . The main fault lay in Kennedy's fluid, informal management style, which placed enormous burdens of coordination and follow-through on the president. . . . He insisted that everything be brought to him. He was governing alone and he was overwhelmed by it. There was little chance for reflection, planning, or anticipation. (p. 50)

The reason these conclusions are important is that they suggest that any analysis of decision-making fiascoes anchored narrowly within the logic of groupthink may fail to weigh appropriately the impact of other subtle political, organizational, and social pressures operating on decision makers.

In that spirit, this chapter has hopefully illustrated how fresh insights may emerge from a sustained reappraisal of a long-dissected case. How might we appraise the usefulness of this second-look approach to the study of decision-making fiascoes more generally? In an influential essay, Mortensen and Cialdini (2010) advocated the use of what they termed a "full cycle" approach to social psychology. According to this approach, researchers conscientiously go back and forth between field and lab in order to obtain a more comprehensive view of a phenomenon of interest. In a similar spirit, I suggest here that qualitative researchers should adopt a "full circle" approach in their inductive work. The willingness to "circle back" to old empirical burial grounds in the hope of discovering missed treasures may be more fruitful than heretofore appreciated.[1] There may, in short, genuinely be new news in old news. In that spirit, the primary aim of this chapter has been to demonstrate that a second-look approach to qualitative studies of major decision-making fiascoes is not only viable but theoretically productive. Just as the "cold case" method used by law enforcement agencies has sometimes led to spectacular successes in resolving even decades-old unsolved crimes, so taking a fresh look at "old" organizational decisions can help us gain fresh conceptual insights and lead us to refined lessons from those insights.

Table 39.1 Examples of Second-Look Studies of Decision-Making Fiascoes

Reference	Research Context	How Innovation Was Used	Outcomes/Results of Innovation
Kramer (1998)	Examination of evidence pertaining to the Vietnam and Bay of Pigs decision-making process	To reassess adequacy of groupthink hypothesis in light of newly released evidence and theoretical strides in decision-making research	Major assumptions made by Janis challenged; identifies neglected non-groupthink-related causal factors; challenges some of the Janis prescriptions of avoiding decision-making fiascoes
Kramer (2008)	Pre-9/11 decision-making environment within U.S. intelligence agencies and the White House	To assess adequacy of official government post-mortem; to apply social psychological and organizational theory and research on judgment and decision-making processes to archival evidence pertaining to the decision environments within the FBI, CIA, and White House	Reevaluation of evidence suggests importance of social psychological processes and intergroup dynamics on the decision-making process
Kramer (2005)	Reexamination of Bay of Pigs decision-making process	To reassess adequacy of groupthink hypothesis in light of further declassifications of post-mortems and additional interviews with surviving members of Kennedy administration	Major assumptions made by Janis challenged; neglect of non-groupthink-related causal factors highlighted; challenge to some of the prescriptions of avoiding decision-making fiascoes
Kramer (2012)	Pre-9/11 decision-making environment in U.S. intelligence agencies and White House	Further reevaluation of evidence in light of newer declassified documents and evidence from interviews with CIA Fellows	Reevaluation of evidence suggests importance of social psychological processes and intergroup dynamics; culture of trust by FBI and CIA in others' capabilities and coverage may have left "blind spots" in threat detection and hindered threat assessment

As a methodology for studying real-world decision-making processes, the logic of second looks resembles in some ways the logic of replication for experiments. The purpose of an experimental replication is to enhance confidence in the validity of the findings of an original experiment—especially one that has yielded particularly surprising or provocative results. The more a given result can be obtained by different researchers in different labs, the greater the confidence in the original result. In a similar fashion, the greater the extent to which independent qualitative researchers can converge on similar conclusions as to what a given body of data demonstrates or implies, the greater the confidence in that analysis and inference.

Note

1 The writing of this chapter, in fact, afforded me another opportunity to take another look at my own original second look at Janis's post-mortem. A preliminary analysis of the Bay of Pigs decision-making process was reported earlier in Kramer (1998). However, the completeness and validity of that analysis were limited by the unavailability of several key reports, including the critical CIA study and an independent study commissioned by the Attorney General Robert F. Kennedy (the so-called Taylor Study). Those documents have now been declassified and their major findings incorporated in the present, updated chapter.

References

Allison, G., & Zelikow, P. (1999). *Essence of decision* (2nd ed.). New York, NY: Addison-Wesley.

Benson, W.F. (2003). *Writing JFK: Presidential rhetoric and the press in the Bay of Pigs crisis.* Austin: Texas A & M University Press.

Burns, J.M. (2006). *Running alone: Presidential leadership from JFK to Bush II.* New York, NY: Basic Books.

Cohen, M.D., March, J.G., & Olsen, J.P. (1972). A garbage can model of organizational choice. *Administrative Science Quarterly, 17*, 1–25.

Dallek, R. (2003). *An unfinished life: John F. Kennedy, 1917–1963.* New York, NY: Little, Brown.

Edmondson, A. (2012). *Teaming: How organizations learn, innovate and compete in the knowledge economy.* San Francisco, CA: Jossey-Bass.

Farnham, B. (1994). *Avoiding losses, taking risks: Prospect theory and international conflict.* Ann Arbor: University of Michigan Press.

Fursenko, A., & Naftali, T. (1997). *One hell of a gamble: The secret history of the Cuban Missile Crisis, Khrushchev, Castro, and Kennedy, 1958–1964.* New York, NY: Norton.

George, A. (1980). *Presidential decision making in foreign policy: The effective use of information and advice.* Boulder, CO: Westview.

Gilovich, T., Griffin, D., & Kahneman, D. (2002). *Heuristics and biases: The psychology of intuitive judgment.* Cambridge, England: Cambridge University Press.

Hackman, J.R. (2011). *Collaborative intelligence.* New York, NY: Berrett-Koehler.

Hart, P. (1990). *Groupthink in government: A study of small groups and policy failure.* Baltimore, MD: Johns Hopkins University Press.

Higgins, T. (1987). *The perfect failure: Kennedy, Eisenhower, and the CIA at the Bay of Pigs.* New York, NY: Norton.

Janis, I.L. (1972). *Victims of groupthink.* Boston, MA: Houghton Mifflin.

Janis, I.L. (1982). *Crucial decisions: Leading in policymaking and crisis management.* New York, NY: Free Press.

Janis, I.L. (1983). *Groupthink: Psychological studies of policy decisions and fiascoes* (2nd ed.). Boston, MA: Houghton Mifflin.

Jones, H. (2010). *Bay of Pigs.* New York, NY: Oxford University Press.

Kahneman, D. (2011). *Thinking fast and slow.* New York, NY: Farrar, Straus, and Giroux.

Kennedy, R.F. (1988). *In his own words: The unpublished recollections of the Kennedy Years.* New York, NY: Bantam Press.

Kornbluh, P. (1998). *Bay of Pigs declassified: The secret CIA report on the invasion of Cuba.* New York, NY: The New Press.

Kramer, R.M. (1989). Windows of vulnerability or cognitive illusions? Cognitive processes and the nuclear arms race. *Journal of Experimental Social Psychology, 25*, 79–100.

Kramer, R.M. (1998). Revisiting the Bay of Pigs and Vietnam decisions 25 years later: How well has the groupthink hypothesis stood the test of time? *Organizational Behavior and Human Decision Processes, 73*, 236–271.

Kramer, R.M. (2005). A failure to communicate: 9/11 and the tragedy of the informational commons. *International Journal of Public Management, 8*, 1–20.

Kramer, R.M. (2008). Presidential leadership and group folly: Re-appraising the role of groupthink in the Bay of Pigs decisions. In C. L. Hoyt, G.R. Goethals, & D.R. Forsythe (Eds.), *Leadership at the cross-roads* (pp. 230–249). Westport, CT: Praeger.

Kramer, R.M. (2012). Institutional trust failures: Insights and lessons from the 9/11 intelligence failures. In R.M. Kramer and T. Pittinsky (Eds.), *Restoring trust in organizations and leaders* (pp. 69–94). New York, NY: Oxford University Press.

Kramer, R.M., Meyerson, D., & Davis, G. (1990). How much is enough? Psychological components of "guns versus butter" decisions in a security dilemma. *Journal of Personality and Social Psychology, 58*, 984–993.

LeoGrande, W.M., & Kornbluh, P. (2014). *Back channel to Cuba: The hidden history of negotiations between Washington and Havana*. Raleigh: University of North Carolina Press.

March, J.G. (1995). *A primer on decision making*. New York, NY: Free Press.

Mischel, W. (2008). The toothbrush problem. *Observer, 21*, 14–15.

Mortensen, C.R., & Cialdini, R.B. (2010). Full-cycle social psychology for theory and practice. *Social and Personality Compass, 4*, 53–63.

Naftali, T. (2001). *The presidential recordings of JFK*. New York, NY: Norton.

Neustadt, R.E., & May, E.R. (1986). *Thinking in time: The uses of history for decision makers*. New York, NY: Free Press.

Prados, J. (2003). *The White House tapes*. New York, NY: The New Press.

Rasenberger, J. (2014). *The brilliant disaster: JFK, Castro, and America's doomed invasion of Cuba*. New York, NY: Scribner.

Reeves, R. (1993). *President Kennedy: Profile of power*. New York, NY: Simon & Schuster.

Schlesinger, A. M., Jr. (2007). *Journals: 1952–2000*. New York, NY: Penguin.

Staw, B.M. (1976). Knee-deep in the big muddy: A study of escalating commitment to a chosen course of action. *Organizational Behavior and Human Decision Processes, 16*, 27–44.

Strober, G.S., & Strober, D.H. (1993). *Let us begin anew: An oral history of the Kennedy administration*. New York, NY: Harper.

Tetlock, P.E. (1991). An alternative metaphor in the study of judgment and choice: People as politicians. *Theory and Psychology, 1*, 451–475.

Turner, M.E., Pratkanis, A.R., Probasco, P., & Leve, C. (1992). Threat, cohesion, and group effectiveness: Testing a social identity maintenance perspective on groupthink. *Journal of Personality and Social Psychology, 63*, 781–796.

Turner, M.E., Pratkanis, A.R., & Struckman, C.K. (2007). Groupthink as social identity maintenance. In A.R. Pratkanis (Ed.), *The social of social influence* (pp. 223–246). New York, NY: Psychology Press.

White, M.J. (1999). *The Kennedys and Cuba: The declassified documentary history*. New York, NY: Ivan Dee.

Whyte, G. (1989). Groupthink reconsidered. *Academy of Management Review, 14*, 40–56.

Widmer, T. (2012). *Listening in: The secret White House recordings of John F. Kennedy*. New York, NY: Hyperion.

Part VII
Multimethods Approaches

40

Mixing Quantitative and Qualitative Research

Sarah Kaplan[1]

In the field of management, there is often a gulf between qualitative and quantitative research. Despite a wealth of literature on mixing qualitative and quantitative methods (Bryman, 2006; Creswell & Clark, 2007; Jick, 1979; Small, 2011), rarely do individual scholars conduct both forms of research, and even more rarely do they present them together in a single scholarly work. Quantitative researchers may view qualitative research as suspect, or only as a means to generate hypotheses to test in quantitative analyses. According to this view, qualitative research is but an intermediate output supporting "empirical" regression analysis. On the other hand however, qualitative researchers often view quantitative work as too reductive. They may only include quantitative data for rhetorical purposes, recognizing that they are outnumbered (no pun intended) in a world dominated by scholars untrained in qualitative methods.

There are many understandings of the words *qualitative* and *quantitative* within various research traditions. For the purposes of this chapter, I take the broadest of definitions of each, where qualitative research is any analysis based on words (e.g., texts, interviews, or field notes from observations) and quantitative research is any analysis using numbers, either descriptively or in regression analysis.

In this chapter, I offer several models of ways that scholars can usefully integrate qualitative and quantitative research with the hopes of expanding the perspectives of scholars in both camps. In doing so, I call existing characterizations of the relationships among the two types of research into question and offer a more nuanced portrayal of the relationship between them. That is, qualitative methods can be used to understand mechanisms that underlie relationships identified in quantitative research as much as they can be sources of hypotheses or constructs for large-n analyses (see Figure 40.1). Further, quantifications of qualitative data or supplemental quantitative analyses may sometimes serve a useful purpose in validating findings. Small (2011) and Creswell and Clark (2007), among others, provide very detailed analyses of mixed-methods research and the various controversies within it. I have a much narrower goal in this chapter: to identify several models for integrating qualitative and quantitative data and analyses into a research paper (or in a research program) (see Table 40.1), highlighting the potential benefits and pitfalls of the various approaches. Through this analysis, I demonstrate that the line in the sand between qualitative and quantitative research may get in the way of interesting and compelling research projects and programs.

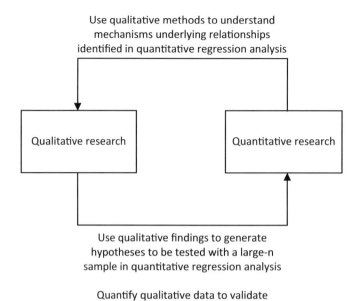

Use qualitative methods to understand
mechanisms underlying relationships
identified in quantitative regression analysis

Use qualitative findings to generate
hypotheses to be tested with a large-n
sample in quantitative regression analysis

Quantify qualitative data to validate
observed patterns

Figure 40.1 Relationship Between Qualitative and Quantitative Research

Table 40.1 Examples of Mixed-methods Papers and Research Programs

Mixing Qualitative and Quantitative Methods in a Single Research Paper	*Mixing Qualitative and Quantitative Methods in a Research Program*
Qualitative before quantitative: Qualitative data to justify the development and testing of a construct • in archival regression analysis (Briscoe, 2007; Canales, 2014; Doering, 2014; Tripsas, 1997) • in a survey (Bresman, 2010; Edmondson, 1999; Ely, 1994; Lounsbury, 2001) • in an experiment (Elsbach, 1994; Ranganathan, 2014) **Quantitative before qualitative**: Survey or archival data-based regressions to establish phenomenon and fieldwork to understand the mechanisms (Bidwell, 2009; Edmondson, 1999; Fernandez-Mateo, 2009) **Quantifying qualitative data** to enrich analysis, validate qualitative insights (Barley, 1986; Kellogg, 2009), or to generate constructs to be tested in regressions (Wageman, 2001)	Lounsbury (1997, 1998, 2001): qualitative fieldwork used to develop a rich understanding of the context, which is presented in a series of papers taking different theoretical angles; qualitative evidence combined with a subsequent survey for quantitative analysis in one paper Kaplan (2008a, 2008b): concurrent qualitative and quantitative studies, iterating between a quantitative analysis of relationships and a qualitative analysis of mechanisms; published as two separate papers, but the emerging insights in each shaped the research strategies and analysis of the other. Mische (2008): rich ethnographic detail combined with social network analysis (based on network data collected as part of the fieldwork); presented in a book format in order to accommodate the richness of the two forms of analysis.

Small (2011) makes important distinctions between complementary and confirmatory purposes for integrating qualitative and quantitative methods and also between sequential and concurrent research designs. When planning research, it is certainly important to think about these choices. However, my own experience, and that of many of the scholars' whose work I describe herein (as told to me in interviews), these purposes evolve over time as the research unfolds. Research intended to be confirmatory ends up offering new, complementary insights. Research that was intended only to be quantitative becomes multimethod as reviewers ask for evidence to elucidate the proposed mechanisms. The published articles or books may not reflect these vagaries of the research process, but researchers engaging in mixed-methods studies may want to be prepared for or attentive to these potential shifts. I will return to these insights in the conclusion of this chapter.

Qualitative Data in Support of Quantitative Analyses

Amongst the most traditional views of the relationship between qualitative and quantitative research is the use of the former to generate hypotheses and constructs to be measured and tested in the latter. That is, there is an outcome that is puzzling (such as heterogeneity in incumbent organizations' responses to technological change or differences in team learning), existing explanations are not satisfactory, and scholars use qualitative evidence to identify potential alternative explanations that are more complete or resolve tensions that exist. Researchers then translate these insights into hypotheses that they then test in a subsequent quantitative, regression analysis. The quantitative component can take multiple forms, from archival data to surveys to experiments.

Using Qualitative Data for the Development of a Construct and/or Model That Is Then Tested in Archival Research

Tripsas's (1997) study of creative destruction in the typesetting industry starts with a puzzle: If a new generation of technology is competence-destroying for incumbent firms, why do some survive and even thrive? She uses a detailed historical analysis of the companies in the typesetting industry—based on company and trade association archives, interviews, personal records of retired employees, industry trade journals, and other sources—to uncover the reason. She found that the differences are due to the degree to which a firm's specialized complementary assets are aligned with the new technological regime. She demonstrated this in a series of tables identifying the technological competencies and complementary assets required for each generation of technology. In the second half of the paper, she used these qualitative insights to generate measures of competencies for each of the firms in a complete dataset of all of the firms and products in the industry over time. (Note that she developed this quantitative dataset using many of the same resources that provided the qualitative insights.) In the regression analysis, she demonstrated that incumbents whose complementary assets were not devalued had higher market shares in new technological regimes than those whose complementary assets lost value. In this study, the qualitative and quantitative analyses were both complementary and confirmatory. The analysis of the qualitative data uncovered relationships and helped to generate constructs for a quantitative analysis that then confirmed the qualitative insights.

Briscoe's (2007) study of professional service workers follows a similar approach. He used a field study of primary care physicians to develop a model of how organizations influence the temporal flexibility of their work. The fieldwork—observations, archival data collection, and interviews with 55 informants—allowed him to identify the primary source of inflexibility (inability to hand off patients at the end of a shift) and locate specific practices associated with bureaucratic formalization that might create more flexibility. This first study uncovered the mechanisms but did not allow Briscoe to rule out other potential factors shaping temporal flexibility. Thus, in the second study, he used survey data on physicians and their organizations in order to evaluate the effect of bureaucratic formalization on three measures associated with temporal flexibility. He did not design or conduct this survey of over 6,000 physicians himself, but rather he was able to obtain it from another researcher who had collected these survey data for other purposes. Matching his qualitative insights with these more comprehensive data enabled him to confirm that bureaucratization was indeed associated with greater temporal flexibility, controlling for other organizational characteristics such as size, type of ownership, and age.

Doering's (2014) study of a microfinance institution explored the ways that escalation of commitment can actually be productive for organizational outcomes. She used ethnographic observations and interviews to provide insights into loan officers' behaviors as they interacted with clients, from which she developed a series of hypotheses. As she noted, such data "are poorly suited to address the frequency of these processes or their long-term, broader consequences for the organization" (pp. 12–13). So, she used a database from the organization on lending and repayment behaviors over time in order to show that delinquent clients who work with original loan officers (who are presumed to escalate their commitment if they keep these clients on the books rather than sending them to collections) are more likely to repay loans on time and take out subsequent loans (evidence of higher levels of performance). This regression analysis enabled her to connect escalation of commitment to performance as well as to account for alternative explanations and selection bias in ways not possible in the field study. In this study, Doering iterated between complementary and confirmatory goals and between qualitative and quantitative data collection and analysis over time. (See Canales, 2014, for a similar style study of microfinance using ethnography and archival evidence from loan databases to understand the tensions between standardization and flexibility in loan management.)

In these examples, qualitative research enabled the researchers to identify a potential explanation not previously explored in the literature and measures that could then be tested in a regression. However, the ways that the scholars made the connections between their qualitative and quantitative data differ. In Tripsas's (1997) study, the sources of data for the qualitative and quantitative studies were highly overlapping. Her comprehensive database of firms and product models was not available off the shelf, so she necessarily had to dig into many forms of archival evidence to construct the quantitative variables for testing the hypothesis she generated from a qualitative analysis of these same materials. For Briscoe (2007), he was able to match insights from his own fieldwork with a previously conducted survey that he could adapt for his purposes. For Doering (2014) and Canales (2014), the ethnographic work was complemented by a database from the same organization.

Using Qualitative Data for the Development of a Construct and/or Model That Is Then Tested in a Survey Designed Based on those Constructs

Edmondson's (1999) paper on team psychological safety started with observations and interviews of eight teams to verify that the constructs of team psychological safety and team learning behavior could be operationalized in her research site. She then administered a survey measuring these constructs to members of 53 teams and a separate survey to recipients of the teams' work in order to measure team performance. As a final step, she then turned back to more fieldwork to conduct a comparison of extreme cases (four high- and three low-learning teams) to the relationships between the two focal constructs. The goal, as she stated, "was to learn more about how they functioned as teams rather than to confirm or disconfirm a model" (p. 370). The most powerful part of this third phase of qualitative research was her use of outliers to show how the lack of psychological safety hindered team learning even in contexts that should have otherwise enabled it.

Similarly, Bresman's (2010) study of external learning by pharmaceutical teams used qualitative data from 94 interviews of members of six teams to develop measures of different forms of external learning—contextual and vicarious—that he introduced subsequently in a complementary survey of 62 additional teams. The survey data then allowed him to examine the performance implications of these external learning activities, showing particularly that vicarious learning only leads to higher performance when coupled with internal learning.

Ely's (1994) study worked slightly differently in that she interviewed and surveyed the exact same sample of people (women in law firms) to understand the impact of the presence of women in upper echelons of management on hierarchical and peer relationships among professional women. She first conducted four to five hours of interviews for each of 30 women professionals from four matched pairs of law firms (matched according to whether the upper management was gender inclusive or not). She then conducted content analysis of the interviews (with interrater reliability tests) to identify the key dimensions of the theoretical mechanisms of interest. She subsequently used the natural language of the respondents to design questions in a survey that each informant completed. This "empathic" approach to survey design increased construct validity. Based on the survey results, she conducted a series of t-tests on the average scores by type of firm in order to confirm that women in firms with few women leaders did not experience gender as a positive basis for identification, did not find senior women to be positive role models, and were more likely to compete with their peers. She complemented these statistical tests with rich quotes from the interviews that showed the grounding of these identified relationships in the lived experiences of the women.

Lounsbury's (2001) study of the introduction of recycling programs at universities started with interviews with program leaders across 60 different universities. In this exploratory study, he found that the implementation of recycling came in two forms, either programs staffed by a full-time recycling coordinator or ones where the responsibilities were added to existing work roles. The fieldwork (in iteration with the literature) suggested several reasons why there might be variation in staffing models for recycling programs. To test these hypotheses, he then conducted a survey of 154 schools in order to confirm the role that status and social activism had in shaping adoption patterns.

Thus, qualitative fieldwork and survey studies can be useful complements (Sieber, 1973, provides an excellent description of these complementarities). Qualitative research can be seen as a precursor to a survey, or a survey can be seen as a supplement to fieldwork. Surveys are very tricky to get right. Assuring the validity of the questions and the scales is essential for generating insight. For those scholars whose initial intention is to do survey research, conducting in-depth fieldwork in order to develop a survey may lead to a more valid set of measures than if they had just pretested a survey designed in the absence of these insights. Fieldwork can also help in the interpretation and theorizing of the survey data. For scholars starting with qualitative fieldwork, such as Lounsbury (2001), the idea to conduct a survey might only emerge during the research process at a point when it becomes beneficial to collect data over a larger number of sites. Surveys can contribute to the analysis of qualitative data from the field by confirming or contextualizing observations derived from a smaller sample.

Using Qualitative Data for the Development of a Construct and/or Model That Is Then Tested in an Experiment

Elsbach (1994) studied the California beef industry in order to understand how organizations can manage perceptions of negative events in order to maintain their legitimacy. Her paper presents three studies sequentially. In the first two, she conducted interviews of those attempting to shape perceptions (15 executives in beef producer organizations and industry associations) and the intended audiences (15 members of the press, nutritionists, and politicians). The analysis of these interviews (as well as of supplemental press articles and press releases) allowed her to produce a typology of different responses to negative events based on the form and content of the communications and to construct three propositions of the relationships between the types of negative events, the types of responses, and their effectiveness.

In the third study, she translated these insights into a vignette-based lab experiment in which she tested the effects on various measures of organizational legitimacy of each of the different types of accounts. The experimental results largely confirm the findings from the two qualitative studies. This combination of studies proves to be effective in a way that none would be on its own. With only

427

15 interviewees for each of studies 1 and 2, the reader might not be convinced of the findings, but complementing these insights with a lab experiment validates the qualitative findings.

A recent study by Ranganathan (2014) on craftsmen and traders of lacquer work in India follows a similar template, using ethnographic evidence to show how different orientations toward work shape prices charged and then conducting a field experiment to validate the findings and hone in on the mechanism (with the counterintuitive insight that the craftsmen will charge less if they think the customer will appreciate the product more).

Coupling fieldwork and experiments is not frequently found in the literature but offers great potential. As Fine and Elsbach (2000) point out, qualitative field data can contribute a richer, contextualized set of theories to test in experiments where lab work alone is a poor proxy for the real world. On the other hand, they argue, qualitative data alone may produce theories that are highly complex and too specific to the case or cases studied. They suggest, as the previous examples illustrate, that coupling fieldwork and experiments in an iterative process can lead to more nuanced analyses and more rigorous understandings of the mechanisms at play.

Starting With Quantitative Data

An alternative model of mixing qualitative and quantitative methods is to start with a statistical regression and then follow with qualitative evidence. This approach can have two effects. The first is to lend face validity to regressions. If the relationships identified using necessarily abstracted quantitative measures make sense in the context of the lived experience of people in those contexts, one can feel more comfortable that the measures capture the constructs they are meant to capture and that the associations (perhaps even causal relationships) identified are not spurious. Second, qualitative analysis may also allow the researcher to explain the underlying mechanisms behind a relationship identified in a regression, ruling out some and offering in-depth elaborations of others.

One example is Fernandez-Mateo's (2009) study of gender disadvantage in contract employment. This study is based on data from the placement records of a temporary staffing agency showing how the gender wage gap evolves over time. She used the quantitative data in a series of analyses to show that men accrue benefits from tenure at a greater rate than do women. She also ruled out a number of possible mechanisms—such as firm-specific skills that develop over time—previously suggested by the literature. In the second part of the paper, she identifies the two remaining possible mechanisms (the supply-side explanation of general skills acquisition and the demand-side explanation of implicit biases). She then used information from observations and 49 interviews at the staffing agency to adjudicate between them, suggesting that implicit bias on the part of employers is the most plausible explanation for the cumulative disadvantages of women in this context.

In an interesting twist on the use of surveys, in Bidwell's (2009) effort to collect survey data using in-person surveys in IT outsourcing, he ended up accumulating a good deal of rich qualitative evidence that emerged in the discussions associated with collecting the quantitative survey data. He used the qualitative data to give richness to the explanations about the differences between contractors and employees and when each would be deployed on a project. And as illustrated previously, Edmondson's (1999) study came full circle, having used qualitative evidence to generate a survey and then returning to fieldwork to understand the mechanisms underlying the effects from the survey-based quantitative analysis.

While it is certainly true that not all quantitative regression analyses demand a qualitative component in the published version of the paper, it is also true that nearly any quantitative scholar would benefit from entering into the field. Even the most high-tech, sophisticated regression analysis can benefit from some fieldwork to assure the regression results make sense and are grounded in reality. This is important because variables used in quantitative studies are always simplifications or approximations of the underlying constructs, and the sanity check with the field helps assure the scholar of the validity of the measures. Unfortunately, few quantitative scholars receive training in qualitative methods and therefore can feel ill-equipped to engage in this complementary work.

Quantifying Qualitative Data

A further model for the relationship of qualitative and quantitative research is in the quantification of qualitative data (see McPherson & Sauder, this volume, for further detail on this subject). Scholars may undertake this for the purposes of conducting subsequent statistical analyses to confirm findings. Quantification may also help to represent qualitative evidence compactly, potentially revealing patterns that might not be visible otherwise.

Barley's (1986) study of the introduction of CT scanners into two hospitals is largely an ethnographic study of the different organizational forms that can emerge from the adoption of the same technology, but he introduced quantitative elements to reinforce or validate his analyses. He based the bulk of the story on his observations of the negotiations about who makes the decisions in the scanning process, and he documents a series of scripts (different by hospital) that were enacted over time. To demonstrate the differences in the two hospitals, he counted the occurrences of these various scripts in his field notes and showed that different patterns emerged in the different contexts.

Over the course of these observations, he recorded 400 radiological examinations, of which 91 were CT scans sufficiently documented to understand whether the radiologist or the technologist was the primary decision maker in the various decisions required by each scan. He calculated the percent of decisions made by the radiologist for each scan (49 scans in one hospital and 42 in the other) and used the plots of these ratios over time to demonstrate not only the shifts toward the technologist over time in each, but also the different rates and phases associated with the different settings. He then offered correlations established in two very simple regressions to support his qualitative conclusions about the differences in rates between the two hospitals and also to validate his identification of the different phases of structuration in each.

In a similar study of organizational change in two hospitals, Kellogg (2009) examined the degree to which new practices associated with work hour reductions (such as handing off patients to doctors coming on in the next shift) were implemented. She counted the different kinds of change mobilization activities in 202 different meetings and the percent of handoffs that occurred in 101 sign-out encounters she observed. She used a comparison of these counts to demonstrate that doctors in the successful hospital engaged in a set of practices that those in the unsuccessful hospital did not.

In Wageman's (2001) study of how leaders foster team effectiveness, she transformed interview responses into quantitative variables by using multiple coders to assess the presence of various team characteristics—several dimensions of team design, self-managing behaviors, and leadership coaching—as being either high, medium, or low. She then matched these quantified data with survey responses and archival information on team performance in a regression analysis in order to conclude that the effectiveness of leaders' coaching depended on how well teams were designed to begin with. In this study, the qualitative data are not presented in a separate narrative but rather only as they are quantified.

Because of the rhetorical power of numbers, scholars are often tempted to generate counts from qualitative, even ethnographic, data. As the Barley (1986) and Kellogg (2009) studies show, such numbers can provide useful confirmation of the patterns developed through the qualitative analysis. In each of these studies, counting is appropriate because the researchers were able to observe repeated equivalent events collected in a systematic way. Other forms of quantification might be more problematic. For example, generating a quantitative rating of degree (of importance, of intensity, etc.) using a Likert scale should be seen as suspect especially if it is generated by the researcher. Better versions of this approach might involve multiple coders not informed of the research question, with tests for interrater reliability (as in Wageman, 2001). Alternatively, one could get the informants themselves to provide a numerical rating through a survey instrument (perhaps used in the context of an interview, e.g., Eisenhardt & Bourgeois, 1988). But, it should be emphasized that good qualitative research does not have to offer quantifications, and indeed, such strategies should only be deployed when it is appropriate and useful in extending the analysis.

Recent trends in quantification of texts, from simple word counts to more sophisticated computer science–based methods such as topic modeling or feature extraction, are another form of quantification of qualitative data (e.g., Kaplan & Vakili, in press). With the increasing availability of electronic texts, these approaches are only likely to grow over time (increasingly blurring the distinctions between qualitative and quantitative evidence and analysis). Some of the early approaches have usefully mixed these quantifications with qualitative evidence, such as in DiMaggio, Nag, and Blei's (2013) study of controversies in arts funding in the U.S. where they use topic modeling to identify topics emerging from over 8,000 newspaper articles and then mobilize these topics in a rich historically informed explanation of how these controversies played out.

Mixing Methods in Research Programs Rather Than Single Articles

These same principles can also be applied within a research program rather than in a single paper. As those who have attempted to shepherd a mixed-method paper through the review process have discovered, it is very difficult to introduce the required detail for each method in a journal-length article. The rewards for succeeding in this endeavor are high, but there are also times when it is more appropriate to iterate between quantitative and qualitative work, focusing single articles on specific data sets and methodologies. The accumulation of these studies over the course of a research program can lead to rich insights that might not always be possible to generate in a single mixed-method article.

An example would be Lounsbury's stream of research on recycling programs. The survey-based study reported previously included only some of the rich detail he gained through the fieldwork that preceded it. In other papers, he took advantage of the more than 160 interviews he conducted to report on how collective entrepreneurship contributed to the creation of a new occupational category (Lounsbury, 1998) and to illustrate different forms of institutional analysis (Lounsbury, 1997). Kaplan (2008b) conducted an ethnography of strategy making in one organization in the communications industry concurrently with a quantitative study of more than 70 firms in the industry over 20 years (Kaplan, 2008a). Each study looked at a different aspect of the role of cognition in shaping how organizations respond to radical shifts in the industry—the first looking at one firm's response to the crash of 2001–2002 and the other looking at the response to the emergence of fiber optics in an industry previously dominated by copper wiring. Insights from the field study that cognition and incentives were tightly intertwined in how decision making unfolded (in a process she called "framing contests") led her to explore how variables measuring CEO cognition and organizational incentives might interact in the large-sample study. As a result, she was able to demonstrate that CEO attention can compensate for poorly aligned organizational incentives. The ethnographic study of the decision-making processes in one organization could then explain why this might be the case.

While in both of these examples the papers were published separately, the research process itself was highly iterative. Rather than splitting up these results into multiple papers, another alternative (taken less frequently in management scholarship) is to write a book that collects these insights together. Mische's (2008) sociological study of mobilization of Brazilian youths combining ethnography and social network analysis is a powerful example of this approach.

Observations About Mixed-Methods Research

Across these examples, the mixing of methods takes two forms: one is confirmation and the other is complementarity (Small 2011). (This is the simplest typology. Greene, Caracelli, and Graham [1989] and Bryman [2006] offer more granular categorizations for those who are interested.) Sometimes the quantitative analysis confirms a pattern observed in the qualitative data, either through quantification of that data or through triangulation in a subsequent study. Or, the qualitative data can offer confirmation of the validity of constructs or mechanisms identified in quantitative research. In complementary studies, qualitative analyses can get at mechanisms underlying relationships identified in regression analyses, or quantitative studies can establish connections to performance of the constructs identified in qualitative studies.

Thus, the popular dichotomy—that quantitative research is deductive and qualitative is inductive or exploratory—is less useful when we consider the research discussed previously. Sometimes qualitative evidence is used to confirm quantitative findings, and sometimes it is used to explore a phenomenon in order to develop hypotheses for quantitative testing. Sometimes quantitative research can be exploratory—for example, is there a relationship between these two variables?—and qualitative research can explain why. In other words, once we mixed qualitative and quantitative methods, we see that each type of research plays a variety of roles. These relationships between quantitative and qualitative data and analysis can be built into the initial research design (e.g., Kaplan's studies which were designed as multimethod from the outset) or may emerge over time (e.g., Lounsbury's survey work which only emerged as he was analyzing his interview data or Fernandez-Mateo's fieldwork, which was instigated by the desire to sort through alternative explanations of her quantitative results). Where one starts may be as much a matter of taste as of any hard and fast rules about matching methods to inductive or deductive research problems.

Sometimes mixing qualitative and quantitative methods is based on the same data and involves different forms of analysis, as in Tripsas's (1997) historical study of the typesetting industry or Barley's (1986) study of CT scanners in hospitals. Other times, the mix requires two different data collection strategies, as in Edmondson's (1999) interviews and surveys or Elsbach's (1994) interviews and lab experiments. Small (2011) defines the former case as "mixed data analysis" studies and the latter as "mixed data collection" studies. The challenge with either case is that the researcher must give adequate treatment to each method. The risk, in the constraining form of a journal article, is in glossing over some of the methodological details in order to save space. But, for a multimethod paper to be convincing, the reader must be privy to the methodological details in the same way he or she would be in a single-method paper. Elsbach's (1994) study is a model here as she presents each of her three studies sequentially, including very rich detail on the data sources and analytical methods; she does not give short shrift to any of the three methodological approaches.

As Edmondson and McManus (2007) have pointed out, mixing qualitative and quantitative evidence does not always lead to better research or a stronger paper. Mixing methods is often worthwhile because it is a useful route to a "full" understanding of a problem. However, in undertaking multimethod research, the scholar risks being a jack-of-all-trades and master of none. In the presentation of research results, if the researcher gives each dataset inadequate treatment, the evidence may remain superficial or unconvincing. Adding qualitative data to a quantitative analysis must serve a purpose other than lengthening the paper. Including quantitative analyses in a rich qualitative paper must be done sufficiently rigorously and add enough insight so as not to appear to be a transparent rhetorical strategy to convince readers who would be presumed to be unconvinced by qualitative data only.

In Western societies, we privilege quantitative knowledge as being somehow more "objective" than qualitative evidence (Denis, Langley, & Rouleau, 2006; Porter, 1995). Mixing methods is often a strategy that qualitative researchers are tempted to deploy for rhetorical reasons in a field (management) where qualitative work is still in the minority. That is, because we are socialized to be convinced by quantitative evidence, many scholars are likely to pursue quantitative research strategies. But, as Cameron (1963) points out, "not everything that can be counted counts, and not everything that counts can be counted." The advantage of the mixed-methods studies highlighted here is that they recognize the value of iterating between that which can be counted and that which cannot in order to generate richer insights about the phenomena of interest.

Note

1 The author would like to acknowledge useful comments from Valentina Assenova, Jillian Chown, Kim Elsbach, Rod Kramer, Michael Lounsbury, Chad McPherson, Matthew Regele, Michael Sauder, Amy Wrzesniewski, and the slump_management research group. Any errors and omissions remain my own.

References

Barley, S.R. (1986). Technology as an occasion for structuring—evidence from observations of CT scanners and the social-order of radiology departments. *Administrative Science Quarterly, 31*(1), 78–108.

Bidwell, M. (2009). Do peripheral workers do peripheral work? Comparing the use of highly skilled contractors and regular employees. *Industrial & Labor Relations Review, 62*(2), 200–225.

Bresman, H. (2010). External learning activities and team performance: A multimethod field study. *Organization Science, 21*(1), 81–96.

Briscoe, F. (2007). From iron cage to iron shield? How bureaucracy enables temporal flexibility for professional service workers. *Organization Science, 18*(2), 297–314.

Bryman, A. (2006). Integrating quantitative and qualitative research: How is it done? *Qualitative Research, 6*(1), 97–113.

Cameron, W.B. (1963). *Informal sociology, a casual introduction to sociological thinking.* New York, NY: Random House.

Canales, R. (2014). Weaving straw into gold: Managing organizational tensions between standardization and flexibility in microfinance. *Organization Science, 25*(1), 1–28.

Creswell, J.W., & Clark, V.L.P. (2007). *Designing and conducting mixed methods research.* Thousand Oaks, CA: Sage.

Denis, J.L., Langley, A., & Rouleau, G.A. (2006). The power of numbers in strategizing. *Strategic Organization, 4*(4), 349–377.

DiMaggio, P., Nag, M., & Blei, D. (2013). Exploiting affinities between topic modeling and the sociological perspective on culture: Application to newspaper coverage of US government arts funding. *Poetics, 41*(6), 570–606.

Doering, L. (2014). Rethinking escalation of commitment: Relational lending in microfinance. Working paper.

Edmondson, A. (1999). Psychological safety and learning behavior in work teams. *Administrative Science Quarterly, June,* 350–383.

Edmondson, A.C., & Mcmanus, S.E. (2007). Methodological fit in management field research. *Academy of Management Review, 32*(4), 1155–1179.

Eisenhardt, K.M., & Bourgeois, L.J., III. (1988). Politics of strategic decision making in high-velocity environments: Toward a midrange theory. *Academy of Management Journal, 31*(4), 737–770.

Elsbach, K.D. (1994). Managing organizational legitimacy in the California cattle industry—the construction and effectiveness of verbal accounts. *Administrative Science Quarterly, 39*(1), 57–88.

Ely, R.J. (1994). The effects of organizational demographics and social identity on relationships among professional women. *Administrative Science Quarterly, 39*(2), 203–238.

Fernandez-Mateo, I. (2009). Cumulative gender disadvantage in contract employment. *American Journal of Sociology, 114*(4), 871–923.

Fine, G.A., & Elsbach, K.D. (2000). Ethnography and experiment in social psychological theory building: Tactics for integrating qualitative field data with quantitative lab data. *Journal of Experimental Social Psychology, 36*(1), 51–76.

Greene, J.C., Caracelli, V.J., & Graham, W. (1989). Toward a conceptual framework for mixed-method evaluation designs. *Educational Evaluation and Policy Analysis, 11*(3), 255–274.

Jick, T.D. (1979). Mixing qualitative and quantitative methods: Triangulation in action. *Administrative Science Quarterly, 24*(4), 602–611.

Kaplan, S. (2008a). Cognition, capabilities, and incentives: Assessing firm response to the fiber-optic revolution. *Academy of Management Journal, 51*(4), 672–695.

Kaplan, S. (2008b). Framing contests: strategy making under uncertainty. *Organization Science, 19*(5), 729–752.

Kaplan, S., & Vakili, K. (in press). The double-edged sword of recombination in breakthrough innovation. *Strategic Management Journal.*

Kellogg, K.C. (2009). Operating room: Relational spaces and micro-institutional change in two surgical teaching hospitals. *American Journal of Sociology, 115*(3), 657–711.

Lounsbury, M. (1997). Exploring the institutional tool kit—the rise of recycling in the US solid waste field. *American Behavioral Scientist, 40*(4), 465–477.

Lounsbury, M. (1998). Collective entrepreneurship: The mobilization of college and university recycling coordinators. *Journal of Organizational Change Management, 11*(1), 50–69.

Lounsbury, M. (2001). Institutional sources of practice variation: Staffing college and university recycling programs. *Administrative Science Quarterly, 46*(1), 29–56.

Mische, A. (2008). *Partisan publics: Communication and contention across Brazilian youth activist networks.* Princeton, NJ: Princeton University Press.

Porter, T.M. (1995) *Trust in numbers: The pursuit of objectivity in science and public life.* Princeton, NJ: Princeton University Press.

Ranganathan, A. (2014). Choosing meaning over money? Evidence from a field audit study with handicraft artisans in southern india. Working paper.

Sieber, S.D. (1973). Integration of fieldwork and survey methods. *American Journal of Sociology, 78*(6), 1335–1359.

Small, M.L. (2011). How to conduct a mixed methods study: Recent trends in a rapidly growing literature. *Annual Review of Sociology, 37*, 57–86.

Tripsas, M. (1997). Unraveling the process of creative destruction: Complementary assets and incumbent survival in the typesetter industry. *Strategic Management Journal, 18*, 119–142.

Wageman, R. (2001). How leaders foster self-managing team effectiveness: Design choices versus hands-on coaching. *Organization Science, 12*(5), 559–577.

41

Counting Qualitative Data

Chad Michael McPherson and Michael Sauder

Introduction

Discussions of the relationship between qualitative and quantitative approaches to social research often focus on their contradictory aspects or the relative strengths of each (for helpful overviews, see Kaplan, this volume; Howe 1988, 1992; Rossman and Wilson 1985). Qualitative research is often portrayed as offering rich context, phenomenological understanding, insight into behavioral complexity, and the opportunity for inductive theory building, while quantitative approaches are cast as promising standardization, control, reliability, and a firmer basis for making causal claims consistent with deductive theory testing (for helpful overviews, see Adler and Adler 1994; Fine and Elsbach 2000; Johnson and Onwuegbuzie 2004).

Focusing on the distinctive strengths of each approach, however, leaves aside questions of how qualitative and quantitative logics intermingle in various aspects of the research process. Although there is a great deal of discussion about the benefits of adopting both qualitative and quantitative approaches in data *collection*—for instance, there is no shortage of published material arguing for the employment of "mixed methods" or triangulating from multiple types of data (Bryman 2006; Jick 1979; Onwuegbuzie and Leech 2005; Rossman and Wilson 1985, 1994)—there has been very little written about the simultaneous use of qualitative and quantitative approaches in data *analysis* (for exceptions, see Maxwell 2010; Miles and Huberman 1994; Sandelowski 2001). In particular, practical, systematic discussions of how qualitative data is quantified, the risks and benefits of applying mixed analytic procedures to qualitative data, and the conditions under which such approaches make the most sense are difficult to find in organizational scholarship.

In this chapter we discuss one form of the quantifying of qualitative data, the development of "counts" in the analysis of data and presentation of findings.[1] After briefly laying out the different ways in which quantification, and specifically counting, enters into qualitative research, we specify some conditions under which employing counting strategies is most appropriate and can best assist theory development. We next highlight the rationales for and benefits of counting qualitative data. We conclude by discussing the potential risks associated with this approach and, more generally, the dangers of equating quantification with validity, reliability, and high standards of evidence.

Quantification in Qualitative Research

The creation of numbers and counts—whether for academic, market, or policy purposes—promotes the appearance of scientific rigor, objectivity, and legitimacy (Espeland and Sauder 2007; Hacking 1985, 1999; Porter 1995). This dominant epistemological position rewards quantitative research and makes it increasingly essential to include in qualitative research, especially qualitative research that is aimed for general audiences. Abend, Petre, and Sauder (2014), for example, find that qualitative articles recently published in the most prestigious journals in U.S. sociology are much more likely to quantify aspects of their methodology than are qualitative articles published in either these same journals 50 years ago or current specialist journals. Their findings suggest that the quantification of methods and data is used to enhance the legitimacy of qualitative research and increase validity in the eyes of generalist audiences.

There are several ways in which quantification is employed in qualitative research. Most commonly, qualitative studies produce and present numbers to describe their methodology. These numbers typically tell the reader, for instance, how many hours were spent in the field, how many pages of notes were taken, how many interviews were conducted, how long the interviews lasted, and how many sites were visited. This type of quantification is often used to demonstrate the rigor and systematic nature—not to mention the time intensity—of the research, and, at least in sociology, is far more common in generalist journals than those specializing in qualitative research (Abend, Petre, and Sauder 2014). In general, quantification used to describe methods is a taken-for-granted practice that's part of the qualitative scholar's repertoire of reporting on research.

What we are interested in here, however, is how the analytical strategy of counting data is used to support, verify, and triangulate qualitative analysis and theory development. Our focus is on specifying when and why counting is useful and the risks that such counting entails. There is considerable variation in the complexity of this form of quantification, ranging from rudimentary counts of the occurrence of observable events or the frequency of word use in textual analysis to more abstract, theory-driven evaluations like the number of times a symbolic practice is interpreted to have been enacted or a concept is invoked in interviews. While there are several rationales and conditions constraining decisions to use counts, quantification strategies can open new possibilities for understanding and interpreting data. The quantification of qualitative data as part of an analytic strategy has entered recent discussions (see, for example, Onwuegbuzie et al. 2009; Sandelowski 2001), but it is far from a commonplace concern in qualitative methods scholarship. For example, very few works discuss practical considerations, such as under what conditions counts might be considered and why researchers might or might not consider creating and analyzing counts. We attempt to move this conversation forward by specifying how the counting of qualitative data can be a productive strategy for researchers.

Conditions Favorable for Quantification and Theory Development

Not all qualitative data lends itself to quantification. There are many instances in which counting is inappropriate for the aims of the research. For instance, when the goal of the study is to identify mechanisms (e.g., Lutfey and Freese 2005), it is often less important to count how many times these mechanisms are cited by research subjects than it is to identify the full range of mechanisms that are in operation. Likewise, the data gathered from open-ended interviews are usually at odds with quantification. Counting the frequency of the mentions of a theme or topic in interviews is often uninformative, and sometimes even misleading, since there is inconsistency in how each interview unfolds (see Gherardi and Turner 1987; Maxwell 2010; Sandelowski 2001). Counting is also ineffective when subjects are not fully aware or vary in their understanding of the structural influences on their behavior; insights do not come from the additive effects of quantities in those studies, but from the researcher skillfully synthesizing and contextualizing social activity—what Katz refers to as the "researcher's imagination" (1987: 392). The point here is that counting, even if it is possible, should not be done just for the sake of constructing quantities.

Given these limitations, when *is* counting an effective strategy? There are a number of rationales for quantifying qualitative data, including when it serves as a strategy for testing or confirming the validity of qualitative findings (see Denzin 1978; Miles and Huberman 1994; Smith 1982), when it is used as a means of triangulating qualitative findings to develop a complete, specified, and valid theory (Onwuegbuzie et al. 2009; Sandelowski, Voils, and Knafl 2009), and when it safeguards against researcher bias. As Rossman and Wilson (1985, 1994) suggest, counting can also be valuable for expanding the theoretical scope or richness of a study when it directs attention to surprising patterns and insights that may not be detected in examining the qualitative data alone. No matter the rationale, however, it is important that the researcher have a clear purpose for constructing counts and guard against unsystematic, poorly devised counting or data mining (see Sandelowski, Voils, and Knafl 2009; Van de Ven and Poole 1990).

More practically, for counting to be effective there must be some justification for identifying discrete instances or cases of particular phenomena. Moreover, researchers should be able to justify that the things being counted are commensurate. Counts may be undertaken—using either all of the data collected or a theoretically and methodologically justified subset—as long as the data can be divided into comparable units; these units may consist of events, periods of time, episodes, types of interaction, activities, types of institutions, or other stable phenomena with substantial comparability (Gherardi and Turner 1987; Miles and Huberman 1994). These discrete observations are comparable because they are repeated over time, they occur under similar conditions, and/ or they take place between similar or similar types of actors (see Martin 2004; Sandelowski, Voils, and Knafl 2009). Some counts, such as the number of interview subjects who identified as being a particular gender or the number of observations that involved specific, defined positions in an organization, are relatively straightforward. However, when measuring more complex phenomena, like episodic events or context-specific interactions, more care is necessary to ensure that the events are similar enough to be categorized together and counted. In effect, the researcher needs to be careful to ensure that the common denominator is being specified correctly, asking if it is possible to effectively isolate both the occurrence *and* non-occurrence of phenomena in time, space, place, or context.

Recent research provides instructive examples of comparable phenomena that lend themselves to counting. Nelson and Schutz's (2007) ethnographic comparison of the techniques providers used at two daycare centers shows variation in child-rearing strategies by class. The points of comparison include the services provided, type of institution, local standards for services, age of children, and periods of observation. Taking advantage of these well-defined contexts, the authors are able to reliably count behaviors of theoretical importance such as how often children are corrected and praised, providers employ various interventions, children call on teachers for help, and specific types of interactions take place among the children.

Calarco (2012) employed similar strategies to examine class-based differences in students' help-seeking behaviors by counting various behavioral observations of four classrooms within a single elementary school. Calarco's quantification is informative because the counts of student behaviors were standardized by the consistency in the duration and type of time spent in each classroom; this regularity provided a common denominator by which reliable comparisons could be made. Similarly, to study the cultural significance in gendered names of youth sports teams, Messner (2000) clearly defined his denominators by event (the opening ceremonies of a summer soccer camp), geographic location (city), and individual characteristics (participant age). These studies all demonstrate ways to effectively create countable categories; they also provide a sampling of the variety of denominators that serve as bases of quantification.

Table 41.1 Uses of Quantification in Qualitative Research Methods

Reference	Research Context	How Innovation Was Used	Outcomes/Results of Innovation
Calarco (2012)	Elementary school children's help-seeking skills and strategies in classrooms	Summarization and evidence: counts of different kinds of children's help-seeking behaviors across classrooms to show students' behavioral differences based upon their categorized class	Comparing students across several classrooms to show how class background is associated with how students seek help from teachers. Results quantify comparative privileges accrued by middle-class students.
Garud and Van de Ven (1992)	Trial-and-error learning in corporate ventures examined to explain innovation during strategic development	Verification and specification: 6 years of qualitative "critical incidents" are coded and quantified and then used in time series equations to test emergent qualitative model	The creation of a strategy process model of how corporations learn in the development of innovations; qualitative analysis is tested, verified, and refined based on predictive quantitative models using longitudinal qualitative data.
McPherson and Sauder (2013)	The management of institutional complexity in the everyday work of a drug court made up of actors from various professional backgrounds	Simplification, evidence, and elaboration: qualitative analysis and theory development informed counts of actors' use of logics as well as the estimation of outcomes for each case deliberated	Quantification shows comparative differences in professionals' abilities to use logics and adopt other professions' logics, reveals patterns of relations between logic usage and adopted courses of action, and shows how logic usage is associated with deviations in severity of court sanctions.
Messner (2000)	Gendered events of 4- and 5-year-old children at a youth soccer opening ceremony	Summarization and evidence: counts of gendered names categorized along three dimensions, highlighting how patterned differences in team naming reinforce gender boundaries	Shows how gender structures reinforce boy–girl categorical differences and how popular culture provides resources for gender category reproduction
Nelson and Schutz (2007)	Ethnography of two daycare centers, examining class-based differences in styles of child care	Summarization and evidence: derived systematic counts of different types of teacher disciplining, praise, and involvement	Comparison counts of various teacher–student and student–student interactions; provides evidence for class-based differences in child-care professionals' strategies and shows mechanism of class reproduction.
Van de Ven and Polley (1992)	Examines trial-and-error learning in development of biomedical innovation in an interorganizational joint venture	Verification and specification: quantified adaptive courses of action taken by entrepreneurs; used counts in time series analyses	Counts used to develop a theoretical model of adaptive learning derived from qualitative analysis; model then tested using quantitative analysis; results show support for and specify model.

Aside from these practical considerations, the *meaningfulness* of counting qualitative data is often dependent on whether there is significant frequency and variability in counted phenomena. In general, quantification is only theoretically meaningful when the phenomena take place frequently enough that researchers can convincingly show the significance in the occurrence and variability of these phenomena. For example, Nelson and Schutz (2007) counted not only the number of times that teachers corrected or praised preschool children, but also the various reasons for corrections (e.g., for being annoying, for safety purposes, and for cleaning up) and praise (e.g., compliance, compliments, and creativity). If we think of a type of phenomenon as a variable with multiple values, the variable's values should be detectible in significant numbers such that there's variance in occurrence across the comparable and discrete events.

It is important to recognize, however, that quantification of this kind involves subjective decisions that originate in the qualitative data. Writing about variability, Sandelowski, Voils, and Knafl (2009) suggest that quantification is often inextricably tied to the qualitative understanding of the data through the construction of categories or gradations of a phenomenon. Srnka and Koeszegi (2007) refer to this as a conversion process involving unitization, categorization, and coding (see also Tashakkori and Teddlie 2003). In other words, the utility of quantification is dependent on the ability of counts to represent the theoretically derived insights produced by the qualitative analysis. Determining what should be counted and how it should be counted is a form of interpretive work that is subjective in practice (Martin 2004; Sandelowski, Voils, and Knafl 2009). For example, before Calarco (2012) counted children's help-seeking behaviors in four elementary school classrooms, she first had to identify the components of help-seeking, which behaviors counted as help-seeking, patterns in help-seeking, and classify the discrete types of help-seeking that would be counted—all decisions based on qualitative analysis.

Counting as an Analytic Strategy

Having discussed *when* it makes sense to incorporate counts into the data analysis, we now turn our attention to *how* counting can enhance data analysis. Specifically, we outline four ways in which quantifying qualitative data can expand or improve qualitative projects: detecting new patterns, providing evidence of the validity of claims, honing theoretical arguments, and providing an opportunity for "analytic triangulation."

While qualitative data can provide rich description and nuanced insight into social processes, the mass and differentiation of the collected data makes it a challenge to identify complex patterns in it (Denzin 1978; Langley 1999; see Smith's 1982 "enumerative induction"). Qualitative researchers are usually faced with extensive—often thousands of pages—of qualitative field notes or interview transcripts containing a multitude of themes, ideas, and potential research directions. Developing counts can help the researcher to organize qualitative data in a way that reveals previously unnoticed patterns of results—patterns that might generate surprising new insights, demonstrate undetected relationships, clarify associations, or, ultimately, unmask the logic behind social processes (Law 2004; Sandelowski 2001; Sandelowski, Voils, and Knafl 2009). Garud and Van de Ven (1992) and Van de Ven and Polley (1992), for instance, develop a dynamic theory of learning during corporate innovation by using quantification strategies (including counts) to detect associations among several quantified variables and then testing theoretical explanations using quantified data (see also Cheng and Van de Ven 1996).

Aside from the identification of new patterns, counting can also be useful for helping researchers verify or question the patterns they have recognized in their qualitative analyses. Researchers adopting qualitative approaches necessarily wrestle with cognitive biases that can limit their ability to see evidence of patterns that do not support emergent findings, existing theoretical orientations, or already formulated hypotheses (Miles and Huberman 1994; Nisbett and Ross 1980). Under the right circumstances, counting can provide reassurance about perceived trends in the data or encourage a reconsideration of held beliefs.

A second way in which counting can bolster a qualitative project is by reassuring both the researcher and the audience of the validity of claims made about and conclusions drawn from the qualitative analysis of the data (Maxwell 2010; Sandelowski 2001). Qualitative researchers often continue their fieldwork until they determine that they understand the phenomena they are studying (for example, the mechanisms that are driving action, the motivations behind certain behavior, and the structural constraints that are shaping activities). The challenge then becomes how to substantiate, both to yourself and to skeptical audiences, what you have come to "know." In situations where they are appropriate, counts can demonstrate the existence and frequency of patterns in ways that complement the presentation of selected examples from the data (for examples, see Calarco 2012; Nelson and Schutz 2007). Even if they only summarize qualitative findings, counts can highlight the complexity of qualitative work (John 1992; Sandelowski 2001).

Counting can also hone theoretical arguments. One way in which it does this is through its previously discussed ability to detect and specify patterns in the data. Doing so is critical for researchers interested in theory building. Quantification and the types of analysis it allows can do more than detect frequencies and show regularities in the data; counting allows researchers, often through the use of statistical methods, to assess variations in observed patterns as well as affirm, specify, or clarify theory built on the analysis of qualitative data (Langley 1999). Combining qualitative insights with those made possible by counting may result in findings that more clearly specify relationships between phenomena, thereby enhancing the theory's parsimoniousness and generalizability (see Daft 1983; Weick 1979). In doing so, counting can close the gap between data and theory (Langley 1999; Orton 1997).

Another way in which counting can extend theoretical arguments is simply by providing a fresh perspective on the data. Counting necessarily involves abstraction from the concrete observations that make up the qualitative data (Tsoukas 1989). While the analysis of qualitative data generally provides the material for rich theoretical accounts based on concrete data (Daft 1983; Weick 1979), it sometimes does so at the expense of simplicity and generalizability (Langley 1999). In creating a framework for counting—operationalizing variables, developing a coding scheme, deciding what counts and what does not—researchers necessarily put distance between themselves and the contextual details of data collection and qualitative analysis. As a result, the process of counting can help to reduce the likelihood that researchers fail to see certain types of evidence, especially disconfirming evidence or evidence that does not fit with the emerging findings and theory from analyses of qualitative data.

Finally, counting can be used to triangulate data and analysis, providing a more complete picture of a process or phenomena as well as helping to enrich emerging theories and frameworks (Rossman and Wilson 1985, 1994). Quantification can be thought of as a means to understand data rather than an end in itself. As such, it is fruitful to approach counting as a set of techniques that can usefully support qualitative analysis, findings, and theory development (see Miles and Huberman 1994). In qualitative research, the most common claims about triangulation—which typically refers to the process by which researchers gather complementary types of data and conduct complementary types of analysis about a topic—involve case comparisons, multiple sources of qualitative data (e.g., ethnography complemented by interviews, focus groups, or informal surveys), or the engagement of multiple data coders in order to assess and strengthen intercoder reliability (see Leech and Onwuegbuzie 2007; Miles and Huberman 1994). Surprisingly, there are few discussions of quantification as a technique to triangulate the findings of qualitative research (but see Onwuegbuzie et al. 2009). Specifically, counting is a form of analytic triangulation in which different analytic strategies are employed to analyze the same set of data. For many of the reasons we discussed previously, counting is a potentially valuable tool for triangulation because it can contribute to the development of accurate but

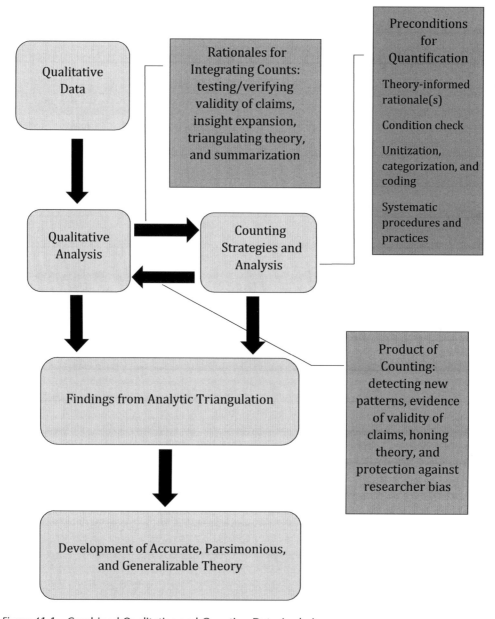

Figure 41.1 Combined Qualitative and Counting Data Analysis

also generalizable and parsimonious theory (Weick 1979; see also Denzin 1978). Triangulating with counts affords not only increased validity of findings through the application of multiple forms of analysis on the same data, but also explanatory theory development (see Figure 41.1).

Take, for example, our recent study of institutional logics in drug court decision processes (McPherson and Sauder 2013). Here, we examine how actors with different professional backgrounds employ institutional logics in day-to-day interactions. Our qualitative data (primarily ethnographic observations and in-depth interviews) provided a number of insights into this process: Operations were steeped in multiple, coexisting logics, these logics were used to construct arguments about case outcomes, and the logics were employed in unanticipated ways (e.g., an actor from one professional background would often "borrow" another profession's logic to make an argument about the case).

Fortunately, our site lent itself to the development of stable counts. We observed 460 discrete case deliberations, each with a consistent cast of professionals and with stable procedural rules. In addition, and in part due to the strict formalization of procedures, we were able to quantify the severity of case outcomes. These conditions allowed us to put numbers on how often logics were invoked, how often each logic was invoked by each professional group, and how much the invocation of logics affected the severity of sanctions.

In this case, counting provided us with the means to verify insights from our qualitative analysis: We could show precisely how often each logic was invoked, by whom, and to what effect. But, even more valuably, these counts led to unexpected theoretical insights. For example, our counts revealed that adopting the logics of other professions was more effective in swaying the court's decision about sanctions than using the logic that would be expected given one's professional background. We believe that we were able to construct a more complete and sharper analytic account of the use of logics by combining independent insights from both qualitative and quantitative approaches—that is, through the employment of analytic triangulation.

Risks of Quantifying Qualitative Data

When weighing the costs and benefits for using counting strategies, researchers should be aware of the risks quantification introduces: (a) the misrepresentation or underutilization of qualitative data by sacrificing complexity of meaning and foreclosing on fruitful avenues of inquiry, (b) the devaluation of information that is not counted or countable, and (c) the fetishization of the quantification of findings.

While the development of counts can help to organize data and reveal new patterns, there is also a risk of losing valuable information if the quantitative trail is followed too myopically. For example, it is not always how often people make an observation that is informative; particularly insightful subjects might offer novel observations that are as important to our understanding of a social process as oft-repeated information. Counts are not well equipped to appreciate these contributions. Similarly, quantification can narrow a study's focus to an unwanted degree. In the same way that becoming wedded to particular theoretical questions early in qualitative data collection can blind one to other theoretical possibilities, developing counts early in the analytic process may foreclose on ideas that emerge in later stages of the project. So, despite the facility shown by counts to focus attention, it pays to be wary of the costs of this tendency to narrow possibilities. Finally, too much attention paid to quantitative analysis and findings can compromise the utility of the qualitative research by either misrepresenting or detracting from the complexity of findings (see Maxwell 2010; Sandelowski 2001). While counts might help simplify and summarize, employing counts necessarily draws audiences' attention away from the richness of the data. It is important not to underestimate the cost of lost complexity and nuance.

A second risk of quantification is that information not amenable to counts may be discounted or ignored. It is worth emphasizing that counts will not accurately capture all, or even most, insights developed through qualitative analysis (Sandelowski 2001; Seale 1999; Stern 1989). Trying to quantify responses from open-ended interviews exemplifies the potential problems of this approach (see Maxwell 2010; Sandelowski 2001); not all topics are covered in every interview, some questions go unasked, prompted responses may have different meaning than those that are unprompted and might be counted differently. The frequency in which statements, keywords, or concepts occur in the data (not only for interviews, but also in the case of analysis of texts) may not be an accurate representation of underlying phenomena. Low frequencies, for instance, do not necessarily dismiss the validity of certain insights. More generally, counts of qualitative data can undervalue particularly illustrative or vivid accounts (Miles and Huberman 1994); may not convey the meaning of events, activities, or practices (for discussions of acontextuality, see Sandelowski 2001; Stern 1989); and can lead to faulty inferences regarding the generality and prevalence of conclusions (Maxwell 2010). All of these risks should be kept in mind when considering whether to quantify. It bears repeating that counts are ideally employed as a complement to rather than as a replacement for qualitative analysis (see Rossman and Wilson 1985, 1994).

A final and more general risk of quantification concerns equating counting with validity, reliability, and convincing empirical evidence. There is a risk that counting might contribute to the fetishizing of quantitative research and findings—reinforcing the ideas that numbers are more legitimate representations of valid research (Abend, Petre, Sauder 2014) and that we can trust them more (Lather 2004; Maxwell 2004; Porter 1995)—while discounting the strengths of the qualitative approach. Qualitative researchers should be cautious about being seduced by the legitimating powers of quantitative findings. Although these numbers can bolster one's own as well as readers' confidence in the findings, they are but one tool for affirming results.

Note

1 We use the terms *counts* or *counting* to stand in for *quantification* and *quantifying* (or *quantitizing*) for the sake of readability, but we caution readers against assuming that *counts* only refers to binaries such as the presence or absence of something.

References

Abend, Gabriel, Caitlin Petre, and Michael Sauder. 2013. "Styles of Causal Thought: An Empirical Investigation." *American Journal of Sociology* 119(3): 602–654.

Adler, Patricia and Peter Adler. 1994. "Observational Techniques." *Handbook of Qualitative Research* 1: 377–392.

Bryman, Alan. 2006. "Integrating Quantitative and Qualitative Research: How Is It Done?" *Qualitative Research* 6(1): 97–113.

Calarco, Jessica McCrory. 2012. "'I Need Help!' Social Class and Children's Help-Seeking in Elementary School." *American Sociological Review* 76(6): 862–882.

Cheng, Yu-Ting and Andrew Van de Ven. 1996. "Learning the Innovation Journey: Order out of Chaos?" *Organization Science* 7(6): 593–614.

Daft, Richard. 1983. "Learning the Craft of Organizational Research." *Academy of Management Review* 8: 539–546.

Denzin, Norman. 1978. *The Research Act, 2nd Edition.* New York: McGraw-Hill.

Espeland, Wendy and Michael Sauder. 2007. "Rankings and Reactivity: How Public Measures Recreate Social Worlds." *American Journal of Sociology* 113(1): 1–40.

Fine, Gary Alan and Kimberly Elsbach. 2000. "Ethnography and Experiment in Social Psychological Theory Building: Tactics for Integrating Qualitative Field Data with Quantitative Lab Data." *Journal of Experimental Social Psychology* 36: 51–76.

Garud, Raghu and Andrew Van de Ven. 1992. "An Empirical Evaluation of the Internal Corporate Venturing Process." *Strategic Management Journal* 13: 93–109.

Gherardi, Silvia and Barry Turner. 1987 [1999]. "Real Men Don't Collect Soft Data." *Trento: Quaderni del Dipartimento di Politica Sociale* 13.

Hacking, Ian. 1985. "Styles of Scientific Reasoning." Pp. 145–65 in *Post-Analytic Philosophy*, edited by J. Rajchman and C. West. New York: Columbia University Press.

Hacking, Ian. 1999. *The Social Construction of What?* Cambridge, MA: Harvard University Press.

Howe, Kenneth. 1988. "Against the Quantitative-Qualitative Incompatibility Thesis or Dogmas Die Hard." *Educational Research* 17(8): 10–16.

Howe, Kenneth. 1992. "Getting Over the Quantitative-Qualitative Debate." *American Journal of Education* 100(2): 236–256.

Jick, Todd. 1979. "Mixing Qualitative and Quantitative Methods: Triangulation in Action." *Administrative Science Quarterly* 24(4): 602–611.

John, I. D. 1992. "Statistics as Rhetoric in Psychology." *Australian Psychologist* 27: 144–149.

Johnson, R. Burke and Anthony Onwuegbuzie. 2004. "Mixed Methods Research: A Research Paradigm Whose Time Has Come." *Educational Researcher* 33(7): 14–26.

Katz, Jack. 1987. "Ethnography's Warrants." *Sociological Methods & Research* 25(4): 391–423.

Langley, Ann. 1999. "Strategies for Theorizing from Process Data." *Academy of Management Review* 24(4): 691–710.

Lather, Patti. 2004. "This *IS* Your Father's Paradigm: Government Intrusion and the Case of Qualitative Research in Education." *Qualitative Inquiry* 10(1): 15–34.

Law, John. 2004. *After Methods: Mess in Social Science Research.* New York: Routledge.

Leech, Nancy and Anthony Onwuegbuzie. 2007. "An Array of Qualitative Data Analysis Tools: A Call for Data Analysis Triangulation." *School Psychology Quarterly* 22(4): 557–584.

Lutfey, Karen and Jeremy Freese. 2005. "Toward Some Fundamentals of Fundamental Causality: Socioeconomic Status and Health in the Routine Clinic Visit for Diabetes." *American Journal of Sociology* 110(5): 1326–1372.

Martin, Aryn. 2004. "Can't Any Body Count? Counting as an Epistemic Theme in the History of Human Chromosomes." *Social Studies of Science* 34(6): 923–948.

Maxwell, Joseph. 2004. "Re-Emergent Scientism, Postmodernism, and Dialogue Across Differences." *Qualitative Inquiry* 10: 35–41.

Maxwell, Joseph. 2010. "Using Numbers in Qualitative Research." *Qualitative Inquiry* 16(6): 475–482.

McPherson, Chad Michael and Michael Sauder. 2013. "Logics in Action: Managing Institutional Complexity in a Drug Court." *Administrative Science Quarterly* 58(2): 165–196.

Messner, Michael. 2000. "Barbie Girls Versus Sea Monsters: Children Constructing Gender." *Gender & Society* 14(6): 765–784.

Miles, Matthew and A. Michael Huberman. 1994. *Qualitative Data Analysis: An Expanded Sourcebook, 2nd Edition.* Thousand Oaks, CA: Sage.

Nelson, Margaret and Rebecca Schutz. 2007. "Day Care Differences and the Reproduction of Social Class." *Journal of Contemporary Ethnography* 36(3): 281–317.

Nisbett, Richard and Lee Ross. 1980. *Human Inference: Strategies and Shortcomings of Social Judgment.* New York: Prentice-Hall.

Onwuegbuzie, Anthony and Nancy Leech. 2005. "On Becoming a Pragmatic Researcher: The Importance of Combining Quantitative and Qualitative Research Methodologies." *International Journal of Social Research Methodology* 8(5): 375–387.

Onwuegbuzie, Anthony, John Slate, Nancy Leech, and Kathleen Collins. 2009. "Mixed Data Analysis: Advanced Integration Techniques." *International Journal of Multiple Research Approaches* 3: 13–33.

Orton, James Douglas. 1997. "From Inductive to Iterative Grounded Theory: Zipping the Gap Between Process Theory and Process Data." *Scandinavian Journal of Management* 13(4): 419–438.

Porter, Theodore. 1995. *Trust in Numbers: The Pursuit of Objectivity in Science and Public Life.* Princeton, NJ: Princeton University Press.

Rossman, Gretchen and Bruce Wilson. 1985. "Numbers and Words Combining Quantitative and Qualitative Methods in a Single Large-Scale Evaluation Study." *Evaluation Review* 9(5): 627–643.

Rossman, Gretchen and Bruce Wilson. 1994. "Numbers and Words Revisited: Being 'Shamelessly Eclectic.'" *Quality and Quantity* 28(3): 315–327.

Sandelowski, Margarete. 2001. "Real Qualitative Researchers Do Not Count: The Use of Numbers in Qualitative Research." *Research in Nursing & Health* 24: 230–240.

Sandelowski, Margarete, Corrine Voils, and George Knafl. 2009. "On Quantitizing." *Journal of Mixed Methods Research* 3(3): 208–222.

Seale, Clive. 1999. "Quality in Qualitative Research." *Qualitative Inquiry* 5(4): 465–478.

Smith, R. B. 1982. "Enumerative Induction: Quantification in Symbolic Interaction." *Qualitative Methods: A Handbook of Social Science Methods* 2: 303–318.

Srnka, Katharina and Sabine Koeszegi. 2007. "From Words to Numbers: How to Transform Qualitative Data into Meaningful Quantitative Results." *Schmalenbach Business Review* 59: 29–57.

Stern, Phyllis Noerager. 1989. "Are Counting and Coding A Cappella Appropriate in Qualitative Research?" Pp. 135–148 in *Qualitative Nursing Research: A Contemporary Dialogue,* edited by J. M. Morse. Rockville, MD: Aspen.

Tashakkori, Abbas and Charles Teddlie. 1998. *Mixed Methodology: Combining Qualitative and Quantitative Approaches.* Thousand Oaks, CA: Sage.

Tashakkori, Abbas and Charles Teddlie. 2003. *Handbook of Mixed Methods in Social and Behavioral Research.* Thousand Oaks, CA: Sage.

Tsoukas, Haridimos. 1989. "The Validity of Idiographic Research Explanations." *Academy of Management Review* 14(4): 551–561.

Van de Ven, Andrew and Douglas Polley. 1992. "Learning While Innovating." *Organization Science* 3(1): 92–116.

Van de Ven, Andrew and Marshall Poole. 1990. "Methods for Studying Innovation Development in the Minnesota Innovation Research Program." *Organization Science* 1(3): 313–335.

Weick, Karl. 1979. "Cognitive Processes in Organizations." *Research in Organizational Behavior* 1(1): 41–74.

42

Combining Qualitative Methods to Study Collective Cognition in Organizations

Ileana Stigliani and Davide Ravasi

Introduction

The study of collective cognition in organizations can be traced back to the early 1980s, when strategic management scholars became interested in the interpretive side of organizations (e.g., Daft and Weick, 1984; Kiesler and Sproull, 1982; Sims and Gioia, 1984; Weick, 1979). These studies mostly focused on the role of managerial cognition in influencing strategy formulation (e.g., Huff, 1982; Porac and Thomas, 1994; Porac et al., 1989) and strategic outcomes (e.g., Barr, 1998; Barr et al., 1992; Thomas et al., 1993). Ever since, a rise of interest toward cognitive processes in organizations has diffused throughout different areas of managerial scholarship, drawing upon advances in cognitive and social psychology (see Kaplan, 2011a, for a more comprehensive review).

Early attempts to study cognition in organizations relied upon graphic representations, collectively referred to as *causal maps* (Huff et al., 1990) or *cognitive maps* (e.g., Barr et al., 1992; Bougon, 1992; Bougon et al., 1977; Fiol and Huff, 1992, Laukkanen, 1994), to visually capture the content and structure of managers' beliefs about key organizational phenomena and their links to decision making.

Despite a call for further research using visual representations to collect and analyze data in organizations (see Meyer, 1991), cognitive mapping was gradually replaced by alternative approaches privileging verbal reporting to visual reporting. In particular, spurred by rising interest in how language constitutes and constructs social reality (Alvesson and Kärreman, 2000), qualitative research on cognitive processes inside organizations turned to examine how conversation, narratives, and accounts shape the convergence around collective interpretations (e.g. Balogun and Johnson, 2004, 2005; Cornelissen, 2012; Donnellon, Gray and Bougon, 1986; Gioia, Thomas, and Clark, 1994; Kaplan, 2008; Maitlis, 2005; Maitlis and Lawrence, 2007; Quinn and Worline, 2008; Sonenshein, 2010).

In recent years, however, the visual dimension in the study of organizational processes has received renewed attention (Meyer et al., 2013). Inspired by a broader material turn in the social sciences (Hicks and Beaudry, 2010), more recent studies have started investigating how material practices and artifacts support collective cognition. This research shows how organizational members typically rely on various artifacts to develop collective interpretations as they formulate strategies (e.g., Buergi, Jacobs, and Roos, 2004; Denis, Langley, and Rouleau, 2006; Heracleous and Jacobs, 2008; Kaplan,

2011b), exchange knowledge across occupational communities (e.g., Bechky, 2003; Carlile, 2002), and develop and evaluate new ideas (e.g., Hargadon and Sutton, 1997; Sutton and Hargadon, 1996). However, while these studies provide robust evidence that material artifacts and practices may support the development of individual and collective interpretations, they tell us less about *how* they do so.

In our study of how designers develop new ideas (Stigliani and Ravasi, 2012), we combined ethnographic observation, grounded theory, and visual narrative analysis to unravel the transition from individual to collective level in prospective sensemaking. We argue that the combined use of these three methodologies allowed us to provide a deeper and more nuanced understanding of how material practices influence the development of collective interpretations. Ethnography helped us map and unpack the material practices designers engage in when developing new ideas. Interviews and grounded theory helped us articulate informants' interpretations of these practices and capture the underlying cognitive processes. Finally, visual narrative analysis helped us systematically track changes in the evolving collective interpretations and link together practices and processes in a longitudinal fashion.

By doing so, our study provides insights into innovative forms of data collection, analysis, and interpretation, which, we argue, compensate the limitations of more traditional approaches to the study of collective cognition (i.e., experimental and natural). In the next section, we review these approaches by explicitly focusing on those studies investigating the links between material artifacts and cognition.

Traditional Approaches to the Study of Materiality and Cognition

Research across the social sciences is directing increasing attention to how materiality and visual engagement with reality influence cognitive work. In reviewing extant research on the topic, we identified different methodological approaches that roughly fall into two main groups: experimental studies and natural studies.

Experimental Studies of Materiality and Cognition

Some cognitive psychologists argue that cognition is "distributed," in that it does not consist only of individuals' mental representations and operations but also interacts with a material environment "rich in organizing resources" (Hutchins, 1995: 2). Central to this perspective is the notion of "cognitive artifacts"—such as calendars, to-do lists, computational artifacts, or simply a string tied around the finger—defined as "artificial devices that maintain, display, or operate upon information in order to serve a representational function and that affect human cognitive performance" (Norman, 1991: 17). These artifacts serve as "cognitive extensions" that facilitate various mental processes by extending the capacity of the brain to store and process information (Clark, 2008; Clark and Chalmers, 1998). Research in cognitive psychology also shows that individuals may acquire and process information verbally or visually and that the strategies they employ have different effects on memory and judgment (Kosslyn, 1976; Paivio, 1971). Visual imagery is also believed to facilitate the comprehension and store of verbal information (Garnham, 1981; Wyer and Radvansky, 1999).

Research on creative cognition—an approach to the study of creativity based on the experimental methods of cognitive science—adds to this line of thinking, suggesting how the exposure to visual stimuli influences the activation of generative cognitive processes (e.g., retrieval, association, analogical transfer) and the creation of pre-inventive structures (e.g., visual patterns, mental models, category exemplars), which are then modified through exploratory cognitive processes (e.g., attribute finding, conceptual interpretation) (Finke et al., 1992).

Collectively, these studies look at artifacts as resources or stimuli to investigate the fundamental mental processes, such as attention, memory, problem solving, and creativity triggered by said artifacts.

Although insightful in unpacking the main mechanisms underlying collective cognition, the results of laboratory experiments cannot be easily transferred and applied to organizational contexts, where complex patterns of interactions among people, and between people and artifacts, unfold over time.

Natural Studies of Materiality and Cognition

Research in the sociology of science has shown how scientists use a variety of tools, documents, and instruments to shape the collective production of new belief structures. Knorr-Cetina (1981), for instance, talked about the scientist as a practical reasoner, the scientific laboratory as "a local accumulation of materialisations from previous selections," and the scientist's work as an activity "consisting in realising selectivity within a space constituted by previous selections" (6). Later on, she developed the notion of "epistemic objects" (Knorr-Cetina, 1999) as objects of inquiry—such as a molecule, a production system, a disease, or a social problem—arguing that the "openness" of these "epistemic objects" facilitates scientific inquiry and the production of new knowledge (Rheinberger, 1997).

In organization studies, research on organizational artifacts has highlighted how physical objects are used to support cognition in situations characterized by a certain degree of ambiguity, and, in some cases, it has traced explicit connection with individual and group-level sensemaking (Bechky, 2008; Pratt and Rafaeli, 2001). The concept of organizational artifact was introduced by students of organizational culture to indicate visible and tangible expressions of a culture (Schein, 1985). Building on this notion, past research suggests how organizational artifacts influence how individuals interpret organizations and organizational members. Organizational artifacts such as logos, buildings, and products influence how stakeholders develop an understanding of an organization (Rafaeli and Vilnai-Yavetz, 2004). Other artifacts, such as office décor, uniforms, and other personal objects represent cues that, combined with preexisting social categories (acting as frames), help members make sense of (and give to) the relative position of other members within the social structure of the organization (Elsbach 2003, 2004; Pratt and Rafaeli, 1997).

Later studies have shown how artifacts affect the social processes through which interpretations are transformed and transferred across different groups and/or professional communities inside organizations (Bechky, 2003; Carlile, 2002, 2004; D'Adderio 2001, 2003; Henderson, 1991, 1998). Because of different backgrounds and experiences, different occupational communities tend to develop different understandings of organizational tasks, which in turn may hamper coordination and collaboration across community. Some artifacts, like drawings, machines, and so forth that are shared by two or more communities can serve as "boundary objects" (Bechky, 2003; Carlile, 2002) that facilitate the transfer and sharing of interpretations and knowledge across communities and help members to make sense of their respective contributions to a common task. Collectively, these studies look at artifacts as ways to store and transmit the social knowledge of a community and to retrospectively reconstruct the meaning structures they embody (see Meyer et al., 2013).

By relying on ethnographic observations and interviews, these studies insightfully pointed out that material artifacts are deeply intertwined in the sociocognitive dynamics unfolding in various organizational contexts. As mentioned earlier in this chapter, these scholars mainly used ethnographic data of how artifacts are used, exchanged, and negotiated to infer the underlying cognitive processes. The limitation that we see in this approach resides in the ability to really understand cognitive processes by inferring them from the observation of practices, rather than explicating these processes by fleshing out the links between cognition and material artifacts and practices. In a similar vein, Edgar Schein discourages students of organizational culture from inferring cultural beliefs from the observation of collective practices, as these practices may reflect situational contingencies or temporary coercion (2010, p. 20).

In the next section, we describe how we approached the study of these links by combining different methods of data collection and analysis.

How We Studied Collective Sensemaking in an Organizational Setting

In our study of how designers develop new ideas (see Stigliani and Ravasi, 2012), we wanted to investigate how material artifacts—and the practices through which they are produced and attended to—facilitate cognitive work in collective sensemaking. We considered a design consulting firm as an appropriate setting to our research purpose because designers often face ambiguity regarding both the solution to the problem they address and the context within which this solution will be implemented (Clark, 1985; Lawson, 2005) and use various types of artifacts, such as drawings, sketches, and models, to support their interpretive processes (Boland and Collopy, 2004; Sutton and Hargadon, 1996). Our findings show the interplay between material and conversational practices in the collective sensemaking process, and in particular show how material practices support the cognitive subprocesses involved in the gradual organization of individual interpretations, and the integration of ill-defined early ideas into more refined shared understandings.

In approaching this study, we followed common recommendations for ethnographic work (e.g., Jorgensen, 1989; Spradley, 1980; Van Maanen, 1979), and we collected data by combining participant observation of three new product development projects; 56 formal semistructured interviews and archival data, consisting in company- and project-related documents; as well as pictures and copies of the material artifacts created by designers during the projects. As explained more extensively in Stigliani and Ravasi (2012), we analyzed these data in three steps, which are discussed in the remainder of this section and visualized in Figure 42.1. Table 42.1 summarizes past studies that adopted similar methods and inspired our research design.

Stage 1: Using Participant Observation to Trace Individual and Group-Level Practices of Sensemaking

Building on the idea that the conversational practices that underpin the production of new knowledge structures are "materially mediated" by textual and representational artifacts (Knorr-Cetina, 1999; Orlikowski, 2007), we began our investigation by carefully mapping the material artifacts that members produced and used in the course of the projects and the practices that they engaged in as they did so. We did so through deep and prolonged ethnographic engagement with our research site, as the first author spent 10 months as a participant observer in three development projects.

Consistent with a practice-based approach to organizational analysis (Feldman and Orlikowski, 2011), we understood practices as recurring, routinized activities aimed at accomplishing a specific

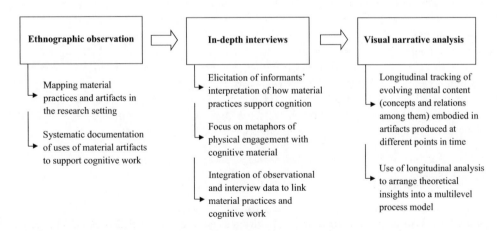

Figure 42.1 A Visual Representation of Our Method

Table 42.1 A List of Past Studies Combining Different Qualitative Research Methods

Reference	Research Setting	Research Method	Outcome
Henderson (1995)	R&D and production departments of a U.S. engineering firm	Observations and interviews were combined with the visual analysis of drawings and prototypes produced and exchanged between the two departments.	The author shows how these visual representations support the social construction of practice-situated and practice-generated knowledge.
Pratt & Rafaeli (1997)	Rehabilitation unit of a large U.S. hospital	Observations were combined with semistructured interviews and archival data.	The authors show how organization members used organizational dress to represent and negotiate issues inherent to the identities of the unit and the nursing profession.
Ewenstein & Whyte (2007, 2009)	UK architectural practice	Observations were combined with visual analysis of the artifacts produce by architects.	The authors show that visual objects mediate interactions between epistemic communities inside organizations and allow the development and sharing of knowledge.
Heracleous & Jacobs (2008)	Strategy development team, business operations team, and technical division of a European mobile telephony provider elephony	Observations were combined with comparative case study.	The authors show how the use of objects like Lego bricks can foster the collective construction of embodied metaphors in the process of strategy formulation.

task and associated with specific artifacts (see Table 3 in the published article). Extracting practices from the general ongoing flow of activities performed by designers was based not only on our observations, but—consistent with the idea of practices as being meaningful to the practitioner—also on what informants consistently referred to and labeled as distinctive subsets of activities.

For example, across the three projects observed, we noticed that during team meetings, designers would engage in the tentative grouping and regrouping of Post-its or cards representing preliminary ideas to trace connections across them and surface possible patterns. For instance, during the initial phase of one project, members used cards including demographic information about the informants they had interviewed (age, number of kids, owned cars) and significant quotes from these interviews. By grouping and regrouping these cards based on variables like daily schedules, lifestyles, aspirations, emotional needs, and purchasing behaviors, members eventually identified three main groups characterized by different needs and consumption patterns. Informants referred to this practice as "bucketing."

Stage 2: Using Grounded Theory to Articulate Cognitive Processes

In a second stage of analysis, we used interview data to investigate the cognitive subprocesses that, according to informants, material practices and artifacts supported and enabled. In our interviews, we asked informants to explain how and why they engaged in these practices and how doing so helped them accomplish their tasks. Following recent research on sensemaking (e.g. Corley and Gioia, 2004; Maitlis 2005), we turned to common procedures for grounded-theory building (Gioia et al., 2012; Locke, 2001) to analyze our data. We used interview transcripts to capture informants' interpretations of the previously mapped material practices, and we used these interpretations to bring to the surface the cognitive processes underlying these practices.

When explaining how the production and use of material objects helped them produce ad refine new ideas, informants repeatedly used metaphorical expressions suggesting their material engagement with abstract cognitive structures (e.g., "organizing thoughts," "parking ideas," "connecting brains"). For instance, informants mentioned how the practice of bucketing, described earlier, helped them "sort things out," an expression that suggested how being able to physically move cards and Post-its around helped group observations and tentative ideas into broader categories based on patterns of differences and similarities (see Stigliani and Ravasi, 2012).

Past research on collective cognition has drawn attention to the importance of metaphors in the negotiation of a consensual understanding of social reality (e.g., Donnellon et al., 1986; Gioia et al., 1994). We used the metaphors that informants spontaneously produced to account for their material practices (embodying their first-order interpretation of these practices) to infer and theorize the underlying cognitive processes (articulated as a second-order interpretation). Metaphors of physical engagement with cognitive structures, in this respect, helped us overcome the common difficulty to articulate one's cognitive processes and vividly label these processes for further analysis.

Stage 3: Using Visual Narrative Analysis to Associate Material Practices to Cognitive Processes

Combining the map of practices resulting from ethnographic observations with informants' accounts of how these practices supported their cognitive work, we produced a multiphase, multilevel grounded model of how material practices support collective sensemaking efforts. This phase largely relied on what we refer to as *visual narrative analysis* (not described in detail in the article, for the sake of simplicity and space saving). We define visual narrative analysis as the investigation of a process through the systematic collection and analysis of the material artifacts produced and used during such process (for a similar method, see Kaplan, 2011b) to document evolving mental structures (concepts, relationships, etc.) resulting from individual and collective cognitive work and embodied in the these artifacts.

Analyzing visual artifacts longitudinally in chronological order helped us reconstruct how new understandings of users, needs, and relevant design attributes were tentatively explored, connected, refined, discarded, and eventually organized around a new "big idea." This analysis, for instance, showed how a pyramidal representation of Maslow's hierarchy of needs inspired the evolving artifacts that eventually allowed designers to bring order in their exploration of consumers' needs by visually (and conceptually) arranging them in a hierarchy. When printed on paper, the idea of a hierarchy of needs lent itself to various visual manipulations as team members collectively attempted to merge ideas and link various insights from early stages, until the group converged on a visual representation of the "vehicle hierarchy of needs" (undisclosed for confidentiality reasons). The new representation was used as a platform to produce further visual artifacts that gradually integrated emerging understandings of user needs, consumer categorization, and product features to outline potential areas of innovation (undisclosed for confidentiality reasons).

The fundamental notions behind Maslow's model, then, triggered the initial idea of hierarchically arranging consumers' needs emerging from earlier field work in a pyramid. But it was the visual representation it inspired that offered an infrastructure to gradually organize insights emerging from the discussion (by providing an implicit relational structure to be filled with content), to keep track of evolving interpretations (as reflected in the numerous tentative representations that the team produced), to facilitate the integration of different members' ideas (as two or more members physically added their ideas to the emerging framework by writing on a common board), and the establishment of visual linkages among different elements of the task (by using a mix of tables and color codes). In other words, it was the embodiment of Maslow's ideas into a more general visual representation that supported organizing thoughts, building on each other's ideas, keeping the bread crumbs, and other cognitive processes that underpinned the collective sensemaking process.

By combining the results of this visual narrative analysis with the results of the grounded theory analysis, we managed to associate the different artifacts produced by designers at different steps of the projects to changes in the evolving collective interpretations, and by doing so, to link together practices and processes in a longitudinal fashion and to produce a more general process model of how material practices support the transition from individual to group-level sensemaking (Stigliani and Ravasi, 2012).

The Benefits of Combining Different Qualitative Methods

The combination of different qualitative methods allowed us to gain a deeper and more thorough understanding of the cognitive processes supported and facilitated by performing certain material practices. Had we used only one single method, we would have probably not captured the links between the different elements of our model. As mentioned earlier, participant observations of how designers work in groups allowed us to identify the micro practices designers engaged in (e.g., browsing and collecting, bucketing). Had we relied only upon the analysis of this one type of data, we would have probably missed the underpinning cognitive processes. As cognition unfolds in people's minds, we needed to triangulate insights from observations (that in the first place hinted at the development of interpretations by designers) with interview and visual data.

Our interviews had an open-ended format in order to elicit informants' cognitive interpretations of their material practices without "leading the witness." Initially, designers were not aware of the unfolding of their cognitive processes, and they simply tended to consider the artifacts they created as simple tools of the trade. As mentioned earlier, when invited to reflect on how these artifacts, and the associated practices, helped them accomplish their tasks, they often used metaphorical expressions. These metaphors proved very useful for us in order to flesh out the links between materiality and cognition, and for informants in order to reach a higher awareness of how the engagement with materiality supports the development of their interpretations. In other words, these metaphors were useful to explain in an analogical way cognitive processes of which designers had only limited awareness and that could not be illustrated in an analytical way. In addition, the use of visual data (in the form of pictures, diagrams, frameworks, sketches) to complement verbal reporting (both as field notes and interview transcripts) helped us "reveal the data at several levels of analysis, and to induce the viewer to think about substance rather than about methodology" (Meyer, 1991: 232).

Given the benefits illustrated, we argue that the combination of traditional qualitative methods and the use of visual data as a complement to narrative data can prove useful in understanding organizational phenomena that involve multiple dimensions (in our case material, verbal and cognitive) and that happen at different levels of analysis (in our case individual and group levels).

For instance, combining ethnographic fieldwork and accurate tracking of visual artifacts may illuminate our understanding of how "strategy tools" come to be and influence decision making in organizations (Spee and Jarzabkowski, 2009). Research on strategy-as-practice (Vaara and Whittington, 2012) has drawn attention to the vast array of artifacts—Porter's Five Forces, portfolio matrixes, scorecards, and so forth—that strategists use to make, illustrate, and justify decisions. Some of these artifacts are available as relatively standardized templates, popularized and supported by textbooks, articles, and consulting practices; others are produced spontaneously by strategists as they address relatively unique and context-specific problems (see, for instance, Gioia and Chittipeddi, 1991). Most of these tools combine concepts and metrics with visual representations of these concepts and the relationships among them. Visual narrative analysis of how these tools are implemented in the context of a specific decision-making process may improve our understandings of how available tools are introduced and adapted in organizations or crafted and developed in the course of strategic planning.

We see a second promising application of this method in the investigation of boundary objects. Past research has focused on the social interactions that unfold around these objects (e.g., Bechky, 2003; Carlile, 2002), but it has not systematically examined whether and how visual and material properties of these objects affect the function they perform. In this respect, a comparative analysis of different objects used in similar settings, or a longitudinal analysis of changing properties of the same object, may improve our understanding of how material artifacts enable interaction at the boundary between different groups and communities.

Finally, we believe that the application of our method to visual or material artifacts produced by informants as part of data collection may open up new and exciting opportunities for the use of artifacts in the investigation of organizational phenomena. Our study applied visual narrative analysis to naturally occurring data—artifacts produced by informants as part of their daily work practices. Consulting practices have begun to explore opportunities to stimulate strategy making by encouraging team members to build complex artifacts to articulate their understanding of the organizational identity and strategy (Jacobs and Heracleous, 2007, 2008). Future research may build on these experiences to develop visual methods of data collection that can be applied longitudinally and/or cross-sectionally to capture cognitive structures and processes that would otherwise be more difficult to access through traditional techniques based on the collection of textual data.

References

Alvesson, M., & Karreman, D. (2000). Taking the linguistic turn in organizational research challenges, responses, consequences. *The Journal of Applied Behavioral Science*, 36(2): 136–158.

Balogun, J., & Johnson, G. (2004). Organizational restructuring and middle manager sensemaking. *Academy of Management Journal*, 47(4): 523–549.

Balogun, J., & Johnson, G. (2005). From intended strategies to unintended outcomes: The impact of change recipient sensemaking. *Organization Studies*, 26(11): 1573–1601.

Barr, P.S. (1998). Adapting to unfamiliar environmental events: A look at the evolution of interpretation and its role in strategic change. *Organization Science*, 9, 644–669.

Barr, P.S., Stimpert, J.L., & Huff, A.S. (1992). Cognitive change, strategic action, and organizational renewal. *Strategic Management Journal*, 13(Special Issue), 15–36.

Bechky, B.A. (2003). Sharing meaning across occupational communities: The transformation of understanding on a production floor. *Organization Science*, 14 (3): 312–330.

Bechky, B.A. (2008). Analyzing artifacts: Material methods for understanding identity, status, and knowledge in organizational life. In David Barry and Hans Hansen (Eds.), *The Sage Handbook of the New and Emerging in Management and Organization*. London: Sage.

Boland, R. J., & Collopy, F. (2004). *Managing as Designing*. Stanford, CA: Stanford University Press.

Bougon, M. G. (1992). Congregate cognitive maps: A unified dynamic theory of organization and strategy. *Journal of Management Studies*, 29(3): 369–389.

Bougon, M. G., Weick, K., & Binkhorst, D. (1977). Cognition in organizations: An analysis of the Utrecht Jazz Orchestra. *Administrative Science Quarterly*, 22(4): 606–639.

Buergi, P., Jacobs, C.D., & Roos, J. (2004). From metaphor to practice in the crafting of strategy. *Journal of Management Inquiry*, 14(1): 78–94.

Carlile, P.R. (2002). A pragmatic view of knowledge and boundaries: Boundary objects in new product development. *Organization Science*, 13: 442–455.

Carlile, P.R. (2004). Transferring, translating and transforming: An integrative framework for managing knowledge across boundaries. *Organization Science*, 15: 555–568.

Clark, A. (2008). *Supersizing the Mind: Embodiment, Action, and Cognitive Extension*. New York: Oxford University Press.

Clark, A., & Chalmers, D. (1998). The extended mind. *Analysis*, 58: 7–19.

Clark, K.B. (1985). The interaction of design hierarchies and market concepts in technological evolution. *Research Policy*, 14(5): 235–251.

Corley, K.G., & Gioia, D.A. (2004). Identity ambiguity and change in the wake of a corporate spin-off. *Administrative Science Quarterly*, 49(2): 173–208.

Cornelissen, J.P. (2012). Sensemaking under pressure: The influence of professional roles and social accountability on the creation of sense. *Organization Science*, 23(1): 118–137.

D'Adderio, L. (2001). Crafting the virtual prototype: How firms integrate knowledge and capabilities across organizational boundaries. *Research Policy*, 30: 1409–1424.

D'Adderio, L. (2003). Configuring software, reconfiguring memories: The influence of integrated systems on the reproduction of knowledge and routines. *Industrial and Corporate Change*, 12: 321–350.

Daft, R.L., & Weick, K.E. (1984). Toward a model of organizations as interpretation systems. *Academy of Management Review*, 9(2): 284–295.

Denis, J. L., Langley, A., & Rouleau, L. (2006). The power of numbers in strategizing. *Strategic Organization*, 4(4): 349–377.

Donnellon, A., Gray, B., & Bougon, M. G. (1986). Communication, meaning, and organized action. *Administrative Science Quarterly*, 31(1): 43–55.

Elsbach, K.D. (2003). Relating physical environment to self-categorizations: Identity threat and affirmation in a non-territorial office space. *Administrative Science Quarterly*, 48: 622–654.

Elsbach, K.D. (2004). Interpreting workplace identities: The role of office décor. *Journal of Organizational Behavior*, 25: 99–128.

Feldman, M.S., & Orlikowski, W.J. (2011). Theorizing practice and practicing theory. *Organization Science*, 22(5): 1240–1253.

Finke, R.A., Ward, T.B., & Smith, S.M. (1992). *Creative Cognition: Theory, Research, and Applications*. Cambridge, MA: MIT Press.

Fiol, C.M., & Huff, A. S. (1992). Maps for managers: Where do we go from here? *Journal of Management Studies*, 29(3): 267–285.

Garnham, A. (1981). Mental models as representations of text. *Memory & Cognition*, 9: 560–565.

Gioia, D.A., & Chittipeddi, K. (1991). Sensemaking and sensegiving in strategic change initiation. *Strategic Management Journal*, 12(6): 443–448.

Gioia, D.A., Corley, K.G., & Hamilton, A.L. (2012). Seeking qualitative rigor in inductive research. Notes on the Gioia methodology. *Organizational Research Methods*, 16(1): 15–31.

Gioia, D.A., Thomas, J.B., & Clark, S.M. (1994). Symbolism and strategic change in academia: The dynamics of sensemaking and influence. *Organization Science*, 5(3): 363–383.

Hargadon, A., & Sutton, B.I. (1997). Technology brokering and innovation in a product development firm. *Administrative Science Quarterly*, 42(4): 716–749.

Henderson, K. (1991). Flexible sketches and inflexible data bases. *Science, Technology, & Human Values*, 16: 448–473.

Heracleous, L., & Jacobs, C. D. (2008). Crafting strategy: The role of embodied metaphors. *Long Range Planning*, 41(3): 309–325.

Hicks, D., & Beaudry, M.C. (Eds.). (2010). *The Oxford Handbook of Material Culture Studies*. Oxford, UK: Oxford University Press.

Huff, A.S. (1982). Industry influences on strategy reformulation. *Strategic Management Journal*, 3: 119–31.

Huff, A.S., Narapareddy, V., & Fletcher, K.E. (1990). Coding the causal association of concepts. In A. S. Huff (Ed.), *Mapping Strategic Thought*. Chichester, NY: John Wiley and Sons, 311–326.

Hutchins, E. (1995). *Cognition in the wild*. Cambridge, MA: MIT Press.

Jacobs, C.D., & Heracleous, L. (2007). Strategizing through playful design. *Journal of Business Strategy*, 28(4): 75–80.

Jacobs, C.D., & Heracleous, L. (2008). Crafting strategy: The role of embodied metaphors. *Long Range Planning*, 41(3): 309–325.

Jorgensen, D.L. (1989). Participant observation. A methodology for human studies. *Applied Social Research Methods Series. Vol. 15*. Thousand Oaks, CA: Sage.

Kaplan, S. (2008). Framing contests: Making strategy under uncertainty. *Organization Science*, 19(5): 729–752.

Kaplan, S. (2011a). Research in cognition and strategy: Reflections on two decades of progress and a look to the future. *Journal of Management Studies*, 48(3): 665–695.

Kaplan, S. (2011b). Strategy and Power Point: An inquiry into the epistemic culture and machinery of strategy making. *Organization Science*, 22(2): 320–346.

Kiesler, S., & Sproull, L. (1982). Managerial response to changing environments: Perspectives on problem sensing from social cognition. *Administrative Science Quarterly*, 27(4): 548–570.

Knorr-Cetina, K. (1981). *The Manufacture of Knowledge. An Essay on the Constructivist and Contextual Nature of Science*. Oxford, UK: Pergamon Press.

Knorr-Cetina, K. (1999). *Epistemic Cultures. How the Sciences Make Knowledge*. Cambridge, MA: Harvard University Press.

Kosslyn, S.M. (1976). Can imagery be distinguished from other forms of internal representation? Evidence from studies of information retrieval time. *Memory & Cognition*, 4: 291–297.

Laukkanen, M. (1994). Comparative cause mapping of organizational cognitions. *Organization Science*, 5(3): 322–343.

Lawson, B. (2005). *How Designers Think. The Design Process Demystified*. Oxford, UK: Architectural Press.

Locke, K. (2001). *Grounded Theory in Management Research*. London: Sage.

Maitlis, S. (2005). The social process of organizational sensemaking. *Academy of Management Journal*, 48(1): 21–49.

Maitlis, S., & Lawrence, T.B. (2007). Triggers and enablers of sensegiving in organizations. *Academy of Management Journal*, 50: 57–84.

Meyer, A. D. (1991). Visual data in organizational research. *Organization Science*, 2(2): 218–236.

Meyer, R., Hollerer, M.A., Jancsary, D., & Van Leeuwen, T. (2013). The visual dimension in organizing, and organizational research. *The Academy of Management Annals*, 17(1): 487–553.

Norman, D.A. (1991). Cognitive artifacts. In J. Carroll (Ed.), *Designing interaction*. Cambridge, UK: Cambridge University Press.

Orlikowski, W.J. (2007). Sociomaterial practices: Exploring technology at work. *Organization Studies*, 28(9): 1435–1448.

Paivio, A. 1971. *Imagery and Verbal Processes*. New York: Holt.

Porac, J.F., Thomas, H., & Baden-Fuller, C. (1989). Competitive groups as cognitive communities: The case of Scottish knitwear manufacturers. *Journal of Management Studies*, 26: 397–416.

Porac, J.F., & Thomas, H. (1994). Cognitive categorization and subjective rivalry among retailers in a small city. *Journal of Applied Psychology*, 79: 54–66.

Pratt, M.G., & Rafaeli, A. (1997). Organizational dress as a symbol of multilayered social identities. *Academy of Management Journal*, 40: 862–898.

Pratt, M.G., & Rafaeli, A. (2001). Symbols as a language of organizational relationships. *Research in Organizational Behavior*, 23: 93–132.

Quinn, R.W., & Worline, M.C. (2008). Enabling courageous collective action: Conversations from United Airlines Flight 93. *Organization Science*, 19(4): 497–516.

Rafaeli, A., & Vilnai-Yavetz, I. (2004). Emotions as a connection of physical artifacts and organizations. *Organization Science*, 15(6): 671–686.

Rheinberger, H.J. (1997). *Toward a History of Epistemic Things: Synthesizing Proteins in the Test Tube*. Stanford, CA: Stanford University Press.

Schein, E.H. (1985). *Organizational culture and leadership*. San Francisco: Jossey-Bass.

Schein, E.H. (2010). *Organizational culture and leadership* (4th ed.). San Francisco: Jossey-Bass.

Sims, H.P., & Gioia, D.A. (1984). Performance failure—executive response to self-serving bias. *Business Horizons*, 27(1): 64–71.

Sonenshein, S. (2010). We're changing—or are we? Untangling the role of progressive, regressive, and stability narratives during strategic change implementation. *Academy of Management Journal*, 53(3): 477–512.

Spee, A. P., & Jarzabkowski, P. (2009). Strategy tools as boundary objects. *Strategic Organization*, 7(2): 223–232.

Spradley, J.P. (1980). *Participant Observation*. Orlando, FL: Harcourt Brace Jovanovich College Publishers.

Stigliani, I., & Ravasi, D. (2012). Organizing thoughts and connecting brains: Material practices and the transition from individual to group-level prospective sensemaking. *Academy of Management Journal*, 55(5): 1232–1259.

Sutton, R.I., & Hargadon, A. (1996). Brainstorming groups in context: Effectiveness in a product design firm. *Administrative Science Quarterly*, 41(4): 685–718.

Thomas, J.B., Clark, S.M., & Gioia, D.A. (1993). Strategic sensemaking and organizational performance: linkages among scanning, interpretation, action, and outcomes. *Academy of Management Journal*, 36: 239–270.

Vaara, E., & Whittington, R. (2012). Strategy-as-practice: Taking social practices seriously. *Academy of Management Annals*, 6(1): 285–336.

Van Maanen, J. (1979). The fact of fiction in organizational ethnography. *Administrative Science Quarterly*, 24(4): 539–550.

Weick, K.E. (1979). *The Social Psychology of Organizing* (2nd ed.). Reading, MA: Addison-Wesley.

Wyer, R.S., & Radvansky, G.A. (1999). The comprehension and validation of social information. *Psychological Review*, 106: 89–118.

43

Highlights of the Hybrid Method

Charles Galunic

Introduction

In 2006, the Academy of Management Board tried to answer the question "what makes research interesting?" (Bartunek, Rynes, & Ireland, 2006). It surveyed its editorial board and asked each member to nominate up to three empirical papers as "exemplars of interesting research" from the past 100 years of management research in any academic journal. Seventeen papers were standouts, receiving two or more mentions from 67 board members, and of these, 12 were qualitative. That 12 of 17 were qualitative papers is considered a major feather in the cap of qualitative methods (and a rallying call for this handbook). What goes unappreciated, however, is that of these 12 papers, 6 were hybrids. Having over one-third of exemplar papers come from a historically rare form of research is remarkable. While it's difficult to estimate how many papers published by management journals these past 100 years used hybrid methods (without sampling and coding a good number of them), it seems reasonable to suspect that the number is lower than one-third (although it is rapidly increasing). Why has a (historically) rare research design produced more than its share of the most remarkable papers? Skeptics could argue that simply the rarity or uniqueness of the method may bias (favorably) the ability of even seasoned scholars to recall and judge "interesting" papers—it may be that board members simply found hybrid papers more interesting because the method itself was interesting, in the sense of being unusual, without it necessarily contributing much to the content of the paper. But I suspect it has more to do with what the hybrid method offers—a more comprehensive exploration of a phenomenon than either method can offer alone, with more opportunities to produce a-ha moments. This is plausible given the top reasons board members gave for finding a paper interesting: counterintuitive findings and the quality of the exposition. It also helps explain why hybrid designs are growing rapidly in popularity in this century (Small, 2011). In this chapter, I will explore some of the features of the hybrid method in management research, with a particular look at those exemplar *AOM* papers as well as my own experience.[1]

First, some background. Hybrid designs are not easy to define (Small, 2011), but for the present purposes I will define them as some combination of deductive and inductive methods. The former involve (typically, rather than exclusively) quantitative data and hypothesis testing, in which the focus is on explaining variance in outcomes, whereas the latter involve qualitative data and theory discovery with a greater appreciation of process, interpretation, and mechanisms (Eisenhardt, 1989a; Mohr, 1982). Hybrid designs incorporate both, in some balance. For example, a phenomenon is explored qualitatively—for example, grounded in rich description from which insights, constructs, and eventually causal propositions are developed—and at the same time quantitatively—for example, key emerging constructs are measured in greater and sufficient number so that their causes and/or consequences can be tested through statistical methods.

Hybrid methods are receiving much more attention today. For example, Edmondson and McManus (2007) provide a compelling framework for thinking about methodological fit in management field research and answer the question of when hybrid methods are most appropriate. They argue that hybrid methods are best for intermediate-aged fields or theories. While it is not always easy to define the inherent characteristics of an intermediate-aged theory (it is a bit like trying to define "middle age" a thorny question), it is at least easier to think of such theories as what remains in the absence of the pure form at either end of the continuum—that is, nascent fields have no established theories, mature fields have well-established and researched paradigms, and anything neither nascent nor mature can be called intermediate. It then seems reasonable that hybrid methods should have the best fit with fields that are neither "green" (for which deep qualitative analysis may be best) nor where construct development is well established but important questions of variance in causes and consequences remain (for which painstaking quantitative methods may be best).

Beyond identifying hybrid designs as some combination of quantitative and qualitative methods, what are some of their features? In particular, what is it about hybrid methods that can help us understand their potential for impact? I will present a few choice features here. The list is not meant to be comprehensive, and it is clearly biased by my own experiences across qualitative, quantitative, and hybrid designs; however, it will mostly focus on the papers the *AOM* board found most interesting. I will also consider some of the weaknesses and risks of this method (see Table 43.1).

Highlights of the Hybrid

The Bull's-Eye: Bold, Audacious Problems With Compelling Answers

Hybrid designs can come with different amounts of qualitative and quantitative elements, including what is likely to be a popular format: the 80/20. This is the case when the vast majority of the study concerns inductive and qualitative analysis (80%) but with a dash of statistics appended (20%), often as assurance that the phenomenon is likely to be true beyond a sample of one or a few. This is also the case when the study is largely deductive and quantitative (80%) but with a side-dish of interviews (20%) to flesh out some of the underlying mechanisms implied but not necessarily displayed through statistical testing. These are legitimate formats that I will come back to, but let's begin with a format that is balanced, hitting a "sweet spot" (50/50) of research opportunity through this method.

Some hybrid designs can offer an impressive balance between two opportunities of this method. The first comes from the inductive element. One of the most important advantages of induction is that it encourages us to ask big, audacious theoretical questions. This is partly because inductive methods are more open-ended (we don't have to guess how the story might end) and so we are more likely to cast our gaze in strange and untraveled directions. It's also because the inductive method tolerates interpretation and the development of new constructs, not just retro-fitting existing concepts, which motivates substantial creative leaps and so tackling large, complex problems.

The common problem associated with such induction is that the novelty and depth of understanding sacrifices robustness and generality. We are left with an interesting occurrence (unique and deeply explored) but so far from being an answer (because the sample is so small) that the findings are far from compelling, even if the question is big and audacious. And yet, hybrid designs in some instances can also deliver remarkably compelling results, exploring not only interesting problems but offering something that, while never providing complete closure (rare, if possible, in the social sciences), satisfies skepticism enough to actually feel compelling. Hybrid methods sometimes hit this bull's-eye of audacious, open-ended questioning in balance with generalizability. For example, this is possible when induction and quantitative (large sample) methods are combined, an excellent example of which is one of the *AOM*'s "most interesting" papers (Barley, Meyer, & Gash, 1988).

Barley, Meyer, and Gash (1988) explore a fundamental issue in management research and education: Do academics influence practitioners (through the diffusion of basic research and deskwork theorizing), or is the influence mostly the other way around (through the politicization of research, as academics cater to the problems managers find relevant)? This is a big, bold research question. Their method is inductive in the first phase—they need to identify a topic that has attracted both academics and practitioners (organizational culture in this case), establish the distinct outlets that belong to each of these communities in the field (through surveying of users and cluster analysis), and then establish the nature of the discourse in each stream (through interpretative coding). While this paper would push the boundaries of what counts as a typical hybrid design—there is no traditional interviewing for grounded theory building as is common in qualitative research—there is also no presumption of knowing, ex ante, the nature of discourse and key constructs within these two communities (indeed, analyzing the texts and output of various authors to grasp how they interpret a topic may be better than interviewing them for their opinion). The second phase of the study then uses various statistical methods on what is an impressive data sample (a nice example of "quantitizing" qualitative data). The results indicate that, while beginning with distinct views on organizational culture, the flow of influence runs from practitioners to academics, and not the other way around. Importantly, the results are based on a large and comprehensive sample that makes generalizability less of a concern. The analyses are also complementary—the effect is additive in this instance, deepening understanding of the mechanisms, rather than the quantitative work just providing a better warrant for belief. In summary, this study not only tackles a bold research question and induces the nature of the discourse within subcultures (itself a finding), but also establishes a sample that makes the ensuing quantitative findings compelling, a good example of the perfect balance that is possible through hybrid designs.

My own experience with hybrid designs was an attempt to find such balance (Bensaou, Galunic, & Jonczyk-Sedes, 2014), using mixed methods both to complement the findings and produce warrants that make the research more compelling. My co-authors and I wanted to understand the strategies organizational actors use for networking. In particular, we wanted to challenge the strong structuralist view that pervades quantitative network analysis (i.e., structural position begets a multitude of human consequences, from pay to power, and so perhaps also the strategies available to individuals) and explore the extent to which agency is at play in how people actually go about forming their relationships and developing strategies for networking. Because of the lack of prior theory, our research goals were best met through an inductive, qualitative design, to allow us to properly ground the emergent strategies in human experience. However, we were uncomfortable with typical case study sample sizes. Would the experiences (cases) of a few professional service workers (our chosen arena) offer a broad enough sample to synthesize networking strategies? We chose instead to interview dozens of professionals across a few companies to improve the reliability of the findings. This meant extra labor, although working as a team improved our efficiency. More importantly, while we induced and coded the raw behaviors in traditional fashion (subjective interpretation aided by grounded theory building), our sample size allowed us to use quantitative methods (cluster analysis) in the second phase of the analysis. Clustering algorithms offered a less subjective method for resolving which data points were closest together (and how many natural clusters existed), and further statistical work was possible to test the distances of clusters on different dimensions. The upshot was that we wanted to induce networking strategies that, while built from grounded analysis, could use quantitative methods to "triangulate" or better confirm the presence of those strategies. Moreover, our design allowed us to test some key antecedents (structure) and consequences of those induced strategies, which complemented each other and we believe provided a more comprehensive and more compelling narrative. The hope is that our use of the hybrid benefited from two key potential benefits of the method: confirmation (triangulation) and complementarity (Small, 2011).

Finally, there is one other *AOM* most interesting paper that comes closest to the "deluxe" version of such bull's-eye hybrid research, Elsbach's study of how organizational legitimacy can be managed (1994). The study exposes a gap between the impression management literature (which focuses on the form that legitimacy seeking expressions take) and institutional theory (which focuses on content and argument). Elsbach wanted to understand how form and content intertwined in the management of organizational legitimacy, as well as the effectiveness of the emerging strategies. To accomplish all this, the paper in fact included three studies that gradually moved the reader from induction to deduction and contributed theoretically in an additive fashion. Study 1 induced a framework describing four prototypical accounts provided by spokespersons, a mixture of form (denial vs. acknowledgment) and content (institutional vs. technical characteristics). Then, study 2 examined the effectiveness of these accounts through qualitative interviews with experts (i.e., using different data sources to offer better confirmation of findings), which was used to construct testable models in study 3 (through the use of experimental methods and vignettes and using a sample of respondents unrelated to the subject matter of studies 1 and 2). The result is not only a careful and detailed study of prototypical expressions, but also a convincing examination of their effectiveness, the latter helping the reader interpret and better understand the nature of the strategies. In all, an impressive, if not intimidating, example of what a well-balanced hybrid method can look like, both motivated by the confirmatory and complementarity potential of the method.

Finishing Touches That Make a Difference

Hitting the 50/50 bull's-eye is an 80/80 chore—that is, it requires a lot of data collection and time to achieve acceptable standards along both qualitative/inductive and quantitative/deductive dimensions. It is also chancy because all of that extreme effort and energy may result in no findings of significance, and while such risk is part of academic life, it is exacerbated by the extreme investment. But hybrid methods can achieve value without aiming for the bull's-eye. As noted earlier, 80/20 designs are possible. These designs provide finishing touches to one mode of research that can make a substantial difference to the contribution of a paper.

Take, for example, Eisenhardt's paper on fast strategic decision making in high-velocity environments (1989b), also one of the *AOM* board's top picks. This paper is mostly and primarily an inductive and qualitative study. Eight microcomputer firms formed the sample, with 53 informants across them, with a focus on the office of the CEO and the top management team. The data analysis was classic grounded theory building using the case method, for which Eisenhardt is well-known (1989a). The results distinguish fast versus slow decision making and provide several nonintuitive findings, for example that fast decision making actually uses more (not less) data and considers more (not fewer) alternatives. But such findings automatically trigger a question in the minds of scholars and managers: Do the processes and outcomes described actually have any impact on performance? While it's nice to find counterintuitive links between fast decision making and collective information processing routines, is there any evidence that these increase performance? Eisenhardt could have appealed to intuition in this instance—it's certainly plausible that faster decisions are better—and left it at that. Instead, she formulated a second research question for the paper and collected some quantitative data on the sample of companies, finding that the faster firms outperformed their slower counterparts, and in multiple ways (from surveying the CEO's to sales growth and profitability figures before and after the study). The contribution-to-data ratio in this instance is high. It did not require a lot of quantitative data to make this assessment, but it provided an important finishing touch to this paper, raising substantially the usefulness or "so-what" factor of the study. Notice that while this didn't appeal to the "confirmatory" benefits of the hybrid, it does draw on the "complementary" benefit.

The 80/20 design also worked well in another of the *AOM* most interesting papers, Barley's CT scanner study (1986). Again, this study is mostly inductive and qualitative, an ethnography of the impact of new medical imaging technology (CT scanners) on the micro-sociology of the workplace. Barley began observations 4 months before the (identical) scanners arrived in two similar community hospitals in Massachusetts, critical to his ability to separate the influence of the CT scanners from legacy systems, processes, and structures. The focus was on the "script" development between radiologists and technologists, first on the use of established technologies (x-ray and fluoroscopic procedures) and then on the use of the highly advanced CT technology. The careful inductive work on the emergent scripts revealed that an identical technology entering two similar institutions can nonetheless result in different outcomes in structuration, with the two departments experiencing a different number of phases in structuration (two for "suburban" vs. four for "urban") and different interaction orders (critically, with different levels of uncertainty and complexity enacted through the role development), resulting in far more decentralization in one department (suburban). That is, while both departments experienced a loosening of control of the radiologists in favor of the technologists (experts in the new machinery), the structural outcomes were in fact different.

Barley then adds a quantitative (and deductive) element to the work. Although both structuration processes proceeded in a sequential manner and gradually eroded the authority of the radiologists, the patterning was not the same, which was visible through graphs depicting the proportion of decisions made by a radiologist over time but then tested through empirical modeling. This showed that the rates of decentralization varied significantly between departments (quadratic model in suburban versus a more linear process in urban). More importantly, it provided persuasive substantiation of a key kernel of the paper's emerging theory—that the process of structuration will influence the outcomes. Compared to the painstaking work of collecting ethnographic data (which took many months), this investment in data preparation and statistical analysis may not seem very much (95/5 may be more appropriate) but it provided a quick test of the implied inductive model, adding depth and credibility to the findings.

Detours in Regular Science

In the papers described previously, the hybrid design preceded the study's execution (or at least this is the impression), including the sequencing of studies (such as in Elsbach's paper). The fact of including both inductive/qualitative and deductive/quantitative elements, and whether this will be a "bull's-eye" or "finishing touch" undertaking, or in what sequence, is usually done in advance. This seems sensible, but I believe it should not be mandatory for good science. Science, like our subject matter, encounters disruptions, and sometimes these may require detours along the planned methodological route. These detours are occasions for rethinking data collection and analysis, and possibly for exercising hybrid designs. A great example is another of the *AOM* board's most interesting papers (Sutton & Rafaeli, 1988). Sutton and Rafaeli were in the midst of examining an intuitive relationship between displayed emotions (courteous and friendly behavior by checkout staff in a chain of U.S. convenience stores) and sales. The presumption is not earth-shattering, as anyone can attest to when they find themselves tipping more a friendly waiter/waitress. Using quantitative field data supplied by the company (through mystery shoppers), they pursued the usual statistical tests. The tests, however, produced a mystery—the display of positive emotions was driving store sales down, not up. More smiles at the till translated into fewer sales, and because of the company's size, a few percentage point drops in sales translated into more than $100 million in lost revenues.

It would have been easy to drop the study. The results were so nonintuitive that they could have been tossed aside as a symptom of bad data, and the data seemed limited in variety (few variables), at best a temptation for data (causation) fishing. Instead, they embarked on an inductive and qualitative study of expressed emotions, visiting many stores, building case studies of customer interaction patterns, conducting interviews with managers and customers, and even working as store clerks. Rather than blindly exploring the remaining quantitative data, they tried instead to understand first-hand what was going on. What they found was intriguing. Positive emotions varied in effectiveness depending on the busyness of the store. For busy stores, rapid processing was best, or as one store manager said, "Customers who are in a long line don't care if we smile or not. They just want us to run like hell" (1988: 475). In slow stores, courteous interactions are more warranted (even expected) and appreciated, including by staff, who may enjoy human interaction in an otherwise lonely setting. With this knowledge in hand, a renewed quantitative analysis ensued, which, first, confirmed that store busyness was a significant predictor of the use of positive emotions, but also that an interaction effect was in play between line length and store sales on the display of positive emotions (in typically slow stores there was a stronger negative impact of line length on the display of positive emotions, suggesting that the lack of experience in these settings of dealing with a faster pace results in a turn to neutral but also negative displayed emotions). This work turned a nonintuitive finding into a deeper explanation of the phenomenon. This was made possible by the use of both deductive and inductive (and deductive again) methods. The result was not only a memorable narrative but also better science than either method alone may have produced.

Another of the *AOM* board's most interesting papers that displays such a detour in normal science is Meyer's (1982) study of how organizations respond to environmental shocks. Meyer had launched a study of 19 general hospitals in a single metropolitan area, all of intermediate size. The study was of contingent relationships amongst hospital strategies, structural features, internal processes, and market conditions, and so presumably (largely) quantitative in nature. But then the population of hospitals was jolted—a major malpractice insurer had revised its coverage of physicians, leading to a huge increase in premiums for individual doctors, which resulted in a massive physicians strike. Meyer used this disruption to adapt both his research question (which now included how organizations respond to external shocks) and, importantly, his design. Meyer argued that simply relying on survey data (and presumably statistical analyses) would "obscure phenomenological aspects of adaptations and introduce biases associated with self-reports" (1982: 516). He therefore added a quasi-ethnographic study of three representative hospitals, introducing rich qualitative data to broader quantitative data, all in an effort to improve the quality of the theory that would emerge, or as he argued, "by juxta-posing qualitative and quantitative modes of analysis, it seeks to compound their discrete advantages, offset their inherent liabilities, and achieve a deeper understanding of adaptation than either method could have produced alone" (1982: 517). The paper finally included statistical analysis of different antecedents as to their relative importance on the different phases of adaptation. The key finding was that ideology and strategic thinking, not so much material resources (slack) and structural features, were important drivers of adaptations. The point is that, once again, we see how a research detour is an occasion to draw upon a hybrid design and, in the process, deliver results which are arguably more robust, compelling, and insightful than would have been possible by one method alone.

Limitations of Hybrid Methods

Research is full of trade-offs (who to survey, how many questions to include and which ones, how long to engage in participant observation, etc.) and this is no less true of hybrid designs. While the promise of the hybrid design is to combine the strengths of quantitative and qualitative methods, there are weaknesses, and ones that are unique to the hybrid method. There are also risks. These are not the same thing. Weaknesses stem from inherent problems in hybrid designs. Risks have more to do with the capacities of an individual researcher and the reactions of other scholars. Both are problematic, but risks are sometimes worth bearing and may change over time as technologies and attitudes develop. I will try to distinguish the two where possible in the limitations I briefly summarize next.

Too Demanding

It is generally true that hybrid designs will require more work (e.g., more data types, more data collection, and more data analysis) than single-method studies. This means not only more work but also more complexity in the formulation of the methodology (for example, how exactly a quantitative study following qualitative work will build on the data to deepen understanding to provide a true complement to the theory). Hybrid designs are not formulaic. Despite my attempts previously to provide some basic taxonomy of (impactful) hybrid research, the potential range of qualitative and quantitative mixes, including how they may be sequenced or nested, is substantial and beyond my purpose here. It is certainly a complex methodological arena, and this may be one reason it is developing into a self-contained methodological field (Small, 2011). Conservative reactions may include specialization (which I will turn to next) or avoiding the method in a single paper, choosing instead to break-up "studies" into separate papers. The problem with the latter is that fields will miss opportunities for tightly integrative research, a discipline on thinking that I believe is missing when papers and methods are loosely coupled. The problem is also that such decoupling may reflect more the incentives in the field—publishing more papers is generally more desirable than publishing fewer papers, and particularly vulnerable are pretenure scholars, who may therefore eschew such methods because of risks rather than the inherent weaknesses of the method. Yes, hybrid methods are heavy, but the outcomes may justify the investments. Elsbach's popular study (1994) could have been split into two or three separate papers, but it is unlikely that it would have had the same impact as the study we do have, which combines methods in one rich paper. Dealing with the risks of heavy manuscripts, however, is a broader problem of scholarship.

Jack-of-All-Trades

Closely related is the need to specialize in methodological, not just field or theoretical, knowledge. Doing hybrid work alone may mean not having enough time and energy to develop specialist knowledge in one method. It becomes hard to be truly cutting-edge in methods. But this is probably true of even researchers who never (ever) contemplate more than one method; focusing on a method is not exactly the same thing as staying on the cutting-edge of that method. Yes, there is a "jack-of-all-trades" risk to the hybrid method, but the upside is that we may gain more rounded scholars.

Epistemological Trade-Offs Are Real

This is the greatest thorn to hybrid methods and a serious weakness. Some mixing is simply incompatible and/or can lead to worse, not better science (Sale, Lohfeld, & Brazil, 2002). Foremost is the cardinal sin of trying to use interpretive or qualitative methods to confirm or test deductive hypotheses (Suddaby, 2006). More generally, it is problematic to begin with positivist assumptions and premises if the intention is to provide "realist" interpretations of social phenomena. Findings can hardly be said to "emerge" if a paper begins by predicting the results. However, there is generally less issue with studies that operate in the other direction, using the platform of qualitative insights to develop and test hypotheses. Indeed, there are good arguments for using both methods in an additive fashion in a single study (Sale et al., 2002). The *AOM* most interesting papers also show that there are clever ways to build hybrid methods (and in both directions, including qualitative work following quantitative analysis) without committing this cardinal sin.

Table 43.1 Highlights of the Hybrid Method

Summary Points	
The bull's-eye: big, audacious problems but with compelling answers	The 50/50 hybrid. A perfect balance between careful qualitative work and compelling statistical testing. Each part captures the essential and complete features of inductive and deductive work.
Finishing touches that make a difference	The 80/20 hybrid. The focus is on either inductive or deductive work, with a modest amount of attention to the other method. This can bring either greater clarity to the mechanisms (80% deductive/20% inductive) or more convincing or robust findings (80% inductive/20% deductive).
Detours in regular science	In the beginning, one method is chosen. However, discoveries during the course of research cannot be explained through that method alone, or punctuated changes in the context open opportunities for complementary investigation, also requiring a new method.
Limitations and risks	Too demanding: It takes more effort and resources to make a hybrid work, which increases risk. Jack-of-all-trades: There is the possibility that researchers may not develop their competencies fully in either method. Faulty epistemology: Done poorly, it may generate biased and unreliable findings. Methodological politics: Research methods can become politicized, which create additional hurdles, and perhaps the biggest "risk," for hybrid methods.

Methodological Politics

There is another risk to not specializing: You may come across specialists in one method who regard methods not "their own" confusing and unacceptable, even irritating and noxious. In fact, you may get reviewers varied by methodology, specialists in each of the underlying crafts, who pull in their own direction and camp. This was the experience of one of my colleagues. His original manuscript, based on a hybrid methodology and submitted to a top journal, tried to provide a balanced explanation of both his qualitative and quantitative methods. His reviewers, however, tended to approach the topic either from a qualitative or quantitative angle—for one camp, the paper was not quantitative enough ("they would ask for things that are just not possible with smaller Ns"), and for the other camp the paper was not qualitative enough ("They were clearly uncomfortable, even annoyed, with a paper that did not follow the conventions of an unambiguously inductive study"). The paper was rejected. Papers are rejected for reasons other than being hybrid, of course, but this paper did eventually find its way into another top journal and is accumulating citations nicely (the key, according to my colleague, was having a strong editor who understands hybrid methodologies). The point is that reviewers may argue compellingly (within their method domain, and of which they believe they are guardians) why your method is not up-to-scratch. Not willing to be convinced that there are methodological trade-offs in order to provide a more rounded perspective, such purist attitudes present a substantial risk to hybrid work.

Conclusions

Hybrid methods may be growing in popularity (Small, 2011), but they still evoke uncertainty and ambivalence in the scholarly world. This may be partly because they are underappreciated, their achievements unrecognized. This chapter is an attempt to point to what the hybrid method is capable of contributing. Hybrid methods, like any methodologies, will have their weaknesses and risks, better and worse examples of how they may be implemented. Although I'm guilty here of sampling on the dependent variable, this chapter examines the positive extremes of this method. It is a notable achievement of this method to be the principal research approach of over one-third of the most memorable papers from the past 100 years of management research in any academic journal. In this chapter, I have tried to understand how the hybrid methodology contributed to those most memorable papers. This is an exercise in looking backward, but I also look forward, offering ways in which future hybrid work can learn from and be modeled on these notable papers.

Note

1 In this short chapter format, I only have the scope to cover some admittedly narrow features. For recent and comprehensive reviews of the hybrid method, see Edmonson and McManus (2007) and Small (2011). See also Edmonson's paper on psychological safety as an exemplar study (Edmondson, 1999). My focus here will be on the *AOM*'s "most interesting" list.

References

Barley, S.R. (1986). Technology as an Occasion for Structuring: Observations on CT Scanner and the Social Order of Radiology Departments. *Administrative Science Quarterly, 31*, 78–108.

Barley, S.R., Meyer, G.W., & Gash, D. C. (1988). Cultures of Culture: Academics, Practitioners and the Pragmatics of Normative Control. *Administrative Science Quarterly, 33*, 24–60.

Bartunek, J.M., Rynes, S.L., & Ireland, R.D. (2006). What Makes Management Research Interesting, and Why Does It Matter? *Academy of Management Journal, 49*(1), 9–15. doi: 10.5465/amj.2006.20785494

Bensaou, B.M., Galunic, C., & Jonczyk-Sedes, C. (2014). Players and Purists: Networking Strategies and Agency of Service Professionals. *Organization Science, 25*(1), 29–56. doi: 10.1287/Orsc.2013.0826

Edmondson, A. (1999). Psychological Safety and Learning Behavior in Work Teams. *Administrative Science Quarterly, 44*(2), 350–383.

Edmondson, A.C., & McManus, S.E. (2007). Methodological Fit in Management Field Research. *Academy of Management Review, 32*(4), 1155–1179. doi: 10.5465/amr.2007.26586086

Eisenhardt, K.M. (1989a). Building Theories from Case Study Research. *Academy of Management Review, 14*, 488–511.

Eisenhardt, K.M. (1989b). Making Fast Strategic Decisions in High Velocity Environments. *Academy of Management Journal, 32*(3), 543–576.

Elsbach, K.D. (1994). Managing Organizational Legitimacy in the California Cattle Industry: The Construction and Effectiveness of Verbal Accounts. *Administrative Science Quarterly, 58*, 57–88.

Meyer, A. D. (1982). Adapting to Environmental Jolts. *Administrative Science Quarterly, 27*, 515–537.

Mohr, L. (1982). *Explaining Organization Behavior*. San Francisco: Jossey-Bass.

Sale, J.E.M., Lohfeld, L.H., & Brazil, K. (2002). Revisiting the Quantitative-Qualitative Debate: Implications for Mixed-Methods Research. *Quality & Quantity, 36*, 43–53.

Small, M.L. (2011). How to Conduct a Mixed Methods Study: Recent Trends in a Rapidly Growing Literature. *Annual Review of Sociology, 37*, 57–86.

Suddaby, R. (2006). What Grounded Theory is Not. *Academy Management Journal, 49*(4), 633–642.

Sutton, R. I. & A. Rafaeli. (1988). Untangling the Relationship Between Displayed Emotions and Organizational Sales: The Case of Convenience Stores. *Academy of Management Journal, 31*, 461–487.

Part VIII

Challenges and Opportunities in Qualitative Methods

44

Confessions of a Mad Ethnographer

Stephen R. Barley

John Van Maanen once told me that when ethnographers get too old to do fieldwork, they start writing about it. John is always good with the quip. On the day he quipped this, I swore I would resist pontificating about fieldwork (at least in print) for as long as possible to sustain my Peter Pan fantasy. In fact, I've made a habit of looking for exceptions to Van Maanen's rule. There is Gary Allen Fine (1996, 1998, 2001, 2004, 2007), just a couple of years older than me, who produces an ethnography every two or three years (and if you count his papers, more often than that). Howie Becker, the eminent statesman of fieldwork, recently wrote a book on playing jazz with Robert Faulkner, himself an ethnographer and professor emeritus (2009). Then, there is the ever pragmatic Aaron Cicourel, who in his late 70s told me he was too old to study young people, so he began fieldwork on Alzheimer's patients and their spouses (2013). But the truth is, exceptions to John's observation are depressingly few. Ethnography may, in fact, be a young person's game. If so, for God's sake don't waste your youth.

Although I have had many invitations to do so, until now I have refused to write about doing ethnography with one exception (Barley 1990a). The exception occurred because the editors of a special issue of *Organization Science* did not want the theory paper that Pam Tolbert and I originally wrote for the conference that fed the special issue. Instead, they leaned on me to write a methods paper about longitudinal field methods. I succumbed by riffing on the methods section of my dissertation. In the end, poetic justice prevailed. The theory paper, which Pam and I eventually published several years later, drew a vastly larger audience (Barley and Tolbert 1997). (To the surprise of both of us, I might add.) All of this is to say that writing the present chapter nearly amounts to Peter Pan admitting that his wings have been clipped. Time will tell. But, as Martin Ruef noted in his recent address to the American Sociological Society, time is getting short; like it or not, I am uncomfortably near the point where the Feds will let me start drawing social security.[1]

Despite the fact that I am now capitulating on my resolution at Elsbach's request (who can resist Kim?), what I am not going to do is tell you how to design an ethnography, gain entry into the field, manage your informants, do an interview, analyze fieldnotes, compare cases, or write a methods section. I am not going to explore the mysteries of coding or the pros and cons of working alone versus in teams. There are plenty of books and papers that address these topics, including some in this volume. I have nothing of value to add to the discourse. Even more certainly, I will not flirt

Stephen R. Barley

with reflexivity in fieldwork. But I am going to tell what John would call a confessional tale of sorts, although I like an aging ethnographer's autoethnographic rant better. The rant will focus on where ethnography (if we want to call it that) in organization studies seems to have arrived over the last three decades and why I think more of us should take a different path. Along the way, I'll note places where I may bear as much or more blame than most for the current state of affairs. Much of what I will say draws on my accumulated experience with reviewers, comments that others have made about their experiences publishing fieldwork, and my own reading of qualitative papers published in the field of organization and management studies. At no point will I back up my critiques with citations or illustrations of offenses. There is no honor in pointing fingers, and there is even less honor in being pointed to. If my approach makes it easier to dismiss my grumblings, so be it.

From Fighting Outsiders to Internecine Skirmishing

Thirty-six years ago when I decided to become an ethnographer, the guardians of epistemological dogma were boogeymen known as "the positivists."[2] Exactly who or what this tribe was remained vague. I am certain the epithet did not refer simply to members of the Vienna Circle and their acolytes, because I don't think most qualitative researchers who invoked the term had ever read Rudolf Carnap and Otto Neurath or even recognized that Karl Popper (1934) was not exactly a positivist.[3] What was not lost on us neophytes in the qualitative camp was that to be called a *positivist* was the academic equivalent of playing "Yo Mama" (for explication see, Abrahams 1962; Lefever 1981). "God help us be anything but a positivist," many of us prayed. In everyday talk, we used the term to slur those who believed in deductive analysis, the testing of hypotheses, and the law of large numbers, unless one could pull off a controlled experiment. According to such individuals—who terrorized us most from the shadows in the form of reviewers—verification, replicability, validity, and, above all, generalizability were commandments that ethnographers willingly broke. So judged, we deserved to be summarily cast from the garden of science.

I vividly remember an eminent organizational psychologist asking me at my first doctoral consortium at the Academy of Management, "What's the difference between you and a journalist?" Flustered, more than a little defensive, and unable to see why good investigative journalism was a problem, I responded lamely, "What's the difference between you and a rock?" It was not my finest moment. Personally, though, as long as positivists behaved civilly, I held little animosity toward them. After all, they were empiricists and at MIT, if you learned nothing else, you learned to worship at the altar of empiricism. Then, as now, I think of good ethnographers as empiricists, too. The difference is that ethnographers like to get up close to the people and settings we study and document phenomena *in situ*, not unlike the naturalists who pioneered the fields of physics, geology, astronomy, and biology centuries earlier. Unfortunately, unlike the naturalists' phenomena, which change slowly, if at all, the dynamics of social life rebel against standing still. When push comes to shove, I came to believe that what the positivists were really asking was for us to provide proof that justified our claims (see Becker 1958 for a similar argument). This did not seem unreasonable; it amounted to nothing more than making a good empirical case for a claim's facticity.[4]

There are many ways for an ethnographer to make a case for facticity. For example, if you are studying the themes that underwrite an organizational or occupational culture, you can show how the themes suffuse multiple domains of activity or how they co-occur in our informants' talk and action. In my first paper, which was on funeral directors, I took this approach (Barley 1983). I used domain analysis to break down the funeral directors' talk about their work using the techniques of cognitive anthropology (Conklin 1955; Frake 1981; Spradley 1979) and then showed that the different domains of talk and action had an identical structure of meaning by mapping them into semiotic charts that revealed connotations, denotations, and the operation of the same metaphorical and metonymical tropes. Soon afterward, I adopted an even better strategy for appeasing the positivists'

466

need for a warrant by sorting and counting behaviors by time period, category of actor, setting, or some other unit of social life that fit the setting and topic I was studying. In short, I used numbers descriptively (and I occasionally used descriptive but almost never inferential statistics) to bolster my interpretations. At the time, this struck me as no big deal. Anthropologists had been using numbers for years to help them make their interpretive cases (Hage and Harary 1983), as had the ecological psychologists clustered around Roger Barker, who were incredibly obsessive fieldworkers (Barker 1963). But apparently the deal was bigger than I thought. I didn't learn this until one afternoon while Royston Greenwood was driving me from the Edmonton airport to the University of Alberta, where I was to give a talk. He accused me teasingly of messing things up for everybody else. I was flabbergasted as to what he meant. Simple, he said, reviewers' now expected qualitative researchers to include counts to support their storylines.

By the late 2000s, the situation had changed: The kicking shoe was on the other foot. There are now many more qualitative researchers in organization studies than there were when I started. This is particularly true in Europe. Moreover, many of these fieldworkers subscribe to epistemologies and ontologies that are different than mine. In full disclosure, I am what Van Maanen called a realist ethnographer (1988).[5] Suddenly, positivists demanding warrants for claims became the least of my troubles. Out of nowhere, it seemed, colleagues and I began to encounter reviewers who told us that it was inappropriate to mix numbers with qualitative data because doing so is inconsistent with the *true* purpose of ethnography. As one anonymous reviewer recently told me:

> To begin, your data analysis strategy seemed at odds with the purpose of an ethnography. Key to an ethnographic analysis is understanding the world according to the people you are studying (Spradley, 1979, The Ethnographic Interview). . . . This concern grew when I saw you comparing percentages of what you found . . . the comparisons seem inappropriate, reflecting a more deductive stance that fails to take into account taken-for-granted meanings [see Pratt 2009].

There is much going on in this statement with which I would take issue, but here I simply want to set the record straight. Pratt (2009) did not say what the reviewer implies. In fact, Pratt wrote early in his essay:

> Qualitative research can be either inductive or deductive or, in very rare circumstances, a combination of both. Finally, it is possible to analyze qualitative data quantitatively, just as we analyze quantitative data qualitatively when constructing stories around the numbers we present. (p. 856)

My point is not that the reviewer was wrong about Pratt, rather I would like to use his or her comment to raise a larger issue. I view this and similar stances I have encountered over the last decade as an indication that qualitative researchers have adopted their own mantles of dogma and that some are out for revenge! On three separate occasions I have been told that I could learn a thing or two about doing ethnography by reading Barley. How should I make sense of such advice? Is the system of double blind reviews working or failing? Do I interpret the advice as, "Damn, they know who I am and they are telling me I'm not as good as I used to be?" (Van Maanen's words echo in my head.) Should I assume that reviewers see something in my work that I never saw and that it's time to read myself hermeneutically? (The echo gets louder.) More problematically, how should I reply? "Thank you for referring me to Barley, I found his papers very helpful" or as I've been tempted to say, "I have consulted Barley and he assures me that he totally agrees with me"? In all cases, I've let the advice slide and said nothing.

But now, the time has come to say a few words. There are lots of ways to do ethnography. Sometimes the resulting analysis is etic, sometimes it's emic. Neither is inherently better than the other. It all depends on what you are trying to do. In fact, the two can be mixed together without the world ending. Moreover, anyone who equates deduction with the use of numbers and induction with their absence should take a course in logic. All ethnographers employ induction, deduction, and sometimes abduction when they work with their fieldnotes. (The same, believe it or not, is true of quantitative researchers.) What ultimately matters are not these issues, but whether the ethnographer makes a coherent, believable, interesting, useful, and hopefully enlightening case. Has the ethnographer convinced you that the social structures he or she may have witnessed actually existed in the world studied? If the objective is to draw you into the perspective of the members of a group, did he or she do so persuasively and effectively? In short, does the narrative hold together empirically? Do the story and the data fit? And if not, how could the ethnographer do his or her job of convincing and communicating better (assuming he or she has sufficient data to do so)?

What is not acceptable is for a reviewer to say that I subscribe to this ontology and you don't, so you are wrongheaded. When we make such demands, explicitly or implicitly, we undercut our claim of being social scientists, which I take to mean that we are dedicated to telling accurate stories that somehow enlighten us about a social phenomenon. I worry that behind such critiques lie battle lines of brewing internecine warfare based on ontology, which unlike epistemology, can rapidly shade into religion. Whatever faults they may otherwise have, at least the positivists understood how to critique a paper, which is why positivists typically spend considerable time worrying about methods and reviewing papers for methodological adequacy.

Methods Sections as a Genre

Our problem is, what ethnographers actually do when they collect and analyze data is not easily explained. Of course, this is true for quantitative research as well. For example, survey researchers who get lower than optimal response rates (and most all do) are obligated to explain why their sample is or is not biased (usually they claim that it's not). To do this they can only rely on the variables that they have at their disposal, most frequently some demographic characteristic of the sample that they can compare to the population from which the sample was drawn. Whether these are the appropriate variables for assessing bias with respect to the dependent variable under consideration is rarely discussed, even though accounts are given for why the variables on hand might be relevant. More troubling, survey researchers rarely tell us why some questionnaires were discarded, and they almost never admit when they have ignored outliers to reveal a correlation that they know the bulk of the data supports. Nevertheless, quantitative researchers have tools and generally accepted rules about how to use these tools as well as knowledge of their tools' limitations.

We are not so fortunate. The only tools we typically have are ourselves, our informants, some paper, and maybe a tape recorder. How we get from our fieldnotes and transcripts to the stories we tell is difficult to explain. Why did we choose to code some things and not others? Why did we treat certain behaviors or comments as similar and others as different, especially when behaviors or talk tend to be multithematic? Our usual answer is: We code and convey what the data support, and to do this we rely on our integrity and our commitment to scientific skepticism. (I realize that there are some qualitative researchers who believe that it is impossible to ever rise above our own subjectivity, so we should wallow in it. I do not subscribe to this doctrine. If I did, I would most certainly quit being an ethnographer and become a journalist, an essayist, or a writer of fiction.)

There was a day when ethnographers could pretty much get by on their integrity, their commitment to veracity, and their deep familiarity with the social scenes they investigated. They didn't have to write extensive methods sections. Some of the foundational papers in our field were like this. Here, for instance, is the entire methods section from Howard Becker's (1952) famous paper on the careers of school teachers in Chicago published in the *American Journal of Sociology*:

The analysis is based on interviews with sixty teachers in the Chicago system. The interviewing was unstructured to a large extent and varied somewhat with each interviewee, according to the difficulty encountered in overcoming teachers' distrust and fear of speaking to outsiders. Despite this resistance, based on anxiety regarding the consequences of being interviewed, material of sufficient validity for the analysis undertaken here was secured through insisting that all general statements of attitude be backed up with concrete descriptions of actual experience. This procedure, it is felt, forced the interviewees to disclose more than they otherwise might have by requiring them to give enough factual material to make their general statements plausible and coherent. (p. 471)

The passage appears as the last paragraph in the paper's introductory section and it is not set off from the rest of the text by the heading "Methods."

Since the 1950s, reviewers have urged ethnographers and other qualitative researchers to pen methods sections that emulate the methods sections of quantitative papers. It is worth remembering that the premise of a methods section is that it will allow readers not only to assess the adequacy of the empiricism but also, in principle, to replicate the study if they so desired. We know that these claims are problematic even in the physical and the life sciences (Collins 1974; Lynch 1985). They are even more dubious, if not laughable, with an ethnographic or qualitative study. Yet, over the years, probably through a process of mimesis, ethnographers and qualitative researchers in organization studies have converged on formulae for writing methods sections that placate reviewers. I certainly share some of the blame for this development because even in my earliest papers I wrote methods sections in which I went to considerable trouble to make what I did seem reasonable, if not replicable (see Barley 1983: 399–402; Barley 1986: 84–86).

What troubles me is not that we write such methods sections. It is valuable to force ourselves to try to be as explicit about what we've done as possible, realizing that we always say less than we can ever say, and not for a lack of space. What does trouble me is that methods sections in qualitative papers have taken on the characteristics of a genre: a type of writing defined by specific stylistic and substantive conventions which only the foolish break. Ritualistic adherence to the conventions has become so expected that adherence to the conventions compete with the paper's content for importance.

In 2003, I indulged my conviction that these conventions were useless. I decided to write a short methods section reminiscent of Becker's, albeit several paragraphs longer. In return, I received a three-page lecture from the editor on the difference between qualitative and quantitative research. I learned my lesson quickly: You either give them what they want or your paper doesn't get published. So, in response to the editor, my co-authors and I explained and justified the now much-longer methods section in our letter on the revisions we had made:

The methods section of our original paper was so brief that it did not allow the reviewers to understand what we had done. The current draft expands considerably on our methodology. Specifically, we make clear that the data we use were part of a much larger ethnographic project that provides the context for our analysis. We offer a more extended discussion of our sample, our coding and our analytic approach. We provide additional counts and cross tabulations to assure the readers that our interpretations were warranted by our data. We also explain how to interpret our numerical data within the constraints of an ethnographic agenda so that readers will no longer hold our counts to the standards of survey data or be tempted to infer that we wish to speak to issues beyond the social world of our informants. We believe that these changes will put to rest the editor's concern that interviews are not appropriate material for an ethnographic approach. We now make clear that the interviews were situated within a larger ethnographic study that involved participant observation. We also emphasize that our focus is on our informants' interpretations of their experience and behavior, which is the purpose of ethnography and for which ethnographic interviewing has long been accepted as an appropriate method.[6]

I have not systematically analyzed the methods sections of qualitative papers published in organization studies, so I cannot define the elements of the genre rigorously or exhaustively enough to provide counts or to say how the genre evolved. (Although this does strike me as the kind of study that ethnographers who have become too old for the field could do. I do not recommend that the more vital waste their time on the endeavor.) Nevertheless, I can offer a preliminary list of conventions that I would expect such an analysis to confirm. (I think this may count as a hypothesis.)

First, an adequate methods section in a qualitative paper must invoke scholars who have previously blessed the path you've taken as kosher. Oracular texts include Berger and Luckman (1967, who by the way did not write about methods), James Spradley (1979), Lofland and Lofland (1984), Yin (1989), Eisenhardt (1989), and of course everyone's favorites, Glaser and Strauss (1969) and Strauss and Corbin (1990). Many authors also think it's a good idea to use the term *grounded*, ideally joined at the hip with the term *theory*. (I certainly stand guilty here.) Second, qualitative researchers frequently provide a count of the pages of fieldnotes and transcripts that they collected (guilty again). Aside from suggesting that the ethnographer has done a lot of work, what do such numbers tell us? How do we know whether those 500 pages of notes are pure gold or verbal dung? Third, it has become *de rigueur* to talk about how one started with first-level codes then moved on to second-level codes and even to third-level codes, aggregating and subsuming earlier codes as one goes along. Sometimes researchers speak of open codes and axial codes following the language of Strauss and Corbin (1990). A more recent innovation is to provide tables containing illustrative examples of passages from fieldnotes and excerpts from transcripts that we associated with each code to demonstrate ostensibly and ostensively the reasonableness of the coding. In recent years, I have also adopted this convention to placate reviewers' demands (guilty). Although I can't prove it, my hunch is that researchers select their best-fitting quote to populate such tables so that readers feel more assured that the code matches the content of what was said or done. (You'd be a fool to do otherwise!)

Now that qualitative researchers have a fledgling genre for writing up our methods, what have we gained? Have we somehow made progress since ethnographers like Becker could get away with a brief paragraph on methods? Practically speaking, I suppose we have devised ways of allaying reviewers' concerns over what we've done, or at least a way of hushing them up. But have we come any closer to conveying an epistemic warrant for our claims or for ensuring that our studies are replicable? Could anyone else who bothered to study the same setting find pretty much the same thing? I doubt it, but not on epistemological grounds. I doubt it on substantive grounds. All social settings are rich and complex: They can support a number of viable analytical foci depending upon the researcher's interests.

Consider, for instance, my work on medical imaging and radiology departments (Barley 1986, 1990b). While I had much to say about the machines, how they were used, and the roles that radiologists and technologists played when using different technologies, I wrote nothing about patients. It's not that the data weren't there or that they couldn't be had (in fact, there is a ponderous chapter in my dissertation on patients); it was just that I wasn't interested in patients. A more humanistic researcher with a different agenda than mine could have easily watched the same exams I watched, the same people I watched, the same technology I watched and have written a paper on how patients experience radiological examinations, particularly if they bothered to interview the patients, which I did not. Such a paper might have focused on the experience of being treated like a biological object, of the indignity of a barium enema, the callousness of radiologists, or the fear of learning that one has a deadly disease or a malformed fetus. In short, the raw data would have been roughly the same, but the researcher's focus would have been different and, hence, the analysis would have been totally different. In the end, I submit we are still where Becker was in 1952. Despite our much more elaborate methods sections, readers still have to assess whether the story holds together, whether it fits the data, whether the data are adequate and convincing, as well as trust that the researcher has acted with integrity and a commitment to scientific skepticism. This is no different than with any other method in any other science. Our indignation with revelations of scientific fraud underscores the importance of our willingness to trust that researchers play the game with integrity.

The Tyranny of Alternate Theories

That two ethnographers could enter the same setting; observe the same actions, events, and actors; and come out with different tales points to a third change I have witnessed over my 35 years as an ethnographer. Early in my career, reviewers focused on the adequacy of the evidence for the tale I was telling. They might, for example, ask for additional proof: Just how many times did you see X or how many people said Y and under what conditions? Sometimes they might ask for comparisons: Were the people who said Y different in important ways from the people who either did not mention Y or who said not Y? Sometimes reviewers asked for quotes or excerpts from my fieldnotes to back up or illustrate a claim I made. If I argued that social dynamics evolved through phases, they wanted to know by what criteria I demarked phases and whether these criteria could be made explicit and potentially observable. Were interpretations mine or were they my informants'? They almost always asked me to shorten my findings section and occasionally they asked me to rule out alternative explanations. What I was never asked to do was adopt an alternative theory, perspective, or organizing construct. In fact, I usually received no feedback on the framing of my paper except for requests to write more clearly and to be more precise about the concepts I happened to be using.

In the intervening years, reviewers' expectations and demands have changed. They have done an about face. I rarely receive any comments these days on my findings or my analysis. Instead, the vast majority of comments focus on the theoretical or substantive frame of the story I want to tell. The logic of such comments boils down to this: "You say your paper is about X, but I think it is really about Y." Diane Bailey and I, for example, had a very difficult time publishing a paper that we eventually called "Teaching-Learning Ecologies" (Bailey and Barley 2011) because some reviewers thought we needed to write about tacit learning. Others thought we should be writing a paper about communities of practice. Still others thought we should be writing about knowledge transfer. None of these suggestions was especially helpful. We were simply trying to show how engineers in two different specialties had very different ways of learning what they didn't know, but needed to know, to do complete some task. We weren't even interested in whether the engineers actually learned what they set out to learn or what someone tried to teach them. The point is that the reviews we received focused on the "proper" theory and concepts rather than the data or their analysis. In a more recent paper, Beth Bechky, Bonnie Nelsen, and I were told that we needed to approach our data from the perspective of discourse analysis rather than as an ethnography of speaking, even though the two approaches have very different histories, objectives, and ontologies (Bechky, Barley, and Nelsen, in press).

Numerous ethnographers I have spoken with complain of being subjected to the same kind of critique. When ethnographers gather and talk about publishing, their complaints can be heated. Interestingly enough, no one complains about positivists anymore because our critics no longer delve into the adequacy of our empirics or the coherence of our storylines; besides, these are easy to handle. Rather, they ask us to reframe our data from a different perspective or theory. One colleague recently confided in me that she was considering giving up field research and returning to quantitative research (surveys and experiments) because she was tired of being told her papers should be about something else. She claims that when she does quantitative research, she never gets such

Stephen R. Barley

requests. The implicit threat in such reviews is that "if you don't tell the kind of story I would have told, I won't recommend your paper be accepted."

There are two problems with this new emphasis on subscribing to the right theory or perspective. First, it cuts against the grain of why one does ethnography in the first place. Ethnographers go into the field to learn how others see their worlds and how their worlds are structured. Few ethnographers enter the field to elaborate, much less test, a theory or perspective. Ethnographers are, of course, interested in variation because variation allows comparative analysis. But the variation that feeds ethnography is defined by conditions, circumstances, and outcomes that are situationally relevant and situationally defined. In the purest sense, ethnographers desire to come back from the field with tales and analyses of how things are among a group of people who are different than us.

To be sure, if we are going to tell such tales in journals, we need an organizing framework, but the framework must mesh with the data. Sometimes a theoretical frame comes from analyzing data (Glazer and Strauss 1965). Sometimes it does not (Blau 1955). But in all cases, the data and the frame must be aligned. Finding a framework or theory that organizes the data without doing it violence can take a long time. In my experience, it often takes years and it usually happens serendipitously (see Barley, 2004: 76–77). One thing I am sure of: With ethnography, the fit between concept and data does not occur because you like a theory and want to apply it to your data. If this is the kind of research you prefer, you should do quantitative work where you can design your methods to your theory.

Second, and more importantly, insisting that a paper adopt a framework different than the one the author prefers only makes sense if the framework better organizes the data. The problem is that unless you are familiar with the data, there is no way you can decide on the framework's relative utility. In the absence of such familiarity, urging an author to adopt a different framework comes dangerously close to admitting, however unwittingly, that organization studies is one of the humanities. In the humanities, interpretations of novels or philosophical works lie in the eye of the reader. Worse yet, if insisting that a paper adopt a different frame amounts to telling the author to write the paper you would have written and if authors were to take the advice, it is easy to see how theories might become fads rather than explanatory or orienting vehicles.

Interviews Versus Observation

The final change I have observed over my career as an ethnographer is an increasing reliance on interviews as opposed to observational data. I can't prove it, but my guess is that the number of observational studies has not significantly declined. Participant observation was never the technique du jour. Rather, I suspect that as qualitative research has become more acceptable, interview-based studies have mushroomed, creating a bias for verbal data. Before I turn to the issues of the preference for verbal data, let me clearly state that I have nothing against interview data and, when used correctly, data on talk is extremely important and often necessary. For instance, if one is studying how informants make sense of their worlds or themselves, interview data are useful. Meaning is to be found in talk. Interviews are also critical components of observational studies, not only because they bring out why people believe what they do, but because they can highlight differences between what people say and what they do. Finally, interviews across a sizable sample of people provide insight into the rhetorics and ideologies to which people subscribe. The truth is, no participant-observer avoids talking with his or her informants, although the talking may not be bracketed in the flow of activity as an interview.

Nevertheless, interviews are dangerous when improperly used. It is important to recognize that interviews may or may not provide evidence of what people do and, for that matter, what they actually think. This is particularly troublesome for one-shot interviews that are done without accompanying observations of behavior. In an interview, people are prone to make themselves look good, to attempt to impress the interviewer, or to provide the kinds of answers they think the interviewer wants. As Spradley (1979) emphasized, if you ask people why they do things, you are sure to get an answer, even if the informants never thought about why they do what they do. To do otherwise would be for informants to reveal themselves as incompetents. If Garfinkel (1967) taught us anything, it is that as social beings, we are always prepared to render our actions and thoughts accountable; otherwise, we look like idiots. Interviews are also poor indicators of what actually goes on in a setting or a line of work. We know that what people say and what people do are often radically different (Bernard et al. 1985). The problem is acute when multiple groups of people are involved in a social scene, but researchers only interview one group of actors (managers, for instance). Failure to collect data from representatives of all groups in the setting can lead researchers to make faulty inferences and draw faulty conclusions.

There are good reasons that the relative number of qualitative papers that rely solely on interviews has probably increased over time. Studies built around interviews are much easier to manage, particularly when researchers have limited time for research. In an era where the number of papers one publishes can matter as much or more than the quality of those papers, interviews definitely trump observational studies. All else being equal, one can do more interview studies per unit time. Interviews also require less commitment from informants than does participant observation. Informants are, therefore, more likely to agree to interviews than they are to participant observation. Finally, interviews give informants more control over what the researcher learns and doesn't learn. It is nearly impossible for people to modify their behavior for the benefit of a researcher when the researcher works in a setting as a participant observer over a long period of time. Of course, informants may initially attempt to perform for the observer, but acting eventually falls away because people cannot afford to neglect their work or other routines forever.

Reliance on interviews may partially explain why certain topics have become more common in organization studies, for instance, identity, sense-making, and careers. Such topics are particularly amenable to analyzing interview data. Conversely, topics that require observation are less frequently studied, for example, work processes, rituals, worker/management relations, situated negotiations, decision making, role relations, and role structures.

The relative infrequency of participant observation in contemporary organization studies bodes ill for our ability to understand workplaces and occupations if work and organizations are changing as greatly as many claim they are. It is worth recalling that participant observation lay at the core of much of the research that defined organization studies as a field during the 1950s and 1960s when organizational theorists built their understanding of bureaucracies (Becker et al. 1961; Blau 1955; Blauner 1964; Burns and Stalker 1961; Dalton 1950; Gouldner 1954; Kanter 1977; Marcson 1960; Roy 1959; Rothlesberger and Dickson 1939; Trist and Bamforth 1951). If the nature of work and organizing is indeed changing, we need more people on the ground studying the day-to-day activities of those who work within these organizations. Only then can we determine if—and if so, how—our theories of work and organization need to change to become more veridical. Simply relying on what we are told, especially by managers, is insufficient. When I was a student, Van Maanen introduced us to ethnography by painting an image of Franz Boas stepping off of a boat on Baffin Island, suitcase in hand, ready for a long stay among the Inuit. For the sake of ethnography and our knowledge of the world, more of us need to undertake the long stay.

Notes

1 For a summary of Reuf's comments on the future of organizational sociology and my eminent demise, see http://orgtheory.wordpress.com/2014/09/03/does-organizational-sociology-have-a-future-the-answer-part-2/.

2 My decision was made at the welcoming party for new Ph.D. students at the Sloan School of Management. I had never heard of Van Maanen before that. But I quickly saw that here was a hippie surfer who got a

doctorate by becoming a cop. How cool was that?! I remember thinking, if you can get a Ph.D. by infiltrating other people's lives and then coming back to tell stories about it, sign me up!

3 For a succinct summary of the history and tenets of logical positivism as formulated by Carnap, Neurath, and others, see Suppe (1977).

4 The careful reader will note that I used the word *facticity* not *fact*, which is an extremely useful and pragmatic ontological hedge.

5 A graduate student of my friend and colleague, Deborah Meyerson, recently told me that Deb had told her that I was the only positivist ethnographer she knew. I don't think a positivist would count me as one of their own, but I must admit I like the irony and tension in the term.

6 You can read the resulting methods section in Evans, Kunda, and Barley (2004).

References

Abrahams, Roger. 1962. "Playing the Dozens." *The Journal of American Folklore* 75: 209–20.

Bailey, Diane E. and Stephen R. Barley. 2011. "Teaching-Learning Ecologies: Mapping the Environment to Structure through Action." *Organization Science* 22(1): 262–85.

Barley, Stephen R. 1983. "Semiotics and the Study of Occupational and Organizational Culture." *Administrative Science Quarterly* 28: 393–413.

Barley, Stephen R. 1986. "Technology as an Occasion for Structuring: Evidence From Observations of CT Scanners and the Social Order of Radiology Departments." *Administrative Science Quarterly* 31: 78–108.

Barley, Stephen R. 1990a. "Images of Imaging: Notes on Doing Longitudinal Field Work." *Organization Science* 1: 220–47.

Barley, Stephen R. 1990b. The Alignment of Technology and Structure Through Roles and Networks. *Administrative Science Quarterly* 35: 61–103.

Barley, Stephen R. 2004. "Puddle Jumping As a Career Strategy." Pp. 69–81 in *Renewing Research Practice*, Eds. Ralph Stablien and Peter Frost. Stanford, CA: Stanford University Press.

Barley, Stephen R., Beth A. Bechky, and Bonalyn J. Nelsen. in press. "What Do Technicians Mean When They Talk About Professionalism?: An Ethnography of Speaking." *Research in the Sociology of Organizations*.

Barley, Stephen R. and Pamela S. Tolbert. 1997. "Institutionalization and Structuration: Studying the Links Between Action and Institution." *Organization Studies* 18: 93–117.

Barker, Roger G. 1963. *The Stream of Behavior*. New York: Appleton-Century-Crofts.

Becker, Howard S. 1952. "The Career of the Chicago Public Schoolteacher." *American Journal of Sociology* 57: 470–77.

Becker, Howard S. 1958. "Problems of Inference and Proof in Participant Observation." *American Sociological Review* 23: 652–60.

Becker, Howard S., Blanche Geer, Everett C. Hughes, and Anselm L. Strauss. 1961. *Boys in White*. Chicago: University of Chicago Press.

Berger, Peter L. and Thomas Luckmann. 1967. *The Social Construction of Reality*. New York: Doubleday.

Bernard, H.R., Peter Killworth, David Kronenfeld, and Lee Sailor. 1985. "The Problem of Informant Accuracy: The Validity of Retrospective Data." *Annual Review of Anthropology* 13: 495–517.

Blau, Peter M. 1955. *The Dynamics of Bureaucracy*. Chicago: Chicago University Press.

Blauner, Robert. 1964. *Alienation and Freedom: The Factory Worker and His Industry*. Chicago: University of Chicago Press.

Burns, Tom R. and G.M. Stalker. 1961. *The Management of Innovation*. London: Tavistock Institute.

Cicourel, Aaron V. 2013. "Origin and Demise of Socio-Cultural Presentations of Self From Birth to Death: Caregiver 'Scaffolding' Practices Necessary for Guiding and Sustaining Communal Social Structure Throughout the Life Cycle." *Sociology* 47(1): 51–73.

Collins, H.M. 1974. "The TEA Set: Tacit Knowledge and Scientific Networks." *Science Studies* 4: 165–86.

Conklin, Harold C. 1955. "Hanunoo Color Categories." *Southwestern Journal of Anthropology* 11: 339–44.

Dalton, Melville. 1950. *Men Who Manage*. New York: John Wiley and Sons.

Eisenhardt, Kathleen M. 1989. "Building Theories From Case Study Research." *Academy of Management Review* 14(4): 532–50.

Evans, James, Gideon Kunda, and Stephen R. Barley. 2004. "Beach Time, Bridge Time and Billable Hours: The Temporal Structure of Technical Contracting." *Administrative Science Quarterly* 49: 1–38.

Faulkner, Robert R. and Howard S. Becker. 2009. *"Do You Know": The Jazz Repertoire in Action*. Chicago: University of Chicago Press.

Fine, Gary A. 1996. *Kitchens: The Culture of Restaurant Work*. Berkeley: University of California Press.

Fine, Gary A. 1998. *Morel Tales: The Culture of Mushrooming*. Cambridge, MA: Harvard University Press.

Fine, Gary A. 2001. *Gifted Tongues: High School Debate and Adolescent Culture*. Princeton, NJ: Princeton University Press.

Fine, Gary A. 2004. *Everyday Genius: Self-Taught Art and the Politics of Authenticity*. Chicago: University of Chicago Press.

Fine, Gary A. 2007. *Authors of the Storm: Meteorology and the Culture of Prediction*. Chicago: University of Chicago Press.

Frake, Charles O. 1981. "The Diagnosis of Disease Among the Subanum of Mindanao." *American Anthropologist* 63: 113–32.

Garfinkel, Harold. 1967. *Studies in Ethnomethodology*. Englewood Cliffs, NJ: Prentice Hall.

Glaser, Barney G. and Anselm L. Strauss. 1965. *Awareness of Dying*. Chicago: Aldine.

Glaser, Barney G. and Anselm L. Strauss. 1967. *The Discovery of Grounded Theory: Strategies for Qualitative Research*. Chicago: Aldine.

Gouldner, Alvin W. 1954. *Industrial Bureaucracy*. New York: Free Press.

Hage, Per and Frank Harary. 1983. *Structural Models in Anthropology*. Cambridge, UK: Cambridge University Press.

Kanter, Rosabeth M. 1977. *Men and Women of the Corporation*. New York: Basic Books.

Lefever, Harry. 1960. "Playing the Dozens: A Mechanism for Social Control." *Phlyon* 42(1): 73–85.

Lofland, John and Lynne H. Lofland. 1984. *Analyzing Social Settings: A Guide to Qualitative Observation and Analysis*. Belmont, CA: Wadsworth.

Lynch, Michael E. 1985. *Art and Artifact in Laboratory Science: A Study of Shop Work and Shop Talk in a Research Laboratory*. London: Routledge and Kegan Paul.

Marcson, Simon. 1960. *The Scientist in American Industry*. Princeton, NJ: Princeton University, Industrial Relations Section.

Popper, Karl. 1959. *The Logic of Scientific Discovery*. New York: Basic Books.

Pratt, Michael. 2009. "For the Lack of Boilerplate: Tips on Writing Up (and Reviewing) Qualitative Research." *Academy of Management Journal* 52(5): 856–62.

Rothlisberger, Fritz J. and William J. Dickson. 1939. *Management and the Worker*. Boston: Harvard University Press.

Roy, Donald F. 1959. "'Banana Time': Job Satisfaction and Informal Interaction." *Human Organization* 4: 158–68.

Spradley, James P. 1979. *The Ethnographic Interview*. New York: Holt, Rinehardt and Winston.

Strauss, Anselm L. and Juliet Corbin. 1990. *Basics of Qualitative Research: Grounded Theory Procedures and Techniques*. Thousand Oaks, CA: Sage.

Suppe, Frederick. 1977. "The Search for Philosophic Understanding of Scientific Theories." Pp. 3–233 in *The Structure of Scientific Theories*, Ed. Frederick Supper. Champaign-Urbana: University of Illinois Press.

Trist, Eric L. and K.W. Bamforth. 1951. "Some Social Psychological Consequences of the Longwall Method of Coal Getting." *Human Relations* 4: 3–38.

Van Maanen, John. 1988. *Tales of the Field: On Writing Ethnography*. Chicago: University of Chicago Press.

Yin, Robert K. 1989. *Case Study Research: Design and Methods*. Thousand Oaks, CA: Sage.

Index

Note: Page numbers in *italics* followed by *f* indicate figures and by *t* indicate tables. Page numbers followed by n indicate notes.

abductive approach 352–3, 468; *see also tabula geminus* (twin slate) data coding
abductive shift point: quasi-deduction and responsive induction with surprise as the abductive shift point 99, 104, *104f–6f*, 106; *see also* inhabited institutionalism
Academy of Management 466
Academy of Management Journal (AMJ) 9–23, 21n3, 28, 29, 141, 168, 288; Citation to Editorial Essays on Qualitative Research In *AMJ* (2004–2012) *10t*; Editorial Forum on Interesting Research survey 9–10; most interesting organization papers 3, 454, 457–60, 462n1; Qualitative Best Paper Winners *15t–18t*; "What Makes Management Research Interesting, and Why Does It Matter" 3; *see also* interesting organizational research/papers
Administrative Science Quarterly (ASQ) 10–23, 21n2, 27, 141, 288; Qualitative Best Paper Winners *15t–18t*
Adria, Ferran 298; "Science and Cooking: From Haute Cuisine to the Science of Soft Matter" (Harvard, Adria, and the Spanish Alicia Foundation) *300b*
Adria, Ferran, Richard Hamilton, and Vicente Todoli, *Food for Thought, Thought for Food 299b–300b*
adventures in qualitative research 311–17; reasons for using established qualitative methods 311; story 1: time and transition in work teams 311–13; story 2: women's career development through adulthood 313–17, *315f, 316f*; visual mapping technique for data analysis 315–17, *315f, 316f*
aesthetics of data: visual elements/context 206–14; aesthetic context and the organization 207–8; aesthetic defined 206; analyzing content and mode of representation 209; *Chicago Wilderness* magazine 207, 208–9, 210; content of the image and mode of representation 208, 209, 212; decoupling (aesthetic context as an alternative story) 207, *210f*, 211–12; discussion 212–13; *Living* magazine (Martha Stewart) 207, 208–9; loose coupling (aesthetic context as complement) 207, 210–11, *210f*; relating aesthetic context to organizational

text 208–9; tight coupling (aesthetic context as representation) 207, 209–10, *210f*; types of visual elements 206, 208
"afterlife" of organizations 83; *see also* unexplored/novel phenomena
Agassiz, Jean Louis Rodolphe 12
American Journal of Sociology 468–9
American Sociological Society 465
AMJ see Academy of Management Journal
Anderson, Philip 112; *see also* entrepreneurial identity formation and development
Anteby, Michel 197; *see also* field resistance (and embrace)
archival data from online communities 215–24; advantages of using 215–16; bankers study 216; challenges of developing process theory with online communities 215–16, 220–1; complicated and evolving ethical matters 220–1; conclusion 222; examples of empirical studies *222–3t*; overwhelming volume of data 221; process theorizing defined 215; process theorizing from online discourse 217–19, *217f*; recursive process theorizing and data collection 219–20; relating to the outside world 219; tech bloggers study 216–17; uncertainty regarding data durability 221
archival research testing 425–46
Argonauts of the Western Pacific (Malinowski) 136
artifacts 444–7; *see also* combining qualitative methods to study collective cognition
Ashford, Susan, "Having Scholarly Impact: The Art of Hitting Academic Home Runs" 19
ASQ see Administrative Science Quarterly
atypical cases *see* extreme/atypical cases
authentic emotions 71–2

Balan, Peter 318; *see also* concept mapping, compared with the NVivo matrix method of analyzing qualitative data
Balan-Vnuk, Eva 318; *see also* concept mapping, compared with the NVivo matrix method of analyzing qualitative data

Bansal, P. and K. Corley: "The Coming of Age of Qualitative Research" 13; "What's Different about Qualitative Research?" 13

Barley, Stephen R. 465, 473n1; "When I Write My Masterpiece" 11; *see also* challenges and opportunities in qualitative methods

Bartunek, Jean M. 3, 9, 77; *see also* interesting organizational research/papers; unexplored/novel phenomena

Bay of Pigs revisited studies (Kramer) 414–18, *418t*, 419n1

Bechky, Beth A. 168; *see also* comparative field data for theory generation

Becker, Howard 468–9, 471

Beckman, Christine M. 262; *see also* ethnography across work/nonwork boundaries

"Becoming a Harvard MBA" longitudinal study (Snook and colleagues) 55, 59–63; analysis 62; background 59; before/after pictures 62, 64n7; data displays 62; descriptive statistics 62; evolution 61; informants 61; interviews 60–1, 64n4; methods 60–2, 63–64n3–7; pilot study 60; psychological instruments 61–2, 64n5–6; research questions 59; research team 59–60, 63n1–2; summary 63; thumbnail sketches 62; timing and context 61; *see also* studying elites in institutions of higher education

beliefs, mirroring 71

Besharov, Marya L. 401; *see also* nonauthor collaborators

best paper winners (*AMJ* and *ASQ*) *15t–18t*

Binz-Scharf, Maria Christina 186; *see also* practice approach to study social networks

bisociation (Koestler) 300–1

Boolean-based method 363, *363f*, 366–7, *367t*; *see also* Qualitative Comparative Analysis (QCA) in narrative data analysis

Boren, Brooke Lahneman 156; *see also* Qualitative Comparative Analysis (QCA)

boundaries 80, *84f*

boundary theory 262; *see also* ethnography across work/nonwork boundaries

brainstorming 272

building richness (five lessons for) 12

Burning Man research (Chen) 34, 37

Camus, Albert 177, 185

captive ethnography (interpretation) 46

"case-based" 24

cases aggregated from prior research 33

case study method *see* extreme/atypical cases

causal ethnography 47

causal mapping *115f*, 119, 444

causal validity 146

central actors defined *252f*, 253

challenges and opportunities in qualitative methods ("Challenges of a Mad Ethnographer" by Barley) 465–75; Academy of Management 466;

ethnographers 465; etic and emic ethnography 467–68; facticity 466–7, 474n4; from fighting outsiders to internecine skirmishing 466–8; grounded theory 470; interviews vs. observation 472–3; the late 2000s 467; methods sections as a genre 468–71, 474n6; positivism 466, 471, 473–4n2–3; problems with subscribing to the right theory or perspective 471–2; the tyranny of alternate theories 471–2

Chen, Katherine K. 33; *see also* extreme/atypical cases

Chicago Wilderness magazine 207, 208–9, 210, 211

circular (nonlinear) process of selecting research question and context 179–85, *180f*, *181t*; *see also* crafting/selecting research questions

Citations to editorial essays on qualitative research in *AMJ* (2004–2012) *10t*

Claiborne, Liz 12

claiming 114

coding *see* live coding and discovery/validation; *tabula geminus* (twin slate) data coding

cognition studies *see* combining qualitative methods to study collective cognition

cognitive maps or causal maps 444

Cohen, Lisa 362; *see also* Qualitative Comparative Analysis (QCA) in narrative data analysis

Coleman, James 27

collaboration *see* collaborative analysis; drawing and metaphor analysis; nonauthor collaborators; team ethnography

collaborative analysis 331–40; the academic-practitioner collaboration 336–7; affective (innovation through positive feeling) *333f*, 335; background/schematic 331–4, *333f*; cognitive (innovation through thought) *333f*, 334–5; discussion 337–8; examples of empirical studies *338f*; physiological (innovation through physical energy) *333f*, 335–6; sensemaking in the qualitative research process 332–3

collective cognition studies *see* combining qualitative methods to study collective cognition

collective turnover *84t*

combining qualitative methods to study collective cognition 444–53; background 444–5; benefits of 450–1; examples of empirical studies *448t*; experimental studies of materiality and cognition 445–6; natural studies of materiality and cognition 446; stage 1: ethnographic observation 445, 447–8, *447f*; stage 2: interviews and grounded theory 445, *447f*, 448–9; stage 3: visual narrative analysis 445, *447f*, 449–50; traditional approaches to the study of materiality and cognition 445–6

"The Coming of Age of Qualitative Research" (Bansal and Corley) 13

commitment *396t*, 397–8

comparative case studies 33, 34

comparative field data for theory generation 168–76; background 168–9; comparative analysis 173–4; comparative research design descriptions 170–2;

conducting comparative field research 172–4; examples of empirical studies *175t*; presenting comparative data 174; publications/demographics 169–70; reasons for producing cool ideas and interesting papers 169; research design and data collection 172–3

complementary and confirmatory purposes (Small) 424–5; *see also* mixing quantitative and qualitative research

computerized visual sorting *115f*, 117–18

concept mapping, compared with the NVivo matrix method of analyzing qualitative data 318–30; achieving saturation or theoretical density 325–6; audit trail 326; background/overview 318, *320f*; coding data into nodes or categories and naming categories 324; comparing the results of two methods 322–7, *324t*, *327f*; concept mapping 322, *323f*, *323t*; developing theoretical insights and providing a visual representation 325; discussion 324; examples of empirical studies *328t*; integrating categories 325; intercoder reliability and research collaboration 326; NVivo matrix method 319–21, *320f*, *321t*; the research question, innovation capability construct, and research methodology 318–19; summary 327–8, *327f*; time required for analysis 326–7

constant comparison 124–5

construct validity 146

context *see* aesthetics of data: visual elements/context; crafting/selecting research questions; innovative approaches and online data analysis; unconventional research contexts (e.g. prisons)

context-first approaches 180–2, *180f*, *181t*; *see also* crafting/selecting research questions

contract corporate ethnography and innovation from entanglement 45–53; background/origins of organization ethnography 45–6, 51n1; causal ethnography 47; critical features 46; defining 46–7; "deliverables" 46, 51n3; elements of 47; on entanglement and innovation 50–1; ethnography as epistemology 46–7; fieldwork and 49, 51, 52n6; goal-sharing 49, 52n7; improvisational nature of 46; *Journal of Business Anthropology* 45; *Journal of Organizational Ethnography* 45; "outsider" input 47–8, 52n4; similarities and differences between traditional and contract ethnography *48t*, 50–1; *Strategic Pragmatism: The Culture of Singapore's Economic Development Board* (Schein) 51n2; study topics 45; symbolic capital 48, 52n5; the Trifecta (a pseudonym) studies 47–50; types of entanglements 46; types of ethnography 46

convergence of data *see* data expansion using multiple sources

converging lines of inquiry 287; *see also* data expansion using multiple sources

conversation studies *see* strategic conversation data

Corley, Kevin G. 331; *see also* collaborative analysis

corporate culture consultants *see* contract corporate ethnography and innovation from entanglement

corporate social responsibility (CSR) 164

counting qualitative data 434–3; conditions favorable for quantification and theory development 435–6, 438; counting as an analytic strategy 438–41; counting/counts (quantifying) terminology 434, 442n1; "enumerative induction" (R.B. Smith) 438; examples of uses of quantification in qualitative research methods *437t*; quantification in qualitative research 435; risk of quantifying qualitative data 441–2; summary of combined qualitative and counting data analysis *440f*; for theoretical arguments 439; for triangulating data and analysis 439–41, *440f*; for verification and validity 438–9

crafting/selecting research questions 177–85; beginnings 177–8; circular (nonlinear) process 179–85, *180f*, *181t*; context-first approaches 180–2; examples of empirical studies *181t*; fundamental social questions (FSQs) 179, 183–4; linear approach in inductive research 178–9, *178f*; philosophical points 178; theoretical understandings-first approaches 182

creative cognition 445

CSR *see* corporate social responsibility

DA *see* discourse archive

data coding *see* live coding and discovery/validation; *tabula geminus* (twin slate) data coding

data collection 19, 128–9, *148f*; *see also* data expansion using multiple sources; ethnography across work/nonwork boundaries; serendipitous opportunities in data collection; strategic conversation data; structural sampling; team ethnography

data convergence *see* data expansion using multiple sources

data expansion using multiple sources 286–97; dimension 1: temporal stance (retrospective, real-time, prospective accounts) 289–90; dimension 2: researcher influence on the data source (co-construction, observation, interpretation) 290–2; enriching theorizing through expansion 293, 295–6; examples of empirical studies *294t–5t*, 296; four-step process for data triangulation and expansion 286, *287f*; implications 292–3, 295–6; interview data 289, 296n1; multiple data sources: a review of the current state of the field 286–8; multiple data sources: leveraging data expansion 288–92, *292f*; providing evidence of triangulation 293; schematic of data sources for expansion *292f*; three forms of data triangulation: time, space, and person 287

data reduction 286

data sources, primary, secondary, and tertiary 129

data to qualitative inductive paper *see* nonauthor collaborators

data triangulation *see* data expansion using multiple sources
Day, Diana 11–12
de alio entrepreneurship 83
DeCelles, Katherine A. 66; *see also* unconventional research contexts (e.g. prisons)
decision autopsies *see* second-look decision autopsies
decoupling 207, *210f*, 211–12; *see also* aesthetics of data: visual elements/context
deductive (quantitative) research 468; defining 454–5; *see also* quantitative data
deductive reasoning 33
"deliverables" in contract ethnography 46, 51n3
demonstrative quote 354; *see also tabula geminus* (twin slate) data coding
de novo entrepreneurship 83
descriptive validity 145, 148, *148f*
digital instrumentation *396t*, 397; *see also* documenting work
discourse analysis 280–1; texts defined 341; *see also* multilevel discourse analysis; strategic conversation data
discourse archive (DA) *217f*, 218–22; *see also* archival data from online communities
discovery *see* live coding and discovery/validation
disidentification 82–3, *84t*
distant actors defined *252f*, 254
distilled ideology 114
documenting work 391–400; background 391–2; examples of empirical studies *393t*; implication 1. from participant observation to participant tracking *396t*, 397; implication 2. digital instrumentation *396t*, 397; implication 3. commitment *396t*; implication 4. privacy *396t*, 398; implication 5. heightened awareness *396t*, 398; mapping the field of documents 394–5, *394f*; studying 392–3, *393t*, *394f*; summary/conclusion *394f*, 399; tracking the process of *394f*, 395–6
drawing and metaphor analysis 238–48; abundance of metaphors in textual data 238; background 238–9; conclusion 246–7; examples of empirical studies *242t*; graduate school example 244, *245f*; ideal leader drawing 245, *246f*; medicated-assisted treatment (MAT) for opiate addiction 239–40; metaphor defined 238; methodologies for 240, *241f*, *242t*; value 1. empirical *239f*, 240–1, *242t*, 243; value 2. collaboration and power-sharing *239f*, 243–4; value 3. pedagogical *239f*, 244–5, *245f*; value 4. representational *239f*, 245–6, *246f*; workplace bullying 240, *241f*
Dutton, J.E. and J.M Dukerich, "Keeping an Eye on the Mirror: Image and Identity in Organizational Adaptation" 13

Edison, Thomas, study of his electric lighting system 127–9
Editorial Forum on Interesting Research survey (*AMJ*) 9–10

editorial essays and editors' forums on qualitative research 10–14, *10t*; *see also Academy of Management Journal (AMJ)*; *Administrative Science Quarterly (ASQ)*
editors *403f*, 406
Eisenhardt, Kathleen and Melissa Graebner, "Theory Building from Cases: Opportunities and Challenges" 12–13
elaborating theory 103–4, *104f–6f*, 106; *see also* inhabited institutionalism
elBulli (Spanish restaurant) 298, *299b*
Eliot, T.S. 177, 185
elites *see* "Becoming a Harvard MBA" longitudinal study (Snook and colleagues); field resistance (and embrace); immersion ethnography of elites; studying elites in institutions of higher education
Elsbach, Kimberly D. 3, 20–1, 465; *see also Handbook of Qualitative Organizational Research* (introduction to this volume)
emergent and open sampling technique defined 252–4
emergent networks: understanding *189f*, 191; *see also* practice approach to study social networks
emotion, in unconventional research context 70–2, *70t*, *75t*
encouragement, in unconventional research context *70t*, 72–3, *75t*
entrepreneurial identity formation and development 112–21; claiming 114; conclusion and future directions 119–20; distilled ideology 114; examples/empirical studies *116t*; method 1. formal observation and narrative analysis *115f*, 117; method 2. computerized visual sorting *115f*, 117–18; method 3. modified full-context repertory grid *115f*, 118–19; method 4. causal mapping *115f*, 119; methods 112–15, *115f*, 117–19; representational rules 120; research design for a qualitative panel study 115–19
"enumerative induction" (R.B. Smith) 438; *see also* counting qualitative data
environmental health and safety management (EHS) system (Eastern University study by Silbey) 147, 151
epistemology, contract ethnography and 46–7
ethics: archival data from online communities and 220–1; ethnography across work/nonwork boundaries and 269
ethnographers 465
ethnographic units 45
ethnography: ethnographic units 45; similarities and differences between traditional and contract ethnography *48t*; types of 46; *see also* challenges and opportunities in qualitative methods; combining qualitative methods to study collective cognition; contract corporate ethnography and innovation from entanglement; field-level ethnography; immersion ethnography of elites;

innovative approaches and online data analysis; team ethnography

ethnography across work/nonwork boundaries 262–71, *266f*; access and recruitment 265–6; benefits of multiple researchers 269–70; complexity of researcher-participant relationship 268; conducting oneself in the home 267; ethical and moral questions 269; field notes 267–8; four key areas of knowledge 264–5; multisited ethnography: benefits for organizational studies 264–5; multisited ethnography: considerations 268–70; multisited ethnography: overview/ examples of empirical studies 262–4, *263t*; multisited ethnography: pragmatics 265–8, *266f*; nature of ethnographic data 268–9; research design 267; study description 264

evaluative validity 153n1

Evans, Joelle 143; *see also* team ethnography

ex morte entrepreneurship 83

expansion of data *see* data expansion using multiple sources

experimental studies of materiality and cognition 445–6

experiment testing *see* mixing quantitative and qualitative research

explanatory approach, for online texts *385t*, 386–8, 389n5

external actors defined *252f*, 253–4

extreme/atypical cases 33–44; analyzing data 40; background 33, 34–5; conclusion 40–1; deductive vs. inductive/case study research 33–4; how organizations concentrate power and reproduce the status quo 38–9, *38t*; how organizations engage in emergent action when the market and state and civil sectors are absent 37; how organizations pursue values via their organizing practices and forms, 36–7, *37t*; how the extraordinary handle the mundanity of organizing dilemmas 35–6, *35t*; misconceptions/objections about research designs 33–4; negotiating access and collecting data 39–40; presenting claims and data 40; reflexivity and 33; types of 33; understanding "what is this a case of?" 35; undertaking research on 39, *39f*

facticity 466–7, 474n4

Fayard, Anne-Laure 45, 381; *see also* contract corporate ethnography and innovation from entanglement; innovative approaches and online data

Feldman, Martha S. 371; *see also* live coding and discovery/validation

field informants 382, *403f*, 407

field-level ethnography 86–95; examples of empirical studies *91t–3t*; field definitions 90, 94; *Journal of Management Studies* 88; micro-dynamics of organizational fields 86, 88; organizational or institutional fields defined 86, 94n1; step 1. finding a site 87–8, *87f*; step 2. capturing the field *87f*, 89; step 3. analysis *87f*, 89–90; texts defined 87; types (field-wide organizations, agreements, and events) 88

field resistance (and embrace) 197–205; business school professors' silences 199–200, 204n1; clinical anatomists' obstructions 199; combining novel and traditional data sources (comprehensive view of the field) 202–4, *203f*; conclusion 202–4; defining field resistance 197–8; evidence of field resistance 198–200; examples of empirical studies 200–2, *201t*; factory craftsmen's denials 198–9; field embrace as alternate and telling data points 201–2, *201t*; a wide and telling variety of field resistance 200

fieldwork 77; contract ethnography and 49, 51, 52n6; team ethnography and 143–5; *see also* comparative field data for theory generation; headings under field; team ethnography

fly-by ethnography (swift) 46

Food for Thought, Thought for Food (Adria, Hamilton, and Todoli) *299b–300b*

formal observation *115f*, 117

"For the Lack of a Boilerplate: Tips on Writing Up (and Reviewing) Qualitative Research" (Pratt) 13

framings, piloting multiple provisional 83–4, *84t*

free-form writing 79, *84f*

"From Higher Aims to Hired Hands" (Khurana) 57–9

FSQs *see* fundamental social questions

full-context repertory grid, modified *115f*, 118–19

fundamental social questions (FSQs) 179, 183–4

Gage, Phineas 12

Galunic, Charles 454; *see also* hybrid method highlights

generalizability validity 146, 150

"The Generative Properties of Richness" (Weick) 12

Gersick, Connie 311; live coding 374–7, *378t*; *see also* adventures in qualitative research; live coding and discovery/validation

Giorgi, Simona 206; *see also* aesthetics of data: visual elements/context

Glynn, Mary Ann 206; *see also* aesthetics of data: visual elements/context

Golden-Biddle, Karen 371; *see also* live coding and discovery/validation

Gorbatai, Andreea D. 251; *see also* structural sampling

Graebner, Melissa E. 272; *see also* strategic conversation data

Graves, Heather 225; *see also* visual rhetoric, analyzing

Grodal, Stine 341; *see also* multilevel discourse analysis

grounded codes 351–2

grounded process theorizing *see* archival data from online communities

grounded theory (GT) 11, 470; strategic conversation data and 282; *see also* combining qualitative methods to study collective cognition;

microhistorical case studies for building grounded theory
GT *see* grounded theory

Hackman, Richard 311
Haedicke, Michael A. 99; *see also* inhabited institutionalism (II)
Hallett, Tim 99; *see also* inhabited institutionalism (II)
Handbook of Qualitative Organizational Research (introduction to this volume):inspiration for 3–4; organization of 4–7; use of 7–8
Hargadon, Andrew 122; *see also* microhistorical case studies for building grounded theory
Hargadon, Andrew and Yellowlees Douglas, study on Edison's development of electric lighting system 127–8
Harmon, Ellie 262; *see also* ethnography across work/nonwork boundaries
Harrington, Brooke 134; *see also* immersion ethnography of elites
Harrison, Spencer H. 286; *see also* data expansion using multiple sources
Harvard Business School *see* "Becoming a Harvard MBA" longitudinal study (Snook and colleagues); studying elites in institutions of higher education
"Having Scholarly Impact: The Art of Hitting Academic Home Runs" (Ashford) 19
Hawbaker, Benjamin 156; *see also* Qualitative Comparative Analysis (QCA)
heightened awareness *396t*, 398
Hirsch, Paul 24; *see also* trends in qualitative organizational research/historical context
historical clock 123
Hoefer, Rolf 115
Ho, K. 139
Huising, Ruthanne 143; *see also* team ethnography
hybrid method highlights 454–62; *Academy of Management* Board's survey of interesting papers 454, 457–60, 462n1; background/definitions of inductive (qualitative) and deductive (quantitative) data 454–5; the bull's eye: bold, audacious problems with compelling answers 455–7, *461t*; conclusions and summary points 461–2, *461t*; demanding nature of 460; detours in regular science 458–9, *461t*; epistemological trade-offs of 460; finishing touches that make a difference 457–8, *461t*; jack-of-all-trades limitation of 460; limitations and risks of 459–61, *461t*; methodological politics and 461

II *see* inhabited institutionalism (II)
immersion ethnography of elites 134–42; *Argonauts of the Western Pacific* (Malinowski) 136; demands on the researcher 139–40; elites and ethnography 135; examples of empirical studies/contributors 136–9, *137t*; the immersion method 135; origins of the method and the influence of organization studies 136; process characteristics of *138f*; prospects for

future scholarship 140–1; rareness of immersion 134; settings for 134
inductive reasoning 33–4
inductive studies/research 3, 468; defining 454–5; *see also* crafting/selecting research questions; data expansion using multiple sources; extreme/atypical cases; qualitative data
inert coding: compared to live coding 373, *373t*; *see also* live coding and discovery/validation
inferential validity 146
informants, finding 81–2, *84f*
inhabited institutionalism (II) 99–111; designing research for 101–8, *101t*; elaborating theory 103–4, *104f–6f*, 106; examples of empirical studies *101t*; genealogy 99–101; moving forward with: case comparison and field-level ethnography 107–8; new institutional (NI) scholarship 100–1; orientation and multilevel analysis 102–3; quasi-deduction and responsive induction with surprise as the abductive shift point 99, 104, *104f–6f*, 106; research cycle 106–7; site selection and research questions 102; the term interactionist 99, 108n2
initial questions: formulating 189, *189f*; *see also* practice approach to study social networks
innovation, contract corporate ethnography and entanglement and 50–1
innovative approaches and online data analysis 381–90; for addressing the contextual challenge in *384t*, 385–8, *385t*; background 381–2, 389n2; blurring offline and online text and context 388; examples of empirical studies *384t*, *385t*; openIDEO and open source software development studies 386–7; relationship between text and context in online qualitative research 383–5, *384t*, *385t*; relationship between text and context in traditional qualitative research 382–3, *384t*; structuralist, explanatory, and virtual ethnography strategies 385–8, *385t*, 389n4–5; WELL study 387–8
institutional theorists 123
interactionist 99, 108n2; *see also* inhabited institutionalism
interesting organizational research/papers 9–23; background 9–10; best papers (*AMJ* and *ASQ*) 14, *15t–18t*, 19, 21n2–3; citations to editorial essays on qualitative research in *AMJ* (2004–2012) *10t*; editorial essays and editors' forums on qualitative research 10–14; grounded theory and 11; pros and cons 19–20; reviewer bias 21n6; theory building and 12–13; theory elaboration and theory generation 14, *15t–18t*, 19; "What Makes Management Research Interesting, and Why Does It Matter" (*Academy of Management Journal's*) 3; *see also Academy of Management Journal (AMJ)*; adventures in qualitative research; hybrid method highlights; unexplored/novel phenomena
intermediate-aged theory 455

interpreting accounts *148f*; *see also* team ethnography
interpretive validity 145–6, *148f*, 149
intertextuality 282
interviews: vs. observation 472–3; *see also* combining qualitative methods to study collective cognition; grounded theory (GT)
Ireland, Duane 3
isomorphic processes 41
iteration 346

jargon, mirroring 71
Jones, Candace 156; *see also* Qualitative Comparative Analysis (QCA)
Journal of Business Anthropology 45
Journal of Management Studies, field-level ethnography 88
Journal of Organizational Ethnography 45

Kahl, Steven J. 341; *see also* multilevel discourse analysis
Kaplan, Sarah 423, 432n1; *see also* mixing quantitative and qualitative research
"Keeping an Eye on the Mirror: Image and Identity in Organizational Adaptation" (Dutton and Dukerich) 13
Kennedy, John F. 411; *see also* second-look decision autopsies
Khurana, Rakesh 54; "From Higher Aims to Hired Hands" 57–9; *see also* studying elites in institutions of higher education
Kramer, Roderick M. 3, 20–1, 411; *see also* *Handbook of Qualitative Organizational Research* (introduction to this volume); second-look decision autopsies
Kram, Kathy 313
Kreiner, Glen E. 350, 361n1; *see also* *tabula geminus* (twin slate) data coding
Kyprianou, Christina 272; *see also* strategic conversation data

Lacey, Rodney 362; *see also* Qualitative Comparative Analysis (QCA) in narrative data analysis
language of images 206; *see also* aesthetics of data: visual elements/context
"lay sociology" (or "theories-in-use") 146
leaders 54; *see also* studying elites in institutions of higher education
Lee, Thomas and Robert Gephart, "Qualitative Research in Organizational and Vocational Psychology" 10–11
Lefsrud, Lianne 225; *see also* visual rhetoric, analyzing
leveraging data expansion *see* data expansion using multiple sources
Levina, Natalia 215; *see also* archival data from online communities
Levinson, Daniel 313–14
"liability of newness" 84; *see also* unexplored/novel phenomena

Lindsay, Noel 318; *see also* concept mapping, compared with the NVivo matrix method of analyzing qualitative data
linear approach to selecting research questions 178–9, *178f*
live coding and discovery/validation 371–80; background/description/defining 371–4; comparing live and inert coding 373, *373t*; conclusion 379; examples of empirical studies 377–9, *378t*; shift I: from team effectiveness to life cycle model (Gersick) 375; shift II: from life cycle to midpoint (Gersick) 375–7
Living magazine (Martha Stewart) 207, 208–9, 212
Livne-Tarandach, Reut 156; *see also* Qualitative Comparative Analysis (QCA)
Locke, Karen 371; *see also* live coding and discovery/validation
loose coupling 207, 210–11, *210f*; *see also* aesthetics of data: visual elements/context

Malinowski, Bronislaw, *Argonauts of the Western Pacific* 136
mapping, causal or cognitive 444
mapping documents 394–5, *394f*; *see also* documenting work
Masterson, Courtney R. 331; *see also* collaborative analysis
materiality and cognition: experimental studies of 445–6; natural studies of 446
matrix method using NVivo software 318–28; *see also* concept mapping, compared with the NVivo matrix method of analyzing qualitative data
Mauskapf, Michael 24; *see also* trends in qualitative organizational research/historical context
Maxwell, J.A. 145–6
Mazmanian, Melissa 262; *see also* ethnography across work/nonwork boundaries
McPherson, Chad Michael 434; *see also* counting qualitative data
medicated-assisted treatment (MAT) for opiate addiction, drawing and metaphor analysis 239–40
Mendonca, Sandra, study on the emergence of steam-powered ships 123–5
metaphor analysis *see* drawing and metaphor analysis
Metcalfe, Mike 318; *see also* concept mapping, compared with the NVivo matrix method of analyzing qualitative data
methodology 19
methods sections 468–71, 474n6
Metiu, Anca 381; *see also* innovative approaches and online data
micro-dynamics of organization fields 86, 88; *see also* field-level ethnography
microhistorical case studies for building grounded theory 122–33; analysis and theory building 130; challenges of 130; constant comparison and theoretical sampling 124–5; data gathering 128–9; description/defining 122–3, 131n1–2; distinctions

of 125; Edison, Thomas's electric lighting system study (Hargadon and Douglas) 127–9; examples of empirical studies *126t*; grounded theory building with historical cases 124–5; history in the making and the making of history 123–4; Morison, Elting and Sandra Mendonca's studies on sail- and steam-powered ships 123–5, 127; primary, secondary, and tertiary data sources 129; prior theory 125; research approach 125–30, *126t*, *128f*; research question 126–7; research setting in time and place 127–8, *128f*; summary 131; U.S. Radio Broadcasting Industry 127

Miles, M.B. and A.M. Huberman, *Qualitative Data Analysis* 28, 286

mixing quantitative and qualitative research 28, 423–33; complementary and confirmatory distinctions (Small) 424–5; definitions of qualitative and quantitative 423; examples of empirical studies *424t*; mixing methods in research programs rather than single articles 430; observations about mixed-methods research 430–2; qualitative data for the development of a construct and/or model that is then tested in an experiment 427–8; qualitative data in support of quantitative analyses 425–7; quantifying qualitative data 429–30; relationship between 423, *424f*; starting with quantitative data 428–9; for validating findings 423

modes of presentation (narrative vs. tables) 25

Morison, Elting, study on the emergence of steam-powered ships 123–5, 127

multilevel discourse analysis 341–9; application of 346–7; background 341–3, *343f*; conclusion 347–8; discourse defined 343; examples of empirical studies *347t*; step 1. historical reconstruction 342, 343–4, *343f*; step 2. intratextual analysis 342, *343f*, 344–5; step 3. intertextual analysis 342, *343f*, 345–6; step 4. contextual analysis *343f*, 346; step 5. iteration and theory development *343f*, 346; texts defined 341–2

multimethods approaches *see* combining qualitative methods to study collective cognition; counting qualitative data; hybrid method highlights; mixing quantitative and qualitative research

multiple sources *see* data expansion using multiple sources

multisited ethnography *see* ethnography across work/ nonwork boundaries

Murmann, J. Peter 11–12

narrative data analysis *115f*, 117; *see also* Qualitative Comparative Analysis (QCA) in narrative data analysis

National Science Foundation 27, 29

natives (field informants and phenomenon experts) 382, *403f*, 407

natural studies of materiality and cognition 446

networks/networking *see* practice approach to study social networks

neutrality (pushing the boundaries of) *see* unconventional research contexts (e.g. prisons)

new institutional (NI) scholarship 100–1; *see also* inhabited institutionalism

NI *see* new institutional (NI) scholarship

nonauthor collaborators 401–10; background 401–2; concierge (process facilitators) *403f*, 407–8; content and process help *403f*; creating your own journey 408–9; customs officers (editors and reviewers) *403f*, 406; examples of empirical studies *408–9t*; friends we are trying to make (wider academic audience) *403f*, 405–6; natives (field informants and phenomenon experts) *403f*, 404; travel companions (a community of practice of qualitative research) *403f*, 404–5; types of helpers and the help they provide (summary) 402–3, *403f*; *see also* collaborative analysis; team ethnography

nonverbal communication 207; *see also* aesthetics of data: visual elements/context

nonwork settings *see* ethnography across work/ nonwork boundaries

NVivo matrix software *see* concept mapping, compared with the NVivo matrix method of analyzing qualitative data; matrix method using NVivo software

observation, vs. interviews 472–3

oil advertising example of visual rhetoric 231–4, *232t*, *233f*, *234t*

O'Mahony, Siobhan 168; *see also* comparative field data for theory generation

online data *see* archival data from online communities; innovative approaches and online data analysis

open and emergent sampling technique defined 252–3

openIDEO study 386–7

open source software study 386–7

organizational or institutional fields: defined 86, 94n1; micro-dynamics of 86; *see also* field-level ethnography

organization research methods 3

Organization Science 288, 465

Osterlund, Carsten 391; *see also* documenting work

participant observation to participant tracking *396t*, 397

parting ceremonies 83, *84t*

PDWs *see* professional development workshops

pedagogical value of drawing *239f*, 244–5, *245f*

"Persuasion with Case Studies" (Siggelkow) 12

phenomenon experts *403f*, 407

Phillips, Nelson 225; *see also* visual rhetoric, analyzing

Plato 177, 184–5

polyvocality 255

postdeath organizing 83, *84t*

positivism 466, 471, 473–74n2–3
post-mortems on post-mortems *see* second-look decision autopsies
"The Power of Rich" (*AMJ*) 11
power-sharing *see* drawing and metaphor analysis
practice approach to study social networks 186–94; conclusions 192; examples of empirical studies *188t*; social network analysis (SNA) background 186–8; step 1. formulating initial questions 189, *189f*; step 2. exploring relational practices 189–90, *189f*; step 3. understanding emergent networks *189f*, 191; step 4. validating and refining theories *189f*, 191
Pratt, Michael 177; "For the Lack of a Boilerplate: Tips on Writing Up (and Reviewing) Qualitative Research" 13; *see also* crafting/selecting research questions
preferred data collection and analysis methods (ethnographies vs. interviews, inductive description vs. deductive coding) 25
prior theory 19, 125
prison research *see* unconventional research contexts (e.g. prisons)
privacy *396t*, 398
private ethnography 46
problem-oriented qualitative research 178; *see also* crafting/selecting research questions
process facilitators *403f*, 407–8
"process-oriented" 24
process theorizing: challenges of with online communities 220–1; defined 215; form online discourse 217–19, *217f*; *see also* archival data from online communities
professional development workshops (PDWs) 11–12
provisional framings, piloting multiple 83–4, *84t*
proximal actors defined *252f*, 254

QCA *see* Qualitative Comparative Analysis
Qualitative Best Paper Winners (*AMJ* and *ASQ*) *15t–18t*
Qualitative Comparative Analysis (QCA) 24, 156–67; advantages of 158; analytical process/steps 158–61, *159f*; applications 161, 164–5; background/description/defining 156–8; conclusions 165; corporate social responsibility (CSR) and 164; examples of empirical studies *162t–3t*; journals studies published in 157; techniques: crisp-set (csQCA), multi-value (mvQCA), and fuzzy set (fsQCA) 156, 158–61; a word of caution 165
Qualitative Comparative Analysis (QCA) in narrative data analysis 362–70; Boolean-based method 363, *363f*, 366–7, *367t*; contest and complement 362–3; data *363f*, 365–8, *366t–7t*; descriptives and 368–9; examples of empirical studies *364t*; fallibilism (Pierce) and 365; philosophical foundations of narrative methods vs. dominant quantitative methods 363–5; summary/conclusion *363*, 369; truth tables for fact checking 366,

366t–7t; using QCA descriptives to address the expected counterfactual 368–9
Qualitative Data Analysis (Miles and Huberman) 28, 286
"Qualitative Research in Organizational and Vocational Psychology" (Lee and Gephart) 10–11
quantitative data: defined 423; *see also* combining qualitative methods to study collective cognition; counting qualitative data; hybrid method highlights; mixing quantitative and qualitative research; Qualitative Comparative Analysis
quantitative research 471–2
quasi-deduction and responsive induction with surprise as the abductive shift point 99, 104, *104f–6f*, 106
quota sampling 259

radical, emergent change *84t*
Ramachandran, V.S. 12
Ravasi, Davide 444; *see also* combining qualitative methods to study collective cognition
reasoning, modes of 80–1, *84f*
recursiveness 123
Redden, Shawna Malvini 238; *see also* drawing and metaphor analysis
reflexive analysis 197; *see also* field resistance (and embrace)
reflexivity 33, 41; *see also* extreme/atypical cases
relational foundations 11
relational practices: exploring 189–90, *189f*; *see also* practice approach to study social networks
representational rules 120
research methods 3; *see also* extreme/atypical cases
research questions *see* adventures in qualitative research; crafting/selecting research questions; practice approach to study social networks
Reuf, Martin 465, 473n1
reviewer bias 21n6
reviewers *403f*, 406
rhetoric *see* visual rhetoric, analyzing
Rindova, Violina 272; *see also* strategic conversation data
Rogers, Kristie M. 66; *see also* unconventional research contexts (e.g. prisons)
Rouse, Elizabeth D. 286; *see also* data expansion using multiple sources
Rynes, Sara L. 3, 9; *see also* interesting organizational research/papers

sailing ship effect 123
sampling *see* structural sampling
Sauder, Michael 434; *see also* counting qualitative data
Sawyer, Steve 391; *see also* documenting work
Schein, E.H., *Strategic Pragmatism: The Culture of Singapore's Economic Development Board* 51n2
Schinoff, Beth S. 331; *see also* collaborative analysis
"Science and Cooking: From Haute Cuisine to the Science of Soft Matter" (Harvard, Adria, and the Spanish Alicia Foundation) *300b*

Science Quarterly 288
second-look decision autopsies 411–20; conducting 413–14, *414f*; examples of empirical studies *418t*; implications/conclusions 417–18; pre-9/11 reexaminations (Kramer) 413, *418t*; revisiting the Bay of Pigs for example (Kramer) 414–18, 419n1; terms/defining 411–12; worth of 414–17
sensegiving 82, *84t*
sensitivity, in unconventional research context *70t*, 73–4, *75t*
sensitizing concepts 353–54; *see also tabula geminus* (twin slate) data coding
September 11 terrorist attacks, pre-9/11 reexaminations (Kramer) 413, *418t*
serendipitous opportunities in data collection 298–307; background and inspiration 298–300; benefits and caveats 305–6; bisociation (Koestler) 300–1; elements and workings of the approach (summary diagram) *302f*; episode 1. a journalist at a contemporary art exhibition featuring the chef (Kassel, Germany) *299b–300b*; episode 2. a sponsor's representative at science and cooking public lectures (Harvard) *300f*; introduction to the "what's cooking" approach to data collection 300–1; spadework and skills (preconditions) 301–4, *302f*; step 1. exploring potential *302f*, 304; step 2. negotiating role(s) *302f*, 304–5; step 3. trespassing into other worlds *302f*, 305; step 4. returning to the case *302f*, 305
Shah, Sonali K. 251; *see also* structural sampling
sharing accounts *148f*; *see also* team ethnography
Sharma, Sarika 391; *see also* documenting work
ship studies 123–5, 127
Siggelkow, Nicolaj, "Persuasion with Case Studies" 12
Silbey, Susan S. 143; environmental health and safety management (EHS) system study at Eastern University 147, 151; *see also* team ethnography
single case studies 33
skills, in serendipity-driven data *302f*, 303–4
SNA *see* social network analysis
Snook, Scott 54; *see also* studying elites in institutions of higher education
snowball sampling 260n3
Snyder, Jaime 391; *see also* documenting work
social network analysis (SNA) 187–8; *see also* practice approach to study social networks
social systems *see* structural sampling
spadework, in serendipitous opportunities in data collection 301–3, *302f*
STATA analyses 28
Stigliani, Ileana 444; *see also* combining qualitative methods to study collective cognition
strategic conversation data 272–85; additional data 278; analytical approaches 278, *279t*, 280–2, *283f*; conclusion/summary 282–3, *283f*; conversation analysis 281–2; conversations defined 272; data collection 274, *275t–7t*, 278, *279t*, *283t*; data

recording and observation mode 274, 278; discourse analysis 280–1; early-stage analyses 280; examples of empirical studies 272–4, *275t–7t*; grounded theory 282; in-depth analyses 280; research questions and insights 273, *283f*; strategic conversations defined 272
Strategic Management Journal 288
Strategic Pragmatism: The Culture of Singapore's Economic Development Board (Schein) 51n2
structural approach, for online texts 385–6, *385t*, 389n4
structural sampling 251–61; background 251–2; benefits of *252f*, 255; central participants defined 253; challenges of *252f*, 255–6; conclusions 260; in the context of qualitative sampling methodologies 259–60, 260n3; defined 253; examples of empirical studies 256, *257t–8t*, 259; investigating the social system from within 253–4; open and emergent sampling technique defined 252–3; polyvocality 255; proximal and distant external actors defined 254; purpose/objectives of 252, *252f*; putting the social system in context 254; sample completion 254–5; technique of 252–5, *252f*, 259–60, 260n3; uses of 251
studying elites in institutions of higher education 54–65; admission practices studies 57; background 54–5; culture and 56–7; elites and elite education 55–7; "From Higher Aims to Hired Hands" (Khurana) 57–9; historical background 55–9; an individual level of analysis 59–63; summary 63; three groups of elites/leaders (intellectuals/ professionals, owners/managers of large corporations, senior government officials) 55; *see also* "Becoming a Harvard MBA" longitudinal study (Snook and colleagues)
Suddaby, Roy, "What Grounded Theory is *Not*" 11
Svejenova, Silviya 298; *see also* serendipitous opportunities in data collection
symbolic capital 48, 52n5

tabula geminus (twin slate) data coding 350–61; as abductive approach to the theory and data interplay 352–3; background/description of approach 350–1; coding process 354–5; examples of empirical studies *358t*; the process *353f*; sample portions of a coding dictionary 359–60; sample transcript page showing codes 358–9; sensitizing concepts 353–4; theory codes vs. grounded codes 351–2; transparency of the process 356–7; two or more coders 355–6
team ethnography 143–55; advantages of 144–5; challenges of 150–1; conclusion 151; distinctions between fieldwork and ethnography 143–4; enhancing validity/reliability and 144–6; environmental health and safety management (EHS) system 147, 151; ethnography across work/ nonwork boundary 269–70; evaluative validity 153n1; examples of empirical studies *152t–3t*;

external and internal generalizability 150; from
individual to team ethnography 143–5; live
coding (Gersick) and 375; step 1. continuously
improving accounts for descriptive validity 144,
148, *148f*; step 2. triangulating across accounts for
interpretive validity 144, *148f*, 149; step 3. refining
conceptual categories for theoretical validity
144, *148f*, 149–50; training ethnographers and
enhancing ethnographic validity through group
collaboration 146–50; types of validity 144–6; *see
also* collaborative analysis; drawing and metaphor
analysis; nonauthor collaborators
texts: defined for field-level ethnography 87; defined
for multilevel discourse analysis 341; *see also*
innovative approaches and online data analysis
Thelma and Louise (film) 19
theoretical arguments, counting qualitative data
for 439
theoretical sampling 34, 124–5
theoretical validity 146, *148f*, 149–50
theories, validating and refining *189f*, 191
theorizing accounts *148f*; *see also* team ethnography
theory building 12–13, 14, 34, 37, 130, 346; *see also*
grounded theory; microhistorical case studies for
building grounded theory
"Theory Building from Cases: Opportunities and
Challenges" (Eisenhardt and Graebner) 12–13
theory codes 351–2
theory elaboration 14, *15t–18t*, 19
theory generation 14, *16t–17t*, 19; *see also*
comparative field data for theory generation
"thick description" 24
tight coupling 207, 209–10, *210f*; *see also* aesthetics of
data: visual elements/context
time frames 127–8, *128f*
top-down ethnography (hiring) 46
Toubiana, Madeline 66; *see also* unconventional
research contexts (e.g. prisons)
Tracy, Sarah J. 238; *see also* drawing and metaphor
analysis
traditional qualitative research, text and context
382–3, *384t*, 389n2
Trefalt, Spela 401; *see also* nonauthor collaborators
trends in qualitative organizational research/historical
context 24–30, 29n1; background 24–5; future
directions 29; period 1. pre-1950 25–6, *26t*; period
2. 1950–1970 26–7, *26t*; period 3. 1970–1985
26t, 27; period 4. 1985–2000 *26t*, 27–8; period
5. 2000–2014 *26t*, 28; Qualitative Comparative
Analysis (QCA) 24; traditional definitions 24
trial-and-error tinkering 317; *see also* adventures in
qualitative research
triangulation of data *see* counting qualitative data;
data expansion using multiple sources; team
ethnography
Trifecta (pseudonym) contract ethnography studies
47–50; *see also* contract corporate ethnography
and innovation from entanglement

truth tables 366, *366t–7t*; *see also* Qualitative
Comparative Analysis (QCA) in narrative data
analysis

unconventional research contexts (e.g. prisons)
66–76; background 66–7; context 66–7;
discussion of risks/conclusion/summary 74,
75t; distinctions between traditional methods
and alternative methods *75t*; emergent theme
67; emotion 70–2, *70t*, *75t*; encouragement *70t*,
72–3, *75t*; examples of empirical studies *75t*;
interviews 67; jointly considering key features 69;
neutrality (pushing the boundaries of) 67, 70–4,
70t, *75t*; other examples/contexts *75t*; perceived
power and privilege differences 68–9, *70t*;
researcher-informer experience gap 68, *70t*; salient
demographic differences separating the in-group
from out-groups 69, *70t*; sensitivity *70t*, 73–4, *75t*;
strong and unfamiliar culture 68, *70t*
unexplored/novel phenomena 77–85; background/
importance of researching 77–8; collective
turnover *84t*; conclusion 84; connecting your
findings 82–4, *84f*; discovering boundaries 80, *84f*;
disidentification 82–3, *84t*; examples of exemplary
papers *84t*; finding informants 81–2, *84f*; finding
instances 78–9, *84f*; free-form writing 79, *84f*;
modes of reasoning 80–1, *84f*; parting ceremonies
83, *84t*; piloting multiple provisional framings 83–4,
84f; postdeath organizing 83, *84t*; radical, emergent
change *84t*; selecting your approach 80–2, *84f*;
sensegiving 82, *84t*; sharpening your focus 78–80,
84f; vocabulary-building 82–3, *84f*, *84t*
universal state theory 313

Vaast, Emmanuelle 215; *see also* archival data from
online communities
validating and refining theories *189f*, 191; *see also*
counting qualitative data; practice approach to
study social network
validation *see* live coding and discovery/validation
validity: team ethnography and 144–50; types of
144–6
value systems (positivist vs. constructivist) 25
Vanguard 12
Van Maanen, John 45, 143–4, 465, 466; *see also*
contract corporate ethnography and innovation
from entanglement
virtual ethnography, online texts and *385t*, 388
visual elements *see* aesthetics of data: visual elements/
context
visual mapping technique for data analysis 315–17,
315f, *316f*
visual narrative analysis *see* combining qualitative
methods to study collective cognition
visual rhetoric, analyzing 225–37; affective turn
226–7; background 225–6; coding scheme
229–31, *230t*; conclusions 234–6; dialogic,
semiotic, and affective phenomena 225; example

(advertisements): conflict oil, ethical oil 231–4, *232t*, *233f*, *234t*; examples of empirical studies *235t*; rhetorical turn 227; step 1. create corpus of texts 228–9, *228f*; step 2. theoretically sample these texts *228f*, 229; step 3. analyze the visual rhetoric and social semiotics embedded in the texts *228f*, 229–31, *230t*; step 4. analyze the interaction between texts *228f*, 231; use of in organizational research 227; visual turn 226
visual sorting *115f*, 117–18
vocabulary-building 82–3, *84f*, *84t*

Walsh, Ian J. 77; *see also* unexplored/novel phenomena
WASP acronym (coined by Baltzell) 140
Weeks, John 45; *see also* contract corporate ethnography and innovation from entanglement
Weick, Karl, "The Generative Properties of Richness" 12

WELL virtual ethnography 387–8
"What Grounded Theory is *Not*" (Suddaby) 11
"What Makes Management Research Interesting, and Why Does It Matter" (*Academy of Management Journal*) 3
"What's Cooking?" data collection approach *see* serendipitous opportunities in data collection
"What's Different about Qualitative Research?" (Bansal and Corely) 13
"When I Write My Masterpiece" (Barley) 11
Willis, Matt 391; *see also* documenting work
work/nonwork boundaries *see* ethnography across work/nonwork boundaries
workplace bullying, drawing and metaphor analysis 240, *241f*

Zaloom, C. 138–9
Zilber, Tammar B. 86; *see also* field-level ethnography